D0226323

THE MAIN DEBATE

THE MAIN DEBATE

Communism versus Capitalism

EDITED BY

Tibor R. Machan
AUBURN UNIVERSITY, ALABAMA

 RANDOM HOUSE   NEW YORK

To Manny Klausner

First Edition
987654321
Copyright © 1987 by Random House, Inc.

All rights reserved under International and Pan-American Copyright Conventions. No part of this book may be reproduced in any form or by any means, electronic or mechanical, including photocopying, without permission in writing from the publisher. All inquiries should be addressed to Random House, Inc., 201 East 50th Street, New York, N.Y. 10022. Published in the United States by Random House, Inc., and simultaneously in Canada by Random House of Canada Limited, Toronto.

Library of Congress Cataloging-in-Publication Data

The Main debate.

Includes index.
1. Communism. 2. Capitalism. I. Machan, Tibor R.
HX73.M333   1986   335.43   86-26015
ISBN 0-394-35820-1

Manufactured in the United States of America

Cover Design: Suzanne Bennett

Text Design: Susan Phillips

Cover credit: "Day and Night" by M. C. Escher, 1938. © M. C. Escher Heirs c/o Cordon Art—Baarn—Holland.

PREFACE

There are numerous books available about capitalism, and others about communism; this volume will not be an addition to either of these sets of literature. I know of no volume that tries to bring together contributions from supporters of both theories of capitalism and communism. That is what this book does. It aims to present a reasonably fairminded face-off.

Capitalist theorists in this book tend toward supporting the kind of political economy implicit in the works of John Locke and Adam Smith. Yet capitalism's supporters may not see eye-to-eye on the system's details. Capitalists in this book tend, also, to stress individuality, believing that individuals possess rights to personal sovereignty and private property that clearly block certain grand social purposes, however desirable these may be. Thus a supporter of capitalism would not favor coercive redistribution of wealth for the sake of advancing the arts or even social welfare for the poor.

Communist theorists in this book are mostly Marxists or neo-Marxists, those who see Marx's understanding of human life as largely correct. They see communism or socialism, understood in Marx's terms, as the most advanced human community. They tend also to emphasize the social or communal side of human nature and understand the human individual as inherently communal: the individual's full development depends on the full development of everyone else.

Capitalists, as understood here, do not regard the United States or Great Britain as fully capitalist systems, though they would agree that these countries have been among the closest to capitalism to date. Consistent capitalism does not admit of government regulation of the economy, subsidies to business, or trade restrictions. Such a system institutes the principles of the right to private property, as understood in the Lockean tradition, throughout the society. For some of the purists even the financing of government would have to be done with at least the implicit consent of the governed, lest the principle of private property be violated in the administration of political justice.

Nor need Marxian theorists regard the Soviet Union or the People's Republic of China as examples of the fully emancipated human community, though some do think certain features of these societies are relevant to an understanding of post-capitalist, socialist human communities. Consistent communism would exhibit a nonhierarchical social structure and would not tolerate the economic exploitation and the degree of private market activity evident in the USSR, for example. As an ideal, such a system embodies the principle of sharing or communal ownership and administration throughout the society.

Presenting such a face-off between defenders of Marxist-inspired communism and individualist market capitalism could help improve the nature of the debate. In most cases it is Marxists who talk about capitalism, while capitalist economists discuss Marxism. I have chosen Marxists to defend Marxist communism and individualists to defend capitalism, with only a few essays that criticize the contrasting system.

The dispute is much broader than the scope of contemporary economics. This work sees the debate as primarily philosophical and practical. But to say more here would risk getting embroiled in the controversies at the outset.

I should explain right at the start that I am a capitalist—not a large property owner but someone who regards capitalism as sound political economy. I don't much like the term—I think it misleads one to think that a community that makes capitalism possible must make business the whole task of life—just as many Marxists don't like the term "communism," for a variety of reasons. I would probably be thought of as an apologist and reactionary by orthodox (Soviet) Marxists. (The Soviet newspaper *Pravda* once dubbed one of my books an apology for warmongering, imperialist capitalism!) In any case, in this book the debate centers not on motivation and explanation but on evaluation and justification.

I have tried to open these pages to the most important and formidable elements of both outlooks. The idea is that students and other readers will benefit from having these selections brought together for them to read and consider.

The structure of the volume is simple. In each section I have alternated essays by theorists supporting communism and those supporting capitalism. Each essay in a pair addresses roughly the same topic, although because of the very basic differences of perspective, this may not be immediately evident. Otherwise the order of appearance is without significance.

The reason I chose the title should also be made explicit: the major philosophical conflict in the world today is between two societies or their leadership, one proclaiming adherence to individualist capitalism, the other to Marxian communism—never mind now the authenticity of these claims. Getting clear about the convictions of those who in fact fully support the two theories referred to in this persistent conflict may well be a vital beginning in any effort necessary to resolve the conflict.

I wish to thank the John M. Olin and Reason Foundations for their financial support of my work on this book. I also want to thank my friend Douglas Den Uyl and my wife Jamie Sinclair for their help. Finally, I want to extend my appreciation to the contributors to this volume, who have all been very cooperative.

TIBOR R. MACHAN
Auburn University, Alabama

CONTENTS

PREFACE Tibor R. Machan v

PART ONE: DIALECTICS 1

Robert Heilbroner   THE DIALECTICAL APPROACH TO PHI-
                         LOSOPHY 2
Ernst Topitsch   HOW ENLIGHTENED IS "DIALECTICAL
                         REASON"? 19

**PART TWO: HUMAN NATURE AND HUMAN
          EMANCIPATION** 39

Bhikhu Parekh   MARX'S THEORY OF MAN 40
Nathaniel Branden   ALIENATION 62

PART THREE: ETHICS AND MORAL FOUNDATIONS 83

J. Roger Lee   THE MORALITY OF CAPITALISM AND
                         OF MARKET INSTITUTIONS 84
Jon Elster   SELF-REALIZATION IN WORK AND
                         POLITICS: THE MARXIST CONCEP-
                         TION OF THE GOOD LIFE 111
Tibor R. Machan   THE CLASSICAL EGOIST BASIS OF CAPI-
                         TALISM 139
Richard Schmitt   THE DESIRE FOR PRIVATE GAIN 162

ix

PART FOUR: HUMAN FREEDOM AND POLITICAL LIBERTY 179

Lloyd Easton   MARX AND INDIVIDUAL FREEDOM 180

Douglas J. Den Uyl   FREEDOM AND VIRTUE 200

Andrew McLaughlin   FREEDOM VERSUS CAPITALISM 217

Lester H. Hunt   ON IMPROVING HUMAN BEINGS BY POLITICAL MEANS 233

PART FIVE: RIGHTS 249

Milton Fisk   PROPERTY RIGHTS 250

Samuel C. Wheeler III   NATURAL PROPERTY RIGHTS AS BODY RIGHTS 272

PART SIX: POLITICAL ECONOMY 291

Leonard Billet   ADAM SMITH AND JUSTICE 292

Thomas Keyes   THE MARXIAN CONCEPT OF PROPERTY: INDIVIDUAL / SOCIAL 311

Paul Craig Roberts and Matthew A. Stephenson   ALIENATION AND HISTORICAL MATERIALISM 331

Geoffrey de Ste. Croix   CLASS IN MARX'S CONCEPTION OF HISTORY 344

PART SEVEN: ECONOMICS 363

John Roemer   EXPLOITATION, PROPERTY RIGHTS, AND PREFERENCES 364

Robert Nozick   EQUALITY, ENVY, AND EXPLOITATION 385

David Schweickart   CAPITALISM, CONTRIBUTION, AND SACRIFICE 410

Eric Mack   IN DEFENSE OF "UNBRIDLED" FREEDOM OF CONTACT 425

PART EIGHT: IMPERIALISM 439

Kai Nielsen   GLOBAL JUSTICE, CAPITALISM, AND THE THIRD WORLD 440

P.T. Bauer   WESTERN GUILT AND THIRD WORLD POVERTY 454

INDEX 473

part ONE

DIALECTICS

When Karl Marx took up his study of political economy, his main criticism of Adam Smith and other classical economists concerned not so much what they said about capitalist systems but what they implicitly claimed for the principles or laws of such systems, namely, universal validity. In our time, too, one of the central conflicts between supporters of capitalism and communism is that the former take their system to be universally sound, while the latter see their vision of a good human community arriving at a different stage of humanity's development. But underneath this dispute is the broader question of just what principles of reality should be applied by students of political economy. Marxian communists are historical relativists, or contextualists, believing that a dialectical principle governs human social development, the primary dialectic being the class conflict that necessarily accompanies our dependence on material—therefore, economic—reality. Individualist capitalists, on the other hand, tend to see human life as involving more permanence, either governed by fairly stable economic principles or at least subject to stable moral and political principles which are rejected at our peril.

Dialectical reasoning most fundamentally divides capitalist and communist. It might be construed as the metaphysical dispute underlying all others. Is the dialectical approach sound or unsound? This is the first issue to which we turn.

1

ROBERT HEILBRONER

THE DIALECTICAL APPROACH TO PHILOSOPHY

One aspect of Marxism that is vital to understand is the dialectical approach. Whether Marx saw it as a general approach to dealing with all facets of reality or merely a principle evident in human social development, it is nevertheless a crucial aspect of the Marxian outlook. It ultimately underlies Marxian class conflict and revolutionary theories, two features of Marxism that are of vital concern. Robert Heilbroner—Professor of Economics at the New School for Social Research in New York City and author of numerous books, among them The Worldly Philosophers *(1959) and* Marxism: For and Against *(1980)—explains what the Marxian dialectical approach involves and means to us. Marx himself gave the most succinct explanation of it in his General Introduction to the* Grundrisse, *in the section entitled "On the Method of Political Economy."*

There is a great temptation to avoid the thorny subject of dialectics and to move immediately to the problem of capitalism with which Marxism is most immediately and deeply concerned. But I think this would be a mistake. All views of the world express philosophical premises, tacitly if not explicitly, and it is often at this half-exposed level that their ultimate strengths or their weaknesses are located. This is particularly the case with Marxism which is self-consciously built on a philosophic foundation whose concepts and vocabulary run through its writings like a colored thread.

Thus the most important reason to begin a study of Marxism with an examination of dialectics is simply to become familiar with a vocabulary that is inseparable from Marxist thought—a task all the more necessary because the vocabulary of dialectics is not generally familiar, even to most contemporary philosophers. Looking through the journals of modern philosophy, especially in the United States and England, one rarely comes across the word *dialectic,* much less a discussion of "dialectical" problems. Indeed, with the exception of a few European or Marxist philosophers, well out of the mainstream, the entire approach is no longer taken seriously.

Another reason to start with dialectics, therefore, is to interpret it to those who believe that its vocabulary is mere obfuscation and pointless complexity. Obviously I do not hold this to be true. As I shall try to make clear, I think there are problems for which we require the special vocabulary and distinct perspective that are called "dialectical"—problems that remain invisible or re-

Reprinted, with permission, from the author's *Marxism: For and Against* (New York: W. W. Norton, 1981).

calcitrant before the gaze and techniques of more conventional philosophic approaches.

At the same time, I also wish to make clear the limitations, as well as the reach, of a dialectical approach. If dialectics is to be explained to beginners, and legitimated to philosophers, it must be rescued from those who use its terminology as an evidence of piety, or who flash its words as a badge of authority. Thus there is an *against* as well as a *for* in my initial undertaking, both aspects of which will, I trust, become clear as we proceed.

1

It would be useful if I could now start straight off with an exposition of dialectics. But I cannot. The reason is that there is no single established meaning for dialectics, and still less so for the dialectics incorporated within Marxism. I am forced to begin, therefore, with an attempt to define our subject by the process of successive approximations, slowly narrowing the circle of definitions until we have established what Marxian dialectics is not, as well as what it is.

The word *dialectics* comes from the Greek term for dialogue, and a residue of give-and-take, of relentless questioning, continues to inform the concept. At the core of all varieties of dialectics, we find a continuation of that incessant querying, that active engagement with the resistant stuff of knowledge, so unforgettably portrayed by Plato in the person and style of Socrates, the great exponent of the dialectical method in classical philosophy.[1]

For Marxism, the legacy of this Greek sense of a dialectical questioning process resides in an "activist" attitude toward knowledge itself. A Marxian approach to philosophy stresses the *production,* rather than the passive receipt of knowledge—the involvement of the act of inquiry in shaping, as well as in discovering, knowledge. Because Marxian dialectics maintains that knowledge is not bestowed but won, it maintains that there is a deep, and indeed indissoluble, bond between what the Greeks called *praxis* or action, and *theoria* or thought—between "doing" and "thinking."[2] Thus, the unity of theory and practice that we have already noted in passing as an integral element of the Marxist commitment to socialism finds its roots in the dialectical insistence that "philosophizing" can only be vindicated and validated by some kind of activity; that reality is not merely what "is," but what we make it.

This activist orientation, as we shall see in our next chapter, is the source of both strength and difficulty for Marxism. But first we must search for an understanding of the ways in which a dialectical vision of things differs from a nondialectical one. Here we must pay heed to another Greek root of dialectical thought, exemplified by Heraclitus, the famous originator of the problem of stepping twice into the "same" river. From this point of view we derive a second basic idea of dialectics, as profoundly important as it is elusive. This is that the ultimate and irreducible nature of all reality is motion, not rest, and that to depict things as static or changeless is to disregard or violate the essence of their being.

We shall shortly see that this concept leads to important conclusions. But I think it useful to halt for a moment at this early stage of our inquiry. For in the idea of immanent change as the fundamental nature of reality, we can already discover both an advantage for dialectics—a perception not available from a nondialectical standpoint—and a limitation.

The advantage is immediately obvious. A Heraclitean depiction of the universe, with its emphasis on the changefulness of all things, strikes the Western mind as an intuitively right approach to reality, in tune with our temperament, our understanding of things. The difficulty comes when we try to subject this intuitively right grasp of things to systematic examination. Then we find that the very characteristic of changefulness that commends a dialectical viewpoint to our imaginations renders it awkward for our cognitive faculties. It is difficult to "think" about change, even if it is natural to imagine it. Heraclitus's river is much more easily discussed in its infinite instants of motionlessness than in its single trajectory of movement. Therefore when we turn to philosophic discussion we find ourselves naturally inclining toward a view of the universe that stops its processes, like so many frames of a motion picture, in order to allow us to examine things as if they were actually suspended motionless in space and time.

Thus, if there is a natural resonance between the dialectical "vision" of existence and our psychological processes, there is a difficulty in subjecting this vision to intellectual inspection. In this disjunction between the imaginative and the ratiocinative properties of our minds lies an important insight, I believe, into the problem of dialectics. Already it makes clear that a dialectical approach offers an entree into the possible nature of things that is blocked to view from a nondialectical perspective; but it also makes clear that the vision we gain cannot easily be turned to use by the procedures of normal inquiry.

2

The conception of the universe as inherently changeful readies us for the next step in the definition of Marxian dialectics. We must now move from Greek origins to the work of Hegel, without question the philosopher who exercised the greatest influence over Marx himself and over the subsequent development of a Marxian dialectics.

Hegel's thought is profound and forbidding, an elaboration on an immense scale of the ideas of Being and Becoming, which manifest themselves through all of nature and history in a vast process of self-transcendence called the dialectic. Marx was greatly influenced by the grandeur and internal dynamics of Hegel's scheme, although not by the primacy that it accorded to *logos,* or pure thought. Describing Hegel as "that mighty thinker," Marx emphasized that his own version of the dialectical method rested on the world of material things, not on that of thought.[3]

In our next chapter we will examine the idea of a dialectic of materialism. But if Marx turned Hegel upside down, he also retained an idea central to the Hegelian notion of dialectics. This was a conception of change as consisting not in mere movement or displacement, enlargement or diminution, but in *qualitative alteration*. In turn this qualitative alteration arose not from the impingement of "forces" on inert things—that would still ultimately rest on a static conception of reality—but from a universal changefulness located "within" things that Hegel called *contradiction*.

Because the idea of contradiction will occupy us for much of this essay, and because the word presents great difficulties for conventional philosophers and equally great temptations for self-serving Marxist use, we must stop to examine the term. In ordinary speech contradiction has a clear meaning: we cannot properly make two assertions with regard to something, if one assertion denies the other. Thus, we cannot say that a stone exists and that it does not exist, referring to the same stone at the same instant. Or rather, if we do make such an assertion, we forfeit any possibility of carrying on what we call a "reasoned" discussion, for one could then assert any number of incompatible and inconsistent things. Thus to declare the illegitimacy of contradictions is simply to lay down one rule for mutual comprehension and discourse.

This kind of *logical contradiction* is not, however, the meaning of contradiction that applies to dialectics. In dialectics, the word does not refer to the simultaneous assertion and denial of the existence of static things; instead, it refers to the nature of those conflicting elemental processes that are believed to constitute the essence of reality itself. As a first rough description of what such a "contradiction" implies, we can resort to another famous Hegelian phrase— "the unity of opposites." Contradictions therefore refer to the idea that all of reality is changeful because it consists, in its very innermost being, of the unstable coexistence and successive resolution of incompatible forces. Thus the fundamental concept of Being itself implies Nonbeing; and from this joining of opposites there issues forth its resolution, Becoming—which also contains a similar contradiction and resolution.

I shall deliberately leave this description vague and unexplored for the moment, because it is an important part of my argument that we understand at an intuitive level what such a conception of "contradiction" means. Later we shall examine it further. Meanwhile, however, we can see that an affinity exists between this general dialectical vision and the tendencies that Marxism will discover in history—an affinity between the contradiction-laden idea of change as Hegel sees it, and the idea of the disruptive, yet creative, unfolding central to the Marxist analysis of history. Thus, even though Marxism is not a "philosophy," it is powerfully affected by its philosophic premises; and its dialectic vantage point conditions, even if it does not fully determine, its social perspective.

3

The idea of contradiction is the open-sesame of a dialectical philosophy, bringing into high relief problems that are indistinct or simply invisible from another point of view. As we shall see, the notion of contradiction gives us insights with respect to Being and Becoming in society—that is, insights into history. But there is also an illumination provided by the idea of contradiction at a simpler level: it enables us to perceive the complex, relational nature of ideas or entities that appear to the undialectical eye as simple or self-contained.

Hegel gives us a famous example of this elucidatory power in his discussion of the terms Master and Servant. The very concept of Master, he shows, implies the opposite of such a concept in the Servant, one who is mastered. Without the idea of one, we cannot form the idea of the other, although each idea "by itself" is the contradiction (the "negation," in Hegel's terminology) of the other.[4] Note that this use of contradiction does not assert that a Master "is" and "is not," which would involve us in the same absurdity as making that assertion about a stone. Rather, the point is that a Master is a being who can only be *defined* or *described* by using a concept that is its meaningful opposite or negation. Without Servants there are no Masters, and vice versa.

What emerges from this dialectical perspective is a comprehension of existence that is of necessity more complex and ambiguous than that which emerges from a nondialectical approach to things. In turn, from this view in which objects are understood to exist in a mutually interacting "relational" context, Hegel constructs an entire theory of knowledge. It would, however, take us away from our main purpose to pursue that matter further. It is enough to note that the idea of contradiction provides the philosophic underpinning for the socioanalysis that Marxism will perform on the social world. For the kind of mutually determined relationship portrayed by Hegel in the example of Master and Servant will be enlarged and deepened by Marx in his examination of the ideas of Capital and Labor, where he will also discover internal contradictions similar to those identified by Hegel, but of much more striking political and historical import.[5]

The relational complexity opened up by a dialectical examination of the world is still, however, a somewhat static application of the idea of contradiction. Closer to the Marxist usage of the term is its application to the flux and change characteristic of the social world. Here the category that corresponds in its relational complexity to a "concept" is a "process"—a sequence of events. The dialectic perspective allows us to call certain processes "contradictory" because they unfold in ways that are both integral to, and yet destructive of, the processes themselves.

An instance may make this clear. In Marx's own work, the concept of contradiction plays its most important role in analyzing the vast sociohistoric process of capitalism itself. For the idea of contradiction enables us to see that there is a certain dialectical "logic" to its historic tendencies, insofar as they emerge from and reflect the contradictory nature of the system. Perhaps the most famous of these self-negating tendencies is one that Marx discovers in the very core subprocess of the system, its accumulation of capital. It is in the nature of capitalism, as Marx describes it, that it must seek to expand, whether through business growth, or by the search for new ways to increase profits, or in financial operations to increase money capital. As we will later see, the struggle for expansion is an integral and inextricable element in the evolution of capitalism as a period of history. At the same time, however, this expansive aspect is constantly undermining the viability of the larger system. The necessity for business growth, for instance, creates the conditions of "anarchic" rivalry that threaten the system with crisis. The insatiable thirst for profits drives the business system into mechanization that augments profits in the short run, but that eliminates them in the long run. The financial manipulations induce, or magnify, economic disorder.

These complicated modes of capitalist operation will be studied when we examine Marx's socioanalysis of capitalism. What needs to be grasped now is that this analysis depicts the capitalist process as not merely beset by "problems," but beset by problems that are the underside of its "successes." In this way, a dialectical perspective, with its central idea of contradiction, reveals the connectedness of social events that might otherwise seem to be only accidentally conjoined.

It is well, however, that we conclude this exploration of the strengths of a dialectical perspective with two warnings. The first is that *the presence of conflicts within social processes does not in itself suffice to establish these conflicts as contradictions*. The social world, like the natural world, is full of opposing forces, most of which have no more "contradictory" significance than the chance encounter of two particles or the clash of two wills. Contradictions refer to those oppositions that are both necessary for, and yet destructive of, particular processes or entities. This is a distinction that we will meet again in considering the application of dialectics to history.

Thus the task of a dialectical inquiry is not to make sweeping statements about the omnipresence of contradictions, but to identify the particular contradictory tendencies, if any, within a given social process. This is not a matter to be taken for granted when beginning from a dialectical point of view. Two dialecticians, examining the same social panorama, may differ on the appropriate concepts or processes within which to seek contradictions, or having agreed on these, may disagree as to the nature of their contradictory elements. In a word, dialectics provides an angle of vision, a lens through which to view society, but it does not predetermine what will be discovered there. These strictures apply in particular to the use of a dialectical vocabulary by some Marxists to establish the very problem that ought to be demonstrated. To use the word *contradiction* loosely, applying it to conflicts that have not been shown to be both necessary for the maintenance and decisive for the destruction of a social process, is to waste the real strength of a dialectical philosophy by debasing it into mere rhetoric.

The second warning is that *a dialectical approach in itself sheds no light on the actual sequences of events through which contradictory tendencies work themselves out*. Even if a dialectical perspective enables one unfailingly to identify the forces of contradiction in any social situation, the perspective does not describe the sequential happenings by which the contradiction works its effects on the social system. For example, the insight that the emergence of large-scale organized enterprise is both an apotheosis of capitalism and an entering wedge of socialism does not describe the particular ways in which large-scale enterprise grows, or the specific manner in which it will affect the ongoing "metabolism" of capitalism, or the precise fashion in which its technology or organization may become the foundation for a planned economic system. Indeed, these are matters about which Marxists disagree as vigorously as non-Marxists.

Thus the dialectical perspective affords insight into relationships, but not into causal sequences. It offers a heuristic—a diagnostic or revelatory—approach but no special technique to implement that approach. Problems that may remain hidden to a nondialectical view are opened for exploration, but the conclusions to which those explorations may lead are not themselves prescribed by the dialectical perspective itself.

For all its elucidating power, the central idea of contradiction remains a problem for many critics of a dialectical philosophy, and before moving on, I wish to explore this problem a little more deeply.

The difficulty arises, I believe, because many critics continue to interpret "contradiction" in its logical, Aristotelian sense in which the contradiction of A is not-A. This easily reduces dialectical usage to violations of sense and meaning, as Sir Karl Popper shows in *Conjectures and Refutations* and elsewhere. But that is not the meaning that contradiction holds as a relational view of the world. The *logical* contradiction (or "opposite" or "negation") of a Master is not a Slave, but a "not-Master," which may or may not be a slave. But the *relational* opposite of a Master is indeed a Slave, for it is only by reference to this second "excluded" term that the first is defined. Paul Diesing clearly describes this usage:

Two concepts are dialectically related when the elaboration of one draws attention to the other as an opposed concept that has been implicitly denied or excluded by the first; when one discovers that the opposite concept is required (presupposed) for the validity or applicability of the first; and when one finds that the real theoretical problem is that of the interrelationship between two concepts, and the real descriptive problem that of determining their interrelations in a particular case.

The same necessity to think in terms of relationships applies to the strictures of Popper and others regarding the "thesis, antithesis, synthesis" type of argument. Popper has no difficulty in showing that a given thesis does not produce an antithesis as its *logical* opposite. But a thesis may indeed produce an antithesis (or contradiction) when it is viewed *as a process to be understood from a relational vantage point,* and not simply as a statement to be asserted and denied. Parenthetically, neither Marx nor Hegel ever used the "thesis, antithesis, synthesis" formulation. We owe the phrase to Fichte.

The most vexing question for a Marxian view of dialectics, to be sure, has to do with the legitimacy of locating contradictions in nature itself. One can ascribe a dialectical—that is, immanently changeful and contradictory—aspect to all reality as a basic, unchallengeable assumption. Unfortunately, that reduces the idea of contradiction to a tautology, of heuristic but not operational usefulness. For if all of nature is contradictory by assumption, nothing is gained by pointing to the contradictory aspect of any particular element within it.

The problem, therefore, is to try to distinguish contradiction as a universal aspect of nature, and contradiction as an identificatory attribute of particular natural or social processes. Here I believe the way out lies in the conception of the "unities" within which contradictions are to be found. Unities are concepts introduced into reality by our minds. The universe itself is simply a flux, with innumerable collisions and interactions that have no unitary character, except insofar as we create such a character by the act of perception and comprehension. For example, the blast and recoil of a gun are "contradictions" only insofar as we relate the motions of particles that we designate as "blast" to the reaction of the mass that we call "recoil." Without the intervention of our intelligence, blast and recoil are no more bound together than any of the infinite simultaneously occurring events in the universe. We can, of course, describe blast and recoil as "contradictions," but in so doing we are not shedding light on the processes of nature, but on the unifying tendencies of our minds.

It is when we turn to the social world that unities become of immediate importance. We can imagine the universe as a swarm of particles, without its thereby ceasing to be a universe, whereas we cannot so imagine society. Without social, political, intellectual, economic, or other unities, the social world has no meaning. Thus we are *forced* to seek unities within the realm of social existence under an imperative different from that by which we establish them in nature, and in the process of creating different kinds of social unities, we discover the contradictory elements they contain. Dialectics thereby has a natural application to the social world that it lacks in the physical one.

One final point. Hegel circumvents the question of whether contradictions exist in nature because he assumes that thought and reality have a common ground in a preexisting "logos." Therefore there exists in Hegel an identity of thought and existence that permits the idea of contradiction to penetrate all of reality without running into the difficulties we have mentioned. It is because Marx and his followers reject this idealist basis of Hegelian thought, that Marxist dialectics encounters the problem of how to relate dialectical thought and natural processes.[6]

4

The emphasis on exploration takes us now to a last definition of dialectics. We have heretofore emphasized the "activist" search for knowledge with its interdependence of theory and practice; the "vision" of an immanently changeful reality; and the idea of contradiction within the categories and processes of social existence. All these are meanings that dialectics carries for Marxism. Now we must add a final dimension of meaning having to do with the pursuit of truth, namely the *method* by which inquiry is carried out.

The distinctive contribution that dialectics makes to methodology consists of its approach to the problem of forming concepts. Marx himself gives us perhaps the most brilliant example of this method when he asks, in the *Grundrisse,* how we can form the ideas with which political economy will operate.

It seems to be correct [he writes] to begin with the real and the concrete, . . . thus to begin in economics, with e.g. the population which is the foundation and the subject of the entire social act of production.

However on closer examination this proves false. The population proves an abstraction if I leave out, for example, the classes of which it is composed. These classes in turn are an empty phrase if I am not familiar with the elements on which they rest, e.g. wage labor, capital, etc. These latter in turn presuppose exchange, division of labor, prices, etc. . . .

Thus if I were to begin with the population, this would turn out to be a chaotic conception of the whole. I would then . . . move analytically toward ever simpler concepts, from the imagined concrete towards ever thinner abstractions until I arrived at the simplest determinations. From there the journey would have to be retraced until I had finally arrived at the population again, but this time not as a chaotic conception of a whole, but as a rich totality of many determinations and relations.[7]

On the face of it, this procedure is clear enough, involving a regress from superficial surface appearances to their underlying elements, followed by a reconstruction of the original datum in a much fuller context. The difficulty arises when we seek the method to implement the methodology—the specific instructions, the algorithms, the handbook of instructions for realizing each step along the road toward abstraction or back to concreteness. For then we discover that crucially important decisions must be made at each stage—deciding which abstract elements to pursue, disentangling "decisive" connections from accidental ones, specifying the process of analysis or reconstitution, judging the final result for its usefulness. What criteria shall we use in deciding, for instance, whether the population should originally be analyzed as consisting of two social classes, or three, or more? In turn, by which criteria will we judge the decomposition of, say, labor into its constituent "determinations" to be accurate or inaccurate, complete or partial? Such questions cannot be sidestepped if the result of the dialectical methodology is to be defensible against attacks from empirical or other points of departure.[8]

Thus, as before, a dialectical approach yields a rich harvest for the imagination, but a scanty one for exact analysis. As an example of the insight it can offer, we should take note of Marx's profound analysis of "the individual"—the analytic focus of so much non-Marxist social science—as "the ensemble of social relations."[9] What appears to be the concrete entity of *an individual* can easily be shown to be a "chaotic conception" unless we pierce the façade of the solitary being to its social roots, and then reconstitute the individual as a person embedded in, and expressing, the social forces of a particular society. At the same time, the procedures for moving from the naive conception of the individual to his or her social determination and back again are left unspecified, so that two dialectical methodologists may well arrive at two different "rich totalities" of the final result—one, for example, emphasizing the socioeconomic roots of gender differences, the other stressing the sociopsychological roots of the same phenomenon. From one point of view, a woman is quintessentially an exploited being who also has female characteristics; from another, a woman is quintessentially a female being who is also exploited.

To be sure, there is an unavoidable element of arbitrariness in all methods of pursuing empirical knowledge. At best we can minimize that arbitrariness by imposing certain rules on the procedures we are allowed to follow. One of these, for instance, is the rule of ordinary logic—a rule that applies equally to dialectical and nondialectical thought. As we have seen, dialectics asserts that contradictions exist, but not in a sense that would violate the precepts of straightforward logic which prevent us from saying Yes and No simultaneously.

Another rule is that of science, which demands that the methods we follow be defensible by certain established canons of procedure. Here, too, Marxian dialectics joins with other approaches to knowledge in insisting on the "scientific" nature of its own procedures, *but it differs from other approaches in the way it defines science.*

The dominant notion of science today refers to a method of obtaining information about the world, a method that can be roughly described as the formulation of refutable hypotheses. There is no doubt that *social* science falls well short of these ideal specifications, but that is not the matter that interests us here. For the idea of science broached by Marx does not lie in devising testable hypotheses, but in a differently conceived task, namely, piercing the screen of appearances to arrive at the "scientific" truth of a concealed essence. "All science would be superfluous if the outward appearance and the essence of things directly coincided," Marx wrote.[10] This is different from the approach of the nondialectical social scientist who does not concern himself with essences at all, indeed, who does not recognize the word.

A dialectical view of social science therefore poses an interpretive task quite different from that of modern day "positivism."[11] The positivist scientist also penetrates surface phenomena to arrive at underlying truths in the forms of "laws" or patterns, but his task is one of peering through *random* disturbances to discover regularities (not essences) presumably concealed within nature. The dialectical observer, on the contrary, tries to find real essences (not mere regularities), such as contradictory relations, by penetrating the *systematic* distortions imposed upon us by society.

These distortions—religious, political, social, economic—affect our vision in ways of which we are mainly unaware. The primary task of the dialectically minded social scientist, accordingly, is to inform us as to the presence and nature of our systematic misperceptions, so that we can discern essences where we would otherwise be deceived by appearances. What is dialectical about this scientific task is, of course, derived from the view that stresses the relational, contradictory aspect of social knowledge—a view that differs markedly from the approach of non-Marxist social science, with its emphasis on "facts" rather than contexts.

This is a powerful conception of science, at least within the realm of the social universe to which it is properly applicable. Indeed, the entire contribution of Marxism to social thought rests ultimately on its effort to penetrate the veil of appearances to discover the hidden essences of things, the web of relations that is the "real" ground of reality and not the surface manifestations that are its façade. *The target of a dialectical methodology is therefore illusion or delusion, not simple ignorance.* Marx's direct use of the word "scientific" was aimed, more than anywhere, at what he called "vulgar" conceptions of society.

Nonetheless, something is lacking from this penetrative method. It is the same lack we have noted before, namely, a rule for separating valid procedures from invalid ones; a test, however difficult to achieve in fact, that would enable us to discard some dialectical results as false. The dialectical approach to methodology leaves us with no means of appraising its results other than by the tests of conventional science, or those of ordinary logic.

The consequence is that Marxism has an uneasy relation to present-day positivist science. It scoffs at the "blatant empiricism" that is the credo of most social science, which it bitingly describes as gathering and collating facts with no theoretical vision to give them meaning and coherence. This is true enough. Yet a Marxist diagnosis of social events is repeatedly forced to establish its own "scientific" nature by subjecting its conclusions to the only testing procedures that we know—namely, those of empirical, positivist-oriented methods.

An illustration may be useful here. Two of Marx's most striking pronouncements, both grounded in his dialectical analysis of the contradictions of capitalism, were the tendency of capital to agglomerate in ever larger masses, and the tendency of the population to be reduced to the status of dependent wage earners. Both have been amply demonstrated by history (and will be discussed later). The "vindication" of these insights, however, rests entirely on recourse to ordinary empirical methods of observation and testing. Take, now, the dialectical insight that the rise of massive enterprise also creates the structural framework for socialism. There has been neither confirmation nor disconfirmation of this contradiction. Until we have such a test, however, it would be difficult even for Marxists to call the insight "scientific," in the sense of penetrating to the essence of things, for we do not yet know if this *is* the essence of things. A dialectical methodology thereby poses a new and striking vision of the truth that we want science to reveal, but gives us no dialectical test of the results of its application.

5

It is time to review our discussion and to hazard a conclusion. To sum up very rapidly the work of our preceding pages, we have seen that dialectics can be described in several distinct, although related ways: as a stance toward the acquisition of knowledge; as a conception of existence that stresses its fundamental and irreducible element of changefulness; as a conception of social entities that reveals them to be a unity of "contradictory opposites"; and as a method of forming concepts as a "rich totality of many determinations," obtained by an interpretative rather than a purely empirical approach to scientific investigation.

It must be apparent that these different meanings of dialectics operate on different planes. Its conceptions of the changeful and contradictory character of the universe are assumptions about the nature of reality. Its active stance and its methodological procedures concern the mode of investigation required to investigate nature as conceived in a dialectical way. And beyond these definitions lies yet another formulation of dialectics, largely confined to Marx's own writings—a formulation that seeks a distinctive method of presentation, designed to reveal the appearances and the essences of its subject matter.[12]

In different ways, and with different applications, all these various approaches to, and meanings of, a dialectical philosophy seem to me to validate it as a mode of thought and to clarify its essential contributions to Marxism. Yet it is also clear that all these dialectical approaches bring with them a sharp sense of limitation. The dialectical view of existence as inherently changeful is intuitively attractive, but intellectually elusive. The identification of contradiction as an element of social reality yields new possibilities for social dissection, but it gives us no means of identifying what those contradictions are. A dialectical methodology has not found a way of reconciling its suggestive mode of forming concepts or of formulating the task of science with its continued reliance on nondialectical techniques to test the validity of its concepts or its science in use.

The question to be faced, then, is whether we can explain this curiously two-sided aspect of dialectics, at once so rich and so poor, so useful and so useless, so powerful and so impotent. I think there is an explanation, if we return to the contrast between the appeal to our imagination and the frustration of our intelligence that we noted at the outset. This initial dichotomy, which we now see repeated in many applications of dialectics, suggests that the contrast is not accidental, but reflects a deep-lying property of a way of apprehending reality, not quite the same as ordinary "thinking" or "knowing."

Thinking or knowing are complex "activities." We can distinguish at least two types of mentation on which we lean heavily in our efforts to organize or to manipulate the world conceptually. The first consists of the formation of a body of common-sense knowledge learned by experience or secondhand, that enables us to deal with life on terms of familiarity. This common-sense organization of thought, by which we "know" that stones fall and trees grow, forms the basis for those more abstract conventions and conjectures to which we give the philosophic names of causality, chance, identity, and the like.

This mode of mentation is indispensable for our ability to live in the world, or to "explain" it to ourselves or others. Yet we know very little about the process of gaining this kind of knowledge, save that it is accumulated slowly and painfully. Moreover, for all the power that common-sense knowledge exercises over our thought, we also know from intercultural comparisons that "common-sense" explanations of events differ widely from one culture to another, and that the world can have many different "natural" or "self-evident" appearances.

Common-sense generalization, acquired in the universal process of socialization, is not, however, the only process of apprehension on which we depend. There is also a powerful kind of mental activity that "obeys" those rules of syntax and word sequence we call logic. When we perform the activity we call *thinking,* we frequently have recourse to these rules that define for us which sequences of utterance are legitimate or right, and which are illegitimate or wrong.

As Piaget has shown with his ingenious experiments, these formal logical steps have also to be learned.[13] The child does not know that the whole is equal to the sum of the parts, or that A must be bigger than C if it is bigger than B and if B is bigger than C. Such relationships are learned, often with great effort, and in some cases poorly: we all know people who cannot think "logically."

Now what is interesting about logical thought—which need not be Aristotelian logic—is that, once having been mastered, its rules master us. Having learned the rules of identity or transitivity, it is impossible to disavow them. Indeed, it is much easier to lie—to distort deliberately what one hears or sees—than to forswear the veracity of a proper syllogism. Since this logic has to be learned, as we have just said, we can only suppose that in some manner the rules of logic reflect the manner in which most adult minds "work."

Together, the common-sense organization of data and the obedience to canonical or logical rules of utterance describe a great deal of the activity we call rational discourse. They do not, however, embrace all our mental activities. Another, very important kind is our ability to perform such mental feats as suddenly "seeing the point" of something (what the psychologists call the "aha!" sensation), or discerning patterns, resemblances, or other relationships that are not discoverable by common sense or by formally structured logic.

Such insights, metaphors, associations, flights of fancy and the like impart a vast energy to psychic life. Indeed, I would venture that all that is "creative"—all that is a departure from received ideas or utterances—derives from this universally shared capability. Our ability to organize data into generalizations does not lead to novel ideas, but tends to solidify and routinize past experience; our pursuit of logic is, by definition, bounded by the rules that imperiously exert their sway. In sharp contrast, every novel conception or generalization, every invention of a new rule for logic, every new "image" of thought, we owe to the mysterious psychic processes that accompany, but are distinct from discursive thought. Metaphors and images and insights bubble up "from below." We have no control over their generation or their acuity, whereas we do not feel so much at the mercy of uncontrollable forces when we try to think in common sense or formal ways. Imagination takes us by surprise, in a manner that cannot ordinarily be said of thinking.[14]

I have taken this detour because I believe that formal dialectics, in all its different forms, is an effort to capture and to reduce to communicable discourse this inventive psychic capacity. The elusive psychic abilities we have discussed probably derive their energies from unconscious and preconscious processes of the mind. But it is not their origins about which I wish to speculate in these last pages, but rather their ramifications in the dialectical views that we have examined.

The connections are, I believe, twofold. First, much "creative" thought hinges on the possibility of discovering analogies, linkages, syntheses and the like between hitherto separated entities. This mental act of "leaping" from one thought to another has an obvious analogue to the idea of relationship, so central to dialectical philosophy.

Second, unlike common sense or logic, intuitive thought (to give a name to the spectrum of imaginative psychic activities) is often ambiguous and "contradictory." Freud, for example, remarks that symbols emerging from the unconscious are laden with ambivalent meanings—love and hate, male and female, etc. Here, as in dialectics, ambivalence refers to "unities" that can only be understood by the interpenetration and support of mutually exclusive concepts. (Freud also remarked on the tendency of certain words to possess contradictory meanings: "Cleave," for example, means both to sunder and to cling.)

The hypothesis, then, is that dialectics is at bottom an effort to systematize, or to translate into the realm of manageable, communicable thought, certain unconscious or preconscious modes of apprehending reality, especially social reality. This hypothesis gives us some clue as to why the exposition of dialectics leaves us satisfied at one level of our minds while dissatisfied at another. Its ideas of flux, contradiction, essence, remain elusive in terms of ordinary reasoned discourse.[15] Worse, the attempt to translate these terms into the structures of ordinary exposition either desiccates them—reducing dialectics to a set of definitions that can be riddled by the application of common sense or logic—or indicates their nondiscursive meaning by an allusive use of words, by recondite vocabularies, by italics that inject a suggestive tone of voice into prose, etc. Ambiguity, the bane of positivism, is the very essence of dialectics.

The result is the blurred and imprecise exposition—blurred and imprecise according to the criteria of common sense or logic—that caused Pareto to remark in exasperation that Marx's words were like bats: to some, mice; to others, birds. This is a statement that Bertell Ollman, who has strongly emphasized the relational core of dialectics, has called a profound insight into the truth.[16]

The same nondiscursive aspect of dialectics accounts, I suspect, for the extraordinary difficulties in communication that have been manifest among writers in this mode. The straightforward transmission of thought is encumbered by a seemingly inescapable tendency to obscurity and indirection. Finally, in the hands of less skilled writers it has produced that disorderly use of words and that talismanic resort to special vocabularies that has made of "dialectics" an excuse for bad thought or a cheap warrant of Marxist identity.

This nondiscursive capacity of mind from which I believe dialectics draws its strength poses a genuine difficulty for Marxism. The difficulty is that the very elements that generate clear communication in ordinary discourse—the relatively clear-cut languages of common sense and logic—are ill-qualified for the presentation of a dialectical view with its focus on the ideas of flux, contradiction, interpretation, etc. The result is a disturbing choice. To use the language of discursive thought (that is, the language built on empirical generalizations and logic) is to use a language that rules out the very ambiguities, Januslike meanings, and metaphorical referents that are the *raisons d'être* for a dialectical view. Dialectics seeks to tap levels of awareness that defy the syntaxes of common sense and logic. To present dialectics as a set of generalizations derived from empirical observation, or as an exercise in logic, is to betray the very purpose for which dialectics exists.

On the other hand, to eschew the language of reasoned discourse confines dialectics to the realm of statements for which no rules of procedure can be found. Dialectical statements may be as valid or important as those of common sense or logic, but their meanings are poorly communicated at the level of what we call rational explanation. From this deep-seated and far-reaching difficulty, I do not believe there is an escape. The perspective of dialectics imparts insights and perceptions to Marxism, but these gifts are, by the nature of the psychic processes to which they owe their existence, resistant to examination by the conventional modes of rational thought.

NOTES

[1] Dialectics in Plato refers mainly to a mode of argumentation that includes refuting an opponent by drawing unacceptable conclusions from his premises. Plato extolls this *"dialectic"* and denigrates "eristic"—what we would call sophistry. See, for example, *The Republic,* Book VII.

[2] Cf. Richard Bernstein, *Praxis and Action* (Philadelphia: University of Pennsylvania Press, 1971), pp. ix, x.

[3] *Capital,* I, Postface to 2nd edition. [All citations from *Capital,* Volume I, refer to the Vintage Books edition, edited by Ben Fowkes, 1977. References to volumes II and III concern the International Publishers edition, 1967.] For a discussion of Hegel's influence on Marx, see Iring Fetscher, *Marx and Marxism* (New York: Herder and Herder, 1971), or for a more controversial view, Lucio Colletti, *From Rousseau to Lenin* (New York: Monthly Review Press, 1972).

[4] *The Phenomenology of the Spirit* (from *The Philosophy of Hegel*) ed. C. J. Friedrich (New York: Modern Library, 1934), pp. 399f.

[5] For an illuminating discussion of Hegelian dialectics, see J.N. Findlay, "The Contemporary Relevance of Hegel" in *Hegel, a Collection of Critical Essays,* ed. Alasdair MacIntyre (New York: Doubleday, 1972). Findlay makes clear that the process of relating an idea and its contradictory opposite often involves our moving to a *higher level of abstraction,* in which the contradictories unite to create a new synthesis—from which, in turn, still larger complexities

can be constructed. I have omitted this dimension of Hegelian thought as unnecessary for our present discussion. I should add that the contradiction e.g. of Master and Servant is by no means confined to their static definitions, but includes their conflictual interactions, which change the nature of both Master and Servant. This is an approach that we will pursue in our next section.

Finally, I should like to call attention to an exploration of the relational aspects of the dialectical view expounded by Richard Norman in "On Dialectic," *Radical Philosophy,* no. 14, Summer 1976. Norman suggests that dialectics can be seen as an effort to resolve the traditional impasse of views that stress matter over mind (materialism) and vice versa (idealism). Dialectics, according to Norman, seeks to resolve this unsatisfactory dualism by beginning with the concept of the *relationship* between mind and matter, a relationship that unites the two in the act of knowing, according the distinctive attributes to each, and reducing neither element to the other. From this relational viewpoint, Norman then examines the ideas of Universals and Particulars and other such famous antinomies, showing how they can be comprehended once we accept the idea of a conceptual contradiction as described above.

[6] Paul Diesing, *Patterns of Discovery in the Social Sciences* (Chicago: Aldine, 1971), p. 212. For an interesting exchange, see Lucio Colletti, "Marxism and the Dialectic," *New Left Review,* Sept–Oct. 1975 and Roy Edgley, "Dialectic: The Contradictions of Colletti," *Critique,* no. 7, Winter 1976–77. See also Sidney Hook, *From Hegel to Marx* (New York: Humanities Press, 1950), pp. 75–76.

[7] *Grundrisse: Foundations of the Critique of Political Economy,* trans. Martin Nicolaus (New York: Penguin Books, 1973), pp. 100–101 (hereafter cited as *Grundrisse*). I have slightly altered paragraphing and punctuation for the sake of clarity.

[8] The most ambitious recent attempt to reduce the dialectical method to a concrete sequence of steps is by Ernest Mandel, *Late Capitalism* (New York: New Left Books, 1975), pp. 16–17, where the method is presented in six stages of regress and reconstitution. Unfortunately, the six steps are described in words that continually beg the question. For instance, the first step (abbreviated) is "Comprehensive appropriation of the empirical material . . . in all its historically relevant detail." But how do we know what is relevant? And is not the decision as to what is and what is not relevant decisive for the path of further analysis? Mandel (or Marx) provide no means of testing this critical step or subsequent steps, so that the use of the dialectical method is not subject to any internal discipline.

[9] Marx, *Theses on Feuerbach, VI;* cf. also *Grundrisse,* p. 265.

[10] *Capital,* III, p. 817. Marx speaks of social inquiry only. Whether there is a Marxist science of nature that differs from conventional bourgeois science is a matter that once agitated Marxists during the years of Stalin's influence, but that has now subsided almost entirely. The question is, of course, related to the relevance of dialectics to nature, a matter discussed earlier herein.

[11] The canons of positivist science are not easy to abbreviate into a footnote. The main tenets of *positivism,* as a philosophic stance, are (1) a concern with empirical matters and an indifference to "metaphysical" ones, and (2) an attempt to draw a strict line between "synthetic" statements which are related to testable, empirical propositions, and "analytic" statements which involve only questions of logic or grammar. (For a clear exposition, see Hollis and Nell, *Rational Economic Man,* [New York: Cambridge University Press, 1975], pp. 4–10). A positivist *science* builds on this philosophical foundation by limiting itself to empirical problems that can be stated in testable hypothetical form. This canon is by no means always observed, but it does at least represent the positivist credo. The main objective of positivist science is accordingly to discover "lawlike" regularities that enable us to make predictive

statements. There is no difference recognized by positivism between the tenets of social and natural science.

Dialectics does not deny the importance or validity of the work of the empirical experimenter, but seeks to expand the conception of the scientist's work beyond the borders of a positivist approach. It would, I think, be bolder in claiming an "explanatory" purpose, and less confident in claiming a predictive one. This seeming paradox is the consequence of the dialectical concern with interpretation and with the continuous "engagement" of the would-be-knower struggling with the elusive appearances and essences of what-is-to-be-known. This does not lead to such clear-cut predictive laws as does a positivist approach. As we shall see in Chapter IV, however, a Marxist perspective can yield powerful prognostications that derive from the discovery of contradictions.

[12] This method is discussed by Marx in "The Method of Political Economy," *Grundrisse*, pp. 100–108, and elucidated in Roman Rosdolsky's superb commentary, *The Making of Marx's Capital* (London: Pluto Press, 1977), pp. 25–55. Briefly, the method parallels the one previously discussed, in proceeding from the abstract to the concrete and then to a larger reconstitution of the abstract. Marx himself uses the method both in structuring the sequence of argument in *Capital* as a whole, and in approaching various subtopics, such as the idea of surplus value and the length of the working day (I, Chapters 9 and 10), or the relation of capital accumulation to its primitive origins (I, Chapters 26–32). It may be that this usage of dialectics is the most significant (although not the only) meaning of the term for Marx himself, but in the larger canon of Marxist work it has become submerged in the other meanings discussed above.

[13] Jean Piaget, *The Construction of Reality in the Child* (New York: Basic Books, 1954).

[14] Cf., Karl Popper, *The Logic of Scientific Discovery* (New York: Basic Books, 1959), p. 32: "My view [is] that every discovery contains an 'irrational element' or a 'creative intuition,' in Bergson's sense. . . ." For a searching treatment of the psychic processes underlying metaphor, see Stanley Burnshaw, *The Seamless Web* (New York: George Braziller, 1970), Chapter 3.

[15] The previously cited example of Mandel (see Note 8 in this chapter) is a case in point. Mandel chastizes the Soviet theorist Smirnov for a definition of method that, in Mandel's words, "fails to take into account the crucial mediation between essence and appearance and thus reduces the problem to a confrontation of theory and empirical matter" (op. cit., p. 17, n. 16). But how is one to know what is appearance and what essence? To this question Mandel offers no answer because, I believe, there *is* no answer, any more than there is an answer to the question: "How should I think creatively?"

[16] Bertell Ollman, *Alienation, Marx's Conception of Man in Capitalist Society* (New York: Cambridge University Press, 1971, 1976), p. 3.

ERNST TOPITSCH

HOW ENLIGHTENED IS "DIALECTICAL REASON"?

Hegel, who first proposed that the dialectical process is not merely sound means of inquiry (à la Plato) but the actual process of reality perfecting itself, thought that the dialectic was a new kind of logic. It supposedly supersedes Aristotle's logic, which rests on the Law of Identity and the view that contradictions are impossible in nature. Marxism embraced this part of Hegel, at least for limited use. But is this not merely a means by which to make it possible to escape all rational criticism of one's theories and policy proposals? If old Aristotle was wrong, can terms such as "freedom," "justice," "truth," and the like retain any integrity? And if they cannot, how can any theory that adheres to dialectical reason be checked for error? How could any follower of such a system be proven wrong? Professor Ernst Topitsch—of the Institute of Philosophy at the University of Graz, Austria, author of Erkenntnis und Illusion *(1979)—argues that in the end one must look with extreme suspicion at claims to higher forms of reason, since they are groundless and usually are disguised claims to power, nothing more.*

> *"Dialectics at bottom is an effort to systematize, or to translate into the realm of manageable, communicable thought, certain unconscious or preconscious modes of apprehending reality, especially social reality. . . . As long as capitalism exists, I do not believe that we will ever be able to declare that Marx was mistaken in his identification of its inner nature."*
>
> ROBERT HEILBRONER,
> *Marxism: For and Against*
>
> *". . . the Dialectical disease. . . ."*
> GOETHE, *sceptically, to* HEGEL (1827)

In his brief but profound essay on the Enlightenment, *"Was ist Aufklärung?"* (1783), Immanuel Kant wrote:

"Enlightenment is man's escape from his self-imposed tutelage. Tutelage means the inability to make use of his intelligence without another's guidance. This tutelage is self-imposed when its cause is not lack of intelligence but lack of the resolution and courage to make use of this intelligence without another's guidance. *Sapere aude!*—Have courage to use your own intelligence—is, therefore, the slogan of the Enlightenment. . . ."

The philosopher continued:

"Laziness and cowardice are the causes why such a large proportion of men, long after nature has absolved them from alien guidance (*naturaliter majorennes*), never-

Reprinted, with permission from the author, from *Encounter*, May 1982.

theless like to remain in tutelage for the rest of their lives; and why it is so easy for others to impose themselves as their guardians. It is so comfortable to be in tutelage. If I have a book that serves me intelligently, a pastor who keeps my conscience for me, a physician who supervises my diet, and so on, I have no need to make any effort myself. I do not need to think, so long as I can pay others will take over the troublesome business for me. . . ."

All too frequently nowadays one hears talk of a "dialectical enlightenment" capable of achieving incomparably more to help man come of age than the "flat" Enlightenment of the 18th century could do. In many places intellectual trends may be observed which, in the name of "critical" or "emancipatory" aims, demand the politicisation of science, i.e. its subordination to the viewpoints of "social relevance." Again and again we hear the assertion that "bourgeois" science is bankrupt and must be replaced by forms of research and thought appropriate to the people, more specifically the working man or the proletariat. These new forms of knowledge are also said to be "higher," to be "dialectical" and completely beyond the power of the mere "abstract intellectual thinking" of middle-class culture to grasp or assess. Such lines of thought not infrequently lay claim to being "new . . . advanced . . . progressive," or some other fashionable term.

In the face of such trust in the ostensibly enlightening and emancipatory function of "Dialectics," however, we must immediately remind ourselves of the massive fact that in wide areas of the world people are being forcibly held in tutelage and prevented from using their intelligence precisely in the name of a "dialectical" ideology. Anyone in these parts of the world who shows too much intellectual independence may be deprived of his freedom and subjected to one or another degrading form of brainwashing. More than that: he actually has to publicly praise this brainwashing (as one of the most famous Chinese philosophers of the present time, the aged Fung Yu-lan, recently did). In these progressive societies the population has fallen far behind the measure of intellectual freedom enjoyed by Kant and his contemporaries under the enlightened royal absolutism of Frederick II or other like-minded monarchs. If the people in these societies conform at least outwardly to the official ideology, they should not be reproached with mental laziness or moral cowardice. Individuals of heroic courage—and they exist there too—cannot be made a universal criterion.

But we can also observe that elsewhere people rush into tutelage of their own free will, without external compulsion, and renounce the use of their intelligence without alien guidance. They cry out for coloured little handbooks that will "serve the movement" and will relieve them of the "troublesome business" of independent thought, or for a proctor who keeps their conscience for them.

One European philosopher, Professor Hermann Lübbe (of the University of Zurich) has aptly described these trends:

"The culture of a new counter-Enlightenment is unmistakably spreading, and the opposite appearance which it manages to produce is slowly becoming transparent. The bearers of the new counter-Enlightenment movement are, of all people, the so-called critical intelligentsia: in the first place the academic intellectuals. We see establishing themselves in our European universities centers of political thinking that boast certain knowledge of the road to salvation, based on a superior disregard for reality, and advanced with a burning moralism and noisy intolerance."

It may seem paradoxical that the dark opponents of Enlightenment in our day should be recruited precisely from the intelligentsia and the current ideological neo-obscurantism should be primarily an academic phenomenon. But this paradox, this apparent paradox, is unfortunately the truth. The sacred texts of the Marxist prophets and fathers of the church are spelled out sentence by sentence with the zeal of the scribes.

"Vetoes on questioning and criticism are propagated: forced professions of faith are instituted: the simple intellectual life in the stabilising confinement of new orthodoxies is gaining in fascination."[1]

But the crown jewel of these endeavours is dialectics, which is supposed to represent a qualitatively higher form of thinking, cognition and knowledge by comparison with mere "bourgeois" science.

But what is this "higher knowledge"? What precisely is this dialectic that is credited with such an enormous capacity for cognitive achievement? The answer to this question is not simple, above all because it has so far proved practically impossible to obtain from the representatives of dialectics anything even approaching a clear statement as to what they mean by it. Thus as much as thirteen years ago Professor Hans Albert commented on the arguments of his debating opponent, Dr. Jürgen Habermas:

"The question of what dialectics really is, what advantages it possesses over other ways of looking at things, has not been answered. We may in any case conjecture that it could conceivably be an unsurpassed instrument for mastery of complex situations, even though the secret of its operation remains hidden. . . ."[2]

Today the question still hangs unanswered in space, and the dialecticians have taken good care not to disclose the secret.

It is no longer possible to escape the impression that a mystery is being protected from the disenchanting assault of scientific criticism. In most cases it is clearly a matter of safeguarding dogmatic convictions from all critical scrutiny by an appeal to an unverifiable, but ostensibly "higher" knowledge. This emerges particularly clearly on the primitive intellectual level of student radicalism. Thus, one German university instructor in Munich has related her recent experience with Marxist students:

"The remark that there are differences between the writings of the young and the older Marx was answered by one of Marx's present-day disciples with the almost despairing cry: 'I'm sure that can be explained with the aid of dialectics!' Dialectics appears here not as a particular method of philosophical thought, but as a magic key that makes it possible to preserve a closed system of theory and practice, a system that remains untouched by modern analytical criticism. This system does not exist in reality: as a theory it is an illusion and as practice a rather grisly deception."

After all this we shall hardly be surprised that the dialecticians are so unwilling to make any detailed statements concerning Dialectics. But this constitutes a fresh difficulty: one has, alas, to try to find out for oneself just what this mysterious and ostensibly superior "method" is all about. In addition one has to be prepared to hear the representatives of Dialectics say—no matter what the outcome of these investigations may be—that the dialectic criticised is not the "true" dialectic. Thus the critic becomes entangled in a kind of game of hare and hedgehog: no matter how sound the arguments he advances against the various thought-forms or ritualistic verbalisms claiming to be "dialectics," his adversary explains with a smile that they have no bearing on "true" dialectics. But no one has ever received (and probably never will receive) an answer to the question as to what "true" dialectics really are.

Now it is quite correct that in the course of the history of ideas from Socrates to Martin Heidegger very different, indeed contradictory things have been meant by this ominous expression. But we are concerned here with that dialectic which since Hegel and Marx has played such an important—and (from the standpoint both of science and of humanity) such a fateful—role in the realm of political ideology and which often lays claim to furnishing "unity of theory and practice." Perhaps it will be productive to start from this claim and the difficulties resulting from it.

The fact is that the search for scientific truth and the politico-ideological leadership of men have different goals in view and employ correspondingly different methods.

Even with animals the procedure of trial-and-error is fundamental to the acquisition and expansion of knowledge, using the word in the widest sense. This was strongly stressed by Konrad Lorenz in his important book *Die Rückseite des Spiegels*.[3] The process involves the pursuit of experiments which may lead either to success or to failure. Successful modes of behaviour are retained and practised; unsuccessful ones are abandoned. This process is developed by humans into a conscious and methodically thought-out construction and testing of ever more demanding hypotheses. In this process, failures are by no means an evil to be avoided at any price, but a practically unavoidable means of discovering the truth. They make possible the elimination of those hypothetical assumptions that do not stand the test. To maintain hypotheses that fail when put to the test is not in the interests of the acquisition of information. Thus the basic attitude here is one of experimental testing, not of dogmatic assertion.

Things are quite different in the domain of politics and ideology, where the aim is to achieve reliable social behaviour and group solidarity. Here the concern is not the truth, but the motivational force of the relevant thought-form, which would be diminished by failure and refutation. This is done by means of various procedures that may be described as "Immunisation Strategies." One of these consists in rendering the thesis immune to inner contradiction. If the pressure of contradictions is frankly admitted, refutation is impossible and any assertions can apparently be maintained against all logical and even empirical objections. This strategy can appear in a psychologically particularly impressive form when an ostensible "logic of contradiction" of this sort is presented as a "higher logic."

But there is also another important difference between the search for truth and social leadership, which has likewise only recently been perceived. Whereas scientific knowledge is *Wertfrei,* devoid of value judgment, ideological leadership systems are rooted in value, since they make assertions regarding the meaning and purpose of the world and of human existence. Here the world order is a profoundly value-related order. It is directed towards the salvation of man, who can derive from it a meaning for his existence, ultimately valid norms for his actions, and possibly also an absolute guarantee for the success of behaviour in conformity with these norms. An evaluating interpretation of the world such as this, which goes back to the dawn of history as known to us and probably way beyond it into prehistoric epochs, cannot, in view of the profound difference between knowing and evaluating, between *erkennen und werten,* maintain its claim to truth; and it has been supplanted by the methods of non-evaluating science. The modern analysis of ideologies has actually demonstrated that such an interpretation of the world order may be supported upon various, indeed any, politico-moral values, which are then "derived" from it with a claim to "absolute" validity in a process of circular reasoning.

Perhaps these brief remarks are sufficient as an introduction, to make clear the politico-ideological function of Dialectics. Even in the early Middle Ages the appeal to a supposed "higher logic" was already an important instrument of authoritarian ecclesiastical domination. One of the outstanding advocates of this doctrine in the 11th century was St Petrus Damiani, who also coined the notorious phrase that Philosophy should be subordinate to Theology as the maid to the mistress—*velut ancilla dominae.* But in order to protect the dogmas even more effectively against all criticism, this flag-bearer of extreme orthodoxy thought up something quite brilliant: ordinary logic is valid only for the realm of creation, but it cannot be applied to God.[4] Thus this defender of the faith became one of the spiritual forefathers of all those who postulate a double logic: a "lower" logic for general use and a "higher" one for more sublime purposes and regions.

At a later date, Hegel too took his place in this tradition. In his view of things, mathematics, formal logic and the exact disciplines are reduced to "mere thinking of the intelligence (*blosses Verstandesdenken*)," above which rises the higher realm of the "thinking of reason (*Vernunftdenkens*)," which is capable of perceiving the world process as a dialectical-teleological drama of self-realisation and becoming self-aware of God. The drama is one of Fall and Salvation. God does not confront the world in a transcendent otherness, but enters into it in a kind of "Fall." He discards the world or alienates himself from it in order, after overcoming this alienation (*Entfremdung*), to return himself, thereby attaining his true perfection and godliness. This produces a kind of circular schema arising from an original, but still imperfect state (Thesis) and leading through a negatively evaluated but necessary interim state (Antithesis) to the perfect end-state (Synthesis). This scheme may also be applied to the historico-social process, where everything held to be undesirable and negative can easily be banished to the second phase (*Antithesis, Entäusserung, Entfremdung*), while what is desirable is ascribed, as "overcoming of alienation," to the third, the redeeming and crowning phase. In this way (as we shall see) both the destruction of Capitalism as well as the annihilation of the Jews in Hitler's gas chambers can be hailed as "the overcoming of alienation (*Aufhebung der Entfremdung*)."

The dialectical and concrete thinking of "Reason" cannot be verified, much less refuted by means of the sciences of "intelligence," which have been denounced as merely abstract and formal. But as to whether, and to what extent, this higher dialectical thinking can be verified by some method—say, with dialectical means—Hegel remained as stubbornly silent as his historically most important pupil, Karl Marx. Precisely the impossibility of verification corresponds to the ultimate purpose of dialectics: i.e. with the help of this "method" to remove dogmatically preconceived convictions from any criticism as to the ostensible content of a "higher knowledge." But the fact that Dialectics is beyond verification also means that it can be manipulated at will. How can there be any means of distinguishing between a correct and an erroneous application of this supposedly higher form of thought? Hence, with its aid, any dogma whatever may be given the appearance of higher or absolute validity.

Incidentally, the practically unlimited capacity of dialectics for just such manipulation had already occurred to Goethe. In a conversation (noted by Eckermann) that took place on 18 October 1827 between the Weimar poet and the Berlin philosopher, the two of them came to speak of the nature of dialectics.

"Basically," said Hegel, "it is merely a regulated, methodical cultivation of the *espirit de contradiction* (*Widerspruchsgeist*), which is an inborn gift in every man and particularly valuable for distinguishing the true from the false."

"Let us hope," interposed Goethe, "that such intellectual arts and skills are not too much misused for the purpose of turning falsehood into truth and truth into falsehood!"

"That does sometimes happen," replied Hegel, "but only with people who are mentally diseased. (*Dergleichen geschieht wohl, aber nur von Leuten die geistig krank sind.*)"[5]

Ever since then it has remained customary for dialecticians of opposing political tendencies to accuse one another of the misuse of the method and even of madness.

How easy it is with this "method" to prove everything and the opposite of everything has not escaped critics. Thus, Wilhelm Windelband wrote of the relationship of Feuerbach's teaching to Hegel's:

"The spectral vagueness with which the concepts of dialectical logic merged with one another made it possible with the same dialectic to construe exactly the opposite of what the master had formulated in it."[6]

In the course of history, this capacity for manipulation has emerged increasingly clearly in the realm of politics. Again and again the empty formulae of Dialectics have proved available for legitimising or combating any politico-moral demand, measure, movement or institution whatsoever. This has been known to 20th-century critics of ideologies for a long time now. For example, Hans Kelsen wrote on this subject in his book *The Political Theory of Bolshevism,* which appeared more than a quarter-of-a-century ago:

"Nothing can show more clearly the futility of the dialectic method than the fact that it enables Hegel to praise the state as a god, and Marx to curse it as a devil; that in applying this method the one affirms that the progressive realisation of reason, by means of war, necessarily leads to the world domination of the German Nation, whereas the other predicts, as the inevitable result of the historic evolution, the establishment, by means of revolution, of the free society of World Communism."

Dialectics can be used for their purposes equally by those in power and by those in opposition. The former glorify the existing system of government as the third (concluding and crowning) stage; the latter dismiss this system as the second (negative) phase that is destined to be overcome, announcing their own assumption of power as a redeeming leap into the third phase. This, too, Hans Kelsen clearly recognised.

"Any historical situation may be interpreted to represent the thesis, or the antithesis, or the synthesis, according to its political evaluation by the interpreter. Thus, the dialectical method may be satisfactory to any political creed. The fact that the dialectical method may be used for any political purpose explains its extraordinary attractiveness, its world-wide spread, comparable only to the success of the Natural-Law doctrine in the eighteenth century."[7]

With the aid of their "higher logic", that is to say Dialectics, the Marxists can talk their way out of all the contradictions that exist so plentifully both within their theory and between this theory and Soviet-Communist reality. The real function of this Dialectic is perhaps most clearly shown by one of Stalin's remarks (in the Political Report of the Central Committee at the 16th Party Congress in 1930):

"We are waiting for the withering away of the state. But at the same time we are for the strengthening of the dictatorship of the proletariat, the strongest and mightiest state power that ever existed. The highest development of state power in preparation of the preconditions for the withering away of state power—that is the Marxist formula. Is that 'contradictory'? Yes it is 'contradictory.' But this contradiction is inherent in life and it completely mirrors the Marxist dialectic."[8]

But this universally available method can also be applied in detail. For example, a dialectical justification was found for the fact that during the War and the post-War period the children of Soviet officials received larger rations than other children.[9] But that is a rather innocuous detail. Alexander Solzhenitsyn, who himself enjoyed an education in Marxist dialectics, reports that this thought-form was used to legitimise the extortion of false confessions by means of torture and the arbitrary sentencing of innocent people. Andrey Vyshinsky, the chief prosecutor in the notorious Moscow Purge Trials (1936–38) and a theoretician of Stalinist justice, especially distinguished himself in this respect.

"Perhaps Vyshinsky, no less than his listeners, needed this ideological comfort at this time. When he cried out from the prosecutor's platform: 'Shoot them all like mad dogs!' he, at least, who was both evil and quick of mind, understood that the accused were innocent. And in all probability he and that master of Marxist dialectics, the defendant Bukharin, devoted themselves with all the greater passion to the dialectical elaboration of the judicial lie: for Bukharin it was too stupid and futile to die if he was altogether innocent (thus he *needed* to find his own guilt!): and for Vyshinsky it was more agreeable to see himself as a logician than as a plain downright scoundrel."[10]

In this way, with the help of dialectical arguments, Marx and his heirs have laid claim to total power, ostensibly to bring about the "true society" of freedom, of plenty, of peace and happiness; but they have never ventured to say anything further about this society and the path towards it. Furthermore, where they have seized power they have subsequently been unable to keep their promises.

This is not only true of Soviet Marxism. Important aspects of the legacy of the Master of Trier have continued to exert an extremely active influence on the various neo-Marxist movements, on the "Frankfurt School" for example. Of course one could not claim that T. W. Adorno or Jürgen Habermas have personally laid any claims to dictatorial power. But one can see in their writings a clear tendency to arrogate to themselves a "higher knowledge" which is supposedly linked with the idea of insight into the nature of "true society" and necessarily inaccessible to the unenlightened gaze of ordinary scientific investigation. As Adorno put it in one of his last writings:

"The idea of scientific truth is inseparable from that of a true society."[11]

What form such a society would take, Adorno never said, neither here nor else-where. Thomas Mann had already drawn his attention to this crucial point (in a letter of 30 October 1952):

"If there were just one positive word in your writings, *Verehrter,* which might provide even only an approximate vision of the true, of the proposed society! This and only this was what was also lacking from *Reflections from damaged life* [the sub-title of Adorno's *Minima Moralia.*] What is and what would be the right society? At one point you quote Lukacs very approvingly, and in general much of what you write seems to point to a purified form of communism. But what will this look like? Russian despotism is misguided, but is communism conceivable without despotism? 'It's not this and it's not that. But what exactly will it be in the end?' says Michael Kramer. . . ."[12]

Adorno still had more than fifteen years to find an answer to this question, but he never gave one; and if he did find one then he took it to the grave with him. The *wahre Gesellschaft* has, therefore, remained a mystery. Confronted with the sensitive and discriminating personality of Adorno, one feels reluc-tant to speak here simply of bluff and swindle. But what is the appropriate word when an author asserts that he has access to special insights which are inextricably connected with knowledge of the "true society," yet stubbornly refuses or is not in a position to give any more precise details about them? In any case what we are dealing with here is the attempt to avoid responsibility for an extravagant claim through the silencing of all critical discussion. In this way a massive dogmatism is concealed under the cover of "critical theory."

In Adorno, Habermas, and other representatives of the "Frankfurt School" such dogmatism is also served by the dialectic, which is also similarly left here in a mystical twilight zone and is never described with even the modicum of clarity which is the precondition for any analytic argument. To illustrate this, here are a few of Habermas' characteristic formulations:

". . . The dialectical concept of the whole . . . transcends . . . the boundaries of formal logic, in the shadowy realm of which the dialectic itself can only appear as a chimera."

"The distinction between system and totality . . . cannot be immediately defined; because in the language of formal logic it would instantly be dissolved, and in the language of dialectics it must be preserved."

"The dialectic cannot legitimate its own value within a dimension it is on the threshold of transcending."[13]

Especially in the final example the intention of the dialectician becomes clear—to dispense with any need to substantiate his propositions to nondialecticians. Such a position has been rightly criticised as "the classic case of an immunisation strategy."[14]

So it has become more and more evident that the dialectician is availing himself of an artificial device in order to declare himself infallible. Thus, according to another critic, a dialectic of this nature is the "attempt ... to free oneself once and for all from often uncomfortable criticism following the principles of a traditional logic by presenting the dialectic itself as a new, higher and at the same time superior logic"; but a "theory that declares itself unassailable thus renders itself uninteresting as the object of empirical and theoretical scientific investigation."[15] In reality the dialectician is not concerned with empirical or theoretical scientific problems; rather, he wants himself and others to believe that he has access to a "higher knowledge" with which extreme claims to power are often combined.

Thus a peculiar light is thrown upon the doctrine of the "non-repressive rational discourse (*herrschaftsfreien rationalen Diskussion*)" which Jürgen Habermas presents as the central condition of democratic and emancipatory thinking. It is just such a discourse which the dialectician necessarily refuses his opponent! Eduard von Hartmann, incidentally, saw that more than a century ago. The agreement on the validity of the proposition of contradiction

"is the *minimum* of common assumption, *without which no argument whatsoever,* at least no modification of falsehood, is *conceivable.* The dialectician, however, smiles at this prejudice which is after all only one of the laws of the formal logic he has thrown overboard, and consequently the essential *minimum* of common assumption is *lacking* [for a rational dispute]."[16]

One can only kneel down in front of a dialectician and humbly accept his revelations, without ever being allowed to entertain the absurd desire to investigate and examine these revelations. It is not by chance that dialectics is the favourite child of mystagogues and dictators.[17]

In order to dispel any misunderstanding I will say once again: it is in no way my intention to impute to Jürgen Habermas any kind of personal craving for political power. But essential aspects of his teaching are supremely well-suited to a strategy which, under cover of "non-repressive and rational discourse" (impossible within the framework of the dialectic), tries to assume total power.

To be sure, the pseudo-scientific character of Dialectics has not remained entirely hidden behind the Iron Curtain.

Particularly in Poland, where a strong tradition of modern scientific theory has existed ever since the inter-War period, a series of courageous thinkers after October 1956 submitted dialectical materialism in general and the dialectic in particular to a positively devastating critique employing the methods of logical analysis. If the representatives of the dialectical scholasticism were able to escape the consequences of their defeat under the protection of Party power, they had at least to make admissions over crucial points that amounted to the abandonment of central dogmas. A precise account of these events exists which, at its high points, is a positive epic of the self-assertion of scientific objectivity against the power of an institutionalised ideology.[18]

Even in the Soviet Union, at the height of the "Thaw", a professor of mathematical logic at Moscow University was able to request the abolition of the Chair for Dialectical Philosophy on the grounds that it was not concerned with any science worth taking seriously. Naturally the chair was not abolished; but the whole episode shows what, for a time, was possible even in Moscow.[19]

Alongside the path that runs from Hegel via Marx to Stalin, however, there is another one, which since 1945 has been covered over in the German Federal Republic by an impenetrable tabu—the path that leads from Hegel to Hitler.

Certainly, we cannot hold the Swabian thinker (born in Stuttgart in 1770) directly responsible for the total National Socialist regime. The totalitarian state, as a specific phenomenon of the 20th century, lay beyond his vision. But the deeper we penetrate into the matter the clearer becomes the extent to which, in my view, Hegel's dialectical ideology of the *Machtstaat* worked its way through Bismarck's empire into the thought-processes of the "Nationalist opposition " to the Weimar Republic.[20]

Soon after the First World War eminent University teachers and influential academics began combating the liberal democracy of the Weimar Republic, in the name of Hegel's political metaphysics in general and of Dialectics in particular, calling down contempt on human rights, cleverly justifying anti-Semitism, and demanding an authoritarian state based on power, militarism and leadership as the "abolition (*Aufhebung*) of alienation."

When this state became a reality in 1933 it was decked out with all the crown jewels of this metaphysics. How far this process went may be demonstrated by a few sentences from an essay, "Idealism as a Basis for the Philosophy of the State", published by Julius Binder, one of the leading neo-Hegelian philosophers of law, in 1933:

"We must understand the state as a reality of the spirit and can then understand it as a reality of freedom. . . . It is the will of the people, who decide upon their life-form, their existence and their reality for themselves and to this extent, as self-determining will, it is an existence of free will. As this free will the state is a reality of freedom, and to this extent a reality of morality."

From these general socio-metaphysical observations the author drew very concrete political conclusions.

"With these remarks I have merely pursued the purpose of bringing the state we call the '*Third Reich*' closer to people's understanding, of showing them that it is not a monstrosity to be seen as mere force ruling over a herd of people who have lost their freedom, but that in spite of its authority, with which it demands for itself the totality of the life of its citizens, it is not unfreedom and compulsion, but freedom made real."[21]

Subsequently, not merely the rule of terror within, but also the racial laws, the policy of military expansion, and the claim of European hegemony were justified with Hegelian arguments. Even in 1944 one author was still able to write:

"But here too the dialectic of the concrete and universal points into the future. . . . History does not represent the existence of nations merely side by side or one after the other; these nations also stand in a dialectically conceived order. Thus, just as in the concrete concept one motive force is pre-eminent, so Hegel recognises nations which, on the basis of 'geographical and anthropological existence', determine their epoch. Hegel speaks only of the domination of this nation, and there can be no doubt that for his period of the Germanic epoch he had the German people in mind. . . . This development is already outlined in reality and science in the European order as a system of leadership under the ordering might of the *Reich*."[22]

The intellectual justification of anti-Semitism constitutes a particularly dark chapter. For example, as early as 1926 Max Wundt, a leading historian of philosophy, bestowed metaphysical consecration on a positively furious hatred of the Jews by means of the idealist dialectic. The Jews are portrayed here as the furthermost extreme of alienation, indeed as the very force of destruction. They are "the dark power of negation that kills what it grasps. Whoever yields to them is given over to death. . . ." Finally, Wundt expressly equated them with the Devil. Because, above all since the Reformation, preservation of the spirit of Christian idealism has been entrusted to the Germans,

"therefore the work of the Devil is particularly active among them, seeking to inhibit and suppress the effectiveness of the spirit of Christ. The Jews, who even in the Bible are called the children of Satan, are the agents of this work of disintegration."[23]

Unmistakable links run from such utterances, which were published long before the Nazi seizure of power, to what was later to become a terrible reality. Perhaps the only reason a dialectical justification was not advanced for the "Final Solution" was because, as a state secret, it was removed from public discussion. It would have been easy enough to construct such a justification from the statements about the Jews quoted above and others like them—for instance, that Jewry, as something "in itself dead" must be rendered literally dead, or that only out of "the death of Death" can life come into being. In this way even what happened in Auschwitz could have been glorified as the "overcoming of alienation."

The objection may be raisesd that all these are merely late corruptions or per-versions of what were originally deep thoughts and noble motives. But pre-cisely the most recent studies of Hegel and Marx have shown how murky were the very sources from which political Dialectics welled forth.

Thus, in the foreword to his important edition of Hegel's lectures on the philosophy of law, Karl-Heinz Ilting has cast much light on the conditions under which the printed version of the *Rechtsphilosophie* (*Philosophy of Law*) of 1820 came into being, the book upon which, above all, the ideology of the *Machtstaat* advanced by the Hegelian "Right" is supported.[24] The facts brought out by Ilting are very revealing, but the interpretation to be put upon them is different from Ilting's.

Hegel was not—as Ilting would have us believe—"liberal" or even "progressive." Nor was he really a reactionary. He was an opportunist. It is true that the philosopher had developed his ideology of the power state even while still young (as Kiesewetter also points out), but he always had a keen nose for the political situation; and when he was appointed to Berlin, he greatly modified his views to fit in with the reformist trend still dominant at that time.

But the political wind changed direction. Reaction got hold of the reins, and Hegel noted with consternation that he had mounted the wrong horse and entered a danger zone. Now, he could have tried to combine the preserva-tion of his material existence with the preservation of his dignity and integrity as a man and a thinker. Kant did this in his clash with the reactionary minister Wöllner; and not a few of the Berlin professors who found themselves in equal peril did so too. But Hegel not merely displayed in another connection a beha-viour which Schleiermacher branded as "squalid," but sought in a mixture of panic and opportunism to curry favour with the new masters philosophically as well. It was a fortunate coincidence that he was just preparing his *Rechtsphi-losophie* for the press. The philosopher quickly revised his manuscript and caused the dialectical rhythm of the self-realisation of the divine idea in the domain of the state to run in a way that harmonised very closely with the new dominant trends of thought. The publication of the resulting text saved him in relation to the authorities; but the reception of the book by critics and pub-lic was icy. Hegel found himself exposed as an opportunist.

This reproach was made against him in a more or less polite form from many at the time. Jakob Friedrich Fries expressed himself particularly bluntly.

"Hegel's metaphysical mushroom did not grow in the gardens of science, but on the dung heap of sycophancy. Up to 1813 his metaphysic bowed to the French, then it became royal Wurtembergian, and now it kisses Herr von Kamptz's horsewhip."

The *Hermes* reviewer was scarcely less harsh in branding the Swabian philoso-pher as the prototype of political "occasionalism."

Such a philosophy can, of course, accommodate itself to whatever happens to be the order of the day. If liberal principles prevail in the world, this philosophy will teach them. If despotism has the upper hand, the philosophy must preach despotism. Enough, philosophers are those people who never get on bad terms with the present, who always declare to be right whatever can be put into effect and curse those who believe things could and should be different."

Hegel later made a timid attempt to counteract this devastating impression by somewhat more liberal utterances. But the *Rechtsphilosophie* in the reactionary form of its printed version of 1820 became a standard work of the anti-liberal and anti-democratic theory of the state, and it was praised as such by Carl Schmitt in 1934. Schmitt invoked Hegel as an important ancestor of the conception of the state then currently desired in the German *Reich*. In his essay "On the Three Kinds of Juridical Thinking" he openly denied his earlier teachings and advocated, with express reference to Hegel, a "thinking based on concrete order", which was to justify the system of government already established by the National Socialists. In this connection he wrote:

"All these currents and trends of the German resistance [against the liberal 'ideas of 1789'] achieved their systematic summation in Hegel's philosophy of law and the state. In this philosophy, thinking based on concrete order comes to life with undiluted vigour."[25]

All this does not merely show up Hegel's character in a somewhat unfavourable light, but also proves that the much vaunted dialectical method was from the outset well suited—and actually employed—deceitfully to give the appearance of higher, indeed absolute, truth and validity to any political doctrines and positions chosen at a given moment for opportunist reasons. So it is that Dialectics even envelops opportunism and squalid self-seeking with the cosmic mantle of the divine idea.

Things are somewhat different, but scarcely better, with Marx. Recent studies[26] have raised basic doubts regarding the legend of the young Marx's humanism, if they have not refuted it altogether. It would appear that the lawyer's son from Trier showed at an early age a strong conviction of his Messianic mission and Caesarian claims to power, mingled with uncontrollable destructive appetites.

Scarcely any character trait of the revolutionary prophet has been so unanimously noted by observers of the most varied political complexions as his unrestrained will to power, his *Machtwille*. Particularly revealing in this connection is the letter from Lieutenant Techow, which has received far too little attention by students of Marxist literature up to now. On account of his participation in the revolution of 1848 this officer had been forced to emigrate and had come into contact with Marx. His account is written calmly and without animosity; in many places it displays unconcealed admiration; at others a note almost of regret is discernible.

During their conversation, Marx—probably urged on by his interlocutor—drank freely of strong wine and was finally *"vollständig besoffen* (completely drunk)."

"This", writes Techow, "was very welcome to me, for he became franker than he probably would have been otherwise. I gained certainty about many things that otherwise would have remained conjecture. Despite his condition, he dominated the conversation right to the end.

"He made on me an impression not only of a rare mental superiority, but also of an important personality. If he had as much heart as intelligence, as much love as hate, I would go through fire for him, despite the fact that he did not merely hint at his complete contempt for me on several occasions, but in the end came right out with it. He is the first and only one among us whom I would trust to rule, whom I would trust even under great circumstances not to lapse into pettiness.

"For the sake of our cause, I regret that this man does not have a noble heart to place at our disposal along with his outstanding mind. But I am convinced that the most dangerous personal ambition has eaten up everything good in him. He laughs at the fools who repeat his proletarian catechism after him, as well as at the Communists à la Willich or at the bourgeoisie. The only people he respects are the aristocrats, the genuine ones and those who are aristocrats consciously. In order to force them out of power he needs a strength such as he finds only in the proletarians; that is why he has modelled his system for them.

"Despite all his assurances to the contrary, perhaps precisely because of them, I have gained the impression that his personal domination is the aim of all his activities. E[ngels] and all his old associates, in spite of many attractive talents, are far below and behind him, and if they ever dare to forget this he puts them in their place with an effrontery worthy of a Napoleon."[27]

This acute characterisation is confirmed by the testimony of countless other authors. Communists and Anarchists like Moses Hess and Michael Bakunin have complained bitterly of Marx's brutally authoritarian and absolutely intolerant attitude that demanded total subservience, and from the other end of the spectrum, so to speak, comes corroboration in the secret report of a police agent dated 1853:

"M. is jealous of his authority as head of the Party; he is vengeful and implacable towards his political rivals and opponents; he does not rest until he has brought them low; his dominant characteristic is a boundless ambition and desire for domination. In spite of the Communist equality he claims to be aiming for, he is the absolute ruler of his Party; it is true that he does everything himself, but he is also the only one to give orders and he brooks no contradiction."[28]

This claim to total power played at least an essential part in determining the revolutionary thinker's view of history and society.[29]

Marx purloined the dialectical schema of self-deification from Hegel and transformed it to suit his own purposes. It is not Hegel's God who renders himself finite or "alienates himself" into the world, in order (along the path through nature and the finite spirit) finally to return to himself; it is rather working humanity that becomes alienated and reified in relation to the world of the products of its labour and comes under their power. This alienation reaches its extreme degree in the proletariat that has been totally deprived of its humanity and turned into a commodity. Then Marx appears—he knows the secret of history, recognises its dialectical laws, and thereby opens to mankind the way *via* Revolution to the elimination of Alienation and hence to the recovery of its true humanity.

In the early days, Eduard Bernstein had already perceived that this was a purely *a priori* construction. Marx, as it were, arranges the whole of human history as a gigantic display around his own person, which thereby acquires the key position of the Paraclete, the illuminator and the redeemer. At the same time, the dialectical laws of history at once lend him the highest moral justification and guarantee him ultimate success.

To be sure, Marx partially filled this construction with empirical material. But at precisely the decisive points he failed to make even a serious attempt to transform it into an empirically verifiable theory, indeed he consciously or unconsciously avoided any such attempt. On the structure of the Socialist society of the future lived in by "man no longer alienated," and on the path that would lead to it, he remained almost completely silent. When Lenin, as a victorious revolutionary, came up against difficulties, he consulted Marx's writings for advice on what to do next. But he sought in vain. Everything further was improvisation.[30]

The very cornerstone of the whole conception, however, is the question of how the socio-economic dialectic is to bring about *die Aufhebung der Entfremdung.* If Marx dodges precisely this point it is bound to suggest that in reality he was not so very concerned about the overcoming of alienation. What we know about his intellectual and political development makes it seem almost certain that, for the creator of historical materialism, the idea of human liberation and human happiness was essentially a pseudo-ethical disguise for immoderate claims to domination and destructive appetites; and that he regarded the proletariat—which in any case he despised—as simply an instrument of his will to power, much as Napoleon regarded his grand armies.[31]

Thus even the young Marx's conception of history and society was chiefly (if not exclusively) *eine Herrschaftsideologie,* an ideology of mastery. Its connections with the later reality of totalitarian Marxism are far closer than is generally assumed on the liberal-left today. Even many Marxist thinkers cannot shut their eyes to this insight. Thus the Yugoslav Svetozar Stojanovic writes:

"It looks as though in future we must apply the theory of the Unconscious more extensively to revolutionary groups. The phenomena of the inversion of ends and means arouse the suspicion that from the beginning different subconscious ends underlay the conscious ends. In such cases the conscious ends, whose axis was the classless and stateless society, serve to cloak the subconscious wish for one's own absolute power."[32]

Certainly, Karl Marx's ideology of mastery achieved massive effectiveness in political reality only through the Bolshevik Revolution, the establishment of a totalitarian bureaucratic state, and its combination with the imperial demands of a "Third Rome." Certainly, terror under Stalin surpassed even that under Lenin, and at this point the Marxist intellectual tradition was reduced to an unprecedentedly primitive level and became encrusted with Byzantine rigidity. But the the facts do not allow the Georgian to be made a scapegoat and held solely responsible for the "perversion" of Marxism from a gospel of emancipation to totalitarian repression. Behind the "emancipationist" disguise, even with Marx himself, an ideology of domination was the concealed guiding force.

Thus historical observation and theoretical analysis are in accord. The ostensibly "higher" logic or process of God's self-realisation turns out to be an imposing and reverence-inducing façade, which generally conceals certain real and thoroughly unsublime motives. Behind the Dialectic that asserts a claim to divinity there may lurk a lust for power and a delight in destruction—or the cowardice and the opportunism of those anxious to supply the power-holders of the moment with a social metaphysics in keeping with their needs or wishes.

I am aware that nowadays hardly anyone speaks of these things, in spite of the truly shattering experiences we have been through with Dialectics, particularly in the political sphere, during the last century-and-a-half and more; we still need an open discussion of this whole disastrous complex of facts. The German universities (of the "bourgeois restoration" since 1945) have done little or nothing to think through what has been experienced and suffered during the past years and to render it intellectually fruitful. The same forms of thought under whose sign important segments of the German cultured classes prepared the way for National Socialism, collaborated with it, or capitulated before it are still put on display—as if nothing had happened—as the crown jewels of speculative profundity to be approached only with the deepest reverence. It never occurred to anyone to test the scientific stability of these thought-forms, and I can assure the reader that it would have been high treason to unfold their *chronique scandaleuse,* as I have attempted here.

The mandarins of German post-War philosophy—from the pastoral representatives of a restorational, semi-theological hermeneutics to the Frankfurt armchair-Marxists—were so dependent upon Hegel's patrimony that a radical disclosure that went to the roots of these facts was bound to represent a serious threat to their own position.[33] Full of fear and bad conscience, they actually found themselves, by remaining silent and glossing over what happened, at least indirectly making common cause with the former dialectical heralds of the Third Reich.

This finally led to what can without exaggeration be described as *the* scandal of the history of ideas in post-War Germany. While diligent historical investigation cast light on the other ideological sources and entanglements of

National Socialism, bringing into view even such obscure figures as the racial phantast Jörg Lanz von Liebenfels, the vast complex of "Hegel and the Third Reich" remained almost entirely wrapped in protective darkness. This made it possible for Dialectics to continue to be lauded as the palladium of a democratic, emancipationist and truly enlightened way of thought and action. For those aware of the texts and contexts, of course, the supposed "dialectical enlightenment" is a mere illusion, if not worse.

Henceforth the issue is enlightenment *about* dialectics, and it is high time to put an end to the intellectual card-sharping. For once again we have to fight with our backs to the wall against an attempt to deprive us of our intellectual and political independence by means of long-outdated forms of thought. To resist this attempt is, in my view, an act of real enlightenment and emancipation.

NOTES

[1] Hermann Lübbe, in *Endstation Terror* (Seewald Verlag, 1978). See also, for a liberal and enlightened warning about similar developments on the British scene, Professor Julius Gould's study, *The Attack on Higher Education* (1977). For a recently published American evaluation: George Friedman, *The Political Philosophy of the Frankfurt School* (Cornell University Press, 1981).

[2] Hans Albert, *Im Rücken des Positivimus?*, reprinted in the omnibus volume *Der Positivismusstreit in der deutschen Soziologie* (Neuwied-Berlin, 1969), p. 304

[3] Konrad Lorenz, *Die Rückseite des Spiegels: Versuch einer Naturgeschichte des menschlichen Erkennen* (Munich, 1973); see also Karl Popper, *Objective Knowledge: an Evolutionary Approach* (1972), and his essay "On the Sources of Knowledge and Ignorance" in ENCOUNTER (September 1962).

[4] Etienne Gilson and Ph. Boehner, *Christliche Philosophie* (Paderborn, 1954), pp. 290.

[5] See the Everyman edition of *Conversations of Goethe* (tr. Oxenford), p. 244.

[6] Wilhelm Windelband, *Die Geschichte der neueren Philosophie.* Vol. II (Leipzig, 1911), p. 393.

[7] Hans Kelsen, *The Political Theory of Bolshevism* (1948), p. 19.

[8] Joseph Stalin, *Werke,* Vol. XII (East Berlin, 1954), p. 323.

[9] S. Ossowski, *Die Klassenstruktur im sozialen Bewusstsein* (Berlin, 1962), p. 231.

[10] Alexander Solzhenitsyn, *The Gulag Archipelago* (1974), p. 101.

[11] Th. W. Adorno in *Der Positivismus-Streit...*, p. 36.

[12] Thomas Mann, *Briefe 1948–1955* (Frankfurt, 1965), p. 276.

[13] Jürgen Habermas in *Der Positivismus-Streit...*, pp. 155, 156, 169.

[14] R. Simon-Schaefer, *Dialektik: Kritik eines Wortgebrauchs* (1973), p. 12.

[15] G. Patzig, "Hegel's Dialectic and Lukasiewicz's Three-Valued Logic" in *History and the Past,* commemorative essays for R. Wittram (Göttingen, 1973), pp. 443–49.

[16] E. V. Hartmann, *Über die dialektische Methode* (Berlin, 1868; Darmstadt, 1963), p. 39.

[17] A very instructive example of the way in which dialectics can be politically manipulated is to be found in Ernst Fischer's book, *Erinnerungen und Reflexionen* (Hamburg 1969), p. 360. Here Fischer relates that he reminded the Director of the Lenin School in Moscow of a promise she had not kept.

"Not without charm, she laughed. 'But surely you're familiar with the laws of dialectics?' 'What has dialectics got to do with not keeping a promise?'

'Oh, you're a poor dialectician. Everything depends on space and time. On reciprocal action. Several months have passed. At that time what I said corresponded to the situation. Since then the situation has changed. What was correct then is no longer correct today. Can't you understand that?'

'No.'

'I'm afraid you'll have difficulties in the future if you don't understand dialectical reciprocal action.' She looked at me mockingly, kindly and unsettling."

[18] Z. A. Jordan, *Philosophy and Ideology: The Development of Philosophy and Marxism in Poland since the Second World War* (Dordrecht, 1963).

[19] K. Marko, *Sowjethistoriker zwischen Ideologie und Wissenschaft* (Cologne, 1964), pp. 84 ff.

[20] I pointed out the facts in my essay *"Die Sozialphilosophie Hegels als Heilslehre und Herrschafts ideologie (Hegel's Social Philosophy as a Doctrine of Salvation and an Ideology of Domination"*), 1967; and my student Hubert Kiesewetter has since clarified this development in detail in a comprehensive study, *Von Hegel zu Hitler* (Hamburg, 1974).

[21] Julius Binder, "Der Idealismus als Grundlage der Staatsphilosophie", *Zeitschrift fur Deutsche Kulturphilosophie I* (1935), pp. 155 ff.

[22] W. Schmidt, *Hegel und die Idee der Volksordnung* (Leipzig, 1944), p. 158.

[23] Max Wundt, *Deutsche Weltanschauung* (Munich, 1926), pp. 191–194.

[24] K. H. Ilting (ed.), *G. W. F. Hegel, Vorlesungen über Rechtsphilosophie 1818–1831* (Stuttgart, 1973), Vol. I.

[25] Carl Schmitt, *Über die drei Arten des rechstwissenschaftlichen Denkens* (Hamburg, 1934), p. 45.

[26] Arnold Kunzli, *Karl Marx: eine Psychographie* (Vienna, 1966); Ernest Kux, *Die revolutionäre Konfession* (Zurich, 1967); Robert Payne, *Marx* (London, 1968); Fritz J. Raddatz, *Karl Marx* (Hamburg, 1976; London, 1979).

[27] The letter was printed in the now inaccessible work by K. Vogt, *Mein Prozess gegen die Allgemeine Zeitung* (Geneva, published by the author, 1859). It is reproduced in H. M. Enzensberger (ed.), *Gespräche mit Marx und Engels* (Frankfurt, 1973), Vol. I, pp. 179 ff.

[28] Quoted in Werner Sombart, *Der proletarische Sozialismus* ("Marxismus"), Vol. I (Jena, 1924), p. 63.

[29] I have developed and explained this interpretation of Marx in my paperback, Ernst Topitsch, *Gottwerdung und Revolution* (Munich, 1973), pp. 177 ff.

[30] Cf. Robert Waelder, *Fortschritt und Revolution* (Stuttgart, 1970), p. 274, and also Melvin J. Lasky, *Utopia and Revolution* (London, 1977).

[31] Arnold Kunzli in his "psychography" (pp. 645 ff., note 23) points out that "in his lifelong correspondence with Engels, Marx contemptuously referred to the workers as *Knoten, Straubinger, eine Bande von Eseln* (hooligans, grousers, a bunch of donkeys) and so on, which may only be the reverse side of his mythologisation. But Marx never escaped from the antithetical attitude towards the proletariat as the chosen people and a gang of hooligans. . . ."

[32] Svetozar Stojanovic, *Kritik und Zukunft des Sozialismus* (Munich, 1970), p. 182.

[33] See also Anthony Quinton's essay in ENCOUNTER (October 1974), "Critical Theory: On 'the Frankfurt School.' "

part TWO

HUMAN NATURE AND HUMAN EMANCIPATION

For an individualist, human beings have a basic need for political liberty, the freedom from the intrusion of others into their lives and property. Once this is secured, the individual may proceed to the task of emancipation, of becoming a mature, self-fulfilled human being. Except for some severely impaired individuals, this task is in everyone's power—indeed, even the issue of poverty versus riches rests, in the end, on this question of individual self-development.

For the communist, however, the economic circumstances of a person's life are extremely limiting. Not until these barriers have been overcome will there be a realistic chance for self-expression. Human beings can only be truly fulfilled when the constraints imposed by being without property and exploited no longer plague the better part of humanity. Alienation is a condition of life for the majority of humanity simply as a matter of the developmental requirements of the human species. Once the development has reached its completion, alienation will no longer obtain and human beings will be truly free. Here the contrasting conceptions of human nature underlying capitalism and communism can be seen to emerge.

Bhikhu Parekh

MARX'S THEORY OF MAN

One of Marxian communism's main feats is to have advanced an idea of human nature that would appear to reject individualism. The doctrine of individualism affirms the autonomy of the individual, the basic selfishness of every member of society, the tendency of everyone to seek his or her own advantage in virtually all areas of social relations. Marxian communism proposes a different idea, one that identifies human nature as fundamentally—albeit not just yet, in the current phase of human history—social. The idea of the whole man, à la Marx, denies the value of the economic division of labor, of the central role of the profit motive, and of other features of capitalism, as Marx understands that system. In its place it forecasts the emergence of the fully emancipated person, one who will seek his or her fulfillment through the fulfillment of all members of society. Professor Bhikhu Parekh outlines the Marxian idea of man. This will enable us to begin with what to Marx and to communists following Marx is most basic in the study of human community life.

Marx's theory of man can be best seen as an attempt to integrate the radical humanism of Fichte and Hegel on the one hand, and the naturalism of Feuerbach on the other. Fichte and Hegel were right, Marx thought, to place man in the centre of the universe and to see history as a process of man's self-creation. Following Feuerbach, however, he objected to their attempt to identify man with his consciousness and to explain human history in terms of its independent dialectical movement. It is man who possesses consciousness and not the other way round, and therefore not human self-consciousness and Absolute Spirit but the sensuous, empirical man which ought to be made the explanatory principle of history. Since Fichte and Hegel took a "topsy-turvy," "Idealistic" and "speculative" view of man their account of human history remained abstract and false. Further, since they denied the reality of nature, human freedom, which they so cherished, lacked a medium of objectification and therefore remained illusory and unreal. Marx thought that Feuerbach's naturalism avoided the Idealist mistake and was more satisfactory. It acknowledged man's essentially sensuous nature, recognised his membership of the natural world, and stressed the empirical basis of all human knowledge. However Feuerbach's naturalism was static and unhistorical, and did not recognise that both nature and man were constantly evolving. It took a passive and "contemplative" view of man and did not stress man's power to create both himself and nature. It remained unable to explain human history. A view of man was therefore needed, Marx seems to have thought, that satisfied two conditions. First, it

Reprinted, with permission, from Bhikhu Parekh, ed., *The Concept of Socialism* (New York: Holmes & Meier Publishers, Inc.). Copyright © 1975 by Bhikhu Parekh.

must combine the valid humanistic insights of Fichte and Hegel and the naturalistic and empirical orientation of Feuerbach. Second, it must combine them not mechanically but dialectically; that is, it must not combine them in the "insipid" (Marx's favourite expression) spirit of "Bourgeois" compromise but in a truly dialectical manner. What Marx meant was that it must be a view of man in which humanism and naturalism interpenetrate, so that it is not merely humanistic *and* naturalistic but humanistic in its naturalism and naturalistic in its humanism. Marx set about to develop such a view.

To anticipate, Marx viewed man basically as a dialectical unity of certain powers or qualities that he shares with other beings in the universe, and certain others that are unique to him. In Marx's own language, man is a dialectical unity of his natural and human being or essence. For analytical convenience we shall therefore divide this paper into four sections. In the first two, we shall examine man's natural and human being respectively. In the third section we shall outline the nature of their dialectical integration, and in the fourth, we shall sketch the "fully" developed human being as he emerges from the preceding discussion.

MAN AS A NATURAL BEING

Marx maintains that sense perception is the sole criterion of reality. Only what is "visible to senses," "observable, visible and therefore beyond all doubt" is real and can be said to exist.[1] Marx calls an object of sense a sensuous or natural being. A sensuous or natural being alone is therefore "real." A non-natural object, an object that is not an object of sense, is "an imaginary being, a being of abstraction" and therefore "a non-being." God, angels and ghosts are by definition non-natural beings and therefore do not exist and are human fantasies. Natural beings are for Marx the sole constituents of the universe.

In places, Marx inquires if all natural beings can be reduced to some underlying ultimate reality of which there are so many diverse forms, and concludes that matter is such an ultimate reality. However, for the most part Marx found the answer and indeed the inquiry itself pointless and uninteresting. Matter was, he thought, an unreal abstraction, never to be encountered in human experience. We see trees, stars, fruits, animals, humans, etc. but never matter as such. Again, to say that everything is matter, Marx thought, was to stress an abstract similarity between vastly different objects at the expense of their differences which alone made them the sort of object they are. He also seems to have thought that the preoccupation with the so-called material substratum tended to be the "one-sided" "mechanical and mathematical" view of matter dominant in Hobbes and others, depriving matter of "impulse, vital life spirit" and "sensuousness."[2] As the term "materialism" has a specific meaning in philosophical circles to-day and can more properly be ascribed to Engels's philosophy, Marx's ontology might be better described as naturalistic rather than materialistic.[3]

Natural beings are basically of three kinds, Marx suggests. First, there are inanimate natural beings, such as the sun, stars, planets, mountains and rivers, that have neither life nor consciousness. Second, there are natural beings that have life but not consciousness. Plants, trees, etc. belong to this category of "living natural beings." Finally, there are natural beings that have both life and consciousness. Animals and humans fall within this category of "conscious natural beings." Marx's use of the term "natural being" is not consistent. Sometimes he refers to all three kinds of being as natural beings; sometimes he confines the term to the last two. Sometimes, again, he calls the last two "living natural beings" and by implication the first, non-living natural beings.

Every natural being, Marx argues, is a specific and determinate being, and therefore has a definite character or nature which constitutes its identify or essence. Marx defines the character of a natural being in terms of the concepts of power *(Kraft)* and need *(Bedürfnis)* and contends that every natural being has powers and needs. Marx does not define powers but seems to use the term to mean a faculty or ability to act and to produce certain results or consequences. Thus the plant has power to grow, the sun has power to help it grow, and man has power to see, to think, to smell, to eat, etc.[4] Marx takes a vitalist, Aristotelian view of nature and contends that every natural being *strives* to realise its powers. He therefore views "powers" as not merely capacities but "impulses," and argues that every power of a natural being has an inherent dynamism. It *strives* to realise itself, and suffers when it is frustrated. For Marx to say that X possesses a power to do Y is to say not merely that he can do Y but also that he *strives* to do Y. A being with eyes not only can see but wants to, has an urge to see, and feels frustrated when blinded or otherwise prevented from seeing. Need, as Marx understands it, corresponds to power and refers to the conditions a natural being must have to express and realise its powers. Once a natural being's actual and potential powers are identified, that is, powers it at present possesses and is in principle capable of acquiring, we can determine its needs. Powers of a natural being are objectively identifiable, and so therefore are its needs.

Marx explains the point by an example. A plant has the power or "faculty" of growth, of acquiring leaves and flowers. Not only can it become a fully fledged plant in all its beauty but also *strives* to become one. When it grows into a fully developed plant, it manifests all its powers, and can be said to have realised its being, its essence. A plant, however, cannot develop its powers without the help of the sun, the soil, water, etc. These objects are required by its very nature or being, and therefore constitute its needs. Without them its powers remain barren possibilities, and its being remains unactualised and eventually withers away. Even as a plant has the power of growth and needs the sun, the sun too has powers and needs appropriate objects. The sun has the power to confer life on living things, the plant included, and this power remains unactualised in the absence of the plant. The sun therefore *needs* the plant in order to actualise its being. To talk of the sun *needing* the plant is obviously odd. While the vitalist view of nature is *prima facie* plausible with respect to organic nature, it makes little sense when applied to inorganic nature. One can interpret a plant's growth in terms of actualisation of its possibilities and say that it suffers when thwarted; but it is difficult to take such a view of the sun, which cannot be said to be *striving* to actualise its potentialities or to *suffer* in the absence of plants. Marx seems aware of this and for the most part confines the vitalist view to organic nature.

To continue with our example: the plant needs the sun, and the sun needs the plant. They are thus interdependent. Each, further, needs other objects as well. The plant needs not only the sun but also soil and water, and likewise the sun needs not only the plant but also soil, flowers, animals, etc. by means of which to demonstrate its powers. Nature, for Marx, is an interlocking system of interdependence, and each natural being is involved in a series of complex and interlocking patterns of relationships with other natural beings.

Since the being of a natural being can be actualised only with the help of objects existing outside it, we can say that the essence of each natural being resides outside itself.[5] In isolation from external objects, it not only cannot develop its powers but cannot even exist. Every natural being is therefore a relational being, and its nature *is* its relationship to external objects. We know a natural being through its relationship to external objects and have no other privileged access to it. Since the nature of a natural being thus lies outside itself, every natural being is an objective being, a being that cannot exist without the presence of natural objects outside it. A non-objective being, a being that is totally self-sufficient, is a non-natural being, and therefore a non-being, a fantasy. Marx concludes that every natural being, by its very nature, is first an objective being, second, a relational being, third, a dependent being, fourth, a needy being, and, fifth, a suffering being, who can suffer when the objects required by its very nature are not available.

Animals can be dealt with in a few words since they are not central to our discussion and are covered by what we shall later say about man. Like any other natural being, the animal is a specific and determinate type of being. It therefore possesses certain definite powers and needs and has its own distinctive ways of relating to external objects. It is more complex and differentiated than a plant but less developed than a man, and therefore has more powers and needs than a plant but less than those of a man. The animal has a definite physiological structure and distinctive sense organs, each of which in turn has a determinate power, a determinate mode of gratification, and distinctive needs. It has eyes and therefore power to see, and needs external objects over which to exercise this power. Similarly it has nose, ears and other sense organs and therefore appropriate powers and needs. As a living being, the animal further has "natural powers of life"—energy, vitality, the power to be active,—and therefore needs the scope to be active, "to hunt, to roam" and to engage in varied types of activity. The animal has the power to recognise other animals of its species, and finds pleasure in their company, and therefore has "the need of companionship." Since the animal as we shall see later, lacks the capacity for consciousness, it cannot and does not possess intellectual powers and therefore its needs are extremely limited. The animal's being embodies a limited range of powers and capacities, and these determine its needs and the range and quality of its relationships.

Qua natural being man is not substantially different from the animal. He too is "a living, real, sensuous, object being" endowed with wants, drives, faculties and powers that can be gratified only through the necessary existence of external objects. Like any other natural being he tries to realise himself, that is, to appropriate objects related to his powers and tendencies. Marx does not draw up a list of these powers and tendencies and gives only a general indication of what they are. Like an animal, he has several sense organs and the powers associated with them. He has eyes and therefore power to see, ears and therefore power to hear, genitals and therefore power to procreate. He is endowed with "natural powers of life" and therefore finds "joy," "pleasure," "merriness" in being active, in playing with nature and its objects, in "exhaling and inhaling all the forces of nature."[6] Like animals, man *qua* natural being has the power to recognise other members of his species and therefore to enjoy their companionship.

Each of these powers and facilities strives for realisation, for fulfillment. Each is an active power, an "impulse," a "tendency," a "disposition" as Marx calls it. It constantly impels man to go out and secure objects with which to gratify it. In Marx's view human senses and their powers are necessarily outgoing. Man's stomach, whose need for gratification we call hunger, impels him to go in search of food; and his genitals, whose impulse and mode of gratification we call sexual impulse, "urge" or "impel" him to look for the person with whom to copulate. Likewise, his eyes and ears have no meaning in the absence of external objects which they can see and hear, and are therefore necessarily outgoing. A "real man of flesh and blood" bubbling with "energy and life" requires the "living world" of nature whose powers he can breathe and from which he can derive nourishment. As to man's power and need of companionship, it by definition requires other men.

As we observed earlier, for Marx each human faculty, power and need is unique. Each of them has its own "essential being" and a determinate and distinctive mode of appropriation and gratification. Each requires a different object for gratification, and can only be gratified in a manner dictated by its own unique nature and that of its correlative object. Take hunger, for example. It requires edible objects, and cannot be gratified by any other kind. Further, these objects, like hunger, possess a distinctive character and must be appropriated in certain ways. Some must be eaten with hand, some with a knife and fork, and so on. Even as hunger by its very nature can appropriate its objects and gratify itself in a limited number of ways, other impulses too can gratify themselves only in certain ways. What is more, the mode of gratification is unique in each case. Sexual urge cannot be gratified in the same way as hunger, for the obvious reason that the two do not and cannot relate to their different objects in the same way. A woman cannot be appropriated in the same way as an edible object. Following this line of argument Marx argues that each sense organ and faculty relates to and appropriates its objects in a totally different manner from every other.

Man then is a being naturally endowed with certain faculties and powers and therefore with definite and identifiable needs. He needs specific objects appropriate to his natural powers and drives, as well as needing the entire world of nature. Because the objects that satisfy his needs lie outside him, he is by his very nature an outgoing, active and striving being, driven by his impulses and needs to explore and manipulate the external world. Since passion "is man's faculties energetically striving after their object" man is by nature "a passionate being," a creature governed by his passions.[7] A striving being constantly runs the risk of failing to obtain the objects it needs; man is therefore a suffering being, capable of pleasure and pain, joy and sorrow. As we observed earlier, man's faculties and desires are of a determinate kind and can appropriate their respective objects only in certain ways. Since limitations are thus built into the very structure of human desires and faculties, man is a "limited and conditioned being."

It is man's needs, which Marx appropriately calls "inner necessity," that constitute the dynamics of human action and give his activity a direction. Because he is a needy being and his needs are objective, man is not and cannot be a purely passive and contemplative being as Feuerbach had imagined, and because his needs have a built-in objective structure, man is not and cannot be a purely active being, furiously and aimlessly going out into the world to appropriate it in its entirety as Fichte had imagined. Human needs are needs for specific objects, and therefore man cannot have a need for something as abstract as wanting to appropriate the world. Man's needs, further, are not contingent, something he happens to have and can do without, but are rooted in his very being. They are, as Marx puts it, "not merely anthropological phenomena . . . but truly ontological affirmations of his being."

Marx's analysis of need and the way he relates it to passion throws an interesting light on the mode of operation of human passion. As we saw above, passion refers to the strivings of human faculties to attain their objects. It is not, therefore, some mysterious force or a chemically produced urge existing independently of concrete faculties and driving them in certain directions. It is at bottom a mode in which a faculty affirms itself. A faculty, in turn, is not an independent and isolated power, but a particular way in which the human person affirms himself. There is, for example, no entity called sexual passion, but only a passionate way in which a human being strives to gratify his sexual impulse. There are therefore as many passions in man as there are faculties. Marx thus does not confine the term passion to the so-called biological passions such as sexuality but uses it to cover every faculty that strives for its object in an intense way. One can have a passion for music or art or natural beauty just as much as for a woman or a man. Marx does not seem to think that some one or more of these passions are naturally stronger than the rest. As all organs are equally natural and important, so are the impulses located in them. If a particular passion is dominant in an individual or society and absorbs its consciousness, that must be due to undesirable social influences and is a cause for concern.[8]

MAN AS A HUMAN BEING

We have so far examined Marx's concept of natural being and outlined what he means by it. As we remarked earlier, man is not merely a natural but also a human being. It is to the analysis of this concept that we should now turn.

Like Hegel and Feuerbach before him, Marx argues that Man's humanity, his human character, consists in those qualities that distinguish him from all other natural beings, above all the animal, which comes closest to him. The discussion of man's distinctive human character therefore involves Marx, as it had involved Hegel and Feuerbach, in tracing the basic differences between man and the animal.

In Marx's view we can discover the essence of a being by examining its behaviour, the way it lives. As he puts it, "The whole character of a species is contained in the character of its life activity."[9] Of "the totality of life-activities"[10] a living being has to undertake in order to stay alive—such as eating, sleeping, drinking and defecating—the one concerned with gaining its sustenance is the most important. It is the activity that it *must* undertake; it occupies most of its time; and in it are absorbed most of its energies. Marx therefore concludes that the way a species produces its sustenance provides a clue to its essential character and identify. As he puts it, "As individuals express their lives, so they are. What they are therefore coincides with their production, both with what they produce and how they produce."[11] The distinctive character of the human species is therefore to be found in man's productive activity. According to Marx, if we compare man's productive activity with that of the animal we find that he differs from it in four basic respects,—that his humanity consists in his possession of four basic features or capacities.[12]

1. Man is a conscious being.
2. Man is a free being.
3. Man is a universal being.
4. Man is a species-being.

1. MAN AS A CONSCIOUS BEING

Like Feuerbach, Marx uses the term consciousness in its rather specialised and narrow sense of self-consciousness. In its ordinary and broad sense consciousness is not distinctive to man. Animals too are conscious. They can and do recognise other animals, distinguish between members of their own species and outsiders, apprehend danger, etc. Feuerbach, however, thought that animal consciousness was so "limited" that it could more properly be called instinct, and that the term consciousness should be reserved for human consciousness. Marx does not argue the point and implicitly accepts Feuerbach's usage.

The animal, he says, is "directly identical" with, "directly merged" into, its life-activity, and is unable to distinguish itself from it. It is unable to see itself as a separate being from its environment and to detach itself from its activities. Unlike the animal, man is able to distance and distinguish himself from his activities, his environment, and even from himself, and is therefore aware of himself as a subject. This is the familiar Hegelian view that man is not a being-in-himself but a being-for-himself and is capable of subject-object distinction.

2. MAN AS A FREE BEING

Man is a free being and the animal is not in two senses. First, Marx argues, an animal produces only when compelled by immediate physical needs, while man can not only produce when he is free from physical needs but produces better when he is so free. What this presumably means is that man can anticipate his needs and therefore produce in advance of his wants, and that he can produce better when he produces at his own pace and at the time of his own choosing than when compelled to do so by immediate needs.

Second, an animal's "product" belongs immediately to its physical body, while man freely confronts his product. What this means is not very clear, but presumably what Marx intends to say is that the animal cannot see its "products" as separate from itself in a way that man can, and that it sees them as in some sense parts of its own body and not as objects in the external world to which it can freely relate.

3. MAN AS A UNIVERSAL BEING

The animal's productive activity is confined to a limited part of nature, while man can take the entire world of nature as his field of action. The animal has a natural *Wirkungskreis,* a hermetically sealed circle of activity tht exhausts the totality of its life-activity and within which "it acts calmly . . . not striving beyond, not even surmising that there is another."[13] Its "consciousness" is "merely an awareness of the *immediate* sensible environment." Human consciousness, by contrast, knows no such limits. Man can make the entire universe the object of his consciousness and will, and can study and manipulate it.

4. MAN AS A SPECIES-BEING

Man has a number of capacities not to be found in the animal. These, which Marx sometimes calls "mental" or "spiritual" capacities, include the capacity to think, reason, judge, act, know, will, imagine, plan, anticipate, etc. Man can for example visualise the end-product of his activity and direct the latter accordingly, while an animal cannot. To use Marx's example,

"A spider conducts operations that resemble those of a weaver and a bee puts to shame many an architect in the construction of her cells. But what distinguishes the worst of architects from the best of bees is this, that the architect raises his structure in the imagination of the laborer at its commencement. He not only affects a change of form in the material on which he works, but he also realizes a purpose of his own that gives the law to his *modus operandi,* and to which he must subordinate his will."

Of all these "mental" capacities, the most important is that for conceptual thinking. It is this that Marx wishes to emphasise in calling man a species-being. Marx's concept of species-being is highly complex; he does not always use the term in the same sense, and he is not always aware of its implications. Although he abandoned the term later, he retained the concept; and the term social being that he later preferred had all the force and meaning of its predecessor. Marx's concept of species-being therefore deserves close analysis.

Marx took over the concept of species-being from Feuerbach, purged it of part of its meaning and invested it with nuances of his own. He used it for the same purpose as Feuerbach—to define man and distinguish him from the animal. Marx was struck by the fact that unlike the animal, man has generic consciousness, the consciousness of being a man like other men, a member of a species, and he felt that this difference could be best conceptualised in terms of the Feuerbachian notion of species-being. Evidently he found the term extremely useful, as he used it on every conceivable occasion during his Feuerbachian period and derived a number of terms from it that are not to be found in Feuerbach. Thus he used such terms as species-life, species-activity, species-powers, species-capacity, species-consciousness, species-objectivity, species-relationship, species-act, species-will, species-bond, species-action and species-spirit.

Let us begin with a few of Marx's remarks where these terms are most clearly explained.

"Man is a species-being not only because in practice and in theory he adopts the species as his object (his own as well as those of others) but, this is another way of expressing it, also because he treats himself as the actual living species, because he treats himself as a universal and therefore a free being."(Quote 1)[14]

"Conscious life activity distinguishes man from the life-activity of animals. Only for this reason is he a species-being. Or rather he is only a self-conscious being, that is, his own life is an object for him, because he is a species-being."(Quote 2)[15]

"In creating an objective world by his practical activity . . . man proves himself a conscious species being, and as a being that treats the species as its own essential being, or that treats itself as a species being."(Quote 3)[16]

In his several other uses of the term, Marx refers to the sexual act as a species-act and man's relation to woman as "a natural species-relationship." He calls the family, community and state "species-forms." He says that in a properly constituted political society, the legislature is the "representative of the people i.e. of the species-will," and remarks that a will "has its true existence as species-will only in the self-conscious will of the people." He says that man's "species-spirit" finds satisfaction only in cooperation between men. He says that the object of man's labour is "the objectification of species-life" and that being alienated from it deprives him of "his real species objectivity."[17]

Quote 1 above is one of the few clearest definitions Marx ever gives of the concept of species-being and reveals a deep tension in his thinking. We shall therefore examine it in some detail.

Marx is here saying that man is a species-being, and the animal is not, in the sense that man can undertake the following five activities which the animal cannot.

First, he can make his species an object of his consciousness; that is, he can study it theoretically. Marx often identifies consciousness with theoretical study.

Second, he can make his species an object of his will. That is, he can pursue its well-being. Marx often identifies practical action with an exercise of will.

Third, he can make the "species . . . of other beings" an object of his theoretical study.

Fourth, he can make other species an object of his practical concern.

Finally, he can treat himself "as the actual living species." That is, man is a being "that treats the species as its own essential being, or that treats itself as a species being."(Quote 3) In other words man is not only conscious of the fact that he belongs to a species but also of the fact that he derives his essence, his distinctive human powers, from his species. Every being in the universe is a species-being in the sense that it derives its being, its essence, from its species. Man differs from them all in recognising this and in being able to act as a conscious representative of his species.

Marx says (Quote 1 above) that the fifth power is "only a way of expressing" the first four. He does not elaborate this remark and it is difficult to see what he means. He could mean that the fifth power *means* (is the same as) the other four. But this is odd, since man's capacity to treat his species as his own essential being and his ability to study and manipulate other species are clearly different powers. It is more likely that he meant to say that the fifth power is a *source* of the other four. There is some evidence to support this view. First, Feuerbach had taken this view, and it is likely that Marx was following him here as elsewhere during his Feuerbachian period. Feuerbach had argued that it is because man is aware of himself as belonging to a species that he acquires the ability to think in terms of species and therefore to classify natural objects. In other words, it is because man can make his own species an object of his thought and will that he can make other species objects of his thought and will. Feuerbach never clearly explained how man acquires the consciousness of belonging to a species in the first instance, and argued rather feebly that he does so by observing that all men share certain features in common, concluding that they constitute a species.

Secondly, Marx says, at one point: "since the human being does not come into the world bringing a mirror with him, not yet as a Fichtean philosopher able to say 'I am myself,' he first recognises himself as reflected in other men. The man Peter grasps his relation to himself as a human being through becoming aware of his relation to the man Paul, who with flesh and blood, and with all his Pauline corporeality becomes for Peter the phenomenal form of the human kind."[18] Although the remark is not as clear as one would like it to be it could be read to mean that for Marx man acquires awareness of himself as a human, i.e. a species-being, by detecting similarities between himself and others, and that it is the species-consciousness so acquired that enables him to deal with the species of other objects in the universe. Marx's reference to "the consciousness which man derives from the species" seems to reinforce the point.

Whatever the origin of man's species-consciousness and the relation between the first four powers and the fifth, it is interesting to examine the totality of the five powers. Man cannot deal with diverse species, including his own, either theoretically or practically unless he is able to group individual objects into species or classes[19] in the first instance. Man's five powers *qua* species-being therefore presuppose a more general power to classify objects on the basis of their shared characteristics. Marx is saying in effect that man is a species-being because he has the power to classify objects into species. The ability to classify is ultimately the ability to form concepts, to abstract the shared features of a group of objects and to make statements of differing degrees of universality. In effect, man is a species-being because he has a capacity for conceptual thinking, for abstraction. We can go even further. For Hegel and for Feuerbach, to formulate the concept of a thing is to pick out its essential features, so that the concept of a thing is a theoretical statement of its essence. Marx shares their Aristotelian view that the essence of a thing lies in its differentia. Man is a species-being because he can comprehend the essence, the being, the species-character, of all the objects in the universe. In other words, the capacity to grasp the essence (or species-character) of all beings, himself included, constitutes man's essence (or species-character). It would seem that Marx, like Feuerbach, is suggesting that man's five species-powers are "differentiations" of his more general power to comprehend the species-character of each being in the universe. In other words, it is because man has this general power that he has the power to make the species-character of his own and other species the object of his theoretical and practical concern.

Feuerbach had described reason, will and love as man's essential and distinctive human powers.[20] Marx's five powers can, with some qualification, be reduced to Feuerbach's three. Of the five, the first four powers are clearly reducible to two, viz. theoretical and practical powers or reason and will. The first and the third refer to man's theoretical capacity, the second and the fourth to his practical capacity. Theoretical intellect or reason enables man to understand the species-character of beings in the universe and the will enables him to subordinate them to his practical purposes. Thus Marx is saying that reason and will are man's powers *qua* species-being and are derived from his more general power of conceptual thinking. Marx does not examine the relationship between reason and will, although he does at one point claim to enunciate "a psychological law that once the theoretical intellect has achieved freedom within itself, it turns into practical energy and directs itself against the exterior reality of the world."[21] His general view of the relationship between theory and practice also indicates that he would link reason and will very closely. Unlike Feuerbach, Marx does not list affection or love as a separate power, but it is implicit in the fifth power listed above. A being who knows his species to be his essential being is naturally capable of treating all its members as his own essential being and therefore of loving them.

Marx analyses the nature of reason further. It is, he says, a source of two other powers. First, it enables man to identify, abstract, analyse, compare and relate general features of objects and to formulate general laws about them; it is therefore a source of man's scientific capacity. Second, it is also a source of man's artistic capability. Since reason can comprehend the species-character of each being, it is able to grasp the distinctive and unique character of each species. It is therefore able to deal with it according to its own "inherent standard," the norms implicit in its nature.[22] In other words, reason enables man to deal with each species in its own terms, without imposing external, *a priori* and alien standards on it. The animal, not a species-being, cannot do this. It lacks the capacity to respect the character and uniqueness of each species. Presented with pearls, for example, it will play with them, but will not appreciate their distinctive character. That is, it deals with each species of beings and objects according to the demands of its own and not their nature. It is this capacity to deal with each species according to its own inherent standards, that is the source of artistic creation. Man alone therefore is able to form things "in accordance with the laws of beauty."[23] For Marx the capacity for conceptual thinking is a necessary presupposition of the capacity for artistic creation.

For Marx, man is a species-being in the sense that he is capable of elucidating the differentia or the essence of objects and of classifying them. By definition he is also therefore capable of elucidating his own essence and of acting as a representative of his species. Sometimes Marx uses the term species-being in its first, wider, sense (for example Quote 1 above); more often, however, he uses it in the second, narrower, sense. This is evident in the second part of Quote 1, in Quote 3, and in almost all other remarks where he uses the derivatives of the term listed above. Thus the term *species-consciousness* refers to man's awareness of being a human being, a member, a representative, of the human species. The term *species-power* refers to that power which is distinctive to the human species. The term *species-act* refers to acts such as loving, cooperating, exchange and sexual intercourse, in which man affirms his species-being, that is, in which he reveals his distinctive human capacity and "completes" or complements other men. The term *species-activity* refers to those organised forms of activity, such as science and art, and, at a different level, "shoe-making" and other activities in which distinctive human capacities are revealed and human needs served. The term *species-form* refers to those organised forms of interpersonal relationship, such as the family, the state and the community, in which men cooperate with each other to realise common objectives. In the same way the term *species-will* refers to the will formed by men in the light of their species-consciousness, that is, the will that aims at the good of humanity; and the term *species-existence* refers to man's existence not as an isolated individual, but as a member of the human species.

We observed that Marx uses the term *species-being* in two senses. The failure to see this has been largely responsible for the mistaken view taken by many commentators[24] that, for Marx, man is a species-being only in a communist society. Marx does occasionally make remarks that lend credence to this view, but they must be seen in their proper context. If man is a species-being only in a communist society, it would follow that he lacks the capacity for conceptual thinking and is therefore no different from an animal, in precommunist societies. But this is absurd since, however alienated capitalist and other societies might be, they could clearly never have been created by animals, and are distinctively human achievements. Further Marx himself says that man "proves" his species-being in controlling nature; since precommunist societies, above all capitalist society, have clearly controlled nature, they have "proved" beyond doubt that their members are species-beings. When therefore Marx remarks that man will be a species-being in the communist society, implying that he is not yet one, he means to use (or must be taken to mean) the term in its narrow sense. That is, he is saying that, although man in the precommunist society has understood and controlled the species of other beings in the universe and thus proved his species-being in the wider sense of the term, he has not so far understood his own essence, and pursued the well-being of his own species, and has therefore not yet become a species-being in the narrow sense of the term. In all precommunist societies man has remained, and will continue to remain, an egoistic, insulated, selfish, individualistic atom lacking full awareness of the fact that he derives his distinctive human powers from his species.

We have seen that for Marx man is a conscious, free, universal species-being. The question then is how these four capacities (powers, characteristics, or differentia) are related. Marx's answer—such as it is—is ambiguous and somewhat muddled. He says (Quote 2 above) that man is a conscious being *because* he is a species-being, but in the previous sentence and elsewhere[25] he says the opposite—man is a species-being because he is a conscious being. Again, Marx seems to be vaguely aware that the animal too is a species-being (in the narrow sense of the term) at least to a limited degree. As he says in *The German Ideology,* the animal has "herd consciousness" and knows which herd it belongs to. A lion, for example, knows that it does not belong to a flock of sheep, and copulates only with a lioness and not with a goat or a cow. The animal has a "need of companionship" and it seeks its companions only among its kind. As if realising this, Marx describes man not as a species-being *simpliciter* but as a "conscious species-being," without appreciating that he cannot then keep referring to man as a species-being *simpliciter* and also that he cannot then derive man's consciousness from his species-being. He says (Quote 1 above) that man is a universal being and therefore a free being, deriving his capacity for freedom from his universality. But he also says (Quote 2) that man is a conscious being and therefore a free being, deriving his capacity for freedom from his consciousness. Quote 1 continues that man is a species-being *because* he is a universal being; but then to say that man is a species-being *is* to say that he can deal with universal features of different species, so that his universality, instead of being a source of his species-being, is partly entailed by it.

It is clear that a man has certain powers that are his as a member of the human species. They include power to conceptualise and theorise, power to will, to plan, to anticipate, to create space between himself and the object of his perception, to act as a representative of his species, to produce according to laws of beauty, etc. In the course of exercising these powers, man develops countless others and builds "the whole world of culture and civilisation." He is able to develop other powers only because he has these basic powers in the first instance. They are therefore his "essential" or "species powers," characteristic of his species and constitutive of his essence. A man who lacks them is not a proper human being and it is only when an animal equipped with these powers evolves that a proper human being can be said to have appeared.

THE DIALECTICAL INTEGRATION

We saw above that man has certain distinctive species-powers. Since they constitute his human essence, he lives a truly worthy human life, only when he develops and exercises his distinctive species-powers and all other powers that grow out of them. The more powers he develops, the more of a human being he is; and he is fully human when he develops all the powers of which the species is capable. As we saw earlier, Marx takes an Aristotelian view of man and his powers. Man not only *ought* to develop and exercise his powers, he in fact *wants* and *strives* to develop them. Man can develop his powers only when he is free to plan his life as he chooses, only when he is "the sovereign of circumstances." As long as his will is subject to restraints imposed by external factors he remains restricted and unable to make free choices. Freedom, meaning absence of all forms of limitation on the human will, is for Marx the most basic demand of human nature and the most essential condition of a fully human life.

Man's striving for freedom brings him into inevitable conflict with nature which necessarily imposes limitations on him. These limitations are of two kinds, external and internal. External nature is not hospitable to human needs; it is harsh and does not spontaneously produce means of man's material sustenance. Its wild and unpredictable forces constantly threaten his existence. Rivers and mountains create natural barriers to man's free physical and social intercourse with his species. Nature has planted limitations in man's very being and thus his internal nature too mocks at his striving for freedom. As we saw in the first section man's natural being is no different from that of the animal. His natural senses are limited, primitive, confined to narrow perceptual areas and guided by crude and immediate needs. He has limited physical strength, limited capacity to anticipate events, and a narrowly circumscribed life-activity. Marx concludes, "Neither nature objectively nor nature subjectively is directly given in a form adequate to the human being."[26]

If man is to live a free and fully human life, he must overcome these natural limitations. He must use his human powers to reshape nature—both external and his own—in the light of his needs. In other words he must humanise nature. It is only as he humanises nature that man properly becomes a human being. The limits of humanisation are the limits of man's freedom and humanity. He can humanise nature by using his theoretical and practical powers of knowledge and will. He can study nature and use his "theoretical knowledge of its independent laws" as "a stratagem for subjecting it to human needs." He cannot change it all at once, because this requires an Archimedean point in some supranatural world, and such a world is not available. What he can do is to change it gradually, consolidating the parts already won and using them as a basis for further conquests. In this way over centuries man becomes a free being. Although Marx is somewhat ambiguous, he seems to think that man can never humanise nature completely. Notwithstanding the fact that nature might one day cease to be a "power in its own right" and man become able to alter its "forms," Marx is convinced that its "particles" or basic "stuff" will always retain their inherent character and continue to be governed by their own "independent" laws. Man's body will always need food, whether he likes it or not. It will continue to feel tired, grow old, decay and die, thus flouting human will. Human freedom is therefore necessarily hedged in with a number of inescapable limitations, eloquently summed up by the phrase, the "realm of necessity." However, man can and ought to try to subdue nature. As his knowledge grows, the limitations that had appeared "natural" and inescapable to one generation will be transcended in another. In this way man constantly pushes the boundary of nature further and further and correspondingly expands the area of freedom.

It is from this perspective that Marx views human history. Its dialectic is the dialectic of the battle between man and nature, between freedom and constraint. Ever since his first historical appearance as a human being proper, man has striven to recreate, to humanise, both his own and external nature. In the beginning his successes were limited; building on them, he was able to conquer further areas of nature, and this enabled him to extend his mastery even further. Over the centuries generations of men, standing on the shoulders of their predecessors, have subdued the wild forces of nature, subordinated them to human needs, eliminated physical and other barriers imposed by nature, transformed their own nature, developed new needs, civilised their intercourse, and have in general brought nature in harmony with their human powers. Human history, to express the point differently, is a story of human "autogenesis," or human self-creation, of man's continual self-transcendence and "coming to be"; it is a story of "the continuous transformation of human nature" and of the universe.[27] To avoid misunderstanding, Marx is not saying that human self-creation is the end, the *telos,* of history. Contrary to the opinion of his critics, Marx firmly rejects all such attempts to anthropomorphise history and to convert a way of seeing it into its hidden aim or end.[28]

Marx's highly suggestive idea of humanisation of nature raises a number of questions. For example, what precisely does it mean? How precisely are the humanisation of man's own nature and of the natural world related? How far can the humanisation of nature go and what are its limits? How is fully humanised nature achieved in history? Who are its agents and what is the logic of its progression? We do not have the space to pursue these fascinating questions and shall have to be content with exploring in some detail the question most relevant to our discussion, viz. the process by which humanisation of nature is achieved and Marx's conception of the fully humanised man.

Marx takes the view that man humanises nature through labour, a purposive and planned activity in which he uses his knowledge of nature to change and modify it. Although Marx is not entirely clear on this point he seems to say that labour involved in the humanisation of nature is of two kinds. Its first and most well-known form is, of course, industry, in which man "works over" external nature and humanises it. Its second and less well-known form is culture, the term which Marx uses a few times in his early writings and not much thereafter and which in my view best describes the type of activity he has in mind.[29] Industry and culture are, of course, intimately related. Industry creates the basis on which culture arises, and conditions its form and structure. Nevertheless I think it is important to realise that Marx assigns culture a distinct role in the process of humanisation of nature.

The way in which industry humanises nature is obvious and need not detain us long. By cultivating land, by building dams, bridges and tunnels, by taming nature's wild and explosive forces, by building machines and factories etc., man subordinates external nature to his needs. He relieves nature of its naturalness, and makes it an integral part of the human world. Man's humanisation of external nature humanises his internal nature too. He develops new interests, new powers, and new needs, and learns to concentrate, to plan, to discipline and regulate his conduct, to cooperate with his fellow men, and to subordinate his fleeting whims and moods. Above all, the humanisation of external nature develops his species-being and unites him with his species. Humanised nature embodies man's human and species powers. In it therefore man encounters not nature but himself, not a nonhuman power but his own species. In dams, fields, bridges and machines, for example, he sees the efforts and creative powers of his fellow men, and feels both a sense of admiration and gratitude to them and a sense of pride in being human. They thus affirm his species-being and give it an objective and secure expression.[30] That nature does not act as a bond between man and his species in capitalist society is a separate question and does not concern us here.

Industry humanises external nature and through that, man's own nature. Man humanises his nature in another way too. He has, as we have seen, several natural senses and powers. In themselves they are primitive. They are gratified by crude objects; they appropriate them in crude ways; they are compelled by needs and approach them in a purely utilitarian manner. Man must therefore humanise them. Marx calls the process of humanising them culture or humanisation of the senses. Although his concept of culture is highly complex and relatively unexplored, we shall deal with it rather briefly.

Even as man has humanised external nature over the centuries, he has also learnt to humanise his internal nature. He has developed culinary skill, the art of painting, music, architecture, games, literature, dancing, etc., all of which collectively constitute culture.[31] These are all different ways of exercising his natural senses in a sophisticated, skilful, human and therefore free manner. Thus the species has developed culinary skill and produced different types of food and different ways of eating them. Man's palate is therefore humanised, and appropriates its objects in a human way, when it is able to appreciate the quality of the food it eats and the culinary skill embodied in it. A man who lacks a sense of discrimination, and sees food as no more than an edible lump, is no different from an animal. His relation to this food is not culturally mediated, and therefore not human but animal. Man's eyes too are humanised[32] when they appreciate beautiful objects—paintings, sculptures, etc.—with a sense of discrimination, feel at home with them, demand to be surrounded by them and feel outraged and insulted by anything that is ugly. An eye to which beautiful and ugly objects look alike and which sees them only as use-objects, is a "crude" "nonhuman" eye and is no different from that of the animal. Man's ears are similarly humanised when they are able to distinguish between noises and harmonious sounds and feel offended by all that is coarse and discordant. Human sexuality is similarly humanised when it does not simply aim at *secretic mechanico* and follow the printed instructions of sex, but is accompanied by romantic love and variation in love-play. Humanised sense is in other words a "cultivated," "refined" or "cultured" sense, a sense that has incorporated within itself all the relevant achievements of the human species and that relates to its object not merely because of its ability to serve a raw human need but "for its own sake," that is, because of the kind of object it is. A cultured man, a man of humanised senses, is for Marx a free man, a man who has emancipated his senses from the tyranny of nature and turned them into organs freely expressing his human powers.

Like his physical or natural senses, man's mental or practical senses such as "feeling, thinking, being aware, wanting, loving" and imagining are humanised when they respond to their appropriate objects in a human way. Marx does not elaborate the point, but it is not difficult to see what he means. Thus man "feels" in a human way when the character, object and mode of his feeling are determined by human considerations. To respond to man's exploitation of cruelty to his fellow men with a sense of indignation is to feel in a human way; to respond to it with indifference or to seek to justify it is to feel in an inhuman way. To will an object or a state of affairs because it promotes human well-being is to will in a human way; to will an object that causes suffering to others is to will in an inhuman way. To be "aware" of the human power embodied in an object and of the human needs it serves is to be aware of it in a human way; to be aware of it only as an object of utility is to be aware of it in an animal *and* nonhuman or even inhuman way.

In a fully humanised man, the senses "have therefore become directly in their practice theoreticians."[33] Although Marx does not elaborate this interesting and rather puzzling observation it is not difficult to see what he means, especially as Feuerbach, from whom he borrowed both the concept and the phrase, had explained it in some detail. As we saw earlier, theory, for Marx, refers to the capacity to understand objects not merely in their natural particularity but also as members of a class. In that the senses of the humanised man do not simply grasp the particularity of objects but also the general species-skills and powers embodied in them and the general human needs they serve, they are appropriating their objects in a theoretical manner. They do not merely perceive their objects but understand them, and see their point; that is, they see through them just as a theoretician does. Human senses, no doubt, do retain their particularity: eyes, for example, can only see and not hear or smell, but their particularity has become infused with universality. In other words they have become what Idealists call a concrete universal. In becoming universal, man's natural senses have become adequate vehicles of his universal nature, "truly ontological affirmations of his essence" and no longer merely his anthropological characteristics.[34] At the end of a long historical process, his natural existence would at last have caught up with his human essence.

From what Marx has said so far, it follows that humanisation of nature, human self-creation is a cooperative process involving the entire species. It is not achieved by a single individual for obvious reasons; nor by a single nation which by its very nature can develop only some human powers and not others and depends on international commercial and cultural intercourse, thus presupposing humanisation of nature in other countries. As Marx puts it, "the liberation of every single individual is achieved proportionately to the extent in which history is completely transformed into world history,"[35] to the extent that the species as a whole has humanised nature. Marx demonstrates this on the basis of a most impressive doctrine that has received surprisingly little attention from his commentators. Marx calls it the doctrine of "mutual completion" and contrasts it with the bourgeois doctrine of "mutual exploitation" or "mutual enslavement."[36]

Man is capable of developing countless human powers, and cannot be said to have become fully human unless he has actually developed them. The individual by himself, however, is too limited to do so, and needs others to "complete" him. I may, for example, be good at painting but have no "sense" for sculpture or poetry. Left to myself I would therefore remain artistically impoverished, unless someone else who was good at sculpture or poetry produced a beautiful object and thereby enabled me to cultivate the relevant capacity. Marx gives the example of a pianist. The "pianist produces music and satisfies our musical sense; perhaps to some extent he produces this sense ... he raises our individuality to a more active, livelier level."[37] Any individual who produces something new educates his fellow men, gives them new capacities, deepens their imagination, and raises their level of existence. In giving them a new "sense," he recreates his fellow men, and brings them closer to becoming species-beings.

Marx develops the point beautifully in his essay on James Mill.[38] Imagine an individual, he says, who produces a beautiful object. His act has four consequences. First, he has objectified his individuality in this object. In the object his personality has become "objective, visible to the senses and thus a power raised beyond all doubt." This is a source of pleasure to him and enriches his life. Second, others will enjoy the object he has produced, and thus he will have the further pleasure that he has satisfied a human need. Third, he has helped others acquire new senses, a new capacity of appreciation, a new power. He has thus been a "mediator" between these men and the species and would be acknowledged by them as "a completion . . . and a necessary part" of their essence. He is thus "confirmed" in their "thought" and "love." Finally, in objectifying a human power, a species-power, he has realised his "human" and "communal" essence. He has created an object that all can collectively share and cherish as an expression of their common essence. It is like a "mirror" out of which human essence shines.

Men become humanised, Marx maintains, through each other's help. In expressing your powers, you benefit and enrich me. Enriched, I am better able to appreciate and criticise your products and to set you higher standards at which to aim. In educating me, you do not suffer any loss; on the contrary you benefit as much as I. Thus we grow together. In human life we constantly appropriate each other. In appreciating your music, e.g., I appropriate your musical sense which now is as much mine as yours. In giving me new senses, you have refined your own. If you had withheld your powers, I would no doubt have suffered a loss, but so would you. Properly defined, individual and social interests always coincide. In helping me become a human being, you become one yourself; in destroying my humanity, you destroy yours too. As Marx puts it, "mutual completion . . . leads to the species-life, to the truly human life."[39] It is therefore as much in my interest as in yours that I should encourage you to become a unique and "truly individual" being. It is only when an individual is unique that he can "complete" others, and both become and help others to become a species-being.

THE COMMUNIST MAN

In the light of the preceding discussion it is easy to see what a fully humanised man, a communist man, is like for Marx. He is a man united with himself, with his species and with nature. He is not a self-divided being caught up in the morbid and paralysing conflict between his flesh and spirit, or between his natural and human being. He does not deny the demands of his nature, but his behaviour is not dictated by them. He has humanised his nature and acquired the capacity to anticipate its demands and to gratify them in a cultured way. He therefore accepts his natural desires but satisfies them as he freely chooses.

Ascetic self-denial on the one hand, and indiscriminate self-indulgence on the other, are both alien to his way of life.[40] He lives a balanced and integrated life in which each dimension of his being finds its proper satisfaction and none is allowed to dominate. Marx's man, further, is united with his species. He possesses all the basic powers distinctive to the human species—the power to conceptualise, theorise, desire, to concentrate and coordinate his energies, to form independent judgments,—and many others that the species has developed subsequently. Although not entirely clear on this point, Marx does not seem to wish to say that every man should become capable of pursuing science, writing poems and novels, composing music, constructing beautiful buildings, painting pictures, etc. He seems to want to distinguish between power and sense, and to suggest that a fully fully developed man should have the "power" to undertake some of these activities and the "sense" to appreciate the rest.

The communist man is energetic and active, constantly striving to objectify his powers. He is a "demanding"[41] man who requires opportunities both to exercise his powers and to acquire those that the species is constantly developing. He is capable of making his own distinctive contribution to the enrichment of his fellowmen and of mediating between them and the species. He has humanised all his senses and relations to the world and is revolted and outraged by anything that reflects inhumanity, meanness, cruelty, suffering and ugliness. He is, further, united with nature and finds delight in its beauty and diversity. Above all, he has "pride" in being human, a sense of "worth" and self-respect, a love of "independence" and a "sense of dignity."[42] He refuses to subject others to his power or to be "subject, devoted, and obedient" to them himself. He is, in short, a cheerful, well-integrated, expansive, outgoing, loving, inwardly rich, cultured, social being who sums up in his life the greatness and wealth of his species. As long as any individual in any society fails to live this kind of life, the species suffers a loss, and its historic task of humanising nature remains unfulfilled.

On the basis of his conception of man Marx works out a fascinating theory of human needs and sketches the outlines of a society in which a fully humanised man is possible. On its basis he launches a powerful and, in my view, essentially sound attack on the christian, liberal and primitivistic conceptions of man. An examination of all these and other aspects of Marx's theory of man is beyond the scope of this essay.

NOTES

[1] *Economic & Philosophic Manuscripts of 1844* Tr. Martin Milligan, Foreign Languages Publishing House, Moscow, 1961, pp. 111, 155f, and p. 170. This work is hereafter referred to as EPM. See also David McLellan, ed., *Karl Marx—Early Texts* Basil Blackwell, Oxford, 1971, pp. 202 and 203.
[2] *The Holy Family* Foreign Languages Publishing House, Moscow, 1956 pp. 172ff. In all the bibliographies of Marx's writings that I have seen, this work is listed as authored by Marx

and Engels. For the sake of historical accuracy and the light it throws on the two men's initial relationship, it must be observed that the title page of the first 1845 edition states that it was written by Engels and Marx.

[3] Z. A. Jordan in *The Evolution of Dialectical Materialism* Macmillan, London 1967 pp. 11ff takes a similar view.

[4] Bertell Ollman offers a careful analysis of Marx's concepts of power and need in his *Alienation* Cambridge University Press, 1973, pp. 75ff.

[5] *EPM*, pp. 156f.

[6] *EPM*, p. 155. See also Marx's description of Fleur-de-Marie in *Holy Family*.

[7] *EPM*, p. 158. I have preferred McLellan's translation in *Karl Marx: Early Texts, op.cit.*, p. 168.

[8] *EPM*, pp. 73 and 116f.

[9] *EPM*, p. 75.

[10] *ibid.* p. 112.

[11] *The German Ideology*, Tr. R. Pascal London, 1942, p. 7.

[12] *EPM*, pp. 75–6.

[13] *Writings of the Young Marx on Philosophy and Society*, ed. and Tr. by Loyd D. Easton and Kurt H. Guddat Doubleday Anchor Book, 1967, p. 35.

[14] *EPM*, p. 74.

[15] *ibid.*, p. 75. I have preferred Bottomore's translation in his *Karl Marx: Early Writings*, p. 127.

[16] *EPM*, p. 75.

[17] *ibid.*, p. 76. Also *Critique of Hegel's Philosophy of Right, ed.* Joseph O'Malley, Cambridge University Press, 1970, pp. 27, 58, 65 and 119; and *Karl Marx: Early Texts, op.cit.* pp. 193ff.

[18] *Capital* Everyman ed. p. 23.

[19] Marx uses the two terms interchangeably.

[20] *The Essence of Christianity*, Tr. George Eliot Harper Torchbooks, 1957, p. 3.

[21] *Karl Marx: Early Texts, op.cit.*, p. 15.

[22] *EPM*, p. 76.

[23] *ibid.*

[24] Ollman, *op.cit.*, p. 116.

[25] *EPM*, p. 58.

[26] *EPM*, p. 158.

[27] For the socialist man, "the entire so-called history of the world is nothing but the begetting of man through human labour." *EPM*, p. 113.

[28] See, e.g., pp. 57, 58 and 63 in T.B. Bottomore and Maximilian Rubel, eds., *Karl Marx: Selected Writings in Sociology and Social Philosophy,* Watts and Co., London, 1961.

[29] *EPM*, pp. 100, 108f, 117, 118f; *cf.* McLellan, *Early Texts, op.cit.*, p. 147.

[30] Marx's constant reference to the human essence of nature shows clearly that nature for him has no rights against man. Its purpose is to serve man's material and "spiritual" needs.

[31] *EPM*, pp. 118f.

[32] *ibid.*, p. 107.

[33] *EPM*, p. 107.

[34] *EPM*, p. 136.

[35] Quoted in Helmut Fleischer, *Marxism & History*, Tr. Eric Mosbacher, Allen Lane, The Penguin Press, London 1973, p. 23.

[36] *Karl Marx: Early Texts, op.cit.*, pp. 194 and 200f. See also his criticism of Bentham and Utilitarianism in general in *German Ideology*.

[37] *Grundrisse*, Tr. David McLellan, Paladin, London 1973, p. 94.

[38] *Karl Marx: Early Texts, op.cit.,* p. 202.

[39] *ibid.,* p. 194.

[40] The attack on asceticism is a recurrent theme in Marx's writings: see, for example, *EPM,* p. 118; *Holy Family,* particularly his sympathetic characterisation of Fleur-de-Marie and denunciation of Rudolph's "moral theology"; and those parts of *Grundrisse* and *Capital* in which Marx makes a powerful case for full satisfaction of human desires.

[41] *EPM,* p. 100, where Marx attacks the "poor and understanding man" who does not ask to appropriate "the entire world of culture and civilisation."

[42] *Karl Marx: Early Texts, op.cit.,* pp. 75f, 189.

NATHANIEL BRANDEN
ALIENATION

While it is mostly Marxists who have given the concept and phenomenon of alienation close attention, Nathaniel Branden, a psychologist—author of The Psychology of Self-Esteem *(1969),* The Psychology of Romantic Love *(1980), and* Honoring the Self *(1984), practicing in Los Angeles—who defends the capitalist socioeconomic system, has produced a distinctive thesis on this topic. Alienation is for him not a by-product of capitalism but a largely self-induced state some persons experience because of the judgments they have made and actions they have taken in life. Branden takes time to discuss the views of neo-Marxist/humanist Erich Fromm, mainly because such a discussion makes it possible for him to drive a wedge between the more prominent Marxian outlook on alienation and his individualist viewpoint. Since Branden also develops some of the main themes of an individualist conception of human nature and shows how it requires a capitalist socioeconomic order, this essay will quickly advance the discussion of this volume.*

> *And how am I to face the odds*
> *of man's bedevilment and God's?*
> *I, a stranger and afraid*
> *in a world I never made.*

In the writings of contemporary psychologists and sociologists, one encounters these lines from A. E. Houseman's poem more and more today—quoted as an eloquent summation of the sense of life and psychological plight of twentieth-century man.

In book after book of social commentary, one finds the same message: modern man is overwhelmed by anxiety, modern man suffers from an "identity crisis," modern man is *alienated*. " 'Who am I?' 'Where am I going?' 'Do I belong?': these are the crucial questions man asks himself in modern mass society," declares the sociologist and psychoanalyst Hendrik M. Ruitenbeek, in *The Individual and the Crowd—A Study of Identity in America.*[1]

The concept of *alienation,* in its original psychiatric usage, denoted the mentally ill, the severely mentally ill—often, particularly in legal contexts, the insane. It conveyed the notion of the breakdown of rationality and self-determination, the notion of a person driven by forces which he cannot grasp or control, which are experienced by him as compelling and alien, so that he feels estranged from himself.

Centuries earlier, medieval theologians had spoken with distress of man's alienation from God—of an over-concern with the world of the senses that

Reprinted, with permission, and revised for the present volume from Nathaniel Branden, *The Disowned Self* (New York: Bantam Books, 1973).

caused man to become lost to himself, estranged from his proper spiritual estate.

It was the philosopher Hegel who introduced the concept of alienation (outside of its psychiatric context) to the modern world. The history of man, maintained Hegel, is the history of man's self-alienation: man is blind to his true essence, he is lost in the "dead world" of social institutions and of property, which he himself has created, he is estranged from the Universal Being of which he is a part—and human progress consists of man's motion toward that Whole, as he transcends the limitations of his individual perceptions.

"Alienation" was taken over by Karl Marx and given a narrower, less cosmic meaning. He applied the concept primarily to the worker. The worker's alienation was inevitable, he asserted, with the development of the division of labor, specialization, exchange, and private property. The worker must sell his services; thus he comes to view himself as a "commodity," he becomes alienated from the product of his own labor, and his work is no longer the expression of his powers, of his inner self. The worker, who is alive, is ruled by that which is "dead" (i.e., capital, machinery). The consequence, says Marx, is spiritual impoverishment and mutilation: the worker is alienated from himself, from nature and from his fellow-men; he exists only as an animated *object,* not as a human being.

Since the time of Marx, the idea of alienation has been used more and more extensively by psychologists, sociologists, and philosophers—gathering to itself a wide variety of usages and meanings. But from Hegel and Marx onward, there appears to be an almost universal reluctance, on the part of those who employ the term, to define it precisely; it is as if one were expected to *feel* its meaning, rather than to grasp it conceptually. In a two-volume collection of essays entitled *Alienation,* the editor, Gerald Sykes, specifically scorns those who are too eager for a definition of the term; haste for definition, he declares, reveals that one suffers from "an advanced case of—alienation."[2]

Certain writers—notably those of a Freudian or Jungian orientation—declare that the complexity of modern industrial society has caused man to become "over-civilized," to have lost touch with the deeper roots of his being, to have become alienated from his "instinctual nature." Others complain that our advanced technological society compels man to live too intellectually, to be ruled by abstractions, thus alienating him from the real world which can be experienced in its "wholeness" only via his emotions. Still others decry specifically the alienation of the artist; they assert that, with the vanishing of the age of patrons, with the artist thrown on his own resources to struggle in the marketplace—which is ruled by "philistines"—the artist is condemned to fight a losing battle for the preservation of his spiritual integrity: he is too besieged by material temptations.

Most of these writers declare that the problem of alienation—and of man's search for identity—is not new, but has been a source of anguish to man in every age and culture. But they insist that today, in Western civilization—

above all, in America—the problem has reached an unprecedented severity. It has become a crisis.

What is responsible for this crisis? What has alienated man and deprived him of identity? The answer given by most writers on alienation is not always stated explicity, but—in their countless disparaging references to "the dehumanizing effects of industrialism," "soul-destroying commercialism," "the arid rationalism of a technological culture," "the vulgar materialism of the West," etc.—the villain in their view of things, the destroyer whom they hold chiefly responsible, is not hard to identify. It is *capitalism*.

This should not be startling. Since its birth, capitalism has been made the scapegoat responsible for almost every real or imagined evil denounced by anyone. As the distinguished economist Ludwig von Mises observes:

Nothing is more unpopular today than the free market economy, i.e., capitalism. Everything that is considered unsatisfactory in present-day conditions is charged to capitalism. The atheists make capitalism responsible for the survival of Christianity. But the papal encyclicals blame capitalism for the spread of irreligion and the sins of our contemporaries, and the Protestant churches and sects are no less vigorous in their indictment of capitalist greed. Friends of peace consider our wars as an off-shot of capitalist imperialism. But the adamant nationalist war-mongers of Germany and Italy indicted capitalism for its "bourgeois" pacifism, contrary to human nature and to the inescapable laws of history. Sermonizers accuse capitalism of disrupting the family and fostering licentiousness. But the "progressives" blame capitalism for the preservation of allegedly out-dated rules of sexual restraint. Almost all men agree that poverty is an outcome of capitalism. On the other hand many deplore the fact that capitalism, in catering lavishly to the wishes of people intent upon getting more amenities and a better living, promotes a crass materialism. These contradictory accusations of capitalism cancel one another. But the fact remains that there are few people left who would not condemn capitalism altogether.[3]

It is true that a great many men suffer from a chronic feeling of inner emptiness, of spiritual impoverishment, the sense of lacking personal identity. It is true that a great many men feel alienated—*from something*—even if they cannot say from what—from themselves or other men or the universe. And it is profoundly significant that capitalism should be blamed for this. Not because there is any justification for the charge, but because, by analyzing the reasons given for the accusation, one can learn a good deal about the nature and meaning of men's sense of alienation and non-identity—and, simultaneously, about the psychological motives that give rise to hostility toward capitalism.

The writers on alienation, as I have indicated, are not an intellectually homogeneous group. They differ in many areas: in their view of what the problem of alienation exactly consists of, in the aspects of modern industrial society and a free-market economy which they find most objectionable, in the explicitness with which they identify capitalism as the villain, and in details of their own political inclinations. Some of these writers are socialists, some are fascists, some are medievalists, some are supporters of the welfare state, some scorn politics altogether. Some believe that the problem of alienation is largely or entirely solvable by a new system of social organization; others believe that the problem, at bottom, is metaphysical and that no entirely satisfactory solution can be found.

Fortunately for the purposes of this analysis, however, there is a widely read writer who manages to combine in his books virtually all of the major errors perpetrated by commentators in this field: psychologist and sociologist Erich Fromm. Let us, therefore, consider Fromm's view of man and his theory of alienation in some detail.

Man, declares Erich Fromm, is "the freak of the universe."

This theme is crucial and central throughout his writings: man is radically different from all other living species, he is "estranged" and "alienated" from nature, he is overwhelmed by a feeling of "isolation" and "separateness"—he has lost, in the process of evolution, the undisturbed tranquillity of other organisms, he has lost the "pre-human harmony" with nature which is enjoyed by an animal, a bird, or a worm. The *source* of his curse is the fact that he possesses a mind.

"Self-awareness, reason, and imagination," Fromm writes in *Man for Himself,* "have disrupted the 'harmony' which characterizes animal existence. Their emergence has made man into an anomaly, into the freak of the universe." Man cannot live as an animal: he is not equipped to adapt himself automatically and unthinkingly to his environment. An animal blindly "repeats the pattern of the species," its behavior is biologically prescribed and stereotyped, it "either fits in or it dies out"—but it does not have to *solve* the problem of survival, *it is not conscious of life and death as an issue.* Man does and is; this is his tragedy. "Reason, man's blessing, is also his curse . . ."[4]

In *The Art of Loving,* he writes:

What is essential in the existence of man is the fact that he has emerged from the animal kingdom, from instinctive adaptation, that he has transcended nature—although he never leaves it; he is part of it—and yet once torn away from nature, he cannot return to it; once thrown out of paradise—a state of original oneness with nature—cherubim with flaming swords block his way, if he should try to return.[5]

That man's rational faculty deprives man of "paradise," alienating and estranging him from nature, is clearly revealed, says Fromm, in the "existential dichotomies" which his mind dooms man to confront—"contradictions" inherent in life itself. What are those tragic "dichotomies"? He names three as central and basic. Man's mind permits him to "visualize his own end: death"—yet "his body makes him want to be alive."[6] Man's nature contains innumerable potentialities yet "the short span of his life does not permit their full realization under even the most favorable circumstances."[7] Man "must be alone when he has to judge or to make decisions solely by the power of his reason"—yet "he cannot bear to be alone, to be unrelated to his fellow men."[8]

These "contradictions," says Fromm, constitute the dilemma of the "human situation"—contradictions with which man is compelled to struggle, but which he can never resolve or annul, *and which alienate man from himself, from his fellow men, and from nature.*

If the logic of the foregoing is not readily perceivable, the reason does not lie in the brevity of the synopsis. It lies in the unmitigated arbitrariness of Fromm's manner of presenting his ideas; he writes, not like a scientist, but like an oracle who is not obliged to give reasons of proof.

It is true that man differs fundamentally from all other living species, by virtue of possessing a rational, conceptual faculty. It is true that, for man, survival is a problem to be solved—by the exercise of his intelligence. It is true that no man lives long enough to exhaust his every potentiality. It is true that every man is alone, separate, and unique. It is true that thinking requires independence. These are the facts that grant glory to man's existence. Why would one choose to regard these facts as a terrifying cosmic paradox and to see in them the evidence of monumentally tragic human problems?

Fromm does not tell us. Nowhere does he establish any logical connection between the facts he observes and the conclusions he announces.

If we are *not* to regard his conclusions as arbitrary—as mystical revelations, in effect—then we must assume that he does not bother to give reasons for his position because he regards his conclusions as virtually self-evident, as irresistibly conveyed by the facts he cites, easily available to everyone's experience and introspection. But if he feels it is readily apparent, by introspection, that the facts he cites constitute an agonizing problem for man—the most appropriate answer one can give is: "Speak for yourself, brother!"

Reason, Fromm insists, and the self-awareness which reason makes possible, turns man's "separate, disunited existence" into an "unbearable prison"—and man "would become insane could he not liberate himself from this prison and reach out, unite himself in some form or other with men, with the world outside."[9]

The following paragraph is typical of what Fromm considers an explanation:

The experience of separateness arouses anxiety; it is, indeed, the source of all anxiety. Being separate means being cut off, without any capacity to use my human powers. Hence to be separate means to be helpless, unable to grasp the world—things and people—actively; it means that the world can invade me without my ability to react. Thus, separateness is the source of intense anxiety. Beyond that, it arouses shame and the feeling of guilt. This experience of guilt and shame in separateness is expressed in the Biblical story of Adam and Eve. After Adam and Eve have eaten of the "tree of knowledge of good and evil," after they have disobeyed . . . after they have become human by having emancipated themselves from the original animal harmony with nature, i.e., after their birth as human beings—they saw "that they were naked—and they were ashamed." Should we assume that a myth as old and elementary as this has the prudish morals of the nineteenth-century outlook, and that the important point the story wants to convey to us is the embarrassment that their genitals were visible? This can hardly be so, and by understanding the story in a Victorian spirit, we miss the main point, which seems to be the following: after man and woman have become aware of themselves and of each other, they are aware of their separateness, and of their difference, inasmuch as they belong to different sexes. But while recognizing their separateness they remain strangers, because they have not yet learned to love each other (as is also made very clear by the fact that Adam defends himself by blaming Eve, rather than by trying to defend her). *The awareness of human separation, without reunion by love—is the source of shame. It is at the same time the source of guilt and anxiety.*[10]

All social institutions, all cultures, all religions and philosophies, all progress, asserts Fromm, are motivated by man's need to escape the terrifying sense of helplessness and aloneness to which his reason condemns him.

The necessity to find ever-new solutions for the contradictions in his existence, to find ever-higher forms of unity with nature, his fellowmen and himself, is the source of all psychic forces which motivate man ...[11]

In *Man for Himself,* Fromm states that only through "reason, productiveness and love" can man solve the problem of his "separateness" and achieve a "new union" with the world around him. Fromm's claim to be an advocate of *reason* is disingenuous, to say the least. He speaks of reason and love as being "only two different forms of comprehending the world."[12] As if this were not an unequivocal proof of his irrationalism, he goes on to speak, in *The Art of Loving,* of the "paradoxical logic" of Eastern religions, which, he tells us approvingly, is not encumbered by the Aristotelian law of contradiction and which teaches that "man can perceive reality only in contradictions."[13] (Hegel and Marx, he asserts—correctly—belong to this "paradoxical" epistemological line.) His discussion of what he means by "productiveness" is scarcely more gratifying.

In *The Art of Loving,* written some years after *Man for Himself,* he declares that reason and productive work, though certainly important, provide only partial and, by themselves, very unsatisfactory solutions: the "unity" they achieve is "not interpersonal," and the "desire for interpersonal fusion is the most powerful striving in man."[14] Fromm pulls an unexplained switch at this point. What began as a problem between man and nature is now to be solved (in some unspecified manner) by human "togetherness." One is not surprised; in reading Fromm, this is the sort of pronouncement for which one is waiting—there is a sense of inevitability about it. Love and love alone, he tells us with wonderful originality, can allay man's terror—"Love is the only sane and satisfactory answer to the problem of human existence."[15]

Only through "relating" oneself positively to others, only through feeling "care and responsibility" for them—while preserving one's personal integrity, he adds somewhat mysteriously—can man establish new ties, a new union, that will release him from alienated aloneness.

The cat is now ready to be let fully out of the bag. The preceding is Fromm's view of alienation as a *metaphysical* problem; its full meaning and implication become clear when one turns to his *social-political* analysis of alienation. In the context of the latter, one can see clearly what sort of "ties," what sort of "union" and what sort of "love" Fromm has in mind.

Every society, as a system of human relationships, may be evaluated by how well it satisfies man's basic psychological needs, says Fromm—i.e., he explains, by the possibilities for love, relatedness, and the experience of personal identity which it offers man.

Capitalism, Fromm declares, has been disastrous in this regard: far from solving the problem of man's alienation, it worsens it immeasurably in many respects. In liberating man from medieval regulation and authority, in breaking the chains of ecclesiastical, economic and social tyranny, in destroying the "stability" of the feudal order, capitalism and individualism thrust upon man an unprecedented freedom that was "bound to create a deep feeling of insecurity, powerlessness, doubt, aloneness, and anxiety."[16]

Scratch a collectivist and you will usually find a medievalist. Fromm is not an exception. Like so many socialists, he is a glamorizer of the Middle Ages. He perfunctorily acknowledges the faults of the historical period—but in contrasting it with the capitalism that succeeded it, he is enchanted by what he regards as its virtues.

What characterizes medieval in contrast to modern society is its lack of individual freedom. . . . But although a person was not free in the modern sense, neither was he alone and isolated. In having a distinct, unchangeable, and unquestionable place in the social world from the moment of birth, man was rooted in a structuralized whole, and thus life had a meaning which left no place, and no need, for doubt. A person was identical with his role in society; he *was* a peasant, an artisan, a knight, and not *an individual* who *happened* to have this or that occupation. The social order was conceived as a natural order, and being a definite part of it gave man a feeling of security and of belonging. There was comparatively little competition. One was born into a certain economic position which guaranteed a livelihood determined by tradition, just as it carried economic obligations to those higher in the social hierarchy. But within the limits of his social sphere the individual actually had much freedom to express his self in his work and in his emotional life. Although there was no individualism in the modern sense of the unrestricted choice between many possible ways of life (a freedom of choice which is largely abstract), there was a great deal of *concrete individualism in real life.*[17]

It is not uncommon to encounter this sort of perspective on the Middle Ages, among writers on alienation. But what makes the above passage especially shocking and offensive, in the case of Fromm, is that he repeatedly professes to be a lover of freedom and a valuer of human life.

The complete lack of control over any aspect of one's existence, the ruthless suppression of intellectual freedom, the paralyzing restrictions on any form of individual initiative and independence—these are cardinal characteristics of the Middle Ages. But all of this is swept aside by Fromm—along with the famines, the plagues, the exhausting labor from sunrise to sunset, the suffocating routine, the superstitious terror, the attacks of mass hysteria afflicting entire towns, the nightmare brutality of men's dealings with one another, the use of legalized torture as a normal way of life—all of this is swept aside, so entranced is Fromm by the vision of a world in which men did not have to invent and compete, they had only to submit and obey.

Nowhere does he tell us what specifically the medieval man's *"concrete individualism"* consisted of. One is morbidly curious to know what he would say.

With the collapse of medievalism and the emergence of a free-market society, Fromm declares, man was compelled to assume total responsibility for his own survival: he had to produce and to trade—he had to think and to judge—he had no authority to guide him, and nothing but his own ability to keep him in existence. No longer could he, by virtue of the class into which he was born, *inherit* his sense of personal identity: henceforward, he had to *achieve* it. This posed a devastating psychological problem for man, intensifying his basic feeling of isolation and separateness.

"It is true," Fromm remarks, "that the capitalistic mode of production is conducive to political freedom, while any centrally planned social order is in danger of leading to political regimentation and eventually to dictatorship."[18] Capitalism, he further concedes, has proven itself superlatively capable of producing goods and of raising men's material standard of living to undreamed-of heights. But a "sane society" must have more to offer man than political freedom and material well-being. Capitalism, Fromm insists, is destructive of man's *spirit*. He offers several reasons for this charge, which are very revealing.

(1) Like Marx, Fromm decries the humiliating predicament of the worker who has to *sell* his *services*. Capitalism condemns the worker to experience himself, not as a man, but as a commodity, as a thing to be traded. Furthermore, since he is only a tiny part of a vast production process, since, for example, he does not build an entire automobile himself (and then drive home in it), but builds only a small part of it (the total being subsequently sold to some unknown, distant party), the worker feels alienated from the product of his own labor and, therefore, feels alienated from his own labor as such—unlike the artisan of the Middle Ages, whose labor could express the "full richness" of his personality.

It is an elementary fact of economics that specialization and exchange, under a division of labor, make a level of productivity possible which otherwise would not be remotely attainable. In pre-capitalist centuries, when a man's economic well-being was limited by the goods he himself could produce with his own primitive tools, an unconscionable amount of labor was required to make or acquire the simplest necessities—and the general standard of living was appallingly low: human existence was a continual, exhausting struggle against imminent starvation. About half of the children born, perished before the age of ten. But with the development of the wages system under capitalism, the introduction of machinery and the opportunity for a man to sell his labor, life (to say nothing of an ever-increasing standard of material well-being) was made possible for millions who could have had no chance at survival in pre-capitalist economies. However, for Fromm and those who share his viewpoint, these considerations are, doubtless, too "materialistic." To offer men a chance to enjoy an unprecedented material well-being, is, evidently, to sentence them to alienation; whereas to hold them down to the stagnant level of a medieval serf or guildsman, is to offer them spiritual fulfillment.

(2) Fromm decries the "anonymity of the social forces . . . inherent in the structure of the capitalistic mode of production."[19] The laws of the market, of supply and demand, of economic cause and effect, are ominously impersonal: no single individual's *wishes* control them. Is it the worker who determines how much he is to be paid? No. It is not even the employer. It is that faceless monster, the market. It determines the wage level in some manner beyond the worker's power to grasp. As for the capitalist, his position is scarcely better: he, too, is helpless. "The individual capitalist expands his enterprise not primarily because he *wants* to, but because he *has* to, because . . . postponement of further expansion would mean regression."[20] If he attempts to stagnate, he will go out of business. Under such a system, asks Fromm, how can man *not* feel alienated?

Consider what Fromm is denouncing. Under capitalism, the wages paid to a man for his work are determined *objectively*—by the law of supply and demand. The market—reflecting the voluntary judgments of all those who participate in it, all those who buy and sell, produce and consume, offer or seek employment—establishes the general price level of goods and services. This is the context which men are obliged to consider in setting the price they will ask for their work or offer for the work of others; if a man demands more than the market value of his work, he will remain unemployed; if a particular employer offers him less than the market value of his work, the man will seek—and find—employment elsewhere. The same principle applies to the capitalist who offers his goods for sale. If the prices and quality of his goods are comparable or preferable to those of other men in the same field of production, he will be able to compete; if others can do better than he can, if they can offer superior goods and/or lower prices, he will be obliged to improve, to grow, to equal their achievement, or else he will lose his customers. The standard determining a producer's success or failure is the *objective* value of his product—as judged, within the context of the market (and of their knowledge), by those to whom he offers his product. This is the only rational and just principle of exchange. But *this* is what Fromm considers evil.

What he rebels against is *objectivity*. How—he demands—can a man not feel alienated in a system where his wishes are not omnipotent, where the unearned is not to be had, where growth is rewarded and stagnation is penalized?

It is clear from the foregoing that Fromm's basic quarrel is with *reality*—since nature confronts man with the identical conditions, which a free economy merely reflects: nature, too, holds a man to the law of cause and effect; nature, too, makes constant growth a condition of successful life.

There are writers on alienation who recognize this and do not bother to center their attacks on capitalism: they damn nature out-right. They declare that man's life is intrinsically and inescapably *tragic*—since reality is "tyrannical," since contradictory desires cannot be satisfied, since objectivity is a "prison," since time is a "net" that no one can elude, etc. Existentialists, in particular, specialize in this sort of pronouncement. (In recent years there has been a growing tendency among certain writers on alienation to call for the abolition of all known social systems, while evading the question of what new system they propose to substitute; they continue, predictably, to reserve their harshest criticisms not for totalitarian political systems but for the American system of semi-capitalism.)

(3) As consumer in a capitalist economy, Fromm contends, man is subject to further alienating pressures. He is overwhelmed with innumerable products among which he must choose. He is bewildered and brainwashed by the blandishments of advertisers, forever urging him to buy their wares. This staggering multiplicity of possible choices is threatening to his sanity. Moreover, he is "conditioned" to consume for the sake of consuming—to long for an ever-higher standard of living—merely in order to keep the "system" going. With automatic washing machines, automatic cameras, and automatic can openers, modern man's relationship to nature becomes more and more remote. He is increasingly condemned to the nightmare of an *artificial* world.

No such problem confronted the feudal serf.

This much is true: sleeping on an earthen floor, the medieval serf—to say nothing of the cavemen—was much *closer* to nature, in one uncomfortable and unhygienic sense of the word.

The above criticism of capitalism has become very fashionable among social commentators. What is remarkable is that almost invariably, as in the case of Fromm, the criticism is made by the same writers who are loudest in crying that man needs more *leisure*. Yet the purpose of the "gadgets" they condemn is, specifically, to liberate man's time. Thus they wish to provide man with more leisure, while damning the material means that make leisure possible.

As for the charge—equally popular—that the multiplicity of choices offered to man in capitalistic society is threatening to his mental equilibrium, it should be remembered that *fear* of choices and decisions is a basic symptom of low self-esteem. To whose mentality, then, do these critics of capitalism demand that society be adjusted?

(4) The development of a complex, highly industrialized society requires an extreme degree of quantification and abstraction in men's method of thinking, observes Fromm—and this, in still another way, estranges man from the world around him: he loses the ability to relate to things in "their concreteness and uniqueness."[21]

One can agree with Fromm in part: an industrial technological society demands the fullest development and exercise of man's *conceptual* faculty, i.e., of his distinctively *human* form of cognition. The *sensory-perceptual* level of consciousness—the level of an animal's cognition—will not do.

Those who assert that the conceptual level of consciousness alienates man from the real world, merely confess that their concepts bear no relation to reality—or that they do not understand the relation of concepts to reality. But it should be remembered that the capacity to abstract and conceptualize offers man—to the extent that he is rational—a means of "relating" to the world around him immeasurably superior to that enjoyed by any other species. It does not "alienate" man from nature, it makes him nature's master: an animal obeys nature *blindly;* man obeys her *intelligently* and thereby acquires the power to command her. (To prevent any possible misunderstanding, perhaps it should be stressed that the foregoing remarks are not intended to imply any hostility or antagonism between man and nature; the notion of such hostility or antagonism would be thoroughly irrational; man is part of nature, a fact that he forgets only at his peril.)

(5) Finally, most alienating of all, perhaps, are the sort of relationships that exist among men under capitalism, says Fromm.

What is the modern man's *relationship to his fellow man?* It is one between two abstractions, two living machines, who use each other. The employer uses the ones whom he employs; the salesman uses his customers. . . . There is not much love or hate to be found in human relations of our day. There is, rather, a superficial friendliness, and a more than superficial fairness, but behind that surface is distance and indifference. . . . The alienation between man and man results in the loss of those general and social bonds which characterize medieval as well as most other precapitalist societies.[22]

Fromm is claiming that there existed, in pre-capitalist societies, a mutual good will among men, an attitude of respect and benevolent solidarity, a regard for the value of the human person, that vanished with the rise of a free-market society. This is worse than false. The claim is absurd historically and disgraceful morally.

It is notorious that, in the Middle Ages, human relationships were characterized by mutual suspiciousness, hostility, and cruelty: everyone regarded his neighbor as a potential threat, and nothing was held more cheaply than human life. Such invariably is the case in *any* society where men are ruled by brute force. In putting an end to slavery and serfdom, capitalism introduced a social benevolence that would have been impossible under earlier systems. Capitalism valued a man's life as it had never been valued before. Capitalism is the politico-economic expression of the principle that a man's life, freedom, and happiness are his by moral right.

Under capitalism, men are free to *choose* their "social bonds"—meaning: to choose whom they will associate with. Men are not trapped within the prison of their family, tribe, caste, class, or neighborhood. They choose whom they will value, whom they will befriend, whom they will deal with, what kind of relationships they will enter. This implies and entails man's responsibility to form independent value-judgments. It implies and entails, also, that a man must *earn* the social relationships he desires. But this, clearly, is anathema to Fromm.

"Love," he has told us, "is the only sane and satisfactory answer to the problem of human existence"—but, he asserts, love and capitalism are *inimical*. "The *principle* underlying capitalistic society and the *principle* of love are incompatible."[23] The principle of capitalism, says Fromm, is that of "fairness ethics," of *trade,* of the exchange of values, without recourse to force or fraud; individuals deal with another only on the premise of mutual self-interest; they engage only in those transactions from which they expect a profit, reward, or gain. "It may even be said that the development of fairness ethics is the particular ethical contribution of capitalist society."[24]

But to approach love with any concern for one's self-interest is—he asserts—to negate the very essence of love. To love an individual is to feel care and responsibility for him; it is not to appraise his character or personality as a "commodity" from which one expects pleasure. To love "ideally" is to love "unconditionally"—it is to love a human being, not for the fact of *what* he is, but for the fact *that* he is—it is to love without reference to values or standards or judgment. "In essence, all human beings are identical. We are all part of One; we are One. This being so, it should not make any difference whom we love."[25]

It should not, in other words, make any difference whether the person we love is a being of stature or a total nonentity, a genius or a fool, a hero or a scoundrel. "We are all part of One." Is it necessary to point out who stands to gain and who to lose by this view of love?

The desire to be loved "unconditionally," the desire to be loved with no concern for his objective personal worth, is one of man's "deepest longings," Fromm insists; whereas to be loved on the basis of *merit,* "because one deserves it," invokes doubt and uncertainty, since merit has to be struggled for and since such love can be withdrawn should the merit cease to exist. "Furthermore, 'deserved' love easily leaves a bitter feeling that one is not loved for oneself, that one is loved *only because one pleases* . . ."[26]

It is typical of Fromm that he should deliver what is in fact (though not in Fromm's estimate) a deadly insult to human nature, without offering any justification for his charge. He assumes that all men, by nature, are so profoundly lacking in self-esteem that they crave a love which bears no relation to their actions, achievements, or character, a love not to be earned but to be received only as a free gift.

What does it mean to be loved "for oneself"? In reason, it can mean only: to be loved for the values one has achieved in one's character and person. The highest compliment one can be paid by another human being is to be told: "Because of what you are, you are essential to my happiness." But this is the love that, according to Fromm, leaves one with "a bitter feeling."

It is the capitalistic culture, he declares, that inculcates such concepts as the "deserved" and the "undeserved"—the earned and the unearned—and thus poisons the growth of proper love. Proper love, Fromm tells us, should be given solely out of the richness of the spirit of the giver, in demonstration of the giver's "potency." Fromm nowhere reveals the exact nature of this "potency," of course. "Love is an act of faith . . ."[27] Proper love should raise no questions about the virtue or character of its object; it should desire no joy from such virtues as the object might possess—for, if it does, it is not proper love, it is only capitalistic selfishness.

But, Fromm asks, "how can one act within the framework of existing society and at the same time practice love?"[28] He does not declare that love is *impossible* under capitalism—merely that it is exceptionally difficult.

To love is to value, healthy love expresses admiration. Love is not alms, but a tribute. If love did not imply admiration, if it did not imply an acknowledgement of moral qualities that the recipient of love possessed—what meaning or significance would love have, and why would Fromm or anyone consider it desirable? Only one answer is possible, and it is not an attractive one: when love is divorced from values, then "love" becomes, not a tribute, but a moral blank check: a promise that one will be forgiven anything, that one will not be abandoned, that one will be taken care of.

To divorce love from values (and value-judgments), is to confess one's longing for the unearned. The idealization of this longing as a proper moral goal is a constant theme running through Fromm's writing.

That the underlying motive is the desire to be taken care of, the desire to be spared the responsibility of independence, is revealed explicitly in Fromm's socio-political "solution" to the problem of alienation.

In order that man may be enabled to conquer his feeling of aloneness and alienation, to practice love and to achieve a full sense of personal identity, a new social system must be established, Fromm declares.

Private ownership of the means of production must be abolished. The profit motive must be forbidden. Industry must be decentralized. Society should be divided into self-governing industrial guilds; factories should be owned and run by all those who work in them.

Why—according to Fromm's social philosophy—should a janitor in an industrial plant not have the same right to determine its management as the man who happened to create the plant? Does not the janitor's personality require as much self-expression as anyone else's?

Under capitalism, says Fromm, men are overwhelmed by and are the pawns of a complex industrial machine whose omnipotent forces and laws are beyond their comprehension or control. Under the decentralized, "democratic" system he proposes—which is some sort of blend of guild socialism and syndicalism—industrial establishments will be broken down into units whose function is within everyone's easy comprehension, with no "alienating" demands made on anyone's abstract capacity.

Under this system, he explains, every person will be provided with his minimum subsistence, whether the person wishes to work or not. This is necessary if man is to develop healthily and happily. However, to discourage parasitism, Fromm suggests that this support should not extend beyond two years. Who is to provide this support, whether they will be willing to do so, and what will happen if they are not willing, are questions Fromm does not discuss.

So long as men are occupied with the problem of survival, Fromm feels, their spiritual concerns—the concerns that really *matter*—are almost inevitably neglected. How can the worker's personality not be impoverished, if he must face daily the necessity of earning a livelihood? How can the businessman develop his creative potentialities, if he is in bondage to his obsession with production? How can the artist preserve his soul's integrity, if he is plagued with temptations by Hollywood and Madison Avenue? How can the consumer cultivate individual tastes and preferences, if he is surrounded by the standardized commodities begotten by mass production?

If one wishes to understand the relevance of epistemology to politics, one should observe what is gained for Fromm by that "paradoxical logic" of which he writes so approvingly. If, as it teaches, "man can perceive reality only in contradictions," then Fromm does not have to be troubled by the conflict between his claim to be an advocate of reason and his enthusiasm for Eastern mysticism—nor does he have to be troubled by the conflict between his claim to be a defender of individualism and his advocacy of political collectivism. His disdain for the law of contradiction permits him to announce that true individualism is possible only in the collectivized community—that true freedom is possible only when production is taken out of the hands of private individuals and placed under the absolute control of the group—that men will cease to be objects of "use" by others, only when they are willing to renounce personal profit and make *social usefulness* the goal of their lives.[29]

Fromm calls his proposed system "Humanistic Communitarian Socialism." Under it, he maintains, man will achieve "a new harmony with nature" to replace the one he has lost—man will enjoy the tranquillity and self-fulfillment of the animals whose state Fromm finds so enviable.

If, often, Fromm is more than a little disingenuous in the presentation of his views, he is, nonetheless, extremely *explicit*. This is what is unusual about him. Most writers of his persuasion twist themselves for pages and pages in order to obscure their advocacy of the ideas—and contradictions—which he announces openly.

His explicitness notwithstanding, he is very representative culturally and should be recognized as such. The recurrent themes running through the literature on alienation—and through today's social commentary generally—are the themes which Fromm brings into naked focus: that reason is "unnatural," that a non-contradictory, objective reality "restricts" one's individuality, that the necessity of *choice* is an awesome burden, that it is "tragic" not to be able to eat one's cake and have it, too, that self-responsibility is frightening, that the achievement of personal identity is a *social* problem—that "love" is the omnipotent solution—and that the political implementation of this solution is socialism.

The problem of alienation and the problem of personal identity are inseparable. The man who lacks a firm sense of personal identity feels alienated; the man who feels alienated lacks a firm sense of personal identity.

Pain is an organism's alarm-signal, warning of danger; the particular species of pain which is the feeling of alienation announces to a man that he is existing in a psychological state improper to him—*that his relationship to reality is wrong.*

No animal faces such questions as: What should I make of myself? What manner of life is proper to my nature? Such questions are possible only to a rational being, i.e., a being whose characteristic method of cognitive functioning (of apprehending reality) is conceptual, who is not only conscious but also self-conscious, and whose power of abstraction enables him to project many alternative courses of action. Further, such questions are possible only to a being whose cognitive faculty is exercised *volitionally* (thinking is not automatic)—a being who is self-directing and self-regulating in thought and in action, and whose existence, therefore, entails a constant process of *choice*.

As a living entity, man is born with specific needs and capacities; these constitute his *species* identity, so to speak—i.e., they constitute his human nature. How he exercises his capacities to satisfy his needs—i.e., how he deals with the facts of reality, how he chooses to function, in thought and in action—constitutes his *personal* or *individual* identity. His sense of himself—his implicit concept or image of the kind of person he is (including his self-esteem or lack of it)—is the cumulative product of the choices he makes.

A man's "I," his ego, his deepest self, is his faculty of awareness, his capacity to think. To choose to think, to identify the facts of reality—to assume the responsibility of judging what is true or false, right or wrong—is man's basic form of *self-assertiveness.* It is his acceptance of the responsibility of intellectual independence, his commitment to the efficacy of his own mind.

The essence of *selflessness* is the suspension of one's consciousness. When and to the extent that a man chooses to evade the effort and responsibility of thinking, of seeking knowledge, of passing judgment, his action is one of *self-abdication*. To relinquish thought, is to relinquish one's ego—and to pronounce oneself unfit for existence, incompetent to deal with the facts of reality.

To the extent that a man chooses to think, his premises and values are acquired first-hand and they are not a mystery to him; he experiences himself as the *active cause* of his character, behavior, and goals. To the extent that a man attempts to live without thinking, to the extent that he attempts to live without awareness of relevant aspects of external reality as well as internal reality, he experiences himself as *passive,* his person and actions are the accidental products of forces he does not understand, of his range-of-the-moment feelings and random environmental influences. When a man defaults on the responsibility of thought, he is left at the mercy of his involuntary, subconscious reactions—and *these* will be at the mercy of the outside forces impinging upon him, at the mercy of whoever and whatever is around him. By his default, such a person turns himself into the social determinists' view of man: into an empty mold waiting to be filled, into a will-less robot waiting to be taken over by any environment and any conditioners.

A strong sense of personal identity is the product of two things: a policy of independent thinking (of living consciously), and, as a consequence, the possession of an integrated set of values. Since it is his values that determine a man's emotions and goals, and give direction and meaning to his life, a man experiences his values as an extension of himself, as an integral part of his identity, as crucial to that which makes him himself.

"Values," in this context, refers to fundamental and abstract values, not to concrete value-judgments. For example, a man holding rationality as his abstract value may choose a friend who appears to embody this value; if, subsequently, he decides that he was mistaken in his judgment, that his friend is not rational and that their relationship should be ended, this does not alter his personal identity; but if, instead, he decides that he no longer values rationality, his personal identity *is* altered.

If a man holds contradictory values, these necessarily do violence to his sense of personal identity. They result in a splintered sense of self, a self broken into unintegratable fragments. To avoid this painful experience of a splintered identity, a man whose values are contradictory will commonly seek to escape knowledge of his contradictions by means of evasion, repression, rationalization, etc. Thus, to escape a problem created by a failure of thought, he suspends thinking. To escape a threat to his sense of personal identity, *he suspends his ego*—he suspends his self *qua* thinking, judging entity.

Moved by feelings whose source he does not understand, and by contradictions whose existence he does not acknowledge, he suffers a progressive sense of self-estrangement, of self-alienation. A man's emotions are the product of his premises and values. But the man who is run by his emotions, attempting to make them a substitute for rational judgment, experiences them as alien forces. The paradox of his position is this: his emotions become his only source of personal identity, but his experience of identity becomes: a being ruled by demons. Such a man does not, in any but a superficial sense, experience his emotions; what he is aware of are seemingly inexplicable impulses—which is not the same thing.

It is important to observe that the experience of self-alienation and the feeling of being alienated from reality, from the world around one, proceed from the same cause: one's default on the responsibility of thinking. The suspension of proper cognitive contact with reality and the suspension of one's ego, are a single act. A flight from reality is a flight from self. Chronologically, a flight from reality follows rather than precedes a flight from self; thereafter, the process becomes reciprocal.

One of the consequences is a feeling of alienation from other men, the sense that one is not part of the human race—that one is, in effect, a freak. In betraying one's status as a human being, one makes oneself a metaphysical outcast. This is not altered by the knowledge that many other human beings have committed the same betrayal. One feels alone and cut off—cut off by the unreality of one's own existence, by one's desolate inner sense of spiritual impoverishment.

The same failure of rationality and independence by which men rob themselves of personal identity leads them, most commonly, to the self-destructive policy of seeking a *substitute* for identity—or, more precisely, seeking a second-hand identity—through mindless conformity to the values of others. This is the psychological phenomenon which I have designated as social metaphysics. In the chapter on "Social Metaphysics," in *The Psychology of Self-Esteem,* discussing the phenomenon of the second-hand identity, I commented on the type most relevant to the present context, the "Conventional" social metaphysician:

This is the person who accepts the world and its prevailing values ready-made; his is not to reason why. What is true? What others say is true. What is right? What others believe is right. How should one live? As others live. . . . (This is) the person whose sense of identity and personal worth is *explicitly* a function of his ability to satisfy the values, terms and expectations of those omniscient and omnipresent "others." . . . In a culture such as the present one, with its disintegrating values, its intellectual chaos, its moral bankruptcy—where the familiar guideposts and rules are vanishing, where the authoritative mirrors reflecting "reality" are splintering into a thousand unintelligible subcults, where "adjustment" is becoming harder and harder—the Conventional social metaphysician is the first to run to a psychiatrist, crying that he has lost his identity, because he no longer knows unequivocally what he is supposed to do and be.

It would never occur to a person of self-esteem and independent judgment that one's "identity" is a thing to be gained from or determined by others. To a person untouched by self-doubt, the wails heard today about the anguish of modern man as he confronts the question "Who am I?" are incomprehensible. But in the light of the above, the wailing becomes more intelligible. It is the cry of social metaphysicians who no longer know which authorities to obey—and who are moaning that it is *someone's* duty to herd them to a sense of self, that "The System" must provide them with self-esteem. When a person defaults on the responsibility of independent thought, and when he cuts himself off from awareness of his own needs, desires, frustrations and longings, then inevitably he experiences himself as dependent on external forces for any sense of personal identity; identity becomes "recognition," "status," a rank or award to be conferred by the omnipotent Others.

This is the psychological root of the modern intellectuals' mystique of the Middle Ages, of the dazed longing for that style of life—and of the massive evasion concerning the actual conditions of existence during that period. The Middle Ages represents the social metaphysician's unconfessed dream; a system in which his dread of independence and self-responsibility is proclaimed to be a virtue and is made a social imperative.

When—in any age—a man attempts to evade the responsibility of intellectual independence, and to derive his sense of identity from "belonging," he pays a deadly price in terms of the sabotaging of his mental processes thereafter. The degree to which a man substitutes the judgment of others for his own, failing to look at reality directly, is the degree to which his mental processes are alienated from reality. He functions, not by means of concepts, but by means of memorized cue-words, i.e., learned *sounds* associated with certain contexts and situations, but lacking authentic cognitive content for their user. This is the unidentified, unrecognized phenomenon that prompts unthinking people today to grant validity to the charge that modern man lives "too abstractly," "too intellectually," and that he needs to "get back to nature." They sense dimly that they are out of contact with reality, that something is wrong with their grasp of the world around them. But they accept an entirely fallacious interpretation of their problem. The truth is not that they are lost among "abstractions," but that they have failed to discover the nature and proper use of abstractions; they are not lost among concepts, they are lost among *cue-words*. They are cut off from reality not because they attempt to grasp it too intellectually, but because they attempt to grasp it *only as seen by others;* they attempt to grasp it *second-hand.* And they move through an unreal world of verbal rituals, mouthing the slogans and phrases they hear repeated by others, falsely imagining that those empty words are concepts, and never apprehending the proper use of their conceptual faculty, never learning what first-hand, conceptual knowledge consists of.

It is a well-known psychological fact that when men are neurotically anxious, when they suffer from feelings of dread for which they cannot account, they often attempt to make their plight more tolerable by directing their fear at some external object: they seek to persuade themselves that their fear is a rational response to the threat of germs, or the possible appearance of burglars, or the danger of lightning, or the brain-controlling radiations of Martians. The process by which men decide that the cause of their alienation is capitalism, is not dissimilar.

There are reasons, however, why capitalism is the target for their projection and rationalization.

The alienated man is fleeing from the responsibility of a volitional (i.e., self-directing) consciousness: the freedom to think or not to think, to initiate a process of reason or to evade it, is a burden he longs to escape. But since this freedom is inherent in his nature as man, there is no escape from it; hence his guilt and anxiety when he abandons reason and sight in favor of feelings and blindness. But there is another level on which man confronts the issue of freedom: the existential or social level—and here escape *is* possible. *Political freedom is not a metaphysical given: it has to be achieved*—hence it can be rejected. The psychological root of the revolt against freedom in one's existence, is the revolt against freedom in one's consciousness. *The root of the revolt against self-responsibility in action is the revolt against self-direction in thought.* The man who does not want to think, does not want to bear responsibility for the consequences of his actions nor for his own life.

Today, of course, capitalism has largely been abandoned in favor of a mixed economy, i.e., a mixture of freedom and statism—moving steadily in the direction of increasing statism. Today, we are far closer to the "ideal society" of the socialists than when Marx first wrote of the worker's "alienation." Yet with every advance of collectivism, the cries concerning man's alienation grow louder. The problem, we are told, is getting worse. In communist countries, when such criticisms are allowed to be voiced, some commentators are beginning to complain that the Marxist solution to the worker's alienation has failed, that man under communism is still alienated, that the "new harmony" with nature and one's fellow men has not come.

It didn't come to the medieval serf or guildsman, either—the propaganda of commentators such as Erich Fromm notwithstanding.

Man cannot escape from his nature, and if he establishes a social system which is inimical to the requirements of his nature—a system which forbids him to function as a rational, independent being—psychological and physical disaster is the result.

A free society, of course, cannot automatically guarantee the mental well-being of all its members. Freedom is not a *sufficient* condition to assure man's proper fulfillment, but it is a *necessary* condition. And capitalism—laissez-faire capitalism—is the only system which provides that condition.

The problem of alienation is not metaphysical; it is not man's natural fate, never to be escaped, like some sort of Original Sin; it is a *disease.* It is not the consequence of capitalism or industrialism or "bigness"—and it cannot be legislated out of existence by the abolition of property rights. The problem of alienation is *psycho-epistemological:* it pertains to how man chooses to use his own consciousness. It is the product of man's revolt against thinking—which means: against reality.

If a man defaults on the responsibility of seeking knowledge, choosing values and setting goals—if this is the sphere he surrenders to the authority of others—*how is he to escape the feeling that the universe is closed to him?* It is. By his own choice.

As to any sense of alienation forced on man by the social system in which he lives, it is not freedom but the lack of freedom—brought about by the rising tide of statism, by the expanding powers of the government and the increasing infringement of individual rights—that produces in man a sense of powerlessness and helplessness, the terrifying sense of being at the mercy of malevolent forces.

As I conclude this essay, I appreciate the fact that the subject of alienatión—self-alienation in particular—is rather more complex than space allows me to indicate here. I have confined myself to only a few essentials, within the context of the Marxian attack on capitalism. A comprehensive discussion of the problem of alienation—alienation from the body, from our feelings and emotions, from our thoughts, from our intelligence, from our mind or spirit, from our highest possibilities—may be found in my comprehensive book on the psychology of self-esteem, *Honoring the Self* (J. P. Tarcher, 1984; Bantam Books, 1985).

NOTES

[1] Hendrik M. Ruitenbeek, *The Individual and the Crowd—A Study of Identity in America* (New York: New American Library [Mentor], 1965), p. 15.

[2] Gerald Sykes, ed., *Alienation,* vol. 1, (New York: George Braziller, 1964), p. xiii.

[3] Ludwig von Mises, *Socialism* (New Haven: Yale University Press, 1951), p. 527.

[4] Erich Fromm, *Man for Himself* (New York: Rinehart & Co., 1947), pp. 39–40.

[5] Erich Fromm, *The Art of Loving* (New York: Harper & Brothers, 1956), p. 7.

[6] Fromm, *Man for Himself,* p. 40.

[7] Ibid., p. 42.

[8] Ibid., p. 43.

[9] Fromm, *Art of Loving,* p. 8.

[10] Ibid., pp. 8–9.

[11] Erich Fromm, *The Sane Society* (New York: Rinehart & Co., 1955), p. 25.

[12] Fromm, *Man for Himself,* p. 97.

[13] Fromm, *Art of Loving,* p. 77.

[14] Ibid., p. 18.

[15] Ibid., p. 133.

[16] Erich Fromm, *Escape from Freedom* (New York: Rinehart & Co., 1941), p. 63.

[17] Ibid., pp. 41–42.

[18] Fromm, *The Sane Society,* p. 138.

[19] Ibid.

[20] Ibid., p. 86.

[21] Ibid., p. 114.

[22] Ibid., p. 139.

[23] Fromm, *The Art of Loving,* p. 131.

[24] Ibid., p. 129.

[25] Ibid., p. 55.

[26] Ibid., p. 42.

[27] Ibid., p. 128.

[28] Ibid., pp. 130–31.

[29] For the most detailed presentation of these doctrines, see Fromm, *The Sane Society.*

part THREE

ETHICS AND MORAL FOUNDATIONS

Both Marxian communism and individualist capitalism have been expressed as purely scientific systems, the former by Marx and some of his closest followers, such as Engels, the latter by the scientific economists who follow, as they see it, the central precepts of Adam Smith. Their conception of science differs, so that in Marxian science there is room for value—but not necessarily *moral*—judgments, while in neoclassical economics, values are seen as subjective, expressing the preferences people happen to have.

But there are also normative versions of these frameworks, and here we encounter these versions laid out in the most up-to-date fashion. What is defined as good, from the viewpoint of Marxian communism? From a capitalist viewpoint, what are the moral supports that undergird the capitalist system? The question that is being discussed here is clearly normative, indeed, ethical or moral: What ultimately makes a life and a community a good one? Why ought one to choose the one system over the other?

While the debate between communism and capitalism is not always put in these kind of terms, it is important to realize that there is a moral dimension to the argument as well.

J. ROGER LEE

THE MORALITY OF CAPITALISM AND OF MARKET INSTITUTIONS

A major concern about capitalism is whether it is compatible with morality and justice, and it is this topic that J. Roger Lee—Associate Professor of Philosophy at the California State University, Los Angeles, and writer of several essays on criminal justice and other philosophical topics—addresses here. How does the market conform to the requirements of morality and justice? How can the case for capitalism answer charges about the obvious possibility of immoral exchanges within markets? What about alienation, especially in the labor market? What of the possibility of pursuing trivial, irreverent, and immoral goals in the marketplace, a possibility that seems, intuitively, to render the market vicious?

Capitalism is the social, political, and economic system which lets rights to property be transferred by market transactions among private individuals, alone or in groups. Systems of thought that oppose capitalism oppose this way of fixing legitimate property claims and substitute other criteria for the legitimacy of property transfers, or prohibit such transfers altogether.

This essay is an account of the morality of capitalism as a political system, and so it is a study of the moral status of market institutions. Within the field of morality we attempt to formulate rational standards that can be used in distinguishing between right and wrong actions and between good and bad things and institutions. To be useful, any moral theory must be able to come up with a reasonable proof of why people should or should not hold particular moral opinions about things or actions. Such a proof should show a reasonable person that the goodness or badness, the rightness or wrongness is demonstrable on the basis of general, plausible principles.

In addition to morality, this essay will discuss markets. A market is a situation in which people can exchange some goods or services for other goods or services. If I place an ad in the local newspaper offering to sell my typewriter and you read the ad, call me, come to my home and buy the machine from me, then that complex situation of newspaper, people reading it, your phone contact, and the exchange in my home constitutes a market.

What situations are *not* markets? Chaotic situations like battles can block cooperation and trade. Also, there are places or times where there are no people interested in trade. It is hard to sell refrigerators on the North Pole; there are no buyers. So there is no market for refrigerators on the North Pole.

Market exchanges have to be voluntary. Nonvoluntary exchanges like theft or taxation are not market exchanges. Those exchanges are not market exchanges, because of their forced nature.

So the difference between the words "can" and "may" is important here.

This essay was prepared by the author for the present volume.

"Can" connotes possibility of achievement, and that is the term which I have been using throughout. "May" connotes the moral or legal permissibility of an action.

Sometimes voluntary market transactions either of a moral or an immoral sort are illegal. In recent years in the United States, the buying and selling of heroin, without prescription, has been outlawed. If I wanted to buy some heroin and you had some you wanted to sell, any transaction that we undertook to satisfy our mutual desires would be against the law. From the standpoint of the law, one *may* not buy and sell heroin. Of course one *can* do it; witness the flourishing heroin trade in the United States. When market exchanges take place contrary to the law, they are said to occur on the black market. If people can voluntarily exchange goods or services, there *is* a market, even if only a black market. Sometimes the force of law is so effective and so far-reaching, however, that people can no longer freely exchange. Then there is no market because of the law. Yet this is rare; more frequently, black markets flourish despite the law.

UTILITARIANISM AND MARKETS

Utilitarianism is a moral theory about the rightness and wrongness of action. In its pure form, it holds that among the choices we have in a given situation, the right action is the one that produces the most good consequences.[1]

For a century after the publication of Adam Smith's *The Wealth of Nations,* both critics[2] and supporters of markets agreed that if the topic was the wealth of nations, then more wealth is realized with unfettered markets than with any known nonmarket alternatives.[3]

There are only two alternatives to market economies. The first leaves economic affairs absolutely uncoordinated and disallows trade. In this system, people may be producing only for themselves or perhaps for a common pool to which they deposit and take as they will or need. I take it as clear that the most elementary economics shows this alternative to be incapable of producing the greatest amount of wealth, so economics does not show it to have a moral defense on utilitarian grounds. It may be laudable on nonutilitarian grounds but that is a different subject which I take up below.

The other nonmarket alternative would be the case of a planned economy, in which markets were suspended yet economic affairs were coordinated in a nonmarket way. First someone[4] makes a decision, about what will be produced and how it will be distributed, and second, that person imposes that state of affairs on the entire community by force.

THE CALCULATION PROBLEM

At the end of the nineteenth century and the beginning of the twentieth, some social theorists came to think that the objective of maximizing wealth could be better served by government administrative boards of central planning authorities who would replace the seeming anarchy of market exchanges with coordinated planning. In this century, such planning boards were established in the Soviet Union and the Fascist states of Germany and Italy. Since then such boards have been imitated in the United States (largely in the depression era New Deal programs), in other European countries and in parts of the Third World. Although this theory had a certain short-run popularity, it had an early theoretical refutation in economics and has been found wanting in practice in the countries that have attempted it.

This alternative to markets faces the difficulty of the *calculation problem,* which is best viewed as an argument showing that there is a vitiating problem that a central planning authority trying to coordinate the affairs of an economy by directives could not meet.[5]

The argument proceeds as follows. On the market, particular economic decision makers proceed to their activities on the basis of knowledge that they have of particular circumstances of need, cost, and availability of resources. Much of the rationality of the economic activities of these individuals rests on this particular knowledge to which they alone have access and use.

The central planners of a planned economy, on the other hand, do not have access to this knowledge of particular circumstances, because they are not present at all the scenes of activity for which they plan. Bereft of this knowledge, their economic planning is relatively uninformed and thus is relatively inefficient. Consequently, it is impossible for a centrally planned economy to function as efficiently as a market economy—it is impossible for the economic central planners to plan wisely.

PRICES

Market prices are an important issue here. Market decisions are effected through and informed by the mechanism of pricing in a given currency, a recognized unit of exchange. Prices are determined by people choosing to rank things as more or less desirable when they buy and sell things. People are guided by prices in their decisions to trade and thereby to redistribute goods and services in the community. As things are used up, new goods and services are produced. Which goods and services are produced is determined by what individuals are willing to exchange their raw material and labor for. The producers know what these desired goods and services are by checking their relative prices on the market.

In a centrally planned, nonmarket economy, individual consumption decisions among the people who buy and sell on the market would not determine which goods and services would be produced, and what their prices would be. Rather, the decrees of the planning board would determine production and pricing. Prices will almost certainly be different from what they would have been in a market because they will be causally determined by the plan, the prices the central planning authority sets for its own purposes.

This leads to an important conclusion. *The information in the prices will be only the information in the plan, in the beginning, before the plan is applied.* Prices in a planned economy cannot inform the planners about the constraints on their plans, about changing circumstances as the plan is implemented, changing desires, changing relative scarcities, technological change, etc. In the market, on the other hand, producers and consumers inform each other of their desires by trading at changing prices. The prices show relative values of goods and services at the start of the production-exchange process and then, as the process continues, the changing prices reflect changing circumstances that have to be taken into account. *Central planners cannot use the prices that they themselves have imposed to inform themselves of these changing factors.* Markets are vast information-flow networks and central planners remove themselves from that information.

So the problem of economic calculation is the following: In the absence of market prices, how will the planning authority get the information that would have been coded in prices in a market economy? A consideration of the lost information involved shows that a centrally planned, nonmarket economy is empirically impossible of achieving. Either it would not realize its goals or what was realized would likely not prove to be as useful to the economy as was originally hoped.

To the extent that we would try to replace the market in order to impose a vision of the good on economic affairs, we will lose our ability to produce that good because we lose our ability to use the information available to us to coordinate production and distribution.[6] That is the difficulty that the calculation problem presents to those who would attempt a utilitarian justification of the suspension of markets in favor of political or community direction of economic affairs for the greatest good. The utilitarian ideal of the realization of the most good probably would not be realized. A utilitarian cannot endorse the planned economy alternative to market institutions.

UTILITARIANISM AND THE CASE FOR MARKETS

This does not mean that a utilitarian must endorse markets either. There is no good reason to think that markets are ideal vehicles for realizing the utilitarian ideal. Ideal utilitarianism, as we recall, requires that the institution that is to be considered right is the one which produces the greatest good for people.

Adam Smith and others held that market economies maximize the *wealth* of nations. But maximum wealth may not be the maximum of good. We count a society wealthy if it contains a large number of the things which *we desire.* But another society in fact could have more of a particular good and yet be less wealthy *from our point of view* if we do not desire the good. Markets are ideal for providing people with the maximum possible set of *desired* goods and services from among those which are technologically possible to produce and distribute. What markets deliver can be different from what is required by utilitarians before markets are shown to be morally desirable. For a moral defense of markets, utilitarianism requires that the market provides the distribution of the set of goods and services that would be maximally productive of the good in the community. Markets need not do that; certainly a society like ours shows that weakness when it lavishes money on producers of pet rocks and comic books while leaving artists and research scientists wanting. A free market can deviate from a system that maximizes the production of good states of affairs, since it maximizes desire satisfaction.

John Stuart Mill made the mistake of equating pleasure (which sometimes is the satisfaction of desire) with the good.[7] When he did this he clouded this important difference between free-market maximization of desire satisfaction and the goal of maximizing the good. This is important for our purposes because most economists try to explain market phenomena in terms of a simplified model of the motivations of the people who trade on the market. They explain the motivation of trading in terms of people's perception of their utilities, saying that people try to maximize those perceived utilities. Market institutions themselves are then evaluated in a utilitarian fashion on the basis of whether they are efficient institutions for assuring that people will maximize their utilities by trading on these markets. Here utility might be taken to be what actually is good for people. On the other hand, utility might be taken to be just what people want, or what pleases them. The economists who discuss these matters tend to follow Mill in running these two separable things together.[8] This is a mistake. The good and the pleasant need not be the same. People can fail to take pleasure in what is good, or they can enjoy what is bad.

But utilitarianism is interesting as a *moral* theory only to the extent that it advocates maximizing what is *good*. If maximizing pleasure or what is desired deviates from this end, then it loses its moral appeal. This is why markets that maximize the desired need not receive a moral endorsement from utilitarianism.

If utilitarianism does not determine whether markets or their alternatives are morally desirable, we reach an important conclusion. If we are to find the moral case for or against market institutions, we must look past utilitarianism to another type of moral theory for the answer to the question, "Which is morally desirable, markets or their alternatives?"

DEONTOLOGICAL CONSIDERATIONS OF MARKETS

A moral theory of right action is called *deontological* if it treats rights or obligations, rather than consequences, as primary in evaluating actions. For example, given a minimal theory of rights, there is good reason for me not to kill some innocent passerby for sport. The minimal theory of rights provides that reason: "It would be a violation of that person's rights to do that." And that reason is sufficient to decide the moral issue without reference to any consequences of killing the innocent, be the consequences good or bad. Not even the anticipated bad consequence of punishment, when anticipated, weighs in the issue.

The moral case is completely settled by the rights claim. The consideration of any consequences cannot either add to or detract from that rights-based claim. Or so deontologists argue.[9]

RIGHT TO SELF-DETERMINATION

Right now, I am acting to promote my well-being by writing this chapter. I hope to sell first publication rights, get money and fame. The time that I am spending securing money and fame is time that I am not spending helping someone else secure their fame or fortune or the minimal requisites of life.

I have a basic moral right to do what I am doing.[10] Generally, there is a fundamental right that each person has: to pursue his or her own welfare without also having the obligation to *promote* (other than by not impeding) others in pursuit of their own welfare. The permissibility of my writing this essay is a particular instance of the application of that right.

Let's advance my chapter writing story into the future. Suppose, despite my best professional judgment now, it turns out that there is no market for this work. I will have written it for naught. Would that future development show that now I did not have a right to write this essay? Would it show that I may be prohibited to write it? The answer to both of these questions is "No." I have a right to write and try to sell this paper. It doesn't matter what the consequences are.

This shows an important feature of my right to pursue my own welfare. What I have a right to do is to undertake actions that I judge to be in my best interest. It does not matter if my judgment is correct or not. If my best judgment is that doing A is in my best interest, and if doing A does not conflict with others' rights, then it is morally permissible for me to do A.[11] People's rights are not just limited to the right to do what in fact is the best choice of action.

The deontological defense of markets appeals to just these rights. It is desirable that there be institutions that maximally allow people to exercise these rights. The deontological case for the free market is that it is such an institution. Because the institution is well-suited to allowing people to exercise their rights, and since alternative institutions would restrict people in the exercise of those rights, the market is a good institution.

PERSONAL FLOURISHING

There is a nondeontological tradition in moral philosophy that some thinkers have shown comes to the same defense of market institutions as the deontological approach. It is the *personal flourishing* tradition, which goes back to Plato and Aristotle in the fourth century B.C. In personal moral philosophy it holds that actions are right if they lead to the flourishing of the person who performs the action. Here the word *flourishing* means what it does in one's garden. The person will develop all of her or his vital potentials. This is a consequence-based theory of right action—what matters is whether the consequence is a state of flourishing or not. But this consequence-based theory leads almost immediately to an endorsement of the right of personal direction of one's life, regardless of the particular results of the exercise of that right.

Human beings have a rational faculty, including a practical rationality that plans action. Just as it is important for plants to have good root networks and healthy leaves, so too it is a necessary condition for the flourishing of individuals that they have and use a well-developed faculty of practical reason. Human beings cannot flourish unless they direct their own actions. Slaves, under the control of a mad scientist who manipulated all of their behaviors by means of electrodes implanted in their brains, might show the excellence or malevolence of the mad scientist; but they would show none of their own qualities, for they would show no self-directed action. From the viewpoint of the personal flourishing tradition, the effective use of practical reason is a necessary but not sufficient condition for people to pursue a correct path. It must also be permissible for them to undertake self-directed action—they must have a right to self-direct their actions.[12]

No one has a right to prevent people from undertaking right actions. No one has a right to block another's undertaking actions in pursuit of their own well-being. From the human flourishing point of view, if I am prevented from acting for my well-being, on the basis of my best judgment of the situation, then I am prevented from acting rightly. The people who do treat me that way are not observing their obligations not to treat me that way. My rights are being violated.

This is the same rights claim in interpersonal relations that the deontological analysis appealed to.[13] So what is compelling in the deontological account is preserved in this version of the personal flourishing account. Since markets are efficient devices for ensuring that societies are arranged to maximize people's being able to act on their best vision of their well-being, then market institutions can be justified on that basis.

COOPERATION

There are other lines of defense of markets. For example, cooperation among people is a desirable state of affairs. When we cooperate, you and I work for our own perception of our well-being, in concert with one another. As a result, our actions to undertake our harmonious ends are reinforced by the actions of the other. Consider the following situation. You find yourself with two copies of the same edition of Kant's *Critique of Pure Reason,* while I have none but want one. I have two copies of the same edition of *Fanny Hill* and you have none, but want one. It would certainly be cooperative for us to trade one *Critique of Pure Reason* for one *Fanny Hill.*

Market exchange, trade, is a form of cooperation, and cooperation is a social enhancement of one's ability to act on one's best judgment of what is right. This result agrees with much of our experience; markets *are* cooperative institutions compared to alternative institutions. Buying a record in a store is much nicer than trying to do anything at either the Department of Motor Vehicles or the post office, isn't it?

The institution most capable of maximally realizing the ends which people actually have in a community is a market. It allows the production of the maximal set of goods and services desired by the members of the community from among the many alternative sets and distributions of goods and services that are technically possible to produce. So, markets are ideal institutions to maximize people's implementing their rights to pursue their own well-being. That is the deontological case for markets.

There are two other useful points to be made about cooperation. First, market institutions allow cooperation without all of the costs that are usually required for cooperation. In my personal life, if I am to cooperate with people intimately, then I must learn a lot about them, their hopes, their past glories and frustrations, their fears, their personal sensitivities, etc. And it is worth doing all this to cooperate with some people, at least. With other people, the personal details can be offputting. We do not come to love everyone we date.

But in the market, I can look out for your desires without even knowing your desires. The fact that someone desires something is communicated to me in the form of prices, as part of the information flow that the market provides. If the price of steel girders goes up, that is evidence to the steel girder manufacturer that more people desire girders. She produces more girders to meet this increasing market. By so doing she facilitates people acting on their self-directed pursuit of the good. She cooperates with them, but without necessarily dealing with or knowing any of the individuals with whom she cooperates.

There is no intimacy in these relations, and intimacy is a good thing. But it is also a good thing that some relations with others do not *require* intimacy. For example, if a friend has a strong desire, and I know it and share a similarly strong desire for him to have what he wants, then I'll move heaven and earth to meet his wish, suppressing all other matters until he has it. That is characteristic of close friendships, but it cannot be characteristic of our relations with all people in need, even all those we could help. Just as there is a low limit to the number of people we can fall in love with, we simply do not have the emotional resources to help all of the people whom the impersonal operations of the market allow us to assist. But by doing business on the market we help them meet their desires anyway, and that is a good thing.[14]

Markets are devices for letting people follow their own best judgment of what is good for them. A capitalistic system does not interfere with people's opting out of the market to a commune, if that is their decision. Communes and other such voluntary, cooperative communities fall under the protection of cooperative relations given in this system. But while people's choice to join such cooperative societies is acceptable, it is questionable that it is defensible as an *enhancement* of cooperation. By withdrawing from the market to the extent that these communities do, they withdraw from a vast cooperation network.

THE PUBLIC GOODS PROBLEM

Economists have developed a problem for the deontological defense of the market presented above. It is called the *problem of public goods* and it has influenced many thinkers, including John Rawls, to despair of the level of cooperation that I have sketched manifesting itself in free markets.[15] Without cooperation, the deontological case for markets unravels, and Rawls and others urge that morality requires that there be some suspensions of markets and that political, constitutional provisions be made to reintroduce cooperation.[16]

A *public good* is a good such that if it is provided to anyone, it is provided to everyone: for example, a guard patrolling a neighborhood street. If one or two of the five people who live on the street finance the guard, then each of the five equally benefit from the guard in the street scaring burglars away from that street. If any benefit, all benefit.

The problem of public goods is that many people will be tempted to "free ride," to get the benefit without paying, counting on others to pay for the public good. Then, it is feared, the public good will not be provided or will be provided in inadequate supply, because not enough people will pay for its provision. Cooperation breaks down in the provision of public goods on the market, so people are to be forced to pay for the provision of public goods, or so the argument goes.[17]

Now free riders can be morally tolerated voluntarily. If I want to ride a coin-operated merry-go-round that can be activated by any one person inserting a coin, then it is irrelevant to me whether there are ten other people already sitting on the thing waiting for someone else to come along and put a coin in it so they can free ride. I'll be willing to put the coin in and not care about the free riders. While the free riders may have character flaws, lacking feelings of benevolence and cooperation, they in no way violate my rights. So I may tolerate them morally. I may cooperate with them and in many cases I will provide the public good.

But then, it is argued, not enough of some public goods like national defense will be provided. Maybe this is so. But it is entirely unclear just how much provision of the public good is to count as enough. And it is essential that the person who is putting the public goods problem forward be able to specify just what this amount is, because he or she is faulting the free market on grounds that it is not providing enough. But our usual account of how much of a good is enough in an economy is identical with the amount the market will bear. So it is difficult to really understand the complaint.

Further, publicly coordinated provision of public goods will inherit all of the difficulties of the calculation problem. We just will not have the information needed to say how much of what is needed to produce when and where.

The perennial political debate over the desirable levels of military expenditure in the federal budget is evidence of this difficulty.[18]

DISCUSSION OF DOUBTS

KEYNES

It is crucially important to make the distinction between these two different kinds of moral justification of the market, the utilitarian and the deontological. This can be seen by a consideration of the attempt of the famous economist John Maynard Keynes to justify interventions in the market.

When Keynes gives *moral* arguments against market institutions, he argues against the utilitarian position. Although he does it as if that were all that was required, we know that it isn't.

He writes:

It is *not* true that individuals possess a prescriptive "natural liberty" in their economic activities. There is *no* "compact" conferring perpetual rights on those who Have or on those who Acquire. The world is *not* so governed from above that private and social interest always coincide. It is *not* so managed here below that in practice they coincide. It is *not* a correct deduction from the Principles of Economics that enlightened self-interest always operates in the public interest. Nor is it true that self-interest generally *is* enlightened; more often individuals acting separately to promote their own ends are too ignorant or too weak to attain even these.[19]

His first sentence is an assertion that rules the deontological case out of court, but without argument. That will not do. Humans do possess rights and they possess them in their choices to buy celery or carrots, in their economic, market activities, as well as in any other context. At the very least we should have strong argument before we give up this position.

Keynes, of course, is right in arguing that self-interested action often is ill-suited to attain its ends. This point was noted above, at the end of my consideration of utilitarianism and markets. And it may even be the case that more desirable goods and services would be provided in some nonmarket society as an alternative, for a time at least.[20] That would be impressive in a utilitarian theory that defined rightness and wrongness in terms of the production of the good. But if we attend to the deontological defense of market institutions and thus to the rights of the individuals involved, which rights Keynes invites us to ignore, then his utilitarian critique falls short of the mark of justifying the suspension of the market.

Not all thinkers who criticize market institutions make the mistake of just criticizing the utilitarian defense of the market. There are other problems raised by thinkers who are not prepared to endorse the market and its attendant justifying feature—freedom of contract. Two such thinkers are Karl Marx and Thomas Aquinas.

MARX

Karl Marx, in his earlier writings, made an influential critique of the entire project of a worker laboring, producing commodities, which are then to be sold. Marx's charge is that production for the market goes against the very essence of human, conscious producers. He maintained that the process involved alienation. It is unclear what Marx himself might have thought of the moral import of alienation. But it is clear that Marx thought such alienated conditions could be done away with in the future, in a communist, nonmarket society.

Alienation. Marx thought that this alienation manifested itself in four ways, all of which spring from a common cause that is also the first form of alienation.

(1) [t]he factor that the worker is related to the *product of his labor* as to an *alien* object. For on this premise it becomes clear that the more the worker spends himself, the more powerful becomes the alien world of objects which he creates over and against himself, the poorer he himself—his inner world—becomes, the less belongs to him as his own.[21]

Marx fails to point out that this form of alienation or estrangement would exist even without a market or without exchange. If I design a product in the world and make it, then *I* am in the product, in some sense. I identify with it but it is not me. One might think, and Marx does think, that this is made worse by the fact that on a market, I then sell the product of my labor or my labor itself. Then the thing that I have made is no longer even proximate to me, is no longer mine. Even though I am alienated, I might have treasured it in some way if it were mine.

The second way that trade on the market is alienating is that (2) the worker's labor itself is sold on the market. Marx maintains that the sort of labor one does for a wage is not labor that fulfills a human nature. He bases this claim on the fact that with wage labor, "as soon as no physical or other compulsion exists, labor is shunned like a plague."[22] We all know of people who have this attitude to their jobs. In contrast some of us have jobs, parts of which at least we enjoy and find personally satisfying.

A reason why selling labor on the market is thought to be alienating is that it involves work under the direction of another. The alienation is intensified, according to Marx, because in exchange for our labor and for the commodities that are the product of our work, we receive money. It is characteristic of money that the money I have is absolutely exchangeable with the money that you have. There is nothing distinctive about any unit of money. In consequence of this, the money I receive for my labor has none of my personality. So I wind up giving up something that has my personality in it for something that does not, and that is further alienating.

This is overblown. If money is estranging, the lack of it is also said to be estranging in these passages. Still Marx has something valuable to say against frustrating work: if the result of selling your labor is a money reward but no personal satisfaction, then it is imprudent to sell your labor in an alienating market transaction if alternatives are available. And prudence is a matter of the morality of human flourishing. There are a great number of markets for my labor that I avoid precisely because I would only encounter alienation in this sense.

Even my job of teaching in college has some aspects that are alienating and fall under Marx's description. A term is spent showing students intellectual joys and sharing in their discovery and early use of insights. But then the end of term can be depressing. The students with whom I have worked to get them to share and enjoy knowledge go away to other courses or out of the university entirely. Rarely does one see them again. When they leave one feels a loss of the joys of sharing and dialogue in which one had invested so much of oneself, so much labor, creating. This is the sort of phenomenon Marx was pointing out. And it is inescapable here because students are human beings whom it is impermissible to own or to keep from going off to independent lives. However, in many areas, my present work does leave me with a feeling of my own accomplishment. Were alienation of either of these first two sorts all that I could expect from my work, I would not do it. And if such alienation was part of all market exchanges, as Marx suggests, then it would be immoral to establish market arrangements in society were nonalienating alternatives available.

In fact, not all market exchanges are alienating in this way. I am writing this essay now. That is labor. I will sell first publication rights to the product of this labor for money. But I will suffer no estrangement through this transaction. A cellist arrives in town, plays a concerto with the local orchestra, is paid and leaves town. Where is the alienation there? Perhaps she does not make close affective ties with any of the orchestra members. But it would have been wrong to expect that on such a short visit. The cellist's close affective ties must come from other contexts. But it is hard to see either type one or type two alienation in this case.

Information and alienation. When I was a youngster I acquired information about which jobs were likely to be alienating and which were not. I then oriented myself to the nonalienating ones. Other classmates of mine did not seem to place a premium on whether alienation of this sort was involved in their work, lots of which paid more than the work that I undertook. There was information available and freedom to decide which types of work we would do. I used it to avoid alienation. Had there not been either information flowing about the character of jobs or the freedom to contract as I and others wanted for jobs, it is very likely that I would not have been able to avoid alienation in Marx's first two senses.

Now—and this is vitally important to the topic of alienation and the morality of markets—the requisites mentioned in the last paragraph amount to saying that unless there had been a job *market* I might not have been able to avoid alienation. Market exchanges, far from *condemning* one to alienation, offer the *possibility of redemption* from it. So markets, *tout court,* cannot be held responsible for alienation; only certain transactions can be held responsible, and they are avoidable, if there is a market.

Alienation and others. The third type of alienation that Marx lays at the door of the market economy is (3) the loss of a sense of dominion over all of nature that is properly ours,[23] and the fourth is an antagonism among people and a failure of a sense of fellow humanness with others. A result of capitalist production and distribution causing alienation of the first two sorts is (4) "the (estrangement of man) from *man.*"[24] Estrangement of the first three sorts show that humans are in conflict on the market, or at least are treating each other in ways that are psychologically distancing. Marx rather overstates this.

The *alien* being, to whom labor and the product of labor belongs, in whose service labor is done and for whose benefit the product of labor is provided, can only be *man* himself. If the product of labor does not belong to the worker, if it confronts him as an alien power, then this can only be because it belongs to some *other man than the worker.* If the worker's ability is a torment to him, to another it must be a *delight* and his life's joy. Not the gods, not nature, but only man himself can be this alien power over man.[25]

There is a moral dimension to this form of alienation. One moral requirement is to be loyal to our sense of our own humanness, and that involves benevolence to others. So if we know that our employees would be working in alienated conditions, employing them could be a failing of this sense of benevolence and shared humanity. To fail at this is in itself to be alienated from the worker as another human being. If the transaction proceeds, then the worker will also be alienated from us because there is little human regard in our relationship.[26]

Now there are exceptions to this. Suppose the worker says to me, "I know that this job is alienating and I appreciate your concern, but I know that this is the best job that I can get for the short run, and so I want it anyway. Just don't expect me to stay on it any longer than it will take me to find different work." In that case, I may concur and employ the worker. That would be an instance of the importance of freedom of contract for treating others as ends in themselves.[27] The deciding factor in whether these workers satisfy this deontological requirement (see the quotation from Kant associated with fn. 42, below) is whether their personal direction of their own lives is honored in the transaction as was discussed above (p. 89). Moral insensitivity to the job-related alienation of prospective employees just comes down to asking another person to live for our own sake, without regard for their personal direction of their own lives.

Evaluation. Different thinkers will evaluate the implications of alienation for the morality of markets differently. It seems that Marx either wants to deny that markets are devices for cooperation of the sort we have sketched earlier, or he is denying that societies ever actually have markets. His only case for denying that markets are devices for cooperation is the importance of the first two kinds of alienation that he stresses.

Yet, as I showed above, markets are devices for *avoiding* alienation. Marx held that the avoidance of alienation would be possible only in communist society. Marx says:

[I]n communist society, where nobody has one exclusive sphere of activity but each can become accomplished in any branch he wishes, society regulates the general production and thus makes it possible for me to do one thing today and another tomorrow, to hunt in the morning, fish in the afternoon, rear cattle in the evening, criticize after dinner, just as I have a mind, without ever becoming hunter, fisherman, shepherd or critic.[28]

This is unclear. What is the relation of myself to the product of my labor in communism? Even if I have a property right to it, won't there still be the alienation of my being externalized in the object which is not me? Yet that is type one alienation.

But most importantly, Marx's future communist society will function without the division of labor because there is social control of production. That social control provides for the production and distribution of sufficient goods and services in the community. It is essential to note that this requires a solution to the calculation problem. And that is why the calculation problem is as important as it is. It is a genuine problem for nonmarket solutions to problems—in this case to the problem of alienation.

Ought implies can. If we *cannot* solve the problem of alienation by communist means then we ought not try. The calculation problem shows that market remedies to alienation, of the sort that I described above as part of my life, are a preferable way to deal with the problem of alienation than the sketch of a communist alternative. Markets are a cure for alienation, not the cause of the problem.

AQUINAS AND JUST PRICES

Karl Marx is not the only nonutilitarian critic of the market. Some thinkers revert to a notion of justice that is centered on individual rights, as opposed to centered on social end-states. St. Thomas Aquinas, though generally utilitarian in his discussion of markets and morals, gives one nonutilitarian ground for calling profit lawful: "when he [the trader] seeks profit, not for its own sake, but as a reward for his labor."[29] Here the use of the word *reward* suggests a natural order of justice in nature. So much work is entitled to so much reward. Various thinkers have attempted to make this notion precise, but without accurate results. Classical economists like Adam Smith believed that labor created wealth as a direct function of time spent. And the last classical economist was Karl Marx, who used the labor definition of value to underlie his theory of capitalist exploitation. Since the workers in factories clearly work and since it is not clear to the workers, at least, that the owners of factories, the capitalists, work, then it looks to be exploitation that the capitalists make money out of the work of their workers.[30]

It is worthy of note that the Marxist moral exploitation theory appeals to this same notion that Aquinas uses. It holds that the capitalist who does not work (according to Marxist theory) receives an unjust reward in terms of profit stolen in the form of surplus labor value from the workers who did produce it. That labor itself, regardless of the terms of the contracts people freely enter into to sell it, has a certain morally *required* return. And those capitalists who are quick to point out the many activities of the owners of industry and the "good-making" characteristics of those activities, accept with the Marxists and Aquinas the legitimacy of this picture of a just fitting of reward with labor. Lucky results are somehow ruled out of moral consideration. And that is unfortunate, because luck plays a big role in business, as in the rest of life.

Subsequent economists have abandoned the labor definition of value and so have abandoned the notion that the economic value of work, and hence its proper rate of return, is independent of the desires and choices of other people. The economic value simply is what it will fetch on the market, and what it will fetch is caused by a complex of factors involving the free choices of trading partners established on the market.[31]

The notion of a correct or moderate price operates as a criterion of justice that is independent of people's free contracting to do what they want with their labor and its products. The deontological defense of markets above is that markets leave people free to pursue their own well-being, according to their best vision of that well-being and of its causes. To say that there is a just price independent of and potentially inconsistent with people's exercise of their right to pursue their own well-being on the basis of their own judgment, is to make justice incompatible with human rights. At best this is to put deontological considerations at war with each other. At worst it is to remove the nonutilitarian concept of justice from its foundation in human rights theory.

The notion of a fair or just price is also imprecise. What is the criterion of moderateness? Profits must first be moderate. But what is the gauge of what is moderate? How could there be a gauge that is not arbitrary? If a person gives incalculable reward to a community, the members of which gladly pay him or her while thinking that they are paying next to nothing for what they get in return, then 200 percent profit would not be excessive. But if that would not be excessive, what would be?

One possible answer has paternalistic implications. We could say that only what is good for you in fact should be rewarded, so we will see to it that you only reward the provisioners of good things. When we say that, we adopt the rights and responsibilities of a parent to the person we address—hence paternalism. If we were to treat individuals other than our dependent children this way, we would be violating their rights to pursue their own well-being by their best judgment. This has no deontological justification.[32] Were we to try a more generalized program of such actions to realize maximal good in a community, then we would lapse back into utilitarianism and we would fall prey to the moral difficulties of that critique of the market, including the calculation problem.

The deontological defense of markets provides a justification of freedom of contract, even of trade, as was shown above. Recently, this freedom has come under a friendlier form of criticism and restriction than the "just price" style of criticism. I have in mind the doctrine of unconscionability in law.[33] Some contracts have been held not to have been freely entered into despite the beliefs of their parties to the contrary, because features of the putative contract show this absence of freedom. Perhaps the parties had unequal bargaining power. In that case the stronger power could have steamrollered the other and there was no free consent on the weaker parties' part. Perhaps the disparity of compensation in the contract would show that no one would freely agree to such terms.[34]

If it were to be shown that there was absence of free consent in a particular trade, that would remove all deontological support from that trade. So this part of law is on the right track in its understanding of the deontological justification of market transactions.[35]

PARTICULAR CASES OF BENIGN PRACTICES

Middlemen facilitate trade and so, cooperation. They do so by coordinating sellers and buyers. A seller and a buyer need each other to do well in their projects. I, for example, need a buyer for a typewriter that I have for sale. I would be glad if a middleman came along and coordinated me with a market. If such a person came to me with a buyer, I would be glad to pay him or her for doing this.

Brokers are special kinds of middlemen. Stockbrokers sell stocks and by doing so coordinate would-be investors with firms that are issuing stocks to raise money for potentially profitable ventures. I only trade with discount brokers, and they charge me only for the execution of orders. This is less than the full-service broker would, who researches firms and associates me with those firms that are reasonably expected to make profits. Whether this falls within or outside what is morally defensible in the market is a question of whether this is an ideal or optimal device for making cooperation possible among people with overlapping purposes.

Speculators, a kind of broker, are people who are paid for taking other people's risks off their hands. If I am a farmer who has planted enough wheat to garner 100,000 bushels, then it will make a considerable difference to me whether wheat is selling for $8 per bushel or for $5 per bushel, when the wheat is harvested.[36] I plan to handle all of my next year's economic transactions from the future income that I will get from selling this year's wheat. That income will determine how much I can eat, whether my children will go to a high-priced college, whether I can afford to have my farm machinery repaired—and so whether I can use machinery in the production of hoped-for future income—and even how much of a crop I can afford to plant next year.

Now if I am a gambler, then I am most likely a person who enjoys risk. I might enjoy betting my future farm well-being on the price of wheat a few months in the future. However if I am averse to taking risks and enjoy security, as so many people do, then I will wish that I could get rid of the insecurity that I have about how much wheat will be worth when I sell it.

Suppose that my best calculations are that I will need $650,000 in proceeds from my wheat in order to meet my financial obligations and to have a little left over for luxuries; $800,000 would be nice, $500,000, a disaster. With only that much income I may have to sell the farm and look for something else to do with my life. Further suppose that I am a risk-averse person and seek security. Then I would like to be out of my risky situation if I could be. It would be nice if I could find someone who would like to buy my wheat for $650,000. If I could, I would sell it to that person gladly.

Such persons are around. Speculators buy "futures contracts" in wheat and other commodities and assets. That is, they assume the risks that others do not choose to hold in the hopes that the future price of the commodity will be sufficiently greater than the present price at which they buy it. Sometimes it is and sometimes it isn't. That's the risk.

So, I sell to a speculator at $650,000 and get the money that I need plus security. As this story is told, it is a completely cooperative affair. The speculator and I have managed to cooperate without necessarily being as intimately connected as friends who cooperated to do things would be. As I say above, as long as there are some intimate, friendly, cooperative arrangements in my life, it is a good for me that the market allows me to cooperate on a broader scale without having that cooperation be contingent on a more widespread intimacy, which I and others would be incapable of effecting. The speculator and I have cooperated to jointly satisfy our desires. This is the sort of activity that the market is good at facilitating.

The speculator has taken my risk off of my hands. In return she or he has no guarantees. But if wheat does sell at $8 per bushel, then the speculator will make $150,000 on my wheat, a profit of 23 percent.

If wheat does sell at $8 per bushel, then perhaps it was a bad thing for me to have sold it at $6.5 per bushel. The speculator sold me what I desired, security. Maybe I ought not have desired it—but I did.

If this were to happen, my situation would be the same as that of the person who desired a commodity and enthusiastically paid more for it than it was in fact worth to her or him. Critics of the profits of speculators either do not recognize this similarity of cases or they do not agree that the moral defense of market institutions trades on preserving freedom of action instead of good results; that it is a deontological and not a teleological issue.

Agents are another often disparaged group of businesspeople on the market. The comedian Fred Allen is reported to have said about Hollywood, "You can take all of the sincerity in this town and stuff it in a flea's navel and still have room left for an agent's heart." Agents are frequently thought ill of. And indeed the agent-client relation in the entertainment industry looks at first almost like a master-slave relation in some aspects. Because of a contract entered into years ago, a film superstar who has his or her choice of million-dollar roles still has to pay 10 percent to an agent who no longer has to work to place the client. Consequently, some clients come to see agents as parasites. But this is a mistake.

An agent is best seen as a combination of a middleman and a speculator. The criticisms of the last paragraph arise from just attending to the middleman role. But the agent is also a speculator. In the beginning, the agent works without return for the client, works to get the client known and works to get the client jobs. But this is risky, a risk that was formerly completely borne by the client. All that work and expense may be for naught, in which case the client will owe the agent nothing. The client gets the agent to assume the costs and risks of promotion of the client. The agent, in turn, is freely accepting the risk as a gamble that 10 percent of the client's future earnings, for a fixed period of time, will be a lucrative return for the effort spent. Whether this falls within or outside what is morally defensible in the market is a question of whether this is an ideal device for making cooperation possible among people with overlapping purposes. And there is no better device.

IMMORAL SITUATIONS AND TRADES

FRAUD

Even thinkers like Ayn Rand who are optimistic about the morality of markets allow that there are some economic transfers which seem to be voluntary but which are immoral. For example, if, misrepresenting myself, I sell you a house I do not own, that would be immoral. Similarly, I defraud you if I sell you a car representing to you that it is in fine condition when I know that it will fall apart within the first ten miles of use. These are indecent, callous cases of fraud, and Rand and others brand them as immoral.[37] Much of the basis of the doctrine of unconscionability, mentioned above, is that such unconscionable contracts can be fraudulent. Rand makes a case that fraudulent transactions involve the initiation of force and are not voluntary and so, by implication, are not market transactions. "Fraud," she writes, "involves a similarly indirect use of force: it consists of obtaining material values without their owner's consent, under false pretenses or false promises."[38] The theory may or may not hold up that fraudulent transactions are forced and so are not market transactions. But whether or not they are the market exchanges that they seem to be at the time that they are entered into, they are immoral.

Here the immorality involved is in treating another as a means to our ends (acquiring the other's property) without treating the other as an end in himself or herself. We pay lip service to the treatment of the other as an end when we volunteer to meet the other's goal of acquiring a car in working condition, for example. We then fail to deliver on our promise to do something consonant with the ends of the other in exchange for securing our own ends.

It would have been acceptable if the other person had granted us this result as a gift. In that case, even without delivering a car or other commodity, I treat the other as an autonomous person with ends if I acquiesce to the other's judgment—even the one to bestow gifts on me.[39] But in cases of fraud, the other has not consented.

OTHER CASES

There are more controversial examples of immoral trades. One which has a popular following and for which some reason can be given is prostitution, the buying and selling of sex. It is probably immoral, in some cases at least, to be a prostitute or to trade with them.[40]

There are also individual cases of selling drugs when one knows that the consequence of the purchaser using the drug, given health or state of intoxication, will be instant death. Knowing that another will die if I sell them the drug is good reason not to sell them the drug.

An action such as a trade on the market might be ill-intentioned. I may sell you perfectly good food while under the mistaken opinion that it is poisonous and that you will suffer great harm as a result of buying and using it. This action clearly is immoral.

Whether any of these immoral practices fall within the deontological defense of the market or not is open to a simple test. The deontological defense was in terms of people having institutions that would allow them to cooperate freely in projects. The simple test to ask about whether the *trades* are moral or not, *as trades,* is to ask whether, if the practices were outlawed, a black market would arise in those trades. In the case of prostitution and drugs, the answer is clearly yes. That is an index that it blocks cooperation among people in pursuit of their ends to outlaw these markets. Conversely, the markets further those ends.[41] On the other hand, outlawing fraud and extortion would not lead to a black market in those practices. So they are not cooperative ventures and do not fall within the scope of the deontological defense of market institutions.

What this shows is that in some cases an action can be correct as a trade and incorrect as a failing to care for the well-being of self or of another. Similarly, something can be immoral both as a trade and as a failing to care for another.

There is nothing unusual about this. Many actions are such that if only part of their character is specified, they would receive praise for that part, while if other aspects were highlighted, they would look onerous. If you provide liver transplants for free or at reasonable fees, that part of your action is fine. But if you don't trouble to get the consent of the donors you use, that part of your transaction is wrong. Breaking a promise is generally wrong, but when a friend's life depends on it, that command of benevolence can so override the wrongness of promise-breaking as to make that the right step to take.

So it is with the morality of market transactions. A number of them may be good as market transactions, yet other considerations like the care of one's character may raise negative considerations that outweigh the positive, and make a particular act wrong. But not wrong *as a market transaction*, wrong as a failure to take care of oneself or another. To find immoral transactions, we have to look to cases like fraud or conspiracy to violate another's rights to life or to property or to freedom to pursue one's own ends.

RACE, SEX, AND ETHNICITY

Treating people uniquely. Racial or ethnic prejudice and sexual discrimination raise moral concerns. Some people prefer dealing with one race, ethnic group, or sex to dealing with another. Women's clubs and black students' clubs exclude men and nonblacks, and part of the motivation for these institutions is racial or sexual discrimination. Now a policy of not recognizing the personal merits or demerits of individual people because they belong to some group is a failure to treat a person as a person, as an end in himself or herself. It is not necessarily to treat a person as a means, because no end need be attained that is specifiable independently of the act. Still, the practice is wrong.

We accept Immanuel Kant's claim that "rational beings are all subject to the *law* that each one must treat himself and every other being *never merely as means*, but always as an end in itself also."[42] That is because we are under a prior obligation, if we are to even know what we are dealing with, to recognize others as individual rational beings with their own individual ends, purposes, and character, not just as members of some group.[43] This is why it is important to take other people's ends into account when dealing with them. And the more fundamental wrong of failing to treat people as unique individuals is what is wrong with racist and sexist behavior.

Justified discrimination. Abstractly, two conditions have to be met for racial or sexual discrimination to be justified and so to fail to be racist or sexist. First, the discrimination must be essential to a common purpose on which people seek to cooperate. Second, that common purpose must be innocent. What I mean here should emerge from a discussion of some particular cases. Consider the following situations.

Imagine a market exchange between two white males that takes place between them only because they excluded a black person, and that that exclusion was done solely because she or he was black. Perhaps one Chinese sold a service to another Chinese, refusing to do the same for an Indian. How should we evaluate such exchanges? As in the other cases in this section, different true descriptions of the exchanges will call forth different moral evaluations of them, positive and negative. First, in the spirit of the deontological justification of markets, such exchange facilitates cooperation among the traders to pursue what they take to be in their interest. So it is praiseworthy on that consideration. But this praise should be withdrawn to the extent that the purpose of the trade was the exclusion of the black from cooperative relations. If that were the sole purpose of the trade, then it would amount to only causing pain and taking pleasure in that bad, and that would have no moral worth—it would fail to be innocent. If, however, it was motivated solely to mutually benefit the traders without reference to the state of the excluded black (say both parties know that they will be optimally satisfied by that exchange of goods and services, relative to all others) then, *as a trade,* the transaction will be justified. Trading that way was a necessary condition for realizing the innocent goals of trade. In between there are the mixed cases of purpose between the good and the bad. Evaluation of the trade will vary proportionally.

Under other descriptions, trade can take on negative characteristics. First, it could be thoughtless. The black person could have been never considered. That would have been wrong. Second, the black could have been considered and not maliciously, as imagined in the last paragraph. But the black could have been considered as a black and not as an individual human being. That still would be wrong.

I offer the above as an outline of the way to evaluate race-sensitive and sexually sensitive behavior. In particular cases the positive or the negative judgment will predominate based on the facts of the case.

For most people gender is an important feature in the choice of a sexual partner. But one's choice of sexual partners is so intimate a feature of one's life, and consequently, so within one's personal authority, that this gender consciousness is widely considered to be perfectly acceptable. Another reason it is so considered is that it excludes people only in one aspect—as a sexual partner—from being treated as a fellow person. And that aspect can, to some extent, be self-contained. My exclusion of you from my sex-life allows my inclusion of you in many other aspects of my life to an extent at least, which ordinarily will exhaust the scope of cooperation that you desire from me. These are considerations that people take to overcome a negative judgment of sexism someone might make against one's choice of a sexual partner. Sexual choice is not the topic of this paper. But I include it as a clear example of what people take to be a case of morally acceptable sexual discrimination.

Were this sexual choice described solely as gender-sensitive choice, it would appear to be sexist and wrong. But that is not all that is at issue in the innocent choice of sexual partners. It falls well within the narrow sphere in which a person has absolute authority over his or her own life. In that area, we may choose among options as we wish and others can have no complaint against us that we have wronged them by excluding them.

Public accommodations. In contrast to morally permissible discrimination, consider the case of what civil rights law calls a "public accommodation." A hotelier or restaurateur offers service to people generally, if the money is there. It is in no way an intimate or essential aspect of that business to be exclusionary. It would be out of character to exclude arbitrarily an individual with money and demeanor from patronage. If such a merchant then were to systematically exclude women or some other group from service, that would be clear evidence that individuals were being treated immorally as members of groups and not as the individuals they are, as ends in themselves. The contrast to the sex partner case is just on this point. As a first approximation, at least, we can say that the negative moral assessment of this case of sexual discrimination is not overcome by positive considerations. The practice is morally wrong.

But suppose you own a restaurant in some part of Africa where Chinese are a persecuted minority. Suppose that the situation where you are is so racist that if you do not exclude the few members of the racially persecuted group in your community, then no one from the racial elite would patronize your restaurant. What then is the morally correct thing to do as a restaurateur? It is hard to say, and I will not attempt to do so here. I am content if I show that there are conflicting moral judgments, either set of which might predominate. In such situations there is a general obligation, first, not to be racist in one's operations and second, to attempt to change the racist attitudes of neighbors. The best way to do that is usually by setting an example—by not discriminating against the Chinese at the restaurant. But in this case we have reason to believe that we would not present an example of integration. The blacks will not eat with the Chinese at the would-be integrated restaurant. Further, if we try this remedy we will be forced to close the restaurant for want of income, and that would help no one. It is unclear what is right here.

Public accommodations that are racially, sexually, or ethnically exclusive are not analogous to the case of the choice of sex partners mentioned above. An analogy to that is afforded by explicitly private clubs. A private club may have exclusivity as a central characteristic. We associate in clubs precisely to restrict the circle of our associates. Sometimes we just don't want to be around everyone, but we would like to be around certain people. Where the people are chosen on the basis of their individual characteristics, there can be nothing wrong with the exclusivity. People are being treated as ends in themselves.

Private clubs. Sometimes private clubs do use racial or sexual criteria of selection. Then the members of the club are using criteria of association that ignore the individual characteristics of both the accepted people and the excluded people. Looked at just that way, it is wrong. But there can be other ways to look at it.

Perhaps the function of the club is to foster a sense of community among women as women. Or perhaps the function of the club is to provide a place for the continuation of Italian customs from the old country, and so it excludes non-Italians. In both of these cases, the function of the club demands ethnic or sexual criteria. So the criteria are good to use to further the purposes of the club. In these cases, the overall moral evaluation of the use of the criteria is affected by the moral evaluation of participating in the purposes of the club. If the purposes are benign, that can minimize the apparent stigma of racism or sexism, even allowing participation in the clubs to be a good thing.

Also important is the place of those activities in one's life. If hanging out at the Polish-American Hall is the only social dimension of one's life, then the ethnic discrimination associated with devoting so much of your social life to ethnically exclusive interactions involves such a major dimension of life as to be a moral failing. On the other hand, if activities at the Men's Athletic Club form only an incidental part of an otherwise diversified social life, then even "good old boy" fun can have an acceptable place in a good life. Presidential candidate Jesse Jackson got in trouble during the 1984 primaries for making anti-Semitic remarks. But he did not get in trouble, on the same occasion, for having selected out a pair of reporters of his own race, suggesting that they spend a short time excluding others of other races so that they could "talk black." That desire for racial exclusivity played so small a part in his life as to be not morally important and it had the added positive feature of relaxation, benign enjoyment, and feeling of kinship. The anti-Semitic remarks he made while in that atmosphere were not so counterbalanced. Public reaction, which identified one of the aspects as benign and the other as reprehensible, was correct.

What justifies market institutions and the trades that occur on them is first, that they allow freedom of a sort required for the treatment of each individual as an end in himself or herself, and second, as an extension of this, that they maximize opportunities for human cooperation. The test that we have used to tell which morally questionable activities fall under this justification, *insofar as they are exchanges,* has been to ask the question: "If a practice was outlawed, would a black market arise to facilitate the practice anyway?" When we apply that test to the issues of sexual or racial preference, if those practices were to be outlawed, the black market institutions that would emerge would have the character of private clubs rather than of public accommodations. That alone does not justify those clubs or the transactions involved with them, although it does show a "good-making" feature they have. But such clubs and transactions might also merit censure. And so, a prima facie justified market transaction may be found to be immoral, all things considered.[44]

NOTES

[1] The classical statement of this theory is G. E. Moore, *Principia Ethica* (Cambridge: Cambridge University Press, 1971), pp. 24–26, 147–148.

[2] Karl Marx allowed for values other than utilities to be realized. That is discussed below.

[3] Karl Marx and Friedrich Engels, for example, writing about the new bourgeoisie market economy, said: "It has been the first to show what man's activity can bring about. It has accomplished wonders far surpassing Egyptian pyramids, Roman aqueducts, and Gothic cathedrals; it has conducted expeditions that put in the shade all former Exoduses of nations

and crusades. . . . The bourgeoisie, during its rule of scarce one hundred years, has created more massive and more colossal productive forces than have all preceding generations together. Subjection of Nature's forces to man, machinery, application of chemistry to industry and agriculture, steam navigation, railways, electric telegraphs, clearing of whole continents for cultivation, canalization of rivers, whole populations conjured out of the ground—what earlier century had even a presentiment that such productive forces slumbered in the lap of social labor?" Karl Marx and Friedrich Engels, *The Manifesto of the Communist Party,* in Lewis Feuer, ed., *Marx and Engels: Basic Writings on Politics and Philosophy* (Garden City, NJ: Anchor Books, 1959), p. 12.

[4] I use the word "someone," because it leaves open all sorts of ways that economies can be centrally directed: by one person with autocratic powers; by a board of such people where the board takes on that power; by a body of regulatory agencies subject to legislative, judicial, and administrative control; or it may even be by the people as a whole, determining by majority political vote what will be imposed on people as a whole—so-called economic democracy. And there are probably other possible ways that "someone" may be interpreted.

[5] The calculation problem, a difficulty for centrally planned economies, was first formulated by Ludwig von Mises in *"Die Wirtschaftsrechnung im sozialistischen Gemeinwesen,"* in *Arichif für Sozialwissenschaften* v. 20 1920 and was developed by Friedrich A. Hayek in many places, but chiefly in his "The Use of Knowledge in Society." Mises' essay is translated and reprinted in F. A. Hayek, ed., *Collectivist Economic Planning* (London: Routledge & Kegan Paul, 1963). This volume collects all of the major papers of Mises and Friedrich Hayek on this topic. References are to this volume unless otherwise noted.

[6] This presupposes, innocuously, that the good is not some such thing as universal destruction or universal suffering, or some other such thing more likely to proceed from inefficient production and distribution of goods and services.

[7] "The creed which accepts as the foundation of morals 'utility' or the 'greatest happiness principle' holds that actions are right in proportion as they tend to promote happiness; wrong as they tend to produce the reverse of happiness. By happiness is intended pleasure and the absence of pain; by unhappiness pain and the privation of pleasure. . . . pleasure and freedom from pain are the only things desirable as ends; and that all desirable things (which are as numerous in the utilitarian view as in any other scheme) are desirable either for pleasure inherent in themselves or as a means to the promotion of pleasure and the prevention of pain." John Stuart Mill, *Utilitarianism,* Oskar Priest, ed. (Indianapolis, IN; Bobbs-Merrill Educational Publishing, 1977), pp. 10–11.

[8] They do this in order to have an effective, value-free test of what is and is not a utility.

[9] This is not to deny that utilitarians could come up with good reasons in another style, supporting this judgment. They can.

[10] It is assumed that I did not have a contractual obligation not to write this paper and that someone else had not copyrighted this paper first, and that I had not promised to do something else at the time, etc. But if anything, including your reading this paper, is ever morally permissible, a similar set of such conditions obtains.

[11] In a particular extreme case like an attempt at suicide, we may interfere with someone because we think that the attempt is not based on the person's best judgment of the situation. But in doing this, we may be wrong. The test is whether after some further discussion the other person freely approves of what we did. If the other person says, "I wanted to do it, I still do, and you had no right to interfere," then they are right.

[12] Two quick technical qualifications: First, it does not follow that because an individual has a need for something in a particular situation in order to act rightly, that person has a right to the needed thing. But the argument I am presenting is about a necessary condition for any

person undertaking any right action, and those elements of universality make the difference. Second, parents have the responsibility to direct children in order to start the development of their practical reason, and then when it is developed, to gradually let the children go off to lives of self-direction.

[13] This style of generation of the relevant rights is attempted by: Eric Mack, "Egoism and Rights," *The Personalist* (Winter 1973); Tibor Machan, *Human Rights and Human Liberties* (Chicago: Nelson Hall, 1975); and Ayn Rand, *The Virtue of Selfishness* (New York: New American Library, 1964).

[14] I am thankful to the editor, Tibor Machan, for these last two points about cooperation and intimacy.

[15] John Rawls, *A Theory of Justice* (Cambridge, MA: Harvard University Press, 1971).

[16] In addition to Rawls, see James Buchanan and Gordon Tullock, *The Calculus of Consent* (Ann Arbor: University of Michigan Press, 1962). Also see Paul Samuelson, *The Collected Scientific Papers,* vol. 3, ed. Robert Merton (Cambridge, MA: M.I.T. Press, 1972), Book 4.

[17] Samuelson, *The Collected Scientific Papers,* Part 12. Also see James Buchanan, *The Demand and Supply of Public Goods* (Chicago: Rand McNally, 1968), Ch. 5.

[18] For an alternative attempt to defuse the public goods problem for the market, see Tibor Machan, "Dissolving the Problem of Public Goods," in T. R. Machan, ed., *The Libertarian Reader* (Totowa, NJ: Rowman and Littlefield, 1982).

[19] John Maynard Keynes, *The End of Laissez-faire* (London: Leonard and Virginia Woolf, 1927), p. 39. Italics and strange capitalization are from Keynes.

[20] In point of fact, as the calculation problem shows, a planned economy will be inherently frustrated by information gaps. And so, except in cases of accident, or self-contained small-scale enterprises, situations that a utilitarian interventionist would appeal to are unlikely to occur.

[21] Karl Marx, *Economic and Philosophical Manuscripts of 1844,* ed. D. Struik, trans. M. Milligan (New York: International Publishers, 1982), p. 108. "The alienation of the worker in his product means not only that his labor becomes an object, an *external* existence, but that it exists *outside him,* independently, as something alien to him and that it becomes a power on its own confronting him." (Ibid.) This of course is directly the situation of the slave in the master-slave dialectic at the beginning of Georg Hegel's *The Phenomenology of Spirit.*

[22] Marx, *Economic and Philosophical Manuscripts,* p. 111.

[23] "Man is a species being, not only because in practice and in theory he adopts the species as his object (his own as well as those of other things), but—and this is only another way of expressing it—also because he treats himself as the actual, living species; because he treats himself as a *universal* and therefore a free being. . . . The universality of man appears in practice precisely in the universality which makes all nature his *inorganic* body—both inasmuch as nature is (1) his direct means of life, and (2) the material, the object, and the instrument of his life activity. Nature is man's *inorganic body*—nature, that is, insofar as it is not itself the human body. Man *lives* on nature—means that nature is his *body,* with which he must remain in continuous interchange if he is not to die." (Ibid., p. 112) It is not clear that this loss of a sense of dominion is directly a function of market activity except remotely insofar as the division of labor facilitates production for trade. It is clear that Marx thinks that the suspension of the market with the coming of communism, bringing social planning of production, will eliminate this form of exploitation.

[24] Ibid., p. 114.

[25] Ibid., p. 115. It is not necessary to Marx's case that the employer take pleasure in the worker's sorry state in alienated labor. The worker is alienated enough even if the employer is either well-intentioned or oblivious to the problems of the worker.

THE MORALITY OF CAPITALISM · 109

[26] It is to be observed that the terms *worker* and *employer* can be replaced by the terms *husband* and *wife* and a critique of certain sexist marriages results.

[27] Again, these are the sort of moral concerns that the robust champion of free markets, Ayn Rand, treated seriously. She has the idealized heroes of one of her novels all swear the following oath: "I swear—by my life and by my love of it—that I will never live for the sake of another man, nor ask another man to live for mine." *Atlas Shrugged* (New York: Random House, 1957), p. 1069.

[28] Karl Marx and Frederick Engels, *The German Ideology* (Moscow: Progress Publishers, 1964), pp. 44–45.

[29] *Summa Theologica,* Question 77, Article 4, conclusion.

[30] First, in fact it is clear that almost all capitalists work, but it is easy to see how one could miss this fact. The work that the capitalist does is different in kind from that of the factory workers. It involves planning to meet the market, arranging financing, etc. From the outside, it may not look like work, but it is. Second, it is unclear whether Marx attached any moral censure to this situation. See William J. Baumol, "Marx and the Iron Law of Wages," *The American Economic Review* 73 (May 1983): 306.

[31] Sidney Trivus, "Dissolving a Muddle in Economics or Dr. Marx Meets Lord Russell," *Reason Papers* 2 (Fall 1975): 7–12; see also his "The Irrelevance of the Subjective," *Reason Papers* 3 (Fall 1976): 94–95. Ayn Rand indicated a conception of economic value similar to this, based on the scholastic notion of objective being, but the relation between the cause of something's being of value and the state of its being of value is less clear in her brief indication of the desiderata of a theory of value compatible with capitalism than it is in Trivus. *Capitalism: The Unknown Ideal* (New York: New American Library, 1967), pp. 22–24.

[32] We could gamble here and act, hoping that on consideration the affected party would approve our action on reflection. But it is a gamble and the rightness or wrongness of our action will come out of that approval or lack of it. Our action, however cannot wait. But see Steven Kelman, "Regulation and Paternalism," in M. B. Johnson and T. R. Machan, eds. *Rights and Regulation: Ethical, Political, and Economic Issues* (Cambridge, MA: Ballinger Publishing Co., 1983).

[33] For a discussion of this doctrine see Lewis A. Kornhauser, "Unconscionability in Standard Forms," *California Law Review* 64 (1976).

[34] Here the deontological principle that freedom of contract is to be preserved is retained. It is defended in spite of what the results of people's free choices were. Results are only appealed to as evidence for or against the presence of free choice.

[35] Whether there are other defects with it as a doctrine of law is a topic that I do not address here. The notion of economic bargaining power is very much more imprecise than I am indicating here. Further, although some courts have been good about this (*Morris* v. *Capitol Furniture and Appliance Co.,* 280 A.2d 775 [D.C. Ct. App. 1971]), there is tremendous opportunity for paternalism in particular cases arising out of different interpretations of what is acceptable compensation. I might think that a certain compensation is acceptable and freely contract for it. A court might have a different assessment of what is worth what and so forbid me to contract here.

[36] It makes a difference of $300,000.

[37] Ayn Rand, *Capitalism: The Unknown Ideal,* p. 333. See also John Hospers, *Libertarianism* (Los Angeles: Nash Publishing, 1971c), pp. 93–94.

[38] Ayn Rand, *Capitalism,* p. 333. There she also treats extortion as indirect use of force.

[39] In some cases, it could be wrong to accept gifts. It might be ignoble or a failing in benevolence to see someone deprive themselves for our benefit.

[40] I only indicate the salient fact that might make this true in some cases. It can be demean-

ing to one's sexuality and thus thwart one's full flourishing. It is a moral obligation not to confuse sexual response with considerations of money and exchange. The psychological consequences of so doing for some people are pretty well documented.

[41] Below, when I discuss racism, I note that cooperation in doing the immoral does not make a justification of doing the immoral. So, although there is a black market for professional murders, that sign of cooperation between A and B who want to have C killed is not to the point, as murdering C is immoral on independent grounds. Further, it is hard to see the envisioned situation as cooperation among people unless C wants to die, then and in that way.

[42] Immanuel Kant, *The Fundamental Principles of the Metaphysic of Ethics,* trans. Otto Manthey-Zorn (New York: Appleton-Century Crofts, 1938), p. 51.

[43] This may be a logical or an epistemic obligation, but as moral judgments turn on an assessment of the facts from the moral point of view, it is not unnatural to say that we are under a moral obligation to take appropriate actions to get the facts right as a part of right action—as part of deciding what is the moral thing to do.

[44] I appreciate financial support of parts of this work from the Center for Study of Public Choice, the Liberty Fund, Inc., and the Reason Foundation.

Jon Elster

SELF-REALIZATION IN WORK AND POLITICS: THE MARXIST CONCEPTION OF THE GOOD LIFE

Marx is not generally treated as a moral philosopher, partly because his account of social history appears to leave little room for a crucial feature of morality, free choice for individuals. But there are those who find a distinctly moral thesis in Marx; indeed, who consider Marxism most potent in its moral or value content. Jon Elster— who is a professor at the Institute for Social Research in Oslo, Norway, and at the University of Chicago, and who wrote, among other works, Making Sense of Marx *(Cambridge University Press, 1985)—is someone who values Marxist thought mainly for the moral thesis it contains. He argues that within Marxism it is indeed the thesis of the vital importance of self-realization in work and in politics that gives the system its basic power.*

I. INTRODUCTION

In arguments in support of capitalism, the following propositions are sometimes advanced or presupposed: (i) the best life for the individual is one of consumption, understood in a broad sense that includes aesthetic pleasures and entertainment as well as consumption of goods in the ordinary sense; (ii) consumption is to be valued because it promotes happiness or welfare, which is the ultimate good; (iii) since there are not enough opportunities for consumption to provide satiation for everybody, some principles of distributive justice must be chosen to decide who gets what; (iv) the total to be distributed has first to be produced. What is produced depends, among other things, on the motivation and information of the producers. The theory of justice must take account of the fact that different principles of distribution have different effects on motivation and information; (v) economic theory tells us that the motivational and informational consequences of private ownership of the means of production are superior to those of the various forms of collective ownerships.

In the traditional controversy over the relative merits of capitalism and economic systems, the focus has been on proposition (v). In this paper, I consider instead propositions (i) and (ii). Before one can even begin to discuss how values are to be allocated, one must consider what they are—what it is that ought to be valued. I shall argue that at the center of Marxism is a specific conception of the good life as one of active self-realization, rather than passive

Reprinted, with permission, from *Social Philosophy and Policy,* vol. 2–3, Spring 1986. Copyright © 1986 by Basil Blackwell Ltd.

* I am grateful to my colleagues in the project "Work and social justice" at the Institution for Social Research for their comments on earlier drafts of this paper. Special thanks are due to Fredrik Engelstad for his guidance in the literature on work satisfaction.

consumption.[1] It is a conception that, with various qualifications and modifications, I am also going to defend by arguing that self-realization is superior to consumption both on welfarist and on nonwelfarist grounds.[2]

It ought to be noted, before I proceed, that it is far from obvious that political theory ought to be concerned with determining the proper conception of the good life. John Rawls argues, for instance, that the goal of political philosophy is to determine the just distribution of primary goods, i.e., the goods that everyone would want in order to realise his or her own conception of the good life.[3] It would be unjustified paternalism if the state were to intervene in order to promote a special conception of the good by influencing the availability of various options or trying to foster the desire for some rather than others.

I have much sympathy for this liberal argument. The idea that someone else than the persons concerned knows what is best for them has a long and unsavory history whose lessons should not be forgotten. Yet liberalism is also and obviously incomplete, in that it totally neglects the *endogeneity of preferences*.[4] Liberalism advocates the free choice of life-style, but it forgets that the choice is to a large extent preempted by the social environment in which people grow up and live. These endogenously emerging preferences can well lead to choices whose ultimate outcome is avoidable ruin or misery.[5] Although this resistible preemption is vastly preferable to a dictatorially imposed conception of the good life, it casts a long shadow on the presumed sovereignty of individual preferences. The political question remains, however, even granting that people do not desire that which would be best for them; how, except in a dictatorial or paternalist fashion, could a change for the better come about? The solution must be a form of self-paternalism: if people do not want to have the preferences they have, they can take steps—individually or collectively—to change them.[6]

Hence, the thrust of the paper is twofold. Substantively, it argues for a certain conception of the good life. Methodologically, it argues that such substantive questions are not outside the scope of political theory. The structure of the argument is as follows. Section II exemplifies and defines the notion of self-realization, argues for the superiority of self-realization over consumption, and tries to explain why people may nevertheless resist its attractions. The following Sections discuss the two main vehicles of self-realization that have been discussed in the Marxist and neo-Marxist tradition. Section III considers the concept of *work* and argues that in spite of the apparent disutility of work, it can be a channel for self-realization. Section IV discusses the neo-Marxist idea that *politics* can provide an outlet for self-realization, through participation in political discussions and decision making. Section V considers both of these vehicles in the light of the Marxist view that the value of self-realization ought to be implemented jointly with that of *community*, i.e., self-realization for others or with others. Section VI, finally, looks more closely at ways in which the desire or opportunity for self-realization could be promoted or blocked by various institutional arrangements. I conclude with some tentative remarks on "how to get from here to there."

II. THE CONCEPT OF SELF-REALIZATION

(A) SOME EXAMPLES AND A PRELIMINARY CLASSIFICATION

Here is a list of some activities that can lend themselves to self-realization: playing tennis, playing piano, playing chess, making a table, cooking a meal, developing software for computers, constructing the Watts Tower,[7] juggling with a chain saw, acting as a human mannequin,[8] writing a book, discussing in a political assembly, bargaining with an employer, trying to prove a mathematical theorem, working a lathe, fighting a battle, doing embroidery, organizing a political campaign, and building a boat.

Activities that for various reasons do not lend themselves well to self-realization can be roughly divided into spontaneous interpersonal relations, consumption, and drudgery. The first class of activities range from talking with friends to making love; they do not lend themselves to self-realization because they are not defined by some further goal or purpose. Consumption activities include eating a meal, reading a book, or paying for the services of a prostitute; the reason why they do not lend themselves to self-realization is spelled out in detail below. Drudgery includes sweeping the streets, working on an assembly line, or (with the qualifications discussed in Section IV) voting in an election; it does not lend itself to self-realization because it very soon becomes trivial or boring.

These classes of activities can also be compared along the dimensions of *purposiveness* and *satisfaction*. In consumption, the purpose of the activity is to derive satisfaction. In self-realization, the purpose is to achieve something, and satisfaction is supervenient upon the achievement rather than the immediate purpose of the activity. Spontaneous interpersonal relations can be deeply satisfying but have no purpose beyond themselves. Drudgery has a well-defined purpose, but is inherently unsatisfying. One should add that the purpose of drudgery normally is to produce something that is satisfying, i.e., a use-value. A final class of activities, therefore, would be those which are inherently unsatisfying and produce nothing or little that is of value. Punishment which took the form of digging ditches and filling them up again would be an example. Some forms of "community work" for the unemployed also approach this category, in that the unemployed are set to do work that society normally does not value enough to pay for.

As these examples indicate, a particular kind of activity may not be confined to a single category. Raising children or having sexual relations, for example, can be drudgery under certain conditions, consumption under others, self-realization under still different circumstances, and spontaneous interaction in some cases. The central features that turn an activity into a potential vehicle for self-realization are that it has an external goal and that it can be performed more or less well—i.e., the goal can be realized to a higher or lower degree—according to independently given criteria. If an activity is to be an actual vehicle for self-realization, its goal must be of suitable complexity—neither so simple as to produce boredom, nor so difficult as to produce frustration. The activity must offer *a challenge that can be met*.

Although self-realization can be deeply satisfying, the satisfaction must not be the immediate purpose of the activity. Self-realization belongs to the general class of *states that are essentially byproducts,*[9] i.e., states that can only come about as the side effect of actions undertaken for some purpose, such as "getting it right" or "beating the opposition." In Section IV below, I discuss how the quest for self-realization through political participation is self-defeating if the political system is not oriented towards substantive decision making. The same danger can arise in self-realization through creative work, if the artist becomes too preoccupied with the process of creation itself.

The main argument of this paper is built around the comparison between consumption and self-realization in terms of their inherent benefits and disadvantages. This approach can be justly criticized as too narrow, since the choice between the two forms of activity ought also to be considered in terms of their impact on spontaneous interpersonal relations, which are an important part of the good life on most people's conception. On the one hand, for instance, the tendency for self-realization to expand into all available time, because of the economies of scale that characterize it, is a threat both to consumption and to friendship. On the other hand, one could argue that friendships based on joint self-realization are more rewarding than those which are rooted in common consumption. I am unable to assess the net effect of these opposed tendencies.

(B) TOWARDS A DEFINITION

In the Marxist tradition, self-realization is the full and free actualization and externalization of the powers and the abilities of the individual. I shall discuss the four components of this definition in the order in which I have just mentioned them. The full motivation behind the definition will only become clear in subsection *(c)* below, where the reasons for valuing self-realization are set out.

(i) *The fullness of self-realization.* The idea that the individual can *fully* bring to actuality *all* the powers and abilities he possesses is one of the more utopian elements in Marx's thought, and certainly not one that I am going to defend.[10] One is constrained to choose between being a jack-of-several-trades and a master of (at most) one. I shall argue that the latter option ought to be chosen, because of the economies of scale that characterize self-realization. It is, however, an important question exactly how a "trade" or skill is to be defined. I argue in Section III below that self-realization through work in a constantly changing society may require the development of general skills that can be harnessed to widely different tasks.

(ii) *The freedom of self-realization.* Even though an individual cannot develop *all* his abilities, he ought to be free to develop *any* of them. The notion that self-realization must be free but cannot be full is captured in a "putty-clay" model of human nature.[11] *Ex ante* the individual should be free to choose which of his many powers and abilities to develop, but *ex post* the roads he did not take become closed to him. The reason why the choice of a vehicle for self-realization must be freely made by the individual is that otherwise it would not be *self*-realization. The individual is both the designer and the raw material of the process. Hence, self-realization presupposes self-ownership, in the weak sense of the right to choose which of one's abilities to develop. If I want to write poetry but also have the potential to become a doctor or engineer, there could be no justification for society to force me—e.g., by means of an ability tax—to choose one of the latter options. It would, however, be justified in creating incentives to channel my desire for self-realization into socially desirable occupations, so long as I am not punished if I choose otherwise. Negative and positive incentives ought to be linked to the activities performed, not to potential activities.

Note, however, that self-realization does not entail self-ownership in the stronger senses of (a) the right to choose when to deploy one's (trained) abilities, or (b) the right to retain the full income one can derive from that deployment. It does not impinge on the doctor's self-realization if he is forced to treat patients in a disaster area or to pay taxes on his income. One may or may not think that some of his other rights would be violated, but that is not the issue here.

The formal or negative freedom to choose any given line of self-actualization ought not to be confused with the positive freedom or opportunity to do so. If I want to realize myself by making epic technicolor films, I may be unable to do so because I lack the material resources, even if nobody actively tries to block my desire. A society cannot guarantee that all individuals get what they need in order to carry out their preferred project of self-realization, since it might then be impossible to match the demand for resources with the supply. It can, however, try to create a large variety of opportunities for self-realization, and good mechanisms for matching desires with opportunities. In doing so, however, it will be constrained by the need to favor (i) forms of self-realization that do not require excessive amounts of material resources, and (ii) forms that lead to the creation of material resources.

(iii) *Self-actualization.* I decompose the notion of self-realization into self-actualization and self-externalization. Self-actualization itself can be analytically depicted as a two-stage process, although in reality the two stages proceed *pari passu.* The abilities and powers of the individual are two steps removed from actuality: they must first be developed and then be deployed. Being able to (learn to) speak French is a condition for knowing how to speak French, and this, in turn, is a condition for speaking French.[12] The actual deployment of the ability is, of course, the *raison d'être* for its development and that which gives value to self-realization.

(iv) *Self-externalization.* The individual has many powers and abilities which may be developed in ways that cannot be observed by others. One may train one's ability to enjoy poetry or wine, but the use of this power is not a part of the public domain. It is consumption rather than self-realization. One may, however, externalize the power by interpreting poetry for others or taking up the occupation of wine taster, in which case the activity becomes a potential vehicle for self-realization. To enjoy wine is not an activity that can be performed more or less well, although one may enjoy the wine more or less. By contrast, professional wine-tasting lends itself to evaluation by external criteria.

(C) WHY VALUE SELF-REALIZATION?

I shall argue that both the self-actualization and the self-externalization aspects of self-realization provide reasons for desiring it. Both of these arguments are welfarist in character, the first directly and the second more indirectly. In addition, I shall argue that even under conditions in which the desire for self-realization does not lead to increased satisfaction, it can be a desirable desire to have on grounds of autonomy.

(i) *The need for suspension of tranquillity.* Leibniz wrote that "l'inquiétude est essentielle à la félicité des créatures."[13] This premise also has a central place in Marx's argument for self-realization.

> It seems quite far from [Adam] Smith's mind that the individual "in his normal state of health, strength, activity, skill, facility," also needs a normal portion of work and of the suspension of tranquillity. Certainly, labor obtains its measure from the outside, through the aim to be attained and the obstacles to be overcome in attaining it. But Smith has no inkling that this overcoming of obstacles is in itself a liberating activity. [Labor] becomes attractive work, the individual's self-realization, which in no way means that it becomes mere fun, mere amusement, as Fourier, with grisette-like naiveté, conceives it. Really free working, e.g. composing, is at the same time precisely the most damned seriousness, the most intense exertion.[14]

The central intuition behind this passage can be stated in terms of the Solomon-Corbit theory of "opponent process."[15] A rough diagrammatic statement of their theory is provided in Fig. 1, which allows us to compare the utility streams derived from episodes of (at least some types of) consumption and self-realization. Let us first define an episode AC—of either kind—as the time from the beginning of the activity to the time when utility is back to the

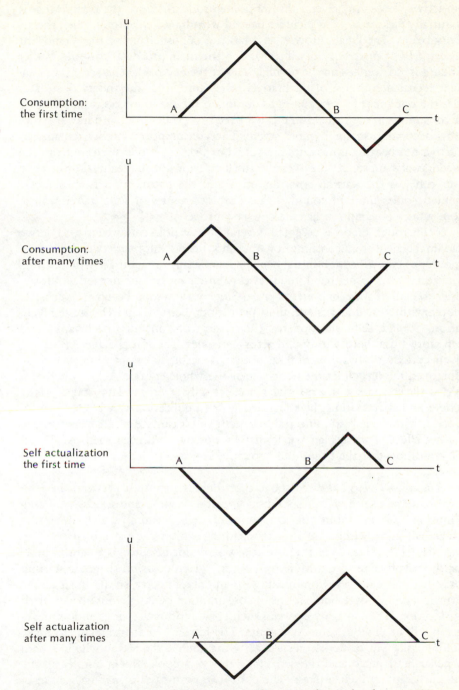

Figure 1. Temporal patterns of utility corresponding to single episodes of consumption or self actualization at early and later stages.

pre-activity level. Any given consumption episode, then, has the pattern that it is initially pleasurable, but includes painful withdrawal symptoms when the activity ceases. The "main process" AB has the opposite sign of the "opponent process" BC. Conversely, in self-realization the main process is painful—"Aller Anfang ist schwer"—and the payoff comes at the end of the episode. If we consider repeated episodes, of qualitatively the same kind, the theory postulates that the opponent process comes to dominate the main process. The pleasures of consumption tend to become jaded over time, while the withdrawal symptoms become increasingly more severe. The consumption activity remains attractive not because it provides pleasure, but because it offers release from the withdrawal symptoms.[16] Conversely, the attractions of self-realization increase over time, as the start-up costs diminish and the gratification from achievement becomes more profound.[17] There are economies of scale in self-realization, while consumption has the converse property.

If this rough model is accepted, several observations follow. First, to derive maximal benefit from consumption, one should search for variety and diversity in order to enjoy the high initial benefits from many different activities. Self-realization, on the other hand, requires concentration on one line of activity in order to exploit the economies of scale. Since variety soon becomes expensive, people with limited means (i.e. most people) do better if they choose self-realization. Second, self-realization has the pattern of "one step backwards, two steps forwards," both within and across episodes. The initial stage AB of any given episode is always painful, although it becomes less painful over time. Moreover, the first times the net effect of the whole episode AC may be negative, while episodes with a positive net effect only emerge at later stages. Many people find that writing their first article for publication is a largely painful process, with a small and uncertain element of pleasure. At later career stages, the net effect of writing an article may be positive, but even then usually on the condition that the beginning is painful.

(ii) *The self and others.* I asserted above that there is a contrast between the temporal patterns of utility corresponding to self-realization and *some types of* consumption. Other forms of consumption, vis., those which represent self-actualization without self-externalization, exhibit the pattern of the bottom diagrams of Fig. 1. Learning to read poetry, for instance, is a painful process; the payoff comes later. Moreover, on any given occasion there are start-up costs that may deter one from picking up a book of poetry, so that instead one turns to a crime novel. Some forms of consumption essentially involve deferred gratification. The similarity between such consumption activities and self-realization will be obvious to many parents. The reason why it is difficult to make children take, say, piano lessons is exactly the same as the reason why it is hard to persuade them to read the first fifty pages of a book which, one feels sure, will then capture their interest. The culprit in both cases is myopia, i.e., resistance to delayed gratification.

To explain why self-realization ranks above such forms of self-actualizing consumption, I shall invoke a Hegelian argument.[18] The most important value for human beings is self-esteem. Self-esteem derives largely from the esteem accorded one by other people. Esteem requires something that can be esteemed, some form of externalization of one's inner self. It is of no avail to be a "beautiful soul" if the soul remains ineffable and mute; the self must be made part of the public domain. This argument is closely linked to the need for external criteria of evaluation. Other people perform the indispensable function of assessing, criticizing, and praising one's performance; they provide the "reality control" without which self-actualization would be like a "private language," a morass of subjectivity. (I return to this issue in V.b. below.)

Drudgery can also be a form of self-externalization that provides esteem and, hence, self-esteem. The fact that one does or produces something that someone is willing to pay for shows that one is being useful and not a burden on others, even when the task itself is inherently uninteresting. This is only indirectly a welfarist argument. It would be simplistic to say that self-esteem is a source of welfare, happiness, or utility. It is, more fundamentally, a condition for the ability to derive welfare from anything. Self-esteem is needed for the motivation to go on with the business of living. When we say that a depressed person suffers from low self-esteem, we mean that it is the cause of the suffering, not its object.

(iii) *Self-realization and autonomy.* In Section VI below, I argue that the lack of desire for self-realization may be due to "adaptive preferences," i.e., to the adjustment of desires to what is possible. In a society with few opportunities for self-realization, it may *for that reason* not be highly valued. With more opportunities, the desire might emerge. Yet we ought to consider the possibility that increased opportunities for self-realization might generate more desires than can be satisfied.[19] If so, the increase in opportunities might make people on the whole worse off in terms of welfare, and yet we might want to say on nonwelfarist grounds that the change was a good thing. For reasons of autonomy, it is better to desire things because they are desirable than to do so because they are available. Many people would agree with this if one used freedom rather than self-actualization as an example, but the argument applies no less to the latter case. To bring the point home, consider an example used by Ronald Dworkin in his rebuttal of welfarist conceptions of equality.[20] Imagine a gifted artist or scientist who, despite his great achievements, is desperately unhappy because he is acutely aware of his shortcomings. Indeed, it is precisely because of his great gifts that he, better than others, can perceive how far his achievement falls short of the ideal. When the circle of light expands, so does the surrounding circle of darkness. It would be simplistic to say that this person should go into another occupation, where he can set his sights lower and not think of himself as a fraud. The achievements of such people are inseparable from their total dedication to what they are doing. Although the darkness makes them depressed, they cannot live without the light. Theirs are lives worth living, though not on grounds of welfare.

D) THE RESISTANCE TO SELF-REALIZATION

Yet there are other reasons, beyond that of adaptive preferences, why people might not desire self-realization. Even when there are available opportunities, people might not take them because of myopia, risk-aversion, or free-riding.

(i) *Myopia.* The fact that self-realization involves deferred gratification, both within and across episodes, must enter importantly into the explanation of why it is not chosen even when its superiority is clearly recognized. As I have argued elsewhere,[21] this is not simply a question of time discounting. It can also, more centrally, be a question of weakness of the will. People may desire life of self-realization and take the first, relatively costless steps towards it, and yet not bring themselves to undergo the painful learning process that is required.

(ii) *Risk-aversion.* I have emphasized that self-realization requires a matching of abilities and tasks to avoid boredom and frustration. It is not, however, a question of choosing a task that is optimally suited to given and known abilities. The situation, unfortunately, is one in which one of William Blake's Proverbs of Hell finds ample application: "You never know what is enough unless you know what is more than enough." The only way for the individual to find the limits of his abilities is, often, to come up against them.

To model the problem decision-theoretically, let us assume that the individual confronts the following situation:

		TASK	
		EASY	COMPLEX
	HIGH	30	100
ABILITY			
	LOW	50	10

The numbers indicate the satisfaction that the individual derives under the different combinations of ability level and task complexity. They assume that matching ability and skill is always preferable to nonmatching, that high-level matching is better than low-level matching, and that the frustration from having chosen a task which is too difficult is worse than the boredom from having chosen one that is too easy. Let us first assume that the choice involves risk, with, say, equal probability that one's ability will be high or low. A risk-neutral individual would choose the complex task, but a risk-averse one might well choose the easy task. Next, assume that the situation is totally clouded in uncertainty, so that no probabilities can be assigned to the various ability levels. In that case, many people would use the maximin strategy of choosing the task which guarantees the highest minimal satisfaction, which again is the easy task. In either case, the conclusion follows that people individually might be deterred from choosing the course of action that would make them better off on the average. In theory risk-pooling could overcome the problem, but it is hard to see how any viable insurance system could be set up.

(iii) *Free-riding.* It must be emphasized that if risk aversion makes people eschew the more demanding vehicles for self-realization, they do not in any way act irrationally. The need for security is not an objectional one. Yet before we conclude that risk-aversion is an insuperable obstacle to self-realization, we must consider another aspect of the problem. Self-realization is not only rewarding for the individual who engages in it. It also provides gratification for those who consume the output of the activity. To the extent that people choose to realize themselves by engaging in scientific or technological activities, they produce medicines that save lives and innovations that make available to everybody and at low cost products that formerly were reserved for an elite. Even those whose efforts at self-realization are frustrated because they overestimated the level of their ability benefit from the activities of those who correctly estimated their ability to be high.

This shows that self-realization is also a problem of collective action. It is probably better *for everybody,* and not just on the average, if all act as if they were risk-neutral, even if they are risk-averse. Yet for each individual, it is always tempting to be a free rider and benefit from the risk-taking of others, while acting in a risk-averse manner. To overcome the free-rider problem, self-realization would probably have to become a social norm, although various other solutions are also possible.[22]

I add two further remarks on this problem. First, it is not clear that even risk-neutral behavior would bring about the socially desirable outcome if the subjective probabilities are correctly formed. Either risk-loving or over-estimation of one's own abilities may be required. The following passage from a book by two cognitive psychologists is well worth reflecting upon:

People sometimes may require overly optimistic or overly pessimistic subjective probabilities to goad them into effective action or prevent them from taking dangerous action. Thus it is far from clear that a bride or groom would be well advised to believe, on their wedding day, that the probability of their divorce is as high as .40. A baseball player with a batting average of .200 may not be best served, as he steps up to bat, by the belief that the probability that he will get a hit is only .2. The social benefits of individually erroneous subjective probabilities may be great even when the individual pays a high price for the error. We probably would have few novelists, actors or scientists if all potential aspirants to these careers took action based in a normatively justified probability of success. We also might have few new products, new medical procedures, new political movements, or new scientific theories.[23]

Second, we may use this occasion to dwell on the distinction between the self-realization of men and that of Man.[24] It is part and parcel of the ethical individualism of Marxism (further discussed in Section V below) that communism ought not to be justified by the prospect of great achievements for Mankind, but by what it offers to each and every individual. It is characteristic of class societies that they allow for the self-realization of Man at the expense of that of most individual men, by enabling scientific and cultural achievements by the few at the expense of the drudgery of the many, while communism in Marx's conception will allow the full and free self-realization *of each individual*. We can retain both the ethical individualism of Marx and the emphasis on self-realization without accepting this utopian conception. The revised version of the ideal is the free and partial self-realization of some, as a result of the attempted self-realization of all, justified by the fact that the benefits of success also accrue to those who fail in the attempt.

III. WORK AS A VEHICLE FOR SELF-REALIZATION

The main tradition in economic thought has looked at work as largely unpleasant, justified only by what it produces.[25] Marx, as we saw in the passage from the *Grundrisse* cited above, had a different view. While he dissociated himself from Fourier's view that work could be made into "mere amusement," he also took exception to Adam Smith's view that work was, necessarily, "a curse." Work, according to Marx, is rewarding *and* painful; moreover, it could not be rewarding without being painful.

Contemporary industrial psychologists have also, from a very different perspective, considered the intrinsic benefits of work. They have almost exclusively discussed the comparative benefits and hardships associated with different forms of work, without asking themselves whether and when work is preferable to its absence, even if income is kept constant. This focus is understandable, whether the concern is with empirical testing or industrial reform, since the option of gaining a full income while not working is not feasible. Yet, from the present perspective, this option can enter usefully into various thought experiments designed to bring out the distinction between motivation and welfare—between what people prefer to do and what is best for them. I argue first that, for several reasons—one of which is self-realization—people may be better off working even if they would prefer not to. I then consider the extent to which the argument from self-realization applies to industrial work in modern societies.

A) THE "DISUTILITY OF WORK"

The very definition of work constitutes a problem. I shall use the term in a broad and somewhat loose sense, to refer to any organized and regular activity whose purpose is to produce use-values or intermediate goods for the production of use-values. It is sometimes made part of the definition of work that it involves some pain or cost, even if only opportunity costs, to the worker. For reasons to be made clear below, I do not follow this usage. Nor is it essential for the definition that work be remunerated.

Why do people work? Serge Kolm has offered the following list of reasons.

- Because of direct coercion, as in forced labor
- In exchange for a wage
- Because of a desire to help and serve others
- Out of a sense of duty or reciprocity
- Out of interest for the work itself
- For the sake of social relations at the workplace
- To show others that one is making a contribution to society or that one possesses certain skills
- Because of the social status associated with work
- To escape boredom
- As play
- Out of habit[26]

The notion of the disutility of work may be considered in the light of some of these reasons for working. Independently of the income from work, a person is usually made worse off by never working than by holding a regular job. Yet given the choice of whether to work or to abstain, with the same income, he might prefer to abstain. This may also be true even if it is rephrased in marginalist terms. For all n, it may be true that, if given a choice between working n hours per week and working $n-1$ hours, a person would always prefer the latter option, yet would be worse off from never working than from working a full week. This situation arises because the person neglects the positive externalities of work or, what amounts to the same, the negative externalities of unemployment. These externalities are not effects on other people, but on the person himself at later times. The situation is an intrapersonal, intertemporal Prisoner's Dilemma.[27]

To understand the precise character of the externality, consider the workplace as a source of friendship and self-esteem. For any n, a reduction in working hours from n to $n-1$ will have little immediate impact on these benefits. A person would not lose his friends or their esteem by working slightly less, and he would gain some leisure. He might well prefer the reduction. Yet the cumulative long-term damage to his social life may be more substantial, and outweigh the short-term gain in leisure. Each hour he is absent from work creates negative externalities for future periods, by loosening his insertion in the web of social relation and reducing his sense of his own worth.

A similar argument applies to the benefits derived from work as self-realization. As I made clear towards the end of Section II, myopia can be a major cause of resistance to self-actualization. Hence, the "marginal utility of work" would have a very different value if it were measured at the beginning of a given task and again when the task approaches completion.[28] Even if one considered the marginal utility of the task as a whole, the value would depend heavily on whether one considered an earlier or a later performance. I conclude that the marginalist approach to the utility of work is ill-conceived, since work tasks are not made up of homogeneous bits, but have a complex temporal structure.

B) THE SCOPE FOR SELF-REALIZATION IN INDUSTRY.

Can work in modern societies provide a mode of self-realization? Marx usually cites art and science as paradigm for self-realization, which is not very helpful. Even though he insisted that communism would be based on large-scale industry and argued against conceiving of work on the model of the artisan, his examples of self-realization fit the latter better than the former. Recent work in industrial psychology is more useful, although it does not, for several reasons, fit my purposes perfectly. For one thing, it takes for granted the property relations and incentive structures of capitalist firms; for another, the central concept of "job satisfaction" is much broader and vaguer than the concept of self-realization (as it is used here.)[29] Reasons of space and competence prevent me from trying to summarize these studies here, but I shall try to restate and discuss some of the findings in terms of the framework set out in Section II above.

A recent survey lists work, pay, promotion, verbal recognition, and working conditions as the main causes of job satisfaction. The first of these is further specified in terms which are quite close to my present approach: "Work attributes that have been found to be related to work interest and satisfaction include: opportunity to use one's valued skills and abilities; opportunity for new learning; creativity; variety; difficulty; amount of work; responsibility; non-arbitrary pressure for performance; control over work methods and work pace (autonomy); job enrichment (which involves increasing responsibility and control); and complexity. While each of the above factors is conceptually distinguishable from the others, there is one element which they share in common, the element of *mental challenge*."[30]

Similarly, one influential writer argues that "Work redesign can help individuals regain the chance to experience the kick that comes from doing a job well, and it can encourage them to once more *care* about their work and about developing the competence to do it even better. These payoffs from work redesign go well beyond simple job satisfaction. Cows grazing in the field may be satisfied, and employees in organizations can be made just as satisfied by paying them well, by keeping the bosses off their backs, by putting them in pleasant rooms with pleasant people, and by arranging things so that the days pass without undue stress or strain. The kind of satisfaction at issue here is different. It is a satisfaction that develops only when individuals are stretching and growing as human beings, increasing their sense of competence and self-worth." He further decomposes the conditions for job enrichment into five elements: skill variety, task identity, task significance, autonomy, and feedback.[31] Clearly, this is a pie that can be cut many ways. There seem to be, nevertheless, some common assumptions and problems that can be related to my concerns here.

(i) *Routine, variety or complexity?* Monotonous, repetitive tasks, by and large, are not conducive to job satisfaction. Monotony can be alleviated by increasing either task variety or task complexity. Increasing task variety can take the form of job rotation in semiautonomous groups, but there seems to be some skepticism about this solution.[32] In terms of the framework used here, the skepticism can be justified by observing that job rotation does not permit one to exploit the economies of scale of self-realization. Variety is a desideratum in consumption, not in work. True, it is better to rotate between several simple tasks than to devote oneself full-time to one of them, but full-time concentration on one complex task is better still.

J. Richard Hackman argues, however, that "not all jobs are suited to all people. Some individuals prosper in simple, routinized work, while others prefer highly complex and challenging risks .... What percentage of the workforce actually desire higher order need satisfaction and so are likely to respond positively to enriched jobs? Some observers estimate that only about 15 percent of rank-and-file employees are so motivated."[33] From the argument in Section II, two objections to these statements follow immediately. First, instead of saying that some people like challenges and others do not, one should say that what *is* a challenge differs across people. Second, the fact that many people do not desire challenging work does not mean that they would not "prosper" in it, once they got over the initial hurdles.

(ii) *Matching workers with jobs.* G. E. O'Brien distinguishes between several strategies for achieving this match.[34] First, one can adapt the tasks to the workers by reform at the workplace. This strategy has the most central place in the literature. O'Brien raises the question of whether economic democracy could be geared to this purpose. In his opinion, this will not be a successful strategy, for the reason, among others, that "The less skill-utilization and influence people have in their jobs, the more likely it is that they see their lives as being determined by others .... This expectation makes it difficult for them to respond initially to changes in jobs or power structures which provide them with more autonomy." I return to some aspects of this problem in Section VI.a below.

Conversely, one may try to fit the worker to the task by suitable hiring criteria. According to O'Brien, "selection psychologists have done well in rejecting applicants with below required skill levels but have been less careful about rejecting applicants whose skill repertoir exceeds the job descriptions." If it is correct, this observation could be explained by the fact that a capitalist firm has no incentive—or may not think it has an incentive—to avoid hiring overqualified workers. If an underqualified worker is hired, both the firm and the worker suffer, but only the worker suffers if he is overqualified.[35]

One may also attack the problem by long-term strategies of planning rather than short-term strategies of adaptation. One of these is to design new factories and organizations so as to facilitate the matching of workers and tasks. The other is "to promote an educational policy which encourages students to have a realistic assessment of their own abilities and the probability of obtaining

jobs which match these abilities." The idea is presumably that with a more realistic assessment, students will decide not to develop abilities the deployment
of which will meet no demand. The argument may or may not be valid, depending on the further assumptions made about individual motivation.[36] In
any case, one must distinguish between two problems. As I mentioned earlier,
no society can provide a guarantee that there will be a demand for a given ability. On the other hand, a good society ought to ensure that for each individual
there is some ability he can develop that will meet an effective demand.

(iii) *Autonomy and feedback.* These requirements from the literature on job satisfaction reflect the interaction between the self and others in self-realization. On
the one hand, the task, to be satisfying, must be freely chosen and performed.
"An employee will not automatically like a task simply because it is challenging or because he has mastered it. He also has to like it for its own sake. This
means that a man must choose the line of work *because he likes it,* not because
someone else told him to like it, or because he is trying to prove something."[37]
On the other hand, the individual needs the recognition and evaluation of
competent others, both to know how well he is performing and to give substance to his self-esteem. The most satisfactory feedback is provided by co-
workers and clients rather than supervisors, since the latter are paid to use profitability rather than quality as the criterion for evaluating work.

The last observation points to a possible conflict between economic efficiency and self-realization. Tocqueville recounts in *Democracy in America* that
he "met an American sailor and asked him why his country's ships are made so
that they will not last long. He answered offhand that the art of navigation
was making such quick progress that even the best of boats would be almost
useless if it lasted more than a few years."[38] With rapid technical change, the
careful attention to detail that characterizes most forms of self-realization is
pointless; conversely, pride in craftmanship may block innovation. The way
out of this dilemma would have to be in the development of *adaptable skills*
that can be harnessed to a variety of concrete tasks and, in fact, be enhanced by
such variety. This would differ from job rotation in that each task would be an
application and extension *of the same skill,* so that the economies of scale would
not be lost.

IV. POLITICS AS A VEHICLE FOR SELF-REALIZATION

Marx did not believe that there would be room or need for conflictual politics
in communism; *a fortiori* he could not promote politics as a channel for individual self-realization. Later Marxists have thought differently, notably Jürgen
Habermas. He suggests that Marx overemphasized *work* at the expense of *interaction,* both in his theory of history and in his philosophical anthropology. The
development of moral competence through rational discussion is a form of
self-realization that ought to be valued as highly as self-realization at the workplace.[39]

Since I have discussed this claim at some length elsewhere,[40] the present discussion will be more summary. It will be organized around two distinctions. On the one hand, politics may be conceived either as a *private* activity, or as one that essentially takes place in the *public* domain. On the other hand, it may be valued either as a *means to some nonpolitical end* or as an *end in itself*. The latter distinction is not an exclusive one; politics may be valued both as a means and as an end. Indeed, the thrust of my arguments is that to be an end in itself, it must also be a means to something beyond itself.

A) PRIVATE POLITICS

According to this conception—memorably stated by Anthony Downs—the essential and almost only mass political activity is that of voting.[41] In Section II, voting was classified as drudgery, i.e., as inherently unrewarding, to be valued only for the outcome it produces. This characterization hides a paradox, however, since it is hard to see how the outcome—an infinitesimally small chance of casting the decisive or pivotal vote—could motivate the act of voting (assuming that it is not compulsory).[42] Where the secret ballot is used, it is not plausible to argue that voting has any consumption value.[43] Nor does it offer any scope for self-realization, since it is not something that can be done more or less well. True, the decision to vote for one party or candidate rather than another may be the outcome of a process of deliberation which can be evaluated according to independent criteria, but to expose oneself to such evaluation is already to take leave of private politics. It is hard to see how voting could be anything else than drudgery, but equally hard to see what motivation it could have as drudgery.

The solution to the paradox is found in a class of motivations that include duty, fairness, internalized social norms, and sheer magical thinking.[44] These attitudes are not easily categorized along the dimensions of purposiveness and satisfaction introduced in Section II. Voting, under normal conditions, cannot be justified by any purpose and does not produce any satisfaction—except that of doing what one believes one ought to do. Then we must ask, however, why one should believe one ought to do something that neither has an extrinsic purpose nor produces intrinsic satisfaction. I am not going to pursue this question here, except to note again that behavior guided by duty or social norms is somewhat recalcitrant to the conceptual scheme used here.

B) A CONTROVERSY OVER ANCIENT POLITICS

The argument that politics is mainly or even exclusively to be valued as a form of self realization has been put forward in discussions of the ancient *polis*. Hannah Arendt, especially, championed the view that politics in the ancient city states was about the agonistic display of excellence and individuality, and nothing else: "Without mastering the necessities of life in the household, neither life nor the 'good life' is possible, but politics is never for the sake of life. As far as the members of the *polis* are concerned, household life exists for the sake of the 'good life' in the *polis*."[45] In plain language, economics is a condition for politics, but not the object of politics. Nor, as far as one can glean from her text, did ancient politics have any other goal which could lend it value as a vehicle for self-realization.

A more ironic version of Hannah Arendt's argument is provided by Stephen Holmes who, when summarizing the views of Benjamin Constant on ancient politics, also appears to deny that ancient politics had any nonpolitical end: "Participatory self-government in the *polis* . . . was an improvised solution to the hoplite's awful problem: a surfeit of leisure time and the terrifying threat of ennui."[46] The goal—escape from boredom rather than self-realization—is more lowly, but the denial of any instrumental value to politics equally explicit.

This view may be challenged on factual grounds, as well as on grounds of consistency. For the first, we may look to the work of Moses Finley. He turns Arendt's view around and argues that: "In the city-states the premise, one might say the axiom, was widespread that the good life (however that was conceived) was possibly only in the *polis;* that the regime was expected to promote the good life; that therefore correct political judgments, the choice between conflicting policies within a *polis,* or, if matters reached such a stage, the choice between *polis* regimes, should be determined by which alternative helped advance the good life. . . . The good life, it should be stressed, had a substantial material component."[47] Elsewhere, asking why the Athenian people claimed the right of every citizen to speak and make proposals in the Assembly, yet left the exercise of the right to a few, he finds that "one part of the answer is that the *demos* recognized the instrumental role of political rights and were more concerned in the end with substantive decisions, were content with their power to select, dismiss and punish their leaders."[48]

My claim is that of these two assertions—most people did not value politics as a vehicle for self-realization; they did value politics as a means to nonpolitical ends—the second would be true even if the first were not. It is inconsistent to value political participation if it is not *about* something. It follows from the argument in Section II that political discussion must have an independently defined goal if it is to provide an outlet for self-realization. The goal must be to make good decisions about what must ultimately be nonpolitical matters. To arrive at a good decision, political discussion must be guided by the norms of rationality; hence, the powers and abilities brought to actuality by discussion are those of rational deliberation. The more urgent and important the decision to be made, the greater the potential for self-realization.

It follows that ancient politics as conceived by Arendt or Constant would be self-defeating. To escape boredom, one must be motivated by some other goal than that of escaping it. What is also—and somewhat inconsistently—emphasized by Holmes and Constant, however, is that constant threat of *war* provided the indispensable, externally given object of ancient politics. The urgency of war concentrates the mind wonderfully, and lends to politics the proper degree of seriousness without which it could neither be a remedy for boredom nor provide a vehicle for self-realization.

Mass political participation, then, can be a form of self-realization, if it takes the form of rational public discussion and decision making about substantive matters. National politics in modern societies involves too many people to provide an occasion for participatory self-realization, while mass demonstrations and similar activities suffer from not being oriented towards decision making. The most promising arenas for this form of self-realization are local government, economic democracy, and democracy within organizations more generally. The conditions under which they lend themselves to self-realization are further discussed in the next Sections.

V. SELF-REALIZATION AND COMMUNITY

According to Hegel and Marx, pre-capitalist societies were characterized by community without individuality. The modern period, conversely, has seen the emergence of frenetic individuality and the widespread disintegration of community. Marx believed that communism would bring about a synthesis of the two values. Although I cannot argue in any detail for this view here, I believe that his conception was inspired by the philosophy of Leibniz, who argued in a similar vein both that each monad differs from all others and that each monad reflects all others from its point of view.[49] On the one hand, people will tend to choose vehicles of self-realization that correspond to their "individual essences," to use a phrase from Leibniz. "Milton produced *Paradise Lost* for the same reason that a silkworm produces silk. It was an activity of *his* nature."[50] The ethical individualism of Marxism requires that "Above all we must avoid postulating 'society' again as an abstraction *vis-à-vis* the individual."[51] On the other hand, the self-realization of the individual must not be an agonistic and antagonistic process, but should take place in and for the sake of the community. According to Marx, self-realization is integrated with community when it is *production for others*. I shall first consider this idea, and then the alternative proposal that the two values might be reconciled in *production with others*.

A) SELF-REALIZATION FOR OTHERS

This ideal is most clearly stated in a passage from Marx's early manuscripts:

Let us suppose that we have carried out production as human beings. Each of us would have *in two ways affirmed* himself and the other person (1) in my *production* I would have objectified my *individuality,* its *specific* character, and therefore obtained not only an individual *manifestation of my life* during the activity, but also when looking at the object I would have the individual pleasure of knowing my personality to be *objective, visible to the senses* and hence a power *beyond all doubt.* (2) In your enjoyment or use of my product I would have the direct enjoyment both of being conscious of having satisfied a *human* need by my work, that is, of having objectified *man's* essential nature, and of having thus created an object corresponding to another *man's* essential nature. . . . Our products would be so many mirrors in which we saw reflected our essential nature.[52]

The text is not transparently clear. It may, perhaps, be read as suggesting a distinction between two ways in which the appreciation of other people enhances the satisfaction I derive from work. On the other hand, I may derive pleasure from the pleasure they derive from my product. This will be the case only when I produce for people I know well, e.g., when I cook a meal for my family. The idea that one can derive pleasure from knowing that one provides a service to "society" is, in my opinion, unrealistic.[53] On the other hand, the critical assessment of other people is needed to tell me whether I am performing well or not. For this purpose, it is crucial that the assessment could be—and sometimes is—negative; "sans la liberté de blâmer il n'y a pas d'éloge flatteur." Family members and friends cannot easily perform this function, since spontaneous interpersonal relations do not go well with this coolly evaluative attitude. Cooking for strangers is more satisfactory. Hence, I suggest that Marx was wrong *if* he intended to suggest—but it is far from certain that he did—that one and the same reference group could perform both functions.

Even if cooking is drudgery rather than self-realization, one might prefer to cook for strangers. Doing or producing something that others are willing to pay for is a source of self-esteem even when the work itself is not challenging or interesting. This may be among the reasons why women often feel the need to escape the close and sometimes suffocatingly ambiguous atmosphere of the family. To repeat, it is not a question of deriving pleasure from the fact that one does something which is socially valued, but of creating the conditions for deriving pleasure from other activities.

B) SELF-REALIZATION WITH OTHERS

An alternative synthesis of self-realization and community would be producing *with* others rather than *for* them. It would be embodied in the work collective rather than in the producer-consumer community. I do not have in mind what one could call *common* self-realization, in which each of several people would perform separate tasks under shared conditions. (Think of a group of scholars working together in a library.) Rather, I refer to *joint* self-realization, in which "the free development of each is the condition for the free development of all."[54] (Think of the players in an orchestra or the participants in a political discussion.) Following the discussion in Sections III and IV, we may distinguish between joint self-realization in work and in decision making. (The players in an orchestra, in addition to playing together, may also decide together which pieces to play and what to do with the proceeds from the concert.)

Consider, first, joint self-realization in the production process. Historically, the trend in the division of labor has been towards greater integration and independence of tasks on the one hand, and ever-simpler tasks with reduced scope for self-realization on the other. The mode of interdependence in modern industry is such that, if A does not do his job, B cannot do his—but it need not be true that the better A does his job, the better B can do his, and certainly not that B's good performance conversely enhances the conditions for A's good performance. And even if this is also the case, it need not be true that both tasks offer indefinite scope for improvement and growth. The conditions for joint self-realization may be observed on a small fishing vessel or in joint authorship, but do not seem to be favored by the nature of industrial work.

Consider, next, participatory democracy at the workplace. The first question that arises is that of efficiency. It is trivial to observe that any implementation of direct economic democracy would have to strike a compromise between the values of participatory self-realization and efficiency. A similar compromise might have to be struck between self-realization in work and efficiency, and in general between any two values one might want to promote. A less trivial statement is that participatory self-realization may actually depend on efficiency. As argued above, the value of participation depends on the degree to which the object of participation is to make good decisions. In the present case, the goal is not to find the decision that would be best if found costlessly, but to make the best decision all things considered, *including the cost of decision making itself*. If enterprises run by direct democracy make a mess of it, the workers will get neither the benefits from efficiency nor from self-realization. Hence, maximal self-realization occurs with a less-than-maximal degree of participation; total direct democracy would be self-defeating.

The market is a device for telling firms how well they perform. Hence, an argument for market socialism, as distinct from state socialism, is that the threat of bankruptcy, like the threat of war, concentrates the mind wonderfully. I would like to illustrate this argument with a piece of personal history. Around 1970, I was somewhat involved with two work collectives, a publishing firm that depended on market success for survival and an academic institution that did not. Although the participatory democracy was much more strenuous and demanding in the first, it was also more rewarding. We gained much insight into the various sub-processes of publishing, and the way they come together in the final product: a book that is bought by someone. After a time, however, strain took its toll and the collective abdicated for a leader. In the second group, the lack of an independent goal and of well-defined performance criteria led to make-believe democracy. Discussion about who had the right to vote on what issues took up an increasing amount of time. The process of self-government turned inward upon itself, with boredom rather than self-realization as the predictable result.

We may contrast direct participatory democracy with representative economic democracy. Direct democracy is strenuous but rewarding, provided that the efficiency constraint is respected. Representative democracy retains the virtue of justice, but does not provide scope for self-realization for the rank and file of workers. The worst system is that which exists when direct democracy degenerates into activist rule, because too many people think the strains of participation exceed the rewards. Activists are not subject to the normal low-cost checks and controls of representative systems, only to the high-cost control of co-participation.

There are two possible ways of coping with the instability of participatory democracy. One is to base the direct democracy on compulsory participation. My view is that, unless it is chosen unanimously as a form of collective self-control, reflecting the fact that self-realization is strenuous and subject to weakness of will, this system would be unjustifiable. It would involve using other people as means to one's own self-realization, and undermine the essentially free nature of rational discussion. The other solution is to have automatic transformation from direct to representative democracy when the level of participation drops below a certain level. If the activists are people for whom decision making is a central form of self-realization, they could offer themselves as candidates in the representative elections. If they simply like untrammeled power, they would not thus offer themselves, which is as it should be.

These remarks apply to political democracy no less than to economic democracy. Under suitable conditions, both can be arenas for joint self-realization. Although in economic democracy the collectivity is one of workers rather than of citizens, it is not oriented toward self-realization in the actual work, but to self-realization in the process of making work-related decisions. This does not mean that the workers perform managerial functions. They engage in a rational, knowledgeable discussion which issues in instructions to the managers. Managers may achieve self-realization individually, by developing and deploying their administrative skills. The self-realization of the workers would, like that of the musicians in an orchestra, be a genuinely joint one. If some of the participants deviate from the rules of a rational discussion, they thereby make it difficult or pointless for others to follow them.[55]

VI. INSTITUTIONS, DESIRES, AND OPPORTUNITIES

What are the institutional conditions that could promote or block self-realization? More precisely, how are the desire and the opportunity for self-realization in work and politics affected by institutional relations within and between firms? This is a question that involves two independent variables and four dependent ones, and in addition we may expect there to be relations between the dependent variables. Here I shall only speculate about some of the connections that may obtain. I first raise the issue of adaptive preferences, already broached in Section II above. I then consider how relations within the firm may affect the opportunity for self-realization, and how relations between firms may affect both the desire and the opportunity. I conclude with some comments on "how to get from here to there."

A) ADAPTIVE PREFERENCES

The absence of self-realization may be due to the absence of a desire for self-realization or to the absence of opportunities. If, in a given society, we observe that there are few opportunities for self-realization and that people do not much seem to want it, it would be tempting to explain the first of these facts by the second. The causal chain could, however, go the other way. Because most people have few opportunities for self-realization, their desires and aspirations might unconsciously adjust to this limitation, to avoid cognitive dissonance. In particular, a high rate of time discounting and a high degree of risk-aversion might emerge endogenously, to make the best elements in the feasible set appear to be optimal even within the wider set that includes opportunities for self-realization as well as for consumption. The idea that self-realization is too strenuous and demanding may be tainted by an element of "sour grapes."[56] On the other hand it may well reflect a respectable, autonomous preference for a quiet life or a life devoted to friendship. We would be able to tell the difference if more opportunities for self-realization were available, for if they were still not chosen, it would show that the desire for a different life style was an autonomous one, or at least one not shaped by the feasible set.

B) DEMOCRACY AND SIZE

Oliver Williamson and others have argued that there are inherent advantages of hierarchy over peer group organization.[57] Hierarchy economizes on the costs of diffusion of information, which is channeled through the leadership instead of being exchanged between all members in pairwise interactions. It imposes a solution on trivial allocation problems that might otherwise have been the object of protracted bargaining. It is more consistent with the monitoring of labor productivity which, although not impossible in the peer group, violates its spirit. These advantages, finally, increase more than proportionally with the size of the group.

To assess these claims, the problem must be stated more precisely. I am concerned with evaluating economic institutions in terms of justice, the scope allowed for self-realization, and psychological stability. Efficiency is not explicitly an issue, but it enters indirectly as a requirement for self-realization, as I argued above. Recall, moreover, that the peer group is only supposed to make major policy decisions, not to supervise the day-to-day activities of all members. It appears to me that all the advantages of hierarchy cited above could be preserved by having some members of the peer group perform managerial functions in accordance with these policy decisions. The difficulty, it would seem, arises at the level of these decisions themselves. Direct democracy is vulnerable to attrition and to plain lack of interest in decision making, e.g., if the workers are fully engaged in self-realization through work. Moreover, with large numbers of workers, it is technically inefficient and hence self-defeating *on its own terms*. To preserve efficiency and economic justice, delegation of decision making to elected representatives then becomes necessary. This arrangement would allow self-realization for these representatives, but not for the rank and file. In the best of all possible worlds, the latter would then be able to achieve self-realization in the work process itself.

Firm size depends largely on technology. To the extent that it is possible to channel technical change in the direction of smaller productive units, it is most urgent to do so in firms where the productive tasks themselves do not offer much scope for self-realization. Because of the economies of scale in self-realization, it is less important to insist on direct democracy where the work itself already offers sufficient challenge. Musicians in an orchestra may well prefer a dictatorial leader, even if he sometimes makes decisions with which they disagree, since this leaves them with more time to concentrate on their work.

c) MARKET OR PLANNING?

The macroeconomic institutions of a society will have a profound influence on both the desire and the opportunity for self-realization. What I shall have to say about the impact on desires will be largely speculative, but I believe the comments on opportunities are somewhat more robust.

Central planning is not favorable to the two modes of self-realization under discussion. To imagine participatory economic democracy in a centrally planned economy is almost a logical contradiction, since it would involve having the same decisions made by two different sets of people. (Imagine, moreover, the complications that would follow from participatory democracy in the planning agencies!) I have also argued that the market performs a useful function for self-realization through work by providing independent external criteria of evaluation, whereas Soviet-type economies have been plagued by the difficulty of finding similarly nonmanipulable criteria. On the other hand, the "market mentality" might work against self-realization by providing incentives to produce profitable junk rather than high-quality products that meet no effective demand. The problem is analogous to the conflict between technical change and self-realization mentioned above, and the solution would also have to be similar: to offer scope for self-realization through general skills of tinkering and improvising.

"Market socialism" with direct economic democracy might also be thought to be, if not a contradiction in terms, at least psychologically unstable. Will not the competition between enterprises be incompatible with the solidarity within the enterprise that is needed to make self-management work? The role of solidarity is twofold. On the one hand, all workers must be motivated to work steadily without shirking. On the other hand, the more qualified workers must accept that the salary gap cannot be too large, i.e., that the labor market must be regulated, since otherwise the motivation of the less qualified might be impaired. I do not know of any evidence that these requirements are incompatible with the spirit of competition. Without going so far as to say that solidarity cannot work unless it is solidarity *against others,* it appears to be a fact of life that intergroup competition and intergroup solidarity often coexist stably.

d) HOW TO GET FROM HERE TO THERE (AND REMAIN THERE)

Consider some possibilities:

		WORKERS UNDER CAPITALISM PREFER	
		CAPITALISM	SOCIALISM
WORKERS UNDER SOCIALISM PREFER	CAPITALISM	(i)	(ii)
	SOCIALISM	(iii)	(iv)

Scenario (i) corresponds to a dominant capitalist ideology: workers don't want to move to socialism, and if they got there they would want to leave it. Scenario (ii) can be seen as an expression of "counteradaptive preferences," created by the fact that both capitalism and socialism have many unattractive and ugly features, so that each of them would generate a desire for its opposite.[58] Scenario (iii) need not similarly be an expression of adaptive preferences. If socialism retains all the options of capitalism, while adding that of self-realization, the desire in socialism for socialism would not be an adaptive one. The preference for capitalism in capitalism would, however, be adaptive. Scenario (iv) would seem totally utopian in the light of recent history. Note, however, that from the observed resistance to moving towards socialism one cannot infer a lack of preference for socialism, since the former might also be due to the costs of transition and the free-rider problem in revolutionary action.

I argue in Section II that the resistance to self-realization is largely due to myopia and free-riding. We now see that the same two obstacles arise in the path towards socialism. I believe that the two problems and the solutions to them are closely related, but that is the topic of another paper.[59]

NOTES

[1] The broader interpretation of Marx that sustains this assertion is set forward in my *Making Sense of Marx* (Cambridge: Cambridge University Press, 1985).

[2] For the notion of welfarism, see Amartya Sen, "Welfarism and Utilitarianism," *Journal of Philosophy,* vol. 76 (1979), pp. 463–488.

[3] John Rawls, *A Theory of Justice* (Cambridge, MA: Harvard University Press, 1971), p. 90ff. I ought to add that there is much in Rawls' book that goes beyond the simple consideration of primary goods. In particular, his discussion of what he calls the Aristotelian Principle (p. 424ff.) has many affinities with the present analysis of self-realization. Yet his arguments for the design of basic social institutions does not go beyond primary goods.

[4] See my *Sour Grapes* (Cambridge: Cambridge University Press, 1983), Ch. III, for the importance of endogenous preference formation to political philosophy.

[5] For an extreme example of how one can "improve oneself to death," see Carl Christian von Weizsacker, "Notes on Endogenous Change of Tastes," *Journal of Economic Theory,* vol. 3 (1971), p. 356.

[6] On the notion of individual and collective self-paternalism, see my *Ulysses and the Sirens* (Cambridge: Cambridge University Press, rev. ed., 1984) Ch. II.

[7] The Watts Towers in Los Angeles were constructed single-handedly by an Italian immigrant, Sam Rodia, over a period of 33 years, out of debris and bric-a-brac that he collected from the streets of the city. (For information see the *Los Angeles Times* for August 12, 1984). They are beautiful in conception and execution, unlike, say, conceptual art, which has mainly the freakish value of stunning novelty, soon fading into boredom. For a discussion of the conditions for self-realization in art, see *Sour Grapes,* Ch. II. 7.

[8] This example and the preceding one were observed at Venice Beach in Los Angeles. They are included to remind us that self-realization is not always channeled into activities that in some substantive sense are socially useful, beyond the value of stunning the spectators.

[9] For a general discussion of this notion, see *Sour Grapes* Ch. II.

[10] Well-known passages in which Marx insists on the fullness of self-realization are found in *The German Ideology,* in Marx and Engels, *Collected Works,* vol. 5 (London: Lawrence and Wishart, 1976), pp. 47, 394.

[11] For this approach to production see Leif Johansen, "Substitution versus Fixed Production Coefficients in the Theory of Production," *Econometrica,* vol. 27 (1959), pp. 157–176.

[12] For a conceptual analysis of abilities and their actualization, see Anthony Kenney, *Action, Emotion and Will* (London: Routledge and Kegan Paul, 1963), Ch. VIII. Kenney's is an Aristotelian concept of self-actualization, to be distinguished both from the Freudian notion of liberating one's repressed thoughts and desires and the Nietzschean one of identifying with one's deeds. For a useful discussion, see Alexander Nehamas, "How One Becomes What One Is," *The Philosophical Review,* vol. XCII (1983), pp. 385–417.

[13] Leibniz, *Nouveau essais sur l'Etendement Humain,* in G. W. Leibniz, *Die Philosophischen Schriften,* ed. Gerhardt (Hildesheim: Olms, 1966 reprint) vol. 6, p. 175.

[14] Marx, *Grundrisse* (Hammondsworth: Pelican Books, 1973), p. 611.

[15] Richard L. Solomon and J. D. Corbit, "An Opponent-Process Theory of Motivation," *Psychological Review,* vol. 81 (1974), pp. 119–145. See also my "Sadder but Wiser? Rationality and the Emotions," forthcoming in *Social Science Information.*

[16] It might be objected that this is a model of addictive consumption, not of consumption generally. With nonaddictive consumption, one cannot assume an increasingly strong opponent process, although the idea of decreasing strength of the main process remains plausible. Since the latter is all I need for my argument, it is not affected by the objection. In any case, there may be an element of addiction (in the sense of an increasingly strong opponent process) in all forms of consumption, although it is usually less dramatic than in the use of drugs, tobacco, and alcohol. The objection might then be rephrased as a question about whether the net effect of a given episode always becomes negative as the number of episodes increases.

[17] There are two exceptions to this statement. First, some abilities might not be susceptible to indefinite development; second, some persons might not be able to develop their abilities indefinitely. Tic-tac-toe, unlike chess, soon becomes boring; a person with poor motor reflexes might find out the hard way that he was not made for chain saw juggling. Economies of scale obtain only if abilities and tasks are suitably matched so as to avoid either of the extremes of boredom and frustration.

[18] See G.W.F. Hegel, *Phenomenology of Spirit* (Oxford: Oxford University Press, 1977), pp. 118, 193, 395ff.

[19] For a more detailed exposition of a similar argument, see *Sour Grapes,* pp. 124, 133ff.

[20] Ronald Dworkin, "What is Equality? Part 1: Equality of Welfare," *Philosophy and Public Affairs,* vol. 10 (1981), p. 222.

[21] "Weakness of will and the free-rider problem" *Economics and Philosophy,* vol. 1 (1985).

[22] For a survey of ways in which free-riding can be overcome, see the article cited in the previous note and also my "Rationality, Morality and Collective Action," *Ethics,* vol. 96 (1985), pp. 136–155.

[23] Richard E. Nisbett and Lee Ross, *Human Inference: Strategies and Shortcomings of Social Judgment* (Englewood Cliffs, N.J.: Prentice Hall, 1980), p. 271.

[24] For this distinction, see G. A. Cohen, "Karl Marx's Dialectic of Labour," *Philosophy and Public Affairs,* vol. 3 (1974), pp. 235–261.

[25] For a full survey, see Ugo Pagano, *Work and Welfare in Economic Theory* (Oxford: Blackwell 1984).

[26] S. C. Kolm, *La Bonne Economic* (Paris: Presses Universitairs de France, 1984), pp. 119–120.

[27] For discussion, see the article cited in note 21.

[28] In some cases, it would also give a different result if measured very close to completion; cp. Byron's "Nothing so difficult as a beginning In poesy, unless perhaps the end."

[29] In the literature on job satisfaction the notion of self-realization is usually discussed with reference to the writings of Abraham Maslow, and dismissed as hopelessly confused. See, for instance, Edwin A. Locke, "Nature and Causes of Job Satisfaction," Marvin D. Dunnette, ed., *Handbook of Industrial and Organizational Psychology* (Chicago: Rand McNally College Publishing Company, 1976), pp. 1307–1309. Although I agree with the criticism of Maslow, I hope that the present discussion shows that the notion is not inherently unamenable to precise analysis.

[30] Locke, *ibid.,* p. 1319.

[31] J. Richard Hackman, "Work Design," in J. Richard Hackman and J. Lloyd Suttle, eds., *Improving Life at Work* (Santa Monica: Goodyear, 1977), pp. 96–162.

[32] Gordon E. O'Brien, "The Centrality of Skill-Utilization for Job Design," K. D. Duncan, Michael M. Gruneberg and Donald Wallis, eds., *Changes in Working Life* (New York: Wiley & Sons, 1980), p. 180. See also Hackman, "Work design," pp. 115, 120.

[33] Hackman, "Work design," pp. 115, 120.

[34] O'Brien, "The Centrality of Skill-Utilization," pp. 180ff.

[35] Hackman, "Work design," p. 117, argues that overqualification also causes loss of productivity via the lack of motivation. This may well be true for some workers and some tasks, but sometimes a higher level of qualification probably leads to superior performance.

[36] Raymond Boudon, *Effets Pervers et Ordre Social* (Paris: Presses Universitaries de France, 1977), Ch. IV, argues that this can turn into a problem of collective action: it may be individually rational for each student to seek higher education, although all would be better off if all flipped a coin to decide. This presupposes, however, that students are motivated by expected income rather than by expected satisfaction, which would also take account of the disappointment and frustration generated by getting a low-education job at the end of higher education. Boudon himself (*ibid.,* Ch. V) has the best treatment of this problem, although, surprisingly, he does not bring his analysis to bear on the problem of educational choice.

[37] Locke, "Nature and Causes," p. 1320–1321.

[38] Alexis de Tocqueville, *Democracy in America* (New York: Anchor Books, 1969), p. 453.

[39] Jurgen Habermas, *Theorie des kommunikativen Handelus* (Frankfurt aM: Suhrkamp, 1981).

[40] In my "The Market and the Forum," in Aanund Hylland and John Elster (eds.), *Foundations of Social Choice Theory* (Cambridge: Cambridge University Press, 1985), pp. 103–132; see also *Sour Grapes,* Ch. II. 9.

[41] Anthony Downs, *An Economic Theory of Democracy* (New York: Harper, 1957).

[42] See notably Brian M. Barry, *Economists, Sociologists and Democracy* (Chicago: University of Chicago Press, rev. ed., 1979).

[43] For a brief discussion and rejection of this possibility, see Howard Margolis, *Selfishness, Altruism and Rationality* (Cambridge: Cambridge University Press, 1982), p. 86.

[44] For further discussion, see my "Rationality, Morality and Collective Action." More instrumental attitudes, such as altruist and utilitarian motivations, might also enter into the explanation of voting, but I believe that their importance is smaller than the ones mentioned in the text.

[45] Hannah Arendt, *The Human Condition* (Chicago: University of Chicago Press, 1958), p. 37.

[46] Stephen Holmes, *Benjamin Constant and the Making of Modern Liberalism* (New Haven: Yale University Press, 1984), p. 60.

[47] Moses I. Finley, "Authority and Legitimacy in the Classical City-State," *Det Kongelige Danske Videnskapernes Selskab, Historisk-Filosofiske Meddelelser* 50:3, (Kobenhavn: Munksgaard 1982), p. 12.

[48] Moses I. Finley, "The Freedom of the Citizen in the Ancient Greek World," in his *Economy and Society in Ancient Greece* (London: Chatto and Windus, 1981), p. 83.

[49] Cp. my "Marx et Leibniz," *Review Philosophique,* vol. 108 (1983), pp. 167–177.

[50] *Theories of Surplus-Value* (London: Lawrence and Wishart, 1963), vol. 1, p. 401.

[51] *Economic and Philosophical Manuscripts,* Marx and Engels, *Collected Works,* (London: Lawrence and Wishart, 1975), vol. 3, p. 299.

[52] "Comments on James Mill." *ibid.* pp. 227–28.

[53] The idea is central in Kolm, *La Bonne Economie.* Although Kolm is right in arguing that such "general reciprocity" would overcome some of the defects of ordinary reciprocity, it would also lose the main virtue of the latter, viz, the warmth and spontaneity of personal relations.

[54] Marx and Engels, *Manifesto of the Communist Party,* Marx and Engels, *Collected Works* (London: Lawrence and Wishart, 1976), vol. 6, p. 506.

[55] Habermas, *Theorie des kommunikativen Handelns;* see also Knut Midgaard, "On the Significance of Language and a Richer Concept of Rationality," Leif Lewin and Evert Vedung, eds., *Politics as Rational Action* (Dordrecht: Reidel, 1980), pp. 87–93.

[56] For a more detailed exposition of this argument, I again refer to Ch. III of my *Sour Grapes.*

[57] Oliver E. Williamson *Markets and Hierarchies* (New York: The Free Press, 1975). For a recent survey, see M. McPherson, "Efficiency and Liberty in the Productive Enterprise: Recent Work in the Economics of Work Organization," *Philosophy and Public Affairs,* vol. 12 (1983), pp. 354–368.

[58] For the idea of conteradaptive preferences, see *Sour Grapes,* p. 111–12. For the idea that capitalism and socialism cyclically generate desires for each other, see John Dunn, *The Politics of Socialism* (Cambridge: Cambridge University Press, 1984).

[59] See the paper cited in note 21 above.

Tibor R. Machan

THE CLASSICAL EGOIST BASIS OF CAPITALISM

Critics of capitalism chide it for its breeding of selfishness, for its theoretical reliance on an egoistic or individualist ethics. But why should that be a liability? Tibor Machan—a philosopher at Auburn University, Alabama, author of Human Rights and Human Liberties (1975) *and editor of* The Libertarian Reader (1982)—*argues that only if a very narrow view of human nature is invoked in an individualist ethics and social philosophy is this criticism really telling. He proposes that this narrow individualism is but a first approximation—based on the eagerness in the sixteenth and seventeenth centuries to mimic the success of mechanistic physics and its attendant (atomistic, mechanistic) materialism—of what in fact is a correct (neo-Aristotelian) ethical egoism. The latter invokes a robust view of human nature. From that it is argued that the proper moral task of each person is to seek personal human happiness in life. Because of the "moral space" such pursuit requires, there are natural rights which, when implemented, give rise to the economic system of capitalism.*

> *Ancient moral philosophy proposed to investigate wherein consisted the happiness and perfection of a man, considered not only as an individual, but as the member of a family, of a state, and of the great society of mankind. In that philosophy the duties of human life were treated of as subservient to the happiness and perfection of human life. But when moral, as well as natural philosophy, came to be taught only as subservient to theology, the duties of human life were treated of as chiefly subservient to the happiness of a life to come. In the ancient philosophy the perfection of virtue was represented as necessarily productive to the person who possessed it, of the most perfect happiness in this life. In the modern philosophy it was frequently represented as almost always inconsistent with any degree of happiness in this life, and heaven was to be earned by penance and mortification, not by the liberal, generous, and spirited conduct of a man. By far the most important of all the different branches of philosophy became in this manner by far the most corrupted.*
>
> Adam Smith
> *The Wealth of Nations*

INTRODUCTION

It is often noted that the natural rights doctrine of, for instance, John Locke, and later the subsequent political economy of Adam Smith as well, rest on a type of egoistic or individualistic philosophy of human life. Both of these out-

This is a revised and expanded version of the author's "On Egoism and Justice," *The Occasional Review* 8/9 (1978).

looks enthusiastically endorse the basic rights to life, liberty, and property of every person. Locke's argument is based on a view of human nature as initially free and equal, from the moral viewpoint, as well as on the idea that human beings' seeking their own well-being is proper to them. No less can be said of Adam Smith's general line of reasoning, albeit put somewhat differently.

After Locke and Smith, many have taken it as a defect that the doctrine of natural rights, and the capitalist economy characteristically linked with it, depend on a kind of egoism. Karl Marx is perhaps the best known among these critics. He disparagingly remarks, for example, that "The right of man to property is the right to enjoy his possessions and dispose of the same arbitrarily, without regard for other men, independently from society, the right of selfishness."[1] Still, there remain defenders of capitalism who in arguing mostly for its economic superiority continue to invoke some form of egoism. It is usually of a psychological type, which holds that persons are naturally motivated to pursue their pleasure or to strive to satisfy their desires (maximize their utilities). And one recent defense of capitalism develops its argument by relying directly on an ethical egoism.[2] It simply cannot be denied then that natural rights theory, which undergirds the idea of a just political system within the Western liberal tradition, requires some type of egoism. But which of these types, if any, has a better chance of success is in dispute. Yet there is reason to suppose that a form of individualism is fundamental to the idea of a just community.

Indeed, one version does appear to be both realistic and morally satisfying, thus combining what practical political thinkers and those concerned with upholding human ideals have demanded of a sound ethical foundation for a human community. This ethical egoism is unusual and unfamiliar since it has a classical pedigree (drawing on but not in full accord with Aristotle's ethics). It will be useful to examine the case for what may be called a classical ethical egoism or individualism.

First, a brief sketch of the argument for this ethics: We as human individuals are responsible for *doing well at living our lives*. This, when understood, implies a system of moral and political principles. It implies morally that each person should aspire to live rationally as a human individual and, politically, that regarding their chosen conduct, everyone must be left free from and should seek protection against intrusions by others. Each person, in short, must be left with a sphere of rightful, defensible authority to make his or her own way about life—e.g., play it safe or take risks, develop or falter, stay apart from others or join with them when this is mutually agreeable. All this rests on a conception of ethics as a firmly based yet contextual system of guidelines required by human beings because they lack automatic, built-in (instinctual) prompters for how to carry on with their lives successfully. In what follows it will also be argued that the human self ought to be understood along not Hobbesian but Aristotelian lines. Then the egoism that emerges will prove to be the best and indeed most noble ethical system on which to ground a sound politics.

Before a more detailed exploration of these issues begins, with an eye to finding the moral grounds for the just social economic order, we should note why there is any particular need for a defense of ethical egoism as the foundation of natural rights and capitalism. It may be possible to defend such a political-economic system on utilitarian or pragmatic grounds or, somewhat more promisingly, on the basis of the requirements of morality itself, never mind what moral system is correct in general. That would save us the trouble of having to commit ourselves to some particular moral system.

First, under some conceptions of morality no natural, negative rights could emerge at all. Consider, for example, altruism, utilitarianism, consequentialism, and conventionalism. Those disallow basic rights in the sense in which we are interested in rights, namely as politically unalienable, fundamental. Focusing as they do on valued results (either of direct action or of agreements), these types of moralities tend to reject freedom of choice, individual or personal responsibility for good conduct. Such moralities ultimately amount to theories of value or of the good. Some of these fail to distinguish between the good and the morally good. Others stress natural duties to others, thus making freedom (or negative) rights wholly subordinate. Since such considerations ultimately control politics and law, these value systems or moral outlooks require that individual negative rights be abridged, even violated.

Egoism is, then, important for hard cases. In these judges or legislatures will need to invoke moral considerations. Especially when rights appear to conflict, moral considerations will have to be invoked to see what the law should do, what public policy should be.

Some believe that conflicts at this level can be dealt with by way of intuition or by reference to general utility, the public interest, etc. Yet even to learn what these mean and whether they are decisive, some moral theory is necessary. What occurs in the arena of practical public affairs may, of course, appear to belie this point. But that appearance may reveal that public policy determination is under the influence of certain metaethical views and not others.

Finally, some say that an egoistically based natural rights system is really utilitarian at heart. The meager truth in this claim is that classical egoism contains consequentialist or teleological features. Principles of social life must, of course, benefit one, produce good results in one's life. But the framework is very different here from the sort that utilitarians rely on because of the centrality of the element of moral agency in this teleological approach to ethics and politics.

BIRD'S-EYE VIEW OF CLASSICAL EGOISM

When defending ethical egoism one faces suspicion right from the start. One version is often used in elementary ethics textbooks as illustration of an unsuccessful, even bogus ethical doctrine. The reason is that the idea of the human self that is involved in the standard version is abhorrent: a purely desire-satisfying, crass "individualist" who has no principles and cares only for promoting whimsical, idiosyncratic private goals.

This is not the form of egoism capitalism needs to rest on, even if it has been associated with it, mostly in economic arguments for the system. In place of the Hobbesian, "atomistic," isolated idea of the human self, the classical idea of the individual, suggested initially by Aristotle's idea of the self-suffi-cient, self-loving human being, is to be invoked.

To secure such a foundation for the individualism that capitalism rests on and supports, we need to discuss the metaphysical issues of causality and human nature.

The first thing then to consider is whether causality permits of diversity, so that it could be possible to consider *persons* (not their will) as genuine causes of their behavior. This would secure a basis for both a naturalistic ethical standard and individual responsibility. As to the former, if we learn that human beings are self-determined in a given respect, this will figure into what we take to be human nature, one possible source of the moral standards they should invoke in their choice of behavior. As for the latter, the reason is that without the possibility of self-determined human conduct, no moral sphere is possible. For someone to be morally required to act in certain ways, he or she needs to be free to choose whether or not to engage in the appropriate con-duct. (This is the main source of the criminal law's insistence that a culpable criminal act be carried out in the state of noncompulsion, volitionally.) The idea that persons are capable of initiating their actions, of genuine free choice, is essential to a moral conception of human personal and social life. The classi-cal individualist or egoist ethics underlying capitalism rests on the idea of human beings as essentially individuals, capable of choosing their conduct within a significant sphere of their lives, based on a standard of good applicable to them as human individuals.

WHY IS EGOISM OR INDIVIDUALISM ABHORRENT?

It will help to consider at this point why egoism or individualism has been found morally objectionable, to the point where in moral philosophy the posi-tion is treated as an instance of antimorality. Indeed, some moral philosophers have come to define the moral point of view in juxtaposition to the egoistic stance.

The skepticism about egoism (not just about whether it's right but even whether it's a bona fide *ethical* theory) rests, in large part, on arguments that attack the dominant or Hobbesian egoist conception of human nature. It as-cribes to egoism a conception of the human self, and identifies as egoistic a system of norms that can be derived from it. The critics hold that any egoism must rest on a Hobbesian idea of the self, and so it is inherently amoral or even antimoral. Virtually all critical discussions of egoism assume that only such a Hobbesian egoism is in contention. And then they disqualify the doctrine be-cause the underlying view of the self is inherently Hobbesian, that is, antiso-cial, atomistic, etc.

Once we consider the alternative, based on a neo-Aristotelian metaphysics, this view of what an egoistic ethics must be need not be accepted. Nevertheless, even in the revised classical egoist position, the basic principle of morality arises from a consideration of what will guide human beings toward living *their* lives successfully, properly, and thus in the end to *their* benefit, since ethics is seen here to arise in response to the question, "How should I live my life?"

Certainly many contemporary moral philosophers hold that the dominant concern of morality lies in determining how one should treat other persons. This predilection toward restricting the moral to the socially relevant may appear to some to be reasonable. It certainly is not self-evidently justified. Philosophers as diverse as Aristotle and Kant disagreed. Of course, standards of an ethically good life will imply how one should treat other persons. And some of the questions that arise about conduct vis-à-vis others will seem at times to center on conflicts between self-interest and the interest of others. But that need not be the best understanding of how morality applies to social life, especially if we consider that the alternative of participating in society is itself one we all face and need to decide on ethically.

Classical egoism approaches conflicts among different persons in terms other than pitting self-interest against self-interest, since the conflict of interest idea of the point of morality is question-begging. It assumes a successful case already made for the morality that discounts any understanding of self-interest as its fundamental standard. And, of course, the concept "self-interest" is problematic. Just what is in one's self-interest is an open issue. Maybe being self-interested is always moral, although it might never be in one's genuine self-interest to do the morally wrong thing. In any case, no such loaded sense of "morally right," e.g., what leads to social cohesion, should be adopted. It clearly flies in the face of Plato's idea, in the *Phaedo,* that rational self-interests will coincide: "Just follow my old recipe, my friend: do yourselves concern yourselves with your own true self-interest; then you will oblige me, and mine, and yourselves too. . . ." (115b).

With some of the familiar antiegoist considerations out of the way, let us consider a sensible version of egoism.

Since the task here will be to present a theory of morality, it will be necessary to proceed by indicating why this framework of morality makes better sense than do others. By reaching this goal, egoism will emerge as a better ethical theory than most believe. It may also be shown to be less difficult to reconcile with the concerns of those who opt for other views because they find egoism antisocial, callous, anticommunitarian.

HOBBESIAN VERSUS CLASSICAL EGOISM

The point of the term "classical egoism" is simple: underlying the egoism of Hobbes and the tradition that follows him, we find a conception of human nature that is reductionist and thus atomistic. The tradition ultimately rejects the objectivity of the classification "human." In this tradition each person is ultimately, actually, an aggregation of bits of matter-in-motion, ergo, a pulsating self-aggrandizing blob of matter pursuing—by following the laws of motion—the task of survival.

More developed versions add certain nuances to this idea, but at heart the story isn't changed. Individuals, the "human" selves or egos, have no specific nature, but each is a sort of bare particular. The human individual is not a determinate instance of the objectively established abstract category "human" but belongs within the human species as a matter of convention, without the benefit of a firm, conclusive justification for that classification. In short, the kind of thing something is taken as is determined by way of a convention or agreement.

Of course, this tradition regards the struggle for self-preservation and aggrandizement as a central human character trait. But this fails to distinguish human individuals from other beings, since everything in the universe possesses such a trait. In other words, within this view human nature is the same as the rest of nature. The reductive materialist viewpoint sees all of nature as the same. Nature is composed through and through of matter in motion and human nature is no different. There is no fundamental difference between the kind of entities human beings are and what other things are, except as that has been established by convention. Human beings are not natural but only conventional kinds.

From this tradition we derive a conception of individuality, selfhood, or ego, which is not anchored in any firm and stable (human) nature. Thus when by this Hobbesian egoistic ethics something is judged to be right, it must be viewed entirely independently of some firm, objective, and independent *universal* standard, depending wholly on individual (or collectively agreed to) wants, desires, or preferences.

And here is the rub: Since a collectively agreed to want or desire can always be changed by someone opting out of the agreement or be changed because the agreement is challenged as unsound, unwise, undesired, risky, etc., it does not provide a rationally binding standard. The updated rational egoistic ethics, based on an idea of "rationality" as calculating means to reach preset ends, may add the provision that "egoistic" must mean concern with a long-range perspective of our goals. But in the end this too makes little difference since the standard rests again on goals set by the agent, quite subjectively, with no way to evaluate them. This makes the standards themselves arbitrary. When coordinated with others in a social setting, they suffice only in the face of effective sanctions, not as rationally persuasive and independently binding guidelines.

But it is likely that the main problem which a Hobbesian egoistic ethics runs up against is that it cannot be reconciled with our general notions about what social ethics involves—noncalculating loyalty, generosity, good will, compassion, etc. All these virtues could find merely a forced expression in this ethics. Why would anyone be generous on such egoistic grounds, other than because some overt or hidden private purpose might be served by it? The same follows for all the other virtues bearing on social life. The impression could never be defeated by this form of egoistic "ethics" that the concern one person could have for another, even in the limited degree expressed through respect for another's right to life or liberty, is no more than care for private advantage or convenience.[3]

Close personal ties for Hobbesian egoists would be impossible except as these may be anchored in their instrumental or pragmatic value. This is where such egoism is reduced to a somewhat robust form of hedonism. As John Rawls says, "Egoists are incapable of feeling resentment and indignation. If either of two egoists deceives the other and this is found out, neither of them has a ground for complaint." Nor could there be "bonds of friendship and mutual trust" among egoists.[4]

It is then virtually a foregone conclusion that any idea of ethical egoism that might have a chance of success has to be prominently distinguished from the sort discussed by almost any moral philosopher.[5] The term "classical" aids in this by philosophically relocating ethical egoism in the tradition of Aristotelian thought. In that tradition the human individual could be viewed differently from the way it is viewed within the Hobbesian framework.[6]

In reply to Rawls we might begin by noting what Aristotle said on the subject of self-love:

. . . if a man were always anxious that he himself, above all things, should act justly, temperately, or in accordance with any other of the virtues, and in general were always to try to secure for himself the honourable course, no one will call such a man a lover of self or blame him.

But such a man would seem more than the other a lover of self; at all events he assigns to himself the things that are noblest and best and gratifies the most authoritative element in himself and in all things obeys this; and just as a city or any other systematic whole is most properly identified with the most authoritative element in it, so is a man; and therefore the man who loves this and gratifies it is most of all of a lover of self.[7]

This is the first clue I wish to advance toward a better understanding of classical egoism. But it may be asked why we call this egoism in the first place. The answer is that in the end the ultimate beneficiary of moral conduct is the agent, in that he or she will be the best person he or she can be. The point of morality or ethics is to provide human beings with a guide to doing well in life, to living properly, to conducting themselves rightly.

WHY MORALITY?

Why should morality matter to us at all? Morality or ethics identifies the standards for living properly or well. This purpose right away shows how ethics must be understood as a kind of egoistic system. The reason is that living for human beings is, at a crucial juncture, an individual task.

This is a crucial point. A human being is by nature an individual, a being whose life is in the power of him- or herself. Whatever level of capacity for self-determination someone possesses, such self-determination is an integral part of his or her being human. As rational animals, living beings with the distinctive capacity to engage in conceptual thought and the need to be guided by such thought in their conduct, human beings exemplify their very humanity in their individual *choice* to be conceptually attentive to their lives.

Of course this is an emergent aspect of a person, one that needs to be honed and sustained initially by others (society), but there is evidence of this individualist role in life from the earliest stage of human existence. The formation of ideas, and coordination of behavior, the planning of life—this is distinctive of human animals. That they behave consciously is an inescapable fact about them. This is true, of course, only of those not crucially incapacitated. And it is quite irrelevant that some signs of such conceptualization are evident in other kinds of animals—their successful living is generally not dependent on exercising such a capacity.

Ethics is part of human life because such life embodies a fundamental role for a system or code of *standards.* It is something we need *as human beings,* given our nature as free and independent living agents (vis-à-vis what we *do*). We must choose to act and need some guideline or source for distinguishing between better and worse alternatives in life. Whereas the rest of the animal world can rely on instincts or drives, we cannot.[8]

True enough, some people appear to get along perfectly fine without reference to moral standards. They appear to be amoral, unconcerned with questions of moral right and wrong. Here, too, however, interpretations can differ. When seriously considered, only sociopaths seem to fit this characterization. Even there some perverse conception of rightness appears to be indispensible because for all human beings, insofar as they are not driven by forces independent of their will, choices made from among a variety of alternatives require a system of ranking. Just because some seem to be choosing randomly it does not mean that they are not using a standard of sorts, even if in the end it turns out to be an inappropriate standard. The inappropriateness of it, however, could very easily show its results in certain conflicts that the person experiences. The racist who nevertheless truly respects some members of the race he regards as generally inferior will likely find himself experiencing inner conflict, e.g., when he is insisting that his friend be admitted to a club that is barred to those of his friend's race. So will the thief who insists that what he has stolen not be taken from him by his fellow thieves.

The freedom to choose, the moral independence at issue here, deals with the fact that no one or nothing drives or moves a person to take many of his or her most significant actions—nor is anything or anyone else responsible for them. Faced with such a state—as far as we know unique to human beings—persons require moral standards or what appear to be substitutes for them (e.g., some pragmatic rule of thumb, such as "Go with the flow"). And when they try to go without a consistent moral system, or when they inconsistently apply it, they are very likely to suffer consequences that have an adverse bearing on their lives, preventing them from flourishing.

EGOISM REVISED

The egoist begins by observing that life is the source of all value. Egoism then predicates any further considerations of what standard one should live by on the fact that only for those who can choose and have chosen, freely, to pursue life are standards of value of *moral* concern. Further, egoism notes that the life that one chooses is necessarily a human life, one's own. The issue that arises next is what is implied in the choice to live one's human life. In short, "How should I (this particular *human* being) live my life?" To which the ethical egoist's answer is that,

To evaluate the alternatives facing one with respect to the (implicit) decision (or choice) to live one's life, one should invoke the criterion: "Whatever will most effectively contribute to one's happiness (i.e., success as a human individual)."

This answer, put a bit laboriously to satisfy our analytic purposes, means, in essence, that given that the life one has chosen to live is that of a human being, a rational animal, one ought to carry on in one's life by considering its nature and its circumstances in a careful, sensible, rational fashion and guide oneself in the light of the results.

Why is that the right answer? Because it provides human beings with the best available means (idea) for conducting themselves successfully, coherently, without inherent complications (though not without sustained effort and attention). It satisfies "Ought implies can" by pointing at a feasible life goal.

An ethical theory is correct if it best serves the purpose such a theory has, namely, making it possible to solve all problems within its area of concern. That is what makes not only an ethical theory but any theory the best one among those advanced.

To tell which ethical theory is the best one—which is all we can ask for at any time—existing ethical systems would need to be fully compared and we would need to see which of them will serve human beings best in pursuing the human good. Before that we would need to determine what is the human good and even before that we would have to ask, What is the good?

This won't all be attempted in full here. Still, we need to give some clues to how we would proceed. Let me note first that the problem of good arises in response to a concern with ranking in relation to some end, goal, or purpose. This is how value or good is tied to living, first of all, which is an end-oriented, goal-directed process. A good hunt, a good meal, a good pine tree, a good summer, a good business, and a good apple—all these rank a particular life-related matter along a continuum between the worst and the best of its kind.

And the way something will be located on that continuum is determined by whether it is more or less fully in accordance with its nature as a living being or as an artifact that pertains to some process of living. A good hunt must (most) consistently and precisely accord with the nature of hunting, and so on with a good meal, pine tree, summer, business, or apple. In each of these cases we are dealing with some ranking in terms of a natural (or assigned) end, goal, or purpose. And of course there is much controversy about a natural end.[9]

Of course there are such cases as good news, good state of affairs, good morning, good tidings, good fortune. In each case, however, analysis indicates that the term "good" is employed in the sense proposed above, even if in a less than direct fashion. "Good news," for example, means that in terms of our aspirations in life, that is, given our goals and well-being, what we hear is ranked high. "Good morning" means that we find things as desired, as far as the condition of the day's beginning is concerned. And so forth. And in each case we need to have a clear enough idea—or at least intimate one—in terms of which we can make sense of our ranking. (Of course we make use of such terms as "good" in all kinds of casual, even frivolous ways, where attempting to perform a strict analysis would be artificial and unnecessary.)

Not all of the issues touched on in this position can be dealt with in full, but some need to be looked at a bit more closely. For instance, as to natural ends, we can say that the only respect in which something might have it is in its being a living entity, such that either as a matter of innate drives (instincts) or self-determination it might either flourish or perish. Given its nature as a living entity, and given the kind of living entity it is, some forms of behavior or action will serve, others hinder, its natural end—i.e., the normal results of its success in life as the sort of thing it is. The basic alternative to this natural end is its demise (before its time, as it were). But there is also the less than full attainment of this end, which is a kind of failing.

It makes sense to designate this as the central sense of the concept of good: completing its nature makes something a good one of its kind. If one wishes to have a sensible, nonsupernatural, nonintuitive sense of what good is, one needs something along the above lines, although it is not possible to fully explore the matter here.

The human good, at its most complete, would be the most fully, consistently realized manifestation of *human* nature. In other words, we would have an excellent human being if we found one who most fully and consistently realized human nature. A distinction between this view and Aristotle's may be noted here: we are here resting human goodness on human nature, not merely human essence. Aristotle's Platonic intellectualism came from his essentialist rather than naturalist conception of the human good. Human nature is richer, less specialized than human essence. When we consider human nature, then a person's individuality is of equal significance to his or her humanity. That would indeed be a good human being, so we now need to ask what human nature is.

A human being is a rational animal—the only rational animal, so far as we know. Any other rational animal would also find itself to be morally bound by edicts derived from its nature, including both its characteristic of being an animal and that of being rational. Being a different sort of animal from human beings would make a considerable difference to the content of the ethics by which it would be bound.

Since any animal must be a determinate being—a specific living, biological entity—human beings must by nature be at least "separated" or spatially unique individuals. But beyond this, because of the constitution of their consciousness—namely, as a faculty capable of self-motivation or initiation of its own functions—individuality in human beings is a central characteristic. The nature of human life is necessarily that of an actual, active individual human being. The failure to heed this point has led thinkers like Marx astray to endorse a conception of human nature that leaves all of humanity—species beings—as its manifestation. This is why the debate between the individualist and the collectivist is at heart a metaphysical debate: What is the nature of the human being, individual or collective?[10]

How does ethics relate to the broader area of value theory, to the nature of the good? It does so by virtue of the fact that the human good is tied to human nature, which involves both life, the source of values, and freedom of choice or of the will, the element of responsibility.

Moral or ethical goodness is a special kind because it involves choice. A good pine tree can be identified as such without any reference to what the pine tree has chosen to do. The same goes for a good knife, sunset, worm, owl. All these things can be good or bad, but that has nothing to do with any choices they might have made.

In contrast, the distinctively human good has everything to do with what individual persons *choose*. Not only are some persons good or bad, as can be pine trees or grizzly bears—that is, they are a good specimen of that kind of thing—but they may be morally good or evil, meaning they are responsible for being either one.

It is this special characteristic of self-responsibility that gives rise to the distinctively human good, i.e., ethics or morality. The morally good is, then, the distinctively human good—or more precisely, that aspect of the human good that is subject to determination by the person, or open to choice.

Now the question arises of which conception of the human moral good makes the best sense. We have thus far noted the broad, so-called formal characteristics of that good, but we need to learn of its substance as well, before we can learn of the connection between ethics and politics.

Classical ethical egoism holds that the best conception of the human moral good is what was noted above, namely, stated in the answer to the question, "How should I live my life?" This is everyone's individual human happiness, within the context of his or her actual life. Rationally navigating through one's concrete circumstances, developing oneself and one's intimate fellow human beings—as far as they will consent—is the most that can morally be expected of persons. (Any more concrete statement would necessarily involve some more special conception of human goodness, applicable to some but not to all persons.) Why is this the answer to the central ethical question?

First, since the human moral good is intimately tied to what a person chooses to do, each individual can only make a determinate, definitive contribution to his or her own moral goodness. One can merely avail to others some opportunities for being good—e.g., one's children, for whom one can be a "role model" or good example. (Here is the truth to the claim that morality cannot be taught or instilled.) Second, knowledge of oneself is most available to oneself, thus who is more likely to be in a position to observe the standards of human moral good, namely human nature, which includes one's own individual identity? Third, because no one else pursues one's own moral excellence.

So over one's own life one has a clear responsibility, while others have the responsibility over theirs. All of this makes it evident that from the moral point of view—i.e., to the extent there is such a point of view—one is responsible to make the best of one's life as an individual *human* being. That seems to be just what makes sense of the moral point of view, and the classical ethical egoist position makes this a coherent and consistent ideal, not, as do other ethical systems, an impossible dream.

But in terms of what standards? Being human, and thus a rational animal, the standard will require the use of reason as well as the satisfaction, mostly through that use, of one's needs and purposes in life as determined by one's humanity *and* individuality. That is, acting rationally, choosing to think clearly and logically and thus following the dictates of one's best understanding of nature, including one's life, is the central moral task in everyone's life.

This will often lead to decisions, policies, and attitudes which will seem anything but egoistic in the customary sense of that term—i.e., selfish. Yet in terms of the classical egoism embraced here they are nevertheless egoistic because by living rationally, one is fulfilling one's nature most consistently and thus becomes a good individual human being, succeeding at the (implicit) choice one has set for oneself.

QUESTIONS ABOUT EGOISM

We now need to discuss some of the issues that would usually arise when considering an egoistic ethics of any variety. These questions will face anyone who proposes an egoistic ethics and are often the substance of criticisms levelled at the capitalist society that egoism supports.

First, why should anyone seek happiness, first and foremost? Second, why should we focus on promoting our distinctive human nature? Third, why should one single oneself out as the beneficiary of one's actions? Lastly, how does all this manage to support natural rights theory?

Let us grant that to live is a matter of (implicit) first choice. Of course, in one respect this is obvious—we could commit suicide. But we could also just let ourselves waste away. What is cruicial is that such a choice is a fundamental one, not itself justified by some other reason but a first choice, initiated by a person. This choice gives reason, therefore, for the rest of one's actions and requires no reason for itself. It is the primary reason, the *first* one, which then calls up the need for morality. It is not a chronological but rather a conceptual point.[11] Having tacitly, implicitly chosen to live (and by the nature of human life, starting as it does with infancy, at first it must be that kind of a "choice"), one is faced with how to go about carrying out that choice or commitment, how to do well at it. And this is where ethics, morality, or a moral code emerges.

To ask why one should pursue happiness is comparable to asking why, if one has set out for New York City, one should choose to get there efficiently. The choice to be happy—which does not mean "to be pleased with everything, to have a fun-filled life" but roughly, "to succeed at one's task of self-fulfillment within the range of available possibilities"—is implicit in the choice to live. That is, one makes the commitment to do so successfully just by choosing to do it in the first place. And as to why that choice should be made, the question is a misunderstanding. One either does or does not make it. (Not making it poses no moral problems, since, to the best of our knowledge, in death one needs no guidelines for success or anything else). To the question, Why should I be moral?, the "answer" is: You, a living human being, are inescapably involved in morality, by your choice to carry on with life. Human life and morality are inextricably linked. Finally, one singles oneself out as beneficiary of one's actions because the bulk of the benefits one can reap in life are worthwhile only if one has personally, intentionally achieved them. Here is where we should appreciate the Aristotelian overtones of the present ethical theory—the right course of conduct must be chosen to be morally meritorious. (Of course, some of the points associated with the theory need not fully accord with Aristotle.) This is true of career, close friendships, artistic excellence, great wealth, reputation, health, friendship, romance, citizenship, etc. To benefit another in cases of dire need or in emergencies could provide some necessary but never sufficient support for the attainment of that person's good human life. Of course, one can benefit from having various values provided by others, but such benefit is always conditional upon what one then does with what one is given. Whereas one's own rational achievements are always and necessarily a source of moral pride, even when unappreciated by other persons or society.

EGOISM AND NATURAL RIGHTS

But why would such an ethics require or imply a system of natural rights to govern social life? The question might also be put as follows: "How can a responsibility for my own success or good justify my being respectful of others' responsibility for theirs?" Yet this familiar way of asking the question is misleading because it makes it appear that I only have a type of accidental concern for my own good. By the present account my own good is identical with my interest, i.e., with what is objectively, rationally of benefit to me as the individual human being I am. Given that rendition of the question, why would one who acknowledged the moral and rational goal of seeking his own happiness also acknowledge the moral and rational goal of others to do the same?

The best way to put the answer is to note that the rational life for an individual in the present context is not the same as that conceived along lines of economic or instrumental rationality alone. A life lived rationally involves, among other things, the recognition of others for what and who they are and the treatment of them accordingly. Rational persons—ones who choose to use their minds—treat doors as doors need to be treated and learn what doors are; eat food that is digestible, and acknowledge that the moon is not made of green cheese. Similarly, when rational persons interact with other rational persons, their nature as moral agents—free and equally morally responsible agents who require "moral space" for living their lives in line with their nature (as the human individuals they are)—will be binding on them. In a way the logical rule of substitution will bind each person to rationally respect the moral space of another. If then egoism requires us to be rational, and rationality requires that we recognize the equal moral nature of others, then rationality also requires that just as we require, so others require the needed moral space for their moral nature.

Whereas ethics guides us individually, socially, professionally, and in other personal, voluntary relations, politics provides guidelines vis-à-vis our conduct toward strangers in whom we lack personal interest.[12] Even if we know nothing of another, the fact that this other is a human being imposes some obligations on us, since we have chosen (at least implicitly) to carry on life within their proximity.

The principles that we need so as to inform us about the requirements of proper conduct vis-à-vis other people are called *individual rights,* which, as Ayn Rand notes, "are conditions of existence required by man's *nature* for his proper survival."[13] And since human nature implies that our conduct in life be rational, our rational social life commits us to respect the equal rights of all persons to live by their own choice as they ought to. This respect implies, also, that we accept that others may fail to choose as they ought to. As lamentable as that may be, it would destroy moral life altogether to fail to respect the sovereignty of their choices in regard to the conduct of their lives.

Classical egoism holds that all persons ought to be rational, i.e., fully exercise their distinctive human capacity. The exercise of rationality, something that is a matter of primary choice and virtue, requires a suitable setting. By their nature they more or less have available this setting. It is one that is capable of being both understood and manipulated.

Other human beings, however, are not always so accommodating or predictable and provisions are needed to secure their cooperation or compliance. They are free to evade such facts as that persons require "moral space," to use Nozick's term.[14] Social morality, political principles, are just these provisions.

The natural rights spell out the conditions for cooperation and compliance among strangers. Nothing more may be forced upon strangers as they relate to each other than to heed these rights. That is because the rest of what they should do pertains to them, to their own moral space, while observation of natural rights is required for the preservation of the moral space of everyone. And so as to avoid the problems that stem from the occasional recalcitrants, institutions to secure the rights in question should be established—ergo, government. (The "should" here comes from the ethical egoist imperative that one ought to do what serves one's interest as an individual human being. To be prudent about what debilitating harm others can do to one is a clear example of an egoistic course of conduct.)

There is a lot more that could be said here, but I have discussed natural rights separately; so let me now turn to some criticism of the sort of ethics on which such rights rest.

REPLIES TO A METAETHICAL OBJECTION

Among the numerous criticisms of egoism one is especially worth mentioning, mainly because it aims to cut very deep. This criticism holds not simply that egoism is unsound but that any ethics that conceives of objective moral values based on human flourishing or full development is misconceived.

In a recent paper Gilbert Harman argues, basically, that an ethics of flourishing—roughly of the sort I have called classical ethical egoism[15]—implies "moral relativism, since what counts as 'flourishing' seems inevitably relative to one or another set of values."[16] He adds that "it is difficult to see how one rather than another conception of flourishing is to be validated simply in 'the nature of things' or in the 'nature' of persons—except in the sense in which different sets of values yield different conceptions of nature or of the nature of a person."[17]

Our discussion earlier already meets some of the points Harman raises, as does my response to him elsewhere.[18] But it will be useful to pay some attention here to the issue of whether he can rest the crucial features of a natural rights doctrine on his conventionalist approach. If there is a serious problem about that, then the present ethical egoist stance will be vital for defending the natural rights doctrine that Harman is also interested in supporting.

Harman seems to hold that negative rights—to life, liberty, property, the pursuit of happiness, or however else such libertarian principles have been spelled out—rest on the social agreement that we may suppose has been reached among us, persons with very different frameworks of value:

The basic protections of morality have arisen as a result of bargaining and compromise, sometimes after serious conflict and even war. For example, ordinary morality draws an important distinction between the weighty "negative" duty not to harm others and the less weighty "positive" duty to intervene to help prevent others from being harmed. So a doctor may not seize and cut up a healthy visitor to the hospital in order to save the lives of several patients by distributing the visitor's organs where they would do the most good. The harm to the visitor is not permitted morally even in order to prevent more harm to others. The healthy visitor has a "right" not to be harmed by the doctor. The patients who might be saved by this organ distribution do not have an equally strong "right" to have a corresponding harm to them from disease prevented. I suggest that this distinction in ordinary morality is a consequence of the fact that morality is a compromise between people of different powers and resources.[19]

It is interesting to note that in Harman the social agreement that gives rise to morality arises out of a kind of social clash. This clearly harks back to Hobbes's idea of natural law, as the result of a rational assessment of how we must cope with the impossibility of simply pursuing our raw self-interest. Yet this view banishes morality rather than clarifies it. If, as I think one would have to accept, "ought (largely) implies can," then morality cannot be analyzed into this kind of sociology. By Harman's account we hold "moral" values roughly as a fox may entertain certain strategies of catching the hen or the elephant may have come to live harmoniously with the birds who feed off the lice on its skin.

Yet, to say that people have reached a compromise—which, after all, is possible even between a murderer and a totally innocent potential victim—is different from saying that this was a sound, morally proper resolution among them. Even accepting various standards of value is something different from the view that various standards of value can be binding on people.[20]

When people show differences in frameworks of value, they could be mistaken, they could be stubborn, they could be rationalizing their perverse aims and objectives—or they simply may be focusing on the diverse, often idiosyncratic implications of what could well be an objective and universal standard of value, binding on us all.

If social agreement could not be the ultimate ground for the existence of basic rights, as Harman would suppose, why would people have these rights? (And it should be noted that although the actual concept of basic human rights has gained currency only in modern times, there are traces of it in ancient political thought. Moreover, simply because a concept has not developed to the level at which it is presently employed, it does not follow that it has not always been valid.[21])

The reason the negative rights to life, liberty, and property are those supported by ethical egoism is that we should *all* strive to live, to be creative and productive, and to attain the kind of happiness suited to human beings (which includes plenty of provisions that the right to private property can secure intact through the complex institution of property law.)[22] The doctrine of natural rights—first described by John Locke and further developed by others—enables us to lay the foundations for and maintain that system of moral space for all individuals. Despite efforts to convince us that Lockean natural rights are alienable,[23] these rights are indeed something human beings have as human beings—in virtue of their inherent moral nature. That may explain why they have been a source of political optimism and inspiration to millions in the hope, possibly, that their clear understanding will fight off the various tyrants who seek to enslave them.

It might be thought that there is a missing premise here that is really too strong for the Lockean natural rights account, namely, that "One has a right to anything required for one's happiness." But the premise here is much weaker, namely, "One has a right to anything required for the pursuit of one's happiness." That is a rather minimal content for a doctrine of rights. It involves only negative rights, since once such negative rights are secured, either via voluntary respect or government protection, the sort of individuals we have argued human beings are can proceed to seek or pursue their happiness in the diverse ways they should.

Of course Harman's kind of criticism is not the only sort that an ethical theory such as the present needs to contend with. Perhaps an even more fundamental objection comes from those who, following the historical materialist interpretation of humanity's development, deny that human beings have any such power of self-determination that moral philosophy assumes. As Donald C. Hodges makes the point,

One of the contributions of a Marxist sociology of ethics has been to explain differences in the content of ethical expressions in terms of the rise and decline of social formations, the separation between work and ownership, labor and leisure, production and consumption.[24]

As Hodges sees it, the tradition of moral philosophy has indeed been serving special interests and exploits the false assumption that "in every instance we have the power to choose freely . . . as if men always had the capacity of behaving otherwise than they did."[25]

The basic challenge then is really that human beings are not just not "in every instance [free] to choose," but that they really never have that choice, mainly because the real conditions of their lives compel them to behave in specific ways. Or, to use Marx's term, they may now and then "subjectively" rise above these conditions, but this matters very little for their role in the major aspects of social life, namely class struggle.[26]

There is no room here to undertake a thorough defense of the assumptions of moral philosophy, namely, that (a) human beings are substantially self-determined, of course always within their context of existence, and (b) their conduct is capable of being evaluated by reference to some standard that is sufficiently universal and transhistorical to form the basis of a sound moral point of view. I have elsewhere made the attempt to defend the former of these assumptions and this essay is itself an effort to shore up the grounds for the latter.[27] Suffice it to note here that however much this might be resisted, any attack on the basic moral nature of human beings must cut in all directions, including in the direction Marx and such followers of his as Hodges might elect. Hodges notes that, "Far from being disinterested in the effort to extend the limits of human knowledge, a Marxist philosophy of ethics is a theoretical and practical instrument of the modern labor movement in its struggle to abolish exploitation . . . [and] . . . poses questions of revolutionary significance [that Marx and Engels conceived as 'descriptive and explanatory tasks of a philosophy of ethics' and to which they] . . . added the strategical and tactical problems of mobilizing for a radical change in social institutions."[28] In short, Marxism, conceived along this orthodox line, explains the role of ethical ideals or the employment of moral judgments and adds to this the utilization of this explanation for promoting radical change. Ethics, then, is a kind of force in history, not a discipline of knowledge aiming to identify standards of moral conduct.

But in all this, surely Marx and Engels and their supporters see themselves as free agents, as in some sense self-determined? They often enough criticize the way others see things—as does Hodges in his entire discussion of this topic—so they implicitly accept that people could behave differently from the way they in fact behave. And they use standards for making this assessment. (Marx's own life is filled, of course, with controversies, indeed moral conflicts, in which he levels very serious charges of immorality against some of his opponents.[29]) So while this does not admit that people are in all cases free to behave differently from the way they do, it presupposes that often enough they are sufficiently free to do so.

That, however, is all that moral philosophy requires. It never assumed, anyway, that "men always had the capacity of behaving otherwise than they do," nor, again, that "each individual is the absolute master of his actions." Rather ethics assumes that in many crucial spheres of human conduct, human beings are capable of choosing what they will do. If they did not, there really would be a situation of "what will be will be," leaving the radical change Marx and Hodges are talking about to history without any direction from human individuals.

In this essay the hard determinism involved in orthodox Marxism is rejected as self-defeating. It would make doing anything concerning the misery of the workers pointless. Nor is it required that human freedom be contrasted with the determinism of the rest of nature—it is just another form of nature's multifaceted manifestation. Self-responsibility, to a greater or lesser extent, is one of the crucial elements of human existence. The question that remains is by what standard this responsibility is best carried out.

SOME IMPLICATIONS OF CLASSICAL EGOISM

The ethical egoism that undergirds the free market has now been explained and defended. One of its main points can be stressed by way of recalling Adam Smith's observation about the nature of virtue:

It is not the love of our neighbour, it is not the love of mankind, which upon many occasions prompts us to the practice of . . . virtues. It is a stronger love, a more powerful affection, which generally takes place upon such an occasion, the love of what is honourable and noble, of the grandeur, and dignity, and superiority of our own character.[30]

Once the distinctive character and essential soundness of classical egoism is appreciated, we can also see why it supports the kind of free institutions that make capitalism possible. But we can go further than that. There are some crucial implications of classical egoism that support certain of the distinctive and special characteristics of a free market capitalist system. I will only summarize these here.

(1) The price system that enables us to learn of the fluctuating demands (preferences, wants, wishes, desires) of the people in a society records not just general needs, which even planners might be able to identify, but also individual values. If classical egoism is right and the values of individuals can with moral justification vary considerably, such a system is vital so as to make possible their efficient attainment. Thus what to some may be a trivial pursuit that free markets make possible but would be strictly limited in a planned society—e.g., purchase of a pet rock or several Rolls Royces—can, in markets, occur without any intervention from either a centralized planning board or a democratic assembly. Some of these pursuits may indeed be objectionable but it is not generally decidable, outside of individual contexts, which these are.

(2) The well-known calculation problem that afflicts planned systems now can be shown to be based on not just inefficiency considerations but on the fact that planning thwarts vital individual pursuits and their efficient satisfaction. Persons must, in a just system, be able to seek their own happiness and the market makes this far more possible than a planned system.

(3) The social choice paradox does not plague a system in which the public sphere is strictly limited to genuine public pursuits. If preferences may only be satisfied via mutual consent rather than democratic public participation, then the social choice paradox is avoided. Only a very definite kind of choice, bearing on bona fide public matters, will bear on public policy decisions and these can be ranked rationally, unlike any attempt to rank indiscriminately aggregated individual values.

(4) The arguments of the public choice theorists, concerning the inevitability of public decision making according to vested interests, will also be taken account of in a system that respects the distinction between the public and private realms based on the strict limitation of the former to what we can clearly categorize as a public matter (justice, defense, etc.).

The crucial point to make about all these is clear: Where the essential or natural moral concerns of human beings must take into account their individual values—where true individuality, not true collectivity (à la Marx), is the human essence (but understood within the context of the reality of human nature)—a market system, which preserves the possibility of individual differences to the greatest possible extent, is morally suitable and a planned system is morally objectionable.[31]

CONCLUSION

Ethical egoism is one serious candidate in providing the fundamental standards of human conduct. But it has been largely misconceived. The underlying conception of the human self is mostly to be blamed for the misconception. Once this conception is revised and we see that the human self is much richer in its dimensions—e.g., sociality is inherently human, provided it is a matter of choice—much of what is lamentable about egoism disappears. What remains, however, is that morality must ultimately enhance the life of the individual who practices it, although the enhancement may be of a complicated sort, not simply the attainment of fame, power, or fortune.

The implication of ethical egoism for social life is, as has been thought, that a system of natural negative rights should govern individuals in their relations with others (although egoism itself implies a much richer social ethics when friends, relatives, colleagues, and even neighbors are involved).

What egoism will not morally tolerate is the sort of "moral" code that makes of individuals resources for others, even for those who are in great need. From the outset, ethical egoism makes this point clear, and that in part may explain its lack of *popularity*. When we consider the political principles that ethical egoism implies, this intolerance of subjugating some for the benefit of others becomes quite explicit.

Whether ultimately ethical egoism is the best ethical system—the right ethics—is something that could only be considered by comparing it with all the other live options. For that, however, we would need to carry out a far more extensive task than there is room for here. Suffice it to conclude for now that ethical egoism or individualism is not an ethics of greed, ambition, or power, but one of self-development. Its political dimension, the doctrine of natural rights, is concerned with making as much room for such self-development, in as peaceful—though not necessarily fraternal or familial—a context as can reasonably be secured.

This may not seem as inspiring a vision as that offered by those who prophesy the remaking of human nature in order to solve the problems actual human beings face. It is, however, more true to the actual nature of human life, as well as to the more measured conceptions of what that life can be and ought to be for human beings.[32]

NOTES

[1] Karl Marx, *Selected Writings,* ed. David McLennan (London: Oxford University Press, 1977), p. 53. "Far from the rights of man conceiving of man as a species-being, species-life itself, society, appears as a framework exterior to individuals, a limitation of their original

self-sufficiency. The only bond that holds them together is natural necessity, need and private interest, the conservation of their property and egoistic person"(p. 54).

[2] Ayn Rand, *The Virtue of Selfishness* (New York: New American Library, 1964) and *Capitalism: The Unknown Ideal* (New York: New American Library, 1967).

[3] James Rachels, "Two Arguments Against Egoism," *Philosophia* 4 (April/July 1974): 297–314.

[4] John Rawls, *A Theory of Justice* (Cambridge, MA: Harvard University Press, 1971), p. 488. See also Kim-Chong Chong, "Egoism, Desires, and Friendship," *American Philosophical Quarterly* 21 (October 1984): 355–56. It is also fair to hold that Derek Parfit's criticism of egoism, in *Reasons and Persons* (Oxford: Oxford University Press, 1984), accepts this narrow conception of the self, one in reference to which the idea of self-interest must necessarily be a matter of aiming for certain future consequences bearing on the person one assumes one will be. Parfit, of course, aims to deprive this form of egoism of its foundation, namely, of the necessarily stable individual who preserves his or her identity through time. But if the self-interest of an individual rests on abiding by a standard of conduct—e.g., rationality—rather than on serving some future self's desires, wants, or interests (concerns), then even in those rare cases where personal identity does not extend through time and one may become several in time, the egoistic conduct consists in doing what is rational, which in turn must take into consideration what the individual is most likely to turn out in the future; if he or she is to become several, then rational conduct will have to adjust to that probability.

[5] Tibor R. Machan, "Recent Work in Ethical Egoism," in Kenneth G. Lucey and Tibor R. Machan, eds., *Recent Work in Philosophy* (Totowa, NJ: Rowman and Allanheld, 1983), pp. 185–202.

[6] See, e.g. David L. Norton, *Personal Destinies, A Philosophy of Ethical Individualism* (Princeton: Princeton University Press, 1976).

[7] Aristotle, *Nicomachean Ethics,* Book IX, Ch. 8, 1168b33. For a thorough discussion of the sense in which Aristotle can be regarded a kind of ethical egoist, see W. F. R. Hardie, "The Final Good in Aristotle's *Ethics,*" *Philosophy* 40 (1965): 277–295, and Jack Wheeler, "Rand and Aristotle: A Comparison of Objectivist and Aristotelian Ethics," in Douglas J. Den Uyl and Douglas Rasmussen, eds., *The Philosophical Thought of Ayn Rand* (Urbana and Chicago, IL: University of Illinois Press, 1984), pp. 81–101. For another discussion, which is addressed directly to those contemporary moral philosophers who regard matters of prudence irrelevant to morality, see W. D. Falk, "Morality, Self, and Others," in H. N. Castaneda and G. Nakhnikian, eds., *Morality and the Language of Conduct* (Detroit: Wayne State University Press, 1965), pp. 25–67. Wheeler makes a point that may be of interest here. "In a certain real sense, no Greek can be labeled an egoist any more than an altruist. The whole issue of egoism and altruism is modern. Indeed, the entire project of attempting to reconcile one's own interests with benevolence or the interest of society as a whole seems clearly to start with Hobbes and the Hobbesian view of man"(p. 97). Some contend, as Shirley Robin Letwin does, that "there is no more room for individuality in Aristotle's *philia* than in Plato's *eros*" ("Romantic Love and Christianity," *Philosophy* 52 [April 1977]: 134). Letwin claims that "because for Aristotle, as for Plato, rationality is the power to recognize a universal order, Aristotle cannot account for rational consciousness that is ultimately unique"(p. 135). Others argue, however, that Aristotle's metaphysics is individualist and makes ample room for the actual, individual being of entities. See Emerson Buchanan, *Aristotle's Theory of Being* (Cambridge, MA: Greek, Roman, and Byzantine Monographs, 1962). If Buchanan is right, the "what it is for a thing to be" of human beings would have to indicate individuality in view of every person's self-determination, something that is distinctive of human beings. (In this regard see David L. Norton, *Personal Destinies* [Princeton University Press, 1976].)

[8] Roger W. Sperry, "Changing Concepts of Consciousness and Free Will," *Perspectives in Biology and Medicine* 9 (Autumn 1976): 9–19. For more on this, see Tibor R. Machan, *The Pseudo-Science of B. F. Skinner* (New Rochelle, NY: Arlington House, 1974), Ch. 6.

[9] Natural ends are to be distinguished from ends that are matters of convention and have no connection with the way we discover something in nature—e.g., the end or objective of a ping-pong game or TV channel selector. In contrast, consider the end served by the heart in the human biological organism, or the objective of the porcupine's stiff, sharp spines mingled with its hair. Contrary to some notions in the history of ideas, neither is it necessary to impute natural ends to inanimate beings if one imputes them to some beings, nor need Aristotle be read as someone who makes that imputation to all of nature. See Allan Gotthelf, "Aristotle's Conception of Final Causality," *The Review of Metaphysics* 30 (October 1976): 226–254.

[10] Marx speaks of "humanity" as an "organic body" or "organic whole." Karl Marx, *The Grundrisse,* abridged edition, trans. David McLennan (New York: Harper Torchbook, 1971), p. 33. For a discussion of the philosophical approach that will secure a basis for abstraction that yields knowledge of human nature, see David Kelley, "A Theory of Abstraction," *Cognition and Brain Theory* 7 (Summer/Fall, 1984): 329–57. See, also, Tibor R. Machan, "Epistemology and Moral Knowledge," *The Review of Metaphysics* 36 (September 1982): 23–49. Suffice it to say here that the theory of human nature involved rejects the realism of universals, thus the presence of metaphysical essences or natures; yet it secures the objective basis for classification as a result of human concept formation, differentiation, and integration. These views rest on Ayn Rand, *Introduction to Objectivist Epistemology* (New York: New American Library, 1979).

[11] Tibor R. Machan, "A Reconsideration of Natural Rights Theory," *American Philosophical Quarterly* 19 (January 1982): 61–72, and "Individualism and the Problem of Political Authority," *The Monist* 66 (October 1983): 500–516.

[12] Ayn Rand, "Value and Rights," in John Hospers, ed., *Readings in Introductory Philosophical Analysis* (Englewood Cliffs, NJ: Prentice-Hall, 1968), p. 382.

[13] Ibid.

[14] Robert Nozick, *Anarchy, State, and Utopia* (New York: Basic Books, 1974), p. 57.

[15] Machan, "Recent Work in Ethical Egoism."

[16] Gilbert Harman, "Human Flourishing, Ethics, and Liberty," *Philosophy and Public Affairs,* 12 (Fall 1983): 312. A difficulty with arguing with Harman arises from the fact that although he mentions many people who advance a version of the flourishing ethics, he does not provide us with any of the arguments in their own terms. Moreover Harman does not fully develop any of his arguments, partly because he is aiming at too diffuse a target to be very specific. It is arguable that no paper with such an ambitious purpose, namely, to dispose in one fell swoop of one of the most promising schools of philosophical attempts to make sense of and to ground ethics, could be complete.

[17] Ibid., p. 313.

[18] Tibor R. Machan, "Harman's 'Refutation' of Flourishing Ethics," *The Thomist* 49 (July 1985): 387–91.

[19] Harman, "Human Flourishing," p. 321.

[20] See T. R. Machan, "Social Contract as a Basis of Norms: A Critique," *Journal of Libertarian Studies* 8 (Spring 1983): 141–45.

[21] For a discussion of how this kind of conceptual evolution clears up some of the misconceptions that have supported moral (historical) relativism, see Hanna F. Pitkin, *Wittgenstein and Justice* (Berkeley: University of California Press, 1972).

[22] I develop some of these points in detail in Tibor R. Machan, "Toward a Theory of Natural Individual Human Rights," *The New Scholasticism* (forthcoming).

[23] A. John Simmons, "Inalienable Rights and Locke's *Treatises*," *Philosophy and Public Affairs* 12 (Summer 1983): 175–204. For a detailed treatment, see Tibor R. Machan, "Human Rights: Some Points of Clarification," *Journal of Critical Analysis* 5 (July/October 1973): 30–38.

[24] Donald C. Hodges, *Socialist Humanism* (St. Louis, MO: Warren H. Green, Inc., 1972), p. 71.

[25] Ibid., p. 63.

[26] Karl Marx, *Selected Writings,* ed. D. McLellan (Oxford: Oxford University Press, 1977), p. 417.

[27] Tibor R. Machan, *The Pseudo-Science of B. F. Skinner* and "Ethics in an Age of Science" (Great Barrington, MA: Behavioral Research Council, forthcoming).

[28] Hodges, *Socialist Humanism,* pp. 71–72.

[29] There is no honest account of Marx's life that does not recount these facts. It is also evident from most of Marx's correspondence.

[30] Adam Smith, *The Theory of Moral Sentiments* (Indianapolis, IN: Liberty Classics, 1769, 1976), Part III, Ch. 3, p. 235. It is interesting to note here that Smith echoes exactly—almost verbatim—Aristotle's view (*Nicomachean Ethics,* 1168b28–33) that "such a man [who 'at all events assigns to himself the things that are noblest and best, and gratifies the most authoritative element in himself and in all things obeys this'] . . . is most of all a lover of self."

[31] Here is where there is a crucial distinction between the socialist idea, according to which, "The human essence is the true collectivity of man" (Marx, *Selected Writings,* p. 126) and classical individualism that sees individuality as an essential part of the nature of man. I discuss these points in detail in my "Rational Choice and Public Affairs," *Theory and Decision* 12 (1980): 229–258, and "Property Rights and the Decent Human Community," in J. Roth and R. Whittmore, eds., *American Ideology and Values* (Washington, D.C.: The Washington Institute, 1986). For an exploration of why planned societies will not suffice as efficient economic systems, see Don Lavoie, *National Economic Planning: What Is Left?* (Cambridge, MA: Ballinger Publishing Co., 1985).

[32] I thank the Reason and Olin Foundations for their support.

RICHARD SCHMITT

THE DESIRE FOR PRIVATE GAIN

Many defenders of capitalism rest their case on the belief that human beings everywhere are motivated to seek their own satisfaction. This idea—variously referred to as the economic man, the utility maximization, or the selfishness thesis—is challenged by Richard Schmitt, a philosopher at Brown University, Providence, Rhode Island, with numerous writings in various branches of philosophy. In his analysis of the underlying social psychology and learning theory of neo-classical economics, Schmitt argues, in essence, that basic motivations differ significantly between different societies and may well be more seriously affected by a society's institutions than defenders of capitalism acknowledge. If these institutions encouraged motives different from the desire for private gain, it could turn out that what the proponents of capitalism have regarded as basic to human nature is anything but that. A society that took different, perhaps humanitarian or altruistic, motives as in need of encouragement and development would look very different from one that rests on what many defenders of capitalism see as fundamentally human.

Capitalism has been attacked and defended on purely economic, as well as political, and on psychological grounds. Marx attacked capitalism for its economic performance, predicting that monopolistic practices would stifle competition, that the gap between the rich and the poor would continue to grow larger and larger and that, finally, the system would break down completely under the strain of progressively worse and more frequent crises. The first of these predictions is widely recognized as valid. The second and third are more controversial. But they retain sufficient force for defenders of capitalism to have put more stress on the political and psychological justifications of the system. Thus they claim that political freedom, for example, can exist only under capitalism.[1] As Woodrow Wilson said: "If America is not to have free enterprise, then she can have freedom of no sort whatsoever."[2] And in terms of the psychological line of defense it is claimed that the desire for private gain is a fundamental human trait which, more than others, spurs men to activity. Capitalism, more than any other form of social and economic organization, gives free rein to this desire. It is, for this reason, peculiarly well adapted to human nature. Whatever capitalism's shortcomings, alternative systems stifle human initiative and thus are even less productive.

This paper will deal with the psychological defense of capitalism.

I

From the very beginning, the theory of capitalism was closely linked to claims about human nature. Adam Smith stressed human "self-love" as a central mo-

Reprinted, with permission, from *Inquiry* 16 (1973).

tive for human actions.[3] Mill makes the link between the desire for private
gain and the economy a matter of definition. He defines Political Economy as
dealing with the "social phenomena in which the immediately determining
causes are the desire for wealth."[4] In our century, since the spectacular, if temporary, collapse of the capitalist economy in the late twenties, and the close
link of major industries to German National Socialism, as well as to repressive
régimes all around the world, both the economic and the political defense of
capitalism have been less persuasive. Current writers are, for instance, ready to
admit that capitalist systems have tended to stifle free competition by means of
monopolistic practices, that they have forced millions to work under extremely
undesirable conditions, that they have not dealt adequately with problems of
poverty. The performance of capitalism is not unambiguously successful.[5] Nor
has it escaped notice that great wealth and right-wing sentiments often go together. Much weight is therefore placed by defenders of capitalism on claims
about human nature. According to Frank Knight

... there is in some effective sense a real positive connection between the productive
contribution made by any productive agent and the remuneration which its
"owner" can secure for its use. Hence this remuneration (a distributive share) and
the wish to make it as large as possible, constitute the chief reliance of society for an
incentive to place the agency into use ... The strongest argument in favor of such a
system as ours is the contention, that this direct selfish motive is the only depend-
able method for guaranteeing that productive forces will be organized and worked
efficiently.[6]

Whatever the shortcomings of capitalism, it is so peculiarly adapted to
human nature that it will, more than any other system, induce people to make
the most efficient use of the productive resources of their nation. For this reason, the performance of a capitalist economy can be expected to be better than
that of alternative systems.

This passage claims explicitly that people, on the whole, strive for private
gain—as much of it as they can get—and concludes from this that capitalism is
the proper form of social and economic organization. But this conclusion follows only if we accept a further, implicit claim, namely that the desire for private gain is not a consequence of the capitalist social and economic
arrangements but, instead, motivates the actions of all mankind. The defense
of capitalism would be totally implausible without this second, implicit assumption.

In this paper I want to accept the first, explicit claim about the pervasive
behavior in our society, but reject the implicit one about the universality of
this behavior. As a consequence, I shall also reject the attendant defense of capitalism.

Let us, first, be clear about what is not at issue.

There has been a good deal of discussion, in recent years, of the connections between motives and causes. It has alternately been asserted and denied
that motives are causes. This controversy is not relevant here.[7] The claim made

by Knight is an empirical one about the pervasiveness of a particular motive, not a conceptual one about all motives. Nor is Knight, presumably, making any ethical claims about the ethical justifications of a perfectly (or imperfectly) competitive market or about the goodness of competing. The defense rests on one normative assumption, namely that an efficient use of resources is preferable to an inefficient one. That, too, is not an ethical claim but an economic one. It is, moreover, not a controversial assumption.[8] For the rest, the argument deals with relations of ends and means: If efficient use of resources is sought, then an economy that appeals to the desire for private gain will come closer to achieving the desired end.

This argument rests on the assumption that the springs of behavior of men under capitalism are no different from what motivates behavior in differently organized societies. As an empirical claim, this is hard to refute.[9] But if we consider the concept of motive with some care, we can see that the behavior of men under capitalism is not caused by the desire for private gain but is, instead, a consequence of living in a capitalist society.

In the course of this paper, I shall argue, in II, that we talk about a person's motives when we need to make clear the links between his actions and the circumstances under which they occur. This is the primary use of talk about motives. Secondarily, we talk about motives, as the sort of links that we find frequently between certain kinds of actions and the range of situations in which these actions normally occur. A particular motive is identified by citing, on the one hand, the action which it motivates and, on the other hand, other actions which we expect from a person susceptible to this particular motivation. Thus individual motives like "ambition" or "desire for private gain" name lists of actions that flow from having these particular motives. We can explain what it is, say, to desire private gain by listing what a person with that motive will do.

Having clarified some important features of talk about motives, I proceed, in III, to apply the results of the preceding section to a specific motive, the desire for private gain. Section IV contains the demonstration that desiring private gain is not a universal human desire but is, on the contrary, just the sort of thing that people will do in a capitalist society. In fact, we call a society "capitalist" because in it one will do the sorts of things by reference to which we identify people's motives as the desire for private gain.

II

There are some obvious questions to be raised about the alleged pervasiveness of the desire for private gain. Economists talk about it a great deal. But when philosophers discuss motives, they mention it extremely rarely and then only with some doubt as to its existence. Professor Anscombe refers to the "desire of gain" as an instance of a popular conception that lacks clarity.[10] We may well ask whether this desire for private gain exists as a distinct motive.

If we decide that such a motive does exist, we need to ask further how it should be described. Economists use a variety of related but not identical expressions. Adam Smith speaks of "self-love," Mill of "desire of wealth." Others speak of a motive for "profit maximization" or a "private profit motive." What are the essential features of this alleged motive and how does it differ from motives more familiar to us?

Finally, there seems considerable implausibility to claiming that the desire for private gain, however it is to be specified in detail, is the all-pervasive motive that economists claim it is. People act from all kinds of motives: ambition, love, resentment, greed or generosity, etc. There is no particular reason to assume that the specific class of actions that economists are primarily concerned with, namely competing in the market for goods and services, should by and large have only one motive and thus be strikingly different from all other classes of human actions. The economists' claim for the universality of the profit motive seems particularly implausible in the light of the fact that no sharp distinction can be drawn between a man's actions in the market place and those outside of it. It is not easy to find examples of behavior that are not "market behavior."

These are empirical questions, of course, but we will not be able to answer them unless we have a fairly clear idea of how one identifies motives, how one distinguishes one motive from another and how one tells when one has anything approaching a complete characterization of a motive.

Philosophers have in recent years spent a good deal of energy on a variety of controversies respecting motives. They have argued whether motives are causes or not, whether all actions have motives or only some, and whether motives are inner, mental goings on or whether to speak about motives is to make predictions about future behavior. But none of these controversies, including the last which addresses itself to the question "what is a motive?", has ever faced the question of identity criteria for motives. Philosophers participating in these controversies begin their papers with a few examples of motives and argue about them. The concept of a motive is generally specified by ostension and not by philosophical analysis. That this is a serious oversight is nowhere more obvious than in the context of the present controversy. A reasonable understanding of the identity criteria for motives shows up the psychological defense of capitalism as a sham. Without such criteria it has seemed to be, at least, plausible.

Philosophers have given a surprisingly varied list of examples of motives:

Character traits as, e.g., ambition, diligence, greed
Long lasting emotions like resentment
Moods like depression
Inclinations like "an interest in symbolic logic"
Feelings like feeling threatened
Mental acts like making a decision
Mental states like intending
Capacities like stupidity

Physical feelings like sexual desire
Convictions like Patriotism
Attitudes like optimism
Needs like being hungry or thirsty
Habits like being punctual

There are several questions concerning identity criteria to be raised about these instances of motives:

(i) What determines whether a phenomenon shows up in one's list of motives or not? I.e. what are the criteria for being a motive rather than something else?

(ii) Given that we have decided that a given phenomenon does belong on our list of motives, what serves to distinguish it from other items on that same list? This question has two subparts:

(a) How do we decide that two motive descriptions are not descriptions of the same motive?

(b) How do we decide that two motive descriptions are descriptions of the same motive?

I) WHAT DISTINGUISHES MOTIVES FROM OTHER PHENOMENA?

The list of motives includes a wide variety of mental or physical phenomena. While all of them may function as motives at one time or another, not every emotion, feeling, mood, capacity or sensation is a motive. Talk about motives fits into a very specific context, namely the context of explaining why someone acted or refrained from acting in specific ways. But we say many other things about people besides trying to explain their actions. We describe, criticize, exhort, flatter, etc. In all those cases we may speak about emotions, capacities, etc. but we are not always speaking about motives. Any of the items on the list may be called a "motive" when we try to explain an action. But any of them can function in contexts where no action is involved. Not all the feelings I have at any moment, or sensations, or capacities have a bearing on what I am doing. They do not function as motives at that time.

Some states of persons function as motives in contexts where they affect action. We refer to motives, therefore, to explain actions. But not all explanations of actions are motive-explanations. "I killed him because he killed my brother"[11] is a perfectly good explanation but does not involve, nor does it require, mentioning a motive. But in many situations we do not feel that an action has been explained adequately if we only know the surrounding circumstances. "I killed him because he asked me for money" is not a transparent explanation. If someone asks you for money, you might give a number of responses that would be more readily intelligible. Any attempt to make that action more intelligible might very well begin with more details about the situation in which I act. ("He was blackmailing me.") One might specify in more detail the character of the other person or the history of our relation. If, after a more complete account of the situation, it still remains unclear why I acted, I may then begin to talk about my motives. Motive explanations serve a very specific function: they bridge the gap between action-descriptions and descriptions of the environment in which the action takes place. Where the relation between the two is not intelligible, talk about motives will often help. "He had asked me for money so many times before. When he asked me again, I flew into a blind rage."

The function of motive explanations, in turn, throws light on the nature of motives. The fact that "I killed him because he killed my brother" is an adequate explanation does not prove, as Anscombe thinks, that there are no motives for the action. The explanation, to be sure, is adequate for us. It might not be for a visitor from a tribe that does not know about revenge. To him we might have to speak about motives. Motives provide the link between the agent's environment and his actions. Given a certain situation, a person may act or he may not act. If he does act he may act in different ways. Whether he acts at all and what he does depends on how he perceives the situation, on his beliefs about the situation as well as on his beliefs about what it is good to do in given situations. His actions are further determined by his needs, by any number of attitudes, by his abilities, his short-term and long-term emotions. All of these go to make up the rather heterogeneous list of phenomena that philosophers provide as examples of motives, because all of them function in similar ways in establishing the connection between a situation and the action a person takes in that situation.

The common feature of all the phenomena that may function as motives is not easy to specify. The temptation to call them "inner" states or events must be resisted. For such a designation seems to suggest that we know our motives by introspection and I shall argue that that is not true. What I shall have to say about motives implies that it is a mistake to differentiate motives from actions as what is "inner" from what is "outer" or public. To draw the distinction between motive and action in that way is not so much false as misleading. Philosophers who have drawn the distinction in that way have done so because they did not reflect sufficiently upon the wide variety of phenomena that function as motives. It will therefore be more useful to mark off the sorts of phenomena that can function as motives by saying that no phenomenon that can be ascribed to a dead body or to a person in a coma for a long time can function as a motive. Such a person has no capabilities, no moods or emotions. His needs and attitudes have disappeared.

With this beginning for a criterion for motives in hand we may now go on to the second question:

II) WHAT SERVES TO DISTINGUISH ONE MOTIVE FROM ANOTHER?

That question has two parts, namely what the meaning is of "same" and of "different" when we speak about individual motives. We know what is meant by "same" as applied to motives if we have some idea of how we identify any particular motive. That question, in turn, subdivides into how we identify our own motives and how we identify those of others.

(a) There is a controversy concerning what sorts of data we use to identify our own motives. On the one hand, some philosophers believe that I introspect to determine what my motive is in any given case. On the other hand, other philosophers want to deny that introspection plays any role in the identification of my own motives. They claim that I identify my motives by my actions actually performed and by my propensities to act in certain ways. A look at the list of the sorts of phenomena that philosophers cite as examples of motives shows that this is a pointless controversy. For, on the one hand, I do know by introspection, by direct acquaintance with myself, that I am hungry and what I am hungry for. I know in similar ways, what I believe, what I intend to do. Insofar as desires, beliefs, and intentions are among the phenomena that may function as motives, it seems clearly true that some of them are known to me by introspection. It is equally clear, if we go back to our list, that not all of the phenomena that sometimes function as motives are known to me in that way. I may know by introspection that I am angry now, but my character trait, irrascibility, is not known by introspection. To say that someone is irrascible is to say that he is often and suddenly angered. One can know that about me only by observing the frequency of my anger and its suddenness. The same is true of capacities. I don't know introspectively that I am intelligent. Neither do I know my attitudes, like optimism, in that way. It is clear that some of the phenomena that may function as motives may be known introspectively and others not.

These observations settle the controversies between those philosophers who claim that I know all my motives exclusively by introspection and those who deny that introspection enters into knowledge of my motives at all. But they do not settle the really interesting question, namely whether I ever know *completely* by introspection what motivated an action of mine.

Some of the phenomena that may function as motives are completely identifiable by introspection. I identify a sudden craving for black bread and cheese by having the craving and in no other way. I do not need to wait until I go into the kitchen to find out what I am hungering for. In fact, I may decide to resist the craving so that it does not motivate any action. I can still identify the feeling however. But the *motive* is not identified by identifying the craving for bread and cheese. It is analytic that identifying a motive is identifying something about me that is connected to an action. To ascribe a motive to someone is not merely saying something about his "inner" states; it implies that he performed an action. Thus identifying a motive involves reference to an action produced by that motive. A motive is therefore not completely identified by introspection, because you also need to identify the action motivated.[12] This fact has escaped notice because motives are most frequently discussed in the context of the explanation of actions, where the action motivated is given to begin with. In such contexts it often seems to philosophers that one can talk about motives without mentioning actions explicitly.[13]

References to actions may be more or less specific. At one end of the spectrum is the reference to an action, any action whatsoever. At the other extreme is the reference to a certain action, performed by a certain agent at a certain place and time, with the smallest time span compatible with anything being called an action. Pulling the trigger takes less time than shooting the gun, beginning to squeeze the trigger takes less time than either. "Beginning to squeeze the trigger" is thus a relatively more specific action-description.

In order to identify any state of the agent as a motive it does not suffice to refer to any action whatsoever, the reference must be to the action brought about by the motive. "He acted from ambition" is incomplete. The motive is completely identified only by "in x-ing he acted from ambition," where any number of plausible candidates can be substituted for "in x-ing", but "in surrendering all chances for satisfying his ambition" cannot. If we identify an actual motive ascribed to an actual person, we need to refer to the actual action thought to be produced by that motive. Talk about motives occurs primarily in explaining actions, specifically by establishing the link between a given action and the surrounding conditions. Parasitic on this sort of talk about motives are situations where we speculate whether someone had the requisite motive to perform an action (for instance, if we do not know whether he did perform the action in question) or where we praise or condemn certain classes of motives (as when we disapprove of being competitive) or say what sorts of motives, generally, move certain sorts of people to do certain sorts of things. In these and similar contexts, we talk about motives as the sort of thing that explains many instances of actions in the most common circumstances. Thus a secondary use of "motive" consists of talking about what is frequently true of agents when they perform certain familiar kinds of actions. It is in this secondary sense that I shall say, below, that motives are identified by lists of actions.

It would be a mistake to argue that motives are completely identifiable without reference to actions motivated and that reference to actions is only needed in order to provide evidence for ascribing a motive to a person. With the same feeling, a considerable range of actions may occur. If I suddenly crave black bread and cheese, but find none in the kitchen, I may go back to my study disappointed or I may decide to make do with white bread. I may go down to the neighbors to borrow some black bread or rush to the store, or begin baking bread. If we claimed that "craving for black bread and cheese" is a complete description of a motive, then we could hardly count "eating white bread and cheese" as unambiguous evidence for ascribing that motive to the agent. What we must do, instead, is to say that the desire for black bread and cheese is such that the substitution of white for black bread is acceptable. That tells us something about the motive. A desire that allows substitutions in the goods satisfying it is different from one that allows no substitutions. Some desires are more specific than others. A desire that can be deferred is different from one that I must satisfy at all costs. Some desires are more urgent than others, some stronger than others. We completely identify motives in these respects only by citing the actions the motives bring about.

The same point can be made about intentions. I can identify intentions introspectively. As motives, I can fully identify them only by speaking also of the actions that I perform in acting on the intentions. For then I must say something as to the specificity of the action intended and how firm my intention is, in the face of difficulties. The same holds for beliefs. I know in many cases what I believe. How firmly I hold a belief and what I regard as instances of the belief, both of which are important when beliefs motivate actions, can be stated only by talking about the actions motivated.

The cases discussed are the most favorable to the view that we know our motives by introspection alone, because they are all cases where the corresponding facts about persons are so identifiable. In many cases inner phenomena are not at all or only very imperfectly identifiable by introspection. In those cases it is much more obviously true that to identify a motive is to identify the action motivated. Playing slot machines, I begin to feel greedy. But my feelings are not specifically feelings of greed, they are feelings of excitement, of deprivation and need which, in different circumstances, I would identify rather differently. The introspectible data in a case like that are not even adequate for identifying the feeling, even for that I need to talk about what I am doing. In order to identify a corresponding motive, talking about actions is even more indispensable. This is more unambiguously the case with those so-called inner phenomena, like character traits, that are not at all identifiable by reference to introspection.

I have, so far, been speaking about identifying my own motives. It turns out that that involves identifying the actions motivated. Since I do not know anyone else's inner states introspectively, identifying the motives of others also requires identifying the actions motivated.[14]

(b) But to identify the action motivated is not to identify the motive completely. One and the same action may spring from a variety of motives. It is that fact that makes motive explanations interesting. How do we differentiate motives if they eventuate in one and the same action? I attack a fellow philosopher intemperately at a public meeting. I defend my action on the grounds that I was motivated by a desire for truth. His views were totally false and needed to be criticized. Others think that I acted from desire to impress my audience, that I was motivated by ambition. One and the same action may be motivated by different motives. How is the difference between them drawn? It is clear, in the light of what has been said, that introspection may enter into the attempt to be clear about my motives but will not suffice to settle the question whether the desire for truth or ambition was behind my attack. For even if there are specifically ambitious feelings and even if, at the time I attacked the man's speech, I experienced some of these feelings, that does not suffice to establish that I did in fact act from ambition. I may well have been motivated by the desire for truth, all the while experiencing some twinges of ambition. Whether that is true is to be decided by looking at lists of actions. There are lists of actions for ambitious persons in particular situations. An ambitious academic does different things from the ambitious politician. There are for any given list, alternative lists. These are lists of what a person, differently motivated, would be expected to do in the same situations. There are complementary lists of situations in which, say, the ambitious man acts and the lover of truth abstains, and those situations in which the lover of truth speaks out but the ambitious keeps his counsel. All of these lists are incomplete. The accusation that I acted from ambition when I publicly attacked a fellow philosopher comes to saying that I can be expected to seek public victories of similar sorts, even in cases where there is no conceivable question of injury being done to the truth. The accusation also implies that I can be expected to be less outspoken in the defense of truth if to do so would interfere with the realization of my ambitions. The ambitious person can be expected to treat those above him in rank and status with deference and be disinterested in persons that cannot help to advance him. We can expect him to continue striving to enhance his prestige or power beyond points where other men would be content with their achievement. He will do work that is intrinsically repugnant to him if it promises to advance his ambitions. For the same reasons he will conquer fear, dislike for persons, fatigue. Love and friendship will weigh less heavily in his deliberations than satisfying his ambition. Here are fairly definite areas on the lists of actions, and situations, in which I can be expected to act, that constitute what we mean by "being ambitious." But to call someone "ambitious" is not to offer to predict all his actions in any conceivable situation. This is so for a number of reasons. Different persons are ambitious to different degrees. One man will ruthlessly sacrifice personal ties to his ambition, another may at a certain point give up his projects for the sake of seeing more of his family. People are, in the second place, ambitious in different ways. Thus the lists that identify their particular form of ambition are slightly different. One man may have his competitor murdered in order to run the rackets single-handedly. Another may try to achieve the same end by political manipulation and legal maneuvering. No list, finally, enables us to answer extravagant questions like "Would he murder his children if that would enable him to become President?" Nor can we tell, even of persons whose motives we understand fairly accurately, how they will react in great crises, in the face of death. To that extent our lists are incomplete and one's sense of what it means for a person to be ambitious remains indefinite.

Motives are, therefore, only in subsidiary ways identifiable by introspection, if at all. To describe a motive is to describe lists of actions that a person so motivated performs in a series of situations and a list of situations in which a person so motivated is liable to act. To say, however, that the lists are incomplete is merely to recognize that the vocabulary we use to identify and discuss motives is beset by vagueness. There are many controversies about a person's motives that cannot be settled.

The preceding argument may, nonetheless, leave one wanting to say something like this: "But surely motives are something different from actions or lists of actions. They are not what a person does, but what occasions his doing what he does." The foregoing account does not deny this, in fact it insists on it. I have been talking exclusively about how we identify motives from other states of persons or how we differentiate one motive from another. I have been talking about how we explain actions, if they are not transparent, simply by reference to the surrounding conditions and how we explain what we are saying about a person when we explain his action by talking about his motives. There is a good sense in which I have not said what motives *are*. In the background of the entire argument is the belief that we do not know what motives are, we only know what they do. To know what motives in general and specific motives are we need to know a great deal more physiology than we do now. What moves one to act is a certain configuration of the body which, at present, we know nothing about. But this does not prevent us from distinguishing and identifying motives by means of incomplete lists of actions. Motives are for us a *je ne sais quoi* which we identify obliquely by talking primarily about actions and, in some cases, also about inner states of which we are aware introspectively.

III

If motives are identified by lists of actions and differentiated from other motives by contrasting lists of actions, there is no better way of answering the questions whether there is a motive properly called "desire for private gains" and what it is, than by listing the requisite actions and contrasting that list with an alternative one. My listing is obviously partial. A much more extensive listing, even of a very incomplete list, is possible. There are different lists for different persons since they are liable to be in different situations. I will suggest some members of the list for academics motivated by the desire for private gain and some of the alternatives:

(a) A person may write a book because a publisher offers to pay him for writing it. He may, alternatively, write one because he wants to, even if he cannot get money for it.

(b) A person may choose his job according to where he gets the highest pay or he may, alternatively, be oblivious to the pay differentials between different jobs.

(c) A man may take administrative work if it pays extra or, alternatively, set more time aside for philosophical reflection even if that means less income.

(d) A person may seek the job that carries more prestige (e.g. teaching graduate students) or, alternatively, he may seek to do what he feels he is most competent to do.[15]

(e) A person may strive primarily for the respect and recognition of his fellow academics or he may, alternatively, seek to win the regard of those he teaches.

The list can be extended on and on.[16] Actions (a), (b), and (c) exemplify a person's using his intellectual interest and expertise as a means toward increasing his income. The alternative actions would be those of people not primarily interested in a higher income. Actions (d) and (e) illustrate operation in the academic market where people compete with each other. They find their justification not in their sense of their own competence but in performing activities that are highly regarded in the market place. The alternative actions are those chosen by a person who judges his own actions and does not judge them by what is currently in demand in the academic market.

For different occupations corresponding lists are easily constructed. People choose whether to work or not to work, what to work at and where, by reference to monetary considerations. They judge the quality of work and the standards by which quality is to be judged by reference to what is well liked, i.e. is most saleable in the relevant market. By extending the list which I began, and constructing other ones, anyone can convince himself that there is in fact a desire for private gain and what it is like. The power of this motive is so obvious that philosophers' doubts about it may well make one wonder what philosophers think they are doing.

But is the desire for private gain a separate motive, say, from ambition or the desire to succeed in one's life work? Given any particular action that can plausibly be said to be an instance of seeking private gain, which thus fits into the list of actions that we would expect someone who is seeking private gain to perform, is there an alternative list in which that same action would also belong, which might be the list for being ambitious, seeking power, or seeking fulfilment in one's chosen profession? Due to the incompleteness of lists, this question is difficult to answer. Insofar as the question does have an answer, we must give a negative one. Whether the desire for private gain is distinct from ambition or seeking fulfilment in one's work is not a question that one can discuss in abstraction from social and historical facts. We must specify the social arrangements under which those people are living into whose motives we are inquiring. In a capitalist society, I shall argue, the desire for private gain is, in fact, what ambition or seeking fulfilment in one's work comes to.[17]

Is the desire for private gain as prevalent as economists claim? Since the question is indefinite, it need not detain us long. The argument in the next section will show that a capitalist society is characterized by the importance of this desire. This is not to say that all the actions or even most of the actions that I perform between getting up in the morning and going to bed at night are direct attempts to satisfy my desire for private gain. But it is to say that a large number of important choices, particularly those connected with one's work, are determined by the desire for private gain.

IV

In a capitalist society, goods and services as well as the means for producing goods and for providing services are owned by individual persons. Distribution of goods and services and productive capacities takes place in the market where individuals buy and sell. In its ideal state the market is perfectly competitive and in equilibrium. If it is perfectly competitive no individual buyer's or seller's activity in the market affects prices. If it is in equilibrium demand equals supply and prices are stable. In practice, equilibrium is the rare exception. Too many forces, like a change in supply due to good crops or natural disaster, and changes in demand due to fluctuations in size of population, errors on the part of entrepreneurs, miscalculations due to limited access to information, constantly keep prices fluctuating. Perfect competition is not attainable due to the large variety of goods and services, due to economies of scale, due to the economic advantages accruing from successful restraints of free competition. Under perfect competition, no individual has a sufficient slice of the relevant market to affect prices. Hence no one's actions in a market directly affect the conditions under which another person must operate in that market. In an imperfectly competitive market, on the other hand, or one that is not in equilibrium, the actions of one participant may affect the conditions under which others must operate. In that case, participants are in competition with one another. At any moment the actions of another may worsen my situation. As a consequence, economic security is at a premium in a capitalist society. The participants in the market not only try to buy cheap and sell dear; they must also constantly be on the lookout to consolidate their position in the market and to ward off potential threats to their position.

In a capitalist society, all goods and services are distributed by means of the market mechanism. This means that people will change jobs, change occupations, will leave their homes and move, if such a change will improve their earnings, or their prospects for future earnings. Employers will replace employees, if that reduces their wage bill. Manufacturers decide what they will produce, not by what people need, but by what will be most profitable to produce. Whether one sells one's labor and gets wages for that, or owns machines and buys labor to produce goods and services, one's decisions are always guided by the consideration of increasing one's earnings. In short, one pursues private gain. The various ways in which a wage-earner or an employer seeks to maintain or improve his position in the market constitute the list of actions to which we refer to explain what it means to seek private gain for people in these positions. Thus to say that a society is capitalist is to say that people's behavior conforms to the lists that define the desire for private gain. Seeking private gain, as defined by lists of behavior, is to operate in a market.

On the other hand, the sorts of things that people do from the desire for private gain can, in the vast majority of cases, only be done in a market economy. In a society where feudal or kinship relations determine the relations of worker to his work, he is not free to seek higher pay in different employment. Where people are tied to a particular plot of land by custom or by law, they cannot move at all. One can discharge a worker in a capitalist society to replace him by a machine but one cannot discharge a serf. Under a guild system, custom and law determine one's occupation and what one produces. One cannot switch products to follow the vagaries of supply and demand. The same is obviously true with reference to the more specific lists, cited earlier, that circumscribe the desire for private gain as evinced in the academic world. Where scholarship is one of the functions of a monastic institution, the individual scholar cannot act as an entrepreneur as he can, and must, when he operates in the academic market place. He is tied to his order. He is bound by rules to its discipline and the guidance of his superiors. At other times scholarship and learning were signs of good breeding, adopted by the aristocracy to distinguish itself from the commercial middle classes to whom it had lost its political power. In such a setting, where the point of being learned is precisely to set yourself apart from the people who trade, being a scholar for pay is out of the question.

None of this prevents a scholar, monk, or learned aristocrat from being, say, more deferential to those in power than to those that are powerless. Here is an action that belongs on the list by which we identify the desire for private gain but also occurs in different settings. But this simply points to the fact that single acts are occasioned by different motives, at various times, or, that we may ascribe more than one motive to a person in the light of only a single action, depending on what other actions we expect that person to perform in the future. One action may occur on more than one list. Entire portions of lists may occur on other lists. Lists specifying the desire for private gain may overlap with lists specifying different motives. But that overlap does not establish the universality of the desire for private gain. On the contrary, as long as large portions of that list can only occur in a capitalist society, it is quite clear that the list by which we identify the desire for private gain is indeed a defining feature of a capitalist economy. Here goods and services are apportioned by the market. This means that people display market behavior pervasively and thus can be said to be motivated by the desire for private gain. This desire is not a universal human trait. It defines capitalist man.

To all of this one may want to reply that the desire for private gain is universal after all, but that in different cultures it manifests itself in very different ways or is, to use the language of this paper, identifiable by reference to very different lists of actions. If one wants to talk this way, one cannot claim, however, that capitalism is defensible for being so peculiarly well adapted to the desire for private gain, because, on the present view, so is every other culture, for it too gives free rein to a list of actions which in that culture, we are told, must be used to identify the desire for private gain. The universality of the desire is here being maintained at the cost of saying that all cultures are equally well suited to its expression.

On the other hand, the defender of capitalism may say that granted there are different lists of actions that identify the desire for private gain in different cultures, nevertheless the motive force behind those actions is always the same. But that claim has been dealt with before. We do not possess any criteria by which to identify that inner force.

NOTES

[1] See, e.g., Milton Friedman, *Capitalism and Freedom,* University of Chicago Press, Chicago 1962.

[2] Quoted in David Horowitz (Ed.), *Containment and Revolution,* Beacon Press, Boston 1967, p. 28.

[3] Quoted in Alchian and Allen, *University Economics,* Wadsworth Publishing Co., Belmont, California 1967, p. 10.

[4] John Stuart Mill, *System of Logic,* Bk. VI, Ch. ix, para. 3.

[5] Frank H. Knight, *The Economic Organization,* A. M. Kelley, New York 1951, esp. pp. 21, 36, 63, 73 and 77.

[6] Knight, op. cit., pp. 11–12.

[7] The psychological defense of capitalism seems to include the claim that the desire for private gain is a necessary condition for a large class of human actions. If one could show that motives are not causes, this would serve to invalidate the psychological defense unless the notion of causation used were to exclude the notion of causes as necessary conditions. The relevance of the question whether motives are causes thus depends entirely on what sense one gives to the concept of cause.

[8] The concept of efficiency has a technical use in economics. It is doubtful, however, that it can be defined, in this technical use, without drawing on the apparatus of the capitalist economic model. To use the term "efficient" in this technical sense in the defense of capitalism would clearly beg the question at issue. The sense in which "efficient" is used in this defense must, therefore, be an informal non-technical one in which the assumption is, indeed, non-controversial, if only because it is rather vague.

[9] See George Dalton (Ed.), *Primitive, Archaic and Modern Economics. Essays of Michael Polanyi,* Beacon Press, Boston 1971.

[10] G. E. M. Anscombe, *Intention,* Clarendon Press, Oxford 1958, p. 18.

[11] Anscombe, op. cit., p. 20.

[12] Having a certain feeling is partial evidence for ascribing a certain motive to oneself. The absence of that feeling, however, is very weak evidence for denying that one has that certain motive.

[13] The most recent instance of this is Paul M. Churchland's "The Logical Character of Action Explanations," *Philosophical Review,* Vol. 74 (1970), pp. 214–36.

[14] J. J. Valberg in "Some Remarks on Action and Desire" (*Journal of Philosophy,* Vol. 62 [1970], pp. 503–19) appears to argue against the sort of view I am defending here. In his formulation the view asserts that the description of a motive must refer to the action motivated. His refutation of that view rests on a very restrictive sense of "refer": "A phrase *P* refers, definitely or indefinitely, only if there is an answer to: 'which thing does *P* refer to?' " (p. 509). The claim here is that only particular things can be referred to. The thesis that I am defending implies that classes and sorts of things can also be identified and, therefore, referred to.

[15] Teaching graduate rather than undergraduate students does not automatically produce higher income. But it carries more prestige and thus improves the person's position in the market place. He is in a better position to bargain and improves his chances to increase his earnings. Thus seeking a job with more prestige is a clear member of the list specifying the desire for private gain.

[16] For instance:

A person will teach what he can get paid to teach. Alternatively, he may refuse to teach anything but what he is competent and/or interested in teaching.

A man may teach although he does not like it and does not find it fulfilling, because he gets paid for it, or he may refuse to undertake any work that does not fulfill him.

A student will accept the authority of professors he does not respect instead of recognizing as authority only those he does respect.

Teachers will be very critical of their colleagues who do not, by publishing (or in other ways), add to the prestige of their departments, or they may respect others for being what and who they are.

In placing graduate students, a department may be primarily interested in placing people in jobs where they will do the department credit, or they may be primarily interested in the well-being of the students placed.

A person may treat college administrators and Trustees with more deference than his students, or he may treat people with the deference that he thinks a particular person deserves regardless of rank in the college hierarchy.

A person will submit his work, and thus himself, to the judgment of his professional colleagues, most of whom he does not know, or he will submit his work to the judgment of those whom he knows and respects.

A person will publish articles because he needs to get security and a raise in pay, or he may publish articles when and if he thinks others will profit from reading what he has to say. [17] The same answer holds for questions concerning the relation of the desire for private gain to the desire for truth, the desire for knowledge, and the desire to be of service to society, and whatever are the motives, more commonly cited, as moving people to become academics.

part FOUR

HUMAN FREEDOM AND POLITICAL LIBERTY

Bourgeois capitalism has always been praised and prized for its liberating tendencies: freedom of trade, freedom of enterprise, freedom of consumer choice—in short, for the negative freedom of securing one against forcible, coercive intrusions from others, including governments. But Marxists have argued that this claim is either an outright distortion or only partially supportable. They have said that the freedom of the individual in capitalist systems, even if they were indeed consistently adhered to, is illusory. Only an appearance of freedom is present in capitalism, while in fact the individual is strictly constrained to make his "free" choices within definite social and economic boundaries.

Supporters of capitalism, however, say that it is the negative freedom capitalism secures—liberty to order one's life and property as one sees fit, within one's circumstances—that makes the individual capable of reaching his or her highest potential in life. It also means that persons can fail to reach this potential, and that is only just, since the moral nature of individuals requires that they be free either to win or to lose, to do good or evil, to succeed or to fail. According to this argument, trying to institutionally achieve their "true freedom," as Marxists do, will only lead to tyranny.

Which idea of freedom is the right one? Who supports individual freedom, communists or capitalists?

LOYD EASTON
MARX AND INDIVIDUAL FREEDOM

To most people in Western societies there is little doubt on one issue, namely, that between the two systems, Marxian communism and capitalism, the latter most effectively secures individual freedom. There may be many troubles in capitalism, many in the West believe, but it cannot be that individual freedom is undermined by it. Loyd Easton—emeritus professor of philosophy at Ohio Wesleyan University, author of Hegel's First American Followers: The Ohio Hegelians (1966) *and editor and translator with Kurt Guddat of* Writings of the Young Marx on Philosophy and Society (*New York: Doubleday Anchor, 1967*)—*argues that Marx stands squarely on the side of individual freedom and that impressions to the contrary are due to misunderstanding. With Easton's essay we find ourselves immediately face-to-face with one of the main contentions between communist and capitalist theorists. This will also serve as a suitable introduction to a question that will recur throughout this volume: What is freedom and what kind of society secures it best?*

Contrary to widespread popular opinion nurtured by "official" Marxism and contrary to much scholarly interpretation, Karl Marx consistently and throughout his life defended individual freedom as a matter of philosophical principle and specific social policy. He was not, as often claimed, ambivalent about individual freedom nor did he compromise it in his conception of democracy as a political form for the emancipation of labor. He was not implicitly or in tendency a totalitarian on the basis of his immense intellectual debt to Hegel or his commitment to a unity in society, to socialism and to the classless society of communism, that would obliterate individual freedom.[1] On the contrary, the following pages will argue that Marx's life-long defense of individual freedom was grounded in the philosophy of Hegel, at first in Hegel's conception of a rational or ethical state freed of certain inconsistencies and permanently on the basis of Hegel's dialectic. Though Marx came to divorce dialectic from Hegel's Absolute Mind under the influence of Feuerbach—a divorce that created certain epistemological problems that were never resolved—he nevertheless adhered to dialectic as the fundamental principle of "development" in society and history, and this was the permanent ground of his defense of individual freedom.

I

At the foundation of Marx's political writings in 1842 was the philosophy of Hegel and Hegel's view of the state. Five years earlier Marx wrote to his father that he had studied Hegel from end to end and fell "into his clutches," resolv-

Reprinted with permission from *The Philosophical Forum*, Volume XII, Number 3, Spring 1981.

ing to seek "the Idea in the real itself" and thus overcome the dichotomy between "is" and "ought" that had disturbed him in Kant and Fichte. This gave Marx a basis for "criticism" that "measures existence against essence, particularly actuality against the Idea." In notes to his doctoral dissertation Marx identified himself with the liberal party of criticism—i.e., the Left-Hegelian party of Bauer, Ruge, and his associates in the Berlin Doctors' Club. The liberal party saw the discrepancy between Idea and actuality not as a deficiency in philosophical thought but rather as "a deficiency of the world to be made philosophical," to be made consonant with the Idea.[2]

In Hegel's philosophy the Idea that Marx resolved to seek in the world was identical with Reason, and Reason was a dynamic process of synthesis or unification in every thought and object, but a unification that preserves its particular elements while transcending and thus negating them as something separate. This transcending, *Aufhebung* in German, is dialectic.[3] It also involves self-determination. To grasp the dialectic, rationality, or idea of anything is to see its self-determination and thus its freedom. On this basis the true or fully rational state—Hegel had in mind the community as a whole, including family and economic life with the apparatus of government as only one element—would be one that most fully achieved a unity, a dialectical synthesis of universality and particularity. In contrast to the Greek *polis* that suppressed individual, subjective freedom, the modern state, Hegel often asserted, "has prodigious strength and depth because it allows the principle of subjectivity to progress to its culmination in the extreme of self-subsistent personal particularity, and yet at the same time brings it back to substantive unity and so maintains this unity in the principle of subjectivity itself."[4] For Hegel a state was rational or realizes its idea to the extent that it realizes a dialectical unity that preserves particularity, and such a realization is at the same time the realization of freedom.

This view of the state was the premise of Marx's discussion of censorship, law, representation, and bureaucracy in his writings of 1842 and early 1843. He viewed the state as "a free association of moral human beings . . . aiming at the actualization of freedom." It is not based on religion but rather "reason in society," "the idea of the whole." It is to be viewed as "the great organism in which legal, ethical, and political freedom has to be actualized and in which the individual citizen simply obeys the natural laws of his own reason, human reason, in the laws of the state."[5] When Marx referred to "natural law" at the basis of enacted law he was not referring to a prepolitical state of nature. Like Hegel he regarded that seventeenth and eighteenth century view as "a fiction," in spite of its endorsement in Spinoza's *Tractatus* from which Marx copied passages in his notebooks of 1841 on democracy and the aim of government as liberty.[6] For Marx law had an objective basis in "reason in society" since the legislator only "expresses the inner principles of spiritual relationships in conscious positive laws."[7]

Marx viewed censorship as violating both elements, universality and particularity, of the unity that should characterize a rational state to actualize freedom. On one side, censorship is based on tendentious laws without objective norms. Such laws cancel equality of citizens before the law and resemble the laws of terrorism created by Robespierre. In an ethical or truly rational state, the view of the state is subordinate to all its members even if they oppose a particular organ of the state. In this respect censorship violates the element of universality in law. But in going beyond acts—the only proper province of law—censorship also impinges on "the sacredness and inviolability of subjective conviction," the element of particularity. Thus it violates both sides of the dialectical unity that is the mark of a rational state.[8]

In condemning censorship Marx further appealed to the principle of development or growth in dialectic, a development that includes diversity. Rather than viewing freedom of the press as a species of free trade, a mere instrument rather than an end in itself, Marx preferred the "truly historical view" that the "reason of history" requires room for new views to meet new needs. Without diversity of opinion and even one-sided development of particular views there can be no social progress. "Without parties," said Marx, "there is no development, without division, no progress." What he most wanted in his criticisms of censorship was a press law that would provide "the positive existence of freedom" as in the United States where freedom of the press exists in its purest form. There is even more reason, he added, for such a law in Germany with its longer history of literature and intellectual culture.[9]

In the year he was writing on censorship Marx vigorously defended individual freedom in other respects. He believed that fundamental law must be "the conscious expression of the will of the people, created with and through it."[10] Thus he unreservedly held the principle of popular sovereignty to actualize "reason in society." In the administration of law Marx argued that judges should be independent of the executive in government. Unlike a censor a judge "has no superiors but the law." Further, Marx held that judicial functions of judge, prosecutor, and defender should be separate rather than in one person and that impartiality in form, due process, is inseparable from the content in law. Since law expresses a "public content dictated by freedom and not by private interest," trials should be public and free.[11] As a corollary of popular sovereignty and in opposition to the state system of Prussia based on corporate interests, Marx held that "Representation must not be conceived as the representation of something that is not the people itself. It must be conceived only as the people's *self-representation,* as a state action which, not being its sole, exceptional state action, is distinguished from other expressions of its state life by the universality of its content."[12]

Marx's views on popular sovereignty, representation, and independence of the judiciary were implicitly a criticism of the actual Prussian constitution and also Hegel's view of the structure of a rational state. Without mentioning his name, Marx was arguing that Hegel's conclusions about the state did not follow from his main premise that a genuine state is a rational unity of universality and particularity. Subsequently Marx made such criticisms explicit and detailed in his "Critique of Hegel's Philosophy of the State," written in Kreuznach in the summer of 1843. Marx anticipated that "Critique" at another important point—namely, bureaucracy. In connection with the economic distress of the Moselle vintagers Marx argued that the bureaucracy, the executive civil servants in Hegel's conception of the state, acquires an interest of its own separate from the people. Far from being a "universal class" unselfishly devoted to the whole community, the bureaucracy appears to be "the state" itself against which the world beyond entirely lacks its disposition and insight."[13] Marx concluded that alleviation of the vintagers' distress required, in addition to action from the state, a universal participation in the interests of the fatherland that would transcend bureaucracy to represent each citizen truly, and such participation further requires a free press.

In these discussions of censorship, law, popular sovereignty, and representation Marx was defending basic principles of liberal democracy but was forbidden by law to say so openly. In his draft reply to the ministerial rescript suppressing the *Rheinische Zeitung* Marx noted that "liberal sovereignty" could be understood as the king's personal quality or as the spirit of sovereignty realized through free institutions and laws, the work of *"a moral and rational commonweal [Gemeinwesen]"* to be realized under every form of state.[14] Within a few months, however, he was openly demanding from Paris that Germany leave the political animal kingdom to enter "the human world of democracy," to achieve "the results of the French Revolution, thus in the final analysis a republic and an order of free mankind." Only the awakening of freedom, the feeling of man's dignity, can "transform society into a community of free men to achieve their highest purpose, a democratic state."[15]

Though Marx would soon call his position "communism" based on an elaboration of "true democracy" and "full human emancipation," he did not thereby reject or abandon the principles of individual freedom he espoused in 1842. Five years later the Communist League in London published its position as follows after Marx and Engels had won the majority to their views: "We are not among those communists who are out to destroy personal liberty, who wish to turn the world into one huge barrack . . . [Let us] put our hands to work in order to establish a democratic state wherein each party would be able by word or in writing to win a majority to its ideas." The League also held that communism required "a period of transition, and indeed a democratic period of transition during which personal property would gradually become merged into social property; for communists recognize the principle of personal freedom."[16] Such a "period of transition" will be considered later under another (and today misleading) label, "dictatorship of the proletariat," but it is already apparent that when Marx wrote in the *Communist Manifesto* that the first step was "to establish democracy," he meant to include individual freedom along the lines laid down in 1842.

In numerous articles in his *Neue Rheinische Zeitung* during the revolution of 1848–49 Marx vigorously defended individual freedom and harshly criticized the Frankfurt assembly when it restricted democratic rights or failed to defend them against the Crown. For example, Marx defended the people's unqualified right to assembly, criticized indirect suffrage in elections, and defended freedom of the press more forcefully than he had in 1842.[17] Three years after the publication of the *Communist Manifesto* and after he had begun to use the phrase "dictatorship of the proletariat" to refer to the political dominion [*Herrschaft*] of the working class, Marx edited the first volume of his writing, including his first essay on censorship and pieces from the *Rheinische Zeitung* of 1842 discussing the nature of the state, law and freedom, representation and bureaucracy.[18] Thus there is ample evidence, and more to come, that Marx's commitment to individual freedom was not confined to his early years but continued in his maturity as part of his commitment to democracy.

II

Thus far we have seen how Marx developed his defense of individual freedom in democracy from Hegel's premise that a genuine state is a dialectical unity of universality and particularity or "reason in society," the Idea in social actuality. His criticisms of Hegel's formulation of that unity in constitutional monarchy were only implicit. With his Kreuznach "Critique of Hegel's Philosophy of the State" the criticisms become explicit.

First Marx turns his attention to Hegel's method to show how his principle of dialectical development is a purely speculative, purely logical affair that mystifies social relationships. Hegel treats the state as a subject, as actual Idea, "lending" itself to family and civil society as particular conceptual spheres. Thus they are "made by the actual Idea," united into the state by "the life course of the Idea." Marx charges that Hegel has mistakenly reversed subject and predicate in regard to the Idea and its content because "development takes place on the side of the predicate," the real content of the Idea. "Family and civil society," Marx explains, "are the real presuppositions of the state ... the really active things; but in speculative philosophy it is reversed." Here Marx was following Feuerbach's attack on speculation that had appeared in the *Anekdota* along with his own first essay on censorship. Marx would now have us look to "empirical actuality" and "common experience" for real development, not development in the "abstract sphere of logic."[19]

But with this critique of Hegel, Marx did not reject or abandon dialectic. Rather he relocated it as the process of resolving contradictions and dualisms, the *Aufhebung* of alienations, within observable social and historical movements. This relocation is commonly identified as Marx's "materialism" in contrast to Hegel's idealism. As with Feuerbach and common usage of the day, "materialism" was primarily a synonym for empiricism, the view that "our knowledge and ideas originate from the world of the senses."[20]

That Marx had not abandoned dialectic but only relocated it is apparent in his subsequent major writings. The *Economic and Philosophic Manuscripts of 1844* praise Hegel for his "dialectic of negativity" and thus for his grasp of "the self development of man as a process ... as alienation and transcendence of this alienation ... he thus grasps the nature of *work*." Hegel's mistake was to treat that process speculatively rather than as development in perceptible historical practice. A year later in *The Holy Family* Marx found a "great scientific advance" in Proudhon's view of the dialectical connection between property and poverty but subsequently criticized him for not having grasped "the secret of scientific dialectic." Hegel's dialectic, said Marx, is "the basic form of all dialectic" after it has been stripped of its mystical form.[21]

Even where Marx most firmly criticized speculative idealism as an explanation of history in favor of empiricism derived from Feuerbach—the first part of *The German Ideology*—we find him adhering to dialectic. Though the premises of his view of history are real individuals, their material conditions of life that can be verified "in a purely empirical way," this means "a real, empirically perceptible process of development under certain conditions." Abstractions must only depict the sequence of such a development, and such a conception of history, starting out from material production, depicts civil society in action dialectically, "as a totality and the reciprocal action of its various sides on one another." From this standpoint Feuerbach's position is now seen to be defective precisely because it lacks the element of historical and dialectical development. For him history can only be "a collection of dead facts as it is with the empiricists." Later Marx was to complain that Feuerbach "has much to answer for" in the disrepute of Hegel's dialectic, in its being treated as a "dead horse."[22]

Finally, in the 1873 preface to *Capital* Marx forcefully declared his allegiance to Hegel's dialectic freed of its "mystification," i.e., its identification with "the Idea" as an independent subject. While others were treating Hegel as "dead dog" Marx declared himself to be "the pupil of that mighty thinker," the first to present comprehensively and consciously dialectic in its "general form of working." In its "rational kernel" dialectic includes affirmation of the existing state of things and the negation of it, its dissolution. It regards every social form as in fluid movement. In essence it is critical and revolutionary. This description of dialectic, it should be noted, emphasizes the process of *Aufhebung,* transcendence that both preserves its elements (affirmation) as it negates them within a new form. By virtue of such transcendence, Marx's statements imply, dialectic not only depicts the constant transformation or revolutionary side of history, but it also provides a basis for criticizing history in the extent to which any social process achieves the integral transcendence, synthesis, or unification that he had earlier called meeting "the demands of reason."

Now there are deep, complicated epistemological problems in Marx's wedding of dialectic in its "rational kernel" from Hegel to the "empirically perceptible process of development" in society and history, and I have explored these problems elsewhere.[23] They center on how one can connect the "necessity" of Marx's dialectic, not to mention "contradictions" and "negations," with sense perception that can support only contingent, probable truths. Such features of dialectic were no problem for Hegel because he was an idealist. For him the substance of all events and objects was idea or thought where "necessity," "contradiction," and "negation" are clearly appropriate. But Marx rejected Hegel's idealism and consequently faced the difficulty just noted. This may explain why he never got around to the systematic treatise on dialectic that he said he intended to write. Nevertheless he adhered to Hegel's dialectic throughout his major writings. It was the framework both for his description and his "critique" of society and history. Within weeks of his first criticism of Hegel's speculative "mystification" he published his view of the task of the critic couched in terms of "demands of reason" expressing dialectical development with continuity. In Marx's words:

Reason has always existed but not always in rational form. The critic, therefore, can start with any form of theoretical and practical consciousness and develop the true actuality of the forms *inherent* in existing actuality as its ought-to-be and goal. As far as actual life is concerned, the *political state* especially contains in all its *modern* forms the demands of reason, even where the political state is not yet conscious of socialistic demands. Everywhere it claims reason as realized. Equally, however, it gets into the contradiction between its ideal character and its real presuppositions. Social truth, therefore, can be developed everywhere out of this conflict of the political state with itself.[24]

Even the most specific problem such as the difference between the estate and representative system, Marx urged, should engage attention because it expresses in a political way the difference between the control of men and the control of private property. In contrast to the dogmatic abstractions in the communism of Cabet and Weitling, "We develop new principles for the world out of the principles of the world." So there is not a blank between past and future. "It is a matter of *realizing* the thoughts of the past."

III

In his statement of the function of the critic Marx outlined his major themes of the later sections of his Kreuznach "Critique of Hegel's Philosophy of the State," the sections following his criticism of Hegel's speculative "mystification." His aim in particular was to show how Hegel's constitutional monarchy was a "contradictory and unjustifiable institution" that did not resolve the contradiction between its ideal character and its real presuppositions, did not provide the dialectical unity of universality and particularity that would fulfill the "demands of reason." For example, in regard to the sovereignty of the monarch, Marx argues that the idealism of the state, its universality, cannot exist in one person because no single person exhausts the sphere of personality. "What kind of idealism of the state," Marx asks rhetorically, "would exist as the communal soul of the state in *one* person, *one* subject, instead of being the actual self-consciousness of the citizens?"

From this Marx concludes that "democracy is the truth of monarchy." Democracy can be conceived in its own terms. It is the generic constitution with a unity of form and content because it is "the constitution of the people," their own work and free product. "Only democracy, therefore, is the true unity of the general and the particular." And it is the "actual universal" so that "the political state disappears in true democracy," i.e., the political state as something separate, no longer applying to the whole.[25]

This view of the "political state" in relation to "true democracy" implies that in modern times, as Hegel perceived and sought to justify as "rational," there is a separation between the state and civil society as the sphere of private property and economic institutions. Hence property is outside community control, outside the "social and ethical ties" of citizenship. In his view of primogeniture and landed property, Marx observes, "Hegel makes citizenship, political existence and political conviction attributes of private property instead of making private property an attribute of citizenship."[26]

In criticizing Hegel's views on representation and the legislative function of the state Marx refines what he said earlier about self-representation of the people, the true universality of content in a rational state, and finds its mechanism in universal suffrage with active and passive voting. With this conclusion he rounds out his conception of "true democracy" as the unity of universality and particularity, Hegel's own criterion of a genuine state.

Here Marx clearly had in mind the preservation of individual freedom and more, its concrete realization in "unlimited voting, active as well as passive." He expected the people to vote on important legislative matters directly and elect representatives who would in turn vote on legislation. Such representatives would be deputies instructed and bound by their constituencies.[27] Further, "true democracy" would mean the dissolution of the bureaucracy, the supposedly "universal class" in the abstract political state that actually functions as a closed society serving its own interest. Instead, administrative and executive functions would be the work of every citizen on a part-time or short term basis.[28]

To distinguish "true democracy" from the political state that would disappear, even the political state as a republic, Marx called it a *Gemeinwesen,* a community or commonweal, the label he had used a year earlier for a truly rational state or self-representation of the people. As involving the disappearance of the political state, "true democracy" anticipates Marx's later position in the *Communist Manifesto* and elsewhere referring to his goal as an "association" where "public power has lost its political character." As involving the dissolution of civil society—the realm of economic activity, private property, and class distinctions in Hegel's system—through "unlimited voting," "true democracy" prescribes the management of economic life and property by "individuals as all" as members of society, and thus an economically classless society rather than one divided into classes.[29] So formulated, "true democracy" anticipates major features of Marx's communism. He did not call his view "communism" until a year later as he analyzed the alienation of labor implied in the classical economics of Ricardo and others,[30] but he had arrived at its main features.

Later we shall see how the principles of "true democracy" with individual freedom were embodied in Marx's defense of the Paris Commune of 1871 as the "political form" for the emancipation of labor in "possible communism" with a basic change from the *Manifesto* in regard to the state. What is now apparent is that Marx viewed the exercise of popular sovereignty through universal suffrage as a revolutionary act, the vehicle of fundamental structural change in society. In this he welcomed what many conservatives in his day feared. He was reading in Tocqueville and Thomas Hamilton that democracy with universal suffrage would immediately lead to "spoliation" of capitalist property by the popular masses.[31] Further, he saw the revolutionary implications of the Chartist movement in England and on several occasions up to 1879 held universal suffrage to be the primary road to socialism in countries with working class majorities.[32]

IV

While Marx was writing his "Critique of Hegel's Philosophy of the State," he was drafting an essay "On the Jewish Question," published a year later in Paris, that developed further his criticism of Hegel on the split between the abstract political state and civil society in relation to individual freedom and on the difference between political emancipation and human emancipation. On this basis Marx explored the distinction between the "rights of man" and "the rights of the citizen" as marked in the French Declarations to conclude that the former are rights of a member of civil society, "of egoistic man, man separated from other men and the community," and that the practical focus of the right of liberty is property. The "rights of the citizen," by contrast, are "political rights that can be exercised only in community with others. *Participation* in the community . . . or state constitutes their substance. They belong in the category of *political freedom*, of *civil rights*."[33] Marx does not discuss the "rights of the citizen" but took them for granted as shown in his earlier conclusions, never repudiated, on censorship, representation, and voting. In the French Declaration of 1793 they include, as Richard Hunt has well documented, rights of participation such as voting and holding office, political equality, free expression, and freedom of assembly.[34] The essential problem, as Marx saw it, is that even in a limited, merely political state such as a democratic republic the rights of the citizen that define individual freedom are cases of "unactual universality." What is needed is their actualization in civil society, and such a step goes beyond mere political emancipation to human emancipation. In Marx's words:

Only when the actual, individual man has taken back into himself the abstract citizen and in his everyday life, his individual work, and his individual relationships has become a species-being, only when he has recognized and organized his own powers as *social powers* so that social force is no longer separated from him as political power, only then is human emancipation complete.[35]

Though Marx has substituted for Hegelian "universality" the notion of "species-being" from Feuerbach—the notion, Marx said in a letter to Feuerbach, of "the unity of man with man ... based on their real differences,"[36] thus itself a dialectical unity—his conception of human emancipation is clearly a case of dialectical *Aufhebung,* a synthesis or unity of universality and particularity, that preserves the rights of citizenship listed earlier. Political emancipation, Marx noted, is itself a great step forward, thus a necessary but not sufficient condition of human emancipation. Human emancipation does not require, as Rousseau thought, the adoption of "alien powers" to transform human nature but only the recognition that man is already a "species-being," so it is a question of organizing his existent social powers.[37] The notion of human emancipation, then, is a particular specification of "true democracy" as related to individual freedom in the rights of citizenship.

Marx was not contemptuous of the rights of citizenship, but he was of the "so-called" rights of man because they conceived individual freedom, equality, and security as functions of private property. He later described capitalism with its private ownership of the means of production as a veritable "Eden of the innate rights of man."[38] In his Kreuznach "Critique" he had already criticized the right to private property as something "inalienable" because it removed property from the "social and ethical ties" of citizenship and made citizenship an attribute of private property. Like Thomas Jefferson, who replaced Locke's natural right of "property" by "pursuit of happiness" in the American Declaration of Independence, Marx held that the right of private property was not inalienable but rather it was a civil right, something that the community could rightfully regulate and control.[39] The grounds for this agreement, of course, were different. Jefferson's was individual reason apprehending natural law and social utility. Marx's, as we have seen, was "reason in society"—a reformulation of Hegel's "Objective Mind"—as law expressing norms of social life that nurtured human dignity in self-determination, freedom.

Accompanying his essay "On the Jewish Question" Marx published another, "Toward the Critique of Hegel's Philosophy of Law: Introduction," to precede a reworking of his unpublished Kreuznach "Critique." After extensive analysis of backward German political conditions, it significantly identifies the proletariat as the means to achieve what he had just called "full human emancipation" and "true democracy." With extensive study of the conditions of the French Revolution Marx finds in the proletariat "a sphere of society having a universal character because of its universal suffering" that can "stand for the notorious crime of society as a whole" like the position of the French bourgeoisie of 1789. The proletariat could now say *"I am nothing and I should be everything."*[40] Further, Marx frequently attended meetings of socialists and workers' associations in Paris where he found that "the brotherhood of man is no mere phrase but a fact of life," and there "history is preparing the practical element for the emancipation of man."[41] Thus he found elements of a new society growing inside the old, a dialectical *Aufhebung* in microcosm.

Marx's view of the proletariat, however, raises a question in relation to his view of democracy as involving universal suffrage and unrestricted voting, the pillars of individual freedom. He recognized that the proletariat was "only beginning to appear in Germany as a result of the rising industrial movement."

If its emancipation is the basis of fundamental revolution in Germany, how could such a revolution be anything but a minority movement requiring a dictatorship or vanguard party of some kind? The answer lies in Marx's expectation of an "acute disintegration of society, and particularly of the middle class, which gives rise to the proletariat."[42] He expected that pauperism would increase geometrically—he had seen such hardship among the Moselle vintagers and Silesian weavers—and agreed with Hegel's earlier observation that with the development of industry "a great mass of people sinks below a certain necessary level of subsistence and thereby loses . . . the honor to exist by one's own activity and labor. This produces the proletariat [Pöbel] which in turn facilitates the concentration of excessive wealth in a few hands."[43] Though Marx's expectation of the emergence of the proletariat as the vast majority of society was grossly mistaken in respect to timing, it was entirely consonant with his adherence to unrestricted voting and majority rule implied in "true democracy." A year later we find him outlining a book on the modern state that would deal with such topics as "individual freedom and public power," "sovereignty of the people," "political parties," and significantly concluding with a line on "Suffrage, the struggle to overcome [Aufhebung] the state and civil society"—all matters of his central concern since 1842.[44]

In 1845 Marx collaborated with Engels on *The German Ideology,* unpublished until 1932, to develop further his view of individual freedom in relation to communism. (Engels later noted that Marx has already arrived at the main features of his view, so the theory "rightly bears his name.") Further developing themes of his *Economic and Philosophical Manuscripts of 1844,* Marx finds the basis of private property, correctly described by modern economists as "the power of controlling the labor of others," in the division of labor. On this basis "man's own act becomes an alien power opposed to him and enslaving him instead of being controlled by him—as long as he remains in natural society, as long as a split exists between the particular and common interest and as long as the activity is not voluntarily but naturally divided."[45] Out of this split the interest of the community takes on an independent form as "the State." It is an illusory communal life but based on classes determined by the division of labor and particularly the domination of one class representing its interest as the universal interest. The proletariat, after becoming such a dominant class, can abolish the rule and existence of classes because it is "the expression of the dissolution of all classes."[46] With this the state as an independent, illusory community dominated by one class is itself transcended. Instead there is a real community where the conditions of existence of all members of society are under their control, conditions previously left to chance with a seemingly independent existence. Marx calls such a community "communism."

In communism personal freedom becomes a reality because the conditions of life are under the control of all the associated members of society. "In previous substitutes for the community," Marx claims, "personal freedom has existed only for the individuals who developed within the ruling class and only insofar as they belonged to this class." With communism, however, individuals participate as individuals "making it impossible that anything should exist independently of individuals."[47]

In arriving at this conclusion Marx crystallized and applied his earlier views of the merely political state as an "illusory universality" and his view of the proletariat as the key to "full human emancipation." His commitment to democracy with individual freedom is implicit in his notion of the control of the conditions of life by the whole community, all members of society. Here Marx anticipates and provides the rationale for his proclaimed goal in the *Communist Manifesto* three years later (and note the priority in his statement): "an association, in which the free development of each is the condition of the free development of all"—and in *Capital* almost twenty years later: "a higher form of society, a society in which the full and free development of every individual forms the ruling principle."[48]

V

The fullest implementation of Marx's view of "true democracy" in relation to individual freedom is to be found in his address to the International Workingmen's Association on the Paris Commune of 1871. That address, however, is itself a highly controversial matter. A few months before the establishment of the Communal government Marx had warned the Parisian workers against any such move as "folly" in the face of German arms and urged them to use existing republican liberty to build up their own organization. After the fall of the Commune he suggested that the whole enterprise had been a mistake, the rising of a city under exceptional conditions. "The majority of the commune," he said, "was in no sense socialist, nor could it be." Conditions for a socialist government were not sufficiently developed.[49] Further, it is often noted that Marx was not historically accurate in his portrayal of the Commune. But none of these observations detracts from the significance of Marx's address as a statement of his political principles bearing on individual freedom. He was primarily concerned with the direction and tendency of the Commune—what it *was to do* on the basis of what it did do—that betokened "a government of the people by the people." In short, he was preoccupied with the *principles* of the Commune. The minutes of the Council of the International reported him as saying: "The principles of the Commune are eternal and cannot be crushed; they will assert themselves again and again until the working classes are emancipated."[50]

What were the basic principles of the Paris Commune? They all have to do with self-government and control of governmental institutions by the people in such a way as to insure individual freedom. The governing assembly was formed of councillors elected by universal suffrage at short terms, responsible to the voters and revocable by them. It was to be "a working, not a parliamentary body, executive and legislative at the same time." Here Marx was apparently striking at a separation of powers that would frustrate the popular will. The police and all other administrative officials as well as judges were to be elective, responsible, and revocable and were to perform their duties at workmen's wages. The aim here was to eliminate "vested interest" and keep public functions from becoming the private property of agents of the central government in bureaucracy.[51]

Other features of the Commune clearly bolstered individual freedom. To end spiritual repression the Commune disestablished and disendowed all churches as proprietary bodies. All educational institutions were opened free to the people and cleared of interference of church and state. Marx later cited the United States as a model in this respect. General legislation to guide inspectors concerning teaching staff and instruction, Marx held, "is a very different thing from appointing the state as the educator of the people."[52] With such freedom in education, scientific inquiry could shake off the fetters imposed on it by governmental pressure and class prejudice. The practices of the Commune, furthermore, assured freedom to criticize the government. "The Commune did not pretend," Marx observed, "to infallibility, the invariable attribute of all governments of the old stamp. It published its doings and sayings, it initiated the public into all its shortcomings."[53]

Marx recognized that there was a pluralism of interests and factions in the Commune. Under the subtitle, "The Communal Revolution as the Representative of all Classes not Living on Foreign Labour," he noted the inclusion of the great majority of the peasantry, the small industrial working class, and "vital elements" of the middle class necessary to production. Of working class parties or political factions, Proudhonists and Blanquists were the immense majority and members of Marx's International Workingmen's Association a minority.[54] Thus Marx's endorsement of the Commune implicitly followed his earlier dictum: "Without parties there is no development; without division, no progress." Certainly he did not think of the Communal government as the instrument of a single, monolithic, all-dominating party carrying out a "dictatorship of the proletariat" that could be exercised, as Lenin said, "by individuals" with thousands of workers in *unquestioning obedience* to the will of a single person."[55]

With the Paris Commune as a model for all industrial centers and even for rural villages, district assemblies were to be formed of delegates from local communes, delegates revocable at any time and bound by a *mandat imperatif* from their constituents, and similarly delegates from district assemblies were to constitute the national assembly in Paris. The unity of the nation, Marx argued, would not be broken, but the old state power claiming to embody the nation's unity, a "parasitic excrescence" independent of and superior to it, would be destroyed. Its legitimate functions—those "necessitated by the general and common wants of the country"—would be restored to responsible agents of society through universal suffrage that would serve the people just as individual suffrage serves an employer to get the right manager or workman in place or remove him promptly if a mistake is made.[56]

What is apparent in this sketch of Communal government is that Marx is applying some of his earlier conclusions about "true democracy" in relation to universal suffrage and bureaucracy. He stresses the "really democratic institutions" of the Commune, and notes that it involves a dialectical transcendence, an *Aufhebung,* of the old state power. It destroys or negates the old state power as a "parasitic excrescence" independent of society, what he ealier called an "illusory community" that is really the instrument of class domination by the few who own the means of production. But the "legitimate functions" of the state remain as the responsibility of society through its agents determined by universal suffrage.[57] In general terms, the Commune achieves a dialectical synthesis of universality and particularity that Marx earlier characterized as a "rational state" or *Gemeinwesen,* Hegel's premise but achievable only in democracy.

The decisive feature of the Commune for Marx was that its "really democratic institutions" made it "the political form at last discovered under which to work out the economic emancipation of labor." It was a lever for uprooting the economic basis of class rule. Its special measure to this end was the surrender of all closed workshops and factories to associations of workmen, under reserve of compensation. This was an "expropriation of the expropriators," said Marx, that would "make individual property a truth by transforming the means of production, land and capital, now chiefly the means of enslaving and exploiting labor into mere instruments of free and associated labor." Such "cooperative production" to supersede the capitalist system with "united cooperative societies" regulating national production on a common plan is nothing else, said Marx, "but Communism, 'possible' Communism."[58]

But cooperative production is not simply a utopian ideal. It is a higher form latent in the present society. Through a series of historic struggles the working class can "set free the elements of the new society with which the old collapsing bourgeois society is itself pregnant." In *Capital* Marx had already referred to cooperative factories as destroying the antithesis between capital and labor by making associated workers their own capitalist. They show, said Marx, "how a new mode of production naturally grows out of an old one." Again, in his Inaugural Address to the International Workingmen's Association Marx referred to the cooperative movement as an even greater victory of "the political economy of labor" than the ten hour bill in England, so important that it should not be left to casual efforts of a few workmen but rather "fostered by national means."[59] With the Paris Commune Marx crystallizes his view of cooperatives as the main feature of the "emancipation of labor" and thus communism.

Two features of Marx's view of cooperative production in communism are noteworthy. First, as in his view of the state he sees cooperative production not as a matter of simple negation of the existing capitalist system but rather as a dialectical transcendence that negates as it preserves. This is apparent in what he says about making individual property a truth with communism and his view that present society already contains elements of the new society, associated labor in unions and cooperatives. Secondly, he sees cooperatives as the economic corollary of the "really democratic institutions" of the Commune. The core principle is self-government with all authority subject to control of those who are affected. Hence both cooperatives and government are simply vehicles of individual freedom. This is especially apparent in Marx's notes on Bakunin's claim in *Statism and Anarchy* that democracy with universal suffrage would still involve domination by a privileged minority, ex-workers representing only themselves and not the people. "If Herr Bakunin were only acquainted," wrote Marx, "with the position of a manager in a worker-cooperative factory, all his illusions about domination would go to the devil."[60]

In his introduction of 1895 to a new edition of Marx's address on the Paris Commune Engels identified the Commune with "dictatorship of the proletariat." "Do you want to know what this dictatorship looks like?" asked Engels. "Look at the Paris Commune."[61] Marx also identified the Commune with "dictatorship of the proletariat" because it fulfilled the requirements of his definition in his *Critique of the Gotha Program* and elsewhere. "Between capitalist and communist society," Marx wrote, "lies the period of revolutionary transformation of the one into the other. There corresponds to this also a political transition in which the state can be nothing but the revolutionary dictatorship of the proletariat." Marx viewed the Commune as a "political transition period" in that the "legitimate functions" of the state were restored to responsible agents of society to serve the people, and within this new political form the emancipation of labor could be realized through a development of cooperative production. Thus there was a revolutionary transition in both the relation of state to people and in the economic structure of society.

Marx used the phrase, "dictatorship of the proletariat," some eight times in correspondence and minor writings. Close examination of these uses reveals that it had no other content than that suggested in the *Kommunistische Zeitschrift* of 1847 referring to "a democratic period of transition"—democracy as dominion of the proletariat, the great majority of society or very soon to become such a majority, enacting measures such as those in the Paris Commune to emancipate labor and achieve communism.[62] In 1850 Marx first used the phrase in a brief "united front" with followers of Auguste Blanqui who advocated insurrectionary seizure of power by a revolutionary minority to establish socialism with deferment of elections. Marx, however, always insisted on dictatorship as dominion of the proletariat as majority *class*, opposed tactics of minority insurrection, and regarded the Blanquists as "alchemists of revolution" who ignored historical development of the pre-conditions of socialism.[63]

Shortly after Marx last used the phrase "dictatorship of the proletariat" in his *Critique of the Gotha Program*, he expressed regret that the program had not been able to demand, in view of legal restrictions, a "democratic republic." Only in such government is there room for universal suffrage, direct legislation, and people's justice as already substantially realized in Switzerland and the United States. But in relation to Germany, then a military despotism, such demands would be irrelevant, only "the old familiar democratic litany" and in the circumstances "pretty little toys."[64] This charge of irrelevance, however, is not rejection of those mainstays of individual freedom in democracy that he had defended from 1842 to the Paris Commune.

VI

There are a number of unresolved problems and gaps in Marx's view of democracy as involving individual freedom grounded in dialectic, the "rational kernel" he always retained from Hegel. Marx never explained how "necessity," "contradictions," and "negations" in dialectic can be reconciled with empiricism that allows only contingent, probable truths. He never freed himself from the purely rationalistic aspect of Hegel's method. This aspect of his thought readily lends itself to the *a priori* "trimming" and oversimplification of history he condemned in others. His use of the dialectic of essence and appearance after restudying Hegel's *Logic* in 1858 implied a theory of internal relations that entails a thoroughgoing monism, effectively cancelling all individuality or particularity and consequently any real pluralism and change.[65]

In Marx's projective description of the "really democratic institutions" of the Paris Commune there are gaps and problematic features that raise questions about the workability and relevance of those institutions for a highly developed and integrated industrial society. For example, he says nothing about the connection of the governing assembly of elected delegates with the union of cooperative societies to plan production, nor does he indicate how that assembly, "executive and legislative at the same time," could operate without a relatively permanent and extensive executive apparatus, a bureaucracy, that would at the same time be under continuous and effective popular control. There is the further question of whether the *mandat imperatif* binding assembly delegates would permit majority rule or even any action at all where delegates had widely differing instructions.[66] Many such gaps and problematic features in Marx's view of democracy reflect his underestimation of the persistence and permanence of political disagreement and his overestimation of the unity of the working class nurtured by his use of dialectic. They also reflect his unwillingness to lay out blueprints for socialism such as the utopians he criticized were wont to do. Such utopianism was invariably linked with authoritarianism or personal dictatorship, and Marx always insisted that the emancipation of the working class must be an auto-emancipation, an emancipation of the working class by itself.

Some of the problematic features of Marx's view of democracy, particularly of the *mandat imperatif* and delegation, may be seen as defects of his virtue, as inadequately developed means to his laudable and overriding end, an apparatus of government effectively and permanently "of the people and by the people," a thoroughgoing and unqualified democracy. "Freedom," said Marx in his last major statement on government, "consists in converting the state from an organ superimposed on society into one thoroughly subordinate to it."[67] He persistently maintained, as we have seen, that such an organ is constituted by universal suffrage and unrestricted voting and entails other forms of individual freedom—freedom of speech and opinion, freedom of assembly, equality of citizenship and freedom to hold office, free education, and freedom of inquiry—that he had defended since 1842 as requirements of society's dialectical development.

NOTES

[1] For allegations of Marx's totalitarianism and ambivalence about individual freedom by J. L. Talmon and others see R. N. Hunt, *Political Ideas of Marx and Engels* (Pittsburgh: University of Pittsburgh Press, 1974), I, 9, 13–14, and the qualified allegation in L.D. Easton, "Alienation and History in the Early Marx," *Philosophy and Phenomenological Research*, 22 (1961), 205—repeated in "Introduction," *Writings of the Young Marx on Philosophy and Society*, ed. and trans., L. Easton and K. Guddat (New York: Doubleday Anchor, 1967), pp. 31–32—now corrected in the pages to follow. I gratefully acknowledge the award of a Fellowship for Independent Study and Research, June–Dec. 1976, from the National Endowment for the Humanities in support of the present essay.

[2] *Writings of the Young Marx on Philosophy and Society*, pp. 46–7, 62–3. Hereafter cited as WYM.

[3] See Hegel, *Logic* (from the *Encyclopedia*), trans. W. Wallace (Oxford: Clarendon, 1975), Sec. 81.

[4] *Philosophy of Right*, trans. T. M. Knox (Oxford: Clarendon, 1942), Sec. 260. See "Additions," *ibid.*, p. 280.

[5] "Leading Article," in WYM, pp. 128–130.

[6] See Marx, *"Le Traité Theologico-Politique,"* ed. and trans. M. Rubel, *Cahiers Spinoza* (Paris: Réplique, 1977), I, 44–49, 56–61.

[7] "Divorce Law," in WYM, pp. 137–40; "Historical School of Law," in WYM, pp. 97–98.

[8] See "Prussian Censorship," in WYM, pp. 77–82.

[9] "Debates on Press," in Marx and Engels, *Collected Works* (New York: International, 1975), I, 162, 167, 174–82. Hereafter, MECW. "Leading Article," in WYM, p. 130. A similar defense of freedom of mind on the basis of dialectical development was presented a few years later by J. B. Stallo of Cincinnati, Ohio. See L. D. Easton, *Hegel's First American Followers: The Ohio Hegelians* (Athens: Ohio University Press, 1966), pp. 70–71.

[10] "Divorce Law," in WYM, p. 144.

[11] "Wood Theft Law," in MECW, I, 260; "Debates on Press," in MECW, I, 166; "Prussian Censorship," in WYM, p. 91.

[12] "Commissions," in MECW, I, 306.

[13] "Moselle Correspondent," in MECW, I, 344. See WYM, pp. 143–48.

[14] MECW, I, 362–63.

[15] "Exchange of Letters," in WYM, pp. 206–9.

[16] Marx and Engels, *Communist Manifesto*, ed. D. Rjazanov (New York: International, 1930), pp. 292, 296–7.

[17] MECW, VII, 16, 48, 437, 251; Marx and Engels, *Werke* (Berlin: Dietz, 1960), VI, 339–42—hereafter, MEW. See Hal Draper, *Karl Marx's Theory of Revolution* (New York: Monthly Review Press, 1977), Bk. I, 286–97.

[18] See Marx and Engels, *Gesamtausgabe,* ed. D. Rjazanov (Frankfort am Main: Marx-Engels Archiv, 1927-), Abt. I. Bd. 1, pp. xi-xii; hereafter, MEGA.

[19] "Critique," in WYM, pp. 151-7. See Ludwig Feuerbach, "Preliminary Theses," in *The Fiery Brook,* ed. and trans. Z. Hanfi (New York: Doubleday Anchor, 1972), p. 154.

[20] Marx, *The Holy Family,* VI, in WYM, p. 392.

[21] WYM, pp. 321, 326, 367, 373; Marx and Engels, *Selected Correspondence,* trans. D. Torr (New York: International, 1942), p. 234—hereafter MESC.

[22] WYM, pp. 415-16, 431; MESC, p. 233.

[23] L. Easton, "Alienation and Empiricism in Marx's Thought," *Social Research,* 37 (1970), 402-27. See also note 65 below.

[24] "Exchange of Letters," in WYM, pp. 213-14.

[25] "Critique," in WYM, pp. 172-5, 166.

[26] "Critique," in MECW, III, 111, 100.

[27] See "Critique," WYM, p. 202; Hunt, *Political Ideas of Marx and Engels,* I, 81-82—hereafter, PIME.

[28] See "Critique," in WYM, pp. 183-85, 190 and in MECW, III, 51; Hunt, PIME, I, 64-66.

[29] See "Critique," in WYM, p. 202.

[30] See "Private Property and Communism" from "Economic and Philosophic Manuscripts (1844)," in WYM, pp. 301-304, 314 where Marx commits himself to communism not in its "crude" form as forcefully universalizing private property and establishing community of women and not as "political," still infected by private property, but as "the *positive* overcoming [*Aufhebung*] of *private property*" involving "the complete and conscious restoration of man to himself within the total wealth of previous development." This implies that communism would preserve not only the productive achievements of capitalism and the hard-won gains of culture and civilization but also forms of individual freedom that characterize political emancipation in a democracy.

[31] See M. Rubel, "Notes on Marx's Conception of Democracy," *New Politics,* I (Winter, 1962), 84-5; Marx, "Jewish Question," in WYM, p. 224

[32] See Marx, "The Chartists," *Political Writings II,* ed. D. Fernbach (New York: Vintage, 1974), pp. 264, 14, and "Speech on Hague Congress," *Political Writings III,* ed. Fernbach (New York: Vintage, 1974), pp. 325, 55-6, where Marx qualifies his statement in the *Manifesto* that socialism can be achieved "*only* by forcible overthrow of all existing social conditions" and his statement in *Capital* that "Force is the midwife of *every* old society pregnant with a new one" (italics mine). Though Marx made no general statement affirming the normal possibility of a "peaceful road" to socialism, Engels' "Introduction" (1895) to Marx's *Class Struggles in France* stressed universal suffrage as the proper "weapon of emancipation" in Germany and Latin nations rather than street fighting for revolution "by one mighty stroke." The growth of working class power through universal suffrage and legal methods, Engels held, can only be checked by revolt of the "parties of order" resorting to unconstitutional force. See Marx and Engels, *Selected Works* (Moscow: Progress, 1970), III, 199-203, and a similar conclusion by Marx in 1879 quoted in D. McLellan, *The Thought of Karl Marx* (New York: Harper and Row, 1971), p. 201 from *Marx-Engels-Werke* (Berlin: Dietz, 1960-), XXXIV, p. 498—hereafter, MEW. For Russia, Engels allowed, the Blanquist tactic of minority, conspiratorial insurrection might have "a certain justification" (MESC, p. 437).

[33] "Jewish Question," in WYM, p. 233; cf. E. Bloch, "Man and Citizen According to Marx," *Socialist Humanism,* ed. E. Fromm (New York: Doubleday Anchor, 1966), pp. 221-25.

[34] PIME, I, pp. 72-3.

[35] "Jewish Question," in WYM, pp. 227, 241.

[36] MECW, III, 354.

[37] See "Jewish Question," in WYM, p. 241.

[38] *Capital,* trans. S. Moore and E. Aveling, ed. F. Engels (Chicago: Kerr, 1906), I, 195.

[39] See Jefferson, "Reflections on Articles of Confederation," in P. Anderson and M. Fisch, eds., *Philosophy in America* (New York: Appleton-Century, 1939), pp. 191–92, 187.

[40] "Toward the Critique," in WYM, pp. 261–2.

[41] "Economic and Philosophic Manuscripts of 1844," in MECW, III, 381.

[42] "Toward the Critique," in WYM, p. 263; cf. "King of Prussia," in WYM, pp. 342–7.

[43] *Philosophy of Right* (trans. mine), Sec. 244.

[44] "Points on the Modern State," in WYM, pp. 399–401; cf. MECW, IV, 666, with misleading translation of *Aufhebung* simply as "abolition"—not the first translation into English as claimed—and p. 719, note 241, strangely omitting "Suffrage" from Marx's concluding point.

[45] "The German Ideology," in WYM, p. 424.

[46] *Ibid.,* pp. 431, 425–26.

[47] *Ibid.,* pp. 460–61, 457.

[48] *Manifesto,* Sec. II, end; *Capital,* I, 649. The authorized English translation of the *Manifesto* also speaks of concentrating all production "in the hands of a vast association of the whole nation," thus giving a handle to nationalization and centralized state ownership, but the original German only says "in den Händen der assozierten Individuen konzentriert."

[49] Marx and Engels, *Writings on the Paris Commune,* ed. H. Draper (New York: Monthly Review Press, 1971), p. 233. Hereafter, WPC.

[50] *Ibid.,* p. 223, indirect quotation made direct.

[51] *Ibid.,* p. 73.

[52] *Critique of the Gotha Programme,* ed. C. Dutt (New York: International, 1938), p. 21. Hereafter CGP.

[53] WPC, p. 83.

[54] See *ibid.,* pp. 159–60, 30–31.

[55] "Immediate Tasks of the Soviet Government" (*Pravda,* 28 Apr. 1918) in *Collected Works,* trans. C. Dutt (Moscow: Progress, 1965), XXVII, 268–71. See E. H. Carr, *The Bolshevik Revolution* (New York: Macmillan, 1951), I, 230, quoting Lenin's defense of "the dictatorship of one party."

[56] See WPC, pp. 74–75, 152–53. In his notes on Bakunin's *Statism and Anarchy,* Marx held that such elections should no longer be regarded as "political" because they no longer entail any domination in the economic relationship among voters. When such domination ceases, the state in "the accepted political sense of the word" disappears, or, as he put it in the *Manifesto,* public power loses its political character. See MEW, XVII, 635 and Hunt, PIME, I, 324–25 for best translation.

[57] Marx apparently did not share Engels' view that a new generation would be able "to throw the *entire* lumber of the state on the scrap heap," for he subsequently referred to "the future state in communist society" whose functions analogous to those of the present state could only be determined "scientifically," presumably on the basis of reliable knowledge of "the general and common wants of the country." Engels, "Introduction," in WPC, p. 34; Marx, CGP, p. 18.

[58] WPC, pp. 77, 81, 28.

[59] *Capital,* III, 521; Marx, "Inaugural Address," *Political Writings,* III, ed. Fernbach, pp. 79–80. Marx objected, however, to provisions of the Gotha Program of the German Workers Party, 1875, on producers' cooperatives as something the state, not the workers themselves, would create. Cooperatives, said Marx, "are *only* valuable if they are independent creations of the workers and not the proteges either of government or of the bourgeoisie." CGP, p. 17.

[60] MEW, XVIII, 635; slightly different translation in Hunt, PIME, I, p. 325.

[61] WPC, p. 35; Marx, *Political Writings* III, Fernbach, pp. 62, 272 and CGP, p. 18.

[62] See Hunt, PIME, I, Ch. 9; H. Draper, "Marx and the Dictatorship of the Proletariat," *Etudes de Marxologie* (Sept. 1962).

[63] See B. Nicolaevsky, "Who is Distorting History?" *Proceedings of American Philosophical Society,* 105 (1961), 218-21; Marx, *Cologne Communist Trial,* trans. R. Livingstone (New York: International, 1971), p. 108; and Easton, *Hegel's First American Followers,* pp. 171, 174-80 on Marx's differences with Blanquists led by August Willich in the Communist League.

[64] CGP, p. 19.

[65] See S. Moore, "Marx and the Origin of Dialectical Materialism," *Inquiry,* 14 (1971), 423-27 and B. Ollman *Alienation* (Cambridge: University Press, 1971), II and III, on Marx's appropriation from Hegel of the theory of internal relations, the view that the links of one thing to others are not contingent, logically independent, but constitutive of its nature or "essence" and thus logically necessary. Ollman notes that Marx never dealt with the problems in this theory—the "stumbling block" of individuation and the relation of concepts, "forms," to sense perception—but claims that they were resolved by Joseph Dietzgen whom Marx "supported." But Marx sharply criticized Dietzgen for ignorance of Hegel and said that Dietzgen's *Letters on Logic* "progressed" backward to Hegel's *Phenomenology.* "I hold the case to be incurable," said Marx (MEGA, Abt. III, Bd. 4, p. 519; MESC, p. 253). Further, Dietzgen never achieved a viable, self-consistent conclusion on the relation of concepts to sense perception and on individuation in multiplicity as shown in L. Easton, "Empiricism and Ethics in Dietzgen," *Journal of the History of Ideas,* 19, (1958), 82.

[66] See J. Plamanetz, *Man and Society* (New York: McGraw-Hill, 1963), II, 384-85.

[67] CGP, p. 17.

Douglas J. Den Uyl

FREEDOM AND VIRTUE

On the issue of the connection between the kind of freedom involved in capitalism and the moral quality of society, not only Marxists but also conservatives have faulted capitalism. The two, freedom and virtue, are treated as antagonists. Even defenders of capitalism, such as economists Milton Friedman and F. A. Hayek, tend to shy away from suggesting that the free market encourages moral virtue. Douglas Den Uyl—a philosopher at Bellarmine College, Louisville, Kentucky, author of The New Crusaders *(1984), and co-editor of* The Philosophical Thought of Ayn Rand *(Chicago: University of Illinois Press, 1983)—argues, however, that the only kind of moral virtue that is worthy of the name is the kind that can flourish in a society that protects and maintains the right to a freedom capitalism is noted for—the freedom of one person from the physical intrusions of others. Any coercive means of attaining benefits must lack moral worth, in view of the connection between moral agency and free choice. This is clearly one of the topics over which there is extensive controversy between communists and capitalists: Must a good human society embrace a Marxian or capitalist idea of human freedom?*

Modern political thinkers have consistently agreed that the goal of social action is freedom. Spinoza, for example, states that "the purpose *(finis)* of the state is really freedom."[1] Rousseau's opening comments of the *Social Contract* indicate that he is concerned with the liberation of mankind. J. S. Mill, in the introductory chapter of *On Liberty,* argues that the conflict between liberty and authority is the central political issue. Ancient political philosophy, on the other hand, is characterized by a rather different attitude toward the purpose of the state. Aristotle, in fact, criticizes the democrat who places liberty and equality above all social values.[2] For the ancients, virtue constituted the end to be sought. It is "for the sake of good actions . . that political associations must be considered to exist."[3] The fundamental political choice, therefore, seems to be between a regime that promotes freedom and one that promotes virtue. Are these mutually exclusive alternatives?

I

If a free society is defined as one in which each person may live his life as he chooses so long as he does not infringe on the rights of others by the initiation of physical force, then the classical attitude on what a political regime should seek to secure would seem to be the most defensible in all cases. Given a society whose institutions conformed to the above principle, there would be no

Reprinted, with permission, and revised by the author, from *Reason Papers* No. 5 (1979). Copyright © 1979 by the Reason Foundation, Santa Monica, CA 90405.

question of the promotion of freedom. A free society could not promote freedom, because that society would already *be* free. That is to say, that freedom would not be something a society or its members could aspire to. Freedom would instead characterize their condition or state of existence. The promotion of freedom only makes sense in societies that are unfree. Virtue, on the other hand, is something that can always serve as an object of one's aspirations. A man may be born free, but he is never born virtuous. For this reason, all societies are in a position to consider the promotion of virtue. Free societies can seek to maintain their freedom, but freedom will not serve as a further goal for the members of that society. The answer given by the ancients to the question of what constitutes the central social goal is, therefore, a most profound one; for, unlike the goal of freedom, virtue is an ever-present concern even in an ideally free society.

It might be objected that people always desire to purge themselves of such social burdens as poverty, disease, and ignorance. We desire to be free of these burdens; and since actions must be taken to achieve this type of freedom, freedom can be promoted in a free society. This objection, however, is not without difficulties. In the first place, it is true that the relief of poverty, disease, and ignorance can serve as goals in any society. Yet freedom conceived in terms of the relief of burdens cannot be a primary sense of freedom. The mere aspiration to relieve certain burdens implies nothing about the context in which those burdens are to be relieved. That is to say, such aspirations would be present in any social context whether the society was rich, poor, politically repressive, politically liberal, etc. And since the aspiration to relieve certain burdens is present in any (actual) society, the criterion of relieving burdens cannot serve as the most essential standard for distinguishing a free from an unfree society. Thus one is compelled to search for a more fundamental conception of freedom that will set the context for legitimizing any secondary senses of freedom. One must be able to claim, in other words, that the institutional arrangements of a society (in which particular goals are sought) are themselves free. The definition of freedom given above qualifies as a candidate for a first-order, or primary, conception of freedom (there may be other candidates). That definition does not suffer from a need for a setting in which the conditions demanded by the definition can be met. The definition itself determines such a setting. In short, the relief-of-burdens view of freedom must be derivative from or dependent upon a more fundamental conception of freedom, since the aspiration to relieve burdens begs one to search for the proper context for that relief.

But suppose we grant that the relief of burdens cannot serve as a fundamental standard for determining which societies are free. Nevertheless, the objection could be re-phrased to read: given a primary conception of freedom, is it not still possible to pursue freedom in a free society by relieving burdens which are admittedly secondary freedoms? This reformulated objection brings us to the second major defect of the relief-of-burdens view of freedom. To relieve burdens requires action, and the mere desire to obtain such relief does not specify the nature of the actions to be taken. We could, for example, solve the problems of poverty, disease, and ignorance simply by doing away with whoever is poor, sick, or stupid. Some knowledge is, therefore, required in order to distinguish between right and wrong actions. Yet once we become concerned with the distinction between right and wrong, we are no longer considering freedom but rather virtue. Right action or virtue can be promoted, but the *actual* relief of burdens cannot. To be without burdens is, once again, to be in a certain existential condition. Actions conducive to securing that condition can be promoted in order to obtain the desired result, but the result itself cannot properly be considered without giving attention to the means necessary for the achievement of that result. Thus, a society cannot literally promote freedom from any burden and cannot properly promote a certain set of means for the relief of burdens without first having a clearly defined set of ethical principles that justify the means under consideration. In some sense, therefore, the relief of burdens presupposes the promotion of virtue—that is, right action.

A second objection to the conclusion that freedom cannot be the central social goal might be that a society could promote freedom by insuring the freedom to *do* certain things, such as obtaining a better job, receiving an education, or having the leisure to travel. The freedom to engage in certain activities, however, is also a second-order view of freedom and suffers the same defects as noted above. The freedom to do X(s) calls for a determination of the context in which X will be done. Moreover, the freedom to an X raises the question of whether X is good for human beings and the question of the appropriate means for pursuing X. Once these questions are raised, one is compelled to search for both a more fundamental conception of freedom and some standards for determining which things are worthy of our aspirations. The latter concern again raises the issue of virtue; for the virtuous person is able to distinguish the good things from the bad.[4]

The foregoing arguments indicate that reflection moves us to transcend the concern with secondary senses of freedom. We must justify that primary context in which our actions will take place and determine those moral principles that establish the permissible within the context. Concern for the relief of certain burdens and the attainment of certain goods must give way to a concern for gaining the wisdom necessary to understand what must be secured to relieve *any* burden or gain *any* good. Wisdom, in this sense, means not only practical knowledge of the means to certain ends but, most importantly, knowledge of those principles that should guide and set the context for all of our actions. Right action is itself dependent upon wisdom; for it would make no sense to claim that one ought to do A and, at the same time, have no conception of why alternatives to A are either wrong or less than satisfactory. Knowledge of moral principles is thus more fundamental than concrete moral acts. In the end, one comes to recognize the myopic nature of doctrines formulated exclusively in terms of secondary freedoms.

The promotion of virtue is of fundamental importance because persons stand in need of standards to guide their actions. A society without a sense of its own fundamental moral principles is one in which the members of that so-

ciety are not able to perceive clearly the worthiness of their actions. Moreover, as indicated above, a society whose sole focus is upon the secondary freedoms is one out of touch (or soon to lose touch) with more fundamental
concerns. The United States is today a country that has lost sight of its
earlier concern with a primary conception of freedom.[5] Instead, the secondary
freedoms now dominate the public consciousness. Since the "pursuit" of
secondary freedom is argued for on moral grounds, the interesting question is
whether a primary sense of freedom is compatible with the demands of moral
virtue. The foregoing discussion has argued for the importance of moral
virtue and has also shown the deficiencies inherent in an exclusive concern
with secondary freedom. Thus, can a primary conception of freedom (such
as mutual non-interference) also set the context for the advancement of virtue in society? In the next section I argue that moral virtue cannot be
achieved by the coercive measures so common in contemporary social life. I
conclude that freedom in the primary sense not only depicts the proper setting
for social interaction, but also specifies the conditions for a meaningful
sense of moral virtue.

II

"Virtue" is a moral term—that is, a term understood within an ethical or
moral context. The nature of the ethical theory one adopts is therefore likely
to determine one's view of virtue. Without developing a full ethical theory
here or even outlining one, I can look into a specific moral question that is
relevant to our present theme. The conclusions drawn below should be sufficient to indicate the necessary connection between freedom and virtue.

Given the assumption that freedom ought to be maintained and virtue
promoted (i.e., given the argument of the first section), the question whether
there might be some conflict between freedom and virtue still remains. This
question arises because freedom, as earlier defined (mutual non-interference),
seems too weak a condition for securing virtue. The apparent weakness of mutual non-interference has led many to call upon certain coercive agencies to act
in behalf of virtue or moral goodness. We shall, therefore, examine the moral
significance of the methods used by that agency which puts checks on our
freedom for the sake of the "morally proper"—namely, we shall examine the
methods employed by government. Government is an institution often utilized by those who seek to undertake moral actions. Certain individuals claim
moral worth or credit for actions that employ the coercive power of government. The question under consideration is whether, in fact, one does deserve
moral worth or credit when utilizing the coercive power of government to
perform certain alleged "good deeds."

If it can be shown that the employment of coercive methods can never be
morally worthy (and is indeed morally unworthy), then freedom and virtue
will not be in conflict *politically,* since it will be for ethical reasons that this
traditional role of government will be criticized. Our primary definition of

freedom, in other words, will not only serve to define the context in which other secondary senses of freedom might obtain, but that definition will also serve to define the ethical context in which virtuous actions must derive their meaning. Thus, mutual non-interference will be primary with respect to both freedom and virtue and will serve as the condition that must be presupposed before any meaningful sense can be given to freedom and virtue. Freedom and virtue, therefore, will be seen as inextricably linked.[6]

Coercion can be defined as the use (or threat) of physical force. There are two types of coercion. The first is initiatory—the initiation of (or threat of) the use of physical force. Most present-day governments are greatly expanding their use of initiatory coercion. Initiatory coercion can be distinguished from the second type—retaliatory coercion, or the retaliatory use of physical force (e.g., self-defense). I cannot undertake here a discussion of retaliatory coercion, except to note that retaliatory coercion may not be inconsistent with the definition of freedom given above. The rights people possess would have little practical significance if it were not possible to ensure the protection of those rights. Retaliatory coercion may therefore be necessary to counter the destructive effects of initiatory coercion. Moreover, retaliatory coercion may be the morally proper response to initiatory coercion.

The argument below will concern only initiatory coercion, which has traditionally been considered consistent with a virtuous and moral society. We shall first examine whether those who initiate coercion (or advocate that initiation) for the sake of some "good" thereby gain or deserve moral worth. We shall then examine whether coercion ought ever to be employed.

The notion of responsibility can be considered the central concept for a proper understanding of morality and human rights. Moral consideration cannot be given to a person's deeds unless that person was responsible for doing those deeds—that is, was the moral agent of the deed. There can be no good or bad deeds without actual doers of the deeds; and in order to qualify as a doer (i.e., moral agent) of a deed, one must be responsible for the deed done. Yet this seemingly obvious point has been almost completely ignored in contemporary society.

A word needs to be said here about the relation of moral agency, or responsibility, to moral predicates (terms such as "good," "bad," "noble," "just," etc. applied to persons and their acts). We have already assumed that if a person is not responsible for taking an action, that person cannot be held morally responsible for the act. "Moral agency" is thus a notion whose full intelligibility necessarily depends upon the notion of responsibility. To be responsible or to act responsibly means to be an adult human being who undertakes an action by his own choice.[7] A person is not held responsible for an act if he was forced to do that act or if he is mentally defective or incompetent. By the same token, if a person does not do an act he is not responsible for the act (e.g., when we find out someone else did the act). On the basis of these conceptual relationships it thus seems reasonable to conclude that if a person did not do an act or was forced to do it, moral worthiness or unworthiness cannot be attributed to that person.

Now just as a man cannot be held responsible for an act he did not do or was forced to do, the act itself cannot be of any moral significance if there are no responsible agents performing the act. In a community of sleepwalkers or zombies, there would be no morally good or bad acts. The reason for this is connected to the slogan "ought implies can." In order for an act to be called good or bad, that act must be of the sort that would allow one to say, "one ought to do this" or "one ought not do that." It would make no sense to tell sleepwalkers or zombies that they ought or ought not do X, because they are not responsible agents—that is, they have no choice in what they do.

To apply the point further: if all the agents involved in an action (call them group A) were performing the action under coercion, "ought" and "ought not" would not be applicable to them *or to anyone else not in group A*. It makes no sense to say of those being coerced (group A) that they ought or ought not do X, since they have no real choice in the matter.[8] Moreover, one cannot propose to anyone outside of group A that he ought to take action X in the same way and under the same conditions that the members of group A are taking the action. The reason for this last statement is that one cannot recommend, "you ought to do X" *and also* (in the "same breath") recommend, "the way you ought to do X is by being coerced to do X." The second recommendation negates the first. When one is coerced to do X, one does not have any choice in doing X; but when one asserts that "one ought to do X" one necessarily implies that the proposed action is open to choice. One *can* choose to be coerced into getting X done; but one cannot be considered to be *doing* X in the sense of being responsible for X.[9] This last line of reasoning points to the following: there is something strange (to say the least) about the proposition, "one ought to be coerced into doing good deed X." The strangeness, I believe, stems from the separation of choice from the applicability of an ought statement. Since moral recommendations presuppose choice, the actions of a coerced party lack moral significance.[10]

It is necessary to point out that actions with no responsible agents may have beneficial or deleterious consequences; thus the actions that produce those consequences might in everyday speech be called good or bad. For example, a sleepwalker might aid someone in his walking, and we might therefore conclude that a "good" action was done. The sleepwalker's "good" action is without any real moral force, however, since it is not possible to say of that action that one ought to perform it.[11]

One may wonder why we should ever be concerned with the moral issue. Why not simply seek to produce benefits and avoid harm? The justification for the necessity of a serious consideration of moral issues is a complicated one and beyond the scope of what can be accomplished here. Nevertheless, I did indicate in section one that to focus only upon secondary freedoms (benefits) ignores certain substantive questions that demand attention. Moreover, unless one is willing to claim that moral virtue is the same as the reception of a bene-fit, a concern for the advancement of virtue in society will necessarily be a con-cern for more than the mere production of benefits. And finally, if choice and morality are inextricably linked, it does not seem possible to escape the moral issue. For even if only a few are producing benefits by coercing the majority of people in society, those few are still acting by choice and thus subject to moral appraisal.[12]

Let us now take the case of a prejudiced white homeowner who refuses to sell his house to a black man.[13] The selling of the house would seem to be good, for if the man could be convinced to sell, he should be praised for over-coming his prejudice. The selling of the house might, furthermore, lead to ra-cial harmony, since those who live in the neighborhood could come to recognize that there is nothing inherently wrong with blacks. Let us also sup-pose, however, that there is a law that prohibits such refusal of sale. In this case there would be four principal actors: the homeowner (H), the black man (B), the police who enforce the law (P), and the legislators who made the law (L). Let us suppose further that because of L, P forced H to sell to B. Now if we ask who is the moral agent (or responsible agent) in the actual selling of the house, we find that our answer to this question must be, nobody. H is not re-sponsible for "selling" the house, because he was coerced into the "sale." L and P are not responsible agents for the "sale," because they did not sell the house, since it was not theirs to sell. B, of course, does not figure into the selling act. We have, therefore, the peculiar picture of the performance of a supposedly good act without any morally responsible agents of the act.

It is true that L and P (and also H and B) are responsible in one sense, namely, *that* the house was "sold." The fact that L and P were responsible that the house was "sold," however, in no way entitles them to any moral credit. In order to discover the reason for this last assertion let us draw a distinction be-tween "responsibility-that" and "responsibility-for." Responsibility-that an ac-tion occurs refers to the causal mode which brought about the action. Responsibility-for an action will include certain features of responsibility-that but adds the moral element of whether and in what sense the agents of the action acted by choice. There can be responsibility-that without responsibility-for. The case of the prejudiced homeowner is one example, and so is the case of the sleepwalker who is responsible-that the lamp fell on the floor, but not re-sponsible for the lamp ending up there. Yet it was noted earlier that there can be good or bad acts only when there is (to use our new term) responsibility-for. It is possible to be confused about whether someone is responsible-that an action occurred or responsible-for that action, but these practical difficulties do not affect the fact that we attach moral significance only to the latter form of responsibility.

To deserve moral credit an action taken by an agent must be a good action. The only way any of the actions in the home-seller example could qualify as good actions would be if one were prepared to accept the notion that there can be morally good or bad actions apart from there being any agent responsible-for those actions. I have previously indicated some problems with this position. Since no one is responsible-for the "selling" of the house, the act of "selling" the house no longer qualifies as a good act (though it may well have conferred a benefit). One cannot say, in other words, that the "selling" of the house is a morally good act and one that others ought to perform. "Ought" has no meaning when applied to H or anyone else in H's position. Even *if* it were possible to say that the fact that the house was "sold" was morally good (which it is not), the fact that no one was responsible-for the "sale" of the house means that no one can claim moral credit for that "sale."[14]

The implications of the above argument are sweeping. If someone claims that he or she is about to do or advocate on moral grounds some action for the "public good," and that coercive methods will be employed to secure the desired end, then the action that results from the coercion and for which the advocate of coercion attempts to claim some moral worth is not a morally worthy action.[15] Thus, a very large percentage of current political events do not deserve to be viewed as enhancing the moral status of those who proposed those events.[16] Having offered some rationale for the impermissibility of ever linking coercion to the morally good, let us now see if coercion must be considered morally bad.[17]

From the homeowner example at least two additional arguments can be advanced on why a society seeking virtue would not want to employ coercion. In the first place, to coerce people is to remove the possibility of moral praise from those being coerced. Thus in a society of complete coercion no one (except perhaps the coercers) could be praised for his actions. By contrast, a completely voluntary society would leave open the possibility that everyone could be praised. Now surely a society in which all have the possibility for praise is preferable to one where none or only some do.

But the response might be that if all have the possibility for praise, all have the possibility for blame as well; and surely it is better to have a social order where some "good" acts are enforced, rather than leave open the possibility that all acts might be evil. The cost of not being able to praise all is worth paying to keep us from lapsing into total depravity. While there is plausibility to this response, the response nevertheless fails on two counts. First, a free society (as defined above) will not lapse into *total* depravity, since no act of initiatory coercion will be allowed (e.g., murder, theft, rape, etc.). On the other hand, once coercion is taken to be appropriate in some circumstances it becomes difficult to see why coercion may not be appropriate in any and all circumstances—thus raising the spectre of totalitarianism.[18] This is especially true if those in positions of authority are convinced that the ends justify the means (i.e., that voluntary participation is not a necessary consideration when formulating social policy), for then it does not matter whether the result is coercively achieved or not. It is true that the fear of totalitarianism may prevent a society from explicitly endorsing a totalitarian end: but fear of totalitarianism is not an argument directed specifically against any new act of coercion that might be proposed. Thus each additional coercive measure may chip away at freedom until the feared end arrives anyway. Therefore, the real possibility of one form of complete moral depravity (totalitarianism) is present in the mixed regime (coercive and free). On that basis it is no longer obvious that the attempts to avoid depravity by allowing some coercion is less costly than not allowing any.

It is only apparent, secondly, that we have a middle ground between freedom and totalitarianism in moral matters. It is true that if left free people may not voluntarily do what is best. But when they are coerced that possibility is removed entirely. And since rewards are proportionate to risk, the mixed social order removes the possibility of a robustly virtuous society in favor of, at best, a social order of thin virtue. Coercion cuts off the possibility of moral peaks for those forced into the "actions" they take. Their "actions" are less laudatory than they could otherwise have been if they had chosen those "actions" voluntarily.[19] Thus *only* a free society holds out the possibility of full virtue, and again it is no longer obvious that the chance for complete excellence is not worth the risks of complete freedom.

The second major argument I wish to make takes a somewhat different tack. In order to assert that coercion is good, one must be able to argue that, at least in some circumstances, coercive acts ought to be undertaken. When one recommends the moral propriety of coercive acts, one implies the following proposition. "One ought to act such that the situation created by the coercive action renders the term 'ought' (or 'ought not') inapplicable to the action to be done by the coerced, no matter what the nature of the action may be."[20] The foregoing proposition is a necessary implication of the recommendation to coerce, because of the argument given in the first part of this second section. To give an example, if a gunman sticks you up, it makes no moral sense to tell you (the coerced) that you "ought" to give the gunman your money; for one of our previous conclusions was that moral oughts are inapplicable to persons who are being coerced. Let us carry our analysis a bit further.

It is possible (a) to translate the word "ought" by substituting the word "good" (any other positive moral value term would work as well for our purposes). For example, when one asserts, "You ought to do X," one normally means that it is good that you do X. Let us (b) also translate "the coerced" in the proposition of the preceding paragraph to "the other party to the relation." If we first apply translation (b), and then (a) with (b), to the proposition under consideration we would move from, "One ought to act such that the situation created by the coercive action renders the term 'ought' inapplicable to the action to be done by the other party to the relation, no matter what the nature of the action may be," to, "It is good to act such that the situation created by the coerced action renders the term 'good' inapplicable to the action to be done by the other party to the relation, no matter what the nature of that action may be." The problem with this translation is that the power of the first "good" of the translation loses its force or meaning by the time we reach a consideration of the results of the action. It seems meaningless, in other words, to say that the first action of a relationship between two people is good (namely, A's coercion of B) if the second act (e.g., B's giving A the money) cannot bear any relationship to the moral quality of the first act. What could the first "good" possibility mean here? Does it make sense to assert that one ought to engage in a relationship with another person, who is necessary to achieve some end, when no matter what that other person does, his actions cannot be called good?

In the example under consideration it is impossible for the actions of A and B to have the same moral status. And if it is impossible for the actions of A and B to have the same moral status, then no positive moral quality can be attached to the relationship between A and B. Since there is a *relationship* between A and B, the only way that relationship could be deemed a good one is if it were *possible* (at least) that the actions of both parties to the relationship could be good—otherwise (if it were not possible) there could be no morally good *relationship* between A and B. In short, coercive acts make it impossible for the term "good" to be applied to all parties to the relationship; and if a positive moral term, such as "good," cannot be applied to *all* aspects of a relationship, then the relationship itself is suspect.

The kind of problem we ran into above does not arise if one begins with the supposition that coercion is bad or that one ought not to coerce. It is, indeed, meaningful to say that "One ought not to act such that the situation created by the coercive action renders the term 'ought' (or 'ought not') inapplicable to the action to be done by the coerced, no matter what the nature of the action may be." (We can, of course, substitute "it is bad that" for "ought not" in the above.) In this last case, the entire force of the "ought not" is maintained. One can use "ought not" either to indicate that something is bad or to indicate that a relevant feature of an action may not be good. We usually use this second sense of "ought not" when we lack knowledge. For example, one might say that one ought not to do X because it is not known whether a relevant feature of that act is bad or good. But in situations in which coercion is used, we do know that a relevant feature of an action *cannot* be called good (by the argument above). Thus, whether "ought not" is applicable to coercive acts because those acts are positively bad or because it is not meaningful to say one ought to coerce, the result is the same—coercive acts ought not to be undertaken. The initial force of the "ought not" generates no paradox. We must conclude, therefore, that the only way to characterize coercion is an action that ought not to be undertaken.

So far we have shown the following: those coerced into an action cannot be said to deserve praise (or blame), only a free society offers the possibility of a completely virtuous society, and a coercive relationship between two parties does not allow both parties to equally achieve the same moral status. With respect to the last point a utilitarian (for example) might say, "So be it. The fact that both parties to the relationship cannot achieve the same moral status does not show that the act of coercion was itself wrong." Yet I believe that the preceding argument does in fact give us a good reason for condemning the coercive act. Coercion is a relative concept, a concept that refers to a *relationship* between two (or more) individuals. Since our argument has shown that the parties to the relationship cannot (no matter what) achieve equal moral status, the only remaining alternative is that those advocating a coercive relationship are advancing a type of moral elitism. I say elitism because, if the coercive act is considered good, the coercer has established a situation in which only the coercer has the opportunity of moral excellence to the exclusion of any others in the relationship. Therefore, the necessary inequity of a coercive relationship is a good reason for abandoning that type of relationship altogether.[21]

But perhaps the objection to my argument cuts somewhat deeper. Have I not assumed all along too close a connection between an evaluation of the act and an evaluation of the person? We often say, for example, that an act was wrong, but the person doing it is excused for such and such a reason. Thus it would seem that we have a case where the act was wrong but there was no responsible agent of the act. Moreover, a utilitarian might say that since all that matters in evaluating acts are the consequences, the coercive or non-coercive character of the act is irrelevant. If an act is good, the act *must* be performed even if coercive measures are needed to secure it.

Before responding to these criticisms I should like to emphasize again that my arguments are meant to apply to initiatory coercion. Incarcerating individuals for violent crimes or enforcing contractual obligations are acts of retaliatory coercion and would have to be dealt with separately. By the same token, my arguments are not necessarily applicable to the relationship between children and adults. They may be, but since it is not clear that children deserve the same moral responsibilities as adults, we shall ignore the question here.

Two meta-ethical assumptions stand behind the arguments advanced so far. I shall not argue for these assumptions, since they are not without their own inherent plausibility; and to argue for more would take us too far afield. Nevertheless, I shall try to outline below some implications of these assumptions as they bear directly on the recent criticisms of my argument. The two assumptions are, 1) actions do not exist apart from actors, and 2) the moral order is instantiated by an act of choice.[22]

It is common in textbooks on moral philosophy to distinguish action morality from agent morality. But if the first meta-ethical assumption is correct, this common distinction is essentially an artificial one. Actions are not "writ large" in some Platonic heaven or Kantian noumenal order. Actions only exist when taken by concrete individual human beings. To assume otherwise is to create a dualism in the moral order comparable to that found in some theories of the mind/body relation. In both cases the human person is divested of unity, since an evaluation of his behavior is subject to two different modes of analysis. Thus it is misleading, at best, to speak of the rightness (or wrongness) of an act apart from any reference to the actor—that is, if the first assumption is correct.

I do not want to be understood as claiming that the distinction between agent and action morality is useless. Just as Aristotle claimed that the distinction between soul and body was useful for analytic purposes, so also analysis may justify the distinction between agent and action morality. It is, for example, often helpful in teaching moral philosopohy to ignore motives and intentional choices in order to help clarify and categorize actions. Yet when we engage in such abstractions we are ignoring part of the reality rather than grasping a different one. That is to say, if we focus on the action to the exclusion of the agent, we are saying, in effect, that "given a normal set of motivations, intentions, and choices, action X is right (or wrong)," or "*ceterus paribus,* action X is right (or wrong)," or "*if* we ignore the agent himself, then action X is right (or wrong)." All these statements indicate that the full reality is not described by focusing on the action alone. Indeed, in the strictest sense the term "action" would include *both* the individual's behavior and his psychological disposition.[23]

As to the second meta-ethical assumption, the moral good is distinguished from the non-moral good by the fact that the moral good is chosen. An animal may achieve the good by catching its prey, but this good is not a moral one because the animal (presumably) did not act from an intentional choice. Rather, the animal was directed by instinct. In contrast, what makes any good achieved by a human being a moral good is the fact that it was chosen. Thus, if we take the agent's motivations on one side and the act itself on the other, it is choice which links the two sides together and instantiates an event capable of moral evaluation. The importance of choice to human morality cannot be overemphasized. Even if we infallibly knew, for example, that God dictates X as good and Y as evil, such knowledge would not become part of the moral enterprise until someone chose to follow or not follow God's dictates.[24]

In applying these meta-ethical principles to the criticisms mentioned earlier, let us begin with excuses. The ordinary analysis of excusing someone runs as follows:[25] the act was wrong, but you are free of blame because of N facts or circumstances. On this analysis the act remains wrong, but the agent is free of blame. Thus cases of excusing seem to cast doubt on my first meta-ethical assumption. But I wish to propose another analysis of excusing—one that accords more readily with that assumption. Under the new proposal, a person is excused when, a) there is some basis for questioning the propriety of an action(s) and b) the person's action(s) is found to be (upon further inquiry) morally right or morally acceptable.

Consider two examples. Jones sees smoke pouring out of a window at the rear of some building. He is unable to take a closer look, so he pulls the fire alarm on the box next to him and calls the fire department. It turns out that the fire department was called needlessly, since the smoke came only from an overheated frying pan. In the second case, Smith is walking through the woods near Brown's property. Brown will not tolerate trespassing, and Smith respects that right. He notices an old stump that marks the edge of Brown's property and steers clear of it. Smith was not aware that that morning Brown bought the property that extended beyond the stump and included the area where Smith was walking. In both cases, Smith and Jones would be excused.

With the Jones example we have a case where Jones did in fact undertake

the morally correct action. Jones acted with the fullest use of his rational faculties and on the basis of the most complete information. Had another person
been present at the time Jones saw the smoke, it would have been appropriate
to say, "you ought to pull the fire alarm" and "you did the right thing by calling the fire department." The truth of these propositions is not changed with
hindsight. The reason we may now feel inclined to say that the false alarm was
wrong (though excusable) is because we compare our judgment of the act in
question to propositions about normal actions (e.g., "calling in false alarms is
wrong"). We forget these "normal" assessments are contingent—that is, *given*
normal circumstances the act is wrong. But under the circumstances discussed,
Jones did the right thing. The Smith example can be analyzed similarly,
though we are less inclined to say Smith acted rightly. We might say instead
that Smith's action was morally acceptable. On this theory, then, excusable actions are those actions called into question by their apparent conflict with
paradigm cases of moral propriety, but where the action is nevertheless found
to be at least morally acceptable. All that has been abandoned in this theory
versus the traditional analysis is the unreasonable demand that we ape the
stance of God when making moral evaluations.

Notice that both Smith and Jones were responsible for the actions they
took. And given the preceding argument, moral evaluations can be given to
their acts. This is quite different from the case of "selling" the house discussed
above. There no one was responsible-for the act of "selling" the house, though
someone was responsible-for the act of coercion that caused the house to
change hands. Thus, unlike Jones who could be praised for taking decisive action under limited conditions, we still cannot praise L for "selling" the house.

The utilitarian might still insist that what is relevant to morality is only
that the act be done by whatever mode is necessary to accomplish that end. In
this case our second assumption is applicable and cannot be ignored by the
utilitarian. If consequences alone were sufficient to establish the moral propriety of an action, then presumably moral evaluations ought to be extended to
animals and machines. They too do things which have consequences. The utilitarian however, apparently wants to restrict the realm of moral responsibility
(and thus evaluation) to human beings.[26] It seems that the most plausible way
to accomplish this is to accept the truth of our second assumption. We would
therefore extend our moral evaluation only to human beings, because only
they choose to act according to the standards demanded by utilitarian theory
(whether act or rule). We expect, in other words, a person to understand what
it means to maximize overall social utility and to make the conscious choice to
be guided by such considerations. Utilitarianism qualifies as a moral doctrine
precisely because it attempts to guide and evaluate actions that human beings
can *choose* to make. If the fundamentality of choice is ignored, there would be
little basis for morally blaming criminals but not tornados for evil consequences. Thus the utilitarian must also recognize that the ascription of virtue
presupposes choice.

While the utilitarian must admit the importance of choice to morality and virtue in some general sense, it still remains true that *this* act of coercion by *this* agent was chosen, and the foregoing arguments have not shown directly that coercion itself is wrong. This last point is accurate. Only a theory of rights could show that coercion itself is unjustified, and no theory of rights has been advanced here. But one must recall what we set out to prove and what has been done toward that end. We have shown that virtue cannot be ascribed to those who act under coercion. Thus the more coercion there is, the less virtuous a society becomes. We have also shown that those who coerce cannot lay claim to the "virtuous" consequences of the coercion, since they were not responsible-for those consequences. They may be praised (or blamed) for the value of the coercive act itself, but not the goodness that allegedly results therefrom. Moreover, coercive relationships are inherently unequal with respect to the moral status of all parties involved. And finally morality cannot concentrate exclusively on the act to the exclusion of considering the choices of the agent of the act.

Now since the overall goal of this essay was to show that freedom and virtue are inexorably linked together, the argument that I have not shown that a particular action of coercion by a particular coercer to be wrong carries little power. In the first place, if the act of coercion is itself good such that we can attribute virtue to the coercer, it must be because the coercer freely chose to coerce. The fact that the action was freely chosen only supports my general theme rather than refutes it. And secondly, we have so limited what a coercer can morally lay claim to that the only possibility left open to those who coerce is that coercion can somehow be *inherently* good. I am willing to rest my case on the evident absurdity of attributing any inherent goodness to any act of coercion.

The foregoing arguments imply that the kinds of governmental initiatives that are justified on moral grounds are not in the best interests of promoting virtue in society. Many contemporary political thinkers conceive of their task as one of balancing the requirements of freedom with those of morality and virtue. This balancing procedure presupposes a fundamental conflict between these two values. Yet if the above analysis is correct, then—fundamentally at least—there is no conflict. Mutual non-interference serves as a necessary condition for both a free and a moral or virtuous, society. If this is so, our task becomes one of seeking voluntary means to secure those secondary freedoms spoken of earlier. This is a demanding task, but one whose undertaking thereby enters the realm of the noble.

NOTES

[1] *Tractatus-Theologico Politicus*. A. G. Wernham (ed.), (Oxford, 1958), Chap. 20, p. 231.
[2] *Politics* 5, 9. 1310a25–38
[3] *Ibid.*, 3, 9. 1281a3–4.
[4] See Aristotle's *Nicomachean Ethics* 6, 5. 1140a24–1140b30.

[5] See my article, "Government and the Governed," *Reason Papers*, No. 2 (Fall 1975), pp. 41–64.

[6] It must be noted, of course, that mutual non-interference does not guarantee a virtuous society, but serves only as necessary condition for a truly virtuous society. Once this primary condition is secured, more would have to be done to secure a fully virtuous society. Though I also believe that a society based upon mutual non-interference is more likely to secure virtue, I shall not argue for that here.

[7] The fundamental significance of choice in morality goes back at least as far as Aristotle. See the *Nicomachean Ethics* 3, 1. 1109b30–33: "Since virtue is concerned with passions and actions, and on voluntary passions and actions praise and blame are bestowed, on those that are involuntary pardon, and sometimes also pity, to distinguish the voluntary and the involuntary is presumably necessary."

[8] I recognize the possibility of certain emergency cases (e.g., war) where the context is so radically altered that our above analysis may not fully apply. For the proper attitude toward such cases, see Ayn Rand, "The Ethics of Emergencies," in *The Virtue of Selfishness* (New York, 1964), pp. 43–49.

[9] It would seem that the foregoing could lead to the following problem: given the general drift of our argument, it appears that one could absolve oneself of moral responsibility by asking to be coerced into an immoral action (e.g., "coerce me into stealing from X"); for if one was coerced, one would not be responsible for the act. This case is only apparently a problem. Basically, there are two ways to consider this case: either one is free to back out of the deal to be coerced (in which case one is not coerced), or one is at core actually being coerced—that is, one is not free to back out or change one's mind. In the latter case one *would not* be fully responsible for what one did (though one may be responsible for initiating the situation). The point is that one's being coerced and one's not being coerced are mutually exclusive states of affairs. One cannot have the characteristics of both states at the same time. If one uncoercedly asks at time t_1 to be coerced at t_2, one is either uncoercedly following the conditions established at t_1 or one is actually being coerced at t_2. One cannot at the same time ask to be coerced and actually be coerced, because whether one is or is not coerced is a decision or action one cannot make oneself. One is coerced only and exclusively as a result of the decisions and actions of others.

[10] I emphasize the qualifications made in note 8 above.

[11] It should be apparent from what has been said that the view offered here is not a utilitarian one. I cannot undertake a critique of utilitarianism here, though something is said later in the essay. It should be clear that the production of benefits does not function as the basis of my moral theory. For more on my own view see, "Ethical Egoism and Gewirth's PCC," *The Personalist* 56 (1975), sec. 1.

[12] Some thinkers, such as B. F. Skinner, have supposed that the leaders themselves could be subject to their own legislation and thus escape being considered any more of a coercer than any other citizen. But this conception is simply a fantasy, since if a society has any authority at all (and it is naive to suppose otherwise, except perhaps in the case of anarcho-capitalism), there will be those in a position to either change (or not apply) the rules or at least keep them in force by choice.

[13] I am not arguing in favor of racial prejudice, which I consider to be wholly immoral. I chose this particular case only so that I would not be open to the charge of selecting examples that gloss over hard cases.

[14] At this point the following questions may arise: if L is not morally praiseworthy for the good act he produced, then would he be morally blameworthy if he coerced another to perform a *bad* act? It could appear by the above argument that he would not be morally blame-

worthy for the resultant bad act. If this is the implication of my argument, then that argument must be mistaken. This is not an implication of my argument, however. In our above case with L, H, P, and B, the mode of action taken by L (ignoring P for the sake of simplicity) ends with H. In other words, the following sort of relation obtains: L (coerces) H (non-coerces) B. This schema helps indicate that L is not the responsible moral agent in "selling" the house and that the mode of activity which L utilizes (coercion) ends with H and not B. Insofar as L is morally responsible, it is with respect to H and not to B. While H must "sell" the house to B, B thus has the option of refusing to take the house. Yet now consider the schema for P coercing R to steal from Q: P (coerces) R (coerces) Q. Because the mode of activity is the same between (P and R) and (R and Q), and because P initiated the sequence, the moral agency of P now extends through R to Q. P is thus responsible for what happens to Q.

[15] The advocacy of coerced actions on moral grounds is quite common among philosophers. For example, the following give but a minute sample of the articles available: Lord Patrick Devlin, "Morals and the Criminal Law," in *Ethics and Public Policy,* ed. Tom L. Beauchamp (Englewood Cliffs, N.J., 1975), pp. 246–48; Burton M. Leiser, *Liberty, Justice, and Morals* (New York, 1973), Ch. 12; Peter Singer, "Famine, Affluence, and Morality," in *World Hunger and Moral Obligation,* ed. William Aiken and Hugh La Follette (Englewood Cliffs, N.J., 1977) pp. 22ff; Jan Narveson, "Aesthetics, Charity, Utility and Distributive Justice," *Monist* 56 (1972): 527–551; J. Brenton Stearns, "Ecology and the Indefinite Unborn," *ibid.,* pp. 612–625; and B. J. Diggs, "The Common Good as Reason for Political Action," *Ethics* 83 (1973): 283–293. Most of the arguments put forth by these authors are stated in impersonal terms—that is, they recommend that certain actions be taken by the state or the government. But since the state is run by individuals, the implications of their arguments are clear: those who contribute to the coercively enforced actions advocated by these authors should consider their acts to be of positive moral worth.

[16] Needless to say, the argument above does not apply to retaliatory coercion, but rather to the initiatory use. I shall ignore those cases where the two sorts of coercion are mixed (e.g., when people are conscripted to defend themselves).

[17] Many references to such arguments could be given, but the positions closest to my own are given in Tibor R. Machan, *Human Rights and Human Liberties* (Chicago, 1975).

[18] The slippery slope argument about the gradual erosion of freedom can be made on legal and economic grounds as well. In the legal area, the role played by precedent is bound to grease the slope. Each case decided in favor of coercive intervention by the state serves as a precedent for many other future cases. And since these other cases will contain features at least slightly different from the original, further intervention (and thus new precedents) will be required to draw these cases in line with the original decision. This is one reason why F. A. Hayek is so concerned to stress the importance of integrity in the legal system (cf. *Law, Legislation and Liberty* [Chicago, 1973] Vol. 1, Ch. 3). On the economic side, intervention in the market causes distortions in the market. These distortions must be corrected either by removing the original cause or with another act of intervention. Since the latter course of action is the overwhelming choice of governments, new distortions are created which must in turn be corrected by more intervention. (cf. Ludwig von Mises, *Planning for Freedom,* Libertarian Press, 1962).

[19] The scare quotes around "action" are designed to indicate my reluctance to call coerced behavior an action. Coercion involves the substitution of one person's will or intention by another's such that the coerced loses his autonomy and becomes, in effect, a tool of the coercer. This is easy enough to appreciate in cases where one is literally physically bound and forcibly placed in circumstances that are not a part of his own choice. But in cases of threat-

ened violence the coercive factors may appear more ambiguous. It does seem that some element of choice or voluntariness is present when one is given the alternative of "your money or your life." Nevertheless, the appearance of choice is largely an illusion. When violence is threatened, one must assume that the threat is serious. Indeed, all too often the threat is carried out no matter what the coerced does. Thus the choices being made are on the part of the coercer who has chosen to threaten rather than initiate violence. He may do so because of a fear of more severe penalties or because of some perverse desire to watch another human being beg for mercy and look frightened. Whatever the motives, taking a coercer's threats seriously implies considering the actions of the coerced *as if* they were being executed under violent compulsion. No other consideration is possible, unless we have grounds for supposing the threats to be made with less than full sincerity. One of the reasons we allow for difference in penalties between threatened and actual violence is that the latter allows for no contingencies. But this difference does not imply that we should lessen our judgment that threatened and actual violence are both equally coercive.

Coercion has sometimes been defined in terms of restricting alternatives or being faced with undesirable alternatives. But surely these criteria are too broad, since natural events and everyday social circumstances can restrict our alternatives or present us with undesirable choices. But even if we were to accept some broader definition of coercion than one constructed in terms of the initiatory use of physical force, there is a hierarchical principle to consider. Physical violence must be considered as the most fundamental form of coercion, because such violence threatens to obliterate the very possibility of any form of moral behavior. Thus to initiate an act of physical violence (e.g., a law) to correct another form of "coercion" (e.g., an employer paying below market wage rates) is to correct a lesser evil with a greater one.

[20] I refer the reader again to note 9 above.

[21] If the coercive act is bad, there is still the inequity. But that is just a further reason for abandoning coercion.

[22] Although I believe in the fundamentality of choice for morality, I am not trying to imply any particular solution to the free will/determination debate.

[23] Eric Mack has made a similar point (albeit more formally) in "Campbell's Refutation of Egoism," *Canadian Journal of Philosophy,* Vol. III, No. 4, June 1974. These kinds of abstractions I am mentioning here are common in other areas besides morality. We can, for example, speak of the color of an object apart from the object itself (or any other such quality or quantity). But here again the separation is merely conceptual and not actual.

[24] More detail on these points can be found in my "Nozick on the Randian Argument," *The Personalist,* April 1978, Section I and II.

[25] To be excused is not the same thing as being pardoned or forgiven. The latter acts presuppose authority, whereas being excused does not.

[26] My point remains valid, I believe, even in those cases where some utilitarians (e.g., Peter Singer) wish to include animals in the set of those who may be affected by the consequences of one's actions. But there is a difference between widening the scope of consequential affectations and making a determination of who is subject to moral evaluation. It is one thing, in other words, to consider the consequences of one's actions upon animals and quite another to hold animals morally responsible for the consequences of *their* actions upon us. Presumably we do not demand the latter, since there is no reason to believe that animals understand the happiness principle (and the norms that follow from it) in such a way that they choose to direct their behavior according to those norms.

ANDREW MCLAUGHLIN

FREEDOM VERSUS CAPITALISM

Continuing with the crucial questions of the nature of liberty and its relationship to the social systems under inspection here, Andrew McLaughlin—a philosopher at Lehman College of the City University of New York, who has done extensive work in the philosophy of science, environmental ethics, and other fields—argues that capitalism is an enemy of genuine human freedom. Following Marx, who in several places indicates his distrust of the kind of freedom endorsed within bourgeois legal and political systems, McLaughlin argues that free trade or exchange, especially in labor, gives only the illusion of freedom to those who partake of it. What instead happens is that the structure of property ownership is itself a kind of limitation of human freedom, a freedom within the practical context of which only a certain limited and often trivial if not debilitating types of choices are possible. According to McLaughlin, communism promises something far more satisfying, namely, human freedom, the escape from necessity, including the necessity of the constraining institutions of capitalism.

It has been suggested by capitalism's proponents that capitalism is itself an element of human freedom. What I want to argue is that capitalism and human freedom are in fact, antithetical. Because I take human freedom to be a moral good, this amounts to a moral argument against capitalism. While capitalism does provide the illusion of a certain sort of freedom, in a more fundamental sense it is a system built upon manipulation and coercion.

Two different types of arguments can be offered about the proper economic organization of society. One can try to argue only in economic terms, suppressing moral considerations as much as possible. (However, no purely "economic" argument on this issue can wholly avoid some value commitments.) Alternatively, one can focus upon moral issues, discussing economic issues briefly and only in passing. Ideally, both the moral and the economic aspects need to be considered, but this would necessitate a very lengthy discussion. The reason why *both* the moral and the economic dimensions of economic organization need to be considered is that while it would be foolish to try to adopt the morally best economic system if it were economically impossible, it would be impossible to justify adopting an economic organization that, though feasible, was morally worse than other available alternatives. Fortunately, it is possible to short-circuit some of the difficult questions of economics by noting the fact of abundance in contemporary post-industrial societies. I want to briefly show why I think that this fact allows one to sidestep the economic questions involved in assessing capitalism.

Reprinted from Dorothy Buckton James, ed., *Outside, Looking In: Critiques of American Policies and Institutions, Left and Right* (New York: Harper & Row, Publishers, Inc.). Copyright © 1972 by Dorothy Buckton James. By permission of Harper & Row, Publishers, Inc.

The economic case for capitalism might be made along the following lines. It has been claimed by some that capitalism is the most efficient mode of economic organization—meaning roughly that the capitalist mode of organization is the one that produces the most economic goods. Now such an argument contains a hidden moral premise concerning the unlimited desirability of economic goods so that it is not "purely" an economic argument. To do justice to this and other economic arguments for and against capitalism raises some difficult questions. To mention only one, what precisely is capitalism? Some theorists equate "true" capitalism with an economic system that has large numbers of relatively small independent producers and consumers and a relatively weak government that does not significantly interfere in the economy. Such a system was reasonably descriptive of some economics in the nineteenth century. However, modern capitalist systems bear little resemblance to that image, because they are typically composed of large producers who can significantly control market conditions. Moreover, governments often attempt to manipulate the economy. Some theorists see this system as capitalism. Which of these two quite different economic systems is to be called capitalism is not an easy question. What does seem clear is that modern technology is conducive to the development of relatively large productive organizations.[1] Whether technology *requires* economic organizations with gigantic corporations is a subject involving difficult questions concerning the nature of technology.[2] Hence, it is unclear whether it is possible to return to nineteenth century capitalism, even if that were desirable. This is but one of the issues that would have to be faced if a wholesale appraisal of the economic arguments concerning capitalism were to be undertaken.

However, as suggested above, the difficult economic arguments can be sidestepped if the fact of economic abundance is granted. It seems clear to me that whatever may be the pressing problems of today, they do not include the problem of economic efficiency. By this I mean that it is no longer necessary to worry about producing the *maximum* or anything near the maximum amount of material goods. Man's productive capacity has developed to the point that it simply is not plausible to claim that morally objectionable social systems must be supported in order for man to produce the material goods necessary for survival—or even the "good life," unless "goodness" is equated with the maximum of material goods. This does not mean that capitalism is not justified. Rather it only shifts the question from one of economics to one of morality. The growth of man's productive capacity widens his options as to economic organization so that what once may have been necessary now becomes a matter for human decision. If capitalism is morally acceptable, then its alleged economic efficiency is fine, but if capitalism is morally objectionable, then given the abundance of material goods, the economic argument becomes irrelevant.

The claim that economic abundance is a fact might be contested. One could point to poverty, both within the United States and worldwide, as evidence that scarcity is still a profound problem. Without pursuing this issue fully, two questions need to be raised about poverty. First, it is obvious that one way poverty could be greatly reduced, if not eliminated, would simply be to redistribute wealth from the rich to the poor. Of course, radical social change and the redistribution of political power are necessary steps toward achieving such a redistribution in the United States. Secondly, what constitutes "poverty" is very much dependent upon the way society is organized and it may be that poverty can be eliminated by simply reorganizing society. An example might make this point clearer. Generally, in the United States a family that could not afford a car would be considered poor. Given the prevailing structure of society, a car is often desirable or necessary because mass transit is inadequate. However, if mass transportation were adequate, then much of the necessity for a car would disappear. Nevertheless, there would still be times when one wanted to go someplace that was not served by mass transit. It is possible to imagine a society that simply provided public cars (built to last, not to become obsolete) located near population centers that were available for use by anyone who needed them. It is true that such a plan would be contrary to the interests of automobile manufacturers, but the benefits for others would be enormous. Life in cities would be greatly enhanced. People would not have to spend so much time working to pay off their cars, nor would they have to spend as much time on an assembly line making the cars. Yet people would still be able to travel when they wanted to. Of course it is obvious that such a transit system would require a radical social change away from capitalism, but notice that such a change would result in the elimination of poverty (at least as far as cars go) while requiring *less* human labor. The general point I am making is that poverty and its causes can be seen as resting within a social context. The amount of material production that is required within capitalism to eliminate poverty is far greater than that required to eliminate poverty within a more humanely organized economic system. This indicates that we may well be in a time of economic abundance right now, and that radical social change rather than increased material production is the solution for poverty. Considerations such as these indicate that economic abundance is a fact—and that fact frees us to appraise economic systems in terms of their moral worth, rather than in terms of alleged "economic necessity."

THE CAPITALIST IDEA OF FREEDOM

Rather than attempt to canvass all the possible moral arguments concerning capitalism, it may be more interesting to look simply at the argument that relates capitalism to human freedom. The basic moral argument put forward for capitalism is that capitalism is itself an essential element of human freedom and, moreover, that such an economic system preserves other dimensions of freedom. Now because I take freedom to be a fundamental human value, if capitalism were an integral aspect of freedom, I would be at least somewhat persuaded that capitalism was a justifiable economic arrangement—but, in fact, I think that capitalism is far from being an element of freedom, and is directly opposed to it. It seems to me that one has to choose between capitalism and freedom since they are mutually exclusive. Showing that this is so will involve first a look at the idea of freedom embodied in the capitalist credo, and then a look beyond this toward a more adequate notion of human freedom.

The most obvious sense in which capitalism might be said to be essential to human freedom, involves the notion of economic freedom. Such a freedom might be defined as the right to use one's resources as one pleases or that one can make economic choices without being coerced in any particular situation. That is, a person can consume what he has, or save, or invest. Of course, this requires some modification since not *every* use of resources will be permitted by the capitalist. For example, capitalist theorists do not grant such rights as the right to form monopolies, or break valid contracts. Milton Friedman and others argue that it is the mechanism of the marketplace in capitalism that translates this freedom into effective social coordination.[3] The freedom involved here is simply the freedom to decline to enter into any particular transaction. The preservation of this freedom is claimed to insure the absence of coercion:

The consumer is protected from coercion by the seller because of the presence of other sellers with whom he can deal. The seller is protected from coercion by the consumer because of other consumers to whom he can sell. The employee is protected from coercion by the employer because of other employers for whom he can work, and so on.[4]

Whether these conditions are significantly present in contemporary capitalism is questionable in the extreme.[5] But present or not, there is a conception of freedom implicit within capitalist ideology that calls for examination. The essential notion of freedom seems to be that a person is free if he is not coerced. This notion of freedom can be applied in all realms, not just the economic. Thus, political freedom, too, can be defined as the absence of coercion in the political realm.

It is important to distinguish this conception of freedom (which is not unique to Freidman) from some of his other views. He thinks that the justifiable role of government is quite narrow, ruling out tariffs, rent controls, minimum wage laws, compulsory old-age insurance, licensing of professions, conscription, national parks or publicly owned toll roads from the realm of legitimate governmental activity. Not all who espouse the fundamental idea of freedom as simply the absence of coercion take such a narrow view of the role of the government. Thus many capitalist theorists think that the government has a responsibility to manipulate the economy to achieve the possibly incompatible goals of the reduction of inflation, full employment and economic growth. But what unites these "left-wing" capitalists and "right-wing" capitalists such as Friedman is the belief that the notion of human freedom can be adequately developed by reference to the absence of overt coercion. This general definition of freedom has been called "negative freedom" which means that a person is free if he is not coerced and "coercion implies the deliberate interference of other human beings within the area in which I could act."[6]

Essentially, then, the ideal of freedom as envisioned by capitalism is one in which a person can do as he pleases without interference by other people. But, of course, all such theorists recognize that *some* constraints must be imposed upon individuals. The traditional suggestion is that a person's actions must be limited to the extent that he cannot take away from other people's freedom to act. Exactly where such a line is to be found is a sticky problem, but one upon which we need not dwell here. The general idea is that one may have to surrender some freedom to act in order to have a viable society. How much freedom and what sorts of actions must be curtailed depend upon empirical questions as to the probable consequences of allowing various sorts of actions to be permitted within society. Berlin states the position of proponents of this sort of freedom well:

Most modern liberals, at their most consistent, want a situation in which as many individuals as possible can realize as many of their ends as possible, without assessment of the values of these ends as such, save in so far as they may frustrate the purposes of others. They wish the frontiers between individuals or groups of men to be drawn solely with a view to preventing collisions between human purposes, all of which must be considered to be equally ultimate, uncriticizable ends in themselves.[7]

This position coincides nicely with Friedman's claim that a free competitive capitalist economy achieves well the goal of giving "people what they want instead of what a particular group thinks they ought to want."[8] This is both the major moral argument for capitalism and a sketch of the ideal of freedom embodied in such an argument, but that ideal needs serious examination. To do this it is first necessary to digress a bit and examine the idea of human choice.

THE DIMENSIONS OF HUMAN CHOICE

One fruitful way of looking at human choice is to separate the choice situation into an objective aspect and a subjective aspect. By the objective aspect, I am referring to the range of alternatives that an agent finds available to him. By the subjective aspect, I am referring to the agent himself, his desires, wants, values, etc. Now a choice can be seen as the result of the interaction between the objective and subjective aspects of the choice situation. What the capitalist idea of human freedom claims is that a person's choice is free (or not coerced) if there is no compulsion by some other person to choose one particular alternative. This view of human freedom is seriously inadequate and overlooks essential elements that must be present in a choice situation before it can really be called free.

In a choice situation a person surveys the alternatives open to him and elects that alternative which best (or adequately) suits him. Which alternative suits him depends importantly upon the subjective element such as his goals, desires, and values. Obviously, it also depends importantly upon what alternatives are available to him. Now one way of coercing someone is to simply structure the situation so that he has only one alternative. One could do this by threatening him with disastrous results (punishment) if he fails to elect the option desired by the coercer. To restrict a person's range of alternatives down to only one option constitutes the extreme case of coercion and coercion can be covertly accomplished by systematically structuring alternatives.

It is possible to deny that even in the most extreme of cases, such as the presence of the threat of death, that a person is not "free." For even the threat of death does not eliminate alternatives—but only substitutes the alternative of death for all but the oppressor's desired alternative. If merely the presence of options implies that the agent is free, then the political prisoner (given the option of death or confession) is still "free." Such a notion of freedom, while of interest to existentialists in analysing the nature of the human situation, has little relevance to the question of economic or political freedom, because we surely want to have a notion of freedom where sometimes people are free and sometimes they are not. But if freedom is taken to be merely the presence of options, then we are always free. Even where there are no "objective" options—such as the prisoner's situation when he is about to be executed—people still have the "option" of the mental attitude they decide to take toward their situation. Such attitudes themselves can become objects of choice—and this means that if freedom is simply the presence of options, everyone is always free, and always will be, at least until there are attitude-determining chemicals that can coerce the mind as effectively as bullets can coerce the body. The upshot is that the mere presence of alternatives is not sufficient to indicate that a person is free.

In the schema of choice that I have adopted here, the capitalist's notion of freedom is that if the range of alternatives is not restricted by other agents, then a person is free. Of course, there is a recognition that there are degrees of freedom and that the necessities of the social system may require that some alternatives be foreclosed, e.g., by attaching punishments to certain types of actions. But it remains true that the essence of the capitalist ideal of freedom is simply that whatever alternatives exist, the degree to which people are free is solely a function of whether other humans prevent an agent from pursuing the alternative of his choice.

What is totally missing in this analysis of freedom is a critical analysis of the types of alternatives open to the agent. This aspect of choice is simply taken for granted by the capitalist and he does not hold up for criticism the ranges of actions open to each individual—yet such a consideration of the types of alternatives is essential in any adequate idea of human freedom. Perhaps this point can be made clearer by looking at one type of coercion that is wholly overlooked by the capitalist idea of freedom.

SYSTEMATIC COERCION

Overt coercion seems fairly unproblematic to define. Someone is coerced when he is threatened with injury unless he acts in some particular way, or refrains from some particular action. But there is another type of coercion that is probably much more important in understanding the degree of freedom within a society. It is extremely difficult to run a society simply on the basis of overt coercion. To do so would require a policeman at every corner and if a society really required that many policemen, it is likely that it would be upon the verge of dissolution. Most forms of social control are much less obvious. Thus, the forces of social pressure, in a small face-to-face community can function much more effectively than can overt coercion, except in extreme cases. Now one important type of coercion involves *the systematic structuring of alternatives that the individual faces in a choice situation.* It is the nature of the alternatives available that is neglected by the capitalist ideal of freedom, yet this is an exceedingly important aspect of coercion. An example may make the nature of this form of coercion clearer.

The following passages are quoted from an *official* Selective Service document entitled "Channeling":

While the best known purpose of Selective Service is to procure manpower for the armed forces, a variety of related processes take place outside of delivery of manpower to the active armed forces. Many of these may be put under the heading of "channeling manpower." Many young men would not have pursued a higher education if there had not been a program of student deferment. Many young scientists, engineers, tool and die makers, and other possessors of scarce skills would not remain in their jobs in the defense effort if it were not for a program of occupational deferments. . . .

The club of induction has been used to drive out of areas considered to be less important to the areas of greater importance in which deferments were given, the individuals who did not or could not participate in activities which were considered essential to the defense of the nation. . . .

Since occupational deferments are granted for no more than one year at a time, a process of periodically receiving current information and repeated review assures that every deferred registrant continues to contribute to the overall national good. This reminds him of the basis for his deferment. . . .

The psychology of granting wide choice under pressure to take action is the American or indirect way of achieving what is done by direction in foreign countries where choice is not permitted. Here, choice is limited but not denied, and it is fundamental that an individual generally applies himself better to something he has decided to do rather than something he has been told to do. . . .

Delivery of manpower for induction, the process of providing a few thousand men with transportation to a reception center, is not much of an administrative or financial challenge. It is in dealing with the other millions of registrants that the system is heavily occupied, developing more effective human beings in the national interest.[9]

A lot of interesting points are made in this document, such as the idea of indirect pressure being more effective as a means of social control than direct pressure. But the essential point to note is that "channeling" is simply a way of

coercing people into various activities by structuring the nature of the alternatives available to them. Such coercion, while not overt and readily visible, *is*
coercion—systematic coercion. Now I do not mean to suggest that such systematic coercion is wholly avoidable—social control is, at least until we develop a wholly voluntary community, simply necessary. What I want to
emphasize very strongly is that any analysis of human freedom must recognize
that systematic coercion is just as real a form of coercion as a club. But if this is
so, this means that an adequate appraisal of how free a person is must involve
looking critically at the range of alternatives that he faces. It is in refusing to
face up to this question that the capitalist idea of freedom shows its inade-
quacy. And, moreover, it is apparent why the capitalist does not focus upon
this dimension of freedom. If he were to look at this dimension, it would become apparent that different social classes have, in fact, widely divergent ranges
of alternatives in their choice situations. The alternatives available to the
worker and those open to the owner are widely divergent. Yet the capitalist
idea of freedom would lead one to believe that the worker and the capitalist are
equally free, because they both can make their choices without overt coercion.
But to call them equally free is to take an important ideal—human freedom—
and twist it into a tacit defense of capitalism.

Marx remarks in the first volume of *Das Capital* that the capitalist needs
"free laborers,"—that is, those who are free in a double sense. First they are free
from the constraints of feudalism with the traditional obligations that prohibit
the worker from changing employers. That is, the system of capitalism requires
that workers can go from one employer to another. *This* is the only sort of
freedom envisioned by Friedman when he touts the freedom of competitive
capitalism as embodied in the worker's freedom from coercion by employers
because he can change jobs (see the quotation from Friedman above). But
Marx presses on to note with irony that the worker in capitalism has also another "freedom." "Free workers" are also free in the sense that they are "free
from, unencumbered by, any means of production of their own." The point he
is making is simply that workers under capitalism find themselves with options
as to whom to work for, but they *are* forced to work. They *must* hire themselves out to those who own the means of production. Their range of alternatives simply is narrowed by the social structure within which they live. And
this must be seen as an important dimension of unfreedom under capitalism.
Moreover, as I will suggest below, to eliminate this form of "unfreedom" in
capitalism would require its abolition.

The essential point that is worth emphasis is that it is not enough to look
at a choice and to decide that it is free if it is not a result of overt coercion.
One must also call into question the nature of the alternatives that are present
within a choice situation. And to talk of meaningful freedom for a person requires that the range of alternatives he can select must be judged adequate.
Human freedom involves much more than simply the absence of overt coercion. While this is one element of freedom, another is the absence of what I
have called systematic coercion. Whether this form of coercion can be wholly

eliminated is a question that requires constructing alternative forms of society and seeing whether they are possible. Rather than trying to do justice to such a vast subject here, let me briefly indicate the direction in which any social system must move if it seriously wants to enhance the realm of freedom through the reduction of systematic coercion.

Any choice that involves ceasing to survive as one of its real alternatives cannot be a free choice, because the choice between labor and starvation is not a free choice. It is not a free choice because the presence of one alternative—death—is such as to *require* the agent to elect one of the other alternatives, and this requirement introduces the objectionable element of coercion. Thus, it would seem that to provide really free choices between alternatives, one must insure that the agent is not only free to elect one of the proffered options, *but is also free to walk away from the deal altogether.* This means that free choices cannot obtain where the question of survival is involved. Consequently, the range of human freedom can be greatly extended by insuring that all have the means for survival. This means that providing the means for the satisfaction of all survival needs is a prerequisite for providing the genuine possibility for human freedom, in the sense under discussion. To a large extent, providing for survival needs eliminates the element of systematic coercion from a social system. The line between survival needs and what might be called psychic needs is not sharply defined. However, the absence of sharp boundaries does not mean that there are no boundaries, and what counts as an item necessary for survival in any given society can be decided with some precision.

The question now arises whether it is feasible under capitalism to provide a reasonable life for every human being, whether or not he has functioned effectively within the economic system. The range of alternatives offered under capitalism for those who do not choose one of the socially defined "productive" alternatives is quite small. Unemployment insurance is only a temporary means of support when a worker has been fired and can find no other suitable job. Hence, this is not really a viable alternative. The various welfare programs do not even come close to providing what amounts to an adequate living. Hence, they are not viable choices, although they are an alternative into which many find themselves forced. The only ones who do voluntarily choose welfare as a means of life are those who have resigned themselves to voluntary poverty and find a suitable life-style. These people have created a viable option out of welfare by changing their own aspirations and values (the subjective dimension of choice) sufficiently to survive on welfare allotments. Indeed, these people—the voluntary dropouts—constitute a significant threat to the capitalist system, in pointing out an alternative life-style. But I want to defer discussion of the subjective aspect of the choice situation for the moment. In essence, the basic coercion on which the capitalist system operates is the necessity to enter into the economy in some way. There are, of course, other coercions (exemplified by channeling) but the basic one is to enter in some way into the market system and earn a living—or else live a life of poverty.

This point might be brushed aside on the ground that the necessity for human labor is a characteristic of the human situation and does not really constitute a basis for objecting to capitalism. The mere fact that to live one must survive, and survival requires labor, is the element of coercion and this is common to all economic systems. There is some force to this objection because it is true that labor is necessary for survival. Nevertheless, it is first important to recognize that this *is* a constraint upon the range of alternatives available to man. Recognition of this fact leads to the idea that freedom really requires the abolition of labor. Consequently, to move toward reducing required labor is to move toward freedom. Absolute freedom *might* not be possible, but the direction toward increasing freedom is clear. Yet capitalism and its image of freedom entirely obscures this.

A second and more important reply that lessens the force of the objection is that capitalism does nothing to diminish this element of systematic coercion and, in fact, thrives upon it. Notice that the fact of abundance makes the *possibility* of the reduction of socially required labor a real one. Yet there is little indication that post-industrial society is moving in a direction that uses the possibility of abundance in a way to enhance human freedom. Capitalism's great contribution, as Marx pointed out many times, was that it made the possibility of abundance real through its immense increase in man's productive ability. The simple reason why capitalism cannot utilize the possibility of abundance to increase freedom is that capitalism is based upon production for profit. Profit is made when goods are sold, hence it is essential for capitalism to have an ever increasing demand for goods. This can be met in several ways—by building cars that rapidly deteriorate, by going to the moon, by fighting wars, building missiles, creating demand for "new and improved" products, and so on. But these methods of creating demand do little, if anything, for increasing human freedom. Indeed, when it is seen that capitalism depends upon ever increasing the demand for goods (hence, the possibility of profit), the American definition of the "good life" as one of never-ending consumption (and thus of never-ending labor) comes to look like a definition of happiness that is highly functional for capitalism. Notice that an alternative principle of production—namely, production for needs—would lead to the gradual reduction in the need for labor as needs were met. Thus, under that principle, the idea of an automobile that lasted for twenty years would be a liberating idea, whereas under capitalism it spells joblessness and hard times. The production for need would lead to an increase in the realm of human freedom, as it would raise the alternative for people that they could choose to work less and pursue other activities. The need for systematic coercion would decline and the realm of freedom would increase.

Yet, even if a policy were immediately instituted whereby every person were entitled to a reasonable life (say a guaranteed income of $7,000 per year) without having to work, its effect upon capitalism is not obvious. It might be that there would be a massive walkout from such institutions as factories or schools, but that might not happen. This latter possibility leads us to the second dimension of any free choice—the subjective dimension. The subjective dimension of choice entails such factors as aspirations, goals, values and desires that lead a person to select one of the alternatives with which he is presented in a choice situation. Thus, in the most trivial of cases, a person is presented with the option of an apple or a pear and he selects one or the other on the basis of his own preferences. Another person, given the same option, might choose otherwise and the different choices would be the result of different subjective preferences.

MANIPULATION

It is when we consider the subjective dimension of human choices that the most profound weakness of the capitalist idea of freedom becomes apparent. As previously quoted, Isaiah Berlin considered negative freedom to involve granting that the ends of people (what I am calling the subjective dimension) are "uncriticizable" in themselves. Now this seems fine and is pleasantly permissive, yet an important issue must be raised. What happens to the idea of accepting people's aspirations uncritically when we raise the question "why do people come to have the desires that they do?" This question becomes rather more pressing when we realize that a complex industrial society with a large number of people depends for its very continuance on the intermeshing of large numbers of individual choices. Now the capitalist argument is that it achieves such coordination without coercion. We have already discussed the element of systematic coercion involved in a society, but I want now to direct attention to an even more profound aspect of social control that goes beyond simply the structuring of alternatives. The socialization process is a process that implants socially necessary values, goals, or aspirations within individuals. By insuring that people come to desire what society wants them to desire, their "free" choices can be influenced. It is this socialization of the subjective dimension of human choice that I call manipulation. Knowing what we do know about the ways society implants values within members of that society, it becomes less reasonable to accept uncritically the particular expressions of preference as necessarily showing what people "really" want. Rather, preferences and values must be subjected to critical scrutiny. Man is molded by his society through many modes of socialization, such as the family, schools, television, religion, films, peer groups, and so on. And lo and behold, at the end of this process he comes out a good citizen, active consumer, and having the aspirations needed by the society. Recognizing these facts requires us, I think, to look rather more critically at the ends people have and not to accept them as "uncriticizable."

The general point about socialization can be made simply by noting how society brings "physiological autonomy" under cultural control.[10] The young infant's physiological autonomy is culturally channeled in at least the following ways: he learns to transform the reduction of blood-sugar levels (hunger) into appetite, which is partially dependent upon external stimuli, and the hunger is directed towards culturally approved foods; he learns to regulate urine and feces evacuation in accordance with culturally acceptable behavior; his emotional reactions are channeled to accord with culturally approved modes of expression. These are but a few of the profound modifications we all learn in going from child to adult. From this perspective, when we ask how it comes to pass that a relatively predictable number of people will desire a new Ford automobile in a particular year, we realize that consumer behavior in the market place is highly conditioned. This does not mean that people are coerced into making the purchases they actually do make, but it does raise the question of why people come to want the things they do want. The manipulation of subjective desires is not coercion, but is rather a much more subtle form of social control.

We should look, then, with a critical eye to the values adults in any particular society have. By looking at those values, we can see that they are a product of the socialization process of a society and, if those values are judged inadequate, then this constitutes a condemnation of the society that produces them. In other words, the question is shifted from the individual to the social level. We look at the sort of person that various societies "grow" and judge societies upon the worth of the types of people they create. The notion of the sort of people societies grow and, in particular, the type of person grown by capitalism is discussed at some length by Erich Fromm. He uses the term "social character" to describe the way in which societies:

shape the energies of the members of society in such a way that their behavior is not a matter of conscious decision as to whether or not to follow the social pattern, but one of *wanting to act as they have to act* and at the same time finding gratification in acting according to the requirements of the culture.[11]

The basic point is that societies *do* in fact socialize their members in ways that cause those people to want what society needs them to want. And this means that we cannot uncritically accept the particular values and desires that people happen to have. If those values are not such as to withstand critical examination, we can decide to restructure society to make other sorts of people. In refusing to raise this question, the weakness of the concept of negative freedom becomes apparent. In fact, if we take freedom to be highly valuable, then we can try to socialize people so that they can be autonomous. This is why I would suggest that, in the name of human freedom, we must subject the society's socialization process to critical scrutiny.

The realm of manipulation becomes most important when a society moves to a stage of relative abundance. When choices are made that relate to physical survival, the needs of each person are fairly clear and not subject to much manipulation—when you are hungry, you need food and it is hard to be convinced to spend money instead upon luxuries.[12] But once choices are to be made that do not have any close relation to survival needs, certain types of social characters are vulnerable to extensive manipulation. For example, the insecure person who derives his self-esteem from his relative status in his neighborhood can easily be convinced that it is important to be "the first on his block to have. . . ." (fill in whatever you want). There is a great deal that could be said about the process of manipulation involved in capitalism. Markets *must* be found for the increasingly numerous goods that are produced— "must" because otherwise there are no profits. This means that abundance is a problem, and people must be forever convinced that there is something more that they "need," something that they are willing to sacrifice some of their money to get. New markets are forever needed. They can be gotten in foreign lands (along with raw materials) or they can be created. The American "fear" of body odor helps to sell deodorant, yet it remains conceivable that we could have a very happy world without such a "fear." But, of course, it is quite understandable how, under capitalism, creating a fear of body odor simply creates a whole range of new products. Rather than dwell at length on this point, I shall simply quote from a quite successful advertising executive who is surprising in his candor:

Feminine hygiene is going to be a big business for agencies. Our stuff, Feminique, is selling well. FDS is doing well. Johnson & Johnson came out with Vespré and it's doing well. The American businessman has discovered the vagina and like it's the next thing going. What happened is that the businessman ran out of parts of the body. We had headaches for a while but we took care of them. The armpit had its moment of glory, and the toes, with their athlete's foot, they had the spotlight, too. We went through wrinkles, we went through diets. Taking skin off, putting skin on. We went through the stomach with acid indigestion and we conquered hemorrhoids. So the businessman sat back and said "what's left?" And some smart guy said, "The vagina." We've zeroed in on it. And this is just the beginning. Today the vagina, tomorrow the world. I mean, there are going to be all sorts of things for the vagina: vitamins, pep pills, flavored douches like Cupid's Quiver (raspberry, orange, jasmine, and champagne). If we can get by with a spray, we can sell anything new. And the spray is selling.[13]

CAPITALISM AND ITS "VALUES"

Rather than trying to canvass all the values that capitalism requires for its existence, I shall only briefly look at two of them. First, capitalism requires a competitive individual, one who gets his satisfaction from outdoing others. Capitalism does not run on love and cooperation. The second value required by capitalism is materialism, or the idea that one becomes happy by possessing more and more material things. Both of these values make a person who is willing to sacrifice most of his waking time to either working to earn money to buy things or using the things he buys.

The training of the individual for competitive behavior starts quite young. The typical elementary schoolroom experience is one of competition. The teacher asks a question and the children put up their hands. The children are excited by the prospect of being called upon and showing that they know the answer, but they are even more delighted by the prospect of being able to correct another child who has given the wrong answer. Slowly, the children learn that their happiness depends upon the other's failure. Thus, they learn to feel bad when another does well. This is simply the sort of training that *must* be carried out if you wish to maintain a stratified society with a pyramid shape. The lovely thing about a pyramid is that it is narrow at the top so there is not much room there. Therefore, "success" is something that can only be had by a few. Hence, it becomes necessary to train people to accept that fact. The way to do that is to train them to be competitive.[14]

The other value that supports the hierarchical structure essential to capitalism is materialism. To train people to judge their self-esteem by reference to the size of the pile of things they accumulate fits in very nicely with capitalism's requirement of ever increasing comsumption. Materialism as a definition of the good life also fits in well with the need for some means of differential reward necessary for a pyramidal social structure because material goods can always be divided into larger and smaller piles, thereby making it possible to dole out different amounts to different people. To see this point clearly, just imagine what would happen to society if we insisted that every person was of equal worth and that the good life consisted in warm interpersonal relations, after the basic physical needs were met.

It is hard to convince someone who is committed to the values of competition and materialism to see the emptiness of the life to which such values lead. It is always hard, in the realm of values, to make progress toward agreement when there is fundamental disagreement. Those who have grown up in America have the whole culture on their side when they respond with disguised hate, when they look at a new car with the throb of desire, when they respond to a friendly gesture with nastiness, and so on. Yet progress can be made. This society and capitalism become a little hard to defend when you strip away the platitudes about "individual achievement" and see how that achievement is rarely an achievement of some personally decided upon goal, but is rather defined in terms of social needs. When a person really becomes conscious of the fact that many of the things that he "wants" are the result of social manipulation, those things lose a little of their charm. Hence, it is important to become conscious of being manipulated. This process of becoming conscious of the shallowness and, finally, loneliness of the competitive and materialistic life can lead to new experiences—of the values of cooperative action and mutual affection. And those experiences lead to further ones. What is required is a new learning process involving the emotions as well as the mind—but once that new learning begins, the values necessary for capitalism no longer have much appeal. Once this process of freeing one's self from the values required by capitalism is begun, one can start to see the terrible poverty involved in the life that capitalism has to offer, not only for the poor and the hungry, but also for the rich and "successful." R. H. Tawney's "tadpole philosophy" provides an alternative perspective from which to view capitalism:

It is possible that intelligent tadpoles reconcile themselves to the inconveniences of their position, by reflecting that, though most of them will live and die as tadpoles and nothing more, the more fortunate of the species will one day shed their tails, distend their mouths and stomachs, hop nimbly on to dry land, and croak addresses to their former friends on the virtues by means of which tadpoles of character and capacity can rise to be frogs.[15]

To work through the manipulation of capitalism leads to the insight that one might decide to be neither a tadpole nor a frog. That's a step towards a new world.

In the end, then, the choice is between capitalism and freedom. Only if the idea of human freedom is made into a trivial concept can capitalism be thought of as a system of freedom. It must necessarily rely upon systematic coercion because it must prohibit the provision of a decent life for all, and to provide such a life would eventually deprive the capitalist of his workers. But even more profoundly antithetical to human freedom is capitalism's need to breed a type of person chained to material goods as tokens of his self-esteem and a person locked into competitive relations with others. It is only in shedding those values that mankind can begin to see a whole new realm of human freedom begin to open up. It is hard to prove, but if we structured a society wherein people were not manipulated, but rather were allowed to grow as they pleased, capitalism would crumble. People, allowed to develop freely, would not have the desires and goals necessary for capitalism. The experience of A. S. Neill at Summerhill school shows this. When students are allowed to learn *what they want when they want to,* they grow up to be happy, yet they are not usually the sort of people that capitalism needs. If this is true, then it brings to light the most fundamental way in which capitalism and freedom are opposed—for capitalism must manipulate people into being what the profit system needs, rather than letting them be.

Unfortunately, the problems of human liberation are more complicated than simply eliminating capitalism. I have tried to argue here that capitalism and freedom, far from going together, are antithetical. But simply to eliminate capitalism would not thereby make people free. There are after all, other forms of society that strive to enslave people to the needs of the social system. When we begin to think seriously about how to arrange ourselves so that we can all be free to be ourselves, we find that we really do not know much. For example, to eliminate capitalism and yet leave untouched sexual liberation for men and women would be to stop short of freedom. But, as we know so clearly now, the difficulties of sexual liberation are profound. It is just too optimistic to think that if we only transcended capitalism toward a more humane economic system, that the problems of human freedom would then be solved. What I can only hope to have shown here is that capitalism *does* stand in the way of human freedom; I can't claim to have discovered all of what stands in the way of humanity becoming fully human.

NOTES

[1] See John Kenneth Galbraith, *The New Industrial State* (Boston: Houghton Mifflin, 1967).

[2] For a summary of much of this problem see V. C. Ferkis, *Technological Man* (New York: Braziller, 1969).

[3] Perhaps the most accessible statement of this position can be found in Milton Friedman, *Capitalism and Freedom* (Chicago: University of Chicago Press, 1962).

[4] *Ibid.,* pp. 14–15.

[5] See Galbraith, *op. cit.*

[6] "Two Concepts of Liberty," Isaiah Berlin, *Four Essays on Liberty* (New York: Oxford University Press, 1969), p. 122.

[7] *Ibid.,* p. 153.

[8] Friedman, *op. cit.,* p. 15.

[9] Quoted from Mitchell Goodman, *The Movement Toward a New America* (New York: Knopf, 1970), pp. 444–445.

[10] The term and this dimension of manipulation are drawn from Lawrence K. Frank, "Cultural Control and Physiological Control," in C. Kluckhohn and H. Murray, *Personality in Nature, Society and Culture* (New York: Knopf, 1954).

[11] Erich Fromm, *The Sane Society* (Greenwich, Conn.: Fawcett Publications, 1965), p. 77.

[12] See Galbraith, *op. cit.,* chapter 18.

[13] Jerry Della Femina, *From Those Wonderful Folks Who Gave You Pearl Harbor* (New York: Pocket Books, 1971), pp. 37–38.

[14] Jules Henry has some poignant descriptions of schoolroom behavior in *Culture Against Man* (New York: Knopf, 1963).

[15] R. H. Tawney, *Equality* (New York: Barnes & Noble, 1964), Ch. 3.

Lester H. Hunt

ON IMPROVING HUMAN BEINGS BY POLITICAL MEANS

One of the crucial charges against Marxian communism consists in arguing that the entire theory requires the remaking of human nature. And while Marx and his followers may think that this remaking will come about naturally, as a matter of the spontaneous emergence of emancipated human beings, critics argue that in fact human nature is stable enough so that for the Marxian "whole man" to come about, he or she would have to be politically created or engineered. Here is where Lester Hunt—a philosopher at the University of Wisconsin, Madison, and author of numerous papers in ethics and in the philosophy of economics—focuses his concerns, by invoking some notions advanced by certain friends of the social system of which capitalism is an economic corollary. Can we improve human beings by force? Is a human being such that his or her "liberation" or "emancipation" can be engineered? Hunt argues that while it may be denied that anyone who makes prophecies about the "new man" really means to advocate forcible remaking of humankind, if human nature is in fact reasonably stable, isn't that the real outcome of adherence to such a "progressivist" philosophy?

> *Some writers have so confounded society with government, as to leave little or no distinction between them; whereas, they are not only different, but have different origins. Society is produced by our wants, and government by our wickedness; the former promotes our happiness positively by uniting our affections, the latter negatively by restraining our vices. . . . The first is a patron, the last is a punisher.*
>
> Thomas Paine
> *Common Sense*[1]

Clearly, there are a number of ways in which one might think that Thomas Paine's remarks restrict too narrowly the ends that laws can legitimately be framed to serve. I will be concerned with one of them. It has been said that the law may be used not only to restrain our vices but to increase our virtue as well: it can make better people of us and thereby positively promote—if not our happiness, necessarily, then—what might be called "the quality of life." Perhaps the most familiar statement of this notion of the legislator as a moral educator is Aristotle's:

. . . we become just by the practice of just actions, self-controlled by exercising self-control, and courageous by performing acts of courage. This is corroborated by what

Reprinted, with permission, from *Reason Papers* No. 10 (1985). Copyright © 1985 by the Reason Foundation, Santa Monica, CA 90405.

233

happens in states. Lawgivers make the citizens good by inculcating habits in them, and this is the aim of every lawgiver; if he does not succeed in doing that, his legislation is a failure.[2]

In other words, the law makes us good by compelling us to act as a good person acts. More specifically, I assume that Aristotle is putting forward the following position:[3] To be a good person is to possess certain virtues, such as courage. To each of these traits there corresponds a certain class of actions, such as courageous actions. The law instills these traits by making us perform the acts that correspond to them. This it does, I assume, by declaring what must be done and offering, by specifying punishments for noncompliance, some extra incentive for doing as it says. In complying with such declarations we gradually form certain habits that either are virtues or are naturally transformed into virtues when we reach a certain level of maturity and enlightenment.

Needing a name for it, I will call this model of how virtues arise "the Aristotelian paradigm." Since the method of moral education it recommends is perhaps the most obvious way in which the state might accomplish this aim, I will call it "the political means of improving character" or "the political means" for short. In what follows, I will argue that the Aristotelian paradigm is an incorrect picture of how character is changed for the better. I will also try to show that, for the same reasons, the political means suffers from certain crippling deficiencies as a means of imparting precisely those virtues it seems most likely to impart. These deficiencies should at least inspire caution in legislators who contemplate using it. If I am right, it is in some contexts misleading to call it an instrument of moral education at all.

I will not claim that what I call the political means is the only way in which the law and the state could possibly make us better.[4] Nor will I claim that it must not play a role in any program of moral education whatsoever. In this way, the case I will make will arrive at a less sweeping conclusion than the most familiar arguments against the political means, which always take the form of showing that the political means should never be used. We shall soon see that these arguments are inadequate, and the need to overcome the most obvious difficulties they encounter will take us directly to one of the most difficult questions of moral psychology: the question of how excellence of character is in fact instilled. Such arguments assume some answer to this question and, as we shall see, it is only by offering a true one that the political means can be plausibly criticized as a pedagogical method. I will offer an alternative answer in which something like the work the Aristotelian paradigm assigns to the state will be performed instead by what Paine called "society." As I do so, I will also offer reasons for rejecting a third alternative, which might be called "the Kantian paradigm," the notion that moral education is accomplished largely by means of the student's own purely autonomous insight. As far as specific policy recommendations are concerned, the case I will make will be unspectacular, but if I manage to shed light on the nature of moral education I think no one should complain.

SOME FAMILIAR ARGUMENTS

One objection to the political means is perhaps more obvious and more often heard than the others. A straightforward example of it may be found in the writings of the American anarchist Albert J. Nock.[5] According to Nock, to control human behavior by means of law is to control it "by force, by some form of outside compulsion." Thus it is incompatible with freedom. Freedom, however, is a necessary condition of "responsibility," because to be responsible, Nock believes, means "to rationalize, construct and adhere to a code of one's own." Responsibility, in turn, is a necessary condition of virtue. Thus the effort to create virtue by law destroys the very thing it is intended to bring about. The political means is therefore simply self-defeating.

This line of reasoning poses a number of problems, not the least of which arises from the remarkably narrow conception of responsibility it employs. If this is what responsibility is, it is surely practiced by very few of the people who actually exist in this world: most people do not live by a code they have constructed themselves, nor even by one they have thought about critically to any large extent. For the most part they accept the principles they live by as social conventions; that is, they accept them because they are accepted by others, who have accepted them for the same reason.[6] This fact presents anyone who holds Nock's position with a dilemma. On the one hand, if this is what responsibility is, social convention is at least as incompatible with it as law is. Thus if Nock's reasoning shows anything about the law it shows that social convention as such prevents people from being responsible. Since such conventions are in large part the basis of human life as we know it, this would seem to mean that most people are not responsible and, presumably, that they have no moral worth. Since such a conclusion must surely seem too harsh even to most cynics, it is a good reason for abandoning this notion of responsibility. But this would destroy the argument as a critique of attempts to create virtue by making it legally obligatory. The argument therefore proves both too much and too little.

We encounter a problem similar to the one confronting Nock's remarks in what is surely the most famous critique of the idea that virtue can be created by enforcing it legally. This is the "fugitive and cloistered virtue" passage in John Milton's *Areopagitica*. In it, he says:

As therefore the state of man now is, what wisdom can there be to choose, what continence to forbear without the knowledge of evil? He that can apprehend and consider vice with all her baits and seeming pleasures, and yet abstain, and yet distinguish, and yet prefer that which is truly better, he is the true warfaring Christian. I cannot praise a fugitive and cloistered virtue, unexercised and unbreathed. . . . Assuredly we bring not innocence into the world, we bring impurity rather: that which purifies us is trial, and trial is by what is contrary.[7]

Like Nock's argument, Milton's assumes a moral theory: virtue requires a certain sort of knowledge, and this knowledge must include acquaintance with models of bad thought and conduct. Thus, it is precisely by attempting to "banish all objects of lust"[8] from the community that law defeats the purpose proposed by Aristotle, which is to make us more virtuous. Milton's alternative is the one expressed in the form of a paradox by the "revised motto" of Mark Twain's "The Man That Corrupted Hadleyburg": "Lead us into temptation."

Milton's argument suffers from a rather serious shortcoming. He wants to say, not merely that the political means of promoting virtue is a bad one, but that at least in some circumstances there is a better one. "Impurity and remissness, for certain, are the bane of a commonwealth; but there the great art lies, to discern in what the law is to bid restraint and punishment, and in what things persuasion only is to work."[9] But why is persuasion ever any better than the law in this respect? To the extent that it works at all, it eliminates temptation from our lives and will presumably produce the same problem he believes to be generated by the law. Indeed, Milton's argument settles on the one characteristic that *all* means to ethical improvement have in common, to the extent that they are successful.[10] If it proves anything about the law it therefore proves the same thing about all of them. It gives no reason for preferring one successful method over another. Since neither Milton nor anyone else wants to oppose all of them, his argument is at best incomplete. Those who like it as far as it goes can only use it as a criticism of the political means if, at least, they find some feature of some alternative, such as convention, which compensates for the effect exposed by Milton, making it a superior method.[11]

A little reflection will show that the remarks of Nock and Milton indicate a problem that confronts any attempt to criticize the political means of improving character. It is obvious that social conventions resemble laws in a number of ways. Any attempt to criticize the political means is in some danger of going too far and opposing reliance on social convention as well. Perhaps, as I have suggested, we can only avoid this danger by indicating some relevant difference between these two ways of controlling behavior. I will try to indicate such a difference in what follows, but first I will attempt to diminish the plausibility of the paradigm suggested by Aristotle's remarks.

VIRTUOUS ACTION

First, it is not difficult to see at least that actions (including abstentions from action) that are done because the law requires them as different in kind from virtuous actions. Whether an action is virtuous or not depends partly on the reason for which it is done: to give something to someone in order to curry their favor is not to be generous. When a lawgiver gives us a law requiring some action that was previously not required by law, he gives us two new reasons for performing that action, and it is for these reasons that it will be performed more frequently than before. First, laws that require us to act in certain ways are widely seen as commands issued by a body of persons having the authority to do so, and thus those who see it this way will see the fact that the law requires something of them as by itself a reason for doing what it requires.

Second, such laws bring with them penalties that make it less desirable to omit the required action than it was before.

It is easy to see that neither of these reasons by themselves can make what we do virtuous. Consider the first one. Suppose that I am a member of a mass movement, an admirer of its charismatic leader. One day our leader issues an order that all members of the movement must give all they have to those in need, and I immediately begin to do it. If this makes me a generous person, then by the same token if my leader cancels his order and forbids us to give to the needy then I immediately cease being a generous person. If he replaces the order with another commanding that we fight the enemies of the movement in spite of the danger involved, I become courageous: if he reverses himself again and commands extreme prudence I become something else. Obviously, virtues—and vices—do not change as easily as authoritative directives do. Such traits are what Aristotle called *hexeis,* relatively permanent dispositions to act in certain ways. Obedience can give one a disposition to act in the same ways, but the disposition is apparently different in kind from those that constitute one's character. Obedience to authority does not generate any virtues by itself.

This is if anything more obvious in the case of the second reason for doing as the laws enjoin. Giving things to people in order to avoid a penalty is no more generous than doing it in order to curry favor.

Separately, neither obedience nor fear of retribution are the sort of reason that virtue requires and they will be equally insufficient when they are combined, as they often are when one does something because the law requires it. What is perhaps more interesting is that what we have seen so far suggests that, in a limited way, Nock was right: virtue does seem to rest on a certain minimal sort of autonomy, if not on the extreme kind he describes. To have a trait like courage or generosity is to act on the basis of one's own notions about the right and the good. This would explain why virtue does not change as easily as the behavior of an obedient person: such notions are themselves relatively fixed characteristics of a person.[12] In acting obediently one acts on the basis of the directives of others, which change much more readily than one's own principles do.

The fact that virtuous conduct is quite different from actions that are done because the law requires them is not fatal to the Aristotelian paradigm. Aristotle himself, in fact, seems to recognize the difference between them.[13] But if authoritative commands and the penalties attached to them can make us better persons by making us act as better persons act then they must, by making us act that way, teach us the notions about what is right and good that make us better people. By considering an example, we can see that, in a way, such methods do teach us ideas of this sort, but we can also see that it does not appear to be true in the way that the Aristotelian paradigm requires.

Let us take an extreme case. Mary's son, Peter, is five years old and no more concerned with the welfare of others than most boys his age. She decides that he will not grow up to be a truly charitable person unless she guides him in that direction. She lays down a rule to the effect that he must give his best toy to any needy child he meets. She knows he is a good boy and generally does what she tells him to do, but to help make sure of it she hints that he will be punished if he disobeys. Eventually he forms a painful habit of doing what the rule says. Before long, though, something unforeseen happens: he conceives a powerful disliking for children who have something "wrong" with them. Children who are lame or blind or sick become more odious to him than broccoli or spinach. This odium is in a way quite rational in the present circumstances and is based on something he has learned: namely, that people with disabilities are bad. He has learned this because his mother *has made it true.* She has altered his situation in such a way that people with disabilities have become bad in the sense that they are now *bad for him,* like poison. Even if, due to a certain natural sympathy with the sufferings of others, he minds sacrificing his interests to theirs less than he would have without it, it remains true that they are destructive of his interests. Since all the most powerfully visible evidence he has on the matter leads to this conclusion, it would actually be irrational of him not to draw it. In a way, he has learned the principle she meant him to learn. She meant to teach him that he should act in a certain way and he has learned it. But she also wanted him to learn that others are worthy of respect and concern. This is shown by the fact that she wanted him to be a charitable person and not simply a compulsive giver. But somehow he has learned virtually the opposite of this.

In the Aristotelian paradigm, the formation of a virtue is the formation of a certain habit. We can see now that this is at best only part of the story of how such traits are formed. Mary has given Peter precisely that habit she would be giving him in teaching him to be charitable, but she has not taught him to be charitable. Peter consistently gives to those in need, but he does so with a resentful, teeth-gritting attitude which, as Aristotle tells us, is inconsistent with virtuous giving.[14] What is missing from this sort of account is an explanation of how the moral educator is to impart to the student an understanding, in terms of notions of what is right or good, of the *point* of the activity in which he is being drilled. Any activity, in order to qualify as a form of education, must give the instructor a certain measure of control over how the student sees things after the activity is completed. I have described Mary as using educational resources—namely, authoritative commands and punishments—which are precisely the ones that the political means employs. As I have described the situation so far, the control that the instructor exercises over how the point is taken seems very poor.

The problem remains even if we alter my admittedly extreme example in ways that make it more realistic. We might suppose, for instance, that Mary attempts to impart a rule about giving that is more reasonable than the one I have her trying to instill. But any rule which requires giving to others would ensure that to some extent Peter's interests come into conflict with the interests of others, thus opening the possibility of his drawing the conclusion I have him drawing. Again, we might introduce into the example the familiar fact that moral education proceeds by precept as well as habituation—that authoritative commands and punishments are not the only means employed. That is, we might have Mary telling her son that the point of all this is that others have dignity and importance as well as oneself, and that their welfare thus merits our concern. But why would he believe this? It is true that her—to him—awesome paternal authority helps to make her pronouncements credible, but all the *facts* she presents him with lead in another direction. So far, she does not seem to have an even minimally reliable method of influencing which way he will go. What is worse, nothing in all this suggests how he is even to understand what such precepts mean. Such assertions are not self-explanatory, and this one conflicts with all the palpable facts she has presented him with, since they point to the conclusion that others are dangerous to him and therefore to be avoided insofar as they need his concern.

Notice, finally, that the story I have told does not in any way assume that Peter possesses an ineradicable, natural instinct to be "selfish." I have made two psychological assumptions about him, neither of which commits me to a controversial theory about human nature. First, I have assumed that he has certain desires—whatever their nature and wherever they come from—which run contrary to the rule he has learned. If this were not so, there would be no point in laying down the rule at all. Second, I have assumed that he really believes the rule he has learned. Due to the regard he has for his mother's authority, he may even be quite incapable of doubting the correctness of the rule. Consequently, he believes that he really ought to give his toys to needy children he meets. This is precisely why they have become so odious to him: whenever one of them appears, he thinks he really must do something that is painful to him, something that is peculiarly painful because he does not see the point of it. Though he believes the rule he must, so far, find it more or less meaningless and even, in a way, absurd.

RULES AND UNDERSTANDING

So far, my efforts to undermine the Aristotelian paradigm rather obviously have something in common with the arguments I considered earlier. I have tried to show that the educational efficacy of the law is limited to the extent that its resources are those singled out by the theory I have attributed to Aristotle. It is already obvious, however, that the same resources are employed in the sort of instruction that occurs in the home, in which we make our initial acquaintance with social conventions. The problem I have posed for the law seems to afflict social convention as well. This is so despite the fact that I have applied a requirement of autonomous moral understanding that is considerably less drastic than the one applied by Nock. Later I will attempt to show that, in fact, such conventions make certain other resources available, in the home and elsewhere, which do meet my less drastic requirement while the political means does not. First, however, I will need to describe in somewhat more detail the problem I have posed.

Both law and social norms serve primarily to regulate our relations with others. Both contain rules which, like the one laid down by Mary in my example, propose that we promote the interests of others. Both also include rules that in various ways require us to refrain from doing things which damage the interests of others. It might be supposed that the difficulties encountered by Mary arise from the fact that she was teaching the first sort of rule, but in fact problems of the same kind are raised by the second sort as well. Rules that prevent us from harming others always either require that we forgo goods we could otherwise secure (by picking pockets, and so forth), or else they require us to give up some good we might otherwise keep (for instance, by refusing to pay our bills). On the whole, it costs us a great deal to observe such rules. In a way, they present other people as threats and obstacles to the pursuit of our own interests. Perhaps even a child can see that we are nonetheless all better off if we all obey rules of this sort. Yet it is rather more obvious that he can see that there is another situation in which he is still better off—namely, that in which everyone else obeys them and he does not. The rules are a help if others follow them and a hindrance if he does.

What is interesting, though, is the fact that, while this is in a way what the rules of morality are like, a moral person does not *see* them that way. If he believes in a rule prohibiting theft, he does not see it as an obstacle to his enriching himself by stealing the purse of the woman standing next to him at the subway station. To see a rule as an obstacle is, in itself, perfectly consistent with believing in the rightness of the rule. I can believe that I really ought to stop for all stop signs and yet be very irritated when one delays me in meeting an important appointment. Why does a moral person not see persons and the moral rules that protect them from harm in this light? The answer suggested by my remarks on the case of Peter is that he "respects" persons in a way that we do not normally "respect" stop signs. Yet the rules themselves do not support any positive attitude toward persons at all, while they do support a certain negative attitude—namely, seeing others as obstructions. On the other hand, while they do not *support* respect, they do *require* it. If we are to acquire any of the virtues expressed by following these rules—honesty, considerateness, and the like—we must somehow acquire respect for others.[15]

It appears that any institution that instills the virtues which both the law and social convention can most plausibly be thought to give us must somehow teach us respect for others. What we need, then, is some insight into what this respect amounts to and how such institutions might teach it. To this end, it will help to draw a distinction—an informal one will be sufficient—between two kinds of rules, one of which I have thus far ignored.

So far, I have treated social norms that are examples of a class of rules that also includes the kind of laws the political means employs: these are rules which tell us what to do and what not to do. In all the examples I have cited, they also, in one way or another, determine the distribution of various goods which, of course, exist independently of the rules that distribute them. Such rules, which might be called "substantive rules," can be contrasted with what I will call "ceremonial rules."[16] Ceremonial rules do not declare who shall have goods of this kind. Indeed, they do not even tell us what to do or not to do. They only specify *ways* in which we can engage in certain activities if we wish or need to. We are quite familiar with such rules in virtue of having observed them. We begin an encounter with others by saying "Hello" and asking how they are, we end it by saying, "Good-bye." We make requests and ask permissions; if granted them, we give thanks. If we do not do such things at the time or place which some substantive rule requires, we make apologies and give excuses. As these examples suggest, the activities these rules might be said to regulate would not exist if rules of this kind did not exist. When we say "Hello" we are engaging in an activity called a "salutation" and, if it were not for the rule which says that we can accomplish it by saying "Hello," and other rules like it, there would be no such thing as a salutation. The same is true of making requests, giving thanks, and all other activities of this sort. Further, these activities are important to us only because of their expressive function and, although it is not always easy to say just what they express, it always has something to do with the agent's appreciation of the person to whom they are done. The lesson of ceremonial observances seems to be that others must be approached gingerly and left with a benediction: we must not assume too much or handle them too roughly.

It is not difficult to see how a child can be brought to learn this lesson by being taught to follow ceremonial rules. Consider the following story. Young Paul wants to play with a pair of binoculars belonging to his uncle John. John has let him use them in the past and, thinking that John wouldn't object to his having them now, Paul takes them. But his mother, Martha, makes it clear to him that this is not the way one goes about getting what someone else has already got: you must ask him for it first, and say "please." Paul asks his uncle if he can please use the binoculars and is immediately told he has done it wrong: one says "may," not "can." If your request is granted, you say "thank you." He soon masters these rules well enough. He cannot doubt their correctness, since he has them on the infallible authority of his mother. He even possesses evidence of their correctness: somehow, people become angry and unpleasant if you take something they have, even if they have no objection to giving it to you, without first saying words like "may," "please," and "thank you." If you say the words, however, they are soothed and happy. There are many ways in which one must avoid jarring people's feelings, and this is one of them. He has learned his lesson.

Yet Paul is really in more or less the same position that Peter was in after Mary laid down her new rule: he has faith in certain principles but does not understand them. Why do people have such volatile feelings about such things in the first place, and why do these words have the apparently magic power to soothe these feelings? If Paul had the sophisticated intellectual resources of a social scientist or a philosopher there would be many answers he could give to these questions. For instance, he might suppose that people are proud of the things they possess because such things show that they have the power it takes to accumulate them. Thus, they hate to have things taken from them because it is a challenge to their power: they would rather give or lend things than have them taken, since giving or lending shows that they have the power to dispose of what they have according to their whims and without any hindrance. Alternately, Paul might think that people simply want to keep in their possession as many things as possible, and that they insist on the practice of asking permission because it enables them to say "no," so that they can maintain the size of their hoard. Because he is only a child, however, Paul cannot indulge in such imaginative speculations. Fortunately, though, he does not need to. It is obvious to him that Martha and John understand the rules he has learned; for him, to understand them is simply to know how adults understand them.

This method of understanding rules, unlike the method in which one relies on one's own imagination, can only lead to one conclusion. These principles are related in definite ways to other ideas that adults use, including especially the notions of "yours" and "mine." The practices of asking, granting, and refusing permission are among those which mark the boundaries between what is yours and what is mine. Paul is aware that he need not seek permission to use something that already belongs to him; he also knows that he need not seek permission in order to come into possession of something which he is being given as a gift, or which he is taking in trade.

Sometimes, though, Paul wants to get to use, on his own initiative, something that is not his and for which he offers nothing in trade. The practices concerning permissions make it possible to accomplish this without simply taking what he wants. The use of this complicated apparatus makes sense to him when he realizes that it is one indication of the fact that, in the adult world, people are ordinarily seen as having a *right* to determine what happens to the things they possess: this is part of what it means to say that these things are *their* things. Asking permission is a practice that makes it possible for Paul to acquire something possessed by someone else without violating that right, which he would be violating if he were to simply take it. If he understands this, he can understand the moves in the game he has been taught in the way that adults understand them. By saying "may" rather than "can" he signifies that he is asking that a right be transferred from someone else to him rather than asking for information. By saying "please" and "thank you" he expresses an appreciation for the fact that the thing he is asking for is not already his by right—that it comes to him, if it does, as a gift. The entire activity, then, expresses a respect for the boundaries between "mine" and "yours"—it expresses a respect for the rights of others.[17] If he comes to see and to pursue the activity in this way, he has acquired in some degree the respect for others that I have said underlies decent relations between people.

The kind of training Paul has undergone is a more effective form of moral instruction than the sort to which Peter was subjected. It is possible, on the basis of what I have said, to explain this fact. The rule Peter learned was one of the substantive rules that regulate our relations with others. It was an example of the sort of substantive rule that governs the distribution of things which, independently of these rules, are regarded as good. Rules of this sort always require that we forgo or relinquish such goods. Consequently, they have a certain tendency to make us see others as threats or obstacles to the promotion of our interests. It was precisely what Peter could see in light of his rule that prevented him from grasping what respect is.

In a limited way, Paul's circumstances were like Peter's; they also involved a substantive rule requiring him to forgo or relinquish something antecedently regarded as good. This is the rule prohibiting one from simply taking things which do not belong to oneself. But of course it was not from this rule that Paul learned respect. He learned it from a ceremonial rule and not from a substantive one. Ceremonial rules in general are relatively costless to follow.[18] It is not in itself against one's interest to ask permission (rather the contrary, in fact). This is true even if one knows in advance that the request will probably be refused. These rules make possible an activity which obviously expresses something, and which is quite mysterious to someone in Paul's position because he does not yet understand what it expresses. As such it *invites* him to try to understand it. We have seen that the practice he is confronted with, and others associated with it, provide him with the materials he needs to succeed. Once he understands it, he also understands substantive rules like the one that prohibits him from simply taking things that do not belong to him: once he comes to see others as having rights, he can appreciate rules that specify what rights others have, and that is what rules like this one do. We have also seen that to understand this practice is, in part, to understand what it is to regard others with respect; it is also clear from what I have said that to come to understand such respect under the influence of a certain sort of authority is, to some extent, to come to possess it.

CONCLUSION

It is time to stop and review the argument I have laid down so far, to see what it has come to. Early on, I said Nock's argument has certain undesirable consequences because of a rather extreme assumption he makes regarding the sort of autonomy required for virtue. These consequences can be avoided if one replaces this assumption with the much more reasonable one that one must act on principles which one understands. The political means however cannot reliably impart this kind of understanding because of the nature of the class of rules of which the relevant kinds of laws are instances: such rules, in general, place barriers in the way of achieving this sort of understanding. There are certain conventions, however, which do have the capacity to impart this sort of understanding. This capacity is sufficient to deliver us from the difficulties that I said were entailed by the assumptions behind Milton's familiar criticism of the political means. It shows that not all ways of promoting decent behavior are equal in this respect; there is one that has virtues which compensate to some extent for whatever limitations they might have in common.

What may we conclude concerning the relative merits of these two kinds of rules as instruments of moral education? It is perhaps important to notice the difference here between what follows and what does not. What follows is that, if they are considered separately, one of them has the character of an instrument of education and the other does not: one tends to lead to the required sort of understanding and the other is apt to block it. However, it is obvious that such instruments are not used separately in the world we live in. As far as what I have said is concerned, it is possible that substantive rules can acquire such a character when they work in the context of a whole system of educational means. It is possible that such rules could contribute something worthwhile to such a system, while other parts of the system overcome the bad effects which, as I have claimed, they are likely to produce. Indeed, we have good reason to believe that such a system is possible, because the one we use to raise our children seems to be precisely of this sort: their behavior is held in place by all sorts of substantive rules while other means of moral education do their work. This is how I have described the case of Paul earlier. It is part of the value of the practices having to do with making requests that they enable Paul to understand certain substantive rules such as the one which prohibits him from simply taking what he wants. Presumably, by helping him to grasp the point of such rules it also enables him to follow them with greater alacrity than before.

As I said at the outset, my argument does not imply that the political means ought never to be used.[19] However, it does imply several other things which were not obvious in the beginning. First, even in the context of the sort of system I have just imagined, the political means has a rather peculiar status: if the system works, it is because the other means function as adequate *antidotes* to the political means. They overcome its ill effects. This in turn suggests a second point. If a legislator is pressing for a new use of the political means, if he is trying to pass a new law to instill a virtue that will improve the way his subjects treat one another, it is not enough for him to claim that the actions enjoined by the proposed law are indeed those which would spring from the neglected virtue itself. The measure he proposes is apt to have effects that run counter to his own purpose and they will be overcome, if at all, by a complex system of beliefs and practices over which he has little control. He must claim the undesirable effects of this measure are not too weighty to be overcome by this system. This is a kind of claim which is obviously capable of being false. It would be false, for instance, if it were made of the rule that I have imagined Mary laying down for Peter. The difficulties involved in making such a claim may not be serious in the parent-child relationship, where it is possible to see all the important effects and easy to change the rule if it does not appear to be a good one. For legislators, who in most states control the behavior of millions of people they can never know, they are much more likely to be formidable. Whether they can be surmounted or not, they should not be ignored.

What I have said here also implies a third and more metaphysical point, one which concerns the relative positions of society and the state in the foundations of the moral life. The Aristotelian paradigm, as I have defined it, depicts the process by which virtue is taught as being fundamentally like the one in which a drill instructor teaches his soldiers to march. I have tried to show that part of the process of acquiring the other-regarding virtues which the law seems most likely to instill is more like learning a language than it is like learning to march or stand at attention, and that ceremonial rules provide the materials for this crucial aspect of moral education. They provide the expressive actions the meaning of which the student must grasp. This suggests that legislators in fact cannot originate such rules. It is impossible for the same reason that it is impossible for the law to originate a new language. The resources of the political means—authoritative commands and punishments—can make people do what the legislator wants them to do, but they cannot make them mean what the legislator wants them to mean by what they do.

To the extent that what people mean is not a product of individual fiat, it seems to arise from social conventions like those which govern the use of language. We do not need to have a theory showing precisely how such rules originate in order to know that they are not made by a specialized social organ which, like the state, imposes its rules on those outside it. They appear to arise somehow from voluntary relations among individuals. In a way, the position I have taken here can be seen as a variant of the theme, which appeared above, that virtue depends on freedom. But it is rather widely different from the variants I considered there. Specifically, I have avoided the assumption that virtue can only arise from purely autonomous individual insight. I have avoided suggesting that the individual must devise his principles himself (by deriving them, perhaps, from the dictates of pure practical reason), or even that he must subject them to critical examination. However, I have supposed that he must *understand* them, and I have tried to show that here the individual relies on the social background of his actions. On this point, Aristotle, with his insistence that man is a social being (*zoon politikon*), seems closer to the truth than an extreme individualist like Kant.[20]

NOTES

[1] In Merrill Jensen, ed., *Tracts of the American Revolution* (Indianapolis: Bobbs-Merrill, 1977), pp. 402–403.

[2] Aristotle, *Nicomachean Ethics,* trans. Martin Ostwald (Indianapolis: Bobbs-Merrill, 1962), 110362-5.

[3] This is not an essay in Aristotle scholarship, and I do not insist that this is Aristotle's position. It seems attractive enough to be worth discussing on its own merits, even if he did not hold it.

[4] For examples of other possible ways, see Aristotle's *Politics* 7, chaps. 13–15 and 17. I have argued elsewhere that the criminal law produces an effect of this kind by removing opportunities for vengeful thoughts and feelings on the part of the victims of crime. But this happens by means of a process that bears no resemblance to what I am now calling the political means. See "Punishment, Revenge, and the Minimal Functions of the State," in *Understand-*

ing Human Emotions, ed. Fred D. Miller, Jr., and Thomas W. Attig (Bowling Green, Ohio: Applied Philosophy Program, 1979).

[5] All quotations in this paragraph are from his short essay, "On Doing the Right Thing," reprinted as an appendix to his *Our Enemy the State* (New York: Free Life Editions, 1973), pp. 93–99.

[6] For a more complete account of what social conventions are and how they work, see my "Some Advantages of Social Control: an Individualist Defense," in *Public Choice* 36 (1981): 3–16.

[7] *Areopagitica,* in *John Milton: Complete Poems and Major Prose,* ed. Merrit Y. Hughes (New York: Odyssey, 1957), p. 728.

[8] Ibid., p. 733.

[9] Ibid.

[10] It is worth noticing that, in Mark Twain's story, convention has precisely the effects Milton says the law has. It creates a sort of virtue which is not genuine and is easily corruptible, simply because it works too well in eliminating temptation. The virtue of Hadleyburg is exemplary only because it has never been subjected to a trial, but this means it is only apparent virtue, because it will fail any genuine trial it meets.

[11] Perhaps I should point out in passing that the issue dealt with in these remarks of Nock and Milton is distinct from that of "the enforcement of morals" as it is presented in the writings of J. F. Stephen and Patrick Devlin, although the two issues are connected in a way. Someone who believes in the enforcement of morals could conceivably agree with Nock and Milton that the law actually makes us worse—he might think for instance that, if we obey the strictures of morality because it is the law, we are doing it for *reasons* which are vicious rather than virtuous. Yet he might think that immoral *acts* are so horrible as such that it is worthwhile to debase people somewhat in order to reduce the frequency with which such acts are done. Where victimless crimes are concerned, this may be an uncomfortable position to hold, but it is not contradictory. It is possible to hold that "morals" should always be enforced while admitting that this would not improve anyone's character.

[12] See my "Character and Thought," *American Philosophical Quarterly* (July 1978), where I argue at length that both virtues and vices rest on such notions. I also attempt to show that beliefs about the right and the good are in fact more difficult to change than other beliefs are.

[13] See *Nicomachean Ethics* 1144a13–18 and 1105a18–1105b18.

[14] *Nicomachean Ethics* 1120a30–31.

[15] In addition, respect seems essential to the value we place upon having these rules observed by others in their conduct toward us. It is obvious that both laws and social norms serve to protect the conditions of our well-being—our property, our health, our "territories," and so forth—against destructive acts on the part of others. It has been pointed out, though, that damage of this kind is not the only evil we perceive in the offenses thus discouraged. Adam Smith remarked that "what chiefly enrages us against the man who injures or insults us, is the little account which he seems to make of us. . . ." We read offenses against us as expressive acts in which the offender shows that "he seems to imagine, that other people may be sacrificed at any time, to his convenience or his humour." Adam Smith, *The Theory of Moral Sentiments* (Indianapolis: Liberty Press, 1969), p. 181. A large part of the value of living in a community in which our rights are observed is the fact that it seems to show that our rights are *respected.* It may be possible for the social and political apparatus to secure such observance solely through fear of the penalties it imposes, but order obtained in this way, even if it were perfect, would be hollow and flat.

[16] This distinction is a reformulation of one made by Emile Durkheim. See chapter 2 of Erving Goffman's *Interaction Ritual* (Garden City, N.Y.: Doubleday, 1967). The account of cere-

monial norms in this paragraph is largely drawn from Goffman. See also his *Relations in Public* (New York: Harper, 1971), chaps. 2 and 4.

[17] Paul can come to this conclusion because it explains a coherent system of practices of which this activity is a part. His reaching this conclusion is an instance of what Gilbert Harman calls an inference to the best explanation.

[18] Of course, this generalization has exceptions, but since the activities these rules make possible are important only because of their expressive function, the exceptions can only be cases in which the meaning of the act is one that one finds unpleasant to express. An obvious case of this is the activity of apologizing, in which we express a conviction that we have wronged the person to whom the activity is directed. Also, in some cultures, there are conventions for greeting religious and political leaders by performing intrinsically self-abasing gestures, like banging one's forehead on the ground. In addition, there may be some conventions that some people find abasing while others do not. It is conceivable, for instance, that some people find it unpleasant to say thank you because it includes an acknowledgment that people other than themselves have rights. If this sort of unpleasantness were a common feature of ceremonial observances then, naturally, the account of moral education I am offering would be no good. However, I doubt that, in our culture at least, they are very common.

[19] It seems obvious that such a position could only be a sensible one if applied to adults. It may turn out that it can only be adequately supported by an argument that is not pedagogical, like mine, but *moral*. It can perhaps only be supported by defending a principle like the one which H. L. Mencken called "Mencken's Law": "When A annoys or injures B on the pretense of saving or improving X, A is a scoundrel." *Newspaper Days: 1899–1906* (New York: Knopf, 1941), pref. This is the sort of argument John Locke gives throughout the *First Letter Concerning Toleration.*

[20] This paper was improved by comments from acquaintances, colleagues, and students too numerous to thank by name, but I should mention that Charles King, John Kekes, Gilbert Harman, Amelie Rorty, Michael Stocker, Morton Winston, and James D. Wallace were good enough to provide comments in writing. An earlier version was presented at the April 1980 Liberty Fund Conference on Virtue and Political Freedom. A fellowship from the Mellon Foundation made writing it much easier than it would have been otherwise.

part FIVE

RIGHTS

Capitalists defend property rights, the right of individuals (as well as freely formed groups of them, such as corporations) to own and dispose of property as they see fit. Communists believe in the abolition of such rights—they identify them as part of a temporary system which, when it has done its historical mission, must give way to a more advanced type of human society.

Are there grounds for holding that property rights are indeed vital to human social life? Is there better reason to think that property rights must be understood along the lines suggested by Marxists? Here is where this dispute is taken up first, although it will be touched upon in other essays throughout this volume.

MILTON FISK
PROPERTY RIGHTS

Capitalism is intimately linked to the idea of property rights. It is often believed that there is something genuinely morally and politically powerful in the idea of these rights, in the sense of its being vital to a decent human community. But what exactly are the property rights that a capitalist system endorses? Do these rights in fact embody the virtues claimed for them? Milton Fisk—who teaches philosophy at Indiana University and is the author of, among other works, Nature and Necessity *(1973) and* Ethics and Society *(1980)—analyzes the idea of property rights as it relates to capitalist institutions and explores some alternative notions in terms of which a different, more equitable social system would be supported. Marx saw property rights as separating man from man, as encouraging people to act arbitrarily with values that are vital to society, and as breeding selfishness. Fisk takes the Marxian task further in his exploration of the nature of property rights in detail from within the Marxian perspective.*

A sharp focus is sometimes helpful in order to get to the bottom of an issue. But when there are issues that on reflection break apart into clusters of sub-issues, sharpening the focus can produce a great deal of harm. Important strands of the central problem get lost and a sense of what the central problem is becomes, beyond a certain point, impossible to recover. Where there is a danger of this happening, it is wiser to adopt a more ample and less analytical style of treatment, even at the risk of losing definiteness of results. One can hint at a general approach while keeping the variety and complexity of the issues in mind.

The property question remains one of the crucial questions of our time. It is far from merely a holdover from nineteenth-century radicalism. Yet focusing the question only upon the rights of individual entrepreneurship would make it impossible to see how the property question could remain a crucial social issue. Marx was indeed right to urge socialists to raise the property question in connection with significant political struggles.[1] But what this question is was never simple and it has grown no simpler since he urged this in 1848.

The focus on the rights of individual entrepreneurship has to be expanded in several ways. On the one hand, there is corporate property to include. This is no longer individual property, but remains private since the corporation is not run for the benefit of the society but for the benefit of those with equity in it. Whether individual or corporate, the kind of property considered here excludes what is often called personal property. This relates to consumption rather than to production, where what counts as consumption rather than production is not fixed absolutely but must be determined in relation to the given

This essay appears for the first time in this volume.

economic system. Personal property, then, is not a matter of rights over facets of the production process. Still, the characteristics of personal property will show variation with changes in productive property.

On the other hand, state property must be included. It is neither individual nor corporate private property since, apart from corruption, it is not held for the private benefit of state officials but to promote whatever end the state exists to promote. State ownership has become a dominant form in much of the world and can no longer be regarded in serious treatments as a freak phenomenon. Rawls, for example, is sensitive to this imperative when he tries to make room, within a reconstructed liberal theory, for just societies that are either small property-owning democracies or forms of market socialism.[2] Leaving such ideal forms of state ownership aside, the actual forms provide plenty of room for raising the property question as a key social question. What rights does the state have through ownership in relation to workers and consumers? Focusing sharply on private property would not only cut off the issues raised by societies where state ownership is dominant but also neglect the role of state property rights in societies where private ownership is dominant.

The general approach to property rights that runs throughout my treatment is materialist. Property rights will be placed within frameworks of economic relations. This approach conflicts with the wide spectrum of approaches starting with preexistent property rights in order then to design a system of economic relations that is ideally "just" because it protects these rights. The materialist approach has the advantage of making clear why the property question remains a crucial social question. Things are different if property rights are independent of social structures. They will be valid then no matter how oppressive certain aspects of the economic relations connected with property might be. Such oppression is not a basis for attacking property rights themselves. Hence challenges to property must be due to simple perversity rather than to the understandable outrage of the oppressed at other aspects of the economic relations. On the view I am taking, however, property rights are not insulated from the economic relations but are valid on the basis of them. Challenges to property rights will ultimately come from the polar forces within those relations that are the basis for polar classes. So the materialist approach accounts both for property rights and for challenges to them.

THE PROPERTY QUESTION TODAY

There has been a dramatic shift in the struggle over property rights in the West since World War II. At first the labor movement had the initiative, setting forth a welfare program that by the early 1970s had by and large been enacted. This program amounted to a considerable limitation upon what had traditionally been taken to be property rights. To insist that part of the income of enterprise be set aside to insure benefits for workers, the unemployed, the sick, and the aged was an attack on property. By the 1980s the initiative had passed to conservative governments and their backers, whose programs were a vindication of property. Those who think of property exclusively in terms of control of the physical means of production will not see this as a shift in the struggle over property rights. But following the interpretation of property rights made here, decisions to increase or decrease income maintenance by the state are decisions that, alternately, limit and expand property rights.

Welfare measures have led to a portion of the wage becoming subject to state control, and thus we speak today of a "social wage" that together with the "private wage" makes up the total wage.[3] The existence of a social wage limits the flexibility of employers in acquiring a factor—labor—for the production of goods and services. In a period of crisis, employers as a collectivity cannot automatically reduce the social wage, which they in large part fund. They would, at such a time, prefer the production of goods and services to take place on the basis of a more accelerated lowering of the total wage than is allowed by the existence of the social wage. The conception of property operative here is not narrowly focused on control of the physical means of production. Rather, it spreads to all the major facets of control linked to production. Thus it spreads not just to the control over the use of equipment and materials but also to control over labor power and the setting of priorities for investing profits.

The conservative regimes of Margaret Thatcher and Ronald Reagan made attacks on the social wage central to their programs. They supported their programs by an appeal to "property"; the wage decision should, they believed, devolve upon employers and be taken away from the state. A key part of the argument is a reversal of the Keynesian doctrine of the role of the state in recovery. Keynes criticized holders of capital for their reluctance to invest during economic stagnation. Because of this reluctance, the state had to jump in to provide a floor on spending and thereby promote recovery. But conservatives have always mistrusted the Keynesian framework, since it openly set about to limit property in order to save the property system. Moreover, that bastardized form of Keynesianism known as the welfare state did not produce recovery in the 1970s. The stage was set in the 1980s for a rejection of state encroachments on property and instead a reaffirmation of property.

The attitude of the trade union movement was equivocal. It scored its victories in gaining welfare measures while assuming that it would still support capital accumulation through limiting its wage demands to equal productivity increases. That assumption was at first seen only in terms of what it meant for good times—but it had an obvious implication for bad times as well. The commitment to capital accumulation by labor means that labor's gain in control over the wage decision is not irrevocable. Thus in the United States, labor made concessions on the private wage and concessions on the social wage as well. The leadership of most major unions in the U.S. advocated private wage concessions in the 1981–83 recession. In only isolated cases did the rank and file reject these urgings. In a dismal display of spinelessness, the AFL-CIO went along with the passage in September of 1982 of the Dole bill, which not only increased taxes on the working class but also involved at least $30 billion in welfare cuts. The limitations upon property rights, involving both the private and the social wage, achieved after World War II by the trade union movement were never intended as irrevocable. The limitations were to stand so long as they were compatible with capitalist goals. We shall see that it is these goals that explain both variations in property rights and property rights themselves.

It has been argued that the welfare state will not be dismantled, since the people not only find it a necessity but also recognize that an attack on the welfare state is favoritism toward business.[4] This optimistic assessment fails to deal with the imposed consciousness that resulted from the struggle for the welfare state. It was sold within a framework of the harmony of the aims of capital and labor. This framework has not been questioned by the political or the trade union leadership. Its acceptance means that people can still legitimize their own austerity by the goal of capital accumulation. This is not to say that defenders of property will dismantle the welfare state. Still, the portion of the total wage made by the social wage may continue to decline through more cuts. In addition, the adequacy of the total wage to reproduce labor—to feed, house, clothe, educate, and transport labor—may remain low not just because of cuts, concessions, and inflation but also because of the sizeable likelihood most workers have of experiencing periods of unemployment. Organized opposition to these losses will be likely to emerge only with a recovery that ends the stagnation that began in the late 1960s.

As one might expect, there is now a concerted attack also on limitations of quite different property rights than those attacked by welfare. In particular there is the attack on unions, whose very existence limits property rights. In the 1920s, under Chief Justice William Howard Taft, the Supreme Court undercut the power of unions by judging their actions conspiracies in restraint of trade, and hence violations of the Sherman Act.[5] The Taft court winked at employer associations that restricted trade with firms that would not adopt the open shop. The Taft court was the staunchest supporter of property; the employer was, for it, king in regard to decisions involving labor. Significantly, the injunction, which originated in English equity courts to protect physical property, was upheld by the Supreme Court as a means of protecting property in the less tangible form of an employer's right to have employees agree not to join a union or of his right to continuous profits uninterrupted by strikes. The militancy of workers in the 1930s overturned the thrust of the Taft court and put union rights ahead of a broad range of property rights. But the tide turned again in the mid-1970s when an emboldened employer class set out to achieve a "union-free environment." The lockout, the weakness of the Labor Relations Board, the failure of the AFL-CIO to pass the Labor Reform Act under Jimmy Carter, and the growth of a multimillion dollar business of pin-striped, attaché-case union-busters were symptoms of the property offensive in the 1970s. The use of Quality of Work Life groups to undercut union authority, the Reagan-Lewis destruction of PATCO over the right to strike, and the Supreme Court's authorization of a company's financial distress as a basis for breaking a union contract have continued the property offensive in the 1980s. Unions limit property rights by denying employers exclusive rights to decide wages, benefits, and conditions of work. They are then a prime target in a property offensive.

Remarkably, the percent of the nonagricultural workforce in unions in 1980 had dropped to the level it was at in 1920. Will it drop from this 19 percent mark to 10 percent by 1990, continuing the plunge from 1920 to 1980? That depends on the resources of the labor movement in countering the property offensive. Once again, the assumption on which union rights were won—that labor and capital are partners—is the key. The goal of the property rights that were limited by unionization—the goal of capital accumulation—was not challenged. In bad times, this means that unions do not assert themselves to protect their rights. It means they extend a helping hand to the embattled employers, in the way Douglas Fraser of UAW did by joining Chrysler's Board, William Winpisinger of the Machinists did when he allowed PATCO to be martyred without calling a strike against the airlines[6], and William Wynn of the United Food and Commercial Workers did by undercutting UFCW Hormel strikers.

We must then look at several aspects of the property question today. First, there are the property rights over which there is conflict. Second, there are the goals of the economic system, which these rights serve. Property rights can be limited in good times for the sake of welfare and union rights, without challenging the goals of the economic system. This limitation is not accomplished, however, without conflict. But in bad times there is a tendency to reaffirm these property rights in order to protect the economic system. Again, this expansion is not accomplished without conflict. A successful defense of welfare and union rights nonetheless calls for more resources than the U.S. or British union movements presently command. One of the resources they need is a critical attitude toward the philosophy of partnership, an attitude that calls for the articulation of new economic goals. The adoption of socialist goals could erode the partnership idea and defeat the property offensive.

Attempts to defeat the property offensive have been a failure in the present period. An exception was the establishment by the Swedish parliament in December 1983 of "wage earners' funds" derived from a 20% tax on profits beyond a minimum level and a tax on wages. Though the funds are limited to acquiring at most 40% of a private company's stock, it was estimated that by 1990 they would control close to 10% of all stocks in private companies. The funds are run by boards dominated by union officials appointed by the government. This development represents a rather weak version of the Meidner Plan, which was adopted by the Swedish Social Democratic Party a decade earlier.[7] In contrast, the failure of the Alternative Economic Strategy of Tony Benn of the leftwing of the British Labor Party to get on the agenda for the 1980s is more typical of the weakness of the resistance to the property offensive.[8]

It is to be noted that property rights would be curtailed rather rapidly by the full Meidner Plan. Private firms would soon end up under the control of the Swedish working class. Stocks purchased with the share of the profits given to the working class would empower it to control decisions on investment, the use of the means of production, and the conditions of work. Thus by limiting the right of non-workers to distribute profits, the Meidner Plan would limit their right to oversee production. Whether letting these rights devolve upon workers destroys capitalism depends on whether this devolution leads to a new form of interaction between firms.[9]

The international nature of the economic crisis has led to a reaffirmation of property in the Eastern Bloc as well. The Polish regime crushed the independent union, Solidarity, which had challenged state property rights on several levels. At first it challenged the state's exclusive right to set the standard of living of labor to fit the state's goals of growth. In August 1980, Polish workers revolted, as they had done before, against increased prices. They then challenged the state's exclusive right to control the workplace through their formation of a union that was designed to be multisectoral, in order to deal with a highly centralized state ownership. To preserve their gains, Polish workers found it necessary to demand, by mid-1981, worker control over management of the workplace. But the assumption accepted by the Solidarity leadership in all these struggles was that the principle of Party control of the state would not be challenged.[10] In the international crisis, the limits Solidarity was imposing on the rights of state ownership were a threat to continued control of the state by the Party. Either state ownership had to be transformed into collective and democratic control of production or Solidarity had to be crushed, as it was on December 13, 1981.

ADJUSTING THE RIGHTS OF CAPITAL FOR THE SAKE OF LABOR

The above idea of a capital-labor partnership can be developed within the theory of rights. This idea implies that property rights can be limited. Thus this partnership has promoted a dialectical view of rights as variable, which has been important in the thinking of trade union officials and progressive capitalists. There is little point in bringing up the unreconstructed free-enterprise ideology, which takes property rights to be uncompromisable. The recent versions of this ideology are directly in the service of the desperate employer and are not a serious development in the theory of rights.[11] But in application to the capital-labor partnership, the theory of rights takes the promising direction of placing rights in a social context, rather than of viewing them as naturally acquired.

The bloody fight between labor and capital in the Western mine fields awoke in John D. Rockefeller, Jr., an urgent need to end the conflict and begin a partnership. In 1914 the miners at Rockefeller's Colorado Fuel and Iron Company engaged in a battle over the right to be represented by the United Mine Workers. Families of some of the evicted miners were subsequently massacred by the National Guard. A year later a Rockefeller Foundation study, headed by the president of Harvard and the former Canadian minister of labor, set forth a plan for employee representation. Rockefeller himself called for labor and management to recognize one another as human beings. "Human relations" based on a common interest had to replace "wantonly wasteful" class conflict. The Rockefeller idea of human relations was the company union, which started at CF & I and then spread to Standard Oil. Significantly, the human relations program was implemented by a corps of permanent industrial relations experts within the Rockefeller empire. Concerned lest the universities should develop programs of trade union studies, Rockefeller inspired and funded in 1922 an industrial relations division of the Princeton Department of Economics.[12]

Behind any such idea of the labor-capital partnership is a view of the good life of the society, that is, of the realization of its common interest. Property rights are limited by the partnership because not limiting them would stir up conflict, making the attainment of the good life impossible. Aristotle contended that, if a single class had its way in ruling a society, it could at best realize what is in its interest but this would not be the good life for the society as a whole.[13] Inevitably then, one must question what the good life or the realization of common interest is. I am not proposing an alternative conception of the good life, but only examining, in what follows, the implications of the conception of the good life needed by those who argue for a labor-capital partnership. My theme is that their conception of the good life already has capitalism built into it and is thus biased against socialism, where a labor-capital partnership is irrelevant.

It has to be recognized that the vision of the good life behind the capital-labor partnership is one of a class-structured life. Realizing the common interest through the partnership is, then, the achievement of a well-ordered class society. After all, a true partnership will involve no threat to the class position on either side of it. Part at least of the good life realized through a capital-labor partnership is a smoothly functioning economy. This is so because of the potential a poorly functioning economy has for ending a class partnership. There is undoubtedly more to this vision of the good life than a healthy economy— Aristotle wanted "noble deeds," and today some would want cooperativeness based on national identity. But without a smoothly functioning economy, class-structured life would have a tendency to fracture. What I am saying is that, when a partnership is seen as a necessary condition for the good life, the good life has to be taken as structured in part by actual economic relations. It is a form life can have in a class-divided society, hence a form that still benefits most of those who are dominant in such a society. The labor-capital partnership, with its mutual limitation of class rights, is called for to shore up, rather than eliminate, this class society. Appealing beyond this to an ideal conception of the good life that excludes relations between classes is of no avail here, since without labor and capital there is no room for a labor-capital partnership.

Ernest Barker has made clear that the partnership needed for the good life is not to mean an end to capitalism.[14] Writing in 1950 in response to the postwar Laborite program of socialization, he insisted on the continuation of the private ownership of capital. There would, though, have to be a recognition that the ownership could no longer be allowed to reduce the worker to the status of a tool. The worker has political rights and rights to personal security that are unrealizable without ending the absolute control of owners of capital over production. A system of partnership must then be devised for the conduct of management. Workers must have "a voice and stake in the undertaking in which they serve." The system of private capital ownership, once restricted in this way, can still provide the advantages of a competitive, decentralized economy. One of the chief advantages of such an economy is, Barker held, its development of personal capacities.

Barker's vision of the partnership led him to recommend as one vehicle of this partnership "a voluntary social parliament" composed of representatives of the working and employing classes. Such a parliament would not involve a devolution of state powers to social associations, as in the more radical Fabian vision. It would, as suggested by Churchill in 1930, be advisory to the state.[15] For Barker, the state cannot alienate its prime function, which is to adjust the rights of different associations, such as capital and labor, in order to create a just blending of those rights. The partnership, then, goes beyond the voluntary social parliament to involve all levels; the state and the firm must also be active in fashioning the partnership. But at none of these levels does the compromising of property rights involve, for Barker, an abandonment of class distinctions or of the aims of capitalism.

The good life is not defined by Barker simply as that which a capital-labor partnership makes possible. There is more to it, for Barker defines the good life by an ethic of human development. To achieve the good life we must, then, aim at the highest development of the capacities of the most people. But is it really possible to say what the highest development of human capacities amounts to without appealing to the economic system that the capital-labor partnership preserves? For Barker the state, on the advice of voluntary bodies, adjusts the rights of property to the rights of workers in order to realize the good life, that is, maximum human development.[16] He notes that it does not adjust these rights by an abstract formula, since different circumstances require different adjustments. We may conclude that the goal of human development would be defeated by adjusting rights so that economic crisis resulted. This would increase unemployment, decrease investment in productive capacity, and reduce welfare spending. These consequences of capitalist crisis would not be compatible with Barker's requirement of human development. This leads, though, to the view that the concept of human development involved in Barker's definition of the good life is not a transcendent one at all. It is human development within the context of a system run for private accumulation.

It is, rather, a concrete conception of human development that lies behind the adjustment of rights that makes for a partnership. This is the conception of human development within the economic system implied by the classes in the partnership. Any ordering of rights—such as Barker's prioritization of liberty over equality—is to be made against the background of this concrete conception of human development.[17] In contrast, Rawls's ordering of liberty before equality takes place in the absence of such a concrete background. The Aristotelian project of a conciliation of classes against a concrete background has disappeared in Rawls, though it was still alive in Barker's search for justice. We can still see in Barker that *legitimate* rights—those trimmed to fit with others in a just arrangement—are relative to the development of humans in a given economic system. The legitimacy of these rights stems from their efficacy in achieving the good life or the fulfilling of common interests. But here the good life is realized at least in part by a class partnership and hence by the development of humans within the form of economy implied by those classes.

It is tempting to think that what Barker has here is a justification for capitalism, and there is no doubt he thought of it that way. For if a necessary condition for the good life is a capital-labor partnership, a necessary condition for it is also the capitalist economy that is the context of that partnership. But the notion of good life involved is already tinged with an economic structure, which is in fact capitalism itself. For what other good life than a capitalist one would require a capital-labor partnership? Barker wanted his view of justice to deal a blow to the socialist aspirations within the Labor Party at the end of the 1940s. But all it did was to show that those socialist aspirations were incompatible with maximum human development realized within the capitalist economy. If we just add the supposition that capitalism is irrevocable, then a partnership makes practical sense and socialist aspirations will be seen as spoiling it. Samuel Gompers, of the AFL, who was an architect of partnership believing in the irrevocability of capitalism, said of the socialists, "Morally you are unsound; socially you are unsafe; and industrially you are an impossibility." From his perspective of labor-capital partnership, he was dead right.

In a similar vein, the recent encyclical on work by John Paul II adopts the dignity of the person as the basis for "adaptations in the sphere of the right to ownership of the means of production."[18] The dignity of the person is subverted by liberal economic philosophy that treats the worker, like land or machinery, as a factor of production. Rather, production must be organized so that it is a means for realizing the worker's humanity. There is, claims the pope in his effort to update the Christian Democratic tradition beginning with Leo XIII's *Rerum Novarum* of 1891, no inevitable conflict between capial and labor. Once adjustments in property rights are made, labor's dignity is compatible with capitalism. One need not abandon capitalism to make production compatible with dignity. For the pope, private ownership promotes personal dignity and is thus to be preferred to any form of socialized property. To make this teaching relevant to the Eastern bloc, John Paul II notes that, since *de facto* state property exists there, it too must be handled according to the principle of human dignity. He rightly notes that state ownership is far from a guarantee that production will be for human realization.

The same consideration applies here as to Barker. The adaptations of ownership rights for the sake of "honest collaboration" do not end capitalism. A dignity of the sort realized through such collaboration will be the dignity of the worker who by producing enriches owners. This gives the worker a secondary role in relation to those who are enriched without work. This secondary status persists even after profit sharing, joint ownership, codetermination at the enterprise level, and a social parliament have been instituted. These are some of the means the pope mentions for adapting property rights to dignity. The dignity appropriate to a secondary role is all that is allowed by honest collaboration with the capitalist class. Thus, as in the case of Barker, this goal—the dignity of the working person—at which the capital-labor partnership aims does not justify private ownership in the form the existence of a capitalist class implies. Rather, the full elaboration of what the pope means by human dignity is impossible without appealing to what work is within enlightened capitalism. There is no independent standard of dignity from which we can derive the conclusion that private ownership of capital is the context in which it will flourish best.

Laborem Exercens tries to avoid identifying capitalism as a part of human dignity by resorting to a transparent equivocation on the term "capital."[19] The collaboration of labor with capital is, in the encyclical, sometimes a collaboration with machines and materials, but it is also sometimes a collaboration with a class whose goal is the private accumulation of the products of others. Of course, there is no conflict with machines and materials, and an honest collaboration with them does not imply any particular class system or any particular economy. The difficulty is that neither can collaboration with physical capital be said to advance human dignity in the absence of a social context that structures such a collaboration. However, when capital is seen as not just physical but also social, collaboration with capital is the acceptance of a social system of production. The dignity achieved by switching from conflict to collaboration is the limited dignity allowed a worker in a system with capitalists. It is the dignity allowed one who produces so that others are individually enriched and acquire social power. This limited dignity is that of the capitalist worker and thus cannot be valued without already valuing capitalism. This dignity does not then justify capitalism; rather capitalism gives it its value.

The pope's position is not an enviable one. As leader of a universalist institution, he both speaks for the oppressed and, as was clear in 1983 in Warsaw and San Salvador, works with the oppressor. A philosophy of capital-labor partnership is then a pragmatic necessity for the universal church. But for the oppressed it is a disaster, since it shows them no way out. The philosophy of property rights needs to be advanced from partnership, conciliation, and honest collaboration to a defense of class rights, to which I now turn.

PROPERTY RIGHTS AS FUNCTIONAL

In the first section I pointed out that the response to the reaffirmation of property in the crisis of the 1980s would depend on the ability of the working class to break with the idea of partnership. In the second section I showed that there is every reason for the working class to break with that idea since a capital-labor partnership allows for only those restrictions of property compatible with the goal of the private accumulation of the products of labor. Now I want to speak about the root of variations in property rights in terms of a functional view of what those rights are. Property rights conform to the relations of production, and cannot then be appealed to in defining those relations of production. The current reaffirmation of property is, moreover, not to be confronted by appeals to return to an earlier partnership, for that partnership has ceased to conform to the relations of production. Rather, the property offensive is to be confronted by a systematic effort to change the relations of production.

It is hard to shake off the physicalist image of property. Locke wanted property to be a feature of the state of nature.[20] It had to be a physical rather than a social relation, as it had been for Hobbes. Thus he generated a physicalist image of property as something with which we mix our labor. He had assumed that labor itself was the laborer's property, but again this had to do with the physical relation of labor to the body. We walk out a boundary to a plot of land, we hold a stone for grinding, we hitch a beast to a load, and, lo, we have created private property for ourselves. The failure of property relations to emerge clearly in prestate communities is sufficient indication that the physicalist image is a gross distortion. All the physicalist image does is to make property into a seeming given that any social arrangement must incorporate. A social arrangement that challenges private property is then stigmatized as unnatural.

Property, though, is not a physical but a social relation. Property follows upon the way a society organizes its production. Changes in productive relations will bring with them changes in property relations. This implies it is wrong to try to explain capitalist productive relations by starting from capitalist ownership. It is also a mistake to try to define class positions by reference to ownership. In both cases the proper order is the reverse.

Nevertheless, there is a tendency among followers of Max Weber to stress the primacy of ownership.[21] The motive behind this tendency is the conviction that control, authority, and power cannot be neglected and that ownership is a basis for control. Thus to assure that control enters one's image of capitalism, one inserts ownership as an independent variable. Fortunately, there is a more adequate way of assuring that control is given its due. The basis of economic power is the day-to-day running of an economic system. The system of productive relations becomes, in other words, *the way things are* for a key part of the population. Habits and expectations develop that support efforts to keep the system running as it has been running. Destabilizing forces, such as a fresh proletariat recruited from the countryside, are then met with institutions intended to control them. This control derives from the unexciting inertia of the way things are within the productive relations. Control, authority, or power as so derived, is harnessed to the goal of reproducing these productive relations. Control is not fundamental but is, when successful, an instrument of stability.[22]

Within this perspective of control as functional for reproducing the productive relations, the key factor is the nature of the activity to be reproduced.

Within capitalism this activity is private accumulation from the production of those who work. Institutions of control stand to this activity as means to end.

As circumstances change—the factory work force becomes larger, the manager ceases to be the owner, or a general decline in profit rates sets in—those institutions of control can undergo dramatic changes while the activity to be reproduced remains largely unchanged. What, though, does this have to do with property?

A property right is a right to control. The reproduction of certain kinds of social activity calls for this kind of right. The physicalist image of property is misleading precisely because property not only doesn't exist without but also is solely directed to social activity. The noble's holding his estate conditional upon the will of the monarch helped reproduce the feudal drive toward the expansion of land holdings by guaranteeing service in fighting wars of expansion. Serf and peasant rights to tools and land within feudalism could reproduce the feudal manner of surplus extraction without undermining it through promoting a labor market. A return to the Roman conception of unconditional property in the late middle ages aided the transition in the towns to a full-blown commodity market. State monopoly of the land in the Islamic empires, which made settled cultivation and development of the land impossible, coincided with a focus on the cities where production, trade, and finance flourished. The goals of capitalism are supported by that aspect of capitalist property that denies workers control over capacity utilization. The transfer of control from legal owners to managers in the monopoly period of capitalism was a change, not an extinction of, the nature of capitalist property that helped reproduce capitalism.

This view of property is based on a distinction that is more analytical than historical. This distinction is that between, on the one hand, an activity that happens to go on in a more or less regular way and, on the other hand, a tendency to support that activity by mechanisms of control directed against possible challenges to it. Such a tendency will take different forms as those challenges themselves change. In applying this analytical framework to capitalism, the accumulation process comes to be viewed as a quasiautomatic activity. Within it one group, the workers, plays the role of working beyond the time needed to reproduce their labor. Another group, the capitalists, plays the role of using what comes from that extra time as a basis for expanding the entire process. This accumulation process is not yet conceived as a process involving property, even though the capitalist has use of the surplus for expansion. Mere use does not amount to property where the activity is automatic, suffers no serious challenges, and hence has within it no tendency for stabilization against such challenges. Since in reality challenges to establishing and maintaining any form of social activity will be forthcoming, that activity will not exist without forms of control for its own defense. For capitalism, private ownership of the means of production becomes an umbrella under which the defense of capitalist activity is mobilized.

There are several things to be emphasized in a general account of property rights. First, it is to be emphasized that we are dealing with a right and hence with something in need of justification. The kind of justification that is appropriate becomes clear only upon looking at the other aspects of property rights. Second, it is to be emphasized that the right has a limited scope. It will not have the same scope as, say, a voting right. Here is where control enters the picture. Property rights are rights to control people and things entering in the process of production. (The relevant forms of control are taken up further on.) Moreover, they are limited in scope in another way. They are the rights only of a certain group within production, those who appropriate the surplus of production. A worker's right to income[23] is then at best a personal property right rather than a productive property right. Finally, it is to be emphasized that the right has a distinctive purpose. Calling it a property right brings attention to this purpose and thus having the purpose is not an accidental fact about it. The purpose turns out to be the key to my materialist account of a property right. The purpose of a property right is to perpetuate the economic system. This purpose is achieved by the control of owners over the property and things entering the process of production. This gives an indication of the kind of justification to be sought, for if a form of control has no tendency to continue the system then there is no right to that form of control. But of course having a justified property right will not imply that the form of control in question guarantees the success of the system. It implies only that this form of control tends to reproduce the system.

Property rights may change with circumstances, since as circumstances change the degree of control needed to reproduce the economy may change. Nonetheless, the property system as a whole may remain the same system even after individual property rights have altered. The system of productive private ownership within capitalism is not destroyed by changing the degree of control capitalists must maintain over the direction of investment. To have this system of private ownership all we need is for those whose role is to appropriate the surplus to have a right to as much control as is needed under given circumstances to continue capitalist production. By contrast, an individual productive property right within the capitalist system is a right of those who appropriate the surplus to a specific form of control of some facet of the capitalist productive process in order that this process can be continued.

This formulation avoids the mistake of the physicalist image of property by putting property in the context of the reproduction of a social activity. It also avoids the mistake of the view that property is an independent variable by attributing to it a functional role within a form of social activity. Moreover, this formulation allows for considerable variations of property rights within a single economic system. For the specific form of the actual control by capitalists over activity linked to production has been drastically changed between early and late capitalism. Another formulation would allow us to situate state ownership, where this is the dominant property form, as control for the reproduction of bureaucratic economic activity. State ownership in a capitalist economy would still involve the same goal included in the definition of private ownership.

One important factor, though, seems to have been left out. Having a justified right to control is one thing, whereas being able to enforce this right is
quite another. The central cases of property systems and property rights involve the power of enforcement. Though this is true, it would confuse matters
to emphasize power before emphasizing rights. The power we are talking
about is a legitimate power and its purchase on legitimacy stems from the jus-
tifiability of the property rights it enforces. Power without right would involve
an enforcement of a form of control that would in no sense tend to reproduce
the economic system. In that case if we spoke of property at all, we would
qualify it as presumptive or fictitious.

A related confusion involves making the state part of the very concept of
property. The idea is that if property rights imply an enforcing power, then it
is only the state that is extensive enough to play this role.[24] Apart from the
error of denying the existence of unenforced rights, this view ignores the fact
that when the state vacillates, owners mobilize their own defense of property.
The bourgeoisie in Latin America has organized its own private gangs of thugs
to turn back land reform programs officially endorsed by numerous states.
There are in fact numerous seats of power—such as, in the U.S., the Pinker-
tons, the Open Shop Association, unmerciful supervisors, business lobbyists,
and of course the National Guard—for the enforcement of capitalist rights
over productive activity.

Though the central cases of property do involve power as well as rights, I
think it is important to emphasize here rights as opposed to power, since social
change involves the emergence of new rights in search of a defense through
power. Around the fringes of the central cases are rights that emerge in transi-
tional periods and on the legal borderline. In the first of the following cases,
power has not caught up with a property right, whereas in the second, defenders of an unjustified property right are complaining about the withdrawal of
power for its enforcement.

(1) In Roman law a distinction reigned between, on the one hand, land,
houses, slaves, and large domestic animals and, on the other hand, other kinds
of property.[25] The former could be transferred to a new owner only by one of
several elaborate formal acts. Such things fell under the heading of *res mancipi*.
This distinction derived from early Roman customs and had little basis in economic reality in the period after Cicero. The person to whom land is sold in
the absence of mancipation is not the *de jure* owner. Yet since this restriction
on the mobility of property might have been appropriate to an earlier feudal
period but was not appropriate to the later period of extended commerce, one
can say that the buyer *really* had a right to the property transferred without
mancipation. Partial recognition of this right came by granting *de jure* ownership after two years of undisputed use. Eventually, a praetor could defend continued use, even within the required two-year period of use, against a
titleholder who had transferred the property without mancipation. Thus the
power to enforce property eventually caught up with the right to property.

(2) When capitalists, in their turn, complain about the denial of their
property rights, what they mean is that the power to enforce alleged rights has

been withdrawn. But often the alleged rights are fictional. Their real rights are defined by what must be allowed if the capitalist system is to be continued and hence their class interest is to be realized. And their interest as a class, as distinct from their interests as competing capitalists, is to maintain the private accumulation of capital through the work of others. When power is withdrawn from a form of control that fails to serve this interest, it is not withdrawn from a real right. Employer contributions to retirement benefits under the Social Security Act, the right of unionized employees to bargain collectively, and the Environmental Protection Act have all been denounced as bolshevism. In each case some aspect of the control over production has been loosened, and to that extent capitalist property rights have been changed. I spoke of this in the first section rather loosely as a "restriction of property rights." But we can now see that this generally means no more than that enforcing earlier forms of control no longer serves capitalism. For there is no evidence to show that these measures have endangered, rather than promoted, the reproduction of capitalist relations. So the restriction of property rights does not mean that they have been ignored, but more often that they have ceased to exist.

Some more needs to be said about the justification of property rights. On the view of partnership in the first part of this essay, property rights must be adjusted for the sake of human development. Apparently, the justification of property rights had a basis beyond the partisan scuffle of classes. It turned out, though, that it was difficult to transcend this scuffle, since in fact classes were brought into the good life through their partnership. The functional perspective on property rights introduced here—in this section—comes out in the open with what was hidden in the idea of adjustment of property rights for the sake of a partnership. On the functional perspective, property rights are justified if the forms of control they allow would in fact tend to reproduce capitalism. Now, the reproduction of capitalism is a key concern in the class interest of those who appropriate surplus. The idea of partnership is to make the reproduction of capitalism a key concern in the class interest of the working class as well. It remains, though, doubtful that the reproduction of capitalism in its recent period is a genuine interest of the working class. It is more certain that the functional character of property rights makes possible a justification of them on the basis of the interests of capitalists rather than workers. The task then of balancing the property rights of owners with the welfare rights of workers is not one that can be accomplished beyond the scuffle of classes on the basis of some neutral conception of the good life.

When welfare gets in the way of capitalist activity, the only ground on which welfare can be supported is the working class itself. Partnership or conciliation is no ground at all, since it is based on the smooth working of capitalist activity. The present fight to protect working-class gains looms up, then, as a fight between the rights of two classes. There is only limited room for compromise on either side, for significant compromise would abandon rights that are legitimate relative to the interests of that side. The reaffirmation of property by capital comes from a sense that now it must "take back" property rights it really did not "need" in more prosperous times. Taking them back means that these rights now exist since the forms of control they cover are now essential for continuing the system. These new rights are then rights capital has in relation to its class interest in reproducing an activity in which it has the use of an alienated surplus. Capitalists have these property rights in relation to their interests, which are not the interests workers have in extending their welfare and control. This relativity of property rights to class[26] follows from the fact that property rights are functional for reproducing capitalist activity which is in the interest of capitalists, not of workers as well.

If there is only limited room for compromise and if each side has its legitimate rights, what happens? Power comes in here. For each side will attempt to deny the other the power to enforce what are its legitimate rights. So far in the 1970s and 1980s, the battle has been one-sided, with workers losing their power to enforce their welfare rights. This is not because in the present crisis of capitalism the capitalists have new property rights that are justified for workers as well. The limits being put on the social wage and unionization are certainly part of the enforcement by capital of its new property rights, but this is no justification for those who bear the brunt of these restrictions. Only a new organizational thrust that rejects the ideology of partnership and hence that is willing to take the risk of making the reproduction of capitalism impossible can generate the power to defend the welfare and union rights under attack.

PROPERTY RIGHTS APART FROM PRODUCTION RELATIONS

What happens to property rights when they are looked at in abstraction from production relations? In this section I shall consider two views of this kind, primarily for the purpose of determining whether they can enlighten us in regard to the property question today.

The first view is a direct consequence of a political strategy for socialism, a version of the strategy of gradualism that is responsive to difficulties that accompany both legal nationalization of the means of production and class revolution. This gradualist strategy involves whittling away the property rights of the capitalist to the point at which the capitalist cannot function. Harrington describes this as "a very practical, unapocalyptic method" of doing away with capitalism.[27] It does not become necessary to deprive the capitalist of legal title in order to have a functional equivalent of socialism. The property rights denied capitalists in this process are taken to be transferred to the state, which acts not for the goals of any class but for the people.

The view of property rights associated with this political strategy is that, taken one by one, they are what they are apart from productive relations. Together, though, property rights can constitute an economic system. Imagine that we could list all the various ownership rights. When all of them are rights of private citizens or corporations and none are rights of the state, we have a pure form of capitalism. The system is a mixed form when only some of these rights have been transferred from private to social hands. When all the ownership rights are socialized, there is a pure form of state socialism.[28] The preservation of the economic system, in this view, no longer provides a goal for which rights are functional; rather, the economic system results from a mere aggregation of rights.

Those social democrats who have developed this socialist gradualism that reduces the economic system to a bundle of rights have correctly emphasized the wide range of rights that can be called rights of ownership. Corresponding to Marx's distinction within the total value of a commodity between surplus value, the value of constant capital, and the value of labor power, it has been customary to distinguish three sorts of ownership directly involved in the *production* of commodities. There is the right to make investment decisions with realized surplus value; there is the right to administer the use of fixed capital to determine the quantity, quality, and mix of products; and there is the right to control the application of labor power to fixed capital through hiring, firing, work schedules, and work pace.

Ownership rights are quite correctly not limited by these theorists to the production process itself. In the first section, I emphasized that the development of the social wage limited property. Control of *distribution* is part of ownership because of its link with production. Without control of distribution, there is a loss of control over production. If the working class wins unemployment benefits, then the capitalist cannot as easily discipline workers by raising unemployment. If the working class wins steady wage gains, thereby effecting a reduction of the ratio of aggregate surplus to aggregate wages, then the capitalist must structure investment decisions to respond to this shift in demand, favoring investment for consumer production in relation to investment for luxury and capital goods production. Thus Adler-Karlsson speaks of three kinds of rights of ownership in regard to distribution.[29] There is the right to decide wages, the right to distribute profits between shareholders and recapitalization, and the right to redistribute wealth through pension plans, profit-sharing schemes, or foundations for community or scholarly projects. When distribution passes out of capitalist control, it will be used to slow private accumulation and thereby place more of the production process under state or worker control.

Finally, there is another area not identical with but linked to production that is important as regards ownership rights—the area of *legitimation*. Crisis management belongs to this area. The state, which is the primary instrument of crisis management, steers a course that is responsive to various immediate interests. The right to decide how to ride out crises is clearly not one left either to individual intrepreneurs or to corporate boards. Also, acceptable levels of economic concentration, the degree of legal ownership allowable in foreign subsidiaries, and the extent to which community values can dominate the goal of profits are all questions of the strength of ownership. Yet each question touches on the legitimacy of capitalism.

Our gradualist socialist thinks that, if enough rights from these three areas—production, distribution, and legitimation—are socialized, then capitalism has been ended in all but name. Quantity is what counts. Before discussing this claim, two issues need stressing. First, the transfer of rights is not so simple a matter once we insist that the rights in the three areas are not all possessed by each and every member of the capitalist class. There is a division of roles within this class, so that all the rights apply only to that fiction called "the global capitalist." The reason this complicates the picture is that some of the roles of the global capitalist may be ones that can be performed only by members of the state apparatus.[30] Thus the private-state contrast becomes misleading as a basis for the contrast between capitalism and socialism.

Second, not all ownership rights belong to the same level, since production is the prime locus of ownership rights, whereas distribution and legitimation give rise to ownership rights on a derivative level. One's right to set wages or to exercise control over the money supply might give one dictatorial power, but unless it is a right that shores up rights capitalists have in regard to production itself, that power is not the power of ownership. When it is convenient for workers to gain more control over the setting of their wages, they do not thereby gain property rights. What happens is, rather, the capitalists lose them.

The point I wish to stress in regard to this version of gradualist socialism is, however, the one on which I based the functional view of rights. It is the point that the strength of capitalism depends not on *how many* property rights the global capitalist enjoys but on the ability of the global capitalist to realize the goal of accumulation through exploitation. In some circumstances, this capitalist goal may be easily realized even when, and maybe partly because, significant restrictions have been made on capitalist ownership. When capitalism is expansive, allowing a spread of control in both the social and economic areas to a citizenry eager to match its monetary gains with more participation is the best policy to win support for continued growth. Moreover, in developing areas of the globe, restrictions on ownership have helped foster indigenous capital. In Mexico, for example, the decision by President Lázaro Cárdenas to nationalize the foreign oil companies on March 17, 1938, was one of the pillars on which capitalist Mexico built its economic miracle immediately after World War II.[31] The gradualist socialist resorts to counting rights rather than to estimating the ability to accumulate capital in order to determine the strength of capitalism. Counting rights can at best tell us in which areas the global capitalist needs control.[32] Rights do not constitute the economic system but are merely indications of its needs.

The present-day reaffirmation of property is partly an expression of a need of capitalism and partly ideological. Old property rights are claimed to be essential now to continue capitalism in the face of the bogey of big government. The property rights at stake belong primarily to the second, the distributional, area. But because the reaffirmation of property expresses a need of capitalism, it is difficult for gradualists to claim now that capitalists do not have the rights they are reaffirming. They have no ground on which to base such a denial. But do they have a program for undermining the power to enforce these new property rights? Do they even have the necessary ideas for formulating such a program? Resistance by the working class to the reaffirmation of distributional ownership rights calls for a rejection of the goal of private accumulation through exploitation. Acceptance of this goal leaves one vulnerable to the argument that, since the old property rights are necessary now for realizing this goal, welfare and union rights should be willingly sacrificed. The gradualist, though, lacks the ideas needed to combat this argument. The reason is that there is no appeal within gradualism beyond the separate rights to the system they bolster. To fight the reaffirmation of property rights it is necessary to fight capitalism, which the gradualist fails to see as anything more than those rights. During the crisis, the gradualist will be unable to comprehend the intensity with which capitalists fight for derivative property rights, such as the distributional ones. A strategy for fightback will have to be structured not as a fight against rights that ignores the system that calls for them, but as a fight against the system that keeps creating property rights.

I come now to the second view that abstracts property from production relations. It tries to understand property entirely at the level of market relations. This view—associated with Pashukanis—is closer to mine than that of the above version of gradualist socialism. It at least puts rights in the framework of a social activity, and it thereby avoids the gradualist socialist's atomism. But the social activity is the market, not the production process.

The distinction between mine and yours becomes crucial, in this view, only when things can be transferred by the market. To speak of an exchange requires that there be clarity as to who owns what. Prior to their becoming easily and widely exchangeable, things had the status of possessions for use but not the status of property. The market, then, both creates and needs property rights. Moreover, as the market becomes dominant in social activity, distinctions between people based on status or occupation lose their importance. People become equal in so far as it does not matter who they are for them to enter into an exchange. Also, the quantity of their property that is exchanged for a given quantity of another's property depends on a universal standard that is blind to who the property holders are. Property rights, with their origin in the market, are borne by equal agents whose family, status, and occupational differences are irrelevant to their natures.[33]

Implicit in this derivation is a criticism of property rights and of rights in general as having the status of fetishes. The criticism is aimed through them at the market system itself. Marx's critique of commodity fetishism[34] is extended here into a critique of property rights and of rights in general. Human nature narrowed to the ability to make market transactions, rights focused on the individual isolated from social combination, and property limited to transferability in accord with a law of value are indeed fetishes. Like all fetishes they do not affect our lives directly but do so only by becoming part of ideology.

But are there no nonfetishized notions corresponding to these fetishized ones of humanity, rights, and property? Focusing on the market leads one to treat exchange value as though it were inherent in commodities. Should we then reject the notion of exchange value as entirely a product of fetishism? We get a corresponding nonfetishized notion by treating exchange value in terms of production relations, which are a necessary complement to the market. This was, after all, Marx's route from commodity fetishism to the labor theory of value. Likewise, focusing on the market may be the source of fetishized concepts of humanity, rights, and property. To understand human nature as something other than an unchanging potential for contracts, one needs to view human nature within the framework of changing production relations. To understand rights as something other than the boundaries isolated individuals protect, one needs to view them as instrumental to the aims of classes and other groups that change as production changes. To understand property as something other than a pregiven potential for transfer, one needs to view it as a shifting set of controls within or around production that tends to advance the goal of production. We are not then locked into the fetishized notions that classical liberal theorists developed. Switching from the market to production relations gives us the way out.[35]

There is another problem with the market approach. The fetishized view of property it derives, in order to criticize market society, fits the free market of equal agents. But it fits neither markets dominated by monopolies, states with large parastatals, nor noncapitalist state-centralized economies. Neumann made the observation, "In the period of monopolization, the new auxiliary guarantee of property is no longer the contract but the administrative act, the form in which the state interferes."[36] There are two questions brought up here. One is whether the contract is still at the heart of property. The other is whether, when the contract changes into the administrative act, there is still property at all.

Pashukanis, writing in 1924 in Russia, held, in answer to the first question, that property still existed in the USSR since the market and hence the contract still determined relations between state enterprises.[37] One can agree that the market played an important role under the New Economic Policy inaugurated by Lenin in 1921. But state enterprises were clearly a new form of property, not to be classed as transferable as between equal agents in a free market. As the state moved, toward the end of NEP, to limit both the foreign and the domestic market more and more, it was not behaving as one among equals in a medium of free exchange.[38] Where there was a contract between enterprises, its place was dropping to a secondary plane in relation to the primary plane of state decision. The contract was no longer at the heart of this system where state property was becoming dominant.

Thus we come to face the second question—without the primacy of the market, is there still property? The question is not merely academic; I want to tie together struggles that might seem to have been historically disparate. The struggles of peasants for land, of workers for unions, of the poor for welfare, and of workers in state enterprises for repossession of what they see as theirs, are all struggles in a world polarized between the "haves" and "have nots."

The "haves" have property in the sense of *dominium;* they have control for the sake of some goal, whether that goal implies giving the market the weight it had in liberal capitalism or not. It is useful to link these struggles as ones that limit control that has an economic aim and, to that extent, it is useful to say they are struggles against property. The property question is, then, still crucial today, though it would no longer be crucial if property derived solely from the interaction of free agents through exchange.

The most promising guide in the struggle against property is a materialist conception of property rights. Property rights express needs a dominant class has for forms of control linked to production in order that certain economic goals can be realized. These rights are neither prior to those economic goals nor derived from the market mechanism for their realization. To be effective, the struggle against property rights—whether as the struggle for welfare measures or as the struggle for a voice in investment decisions—must be joined with the struggle against the economic goals of the dominant class. Otherwise, the struggle against property rights becomes reformism. Conversely, the struggle against these goals, which today is the struggle for socialism—is rooted in the struggle against property. Otherwise, the struggle for socialism becomes utopian. At present, though, these two struggles are far apart.

NOTES

[1] Karl Marx and Friedrich Engels, *The Communist Manifesto,* Part 4, in Karl Marx and Frederick Engels, *Collected Works,* Volume 6 (New York: International Publishers, 1976), pp. 518–519.

[2] John Rawls, *A Theory of Justice* (Cambridge, MA: Harvard University Press, 1971), Section 42.

[3] Ian Gough, *The Political Economy of the Welfare State* (London: Macmillan, 1979), pp. 116–117.

[4] Frances Fox Piven and Richard A. Cloward, *The New Class War* (New York, Pantheon, 1982), p. 44.

[5] Irving Bernstein, *The Lean Years* (Boston: Houghton Mifflin, 1960), Ch. 4.

[6] See William Winpisinger, "PATCO Strike: Another Union's Role," *Boston Globe,* September 17, 1981, Section 1, page 14.

[7] John D. Stephens, *The Transition from Capitalism to Socialism* (London: Macmillan, 1979), pp. 188–194.

[8] Tony Benn, *Arguments for Socialism,* (Harmondsworth: Penguin, 1979).

[9] David Schweickart, *Capitalism or Worker Control* (New York: Praeger, 1980), pp. 70–74.

[10] Colin Barker and Kara Weber, "Solidarność: From Gdansk to Military Repression," *International Socialism, 15,* Winter, 1981.

[11] Milton Fisk, "Property and the State: A Discussion of Robert Nozick's *Anarchy, State, and Utopia,*" *Noûs* 14 (1980): 99–108.

[12] Bernstein, *Lean Years,* pp. 157–169.

[13] Aristotle, *Politics,* Book III, Ch. 13.

[14] Ernest Barker, *Principles of Social and Political Theory* (London: Oxford University Press, 1951), Book VI, Section 5.

[15] Barker, *Principles,* Book II, Section 7.

[16] Barker, *Principles,* Book IV, Section 1.

[17] Barker, *Principles,* Book IV, Section 3, p. 159.

[18] John Paul II, *Laborem Exercens,* 1981, Part III, Sections 14–15.

[19] John Paul II, *Laborem Exercens,* Part III, Section 13.

[20] John Locke, *Second Treatise of Civil Government,* Section 27; also C. B. Macpherson, "Liberal-Democracy and Property," in *Property,* ed. C. B. Macpherson (Toronto: University of Toronto Press, 1983), pp. 199–207.

[21] E.g., Anthony Giddens, *A Contemporary Critique of Historical Materialism* (Berkeley: University of California Press, 1981), Ch. 5. The same insistence on putting control and hence ownership in "the base" leads to the confused definition of feudal relations of production by Perry Anderson, *Lineages of the Absolute State,* (London: New Left Books, 1974), pp. 404–405.

[22] John Westergaard and Henrietta Resler, *Class in a Capitalist Society: A Study of Contemporary Britain,* (Harmondsworth: Penguin, 1976), pp. 142–143. See also Steven Lukes, *Power: A Radical View* (London: Macmillan, 1974), Ch. 4.

[23] Philip J. Levine, "Toward a Property Right in Employment," in *Property: Cases, Concepts, Critiques,* eds. L. C. Becker and K. Kipnis (Englewood Cliffs, NJ: Prentice-Hall, 1984), pp. 116–119.

[24] *Pace* Macpherson, "The Meaning of Property," in *Property,* ed. Macpherson, p. 4.

[25] John Crook, *Law and Life of Rome* (Ithaca, NY: Cornell University Press, 1967), Ch. 5.

[26] Milton Fisk, *Ethics and Society* (New York: New York University Press, 1980), Part V.

[27] Michael Harrington, *Socialism* (New York: Bantam, 1973), p. 362.

[28] Gunnar Adler-Karlsson, *Reclaiming the Canadian Economy* (Toronto: Anansi, 1970), pp. 39–40.

[29] Adler-Karlsson, *Reclaiming the Canadian Economy,* p. 53.

[30] Nicos Poulantzas, *Classes in Contemporary Capitalism,* trans. D. Fernbach (London: Verso, 1978), p. 187.

[31] Nora Hamilton, *The Limits of State Autonomy: Post-Revolutionary Mexico* (Princeton, NJ: Princeton University Press, 1982), Ch. 7.

[32] *Pace* Stephens, *The Transition from Capitalism to Socialism,* p. 25.

[33] Evgeny B. Pashukanis, *Law and Marxism: A General Theory,* trans. B. Einhorn (London: Ink Links, 1978), Ch. 4. Another market rather than production based view of property is that of Macpherson, "The Meaning of Property," in *Property,* ed. Macpherson, pp. 1–13.

[34] Karl Marx, *Capital,* vol. I, Part I, Ch. 1, Section 4 (New York: International Publishers, 1967).

[35] Bob Jessop, *The Capitalist State* (New York: New York University Press, 1982), pp. 84–90.

[36] Franz Neumann, *Behemoth: The Structure and Practice of National Socialism, 1933–1944* (New York: Harper & Row, 1966), p. 257.

[37] Pashukanis, *Law and Marxism,* p. 131.

[38] E. H. Carr, *Socialism in One Country, 1924–1926,* vol. I (London: Macmillan, 1958), Part II, Chapter VIII.

SAMUEL C. WHEELER III

NATURAL PROPERTY RIGHTS AS BODY RIGHTS

Why do we have property rights, if indeed we do have them? This is the question that concerns Samuel Wheeler, a philosopher at the University of Connecticut, Storrs, whose work has concentrated mainly on topics in metaphysics and the philosophy of language. Anticapitalists tend to believe that if there are any such rights, they are in fact only useful fictions, allowing capitalism to gain momentum (through legitimacy) during its historical phase. But such rights are said not to be universal, absolute, unalienable or anything of the sort, as defenders of the capitalist system often maintain. Wheeler proposes that this criticism fails to appreciate the very basic issue that is at stake in the discussion about property rights: that these rights are logical, metaphysical extensions of the right an individual has in his or her body. According to Wheeler, this kind of individual sovereignty is very basic indeed, and if property rights derive from it, surely the right to private property cannot be construed as something temporary and fictitious.

This paper presents a derivation of property rights from rights we have with respect to the use of our bodies. The first sections of the paper establish that *if* we have natural moral rights to move and use our bodies, then there are natural moral rights to property as well. It is also argued that there is no upper bound on the amount of property a person can have a natural right to by this derivation. The fourth section of the paper argues that the antecedent of the conditional is true—that we do have a natural right to move and use our bodies. The last section of the paper discusses the relation of natural property rights to social institutions and practices.

This paper embodies two simplifications:

(1) This paper does not claim to deal with problems of conflicts of property rights. In particular, a host of thorny problems about what rights a person has with respect to things acquired legitimately from someone who acquired them illegitimately, things whose acquisition was effected by use of illegitimately acquired goods, and so forth, are not dealt with. The paper claims to establish only prima facie property rights by showing how, if no one else's rights are violated, a person can have a property right in a thing. I haven't tried to give a complete account of what the condition "if no one else's rights have been violated" amounts to. So, in effect the paper establishes property rights for the idealized situation in which things to which no one else has a right, or whose acquisition-history violates no rights, become private property. Given this idealization the derivation of property rights which follows may not establish property rights to some of what we regard as our possessions.

Reprinted by permission of the author and of the editor of *NOÛS* 16 (1980): 171–193. Copyright © 1980 by Indiana University.

(2) This paper gives no detailed account of initial acquisition-rights. Subject to the Lockean Proviso that there be "enough and as good left in common to others,"[1] it suffices for this paper that a person can without violating rights do as he wishes with what is unclaimed or discarded. Roughly, with respect to initial acquisition, the paper is only concerned with how, given that it doesn't violate any rights to do as we wish with unclaimed or discarded things, we can acquire natural property rights in such things.

As a final preliminary remark, I should note what may be apparent to many readers: The inspiration for the paper is Robert Nozick's *Anarchy, State and Utopia*.[2] My intention is to fill in a justification of property rights that is lacking there.

1. NATURAL BODY RIGHTS

By a natural right I will mean a "right one has independently of institutional arrangements."[3] If a person has a natural right to move and use his body, then it is morally wrong for another to force him to move his body or for another to use his body in ways the person doesn't choose, at least in standard cases. If a bunch of people grab you and clamp you inside a robot which moves your body in ways they choose, then your rights to exclusive control of the motions of your body have been violated whether it hurts or not. If someone decides that your head would make a good door stop and removes it from your exclusive control for that purpose, your rights have been violated, since you have natural moral rights to the exclusive use of your body. Furthermore, it is morally all right for a person to move and use his body as he pleases, unless such motions and uses would violate another's rights. Natural body rights, then, involve the impermissibility of someone else's interference with the motions and uses of your body and the permissibility of your uses and motions of your body.

Alan Gibbard, in arguing that property rights cannot be "grounded in principles of natural liberty,"[4] has posed the problem of justifying property rights as one of showing some grounds for depriving someone of a right without that someone's consent. The rights in question are everyone's prima facie equal right to use the things in the world. With respect to things in the world, Gibbard has argued that no transformations one agent brings about of a thing in the world justifies depriving others of their right to use that thing without their consent. Since everyone has an equal right to everything, there is no natural right to private property, according to Gibbard. Social considerations may overrule this natural right of everyone to everything, but only in such a way as to give rise to encumbered property rights.

The existence of natural exclusive rights to move and use our bodies constitutes an exception to the principle that each of us has equal prima facie rights to move and use any thing in the world. Rather than treating private property as justified deprivation of the rights of others, this paper begins with this exception to equal rights of everyone to everything and shows how private property rights are extensions of this exception. Since other people, prima facie, have no rights to the use and movement of our bodies, no deprivation of rights needs to be justified either for the bodies themselves or for the extended bodies argued for in the paper.

I will argue in the fourth section of the paper that we do each have special exclusive rights to move and use our bodies and to exclude other persons from moving and using our bodies. For the moment though, I take as a premise that everyone doesn't have equal prima facie rights with respect to all entities in the world because each of us has exclusive prima facie rights to move and use his body.

Intuitively, our special rights with respect to our bodies are independent of several contingencies. In bringing out these intuitions, I am expressing the only data we have that these rights *are* independent of these contingencies.

(1) In the first place, our special rights with respect to our bodies do not depend on the relative equality or efficacy of our bodies. If we were much larger or more excellent physically, we would still have these special rights. If only one of us has a better body, he has every special right with respect to his body that we have with respect to ours.

This last claim needs support, since it countenances a kind of inequality. Suppose that in an isolated society of midgets, there is one normal sized person. That normal sized person has the same rights with respect to his body that we have with respect to ours. Being born into a society of midgets can't reduce a person's rights, since such birth isn't his fault or choice. But our existence as normal sized persons external to this isolated society is morally irrelevant to the normal sized person's rights in that society. Whether normal sized persons exist elsewhere or not, a normal sized person has exclusive prima facie rights to move and use his body. So inequalities among bodies do not affect the fact that each person has special exclusive rights to move and use his body.

The principle of the above argument is that a person can't lose a natural right against his will except by actions that are his fault or choice. This claim is not limited to relative size, strength, or talents. The only two-armed person, the only four-armed person, the only adequately furry person, or the only person able to do his own photosynthesis likewise have exclusive prima facie rights to their bodies' motions and use.

The independence of body rights from contingencies of size, strength, and capacities is compatible with the dependence of some consequences of those rights on contingencies of relative size. The right itself has an essence which can be confused with accidental consequences of that right in a given situation. That is, I (accidentally) have a right to exhale in class in part because my exhalations are (by accident) not fatal in the concentrations to which other members of the class are exposed. If the situation were different, I would not have this derivative right, though I would have the underlying basic rights from which the right to exhale around others, given the actual situation, is derived. What is contingent is that exhalation is not a threat.

Thus, for instance, my right to move my body over public bridges might disappear if I were very large. This sort of change of rights to bodily motions with change of bodily size, though, isn't an essential change, but rather the falsifying of the antecedent of a "conditional" right we now have. Such an antecedent in this case might be 'If one's use of a bridge cannot be expected to destroy it. . . .' Actual cases in which ordinarily true antecedents about a lack of threat break down occur in the case of contagious diseases, where we do restrict people's motions and exhalations because they are threats. Nozick handles such questions in Chapter 4 of *Anarchy, State and, Utopia.*

(2) The second kind of morally irrelevant contingency involves the difficulty of removal and transfer of parts of bodies. The fact that the removal of parts of our body is often accompanied by a sensation of pain isn't essential to our right to use and move our body. Our natural rights have been violated when an arm is taken for food even if it doesn't hurt. The non-routiness of removal and transplant of body parts is similarly morally irrelevant to our rights with respect to our bodies. If we now have special exclusive rights to the use of our arms and legs, developments in medical technology which allowed us to pluck them off and store them for later use or donate them to the armless would not remove that right. The principle here is that if we have a right at one time, changes in what people can do can't remove that right.

Related to the moral irrelevance of this contingency is the irrelevance of the fact that we have bodies constructed of protein in the "natural" way. If we were constructed of wires and electric motors, then, given that we were agents, we would have the same rights with respect to plastic and metallic bodily parts that we do with respect to protein parts. In the same way, if our conscious nervous system took over some of the functions of tissue construction now done automatically, we would have the same rights with respect to parts of our body so constructed that we do with respect to our "naturally" constructed parts. Suppose we learned how to take some egg whites, soy beans and vitamin pills, put them into a blender and make an attractive bicep which could be implanted in an arm. We would have all rights with respect to such a bicep which we have with respect to our present biceps.

(3) Not only is it morally irrelevant that parts of the body can't be detached routinely or without pain, it is also irrelevant that parts of the body are standardly attached at all or even have sensation and "agent-type" control. I'll first argue that sensation and agent-type control are irrelevant and then argue that attachment is irrelevant.

Sensation and agent-type control are *actually* lacking in many parts of the natural body. We don't have pain-sensitive nerve endings in our brains, for instance. Much of our control of our brains is *via* other agents we've hired, i.e. neurosurgeons, not agent-type control. If we were abnormal in this respect, so that most people had to have anaesthesia for brain surgery and could do their own lobotomies from the inside, surely our rights not to have our brains interfered with wouldn't be diminished. In the same way, the fact that we are not all adept enough at yoga to control our heartbeat, digestion, and hormome production doesn't make our rights in relation to our hearts, gastro-intestinal tracts, and glands any less. Neither sensation nor control in a direct "agent-type" way is essential to an entity's being a part of the body. Thus the fact that a person has sensation and agent-control of a body part can't be what makes another's use of that body part against a person's will a wrong.

It might be argued that sensation and agent-type control matter in the case of a body part in which there is normally sensation and agent-type control. But for one thing: this deprives paralyzed people of rights which they plausibly have. A person with damage to his leg nerves who has no sensation in or control of his leg below the knee still has his rights violated if we painlessly remove it, whether or not he is able to hobble around on it.

If having normal sensation and control is what matters, we have the further problem that what is normal seems to be quite accidental. Some can wiggle their ears. Yogi's can do all sorts of things. If these skills were more widely taught, and so became normal, surely we who lack those skills wouldn't *lose* some prerogatives.

To see the irrelevance of sensation and agent control more clearly, imagine installing sensors and control devices in a model airplane and, rather than having the dials and push buttons ordinarily associated with radio controlled model building, having these controls and sensors hooked up to the agent's motor and sensory nerves. In such a variation of model airplane technology, the agent senses his plane's altitude, etc., directly rather than by looking at dials, and makes his plane bank and roll in the way he moves his fingers. (This would take some practice, like wiggling the ears.) On the view that special body rights are special because of agent-type control and sensation, the person who went to the trouble of installing this very elaborate setup would have rights with respect to his model airplane that I lack with respect to mine. But this is intuitively false. We each have equal rights with respect to our planes. His elaborate organic control box doesn't make his plane more special to him than mine is to me. Our natural rights with respect to our bodies, then, are not essentially connected with sensation and agent-type control.

Attachment might seem to be the feature of body parts that is essential to the special rights we have with respect to our bodies. I will argue that attachment doesn't gain us rights and that detachment doesn't diminish our rights.

Suppose that in 1981 Cadillac offers as an optional replacement for seatbelts a specially constructed protein car, all of whose parts are attached by ligaments, etc., just as a natural body is. This car is designed so that, when the driver sits in it, his skin in contact with the seat dissolves and the material of the seat sends tendrils into his body very quickly. There is some fluid interchange, etc., just as in the case of graftings. (For driver convenience, the process is brief, painless, and reversible by a push button.) It would seem that this option doesn't give the driver of the Cadillac special rights to it which the driver of a Cadillac without such an option lacks. Of course, just as we must allow a person to release his shoulder belts before removing him from a car, so we must allow this person to become detached from this specially equipped car. (And, if we've taken someone's arm by eminent domain, we must allow the person to take procedures which will make removal of his arm as painless and as harmless as possible.) "Organic attachment," then, doesn't seem to be the source of special prerogatives with respect to bodies, since there can be attachment without a difference in the rights we have with respect to things.

That detachment doesn't diminish rights can be seen by considering the following deviation in human physiology: Reed, of the Fantastic Four,[5] is able to form what amount to pseudo-pods. For instance he can reach out one hundred feet with a hand, expand the surface for his hand to about twenty square feet, and grab a criminal on the run. (As I understand it, the volume of his body remains constant.) Consider the situation when he's reached as far as he can. Presumably, the ultimate stretch leaves his hand connected to the rest of his body by one motor and one sensory nerve bundle. This long strand still constitutes attachment and allows natural agent-type control. A modified version of this, which would allow for still longer reach, would use just a single fiber of, say, ligament-tissue. What might suffice in this physiology, if Reed is to use his hand in an agent-type way, would be a pair of tiny radio transceivers in the hand and trunk to get the hand to do the right thing and to "report back." The hand is still attached, but the attachment no longer seems important, since it doesn't have the strength to hold the hand from further separation. In fact, Remote Man, a crime fighting rival who dispenses with the connecting fiber, would seem to have a hand with the same moral status as our modified Reed. When we switch over to total radio control without the connecting fiber, nothing essential is changed. Remote Man has hands with much longer range, and those hands are still part of his body, with all rights accruing thereby. But his relation to those hands is exactly like that of the second model airplane owner. So it appears that attachment is not essential to whether a thing is part of our body or whether we have body rights with respect to it.

Since neither sensation and agent-type control nor attachment is essential to body rights, at least the burden of proof is on someone who claims that the disjunction is essential. If Remote Man should decide to replace his neural hookups to his hands with a system of dials and push buttons, it would seem that this modification wouldn't change his rights with respect to his hands.

The above arguments indicate that "control" in any very clear sense, agent-type or otherwise, is irrelevant to body rights if agent-type control is irrelevant. No moral difference attaches between a system in which arms are moved by a generally reliable set of dials and switches and one which often breaks down. Since nothing about radio waves is morally privileged, a system in which winged couriers are hired to fly back and forth from trunk to arm is likewise morally on a par with more usual systems of arm movement. If unreliable switches don't diminish rights any more than certain nervous diseases, neither do unreliable couriers hired for the same job. Any number of intermediaries between a direct "act of will" and a motion of the hand leave body rights intact. If the couriers and their subcontracted couriers are corrupt shirkers, the actual control I have over my body can become more normative than real. (Rather like the control I had over my Arabian oil refinery.)

(4) The final independence from contingency concerns bodily surpluses. Intuitively we have the right to exclusive use of our bodies even when we have more body than we need or are likely to need. In a way, this follows from the point that inequalities among bodies are acceptable and compatible with everyone having special exclusive rights to use and move his body as he sees fit. After all, having a body with larger and stronger biceps than most other people gives a person a surplus of strength—more than he really needs, an envious weakling might claim. Furthermore, most of us have two kidneys and could get along with one. The chances of needing that extra kidney are really rather small, compared to the chances of needing an extra car, for instance. If a person has exclusive rights to his extra kidney when he has two, though, he has such rights when he has five. So, if we have an exclusive natural right to the movement and use of our bodies, we have that right even when we have a surplus.

II. THE DERIVATION OF PROPERTY RIGHTS

Rights are instances of principles. To *derive* a right is to show that whatever moral principles apply to a clear case in which there is the right, apply also to a new case in which the right is not clear. If no moral distinction can be drawn between the cases, then if there is a right in the one case, there is that right in the other case as well.

The derivation of property rights from rights with respect to our bodies depends on observing that *things* can become part of our bodies. If a person has used some unappropriated and *therefore no-one's food* and converted it to protein, he now has the right to exclusive use of that protein. The difference from Gibbard's case of the cleared and planted cornfield,[6] to which everyone seems to have a right (since they haven't given their permission for the right to be removed) is only that, in the case of conversion into protein, something is incorporated into a person's *body*. If we do have special exclusive rights with respect to our bodies, this kind of incorporation is one way of making non-property into private property. That is, incorporation into a body turns what everyone has a right to use into something only one person has a right to use, if we have exclusive rights to move and use our bodies. The argument below claims that Gibbard's cornfield case is not significantly different from the conversion to protein case, and that the industrious farmer has the same rights with respect to his cornfield that you have with respect to your arm.

To begin this argument, remember that nothing is special about internal unconscious processes as far as moral rights go. Similarly, whether a bodily part is made of protein is morally irrelevant, as we have argued. Suppose a person could eat twigs and branches and grow a wooden leg. This wooden leg would have the same moral status as our protein legs. Since there's nothing special about internal processes either, a person who used some unwanted stuff from the dump and built himself an artificial leg with it would have a leg which was morally equivalent to our "natural" legs. A transformation of non-property-stuff to which everyone had a right, into a private leg to which exactly one person has rights seems to have been accomplished without the consent of those who *had* an equal right to that stuff in the dump. Building artificial limbs is morally equivalent to eating food.

Some of the things in the world to which everyone has an equal right can be removed from that domain without the consent of those whose rights are diminished, if no one's special rights have been violated. In the case both of building and attaching an artificial limb and that of eating an apple from the woods, something unclaimed has been taken out of the public domain. So far, only the limited number of things that can be made into artificial or real limbs seem to be able to be thus appropriated. The following arguments show that, once artificial limbs are permitted as parts of bodies, nothing stops a person's incorporation of virtually anything.

Artificial arms and legs made from unwanted or unclaimed stuff seem to be morally equivalent to our bodies. But the same holds true of a member of an armless society who builds himself a pair of arms. Since our natural and artificial arms are ours to do with as we please, so are this person's arms. The fact that arms aren't a "natural" part of the bodies of his fellows doesn't deprive him of the exclusive right to the use and motion of his arms. As we have argued above when imagining this society to be isolated, our existence is morally irrelevant to this person's rights. So whether an artificial body part is a makeshift for one "found in nature" is irrelevant to our rights with respect to such a part.

I've already argued that detachability and whether a body part is surplus or not are morally irrelevant. So the person with two artificial arms can leave them at home if he wishes and still have exclusive rights to their use, just as if we could detach our natural arms (perhaps in order to wear a new style sweater). Those arms lying on our dresser are still ours, given that we have the exclusive right to move and use our body. I have also argued that the lack of pain that loss of an artificial arm gives is irrelevant. A sensation can't create a right. That artificial arms can also be far better than any normal arm without significant moral difference from fleshly arms follows from the permissibility of inequalities in bodies.

If an artificial body part doesn't have to be *natural* for our group for us to have body rights with respect to it, then an artificial version of anything that someone *could* have as a body part can be something we can acquire an exclusive right to. This is true even if it's like a remote-control artificial arm which is detached at all times. If detachability is all right for preserving body rights, usable body parts need never be attached. For instance, men are not usually born naturally furry enough for protection from cold and embarassment. So legitimately acquired clothing is for moral purposes artificial fur, i.e., an artificial and always detached body part. Since an animal could have very rapid and adaptable molting, and thus could have what amounts to spare furs just as we have spare kidneys, nothing prevents exclusive rights to whole wardrobes as artificial body parts.

In the same way, turtles and snails have shelters which grow as parts of their bodies. We genetically defective humans have designed artificial shells with pleasant features lacking in the nicest turtle shells. In principle, nothing morally distinguishes my mansion from an artificial arm several times defter and stronger than any natural arm. Since nothing morally distinguishes such an artificial arm from a natural arm, my mansion is, at least morally speaking, a part of me. (The physical and emotional damage to me at its removal may be as intense as that I feel when I've lost a finger.)

Extensions to most other useful things a person might own should be obvious. We could be telepathic, naturally musical, very fast on our feet, have luminescent protuberances, and have a very accurate sense of time. We could, similarly, have a capacity for using very flexible stored material to build parts of our body as they were needed, much as we store fat. (Justifying ownership of money will require the section to follow on transfer rights, but the morally relevant description of money is that it is just a kind of social artificial body part construction material.)

No limitation is in sight with respect to usefulness, either. Diamonds and sequined dresses are for moral purposes artificial plumage. Since my pretty eyes are mine to move and use as I please, your lavender sunglasses are likewise yours. You must not use mine and I must not use yours without your consent.

The argument so far makes the claim that there is no line between what's part of the body of a person and what is his property. In most actual cases, things seem to group themselves into body parts and things that are not body parts. This grouping, though, is accidental and doesn't reflect any real difference in moral or metaphysical kind. An analogy: Suppose that there is in fact an undiscovered genetic continuum. That is, there are physically possible animals such that each of them looks to be of the same kind as the next on the continuum but the first in the sequence is a "paradigm rabbit" and the last a "paradigm squirrel." We can imagine the intermediates as either undiscovered (by accident) but around, as very rare, or as merely possible. If we had different obligations toward rabbits and squirrels (e.g. there are circumstances when it is permissible to kill a rabbit for food but none in which it is permissible to kill a squirrel), there would have to be a point at which a moral line could be drawn with some metaphysical backing. That is, at some point in the sequence, animals have a property which makes killing them wrong. But if the variations are continuous or close enough so that it is correct to treat adjacent elements in the same way, then the differences in moral judgements of obligation are not justifiable, since rights and obligations must depend on principles.

I don't claim that this type of argument applies for moral argument in general. I don't, for instance, hold that it applies to "good" and "ought" arguments. That is, if the consideration that applied were "the shorter a thing's tail is, the *worse* it is to kill it," then there could be significant moral differences between squirrel and rabbit killing even though no sharp line separated them.

But this consideration against rabbit killing is a guideline and not an absolute, since circumstances can make a given killing of a paradigm rabbit a good thing to do. "Good," roughly speaking, is an attributive under which lies a continuous dimension, unlike "has a right." Questions about whether an act is good are questions of whether an act is *better than* an alternative, roughly. But "better than" can be a dimension, so that insignificant changes can add up to one alternative outscoring another.

"Right" is not an attributive[6] and has no underlying dimension. Features relevant to rights are present or absent in a case. Violations of rights are all wrongs, but some wrongs are worse than others.

Further features show that "right," "wrong," and "is obliged" are logically different from "good," "bad" and "ought".[7] When a right has been violated, a wrong has been done even when it is outweighed by considerations of good and bad, or by conflicts with other rights. On the other hand, if it is good, other things being equal, to have pleasure, a particular case of having pleasure which has bad consequences may be no longer good at all.

That is, rights and obligations do not disappear when they are overridden, whereas good and "oughts" do. This, I have argued,[8] is because goodness and "ought-sentences" are governed by guidelines roughly analogous to probability principles, in which "it is probable that Q, given P" and "it is probable that not Q, given P and R" can both be true, whereas rights and obligations are governed by principles analogous to universal quantifications, in which "(x) $(Fx{\rightarrow}Gx)$" and "(x) $(Fx \text{ & } Px \text{ & } - Gx)$" cannot both be true.

These two distinctions are connected in the following way. If a "$(x)(Fx{\rightarrow}Gx)$"—type principle explains the right of b to c, then if b lacks a right to d, F must be present in one case and *absent* in the other. Thus any transition from having a right to lacking a right must be a loss of a property morally significant by itself. On the other hand, if a "given feature Q, doing a is good" principle can explain why it is good for Jones to do a, "given features Q, Rl ... Rn, not doing a is good" could explain why it was *not* good for Jones to do a even though no one of Rl ... Rn *by itself* is morally significant. Furthermore, [Q, Rl ... Rn, Rn 1] might again make it *good* for Jones to do a. Ri has no moral significance, in isolation, then, but only given a "context." So a transition-property in the case of "good" need have nothing intrinsically moral about it.

If rights *can* be overridden by considerations of utility, then a wrong has still been done, but it will be a wrong that ought to have been done because it was a good thing. In establishing property *rights,* then, we are not establishing the inviolability of property but rather showing that a wrong is done when property is taken away from its rightful owner. How bad violating someone's property rights is in a given situation *may* depend on the circumstances of the case and the magnitudes of the goods to be derived from such violation. There may well be circumstances in which violations of someone's property rights is a good thing and so ought to be done. (Thus what politics my view of property commits one to depends on how and whether one thinks that rights can be overridden by utility. That is, rights and their violation must somehow fit into an overall account of what it is good to do. Violating rights, at least on the whole, must be a bad thing, so that these families of moral facts fit together. I have no satisfying answer to the question of how the two sorts of principles cohere to tell us what it is moral to do.)

Thus, since rights require principles of the "$(x)(Fx{\to}Gx)$" kind in which "F" is not a degree-term, the argument that, if no line can be drawn between cases, the right is still there, holds. That is, "derivation" by *principles* requires that significant moral distinctions be drawn between cases. To justifiably ascribe a right in one case and withhold it in another requires that some *property* which distinguishes the two cases in a morally relevant way be appealed to. No such *lines* need be drawn in the case of goods and bads, since there is an underlying dimension on which they are attributives. (So, for instance, gentle spanking of a child for obnoxiousness can be a good thing in the circumstances while bludgeoning her is not a good thing, even though perhaps is a continuum of ergs expended between gentle spankings and bludgeonings. Roughly, even though an erg is not a significant difference, a single erg's difference can distinguish a good chastisement from one that ought not to have been done.)

I have sketched some of the intermediate stages between paradigm bodies and paradigm non-bodies to show that some moral rights and obligations with respect to one apply also to the others. If there are principles which fail to apply to paradigm non-bodies, there must be a line to be drawn. If there is a line to be drawn, it must be drawn somewhere, and I can see no justification for any such line. Each stage is morally indistinguishable by principles from the next. Your property *is* your body.

III. THE USE OF THE BODY: TRANSFER RIGHTS

Thus far we have argued that, given that a person has an exclusive right to the use of his body, he can have anything he has incorporated out of unwanted stuff. Precisely what it takes for there to be "incorporation" is something that we can ignore for purposes of this paper. For our purposes, obvious cases of making things, clearing fields, and so forth will do. I believe that incorporation is a real relation, if persons are real, but I am not prepared to specify its truth-conditions. In a state of nature where there is unincorporated stuff, such unincorporated stuff can be made into parts of a body and thus become a person's private possession. To get fabulously wealthy, though, a person needs to acquire another person's stuff, since life is too short for enough of the above kinds of manufacture, and since, in fact, unincorporated valuables are hard to find. The legitimation of fabulous wealth, then, requires that transfer rights of property be justified and derived. (Legitimation requires only that a right is established, not that it be shown that fabulous wealth *ought* to be encouraged or that it is a good thing.)

Transfer rights are derived from our right to *use* our bodies. What are the uses of the body to which a person has exclusive rights? We can use our fingers as dike plugs, our arms as paperweights, signal devices and so forth. We can use one body part to make another. A common medical procedure is to take a vein out of a thigh and use it to replace a damaged vein elsewhere. If technology advanced, it might be possible to transform a person's spare kidney into a liver. Any use a person makes of his body, including getting a better body, is his exclusive prerogative, if it doesn't violate others' rights.

A social way of using one's body would be using parts of it as items of trade. This is morally no different from using up a lot of stored body fat in the effort required to build an artificial arm using only your feet. Imagine an unfortunate who not only has the task of building an arm in such conditions, but burns up body fat and muscle tissue from specific locations rather than diffusely as we do. That is, in order to build his artificial arm he has to burn up a buttock, for instance. Such a person is using, by divesting himself of, one body part in order to get another one. Part of the body is sacrificed to create or acquire a more needed part. It would seem that such a person has the right to use his body this way, if we have the right to burn body fat for our ends. The social procedure of trading is to be described for moral purposes as essentially the same procedure.

So, suppose you need a kidney and I need an arm. You have an arm you can get along without and I have a spare kidney. If we both have a right to use our bodies as we see fit, it seems that we can trade one part for another, using an arm to get a kidney and vice versa. If we can use body fat or burn up a buttock to gain an external arm by building, we can use an arm to get a prefabricated kidney by trade. When we use a bodily part this way, we voluntarily let someone incorporate a part of our body into his body.

What holds of natural body parts, though, holds equally for artificial body parts. Furthermore, if you have flexible artificial part-building material, you can trade that for body parts, that is, buy them with money.

If you have the right to use your body as you please, no outside agent can decide when you're making a fair trade. If you have special rights with respect to your body, you have the right to make trades for any purpose you please and for any item someone is willing to trade you, barring fraud, etc. So you can trade an arm for a kiss, using a body part to get pleasure. If you can trade an arm for a kiss, though, you can trade an arm for the pleasure of having someone else have your arm. You can give away body parts at will. If this is a use to which your body rights guarantee that you have a right, then the recipient acquires body rights to these gifts just as firmly as you had them. That is, if such gifts and trades are legitimate uses of the body, then the recipient of a traded or donated item can have exclusive rights to it just in virtue of the donor's right to use his body. ("Weaker" sorts of gifts are, of course, allowable also. How much of a property right is transferred depends on the agent and the relevant contracts, social and personal.)

If any rights we have with respect to our natural bodies are also rights we have with respect to artificial parts, we can trade or give houses, money, clothes, diamonds, or whatever. By astute trading or by the lucky accident of being well-loved or well-born, a person can have exclusive prima facie rights to the use and movement of any number of things whatsoever.

As I have said, it may be that these rights really are just prima facie and that some considerations may override them. For example, it may be that the uncharitable owner of the world's total food supply can legitimately be coerced into parting with some of his property. Such a violation of property rights, though, is on a par with taking the flesh of the only robust person against his will to feed the starving. Each such overriding of property rights must be justified against a strong prima facie right of persons to control what they legitimately have as body parts. I have no idea *how* principles of good and bad can suffice to make it the case that we ought to violate another's rights.

Furthermore, that a thing has been incorporated into a person's body only gives him a property right to it, even prima facie, if its incorporation violated no one else's rights. If I take your arm while you're asleep, and attach it to myself, I don't have a property right to it, since it's not clear that it's really part of *my* body. This paper takes no position on what steps you're entitled to take by way of recovery of the arm or the money I earn by use of the arm. If I innocently buy your arm from someone, now dead, who stole it from you in your sleep, subtler problems of rights and compensation arise. The above theory deals directly only with property whose history doesn't contain such injustices. Much actual "property" may well be a result of assiduous employment of goods with such tainted histories. Thus the theory as developed so far may say little about who owns what in the real world.

IV. THE TRUTH OF THE ANTECEDENT: OUR RIGHTS TO OUR BODIES

The derivation of our rights with respect to our bodies depends on finding some still more basic right which entails our right to move and use our bodies. I argue that our right to move and use our bodies as we please, and the obligation others have not to move, use, or transform our bodies against our will, is essential to our right to exist as agents at all. If we have a right to exist, then we have a right not to have our agenthood terminated. I will show that, if we have a right not to have our agenthood terminated, then we must have a right to the exclusive use and movement of our bodies, natural and extended.

To begin with, suppose that two-substance dualism is false, so that, at least, destroying a brain destroys a person. If we do not have exclusive rights to move, use, and transform our bodies, another could legitimately and permissibly eat our brain for supper, or transform it into viscous paving material. If another quicker person has equal right to use and move your body, it seems that he can move your brain out of your head and use it for paving material. But this gives him the right to destroy you. When your body is sufficiently transformed, you're gone.

The obvious strategy to avoid body rights and keep equal rights to all entities for all people without making such agent-termination permissible is to propose a rule such as: "It is permitted to use any thing one pleases, but one must not terminate an agent's agenthood." To begin to see what is wrong with this rule, we should note that many uses short of using a person's brain for paving material in effect eliminate agenthood. If I'm a powerful telepath and decide to transform Jones in ways which do not kill the organism, for instance by shaping his will to fit mine so that my dishes get done without effort on my part, I've destroyed Jones' agenthood. Similarly, a person's agenthood is effectively destroyed in most cases if you just transform his arms and legs and muscle into hamburger.

Eliminating agenthood seems to be a matter of degree. No line obtains between diminishing an agent's power and making him no agent at all. If we chop off a section of a finger, we might say that the agent is still there, able to affect the world. In fact, it would seem that any minute diminution of an agent's body would be such that, if the agent were there before the diminution, he would be there after it. But if no such diminution eliminates the agent, the agent can act without a body, which is false. Thus the only *principle* which could give a person the right to be an agent would give a person a right to be as much of an agent as he is, if eliminating agenthood is essentially vague and also violates rights.

If a person has a right to be an agent, he must have a special right to whatever body he has, since no narrower rule can be justified. A person's special right to his body is just his right to be. Since a person does have a right to be an agent, and since exclusive rights to movement, use and transformation of some of his body is essential to his agenthood, and since no moral justification exists for drawing the line anywhere, a person has exclusive rights to all of his body. This argument doesn't give agents the right to use whatever power they have, if that power involves usurpation of another's body.

It may be objected that theft of "surpluses" doesn't diminish agenthood. But surpluses can be used both to acquire more stuff and as "insurance" for various risky activities. If I have only one kidney, I can still risk it playing football, but it's not usually rational to do so. If being an agent involves planning for the future, and actions are constrained by possible future needs, then theft of surpluses diminishes agenthood. In any case, what counts as a surplus is vague and interest relative, by obvious arguments.

The same considerations apply to "artificial" body parts. You can kill an eskimo just as effectively by transforming his clothes to dust as by transforming his brain to pavement. You may diminish a person's agenthood just as much by taking his car as by taking his right eye. Property, i.e., artificial body parts, can be just as important to our agency as "natural" body parts. If the right to agenthood is what preserves rights to bodies, and no line can be drawn between permissible and impermissible body reductions, then a person has rights to all of his property by the same argument. No significant moral difference in kind obtains between eliminating my ability to play softball by taking my knees away and eliminating my ability to play the market by taking my money away. Crimes against property are just crimes against persons which tend not to produce immediate sensations of pain. Theft, taxation, and disembowelment are different forms of the same kind of violation of rights.

V. SOCIAL INSTITUTIONS AND PROPERTY RIGHTS: A CURSORY TREATMENT

Many people hold that property and property rights are essentially social, so that the most a derivation such as the above can show is what pre-institutional property rights might be. Since I hold that incorporation and property rights are natural, i.e., independent of institutions, the arguments to the opposite conclusion must be dealt with. The basic current form of the argument says that, since property and property rights are logically connected to other persons, rights are essentially social. Furthermore, if rights belong to people essentially, then people are essentially social entities and it doesn't really make sense to derive "rights" for them in an individualistic, a-historical way. I'll deal with the social nature of rights, which implies that what your property rights are depends on what your society is, and then discuss the claim that persons are essentially social.

Property rights *are* social in the sense that an agent in isolation has in fact exclusive use of everything and so has no call to enforce any rights. This though, entails neither that what rights a person has varies from society to society nor that those rights are properties of an individual who is of necessity social.

First, the non-relativity argument: Murder, torture for fun, and enslavement are violations which likewise require other persons. Intuitively, though, the rights that such acts violate are differently enforced in different societies. A society which condones killing someone, if a majority in it so vote, is not a society in which such killing does not violate rights. It is an unjust society, one whose laws do not protect certain rights. So the claim that rights can't be logically independent of some society does not show that rights vary from society to society.

I regard rights as necessary conditional features of persons *qua* persons. I will argue later that "person *qua* person" is a notion which is metaphysically independent of "society." How can there be essential features of persons which are logically connected to societies unless the person is essentially social and the features dependent for their reality on the society the person is in? The following argument should make this independence clear and should clarify what a necessary conditional feature is:

(1) Brontosauri are essentially over seven tons (suppose).
(2) Chipmunks are essentially under one pound.
(3) Necessarily, any brontosaurus outweighs any chipmunk.
(4) Brontosauri have an essential feature which is logically connected to chipmunks, i.e., which cannot be made sense of apart from the concept of a chipmunk.

(5) Brontosauri are inconceivable apart from chipmunks, if necessary features follow from every adequate concept.

(6) The weight of a brontosaurus is something he has only in relation to chipmunks.

The absurdity of conclusion (5) will be used to argue that persons are not essentially social even though some of their essential features are logically connected to society. That of conclusion (6) I now use to argue that rights are properties of persons apart from societies in the same way that a brontosaurus' disposition to outweigh any chipmunk is a feature it has in itself which doesn't depend on the being of chipmunks. The argument depends on noting that another description of exactly the same feature doesn't make reference to chipmunks. Outweighing chipmunks is a feature that derives from brontosauri necessarily weighing over seven tons. Brontosauri, in virtue of their necessary weight, are such that, if there are chipmunks, then in virtue of necessities about chipmunks each brontosaurus necessarily outweighs each of them. Logical connections between features are connections between features under a description. Any two kinds with distinct essences can be "logically" connected in this way by an obvious argument. I would argue that a person's rights derive from his being a rational agent. A rational agent is necessarily such that, if he's in contact with other rational agents, he should be treated by them in certain ways. This feature gives him his rights. But this no more shows that he or his rights depend on other agents than the analogous argument shows that a brontosaurus' weight depends on chipmunks.

The derivation of rights from rational agenthood is, admittedly, tricky, and I refer the reader to Kant for a good sketch. The importation of a society, though, seems not to reduce the problem. If one person can't have rights, how can a lot of people help?

For many people, the flaw in the derivation of society-independent rights from rational agenthood is that rational agenthood is, arguably, impossible without the support of the society. An entity cannot be a rational agent outside of a society. This, along with the argument that rights are essential to man, rights are essentially social, so man is essentially social, is one of the main rational supports of the view that individualist approaches to ethical and social philosophy are misguided.

Rights, on any account, derive from the nature of man. The real reason a defender of a social basis for property rights thinks property rights are social fabrications is that he thinks all rights are social fabrications, because the nature of man is to be a social entity. A well regarded argument for this claim takes the nature of man to be rational agency and argues that being a rational agent requires social support. To be a rational agent requires being something which represents states of affairs truly or falsely, and plans on the basis of such representation. To represent a state of affairs is to have terms or thought tokens which pick out properties and objects, i.e., which refer to properties and objects. A term's reference is determined by what it is applied to—i.e., what a culture means by "toad" depends on what things they call toads. The culture's use of a term, its dispositions to apply the term, determine what the term is true of. Roughly, then, the content of a concept determines its referent. When this theory of reference is applied to an isolated individual, though, it becomes impossible for that individual to state falsehoods. If what he says determines what he's talking about, and this determination proceeds by making what he applies the term to something to which the term applies, then the person can say nothing but truths, by the very nature of what "applying to an entity" is. That is, there is always some extension which fits exactly the person's use of a term, so that, by the principle that reference is a function of use, no alternative utterance the person might have made could be false. But unless there is some possibility of uttering falsehoods, there can be no uttering of truths.

On the "meaning is use" theory, then, the unit for determining reference and therefore truth must be the response patterns of groups of people, so that a kind of majority rule can determine a reference and a correctness of response relative to which an individual can deviate. So if rationality requires representation of truth and falsity, and such representation requires a history of membership in a society, rational agenthood is possible only in a society. So if man is essentially rational, he is essentially social.

What is wrong with this argument is that it rests on a mistaken theory of reference.[9] Reference does not work by matching dispositions to respond with the objects which would elicit those dispositions. The "meaning is use" theory is a theory that internal features of concepts determine reference, so that, to determine reference, we check a culture's head, check the world, and see what matches what. This theory has been attacked[10] and shown to be self-contradictory.[11] Reference depends on what is in the world, what kinds there actually are, not on what sets of things our response patterns would pick out. If a whole culture would be fooled by artificial diamonds made of synthetic abrozite, that doesn't mean that their term "diamond" refers to diamonds and abrozite. So an individual can have his own language apart from a society. Once this isolated speaker names a certain substance "gold," then, if what he next applies the term to is not of the same kind, he has said something false. Reference is up to us when we're baptizing, but reference of general terms[12] is to kinds, and what is another element of the same kind is not up to us or to the contents of our concepts, but rather up to nature.

So an entity can be a rational agent without being part of a society. If rights devolve from the essential nature of man and man is only accidentally social, rights cannot be social fabrications. Societies can only protect or fail to protect rights that are there.

In any case, my derivation is primary and prior to any historical account. If persons really exist, they have a nature. If there are no reasons to think that their nature is social, then none of their rights can be dependent on what society they live in. All persons have the same essential features which are their rights. So historical accounts of rights are just accounts of how societies have come to recognize and disavow certain rights (rather like the history of science). Capitalism may be doomed historically, at least for a while, but this no more shows that it is mistaken than the inevitability of the dark ages showed that Archimedes and Euclid were wrong. There is no reason to think that great discoveries necessarily stay believed, apart from confidence in some mystical progress.[13]

NOTES

[1] Locke, John, *Second Treatise of Civil Government,* Sec. 27 (Henry Regnery Company: Chicago, 1955): 22.

[2] Nozick, Robert, *Anarchy, State, and Utopia,* (Basic Books, Inc.: New York, 1974).

[3] Gibbard, Alan, "Natural Property Rights," NOÛS (1976): 77.

[4] Gibbard, p.85.

[5] *Fantastic Four* (Marvel Comics Group: New York, November 1968) *passim.* Plastic Man had similar talents.

[6] Gibbard, pp.79ff.

[7] For an explanation and theory of attributives see Sam Wheeler's "Attributives and Their Modifiers," NOÛS 6(1972): 310–34.

[8] See "Inference and the Logical 'Ought'," *loc. cit.* This is borrowed from Donald Davidson's "How is Weakness of the Will Possible," in *Moral Concepts* ed. by Joel Feinberg (London: Oxford University Press, 1969).

[10] Kripke, Saul, "Naming and Necessity," in Davidson and Harman, eds., *Semantics of Natural Languages* (D. Reidel: Dordrecht, Holland, 1972): 253–5.

[11] That this is the import of Kripke's argument is argued in Sam Wheeler's "Reference and Vagueness," *Synthese* 30 (1975): 378–9.

[12] If reference is a real relation, then whether a term is a general term will be a fact of nature, not an artifact of a "general term language game."

[13] I thank the following people for helpful comments on earlier versions of this paper: David Braybrooke, Roger Gottlieb, A. S. McGrade, Joel Kupperman, Robert Nozick, Michael Simon and John Troyer.

part SIX

POLITICAL ECONOMY

Adam Smith and Karl Marx were both concerned with political economy, not just with the purely formal principles of economics, as these are conceived of by many neoclassical economists and some contemporary Marxists. What general views did Smith and Marx advance on the relevant topics of political economy—such as justice, ownership, liberty, and personal autonomy? What general criticisms can be made of these positions, and what developments can be advanced from them?

Here we do not so much see a direct face-off between the two competing schools of thought, but a scholarship within different outlooks, based on the research of scholars who have occupied themselves with the study of Smith's capitalism and Marx's communism, as well as with the implications of these systems for understanding various areas of political economy.

LEONARD BILLET

ADAM SMITH AND JUSTICE

There is much debate about whether Adam Smith meant to defend merely a practically useful economic system, with little or no genuine concern for justice, or whether his main concern was with human justice, out of which grew his advocacy of a largely free economic system. Leonard Billet—who has taught political science at the University of California at Los Angeles and has written other essays on Adam Smith's moral philosophy—regards Smith as a champion of justice, one who saw the kind of liberty under which capitalism flourishes as essential to such justice. In the exploration of the differences between our two systems, it will be useful to look at one of the principal defenders of the system of capitalism.

The Wealth of Nations is fundamentally concerned with the question, what is a just economy? References to justice and injustice, equity and oppression appear so frequently in Adam Smith's treatise that it is surprising to note the absence of the just economy theme in scholarly commentary on *The Wealth of Nations.*[1] Yet the persistent moral and political elements in his political economy are neither paradoxical nor ornamental. Adam Smith considered his treatise to be a work of political science and an instrument of political reform. He had intended to write a comprehensive work on jurisprudence or "the theory of the general principles which ought to run through and be the foundation of, the laws of all nations," which, he said, was "of all sciences by far the most important."[2] Smith referred to *The Wealth of Nations* as a partial fulfillment of his grand design.

In order to comprehend the basic moral and political framework of Adam Smith's economic thought, one must refer to his first book, *The Theory of Moral Sentiments,* published in 1759. It is in this work that Smith most explicitly argues the unique importance of justice for understanding the nature of society and government. "Justice," he asserts, "is the main pillar that upholds the whole edifice. If it is removed, the great, the immense fabric of human society . . . must in a moment crumble into atoms."

Society may subsist, though not in the most comfortable state, without beneficence: but the prevalence of injustice must utterly destroy it.[3]

Since the rules of justice are the foundation of social order, the central theme of political inquiry, including political economy, must be the nature of justice.

According to *The Theory of Moral Sentiments,* the moral nature of man and his intrinsic sense of justice make society possible, necessary and desirable: possible because all community must be based on some shared standards of right

Reprinted, with permission, from Fred Glahe, ed., *Adam Smith & The Wealth of Nations* (Boulder, Colorado: Colorado Associated University Press). Copyright © 1979 by Leonard Billet.

and wrong which can be enforced, necessary because man cannot be his social and moral self apart from society, and desirable because only in society can the potentialities of his nature be more fully developed. The "natural sense of justice," ultimately founded on the "general fellow feeling which we have with every other man, merely because he is our fellow creature,"[4] instills in mankind a rejection and resentment against unmerited injuries whether done to oneself or to others. Smith's conception of justice, like Plato's, presupposes that certain things are *due* to people. His notion of justice, however, is much more narrowly defined than Plato's. Both thinkers perceive justice as inhering in the polity, for Plato because political and moral community are the same, and for Smith, because they are not. Justice, in Smith's view, is essentially concerned only with that part of what is morally due mankind which ought to be enforced by governing authority; it is therefore the virtue "of which the observance is not left to the freedom of our wills, [and] which may be [legitimately] extorted by force."[5] For Smith, the basic question raised by justice is: which rules and institutions are most appropriate to human society, and in particular, to the economic order of production and consumption?

Smith's political economy is predicated on the theory of the nature and significance of justice presented in his work on morality. *An Inquiry into the Nature and Causes of the Wealth of Nations* is an attempt to express "the rules which the natural sense of justice would dictate" for the economic order, so that they might be embodied in positive law. Adam Smith referred to his own system of principles and institutions as the "liberal plan of equality, liberty and justice,"[6] "the natural system of perfect liberty and justice,"[7] and the system of "natural liberty and justice."[8]

More than ever, Smith's "liberal plan" needs to be reexamined from the perspective of its moral and political foundations. The following considerations on the moral justifications for economic liberty and their relationship to labor and capital, the role of government within the system of natural liberty and the powerful anti-colonialism of *The Wealth of Nations* are intended to be a contribution to this undertaking.

JUST LIBERTY

Everyone knows that Adam Smith is the apostle of economic liberty. However, few seem to recognize that, for Smith, liberty, competition, and the market process are derived from and subordinate to principles of social justice. Justice necessarily circumscribes liberty, and the unrecognized central theme of *The Wealth of Nations* is *just* liberty. Smith believed that just liberty is a necessary condition for the most creative and efficient production. Underlying this belief is the prior question: why is liberty morally necessary in the economic order? To answer this question, one must begin with his view of man and society, for like all justice theorists, he analyzes and evaluates social rules and institutions in relation to their appropriateness to human nature.

For Smith, human nature is complex, multi-dimensional, inherently conflictive and incapable of perfection. Innate social or "fellow-feeling" capacities necessarily lead mankind to be concerned with the situation and views of others. From this bond the *possibility* of justice is derived. On the other hand, powerful anti-social elements and capacities such as "envy, malice and resentment," "hatred, anger, [and] spite . . . drive men from one another." Though man is a "rational creature" and reason is "capable of counteracting the strongest impulses of self-love,"[9] reason is hard to sustain and mankind is prone to be blinded by passions and the "misrepresentations of self-love." Above all, humans are active, creative, imaginative and choosing beings, i.e., 'self' expressive individuals. Each person has his own inner "principle of motion."[10] From these complexities, the *necessity* for justice is derived.

Smith believed that "man's natural love for society," moral socialization and the enforcement of just laws could contain and inhibit the expression of anti-social tendencies while permitting the social, prudent and humane virtues to develop. But if governing authorities presumed the governed to be like pieces on a chess board—rightfully moved by the will and force of others—people could never fully be 'themselves' or realize their potentials. Self-expression and self-determination in the economic order, as well as in political and religious life, are considered to be essential constituent principles of just social institutions.

Smith's view that the imaginative, choosing and self-expressive nature of man requires just economic liberty also helps to explain the oft-overlooked moral basis of self-interest in *The Wealth of Nations*. This principle of action is a necessary foundation for a just economy precisely because he sees that self-interest is intrinsically connected with choice, reason and self-determination. To the extent that the individual is free to own and use his labor and capital resources, to that extent he will be free to be guided by his own conceptions and desires regarding purpose and benefit. As Smith views it, the choice lies between self-determined and "other-determined" interest as a moral foundation for economic activity. Furthermore, self-interest, the active form of proper self-love, is not a vice. Proper self-love or prudence, "the care of health, of the fortune, of the rank and reputation of the individual," is sharply distinguished from avarice or greed. In addition, economic self-interest coexists with the benevolent other-regarding passions which are also intrinsic expressions of the human personality.

Economic self-interest is assumed to operate within a context of moral rules, religious beliefs and the restraints of civil law and justice which have as one important purpose, among others, preventing human beings from injuring each other. These powerful forces are not suspended in *The Wealth of Nations,* although the focus on economic order and self-interested activity has misled many into ignoring them. These forces inhibit immorality and injustice by directly affecting the character of the inner man through education, socialization and indoctrination or by the threat of punishment, religious as well as civil. It is within this context that "every man, as long as he does not violate the laws of justice, is left perfectly free to pursue his own interest his own way, and to bring both his industry and capital into competition with those of any other man, or order of men."[11]

Economic institutions, unlike these other more important social structures, cannot *prevent* evil. But certain kinds of economic order can channel the operation of self-interest in such a way that its consequences are beneficial to society as well as to the individual. This is the purpose of economic liberty and the competitive market. Smith thought that the great defect of feudal, mercantilist and other economic arrangements was that they created, encouraged or supported opportunities for a few to aggrandize themselves at the expense of the "great body of the people." His reliance on self-interest "expresses his faith in the value of the individual and in the importance of freeing the individual man from the fetters of outworn economic institutions."[12]

According to Smith, the pursuit of self-interest or prudential behavior is itself an already socialized process (i.e., based on taking others into consideration) as J. R. Lindgren has demonstrated. Those involved in economic activity tend to subordinate the impulse of their self-loving passions in accordance with public opinion, and to conform to the expectations of others through a desire for praise. "They regard the pursuit of riches not as the most efficient way to maximize their own satisfactions, but simply as the right way to behave."[13] Even within the context of prudential activity directed towards the pursuit of wealth, self-interest is not exclusively self-orientation in regard to the *results* of such efforts. Self-interest is perfectly consistent with, indeed is often the inspiration for, persons using their goods or resources for the benefit of others through support of the arts and sciences, education, political movements, religious activities or institutions, etc.

The Wealth of Nations also justifies the competitive free market economy as a long-range solution to the important problem of correcting and reforming maldistributions of wealth arising from past injustices. Smith thought of the system of natural liberty as a method of "rectification of injustice in holdings," to use the philosopher Robert Nozick's term. Nozick has argued in a recent work that a comprehensive theory of justice must have, as one of its elements, a principle for rectifying past injustices involving the acquisition and transfer of property.[14] Smith believed that the operation of a market economy accompanied by the abolition of legal privilege, monopolies, corporations, laws fixing wages and inhibiting mobility would tend gradually to reform and redistribute both land and other forms of wealth in the direction of a more equitable and widespread system of ownership.

In Western Europe, the ownership of landed property was, in large part, the unjust heritage of conquest and usurpation, according to Smith. Laws such as entail and primogeniture hindered economic processes from "reforming" or breaking up and dispersing these originally unjust concentrations of property and power. "They prevent the division of great estates, and thereby hinder the multiplication of small proprietors [and] keep so much land out of the market, that there are always more capitals to buy than there is land to sell, so that what is sold always sells at a monopoly price."[15] Such regulations were "founded upon the most absurd of all suppositions, the supposition that every successive generation of men have not an equal right to the earth and all that it possesses."[16] Abolishing restrictions on land ownership and its marketability would extend the possibilities of proprietorship to greater numbers of people who could purchase land with wealth more justly accumulated. While all the evils of the past could not be immediately rectified, the ownership of land and other forms of wealth could eventually be broadened considerably and put on new and more just foundations. With the extension of small proprietorship, which Smith considered the most desirable type of property system, the great estates and aristocratic families might wither away, a process which undoubtedly would be hastened by habits and a way of life more conducive to spending than producing wealth. Through the market process, land could be "transferred" to people of more modest means who were able and desirous of using it productively.

Perhaps even more important, Smith believed that wealth derived from commercial and manufacturing activities was also, in significant part, the product of social injustices. Class legislation, legal privileges and monopoly rights in trade and production distorted the "natural proportion ... between judicious industry and profit." He looked to competition and the market principle to halt the growth of unjustly accumulated wealth, to undermine politically determined sources of economic advantage and to prevent the entrenchment of established industry which, he thought, always has a tendency to seek official "protection," i.e., legal means of preservation from the possibility of competitive displacement. Since most wealth founded on legal privileges could not long be expected to withstand free competition, the system of natural liberty would tend to operate to transform and to weaken the power of the past over the present and future.

The Wealth f Nations' negative evaluation of the joint-stock company or corporation is best understood in this perspective. To Smith, the corporate form, a special and unique creation of positive law, was inherently fraught with serious dangers. Corporations were very attractive to investors because they promised a "total exemption from trouble and risk beyond a certain sum," were able to "draw to themselves much greater stock than any private copartnery," and could undertake activities beyond the capabilities of small numbers of individuals.[17] But this very limitation of liability and 'artificial' concentration of resources gave the corporation an unfair advantage over non-corporate and smaller owner-operated enterprises, which are the necessary mainstay of a competitive free market economy. Though it might be advantageous or profitable to the individuals involved, Smith did not think the corporation was generally a socially advantageous institution. It created and perpetuated a class of proprietors or investors "who seldom pretend to understand anything of the business of the company; and when the spirit of faction, happens not to prevail among them, gives themselves no trouble about it, but receive contentedly such half-yearly dividends, as the directors think proper to make them."[18]

Smith did not believe the law should encourage "ownership divorced from management" or benefit without responsibility. Both monopoly and the corporate form tended to erode the multiplication of ownerships, the diffusion of independence and interdependence of enterprise, the dispersal and diversification of capital and labor and of opportunities for creativity and access to productive activity which he considered to be essential aspects of a just economy. From the point of view of a more egalitarian, creative and efficient, freely competitive and responsible economy, Adam Smith saw no moral basis for the corporation and the unrestrained development of corporate privilege.

LABOR AND CAPITAL

When Marx commented in his early writings that Engels was correct in calling Adam Smith the "Luther of political economy," he was referring to Engels's recognition that *The Wealth of Nations* represented a radically new political economy "which recognized labour as its principle" and which understood that "labour is the sole essence of wealth."[19] The very opening sentence of Smith's treatise asserts the fundamental role of labor in the productive life of every community.

The annual labour of every nation is the fund which originally supplies it with all the necessaries and conveniencies of life which it annually consumes, and which consists always either in the immediate produce of that labour, or in what is purchased with that produce from other nations.[20]

Although Adam Smith was not the first to notice the importance of labor, he decisively liberated economic thought from certain sterile notions about the nature and causes of wealth by placing labor and its productive powers in the center of the creative process. "It was not by gold or silver, but by labour, that all the wealth of the world was originally purchased."[21]

Smith considered labor to be not only the source and cause of wealth, and the "real measure" of exchangeable value, but ultimately the "real wealth of the society."[22] Though aware of the dark side of the division of labor, especially the threat of moral and intellectual stultification which accompanied its growth, he nevertheless considered it to be indispensable to raising the living standards of the vast majority of the people.

For Adam Smith, the activity of labor, the division of labor and the productivity of labor are not only 'technical' conditions of economic life and progress, they are the moral bases of economic activity and institutions. Labor or "strength and dexterity," "toil and ingenuity" is an essential aspect of human self-expression and societal development. Therefore, that system of political economy is most just which allows the greatest scope for persons to labor in accordance with their capacities and aims, and which, as much as possible, enables them to gain the reward or "produce" of their labor.

The human capacities of strength and skill, imagination, toil and ingenuity are the ultimate foundation for all just ownership of property, according to

Smith. "The property which every man has in his own labour, as it is the original foundation of all other property, so it is the most sacred and inviolable."[23] Natural differences in the ability and/or willingness to labor, an existential reality, is the fundamental source of inequality of property. Thus, labor is the natural and just basis for inequality of property. Inequality, however, tempts some to commit acts of injustice against property, no matter how legitimately it has been acquired through toil and effort. It is therefore necessary that the "valuable property which is acquired by the labour of many years, or perhaps of many successive generations" be protected from the "injustice" of others "by the powerful arm of the civil magistrate."[24]

Just ownership of property is ultimately a consequence of human self-possession and self-expression. Smith views property, where it is morally defensible, to be based on the ideas of justice, self and labor. Freedom includes the possibility of acquiring property and Smith held to the view (of Montesquieu) that where men are able to own property, they are not likely to be the property of others. And if, unlike Marx, he does not consider labor as *the* expression of man's humanity, it is nevertheless a kind of human expression which is of decisive practical and moral significance in economic life.

Given Smith's emphasis on the significance and value of labor, the concern over the position and condition of the laboring classes which pervades his treatise should not occasion great surprise. It is true that Smith viewed labor as "the principal claimant, among the several producing groups in society to the sympathies of both the social scientist and the public administrator."[25] What is puzzling to some is his acceptance and justification of capital and profit. Was it not Smith himself who stated:

In that original state of things, which precedes both the appropriation of land and the accumulation of stock, the whole produce of labor belongs to the labourer. He has neither landlord nor master to share with him.[26]

Yet, in "commercial society" the labourer cannot enjoy the whole produce of his own labour but "must in most cases share it with the owners of the stock who employs him." According to Heilbroner, this acceptance of capital and profit clearly indicates Smith's ideological narrowness and the "essentially 'class-bound' nature of his social vision."[27]

Perhaps so, but when Smith abandons the "original state of things" in which the laborer enjoyed the whole produce of his labor, apparently without much regret, it is because he believed that the "fall" into capital, wages and profit is 1) a natural (uncoerced) result of the previous social condition, and 2) a necessary condition for increasing the living standard of the laborer. First, according to Smith, capital and profit are legitimate consequences of the human ability to reason and calculate. Under social conditions where people are able to own and control their own labor and its products and are desirous of and free to improve the material conditions of life, capital and profit tend to develop. The idea and process of "exchange," which brings motivation, calculation and reason into creative relationship with one another, provides a proximate moral basis for capital and profit. While much notice has been taken of the "propensity to truck, barter, and exchange one thing for another" as the "principle which gives occasion to the division of labor," the role of exchange as a significant basis for Smith's moral economy of liberty and justice is less widely appreciated. Though exchange may not appear to be a moral notion, in fact its normative connotations are critical both to Smith's and Marx's political economy.

For Marx, the very idea and activity of a calculated exchange of goods and services involves a distortion of man's true nature. In his view, the only acceptable "labor" is that which involves an expression of man's being for the purpose of directly fulfilling his "needs." Exchange is essentially sordid. It is by the standard of a future exchangeless, though still productive world, that Marx condemns the economic ideas and arrangements of his time and most of previous history. But if for Marx exchange violates "being," for Smith it can express an important aspect of man's creative nature and may therefore serve as a legitimate foundation for economic order and progress. And while for Marx exchange is a form of slavery, according to Smith the natural human ability to exchange one's labor and its products actually has become the instrument for gradually freeing mankind from arbitrary dependence upon others for their subsistence, i.e., from slavery and feudal institutions. In past ages, he argued, the livelihood of the vast majority of people depended on the will and power of wealthy individuals or institutions. Whereas "in the present state of Europe," though a rich and powerful person contributes to the support of very many people, "they are all more or less independent of him . . . because generally they can all be maintained without him."[28]

In an exchange society, every person through the possession of his own labor is naturally provided with something valuable and productive that *he* controls and can use for his own benefit in the light of his own determinations. The universal possession of the ability to labor dictated universal freedom to employ one's labor. Labor and exchange tended to undermine arbitrary and unjust inequalities of wealth. Labor and liberty would bring "comfort and conveniences" to the masses. With higher living standards, and widespread education, a greater equality of opportunity for individuals and societies to freely develop would result. For Adam Smith, the larger meaning of the principle of exchange (and the division of labor) was that it had the potential to deliver man from subordinated dependence to a more egalitarian interdependence. He believed that this was the economic direction in which European society had been moving since the Middle Ages.

The fact that opportunities to use one's own resources are inevitably structured and ordered by society underlay Smith's attack on the political economy of his day for unjustly restraining these opportunities for many, especially the laboring classes. Man's desire for more control over his own life, for greater and more equal opportunity and for freedom from servility and arbitrary dependence on others for his livelihood, remained unfulfilled. Smith urged the adoption of the principles of natural liberty in order to greatly enlarge the scope and strengthen the progress towards independence and interdependence.

When the principles of liberty and self-determined interest are combined with those of labor, exchange, and legitimate inequality of property, capital and profit are likely to result, according to Smith. Though inequality of property does not necessarily lead to capital, it is a basis for capital or that part of a person's or society's wealth employed to produce additional goods. If this process of capital accumulation or reproduction is prohibited or hindered, then the living standards of an individual or a society must remain at the same or nearly the same level.

Capital is not necessary "in that rude state of society in which there is no division of labour, in which exchanges are seldom made, and in which every man provides everything for himself."[29] Labor is central to production, prior to capital and to ownership of property and is itself the source of property, inequality and capital. All economies produce goods though they do not necessarily produce capital. Every economy must have workers but need not have capitalists.

But *The Wealth of Nations* emphatically stresses the importance of capital and capital accumulation to the development of the productive processes of society. The desire to *increase* the production of goods and services, the desire for "development" in other words, and the aim of enhancing the productive powers of labor and the social abilities of man to cooperate and exchange, which is the core of that process, inevitably brings capital into the very center of economic life. The division of labor, Smith emphasized again and again, was the immediate source of improvement and wealth. To it was owed the "invention of all those machines by which labour is so much facilitated and abridged." Every established division of labor and every step forward in specialization, cooperation, and improving the tools of production requires an accumulation of capital, according to Smith. Increased capital investment per worker is the basis for increased output per worker. Furthermore, capital accumulation and investment increase the demand for labor and therefore the wages of labor. Higher wages provide an incentive for owners to improve the productivity of labor resulting in lower prices for consumer goods, thus indirectly augmenting the purchasing power of the working class.

Smith's fundamental concern respecting productivity was the relationship between a "given" amount of labor or industry and its output. The purpose of capital was to "facilitate and abridge," not to increase the intensity of labor or the length of the working day, as Marx supposed. The justification for capital was that either a "smaller quantity of labour produce[s] a greater quantity of work," or that the "same quantity of industry produces a much greater quantity of work."[30] Capital contributed to the benefit of individuals and to the social good by putting greater numbers to work at higher wages and by encouraging more efficient organization and "automation." Only the advantageous employment of capital made it possible for a nation to "maintain the

greatest quantity of productive labour, and increase the most, the annual produce of the land and labour of that country."[31]

In essence, the laborer is better off when he does *not* get the whole produce
of his labor. "In a savage nation every one enjoys the whole fruit of his own
labour, yet their indigence is greater than anywhere."[32]

Compared, indeed with the more extravagant luxery of the great, his accomodation
must no doubt appear extremely simple and easy; yet it may be true, perhaps, that
the accomodation of an European prince does not always so much exceed that of an
industrious and frugal peasant, as the accomodation of the latter exceeds that of
many an African king, the absolute master of the lives and liberties of ten thousand
naked savages.[33]

Because of the increased productivity of labor, based on the institutions of exchange, capital, and profit, the laborer has traded his own little mud pie for a
slice of a larger and more nourishing cake.

THE ROLE OF GOVERNMENT

It is true that *The Wealth of Nations* is primarily concerned with removing obstacles to economic liberty and competition and not with the problem of legislation directed towards the protection and operation of a system not yet
completely established. Since these obstacles were in large part legal and political, prompted by special interests and founded on an inadequate understanding
of economic relationships, Smith was preoccupied with exposing injustices and
explaining the nature of competitive market principles.

Free, however, from the belief in the perfection of man's nature, Smith
could not but be free from the idea of the perfection of the market economy
and its supposed ability to provide *all* the "goods" required by a good society
or even all those services necessary to sustain the system of natural economic
liberty itself. A philosopher who thought that due to the "prejudices of the
public" and "what is more unconquerable, the private interests of many individuals," to expect the complete establishment of his system was "as absurd as
to expect that an Oceana or Utopia should ever be established,"[34] may be accused of undue pessimism, but he is unlikely to assume that those same forces
of prejudice and interest would disappear with the growth of economic liberty.
Further, if we remember that, according to Smith, the established interests,
"the merchants and manufacturers" in particular, are always and everywhere
engaged in a "conspiracy against the public, or in some contrivance to raise
prices" and that the interest of the employers of capital "is always in some respects different from, and even opposite to, that of the public,"[35] it is clear that
preserving and protecting competition and the free market must ever be a concern of government. As Skinner has noted, Smith recognized that the functions of the state "are quite indespensible."[36]

The Wealth of Nations is concerned with *effective* and not merely "formal" economic justice and liberty. Smith exposes and aims to reform all those public policies, institutions, laws and rules of taxation which, 1) help to create, encourage or sustain enterprises or incorporations of capital or labor which can escape the competitive pressures of the market place and impose an unjust and "absurd tax on their countrymen" through higher prices and profit, or 2) which effectively restrict access to certain types of employment and investments or new uses of capital and other factors of production, thereby preventing or inhibiting alternative goods, methods or processes from arising and competing with established ones.

It would therefore be erroneous to argue that *The Wealth of Nations* was only concerned with injustices arising from "legal" as distinguished from "market" monopolies or imperfections or that Smith proposed to accept oppressive or unjust practices provided only that they somehow originated in a competitive market situation. Furthermore, it must be remembered that, for Smith, the system of natural liberty practically excluded the enormous and entrenched concentrations of economic power and resources made possible by the corporate form; it did not have "regulatory" agencies involved in sustaining high prices and profits and inhibiting change, and it was open to almost unrestricted foreign trade and competition. Very few industries, in these circumstances, could attain the kind of market position which would enable them to oppress the public. Nevertheless, injustices, whatever their origins, can only continue where the law permits and protects them. Since government has the responsibility of "protecting, as far as possible, every member of the society from the injustice or oppression of every other member of it,"[37] government is obliged to prevent, correct or ameliorate economically oppressive practices and institutions.

Jacob Viner and other scholars have recognized that Adam Smith made many "exceptions" to his general argument for economic liberty. Spengler has commented that "Smith's definition of what the state could do was quite elastic and his list of specific tasks which the state should perform was rather long."[38] Viner explains this by suggesting that, at times, "Smith conveniently forgot the principle [of natural liberty] and went beyond the limits set in his formal discussion to the proper activities of government."[39] Spengler more accurately points out that because Smith's thoughts on the tasks of government are not all in one place and because his emphasis was on the virtues of economic liberty, he "left the impression of circumscribing the role of government even more than he in fact proposed [a] misleading impression which set the tone for subsequent writers."[40] The implications and significance of the specific tasks assigned to government and of these exceptions to natural liberty in *The Wealth of Nations* are best understood as related not to Smith's forgetfulness, eclecticism or elasticity of principle but to a consistent vision of a just and desirable economic order comprehensive enough so that "considerable controlling duties given to the State"[41] could have a natural and constructive place within it.

Since "consumption is the sole end and purpose of all production; and the interest of the producer ought to be attended to, only so far as it may be necessary for promoting that of the consumer,"[42] one principal guide for the role of government within the system of natural liberty that seemed to have a prominent place in Smith's mind was that of protecting the consumer. *The Wealth of Nations* argues that the release of productive energies and resources brought about by greater competition and a freer market would serve the consumer and help him to exert a "real and effectual discipline" over the producers in a way which "restrains his frauds and corrects his negligence."[43] But in asserting that economic liberty was necessary to protect the consumer, Smith did not argue that it was in all cases sufficient. He was aware of the problem of recognizing and dealing with bad workmanship and inferior quality goods. The exposure of such articles to public sale, he maintained, was often "the effect of fraud" and he suggested that "regulations are necessary to prevent this abuse," citing with approval such examples as the sterling mark on silver and quality stamps upon linen and woolen cloth as giving the purchaser "much greater security."[44] Where the public could easily be fooled by appearances, government should require that goods be labelled and information provided so that persons would know what they are purchasing. Legislation directed toward aiding intelligent consumer choice and the prevention of misleading representation and fraud was not viewed as an unwarranted interference with just liberty.

Smith's discussion of banking practices in Book 2 of *The Wealth of Nations* illustrates some of the concerns which he thought justified public intervention and regulation of certain aspects of commerce and production. The unrestrained liberty of issuing very small denomination bank notes or paper currencies encouraged the founding of a great many tiny and financially insecure banks whose "frequent bankruptcies ... occasion a very inconsiderable inconveniency, and sometimes even a very great calamity, to many poor people who had received their notes in payment."[45] He therefore proposed that bankers be prohibited from issuing such currency notes, even if "all his neighbors are willing to accept them," though "it may be said" that this "is a manifest violation of that natural liberty which it is the proper business of law, not to infringe, but to support."

Such regulations may, no doubt, be considered as in some respect a violation of natural liberty. But those exertions of the natural liberty of a few individuals, which might endanger the security of the whole society, are and ought to be, restrained by the laws of all governments; of the most free, as well as of the most despotical. The obligation of building party walls, in order to prevent the communication of fire, is a violation of natural liberty exactly of the same kind with the regulations of the banking trade which are here proposed.[46]

These are only a few examples of Smith's recognition that, whatever the fundamental desirability of encouraging economic self-expression, the pursuit of individual and group interest did not always spontaneously result in morally or socially acceptable consequences. Provision of appropriate legal remedies for injury and an "exact" and "impartial" administration of justice in the economic order are also essential functions of government in Smith's paradigm. Without proper legal remedies or when the administration of justice was corrupted, a just economic liberty could not be realized. An "unqualified adherence to the principles of *caveat emptor* was apparently not a necessary implication of Smith's laissez faire doctrine."[47]

Another important area of government activity, namely, appropriate public works and institutions, is justified by reasons quite different from those which aim to correct or restrain the defects or "excesses" of self-interested endeavors. Adam Smith never refers to the legitimate provision of public services as involving "violations of natural liberty." On the contrary, he argues that public authority must undertake the task of providing those highly desirable services which the free market cannot or does not provide. Government is responsible for

erecting and maintaining those public institutions and those public works, which though they may be in the highest degree advantageous to a great society, are however, of such a nature, that the profit could never repay the expence to any individual or small number of individuals, and which it therefore cannot be expected that any individual or small number of individuals should erect or maintain.[48]

When certain services which are also in the public interest cannot be financed by the contribution of those who are most immediately benefitted, "the deficiency must in most cases be made up by the general contribution of the whole society."[49] Smith is not hostile to public institutions, but he seems to believe that public works and services must be defended on moral as well as utilitarian grounds; they ought to be so clearly necessary and desirable that citizens "without injustice" may be required or coerced into paying for them. While his views of the role of government on this question are not dogmatic, they place a much heavier burden on the moral wisdom of public authority than is commonly appreciated.

Smith proposed two distinct though overlapping principles as the basis for public services. One countenanced social overhead capital or public works for the primary purpose of facilitating commerce and industry. Transportation and communications facilities, roads, bridges, canals etc., classic examples of this type of public enterprise, were "no doubt beneficial to the whole society, and may, therefore, without any injustice, be defrayed by the general contribution of the whole society."[50] His primary concern respecting this category of publicly financed facilities was that, as much as possible those who use them ought "to pay for the maintenance of those public works exactly in proportion to the wear and tear which they occasion to them. It seems scarcely possible to invent a more equitable way of maintaining such works."[51] The necessity for a cost-benefit relationship would also help to ensure that public works were built where they were the most needed and valuable to the community. A concern for equity as well as efficiency guides his entire discussion of the role of government in providing social overhead capital, including the problems of appropriate management for public enterprises and the question of local finance and control.

Smith's defense of a second type of public service reflects an awareness in regard to certain socially desirable institutions, that those who are most immediately benefitted by them may be too poor to pay for them. The community, for example, has an interest in seeing that all children obtain a certain level of education. Every society, Smith maintained, requires an appropriate kind of moral and intellectual character in its members. But in civilized societies, economic growth, which is necessarily connected with increasing division of labor and specialization, tends to confine the skills of working people "to a few very simple operations" and therefore to "benumb the understanding" of the laboring poor. In developing societies, the "invisible hand" apparently does not produce a requisite level of moral and intellectual vigor. On the contrary, it tends to produce large numbers of men "without the proper use of the intellectual faculties" and therefore "deformed in an essential part of the character of human nature."[52]

In Smith's view, the "attention of government" was necessary if individuals were to be protected against the moral and intellectual stultification resulting from a premature introduction to labor. His thoughts on public education for children perhaps best exemplify some of the general criteria which he believed should guide public provision of services in a just economy. First, there must be an identified need of uncommon importance which is not being fulfilled because it is beyond the means of those immediately benefitted. Second, public authority should not undermine the freedom and ability of families or individuals to provide for their own needs in their own way and with their own means, to the extent possible. Third, public money should not be employed to displace or compete unfairly with private institutions and services. Fourth, private and public means and controls should be combined whenever possible. For example, even in publicly provided schools, parents should be responsible for some direct payment to the school in order to encourage the diligence of teachers and furnish an avenue of influence for the parents.[53]

But perhaps the most important aspect of Smith's discussion of education is the implication that government is responsible for correcting or offsetting the deleterious consequences of commercial society when such consequences derive from the very nature of a complex, specialized and interdependent free market economic order. The significance of this idea for guiding the organization and regulation of certain functions of government within the system of natural liberty, i.e., for harmonizing to a greater degree the elements of justice, liberty, and equality, has been almost entirely overlooked. Smith emphasized certain harmful tendencies resulting from industrial progress not to condemn commercial society and the division of labor, but to urge public attention to remedying its shortcomings. In light of Smith's ideas on the role of government within the system of economic liberty, as well as his emphasis on considerations of justice which so pervade *The Wealth of Nations,* it is hard to imagine that he would object to a vigorous involvement of public authority in such problems of modern economic life as unemployment, health, pollution, etc., though he might well object to many particular methods of amelioration as unjust, unwise or inefficient.

ANTI-COLONIALISM

Adam Smith's opposition and hostility to colonialism and imperialism is of particular significance. *The Wealth of Nations* was the first great anti-colonialist and anti-imperialist tract, in the modern sense of those terms, referring to that particular combination of unwelcome and oppressive authority and economic exploitation imposed by some states on other territories or peoples. This is evident not only in Smith's critique of mercantilism, the theoretical basis of seventeenth- and eighteenth-century colonialism, but in his direct attack on the morality as well as the economics of colonial imperialism. The anti-colonialist theme is an important part of his lengthy chapter on colonies in Book 4. This theme emerges in the first book and persists until the very last page of Smith's work. Yet his real stature as an anti-colonialist thinker is little known. Marxist-Leninist analysis is actually a latecomer to the school of anti-colonialism and it has preempted and obfuscated much of the subject in part because its powerful antecedents in Smith's political economy have been ignored and its implications unappreciated. Had those who were concerned with international economic injustice paid due attention to his analysis, it might have been much more difficult to establish the erroneous view that modern imperialisms are expressions of economic liberty rather than negations of it.

The twin themes of Smith's liberal anti-colonialism are injustice and disadvantage. Colonialism was unjust and harmful both to the dependent peoples and to the colonizing nations. It was commercially destructive and financially disastrous. *The Wealth of Nations* provided a detailed critique of British attempts to restrict and exploit the American economies. Under these unjust and absurd policies, higher rates of profit took precedence over the national interest. The advantages which colonialism procured to a "single order of men" was "in many different ways hurtful to the general interest of the country."

To found a great empire for the sole purpose of raising up a people of customers may at first sight appear a project fit only for a nation of shopkeepers. It is, however, a project altogether unfit for a nation of shopkeepers; but extremely fit for a nation whose government is influenced by shopkeepers. Such statesmen, and such statesmen only, are capable of fancying that they will find some advantage in employing the blood and treasure of their fellow-citizens to found and maintain such an empire.[54]

A just economy does not buy special privileges abroad for capital owners and investors with the "blood and treasure" of its citizens.

Although he assessed the net impact of British exploitation of North American as "not ... very hurtful," because due to cheap land and the very high wage rates of labor in the colonies they could import almost all the manufactured goods they needed cheaper than they could produce them for themselves, Smith condemned British policies as "unjust" and "impertinent badges of slavery imposed upon them, without any sufficient reason, by the groundless jealousy of the merchants and manufacturers of the mother country."

To prohibit a great people ... from making all that they can of every part of their own produce, or from employing their stock and industry in the way that *they* judge most advantageous, is a manifest violation of the most sacred rights of mankind.[55]

The burning issue of the American colonies provoked the anti-colonialist insistence that only justice, liberty, equality and consent were an acceptable basis for a resolution of the conflict between Britain and her contentious offspring. In proposals which illustrate a radical imagination and insight, Smith argued that Britain ought to seek genuine union with her North American colonies, whose leaders were, at that very time, "contriving a new form of government for an extensive empire, which, they flatter themselves, will become, and which, indeed, seems very likely to become, one of the greatest and most formidable that ever was in the world."[56]

There is not the least probability that the British constitution would be hurt by the union of Great Britain with her colonies. That constitution, on the contrary, would be completed by it, and seems to be imperfect without it.[57]

The principle of representation would make such a union possible. Even under taxation with representation, however, the Americans would undoubtedly be concerned about being neglected, given their distance from the seat of government. Since representation ought to be in proportion to taxation, this distance would not very likely be of long duration.

Such has hitherto been the rapid progress of that country in wealth, population and improvement, that in the course of little more than a century, perhaps, the produce of American might exceed that of British taxation. The seat of empire would than naturally remove itself to that part of the empire which contributed most to the general defence and support of the whole.[58]

Such was Adam Smith's view of the best solution to one instance of colonialism; a first "British Commonwealth" based on constitutional liberty, representation and economic freedom.

In a preview of what was to be one of the most important arguments for real union to be found many years later in the *Federalist Papers,* Smith contended that the North American colonies would in point of happiness and tranquility, gain considerably by a union with Great Britain. It would at least deliver them from those rancorous and virulent factions which are inseparable from small democracies, and which have so frequently divided the affections of their people, and disturbed the tranquility of their governments, in their form so nearly democratical.[59]

A union of Great Britain and her colonies might indeed be difficult but the problems were not insurmountable. The greatest ones "perhaps arise, not from the nature of things, but from the prejudices and opinions of the people on this and on the other side of the Atlantic."[60]

The force of these prejudices led Smith to propose a second equally dramatic solution: total independence.

Great Britain should voluntarily give up all authority over her colonies, and leave them to elect their own magistrates, to enact their own laws, and to make peace and war as they might think proper.[61]

He was not at all hopeful of the adoption of this solution by his government or fellow citizens, however, for he believed that due to national pride and the prospective loss of opportunities for position, wealth and distinction "no nation ever voluntarily gave up the dominion of any province, how troublesome soever it might be to govern it, and how small soever the revenue which it afforded might be in proportion to the expense which it occasioned."[62] Nevertheless, justice and wisdom dictated either voluntary union or independence. The imposition of authority meant hostilities between the colonies and "the best of all mother countries."

For Smith, the modern idea of colonialism violated the precepts of natural liberty and justice. Colonial relationships invited oppressive policies and laws and were in fact an enormous political, military and financial burden to the community, however profitable they might be to certain political and business interests. Great Britain "derives nothing but loss from the dominion she assumes over her colonies." The economics of colonialism were absurd. Britain, Smith asserted, was, "perhaps, since the world began, the only state which, as it has extended its empire, has only increased its expense without once augmenting its resources."[63] The British people ought not to support and could ill afford such an "empire." Either it should be reconstituted on a more just and equitable basis or the "golden dream" of empire abandoned and Britain should "endeavour to accomodate her future views and designs to the real mediocrity of her circumstances."[64]

The Wealth of Nations represents a "radical" political-economics; radical in the sense of being grounded on the moral roots of social relationships and radical in the sense of rooting economy in a political-moral context. Like most classics of political and economic philosophy, Smith's treatise has the virtue of combining the pursuit of truth with the pursuit of just reform. *The Wealth of Nations* is not the last word on the just economy, but it is one of the first. The nature of a just economic order remains the central question of political economy.

It is a paradox in contemporary understanding that Marx, who never speaks of justice and injustice, but of science and the laws of motion and development, is everywhere known for the passionately moral character of his language and thought. Smith, on the other hand, who acknowledges the normative problem of justice as central to social analysis, is usually thought to represent an economic science bereft of moral concern.

Nevertheless, Smith's principles of political economy are fundamentally moral principles. They are favorable neither to robbers nor to barons. They are basically concerned with enhancing the possibilities for individual and societal development, minimizing class privilege, ensuring that governmental activity serves the public interest, protecting those unjustly harmed by modern economic life and preventing and rectifying exploitative relationships between people and nations.

NOTES

[1] References to Adam Smith's writings are to the following editions: *The Wealth of Nations,* Cannan ed., (New York, Modern Library, 1937) cited hereafter as WN; *The Theory of Moral Sentiments* (New York, A.M. Kelley, 1966) cited hereafter as TMS; and *Lectures on Justice, Police, Revenue and Arms,* Cannan ed., (New York, A.M. Kelley, 1964), cited hereafter as *Lectures.*

[2] TMS, p. 31.

[3] TMS, p. 125.

[4] TMS, p. 130.

[5] TMS, p. 114.

[6] WN, p. 628.

[7] WN, p. 572.

[8] WN, p. 141.

[9] TMS, p. 194.

[10] TMS, p. 343.

[11] WN, p. 651.

[12] Glenn R. Morrow, "Adam Smith; Moralist and Philosopher," in J.M. Clark et al., *Adam Smith, 1776-1926* (New York: A.M. Kelley, 1966), p. 167.

[13] J. Ralph Lindgren, *The Social Philosophy of Adam Smith* (The Hague: Martinus Nijhoff, 1973), pp. 54-55.

[14] Robert Nozick, *Anarchy, State, and Utopia* (New York: Basic Books, 1974), see esp. pp. 152-53, 208.

[15] WN, p. 392.

[16] WN, p. 363.

[17] WN, p. 699-700.

[18] WN, p. 699.

[19] Karl Marx, *Early Writings,* T.B. Bottomore, ed., (New York: McGraw-Hill, 1964), pp. 147-48.

[20] WN, p. lvii.

[21] WN, p. 30.
[22] WN, p. 249.
[23] WN, p. 122.
[24] WN, p. 670.
[25] P.J. McNulty, "Adam Smith's Concept of Labor," *Journal of the History of Ideas* 34 (July-September 1973): 346.
[26] WN, p. 64.
[27] R. Heilbroner, "Decline and Decay in *The Wealth of Nations*," *Journal of the History of Ideas* 34 (April-June 1973): 260.
[28] WN, p. 389.
[29] WN, p. 259.
[30] WN, pp. 86, 260, 271.
[31] WN, p. 566.
[32] *Lectures,* p. 162.
[33] WN, p. 12.
[34] WN, p. 437-38.
[35] WN, p. 128, 250.
[36] Andrew Skinner, *Adam Smith and the Role of the State* (Glascow: University of Glascow Press, 1974), p. 8.
[37] WN, p. 699.
[38] J.J. Spengler, "The Problem of Order in Economic Affairs," *Southern Economic Journal* 15 (July 1948): 16.
[39] Jacob Viner, "Adam Smith and Laissez-Faire," in J.M. Clark et al., *Adam Smith,* p. 150.
[40] Spengler, *Problem of Order,* p. 161.
[41] A.L. Macfie, *The Individual in Society* (London: Allen and Unwin, 1967), p. 77.
[42] WN, p. 625.
[43] WN, p. 129.
[44] WN, p. 122.
[45] WN, p. 307.
[46] WN, p. 308.
[47] Viner, *Adam Smith,* p. 145.
[48] WN, p. 681.
[49] WN, p. 768.
[50] WN, p. 767.
[51] WN, p. 683.
[52] WN, p. 740.
[53] WN, p. 716–40.
[54] WN, p. 579.
[55] WN, p. 549, my emphasis.
[56] WN, p. 588.
[57] WN, p. 589.
[58] WN, p. 590.
[59] WN, p. 897.
[60] WN, p. 589.
[61] WN, p. 581.
[62] WN, p. 582.
[63] WN, p. 586.
[64] WN, p. 900.

THOMAS KEYES

THE MARXIAN CONCEPT OF PROPERTY: INDIVIDUAL/SOCIAL

Much of what is distinctive about communism stems from Marx's clear-cut announce-ment that this system presupposes and requires the abolition of private property. But having things, being able to say what happens to what one owns seems rather vital to most of us. What then did Marx think about property or ownership? Thomas Keyes takes us through the many-faceted discussions of Marx on this crucial aspect of com-munist theory and develops on original and rare treatment. When finished with Keyes's detailed research and argument, you will be much clearer than before about what Karl Marx actually believed about the institution of ownership.

The concept of property is central to Marx's social and political philosophy as well as to his theory of history. In the *Communist Manifesto,* he underlined its significance when he stated that, "The theory of the communists may be summed up in the single sentence: Abolition of private property" (CM, MECW 6:498).[1] This article is an attempt to clarify Marx's crucially important notion of property and to present the kinds of personal and collective owner-ship that he envisaged would obtain in postcapitalist society. I shall begin by summarizing Marx's persistent demand that property be defined within the context of production and then will try to explain and briefly give his reasons for the abolition of private property. After that, I shall define and examine the notion of individual/social property that Marx believed would be present in future society. Finally, I shall reconstruct his arguments in favor of individ-ual/social property (which indirectly will provide a sketch of Marx's vision of communism), and will close with a few concluding remarks.

PROPERTY AND PRODUCTION

It is common to use the term *property* to refer to objects of ownership ("That car is my property") and to certain legal rights ("This is my cake and I have a right to eat it"), but Marx contends that it is a profound mistake to consider either of these usages as primary. He insists that "to try to give a definition of property as of an independent relation, a category apart, an abstract and eternal idea, can be nothing but an illusion of metaphysics or jurisprudence"(PP, MECW 6:197). For Marx, the general concept of property must be defined within the context of production, a context which is at once both social and historical. "Property thus originally means no more than a human being's rela-tion to his natural conditions of production as belonging to him . . ." (G:491).

The reason Marx demands that the connection between property and pro-duction be observed is that he believes all types of material production are es-

This essay was prepared for the present volume by the author.

sentially ways of appropriating nature by individuals or groups within and through specific forms of society. In fact, he contends that "there can be no production and hence no society where some form of property does not exist" (G:88). An appropriation that does not at the same time make something into property is a contradiction in terms. Thus, according to Marx, all production presupposes some type of property—this does not mean that property exists prior to production, only that it is inseparable from it. Property is the realization of man's productive labor and so, whether it be cars or cakes or any other object, the question of ownership and rights are secondary and derivative from the process of production.

There are two other characteristics of property in the context of production: the first is that it always involves certain social relationships and the second is that it is historical. In other words, as human beings "develop their productive faculties, that is to say, as they live, they develop certain relationships among themselves, and ... the nature of these relationships must necessarily change with the modification and growth of these productive faculties" (L:49).

The main reason property entails social relations is its triadic character. Not only is it a relation between (1) an object and (2) its owner, but it also includes (3) a group or society that is willing to recognize and sanction a more or less exclusive relation (regarding possession, use, and disposal) between (1) and (2). This mediation by society is indispensable, for without its recognition that a particular object belongs to a specific individual or group there would only be possession, not property. It is for this reason that, strictly speaking, animals only possess objects rather than own them. The same is true of isolated individuals; according to Marx, "An isolated individual could no more have property in land or soil [or any other thing] than he could speak" (G:485). Marx's point, of course, is that property (as well as language) is a product of a community of social beings.

Property also has an historical, dynamic quality: "All property relations in the past have continually been subjected to historical change consequent upon the change in historical conditions" (CM, MECW 6:498). This is due to the inexorable links among property, its attending social relations, and the growth and development of the forces of production. For Marx, each of the great economic epochs of history (e.g., the communal, ancient, Asiatic, feudal, and capitalist) had its own particular type of property and attending social relations, and so "in each historical epoch, property has developed differently and under a set of entirely different social relations. Thus, to define bourgeois property is nothing else than to give an exposition of all the social relations of bourgeois production"(PP, MECW 6:197).

In sum, therefore, the general concept of property for Marx can only properly be defined within the context of production, a context that involves certain historically evolving social relationships that are inseparable from a mode of production.

THE ABOLITION OF PRIVATE PROPERTY

One of the most well-recognized aspects of Marx's thought is his call for the abolition of private property. The meaning of this expression, however, is as misunderstood as it is familiar. Many mistake it as a call for the complete prohibition of all forms of personal private property. This misunderstanding is due in large part to the unfortunate translation of the complex and technical German term *Aufhebung* into the relatively simple English word *abolition*. The term *Aufhebung*, which Marx borrowed from Hegelian philosophy, signifies a tripartite development that involves an abolition (the negative element), a preservation (the positive element), and a resulting transcendence (the transformative element). In what follows, I shall examine how these elements apply to capitalist private property.

First, as I mentioned above, Marx's call for the *Aufhebung* of private property does not mean a complete abolition of individual private property. All possessions would not be reduced to common property by this *Aufhebung*. In fact, he labels any such simplistic and total abolition of private property a "crude communism," and rejects it out of hand as a thoughtless proposal because it would eliminate such positive factors as talent and personality development as well as essential institutions like marriage and the family (Cf. EPM, MECW 3:293–297).

Furthermore, it is not all property, nor even all types of private property, that Marx wants to abolish—he specifically targets capitalist private property. This type of property is characterized by the private ownership of the means of production (e.g., factories, agricultural land, vital natural resources, etc.). For Marx, capitalist private property "exists only where the means of labor and the external conditions of labor belong to private individuals" (C, I:761).

Marx offers numerous reasons to justify the *Aufhebung* of this type of property, but in the following passage he singles out one of the most important.

We by no means intend to abolish this personal appropriation of the product of labor, an appropriation that is made for the maintenance and reproduction of human life, and that leaves no surplus wherewith to command the labor of others. . . . Communism deprives no man of the power to appropriate the products of society; all that it does do is to deprive him of the power to subjugate the labor of others by means of such an appropriation (CM, MECW 6:499).

In other words, Marx would disallow capitalist activities because the supporting rights of private property not only sanction but actually encourage individuals to subjugate and exploit the labor of others for their own personal gain. So for Marx the "distinguishing feature of communism is not the abolition of property generally, but the abolition of bourgeois [capitalist] property" (CM, MECW 6:498).

Accordingly, the negative element of this *Aufhebung* entails a total annulment of the private ownership of the means of production—a type of property that "is the final and most complete expression of the system of producing and appropriating products, that is based on class antagonisms, on the expropriation of the many by the few" (CM, MECW 6:498). It is this sort of property that degrades and alienates individuals and frustrates their attempts at self-fulfillment.

The positive element of the *Aufhebung* in question consists of the preservation of that aspect of private property that is fundamental to the development of an individual's personality and self-realization. Marx puts it this way: "The meaning of private property [apart from its negative elements found in the capitalist form] . . . is the *existence of essential objects* for man, both as objects of gratification and as objects of activity" (G:159). Clearly, for example, the painter needs her own exclusive canvas, paints, and brushes to complete her work, as much out of convenience as out of necessity. Indeed, all of us require certain objects of "gratification and activity" for our self-development—objects over which we need to exercise more or less exclusive property rights in possession, use, and disposal.

Finally, let us consider the transformative element. Just as in any *Aufhebung,* the dual actions of annulment and preservation lead to a transcendence of some kind. In the case of capitalist private property, its *Aufhebung* results in a new economic order, one with radical social and political implications. It does so because a change in the type of property only occurs when accompanied by a change in the mode of production and the social relationships among the producers. To be more specific, the new forms of property that Marx anticipated for future communist society could not be established were it not for the tremendous growth and development of production and wealth under capitalism. As Marx explains, "If we did not find concealed in society as it is the material conditions of production and the corresponding relations of exchange prerequisite for a classless society, then all attempts to explode it would be quixotic" (G:159). This is why a communist revolution during the middle ages (or any earlier period) would have been impossible.

This *Aufhebung* of private property leads not only to a change in property but, just as importantly, to a transformation in the social order. "In place of the old bourgeois society, with its classes and class antagonisms, we shall have an association, in which the free development of each is the condition for the free development of all" (CM, MECW 6:506). Accordingly, (1) our attitude toward the private ownership of the means of production will change; we shall see ourselves as beneficent stewards rather than egoistic captains of industry.

From the standpoint of a higher economic form of society, private ownership of the globe by single individuals will appear quite as absurd as private ownership of one man by another. Even a whole society, a nation, or even all simultaneously existing societies taken together are not the owners of the globe. They are only its possessors, its usufructuaries, and, like *boni patres familias,* they must hand it down in an improved condition (C, III:776).

(2) Moreover, the goal of labor in society will also change: "In bourgeois society, living labor is but a means to increase accumulated labor. In communist society, accumulated labor is but a means to widen, to enrich, to promote the existence of the laborer" (CM, MECW 6:499). (3) Finally, as we shall see in a later section, this new system of property and production will lead to a more complete realization of equality, justice, freedom, and self-fulfillment.

INDIVIDUAL/SOCIAL PROPERTY

I have chosen "individual/social property" as the label to designate Marx's notion of future property because it seems to capture his meaning as well as any he employed. "Communist property," "socialized property," or "collective property" (all of which Marx uses at times) are terms I have purposely avoided because they give the false impression that personal, individual property will be excluded. The individual form of property is just as essential for self-realization as social property and so Marx insisted that, "We by no means intend to abolish this personal appropriation of the products of labor, an appropriation that is made for the maintenance and reproduction of human life, and that leaves no surplus wherewith to command the labor of others" (CM, MECW 6:499).

Perhaps the simplest and briefest way of presenting the meaning of individual/social property is to contrast it with the forms of property within capitalism, namely, private/public property. First, individual property differs from capitalist private property in that it excludes the private ownership of the means of production; that is to say, it excludes that type of property that fosters a class system that enables one person (or group) to enslave and exploit others. Second, social property differs from public property in that the former includes all the means of production and is under the complete and democratic control of the community.

Marx has little to say regarding the entitlements of ownership that will obtain in postcapitalist society. Yet from the previous discussion concerning the types of property that will be preserved, it it possible to outline a set of entitlements consistent with his position. First, the owner of individual property will be entitled to the exclusive possession, use, and disposal of that property within socially agreed upon limits. Second, the entitlements of the collectivity to its social property will include the ones listed above as they relate to the means of production. This will especially entail control by the collectivity of what will be produced, how, by whom, and where it will be produced, and the ways in which the products will be distributed.

Earlier in the paper, I explained Marx's view that property is a social phenomenon that is inseparable from a mode of production and its corresponding social relationships. This means that a change from capitalist property to communist (individual/social) property will involve a radical change in the ways in which things are produced and the types of social organization necessary to produce them. Marx mentions some of the differences in the *Grundrisse;* there he states that capitalist production

... is not *directly* social, is not "the offspring of association," which distributes labor internally. Individuals are subsumed under social production; social production exists outside of them as their fate ... social production is not subsumed under individuals, manageable by them as their common wealth. There can therefore be nothing more erroneous and absurd than to postulate the control by the united individuals of their total production, on the basis of *exchange* value. . . . The *private exchange* of all products of labor, all activities and all wealth stands in antithesis not only to a distribution based on a natural or political super- and subordination of individuals to one another ... but also to free exchange among individuals who are associated on the basis of common appropriation and control of the means of production (G:158–159).

Other major differences are that capitalist private property presupposes an economic system based on the struggle and antagonism of classes, where production is controlled by the wealthy few to the detriment of the many, and where social relations are marked by domination, exploitation, and alienation. In Marx's vision of communist society, on the other hand, there will be a classless society where production is democratically controlled by its members for the self-realization of social individuals, and where social relationships are marked by cooperation, support, and mutual respect.

THE ARGUMENTS FOR INDIVIDUAL/SOCIAL PROPERTY

As noted, Marx did not wish to fully abolish private property. He did not think that property relations in postcapitalist society will retrogress to a sort of primitive communal form. Rather, he maintained that the capitalist form of property would be superseded by individual/social property, as was explained. This new form of property needs, however, to be justified, and that is the task of the subsequent portions of the present essay. I will attempt to reconstruct for Marx a number of arguments in favor of this form of property, showing that this is indeed the sense in which the concept of property needs to be understood within the Marxian framework.

But before proceeding to these arguments, a few introductory remarks are in order. To begin, the arguments presented here will be more social, political, and moral in nature than economic. In fact, they will try to ground the claim that true freedom, justice, and self-realization can best be attained within a network of individual/social property relations. This is not to say that economic advantages will not accrue within this new system. Indeed, Marx believed that in a planning economy many of the traditional problems that plague capitalist economics, such as over- or underproduction, inflation, unemployment, recessions, depressions, etc., would simply dissolve. In postcapitalist society, the study of traditional economics will be as meaningful and relevant to individual and social planning as alchemy is to chemistry.

Also, it is important to point out that Marx never explicitly formulated his arguments for the type of property relations he believed would be in place in communist society. They must be reconstructed from passages scattered throughout his published and unpublished works. The lack of any extended, systematic treatment by Marx on the subject makes my task, therefore, more interpretative than simply expository. With that caveat in mind, let us proceed to the arguments.

THE ARGUMENT BASED ON FREEDOM

This argument for individual/social property derives a great deal of its force from the contrast of Marx's concept of freedom with the one he sees as inherent in capitalism. A large part of this section will be devoted to uncovering and explaining his notion of freedom and then showing how it can best be achieved within a system of individual/social property.

Marx stresses that the freedom that obtains in capitalist society is merely formal. In other words, for the worker, it amounts to a freedom to sell his labor to whoever will buy it. Marx speaks ironically of this context where the sale and purchase of labor-power occurs as "a very Eden of the innate rights of man." Here freedom exists "because both buyer and seller of a commodity, say of labor-power, are constrained only by their own free will. They contract as free agents, and the agreement they come to, is but the form in which they give legal expression to their common will" (C, I:176).

The cause of Marx's irony is the fact that the worker is *forced* to sell his labor, and is exploited in the process. "It takes centuries," says Marx, "ere the 'free' laborer, thanks to the development of capitalistic production, agrees, i.e., is compelled by social conditions, to sell the whole of his active life, his very capacity for work, for the price of the necessaries of life, his birthright for a mess of pottage" (C, I:271). It turns out that the only area in which the worker is "free" is in the original agreement to work; he certainly is not free to determine what or how to produce or when, where, with whom or under what conditions the production should take place. Even the agreement to work is not really free, according to Marx, because the worker must sell his labor-power to a capitalist or starve—not much of a choice, he thinks. This is why Marx claims that:

It must be acknowledged that our laborer comes out of the process of production other than he entered. In the market he stood as owner of the commodity "labor-power" face to face with other owners of commodities, dealer against dealer. The contract by which he sold to the capitalist his labor-power proved, so to say, in black and white that he disposed of himself freely. The bargain concluded, it is discovered that he was no "free agent," that the time for which he is free to sell his labor-power is the time for which he is forced to sell it, that in fact the vampire will not lose its hold on him "so long as there is muscle, a nerve, a drop of blood to be exploited." For "protection" against "the serpent of their agonies," the laborers must put their heads together, and, as a class, compel the passing of a law, an all-powerful social barrier that shall prevent the very workers from selling, by voluntary contract with capital, themselves and their families into slavery and death (C, I:301–302).

A more far-reaching difference, however, between Marx and the capitalist lies in their respective conceptions of freedom. For Adam Smith, freedom is primarily a negative quality. It is an absence of restraint or coercion, a "freedom from" compulsions and prohibitions alike. The connection between this sort of freedom and *laissez faire* capitalist economics is instructive. It consists of the way in which those who hold solely to the negative notion of freedom regard labor. "In the sweat of thy brow shalt thou labor! was Jehovah's curse on Adam. And this is labor for Smith, a curse. 'Tranquility' appears as the adequate state, as identical with 'freedom' and 'happiness' " (G:611). Marx does not question the validity of defining freedom, in part at least, as the absence of coercion and restraint. He does, however, question the implication that Smith draws from this negative notion, namely, that labor is a sacrifice and that the really "free" person is the one unencumbered by work.

It seems quite far from Smith's mind that the individual, "in his normal state of health, strength, activity, skill, facility," also needs a normal portion of work, and of the suspension of tranquility. . . . But Smith has no inkling whatever that this overcoming of obstacles is in itself a liberating activity—and that, further, the external aims become stripped of the semblance of merely external natural urgencies, and become posited as aims which the individual himself posits—hence as self-realization, objectification of the subject, hence real freedom, whose action is, precisely, labor (G:611).

This brings us to Marx's concept of freedom, one much richer than the negative notion of "freedom from" mentioned above. According to Marx, freedom also has a positive element, a "freedom to" in the dual sense of (1) "autonomy," which is to say, giving law to oneself (including, but not limited to the moral sense), selecting one's own goals, and giving law to nature, in the sense of controlling it through knowledge and experience in order to meet the physical needs of society with the least expenditure of time and energy; and (2) "ability to do," that is, possessing the material (economic) and sociopolitical conditions necessary to permit individuals to bring their goals to fruition, thereby furthering their own self-realization.

To explain this positive notion of freedom more fully, it is necessary to examine the distinction Marx draws between the realm of freedom and the realm of necessity. Strictly speaking, for Marx, individuals are only truly free when they are no longer burdened by the need to produce the material necessities of life. "In fact, the realm of freedom actually begins only where labor which is determined by necessity and mundane considerations ceases; thus in the very nature of things it lies beyond the sphere of actual material production" (C, III:820). But this "realm of freedom" is not a condition of carefree idleness; it is a state of being, of doing; it is creative activity with self-realization as its purpose. According to Marx, "Labor becomes attractive work [when] the individual's self-realization [is the goal], which in no way means that it becomes mere fun, mere amusement. . . . Really free working, e.g., composing, is at the same time precisely the most damned seriousness, the most intense exertion" (G:611).

Nevertheless, Marx recognized that this aspect of freedom was an ideal that could be met only partially. The material production of the needs of society will continue to limit the amount of free time individuals have for creative activity. He was perfectly aware of this and never predicated the existence of freedom in postcapitalist society on full automation of noncreative labor. Instead, he insisted that: "The shortening of the work-day is its basic prerequisite" (C, III:820).

Freedom of a different, more limited sort, however, can be achieved even within the realm of necessity (i.e., the realm of the material production of necessities). It consists of gaining rational control over the physical and economic conditions of existence. Marx explains what he means by the "realm of necessity" and describes the freedom possible therein as follows:

Just as the savage must wrestle with Nature to satisfy his wants, to maintain and reproduce life, so must civilized man, and he must do so in all social formations and under all possible modes of production. With his development this realm of physical necessity expands as a result of his wants; but, at the same time, the forces of production which satisfy these wants also increase. Freedom in this field can only consist in socialized man, the associated producers, rationally regulating their interchange with Nature, bringing it under their common control, instead of being ruled by it as by the blind forces of Nature; and achieving this with the least expenditure of energy and under conditions most favorable to, and worthy of, their human nature (C, III:820).

To summarize briefly, Marx's concept of freedom has a cluster of meanings: (1) the absence of restraint or coercion, in the sense of not being compelled or prohibited, (2) autonomy, both in the control of one's own objectives (self-direction) and in the control of the environment (both physical and social), and (3) ability, in the sense of having the capacity to achieve the goals one has chosen. To use Marx's example, it would mean possessing the power or ability to do creative labor, such as composing a work of art.

One final point needs to be made on this matter. According to Marx, freedom in the fullest sense can only be achieved in and through community life. "Only within the community has each individual the means of cultivating his gifts in all directions; hence personal freedom becomes possible only within the community. . . . In the real community the individuals obtain their freedom in and through their association" (GI, MECW 5:78).

Marx's concept of freedom, especially its positive elements, forms an argument for individual/social property in the following ways. First, freedom, as described in the realm of necessity, constitutes the rational control over nature and the processes of production, and as such, it demands an association of producers. In a society based on capitalist property, control in this sphere is found only with those who own the means of production. As a result, the majority of individuals are unfree in this sense because they lack the decision-making powers that accompany ownership. Thus, it is only by the common ownership (social property) of the means of production that everyone is afforded the opportunity to decide what should be produced, how it should be produced, and by whom. While this does not automatically make the individuals in this sort of society free (since there is no guarantee that their democratic control of production will result in its rational regulation), it does offer a necessary condition for such freedom.

Secondly, freedom, in the sense of political autonomy, can also add to the argument for individual/social property, since economic freedom is a condition for political freedom. It is only with equal shares in the power base that the real exercise of democracy has any meaning. This equal power depends upon equal shares in the ownership of the means of production.

Finally, freedom as the ability or capacity to accomplish one's goals can only really be a universal possibility under a system based on individual/social property. The reason for this is twofold. First, as Marx has already pointed out, one of the conditions for freedom of self-development is having enough free time from subsistence labor to devote to it. In capitalist society, free time is frequently too little and too late (if at all) for creative, self-fulfilling activity. This need not, nor should it be the case.

The intensity and productiveness of labor being given, the time which society is bound to devote to material production is shorter, and as a consequence, the time at its disposal for the free development, intellectual and social, of the individual is greater, in proportion as the work is more and more evenly divided among all the able-bodied members of society, and as a particular class is more and more deprived of the power to shift the natural burden of labor from its own shoulders to those of another layer of society. In this direction, the shortening of the working-day finds at last a limit in the generalization of labor. In capitalist society spare time is acquired for one class by converting the whole life-time of the masses into labor-time (C, I:530).

The second condition for this aspect of freedom is open access for all to the facilities and resources needed to develop the requisite skills for self-fulfillment. Under capitalism, Marx argues, these facilities and resources are open only to the wealthy few. Under a society based on individual/social property, they will be available in equal shares to all those who desire to take advantage of them. Again, it should be pointed out that Marx's proposal will not guarantee this sort of freedom. After all, if freedom in the negative sense is to be respected, no one has the right to force another to develop his or her talents. All that can be done is to provide the necessary conditions, and this is precisely what a system based on individual/social property would do.

THE ARGUMENT BASED ON JUSTICE

The area of concern in this argument based on justice will be limited specifically to distributive justice, i.e., to the way in which the goods and burdens of society should be distributed. I shall present Marx's concept of justice and attempt to show that its fulfillment requires the adoption of individual/social property.

Marx's major criticism of capitalism, from the standpoint of distributive justice, is that it unfairly exploits the worker. His account of exploitation is too technical and lengthy to present for our purpose, so I shall simplify it. Essentially, his point is that there is a portion of the working day for which the capitalist fails to pay the worker the equivalent value of his labor. Marx maintains that: *"The value of the product is constituted by labor done, including that not paid for;* but *wages* only express *paid labor,* never all labor *done"* (G:570–571). His judgment that this unpaid labor is immoral is unequivocal; he calls it "stealing," "robbery," and "theft." Of course, exploitation is not unique to capitalism; the slave in ancient society and the serf in feudal society were also exploited. However, one of the most important aspects that distinguishes capitalist exploitation from earlier forms is that it is concealed by the labor contract, which makes the exchange between the laborer and capitalist appear as if it is a free and fair transaction.

Given all of this, it would seem that Marx would have readily agreed with a key provision of the *Gotha Program* (a general statement of purpose meant to unify the two factions of the German socialist movement), which stated that "all members of society have an equal right to the undiminished proceeds of labor." But this is not the case. Instead, he offers two distinct standards of justice, one which should apply in what he calls "the first phase of communist society," and another in "a more advanced phase of communist society."

Marx's formal principle of justice is equality of treatment for equals, or, to put it more contemporaneously, dealing with similar individuals in similar cases similarly. This formal principle will hold for both of the material principles I shall now present.

In the first phase of communist society, the means of production will be collectively owned and controlled by all of the members of society. Here the material principle of justice, according to Marx, should be: to each according to his labor after certain necessary deductions have been made from the total social product. These deductions are of two different sets. The first pertains to the economic necessities within the *realm of production:* (1) "cover to replace the means of production used up," (2) "an additional portion for the expansion of production," and (3) "a reserve or insurance fund in case of accidents, disruption caused by natural calamities, etc." (CGP:344). The second set of deductions are made for physical and social necessities within the *realm of consumption:* (1) "the general costs of all administration not directly appertaining to production," (2) "the amount set aside for needs communally satisfied," and (3) "a fund for people unable to work, etc." (CGP:345). After these de-

ductions have been made, "the individual producer gets back from society
. . . exactly what he has given it" (CGP:346). Although necessarily vague, he
gives us a general idea of what he means in the following passage:

For instance, the social working day consists of the sum of individual hours of work.
The individual labor time of the individual producer thus constitutes his contribution to the social working day, his share of it. Society gives him a certificate stating
that he has done such and such an amount of work (after the labor done for the
communal fund has been deducted), and with this certificate he can withdraw from
the social supply of means of consumption as much as costs an equivalent amount
of labor. The same amount of labor he has given to society in one form, he receives
back in another (CGP:346).

Marx is quick to point out that this principle of distribution based on each
individual's productive output is similar to the one employed in capitalism.
Nonetheless, the differences are radical. The means of production will be socially, not privately, owned and, therefore, the individual will contribute only
his labor. Furthermore, personal ownership will be limited to individual means
of consumption. Under these conditions, instead of the capitalist unjustly appropriating a part of the total social product for his personal gain, each will
receive his own individual share (based on the labor he has contributed), plus
the indirect benefits to society as a whole from the necessary deductions. Finally, these conditions make it impossible for anyone to buy and exploit the
labor of others. Making exploitation impossible will thereby eliminate the key
source of injustice that has plagued all past societies.

In spite of all of this, Marx still contends that this standard of justice applicable in the first phase of communism is inadequate, although unavoidable. It
still suffers, he says, from a "bourgeois limitation" of giving each producer a
right to goods and services proportional to his or her own labor. He considers
this a bourgeois limitation for two reasons. First, distributing goods on the
basis of labor output "gives tacit recognition to a worker's individual endowment and hence productive capacity as natural privileges" (CGP:347). Marx
was not a radical equalitarian proponent of strict equality of results and so
agreed that certain inequalities in distribution are justifiable. However, if an
unequal distribution in shares is to be just, it must not be based on attributes
or qualities beyond a person's control and responsibility. Labor output is dependent, to some degree, upon a person's genetic endowment and early child-
hood training, and since these are outside one's control, they ought not to be
used—if it can be helped—as a basis for distribution.

The second reason Marx cites for objecting to this standard of justice is
that it ignores need. "One worker is married, another is not; one has more
children than another, etc., etc. Thus, with the same work performance and
hence the same share of the social consumption fund, one will in fact be receiving more than another, one will be richer than another, etc." (CGP:347).

Hence, for Marx, any standard of distribution that rewards "natural privileges" and ignores individual need is faulty—even though it may be unavoidable.

Marx regards these defects as inevitable during the transition from capitalism to a more advanced phase of communism. He claims that they are unavoidable because: "Right [in this context, read "distributive justice"] can never rise above the economic structure of society and its contingent cultural development" (CGP:347). He is making two points here. The first is that all of the needs of each individual cannot be satisfied unless there is a considerable amount of wealth available, and presumably this will not be the case in the first stage of communism. Second, the cultural milieu from which this first phase of communism will emerge must also be considered, viz., a society of individuals who have been conditioned under capitalism to be primarily egoistic. This sort of person needs personal incentives in order to work, so that an appeal solely to the good of the community will hardly suffice. Thus, he rightly insists that a material principle of justice, if it is to be practically applicable, must take into account certain economic, social, and political limitations. To paraphrase Kant, the "ought" of justice implies the "can" of the society in question.

According to Marx, it will only be possible to eradicate the defects listed above in a more advanced stage of communist society. In this more developed stage, the following material principle of justice should obtain: "From each according to his abilities, to each according to his needs!" (CGP:347). Marx takes pains to stress that this principle ought (and therefore can) only apply given certain conditions. Namely,

... when the enslaving subjugation of individuals to the division of labor, and thereby the antithesis between intellectual and physical labor, have disappeared; when labor is no longer just a means of keeping alive but has itself become a vital need; when the all-round development of individuals has also increased their productive powers and all the springs of cooperative wealth flow more abundantly ... (CGP:347).

Neither of these standards of justice is possible within a system based on private property; they both require that the means of production be collectively owned. This is why the adoption of individual/social property is a necessary condition for either of Marx's standards of justice. For Marx, such high-sounding phrases as "undiminished proceeds of labor," "equal right," and "just distribution" (phrases used in the *Gotha Program*) are "only a load of obsolete verbal rubbish" (CGP:347) if the conditions of production are not transformed. It must be remembered that the mode of distribution is dependent upon the mode of production.

The distribution of the means of consumption at any given time is merely a consequence of the distribution of the conditions of production themselves; the distribution of the latter, however, is a feature of the mode of production itself. The capitalist mode of production, for example, rests on the fact that the material conditions of production are in the hands of non-workers in the form of property in capital and land, while the masses are only in possession of their personal condition of production, labor power. If the elements of production are distributed in this way, the present distribution of the means of consumption follows automatically. If the material conditions of production were the cooperative property of the workers themselves a different distribution of the means of consumption from that of today would follow of its own accord (CGP:348).

In other words, a particular mode of production with its property relations imposes certain practical limits on the types of distribution schemes that are possible. This is why Marx's "from each according to his abilities, to each according to his needs" is impossible under a capitalist mode of production and system of property.

As a final note, Marx would be overstating his case if he thought that a *just* distribution "would follow of its own accord," given a mode of production consistent with individual/social property. It wouuld be more accurate to claim that this new form of property (and production) is a necessary, but not sufficient condition for just distribution.

THE ARGUMENT BASED ON SELF-REALIZATION

The argument based on self-realization is the most general and perhaps the most important of the arguments for individual/social property. While the preceding arguments based on freedom and justice are important in their own right, they also serve as a groundwork for what Marx variously calls "self-realization," "self-creation," "full development," and "objectification." These terms express the very antithesis of alienation. They point to what Marx considers to be the true goal or purpose of human life, namely, the dynamic process of becoming or self-fulfillment of the individual within communal life.

In this section I shall examine Marx's concept of self-realization, contrasting it with its opposite, alienation. It will be argued throughout that the possibility of self-realization for every member of society can best be accomplished within a system based on individual/social property.

According to Marx, the activity by which man realizes or fulfills himself is labor. He credits Hegel with recognizing the importance of labor in the process of human development and states that since "Hegel conceives the self-creation of man as a process . . . he thus grasps the essence of *labor* and comprehends objective man—true, because real man—as the outcome of man's *own labor*" (EPM, MECW 3:332–333).

In a very rudimentary sense, labor as self-realization is the transformation and appropriation of nature to meet the basic requirements of survival. Marx expresses the universality of this sort of labor by saying that "it is the everlasting Nature-imposed condition of human existence and therefore is independent of every social phase of that existence, or rather, is common to every such phase" (C, I:184). In this most general sense:

Labor is . . . a process in which both man and Nature participate, and in which man of his own accord starts, regulates, and controls the material re-actions between himself and Nature. He opposes himself to Nature as one of his own forces, setting in motion arms and legs, head and hands, the natural forces of his body, in order to appropriate Nature's productions in a form adapted to his own wants. By thus acting on the external world and changing it, he at the same time changes his own nature. He develops his slumbering powers and compels them to act in obedience to his sway (C, I:177).

Labor is, however, more than just the process by which man satisfies his basic needs. In a higher sense, human labor, as opposed to animal labor, is a free, consciously purposive activity, one in which standards other than mere efficacy and functionality are applied. It is *free* because "man produces even when he is free from physical need and only truly produces in freedom therefrom" (EPM, MECW 3:276). It is *consciously purposive* because, unlike the constructions of animals, which are determined largely by instinct, man's constructions are the result of freely formed plans—plans that originate in the imagination and are carried out in reality with a purpose he himself has chosen. As Marx states:

. . . what distinguishes the worst architect from the best of bees is this, that the architect raises his structure in imagination before he erects it in reality. At the end of every labor-process, we get a result that already existed in the imagination of the laborer at its commencement. He not only effects a change of form in the material on which he works, but he also realizes a purpose of his own that gives the law to his *modus operandi,* and to which he must subordinate his will (C, I:178).

Furthermore, the objects of man's labor are not limited by the particular needs of his own species; he produces universally and according to standards such as beauty. "An animal forms things in accordance with the standard and the need of the species to which it belongs, whilst man knows how to produce in accordance with the laws of beauty" (EPM, MECW 3:276–277).

We have seen so far what Marx considers to be the essence of labor. Let us now turn our attention to his view of its purpose. According to Marx, the purpose of labor is the satisfaction of needs, both natural and created. Two different categories of needs and their corresponding types of labor can be distinguished. The first is sustenance, providing for the material necessities of human life, i.e., "labor to earn a living" (EPM, MECW 3:220). The second category is the need for self-realization of development, labor as "the enjoyment of . . . personality and the realization of . . . natural abilities and spiritual aims" (EPM, MECW 3:220). It would appear as if the latter could be achieved only within the "realm of freedom," where the worker is no longer burdened with the production of necessities. Strictly speaking, this is true for Marx. Yet, just as he allowed for a limited sort of freedom in postcapitalist society within the "realm of necessity," he also allows for a limited type of self-fulfillment within this realm. While the present-day worker is often one-dimensional in his labor and, consequently, in his talents, he will be replaced in communist society "by the fully developed individual, fit for a variety of labors, ready to face any change in production, and to whom the different social functions he performs, are but so many modes of giving free scope to his own natural and acquired powers" (C, I:488).

Nevertheless, the purer sort of self-realization occurs not inside this sphere of the material production of necessities, but in the "realm of freedom." Here labor is self-creative and an end-in-itself. It is an intrinsic good wherein "the external aims become stripped of the semblance of merely external natural urgencies and become posited as aims which the individual himself posits—hence as self-realization, objectification of the subject, hence real freedom, whose action is precisely labor" (G:611). Thus, for Marx, the true goal of human beings is self-realization through labor and characterized by "freedom and happiness" (G:611). In his vision of future society, the focus of life will be on *being* rather than *having,* and in the following passage he describes the properties of a really "wealthy" person.

When the limited bourgeois form is stripped away, what is wealth other than the universality of individual needs, capacities, pleasures, productive forces, etc., created through universal creative exchange? The full development of human mastery over the forces of nature, those of so-called nature as well as of humanity's own nature? The absolute working-out of his creative potentialities, with no presupposition other than the previous historic development, which makes this totality of development, i.e., the development of all human powers as such the end in itself, not as measured on a *predetermined* yardstick? Where he does not reproduce himself in one specificity, but produces his totality? Strives not to remain something he has become, but is in the absolute movement of becoming? (G:488).

The discussion thus far has focused on a general elaboration of the ideal of labor, the process by which man develops and fulfills himself. In an effort to flesh out this general ideal a bit more, I shall contrast it with the alienating and nonfulfilling labor that typifies capitalist production. Since alienation takes on a number of related forms, I shall briefly describe each and contrast them with the corresponding elements of self-realization.

(1) The first form of alienation is the worker's relationship to the product of his labor. The objects that he creates are alien to him because they belong to another and, therefore, are out of his control. As a result, his product "exists *outside him,* independently, as something alien to him, and it becomes a power on its own confronting him. It means that the life which he has conferred on the object confronts him as something hostile and alien" (EPM, MECW 3:272).

Instead of being controlled by the worker, the product of labor is controlled by two outside forces, the capitalist and the economic "laws" of the marketplace. Both of these forces, Marx argues, act in ways inimical to the worker, so much so that: "In the sphere of political economy ... the realization of labor appears as *loss of realization* for the workers; objectification as *loss of the object* and *bondage to it;* appropriation as estrangement, as *alienation"* (EPM, MECW 3:272).

The elimination of this sort of alienation can only be achieved if the workers themselves collectively own the means of production. From their collective or social ownership comes the right to control democratically the major elements of production, especially, what and how much is to be produced, the way in which it is to be produced, by whom, and the system of distribution. Only in a planning economy of associated workers are the members of society thus able to dissolve this form of alienation, and thereby achieve one of the key aspects of self-fulfillment—freedom.

(2) Marx refers to the second form of alienation as "the relation of the worker to his own activity as an alien activity not belonging to him . . ." (EPM, MECW 3:275). There are two meanings attached to the notion of activity being alien because it does not "belong" to the laborer. In both senses a "loss of self" is involved because "As individuals express their life, so they are. What they are, therefore, coincides with their production, both with *what* they produce and with *how* they produce" (GI, MECW 5:31–32).

The first and most obvious meaning is that the worker has sold himself—his activity—to his employer. In so doing, he has relinquished his right to determine his own activity and therefore surrenders his being by selling his activity. It "belongs" to the capitalist; and so he, not the worker, governs what will be produced and in which manner. In this situation, the laborer is not self-directed, and, consequently, his activity fails to reflect his interests, personality, or creativity.

The second meaning of the laborer's activity as not "belonging" to him cuts more deeply than the first. According to Marx, the worker's labor does not belong to him, because "it does not belong to his essential being" (EPM, MECW 3:274). Which is to say, in the act of production, "he does not affirm himself but denies himself, does not feel content but unhappy, does not develop freely his physical and mental energy but mortifies his body and ruins his mind" (EPM, MECW 3:274). Instead of self-realization, his work is self-sacrifice; instead of satisfying the greatest need, the need to develop oneself, it is "merely a *means* to satisfy needs external to it" (EPM, MECW 3:275).

For the most part, our discussion of the alienation of activity has been on a rather general level. In his later writings, especially in *Capital,* Marx addresses the more concrete manifestations of alienation. There he points out the wretched working and living conditions of his time: the long hours, the unsanitary and dangerous working environment, and the statistics revealing the foreshortened lifespan of the modern worker due to the abuses to which he was subjected. He also speaks of the mind-deadening divisions of labor (both in the sense of the task being divided into smaller segments, and in the sense that his whole life is restricted to just one sort of labor) in which the activity itself is more animal- and machine-like than human. This is the sort of labor in which the worker becomes mutilated and fragmented, degraded to the point of being a mere appendage in the mechanical process, and estranged from his physical and intellectual potentialities.

In contrast to alienation, we have, in passing, presented a number of elements that constitute self-realization. The abolition of private property will, Marx believes, not only eliminate alienation, but it will also make available the conditions for full human self-development. "The positive transcendence [*Aufhebung*] of *private property*," he writes, "as the appropriation of *human* life, is therefore the positive transcendence of all estrangement—that is to say, the return of man ... to his *human* i.e., *social* existence" (EPM, MECW 3:297).

(3) The final form of alienation is the estrangement of man from man which is, says Marx, an immediate consequence of the previous forms. "What applies to a man's relation to his work, to the product of his labor and to himself, also holds of a man's relation to the other man, and to the other man's labor and object of labor" (EPM, MECW 3:277). The important and far-reaching way in which this form of alienation manifests itself is in the division between public and private man.

Marx explains that with the advent of capitalism and with the attendant transformation from feudalism to modern society, a schism developed between the political state and civil society. The general interests of society as a whole are supposed to govern in the realm of the political state, while the private interests of each individual are to reign in civil society. Were there no conflict between these spheres of interest, this division would be of little concern. In modern society, however, the aims of the collectivity and that of the individual are often at odds. In this situation of conflict, the individual becomes a schizophrenic. On one hand, he is asked to lead the life of a public person, one concerned with the welfare of his fellows—a more or less altruistic life. Yet, on the other hand, he is told that he must provide for himself and his own family even at the cost of others, that he must be a private person, an egoist. In this context, says Marx, "man—not only in thought, in consciousness, but in *reality, in* life—leads a twofold life, a heavenly and an earthly life: life in the *political community,* in which he considers himself a *communal being,* and life in *civil society,* in which he acts as a private individual, regards other men as a means, degrades himself into a means, and becomes the plaything of alien powers" (JQ, MECW 3:154).

The dominant half of this schizophrenic man of modern society is the private individual, the egoist. This, according to Marx, is to be expected because the mode of production (the economic life of society) conditions the political environment. The dominance of civil society over the political state can be seen, Marx asserts, in the early constitutions of France and the United States. In both, "the so-called *rights of man* ... are nothing but the rights of a *member of civil society,* i.e., the rights of egoistic man, of man separated from other men and from the community" (JQ, MECW 3:162).

The emancipation accomplished in these constitutions, while certainly an advance over precapitalist conditions, is still incomplete. It divides the individual by giving him conflicting roles that he is expected to play simultaneously. In contrast to this, Marx describes true, human emancipation as occurring

Only when the real, individual man re-absorbs in himself the abstract citizen, and as an individual human being has become a species-being in his everyday life, in his particular work, and in his particular situation, only when man has recognized and organised his *"forces propres"* as *social* forces, and consequently no longer separates social power from himself in the shape of *political* power only then will human emancipation have been accomplished (JQ, MECW 3:168).

Just as the political freedoms guaranteed in capitalist society were a *sine qua non* for its growth and development, so too, economic freedoms (such as freedom from lack of the necessities of life, freedom to actively participate in the decisions of the workplace, freedom to obtain the conditions of creative labor, etc.) will be the foundation of postcapitalist society. Political emancipation is one of the legacies of capitalism; human emancipation will be one of the legacies of Marx's vision of communism.

CONCLUSION

Marx believed that a communist mode of production with its corresponding individual/social property would overcome the abuses of class domination, exploitation, and alienation found in capitalism. It would usher in an epoch of human emancipation marked by true freedom, justice, and self-realization. Moreover, he considered the task of bringing this about as a moral obligation. It is, he says, a *"categorical imperative to overthrow all relations* in which man is a debased, enslaved, foresaken, despicable being . . ."* (EPM, MECW 3:182).

In closing, it is instructive to note that present-day communist systems have failed to accomplish some of the most essential goals of Marx's vision of future society. Their failure, I think, can be traced in large part to the abandonment of his concept of individual/*social* property by replacing it with individual/*state* property. State property is the collective ownership of the means of production by an elite group. In this situation, the means of production have become a powerful instrument of class domination by the party over the exploited and alienated workers. In place of workers' self-governance over their social, political, and economic conditions, we find a highly centralized, extremely powerful, authoritarian and coercive regime that is becoming stronger rather than "withering away." Yet this betrayal of Marx is not inevitable and it is not more utopian for the modern worker to strive for economic freedom than it was for the early bourgeois to strive for political freedom.

NOTES

[1]Each citation begins with an abbreviation of the work from which the quote is taken and will be followed by a MECW reference if contained in the *Karl Marx Fredrick Engels Collected Works* series. For example, (CM, MECW 6:498) stands for *The Communist Manifesto*, found in *Karl Marx Fredrick Engels Collected Works*, volume 6, page 498. See list of abbreviations below.

LIST OF ABBREVIATIONS

C	*Capital*
CM	*The Communist Manifesto*
CGP	*Critique of the Gotha Program*
EPM	*Economic and Philosophic Manuscripts of 1844*
GI	*The German Ideology*
G	*Grundrisse: Foundation of the Critique of Political Economy*
JQ	*The Jewish Question*
L	*The Letters of Karl Marx*
PP	*The Poverty of Philosophy*
MECW	*Karl Marx Fredrick Engels Collected Works*

REFERENCES CITED

Marx, Karl and Engels, Frederick. *Karl Marx Fredrick Engels Collected Works,* Vols. 1–12. New York: International Publishers, 1975—.

Marx, Karl. *Capital,* Vols. 1–3. Edited by Fredrick Engels. New York: International Publishers, 1967.

———. *Grundrisse: Foundations of the Critique of Political Economy.* Translated by Martin Nicolaus. New York: Vintage Books, 1973.

———. *The Letters of Karl Marx.* Edited by S. Padover. New Jersey: Prentice-Hall, 1979.

———. *Karl Marx: The First International and After.* Edited by D. Fernbach. New York: Vintage Books, 1974.

PAUL CRAIG ROBERTS AND MATTHEW A. STEPHENSON

ALIENATION AND HISTORICAL MATERIALISM

The concept of Marxian alienation has been interpreted mostly in humanistic terms. In their essay, Paul Craig Roberts—who holds the William Simon Chair in political economy at Georgetown University's Center for Strategic and International Studies, and wrote Alienation and the Soviet Economy (1971) *and numerous essays on economics, ethics, and foreign policy—and Matthew A. Stephenson—Chairman of the Department of Economics at Wofford College, South Carolina, who has published in numerous journals on topics in the history of economic thought—provide a different view. They provide an interpretation of this concept that explains the Marxian content of central economic planning.*

Marx's greatest dislike for capitalism came from his belief that its chief organizational characteristic—production for sale in the market—made it anarchic and unplanned. Consequently, people are at the mercy of blind forces of their own making. Liberation from the market requires central economic planning, which in practice means massive state regimentation of the economy, from which result numerous lessons about the nature of Marxian socialism and communism.

Perhaps no aspect of Marx has been more widely misinterpreted than his concept of alienation. Others who have found alienation to be a theme in Marx's writings have erred in explaining one result of commodity production, alienation, in terms of other results, greed or private property, or they have interpreted it from an "idealistic" standpoint[*] that is inconsistent with Marx's concept of historical materialism.[1] Their critics have correctly pointed out the incompatibility of "idealistic" concepts of alienation with historical materialism,[2] but some erroneously concluded that a concept of alienation is not present in Marx's later writings. The discussion of Marxian alienation can be faulted for explaining one result in terms of other results, and for misunderstanding the issue of whether a concept of alienation is compatible with historical materialism.

Our interpretation[3] finds the source of Marxian alienation in exchange or the commodity mode of production, just as we have derived every other aspect of capitalism of which Marx was critical from commodity production. Marx's

Reprinted from *Marx's Theory of Exchange, Alienation and Crisis* by Paul Craig Roberts and Matthew A. Stephenson. Copyright © 1973 by the Board of Trustees of the Leland Stanford Junior University. Reprinted by permission of Praeger Publishers.

[*] An "idealistic" concept of alienation is one that gives man's consciousness or psychology the role of a determinant. Marx referred to this view as a "fantasy," because it sees "the relationships of men, all their doings, their chains and their limitations [as] products of their consciousness." *The German Ideology* (New York: International Publishers, 1947), p. 6. According to Marx, this view suggests that man can change himself merely by exchanging one consciousness for another. To Marx, this view is foolish, because man's consciousness is determined by the mode of production: "the nature of individuals thus depends on the material conditions determining their production." *Ibid.*, p. 7.

concept of alienation is materialistic—as it must be, given his materialist concept of history in which the institutions and consciousness of men (ideology in the classical Marxian sense) in any historical period are determined by the economic organization of society. In Marx's words: "The mode of production of material life conditions the general process of social, political, and intellectual life. It is not the consciousness of men that determines their existence, but their social existence that determines their consciousness."[4] Therefore greed is a derivative, not a determinant, in Marx's analysis of capitalism. Greed or money worship cannot then be the source of Marxian alienation; instead, it is a condition socialized into man by the ideological superstructure that results from the commodity mode of production.

There was no change in Marx's concept of the source of alienation from the *Manuscripts* in 1844 to *Capital* in 1867. In both works alienation is said to occur when men are mutually independent and engage in market exchange, and when men are subject to the market—something over which they have no control—as to an alien force. The lengthy discussion of the nature of commodities and the commodity mode of production in *Capital* is prefigured in the 1844 *Manuscripts,* in which Marx says that he has "considered the act of estranging practical human activity, labor, in two of its aspects. (1) The relation of the worker to the *product of labor* as an alien object exercising power over him. . . . (2) The relation of labor to the *act of production* within the *labor* process."[5]

Marx says that in a capitalist economy "labor produces not only commodities: it produces itself and the worker as a *commodity*—and this in the same general proportion in which it produces commodities."[6] As a result, the worker "is looked upon as a supply of a *commodity* like any other. . . . his human qualities only exist for capital *alien* to him."*

Marx is unequivocal in explaining that alienation is a consequence of the very act of production. The act of production is the act of producing commodities. Marx's criticism of economists has been generally misunderstood. It does not turn on drawing the implication of exploitation from the labor theory of value. Rather, Marx mainly criticizes economists for neglecting the organizational implications of commodity production. He says that *"political economy conceals the estrangement inherent in the nature of labor by not considering the direct relationship between the worker (labor) and production."*[7] Here Marx is saying that political economy conceals alienation by not considering that exchange separates production from use. All of Marx's economic writings from the *Manuscripts* through *Capital* have as their basis the examination of the relationship between the worker and the process of production. It is precisely this relationship which is the focus of Marx's analysis of alienation in the *Manuscripts*. He wrote:

---

* Marx, *The Economic and Philosophic Manuscripts of 1844* (New York: International Publishers, 1964), p. 120. Note that in the *Manuscripts* Marx refers to the worker as a commodity. He did not make the distinction between labor power which is a commodity and labor which is the use of labor power until later. In the *Grundrisse* he differentiated between the slave who is a commodity and the worker who sells his labor power as a commodity but is not himself a commodity. He retains this distinction in *Capital.*

When we ask, then, what is the essential relationship of labor we are asking about the relationship of the *worker* to production.

Till now we have been considering the estrangement, the alienation of the worker, only in one of its aspects, i.e., the worker's *relationship to the products of his labor.* But the estrangement is manifested not only in the result but in the *act of production,* within the producing activity, itself. How could the worker come to face the product of his activity as a stranger, were it not that in the very act of production he was estranging himself from himself? The product is after all but the summary of the activity of production. If then the product of labor is alienation, production itself must be active alienation, the alienation of activity, the activity of alienation. In the estrangement of the object of labor is merely summarized the estrangement, the alienation, in the activity of labor itself.[8]

In the *Manuscripts* Marx emphasizes that the dehumanizing of the worker occurs because of commodity production: "Production does not simply produce a man as a *commodity,* the *human commodity,* man in the role of *commodity;* it produces him in keeping with this role as a *mentally* and physically *dehumanized* being.—Immorality, deformity, and dulling of the workers and the capitalists.—Its product is the *self-conscious* and *self-acting commodity* ... the human commodity."[9]

It should be clearly understood that Marx's references to dehumanization and the plight of the individual do not mean that his concept of alienation is the same as the contemporary psychological and sociological concepts of it. Alienation of the sort Marx conceived cannot be treated by therapy for the worker and reform of the system; only a revolutionary change in the mode of production can overcome it. According to Marx, alienation is a consequence of objective economic conditions—the separation of production from use that characterizes the commodity mode of production. As Tucker has correctly observed, Marx "does not consider himself to be dealing with a psychiatric phenomenon. He regards himself as engaged in a criticism of political economy and believes that he has grasped and analyzed a fact of the economic life per se."[10] Marx states the relationship between alienation and economics several times in the *Manuscripts.* For example:

It is hardly necessary to assure the reader conversant with political economy that my results have been attained by means of a wholly empirical analysis based on a conscientious critical study of political economy (p. 63).... We have proceeded from the premises of political economy (p. 106).... We took our departure from a fact of political economy—the estrangement of the worker and his production. We have formulated this fact in conceptual terms as *estranged, alienated* labor. We have analyzed this concept—hence analyzing merely a fact of political economy (p. 115).... political economy has merely formulated the laws of estranged labor (p. 117).

Some have argued that Marx jettisoned the concept of alienation after he had worked out the notion of historical materialism. Perhaps they have read an "idealistic" concept of alienation into Marx. It should be clear that Marx's concept of alienation is materialistic and as such is compatible with historical materialism. He did not drop the concept, but he found it difficult to use the term "alienation" because it had already established idealistic connotations among his socialist rivals and meant to many that man already possessed his true innate human nature to the full and was only prevented from enjoying it because of his bondage to religion or the capitalist.

In Marx, man's realization of his true human nature is a process of becoming. Man as a species has a true human nature, and it is innate in the possibilities of the species, although of course it is not innate in individual men in the stages of "prehistory." When communism arrives (the end of prehistory), mankind achieves the potential inherent in the species. The relations between men become (again) convivial (that is, there is directly associated production), and the relation of man to nature and to his own institutions is scientific. When Marx finds that man is alienated under commodity production, he is comparing him both to a past state and to a future one. In neither pre- nor post-capitalist systems is there separation between production and use. Instead there is directly associated production with convivial relations between men and community control over economic life. Some have interpreted Marx's scheme in terms of fall and redemption. It is partially redemptive in that the convivial relations and community control over production which were destroyed by exchange are supposed to be restored under communism, but the basis for the directly associated production is different in pre- and post-capitalist systems. In a pre-capitalist system conviviality is rooted in community tradition and ritual; in the post-capitalist system it is rooted in a scientific consciousness. Since economic life controls human consciousness, society cannot have control over itself until it controls its economic life. Under capitalism, the control man gains over nature through technology is offset by the control his economic organization has over him.

Those who find in the *Manuscripts* a Marx different from the Marx of *Capital* have overlooked this paragraph from the *Manuscripts:* "Now, therefore, we have to grasp the essential connection between private property, greed, and the separation of labor, capital, and landed property; between exchange and competition, value and the devaluation of men, monopoly and competition, etc.— the connection between his whole estrangement and the *money* system."[11] Here in this concise paragraph Marx outlined his life work. In our work we have shown how Marx grasped the "essential connection" between these categories. He derives every aspect of capitalism from its mode of production. He does not derive one aspect of capitalism from one thing and another aspect from another thing. Neither does he proceed, as do many interpreters today, by deriving one aspect of capitalism from another; he does not explain one result in terms of another result. His uniformity of treatment of all aspects of capitalism is complete and does not exempt alienation. Let us now follow Marx's treatment of alienation from the 1844 *Manuscripts* through the *Critique of Political Economy* and *Capital.*

In the manuscript "Estranged Labor," Marx specifically denotes four aspects of man's alienation. First, there is the alienation of man from the product of his labor. The product of labor dominates man and not vice-versa. It has an existence independent of man as something alien to him and becomes a power that confronts him.

Second, man is alienated from labor itself—that is, from productive activity. Work becomes an activity that is external to, and independent of, the worker and an activity in which the worker finds no fulfillment. A worker does not produce use-value directly for himself or his community but exchange value for his employer. The external character of work for the worker is shown by the fact that it is not his own work but work for someone else, that in work he does not belong to himself but to another person.[12] The results of his own activity accrue to him only in his leisure; in what should be the most human of all activity—work—he is alienated.

The third aspect of alienated labor follows from the preceding two. Man is alienated from himself, his mental life, and his human life. Man's "life activity"—his labor—appears only as a means to satisfy his needs—that is, to make a living. But a man's work is his life; therefore, "life itself appears only as a *means to life*."[13]

Marx finds the fourth characteristic, that man is alienated from other men, to be a direct consequence of the other three. "What applies to a man's relation to his work, to the product of his labor, and to himself, also holds of a man's relation to the other man, and to the other man's labor and object of labor."[14]

In *A Contribution to the Critique of Political Economy,* Marx discusses the characteristics of labor that produces commodities. Labor that produces commodities is labor devoid of any quality. The individuality of labor is lost, and the specific forms of labor are lost because of their abstraction into money. Labor that produces commodities is labor that creates exchange value for the employer instead of use-value for the laborer. And, finally, labor that produces commodities "causes the social relations of individuals to appear in the perverted form of a social relation between things."[15]

Man is alienated from the objects of his labor, the work process, and from his own being when his labor loses its quality and when his labor is expended in producing for the market. Man is alienated from other men when his labor results in the personification of objects. Clearly, labor that creates commodities is alienated labor.

These characteristics of labor that produces commodities are revealed in the antitheses and contradictions which, in *Capital,* Marx finds to be inherent in commodities. In commodities are "the antithesis [between] use-value and [exchange] value; the contradiction that private labor is bound to manifest itself as direct social labor, that a particularized concrete kind of labor has to pass for abstract human labor; the contradiction between the personification of objects and the representation of persons by things."[16]

The various aspects of alienation given in the *Economic and Philosophic Manuscripts* are immanent in the nature of commodities. The contradictions and antitheses present in commodities, which are analyzed in *Capital,* are manifestations of alienation. The alienation of man from the product of his labor, from the work process itself, from his own being, and from other men is manifested in the contradictions between use-value and exchange value, individual labor and social labor, particular concrete labor and abstract general labor, and the personification of objects and representation of persons by things—all contradictions being inherent features of commodity production.

It is possible to pair single aspects of alienation with single contradictions immanent in a commodity. The alienation of man from his fellows is implied in "the personification of objects and the representation of persons by things."

The contradiction between use-value and exchange value implies the alienation of man from the objects of his own labor. Use-values follow from man producing directly for himself, his family, or his community; exchange values follow from man producing for the impersonal market through which the specific products of a man's work can serve other (unknown) men as use-values only after being exchanged.

The contradictions between individual labor and social labor and between specific concrete labor and abstract general labor imply the alienation of man from the work process. Marx says that labor which creates exchange value (commodities) is abstract general labor. From the viewpoint of the market it is immaterial who the individual worker is or whether he is a tailor or a carpenter. The specific concrete character of labor is lost by its abstraction into money.

The alienation of man from his own being follows from his alienation from the product of his labor and the work process. According to Marx, since man realizes himself in work, alienation from the products of his work and from productive activity results in alienation from his own being.

Alienation is immanent in Marx's concept of the two-fold character of labor embodied in commodities. In *Capital* he emphasized the importance he attached to this concept: "I was the first to point out and to examine critically this two-fold nature of the labor contained in commodities. As this point is the pivot on which a clear comprehension of Political Economy turns, we must go more into detail."[17] Labor that produces only use-values is not alienated labor but "a necessary condition, independent of all forms of society, for the existence of the human race."[18] Labor that produces commodities produces use-values only indirectly by producing exchange values. Exchange, which separates production from use, separates labor from the direct production of use-values.

Alienation begins when the purpose of production changes from direct use to exchange. In keeping with Marx's method, alienation is not a condition that engulfed man the moment the first commodities were produced. Just as the commodity mode of production evolved gradually, alienation evolved as exchange become predominant. Alienation became a general human condition with the appearance of labor markets in which men sell their labor power.

In capitalism, labor—man's human activity—cannot take place unless labor power is first sold in the market. Since man cannot even work unless he first sells his labor power, his loss of control over his life activity, the production process, himself as a laboring man, and his relations to other men, is total. This loss of control makes him powerless. If market conditions are such that labor power cannot be sold, then labor cannot be performed at all.

Marxian alienation is specific to systems in which exchange is predominant. This means that Marxian alienation characterizes the economies of the Soviet Union and East Europe. In these economies, labor power and the products of labor are commodities. If, as we believe, the natural structure of modern economy is polycentric,[19] exchange cannot be transcended, and Marxian alienation, if it is not a purely intellectual construction, is merely a fact of life.

One should not jump to the conclusions that by "alienation of man from the objects of his own labor" Marx is merely emphasizing exploitation of the worker and that by "alienation from the work process" Marx merely meant that the worker suffered under the monotony of the assembly line. It is clear in Marx that there can be exploitation without alienation, as in feudal exploitation.[*] Indeed, according to Marx, in *every* form of economy (including communism) men have a part of their product expropriated. Marx does not treat surplus value as unique to capitalism. In the Asiatic, ancient, and feudal economies, there is a ruling class that lives by appropriating surplus value. Under communism, surplus value takes the form of use-value for the community: the individual is exploited by the community rather than by other individuals. Whereas exploitation is a characteristic of all economies, alienation is unique to capitalism because exchange as the predominant mode of production is unique to capitalism.

Having found alienation to be an inherent feature of commodity production, Marx proceeded to analyze the development of the capitalistic system. The contradictions and antitheses of that system, which Marx found revealed in such phenomena as crises, follow directly from the contradictions and antitheses immanent in commodity production, which in turn are manifestations of the various aspects of alienation. Although Marx made many references to the individual's plight, *Capital* is not a study of the psychological and sociological features of alienation. Marxian alienation is a feature of a particular mode of production, and it was the study of that mode of production which was the major work of Marx's life.

To summarize, we have shown that since labor which creates commodities is alienated labor, the contradictions in the relations of production of commodities reflect the characteristics of alienated labor. In the *Manuscripts,* Marx gives the characteristics of alienated labor. In the *Critique of Political Economy* and in *Capital,* he gives the characteristics of labor that produces commodities. We see that the characteristics of labor which produces commodities are the characteristics of alienated labor, and we conclude that commodities are pro-

---

[*] Exploitation is, as pointed out, the extraction of use-value beyond what is necessary to maintain and reproduce the worker and his family, whereas alienation is a consequence of exchange and is immanent in the *separation* of production from use.

duced by alienated labor. In *Capital*, Marx gives the contradictions inherent in the commodity mode of production. We see that these contradictions are manifestations of alienation, and we conclude that Marxian alienation is embodied in the phenomenon of commodity production.

This essay has presented an interpretation of Marxian alienation that stands on its own. Nevertheless, some readers might ask how it fares when confronted with the prevalent interpretation that the division of labor is the source of alienation and is abolished under communism.[20] It is certainly true that Marx said that the specialization and division of labor within manufacture "converts the laborer into a crippled monstrosity, by forcing his detail dexterity at the expense of a world of productive capabilities and instincts";[21] that "it is a result of the division of labor in manufactures that the laborer is brought face to face with the intellectual potencies of the material process of production, as the property of another, and as a ruling power";[22] and that "some crippling of body as a whole. Since, however, manufacture carries this social separation of branches of labor much further, and also, by its peculiar division, attacks the individual at the very roots of his life, it is the first to afford the materials for, and to give a start to, industrial pathology."[23]

Our interpretation is not contradicted by this emphasis. What has misled others is their identification of the division of labor within the factory with the social division of labor and with the capitalist mode of production itself. However, Marx differentiates between (1) the division of labor within society (the social division of labor), (2) the division of labor within the factory, and (3) the mode of production upon which a social division of labor is established.

According to Marx, the division of labor in capitalist society "is brought about by the purchase and sale of the products of different branches of industry,"[24] that is, by exchange. What then establishes "the connection between the detail operations in a workshop?" Marx says it comes about from "the sale of the labor power of several workmen to one capitalist, who applies it as combined labor power."[25] Marx ends his section in *Capital* on "Division of Labor in Manufacture and Division of Labor in Society" by saying perfectly clearly that, whereas a social division of labor is a characteristic of every economic formation of society, "division of labor in the workshop, as practiced by manufacture, is a special creation of the capitalist mode of production alone."[26] The crippling division of labor within the factory is then merely another result of the commodity mode of production, and not a determinant in Marx's system. It is production for market that produces the minute division of labor within the factory.

Marx, like Engels, contrasts the order within the firm with the anarchy of the organization between firms.[27] Once the social division of labor is established by a plan in an orderly way, like the division of labor within the firm, the anarchy of the market disappears along with exchange. When exchange is abolished, so is detail labor (the performance of "one and the same simple operation" by *a laborer all his life*). But neither the division of labor within society nor within the firm is abolished. Rather the effect of detailed labor on the individual is *evaded* by a social plan that rotates the work force through the various tasks.

In Marx's scheme there are really only three general social divisions of labor, each corresponding to a general mode of production. These are: (1) pre-capitalist production for direct use which has a social division of labor rooted in hereditary tradition (this general category contains Marx's specific historical forms of Asiatic, ancient, and feudal); (2) commodity production with a social division of labor established through market exchange; and (3) post-capitalist production for direct use in which a complex division of labor is not abolished but controlled by means of a social plan. Thus, the plan of the socialist or communist society is the mechanism for ending crises, alienation, the creation of private property through exchange, the individual's exploitation of individuals, and detail labor.

Marx sometimes uses the term "division of labor" in opposition to the organization of labor or the "directly associated labor" that characterizes the community which does not produce commodities; that is, he sometimes uses "division of labor" as a proxy for "mutually independent producers" or commodity production. Those who find division of labor to be the source of alienation perhaps have this use of the term in mind.

Others who have offered interpretations of Marxian alienation have found Marx to be a humanist.[28] Does our writing about Marxian alienation mean that we think Marx was a humanist?

We do not profess to know whether Marx was a humanist. Those who do claim to find a humanist in the young Marx of the 1844 *Manuscripts* would be on more solid ground if they gave some attention to the even younger Marx of 1843, who wrote that criticism "is a weapon. Its object is an *enemy* it wants not to refute but to *destroy*. . . . Criticism is no longer an *end in itself* but simply a *means*. Its essential pathos is *indignation,* its essential task, *denunciation."* Marx goes on to say that criticism is hand-to-hand combat, "and in such a combat the point is not whether the opponent is noble, equal, or interesting, the point is to *strike* him."[29]

Lenin would have found in these statements of the young Marx full support for the stand he took when charged by his own party with "conduct impermissible in a Party member." At his trial Lenin unflinchingly admitted that his choice of obnoxious phrases was "calculated to evoke in the reader hatred, aversion, and contempt . . . calculated not to convince but to break up the ranks of the opponent, not to correct the mistake of the opponent but to destroy him, to wipe his organization off the face of the earth. . . . Against such political enemies I then conducted . . . a fight of extermination."[30]

Those who find a humanist in Marx must also confront the remarkable account given by Hammen, which in effect portrays the young Marx as a good "Leninist" who selected the humanist vocabulary of the 1844 *Manuscripts* because it was in keeping with his "requirement that the revolutionary class be portrayed as representing the 'total loss of man,' with the victory of communism effecting the 'full recovery of man.' Concurrently, the existing bourgeois order had to be made to appear responsible for the enslavement, degradation, and estrangement of man."[31] Once a humanist vocabulary no longer suited his tactics, Marx abandoned it, and that is one reason why the 1844 *Manuscripts* were never published by Marx during his lifetime.

In our view, even if those who find the 1844 Marx a humanist can survive the 1843 Marx and Hammen's interpretation, they are still nowhere. The question does not turn on what sort of man Marx was, but on the programmatic implications of his work. That is why we ourselves have focussed not on Marx's personality but on the logic of his thought.

According to Marx, morality is only a mask for class interest. Thus, for Marxists, good will cannot be an effective force in history. Since each class acts in its own class interest, there is no humanistic basis upon which to unite classes and cultivate effective reforms. If there are as many specific moralities as there are class interests, what mediates between moralities? Marx answers that the mediator is violence. Lenin explicitly developed this doctrine of violence. According to Lenin, "the scientific concept of dictatorship means neither more nor less than unlimited power, resting directly on force, not limited by anything, not restricted by any laws, nor any absolute rules. Nothing else but that."[32]

Lenin's doctrine of violence was widely acknowledged by the Communist Party. For example, in 1928 Grigori Pyatakov, later a victim of the doctrine, recognized and approved it: "According to Lenin the Communist Party is based on the principle of coercion which doesn't recognize any limitations or inhibitions. And the central idea of this principle of boundless coercion is not coercion by itself but the absence of any limitation whatsoever—moral, political, and even physical."[33] Marx's reasoning, which leaves violence as the mediator between classes, leads logically to violence as the mediator between the Party and the people (Leninism), and even further to violence as the mediator between the Party and its members (Stalinism).

By showing that Stalinism is a logical derivation from the structure of Marx's writings, we do not mean to say that Marx was a Stalinist. Had Marx been in Stalin's historical position, he might have suspended his logic of violence in the interests of humanism, and perhaps Marx's view of communism has humanistic elements. The point is that Marx does not rely on humanism as the method by which to reach a humane communism. Indeed, parenthetical humanistic remarks notwithstanding, humane methods play no role in any part of Marx's account of historical change, neither in the transition from feudalism to capitalism nor in the transition from capitalism to communism. It is a strange humanist who does not rely on good will among men and humane methods of social change, but instead predicates violence as the force of history.

Eugene Kamenka, a Marxist philosopher who has published two studies on Marxism and ethics, begins one book by acknowledging:

The rejection of any appeal to "abstract" moral principles was for many decades one of the best-known features of the work of Marx and Engels. Marxism was distinguished from utopian socialism precisely by reference to its *scientific* character, to its refusal to confront society with moral principles and moral appeals. "Communists preach no morality at all," Marx wrote (characteristically) in the *German Ideology* (1845–46).... Throughout the remainder of his life Marx would object bitterly to any attempt to base a socialist program on "abstract" moral demands embodied in such terms as "justice," "equality," etc.[34]

In his other study Kamenka states that "in the class society, the common interest is an illusion" and that "Marx's theory largely displaced and discredited" the "emphasis on the directing role of moral ideals."[*]

Engels, who is often superior to Marx in stating their common position clearly and simply, lets us see that whatever revision of Marx Lenin might have made, he did not revise the role of violence. Neither was Lenin the first to declare that good will does not exist as a basis for politics. Engels writes:

Since the rising of class antagonism, the evil passions of men, greed, and imperiousness serve as the levers of historical progress, of which, for example, the history of feudalism and the bourgeoisie affords a conspicuous proof.[35]

Practical self-control with regard to ourselves and love, always love, in our intercourse with others are therefore the foundation rules of Feuerbach's morality, from which all others lead, and neither the enthusiastic periods of Feuerbach nor the loud praises of Starcke can set off the thinness and flatness of this pair of utterances.[36]

Engels says that moral theories of Feuerbach are

as powerless as Kant's "Categorical Imperative." As a matter of fact, every class, as well as every profession, has its own system of morals and breaks even this when it can do it without punishment. And love, which is to unite all, appears today in wars, controversies, lawsuits, domestic broils, and mutual plunder.[37]

But love, yes love, is particularly and eternally the magical god, who, according to Feuerbach, surmounts all the difficulties of practical life and that in a society which is divided into classes with diametrically opposing interests. The last remnant of its revolutionary character is thus taken from his philosophy, and there remains the old cant—'love one another.'[38]

The unbridled scorn that Engels pours on a "universal intoxication of reconciliation" is sufficient to have inspired Stalin's bloodiest thought and deed.

---

[*] *The Ethical Foundations of Marxism* (London: Routledge and Kegan Paul, 1962), pp. 139, 143. Nevertheless, Kamenka seems to ascribe a "moral" tone to Marx. Perhaps it is the tone of "moral inversion." For this concept see Michael Polanyi, "Beyond Nihilism," in *Knowing and Being*, edited by Marjorie Grene (Chicago: University of Chicago Press, 1969).

In the world today there are two distinct movements desperately struggling to revise Marxism into humanism. Neither movement has as its purpose the scholarly interpretation of Marx. The participants in both movements have as their purpose the use of Marx as a weapon against the social, economic, and political systems in which they live. In the communist lands of Eastern Europe and in the Soviet Union itself, "Marxian humanism" is fighting against the Communist Party of the Soviet Union to throw off the economic irrationality, cultural vacuity, totalitarianism, and terror of scientific Marxism. In communist lands "Marxian humanists" are fighting to erect humane sentiment and civic law as mediators between the rules and the people.

In the nations of Western Europe and the Americas, "Marxian humanism" is a mask for, and a repackaging of, the old attacks against the traditional liberties and human feelings which "Marxian humanists" in communist lands are fighting to restore. Left-wing radicals and ideologues in the West find in the concept of alienation a subtler and more effective weapon against contemporary Western societies than the old Marxian slogans. The Polish philosopher and former Stalinist Leszek Kolakowski recently acknowledged the diametrical opposition of the two movements of "Marxian humanism":

The Polish students who demonstrated in March 1968 were simply claiming the traditional liberties—freedom of speech, of press, of learning and assembly—which to some elements of the New Left are nothing but "treacherous bourgeois snares." A Polish friend of mine recently wrote to me from Sweden saying that whenever he had dealings with the New Left he seemed to be watching a film of which he already knew the end. That is exactly how I feel. The kind of language that was used in the past to justify the most brutal oppression is now being repeated as though nothing had ever happened.[39]

NOTES

[1] Daniel Bell, for example, finds the source of alienation in private property and the division of labor, with exploitation and dehumanization being the features of alienation. Robert Tucker, for example, finds the source of alienation in greed. In a later work, Tucker finds the source of alienation in the division of labor. See Bell, "The Debate on Alienation," in *Revisionism: Essays on the History of Marxist Ideas*, edited by Leopold Labedz (New York: Praeger, 1962). See Tucker, *Philosophy and Myth in Karl Marx* (Cambridge: Cambridge University Press, 1961), and *The Marxian Revolutionary Idea* (New York: Norton, 1969). Unlike Tucker, Bell does not find alienation to be a concern of the mature Marx. See Bell, *The End of Ideology* (Glencoe: The Free Press, 1960), p. 344.

[2] See Sidney Hook, *From Hegel to Marx: Studies in the Intellectual Development of Karl Marx* (Ann Arbor: University of Michigan Press, 2nd ed. 1962), and "Marxism in the Western World: From 'Scientific Socialism' to Mythology," in *Marxist Ideology in the Contemporary World,* edited by M. Drachkovitch (New York; Praeger, 1966). See also Hook, *Slavic Review,* Vol. XXI, pp. 552–53, and Vol. XXII, pp. 189–90.

[3] See P. C. Roberts and M. A. Stephenson, "Alienation and Central Planning in Marx," *Slavic Review,* Vol. XXVII, No. 3 (September 1968); "A Note on Marxian Alienation," *Oxford Eco-*

nomic Papers. Vol. 22, No. 3 (November 1970); and P. C. Roberts, *Alienation and the Soviet Economy* (Albuquerque: University of New Mexico Press, 1971).

[4] Karl Marx. *A Contribution to the Critique of Political Economy* (New York: International Publishers, 1970), pp. 20–21.

[5] Karl Marx. *The Economic and Philosophic Manuscripts of 1844* (New York: International Publishers, 1964), p. 111.

[6] *Ibid.,* p. 107.

[7] *Ibid.,* pp. 109–10.

[8] *Ibid.,* p. 110.

[9] *Ibid.,* p. 121.

[10] Robert C. Tucker, *Philosophy and Myth in Karl Marx* (Cambridge: Cambridge University Press, 1961), p. 145.

[11] Marx, *Manuscripts,* p. 107.

[12] *Ibid.,* p. 111.

[13] *Ibid.,* p. 113.

[14] *Ibid.,* p. 114.

[15] Marx, *Critique of Political Economy,* p. 34.

[16] Karl Marx, *Capital* I. (New York: International Publishers, 1967), p. 114.

[17] Karl Marx, *Capital* I. p. 41.

[18] *Ibid.,* p. 42.

[19] See Roberts, *Alienation and the Soviet Economy.*

[20] See, for example, Robert C. Tucker, *The Marxian Revolutionary Idea* (New York: Norton, 1969).

[21] Marx. *Capital* I. p. 360.

[22] *Ibid.,* p. 361.

[23] *Ibid.,* p. 363.

[24] *Ibid.,* p. 355.

[25] *Ibid.*

[26] *Ibid.,* p. 359.

[27] *Ibid.,* p. 356.

[28] For example, see Erich Fromm, *Marx's Concept of Man* (New York: Ungar, 1961), and Gajo Petrovic, *Marx in the Mid-Twentieth Century* (Garden City, New York: Doubleday Anchor, 1967).

[29] Karl Marx, "Toward the Critique of Hegel's Philosophy of Law," in *Writings of the Young Marx on Philosophy and Society,* translated and edited by Loyd D. Easton and Kurt H. Guddat (Garden City, New York: Doubleday Anchor, 1967), pp. 252, 253.

[30] Cited from Bertram Wolfe, *Three Who Made a Revolution* (New York: Dial Press, 4th rev. ed. 1964), pp. 355–56.

[31] Oscar J. Hammen, "The Young Marx Reconsidered," *Journal of the History of Ideas,* Vol. XXXI, No. 1 (1970), pp. 113–14. See also his *The Red 48ers.*

[32] V. I. Lenin, "A Contribution to the History of the Question of the Dictatorship" (October 20, 1920). *Collected Works,* 4th Russian edition. p. 326.

[33] Cited from Robert Conquest, *The Great Terror* (London: Macmillan, 1968), p. 128.

[34] Eugene Kamenka, *Marxism and Ethics* (London: Macmillan, 1969), pp. 4–5.

[35] Frederick Engels, *Feuerbach, The Roots of the Socialist Philosophy* (Chicago: Charles Kerr, 1906), p. 84.

[36] *Ibid.,* pp. 85–86.

[37] *Ibid.,* pp. 89–90.

[38] *Ibid.,* p. 89.

[39] "An Interview with Kolakowski," *Encounter* (October 1971) pp. 46–47.

GEOFFREY DE STE. CROIX

CLASS IN MARX'S CONCEPTION OF HISTORY

The study of Marxian communism has produced some fascinating work on ancient human institutions, and Geoffrey de Ste. Croix—of New College, Oxford, who has written extensively on Marx's concept of class—is here making a contribution to such work. Much scholarship has been inspired by Marx's very numerous ideas, but this work is often too technical for the general reader. In this case the question that is being explored is whether the phenomenon of class relationship may be identified in ancient cultures, particularly in the Greek world. Ste. Croix presents to us his argument —somewhat condensed here from his several longer discussions—that here indeed the Marxian analysis has much to recommend it.

It is both an honour and a pleasure for me to be speaking here today.* It is an *honour* to have been asked to give the annual lecture in memory of Isaac Deutscher, a man who always resolutely pursued his own line of thought with the greatest courage, and throughout his life tried to tell the truth as he saw it, undismayed by attacks from whatever direction. (I greatly regret that I never had the good fortune to meet him.) And it is a *pleasure* to be allowed to give this lecture at the London School of Economics, where (you may be surprised to hear) I actually had my first academic post, and taught for three years in the early 1950s—though perhaps 'taught' is something of a euphemism, because my field of interest as an Assistant Lecturer in Ancient Economic History was rather far removed from anything prescribed by the syllabus; and indeed I was sometimes made aware by some of my colleagues in the Economic History Department (very politely, of course) that I was really a bit of a nuisance, occupying a post which, but for my presence, might have been filled by some genuinely useful person, who could have taken on some of the burden of teaching the syllabus, as I, alas, could not. Well, I did my best to find someone who might be interested in what I had to offer; but when I went around, asking people in different departments whether I might think of giving lectures that could conceivably interest their students, they prudently rejected my advances. And then, suddenly, to my great delight, I was slotted in, if only in a very small way. I received a letter from the Professor of Accounting, Will Baxter (one of the leading authorities on his subject in the English-speaking world), asking me to lecture in his department. 'We'd very much like to know', he said, 'about accounting by the Greeks and Romans, and in particular if they had double-entry: things like that.' Of course, I knew nothing whatever about the subject of ancient accounting, any more than most other ancient historians; but I duly got it up. I had to do a vast amount of work on it from

Reprinted, with permission, from *New Left Review,* No. 146 (1984).
*Isaac Deutscher Memorial Lecture, November 28, 1983. At the editor's request this lecture is printed almost exactly as it was delivered, with the addition of some footnotes giving references.

original sources, as I found that there was hardly anything in the modern books that was any good at all. But I did find an astonishing amount of first-hand evidence, not only in the literary sources and the law-books, but also in the inscriptions and above all the papyri. I wrote a piece which is, I think, the only general study of the subject that makes use of all the various kinds of source material.[1] (It still seems to be cited as the standard account.) I also gave some lectures at the School, both on ancient accounting and on some kindred subjects like the ancient bottomry and respondentia loan (the precursor of marine insurance):[2] these were attended by the professor and his staff, and some ancient historians from other colleges, though not, as far as I could discover, by any undergraduates of the School itself. And even after I had left London for Oxford, thirty years ago, I was invited to come back and give a lecture at the School each year on ancient and mediaeval accounting, until the late 1970s.

I shall not be giving full references today to the various published works I have occasion to cite; but they can virtually all be identified easily, either from my recent book, *The Class Struggle in the Ancient Greek World,* sub-titled *From the Archaic Age to the Arab Conquests* (I shall refer to it as 'my Class Struggle book'), or from a paper I am contributing to the forthcoming 'Colloque Marx' in Paris, the proceedings of which will be published in due course.[3]

I hope you will forgive me if I now launch right into some personal reminiscence, which is in fact highly relevant to the subject of this lecture (namely, the nature of class in Karl Marx's conception of history), because it explains an important part of the process of intellectual development which led me to my present position.

I knew nothing whatever about Marx until the middle 1930s, when I was in my mid-twenties. After a thoroughly right-wing upbringing, I had qualified as a solicitor and was working with a Westminster firm, and—under the impact of the rise of fascism—I had just begun to become interested in the Labour movement. Even then, although I was deeply impressed by the Marxist interpretation of history, in so far as I had discovered anything about it (I knew precious little, really), my ideas remained confused. In particular, although I was very willing in principle to accept Marxist ideas about class and class struggle, which made a powerful appeal to me as soon as I became aware of them, there were difficulties even in that area which I was unable at that time to deal with satisfactorily. I had already come to think of myself as a Marxist (although I suppose 'come to *feel* myself a Marxist' would really be more accurate); but as yet I was ill-equipped to engage in controversy. For example, I could not as yet produce an effective answer to the argument that it was dishonest to speak of 'the working class' in the way many people on the Left did then, and still do, as if it were a united body, carrying on political activity in unison, with a common purpose and a real 'class consciousness'. I remember being reproached by a friend, who was active in the Communist Party, with having no faith in 'the revolutionary consciousness of the proletariat'. I don't expect I had the confidence to reply then (as I would now) that the proletariat certainly has a *potential* 'revolutionary consciousness' which events could one day make actual; but I do remember feeling, even then, that to speak of a 'revolutionary consciousness' as if it were *already actual* in the British working class was self-delusion. Above all, I had no answer at that time to non-Marxist friends who pointed out to me—*rightly*—that in the eyes of Marx, class and class conflict were fundamental, and who then went on to insist—though here, as I *now* realise, *wrongly*—that this *necessarily* entailed that a class should have a consciousness of common identity, a *class consciousness,* and that it should regularly participate in common political activity. These people then pointed triumphantly to the fact (for it is a fact) that in most countries throughout the world in modern times these two characteristics do not exist to a sufficient degree—particularly not for the working class, in the most advanced countries, and above all the one in which capitalism is most fully developed: the United States, where politics in the main are not conducted according to class alignments or in class terms. From this my non-Marxist friends drew the conclusion (as so many people of course still do today) that the concept of class itself, and in particular the Marxist theory of the importance of class conflict (class struggle), has little or no heuristic or explanatory value and does not enable us to understand the contemporary world, and that the Marxist analysis of modern society therefore fails.

I hope I have conveyed the fact that the whole argument I have just been describing rests upon certain *presuppositions* (which I now realise are false): namely, that we must regard both class *consciousness* and *regular political activity in unison* as *necessary* features of class and class conflict, with the consequence that when these features are not present the Marxist class analysis cannot be applied. Today, if we do not reject these false presuppositions, it will be even harder for us to deal with the arguments I have just outlined, for it is a fact that at the General Election in June 1983 only a minority of the British working class who voted at that election voted for Labour while something like a third or more, depending on one's definition of working class, voted for the Conservative Party, led by a woman with deeply reactionary opinions, thoroughly opposed to their interests. We are now told more insistently than ever by people of right-wing views (are we not?) that a Marxist class analysis of society is becoming *increasingly* inappropriate.

I know *now* how to deal with the arguments I have outlined; but in the 1930s I had not realised that they depended upon false presuppositions, and (as I shall explain) it was only when I became an ancient historian that I discovered why those presuppositions had to be decisively rejected.

Before I had solved these and certain other problems came the war, during which I decided to forsake the law when I came out of the RAF, take a degree, and try to go in for some kind of teaching. I had left school at fifteen, after spending most of my time there on Greek and Latin, and although I had forgotten much of what I had learnt of those languages I hoped that at University I would be able to study Greek and Roman *history,* of which I knew little or nothing. As was the wont in those days, my school study of Classics had centred on a few standard literary texts (treated above all as a taxing series of grammatical and stylistic problems), and of course on trying to write Latin and Greek prose, and even verse, in the style of the same standard authors. Although I cannot recall ever finding the slightest interest or significance in that kind of activity, I had been rather good at it, and I felt sure that with the historical perceptiveness I had since acquired, I might be able to find special significance in Greek and Roman history. I was not disappointed. I was extraordinarily fortunate, at University College, London, in being taught mainly by Professor A.H.M. Jones, who from my point of view has made the greatest contribution to ancient history of anyone writing in English since Gibbon—although he never in his life, as far as I know, read a word of Marx. I took my first degree when I was 39, and after a year's research I came to the LSE in 1950, as I have mentioned already.

Now, it is true that a Marxist approach can invest the study of history with a degree of understanding and a fascination which for me is otherwise unattainable. But the trouble with history is that it is largely concerned with brute facts, which, insofar as they are discoverable, have a terrible way of revenging themselves on the practitioner who pretends that they are not as they really were. I know there are many self-styled historians who are made uncomfortable by, and even try to repudiate, the statement that history is concerned with facts—I need not rehearse their arguments, which some of you will have heard all too often. I will only repeat a splendid remark (which I have quoted in my Class Struggle book) by Arthur Darby Nock, a leading authority on Hellenistic and Roman religion who migrated from Cambridge, England, to Cambridge, Massachusetts, and who wrote: 'A fact is a holy thing, and its life should never be laid down on the altar of a generalisation.'[4] For *ancient* history overall there are far fewer facts reliably available than for more recent times. And that makes me think of a well-known maxim formulated in relation to a very different discipline which I often wish could be well rubbed into ancient historians: 'Whereof one cannot speak, thereof one must be silent.'[5] If this principle were regularly applied in the field of ancient history, especially early Greek history, rather a high proportion of the flood of speculative material which pours out from the printing-presses of Europe and some Transatlantic and Antipodean countries would soon dry up.

Studying the sources for Greek and Roman history, I soon found that although a Marxist approach brought new insights, it appeared to come up against precisely the same difficulties as those I have mentioned already as having troubled me in relation to the contemporary world, and indeed in a decidedly more acute form. The reason why the situation looked worse for antiquity was that Marx and Engels always regarded slaves as a class;[6] and yet of all those groups in history which seemed to have the right to be regarded as classes in Marx's sense, it was precisely Greek and Roman slaves who most conspicuously lacked the qualities which, as I have explained, I had been led to imagine as essential ingredients in class: namely, class consciousness, and political activity in common. To a greater extent than, for example, the negro slaves of North, Central and South America and the Caribbean, a Greek or Roman slave household was often quite deliberately drawn from slaves of very different nationalities and languages. (Acquiring an ethnically and linguistically diverse set of slaves is urged upon slaveowners by a whole series of Greek and Roman writers, whom I have quoted in my Class Struggle book.)[7] The heterogeneous character of a given set of slaves would make it difficult for them even to communicate with each other except in their master's language and would of course make it much harder for them to revolt or even resist. It is no surprise to find ethnic and cultural differences playing a major part in promoting disunity in the few great slave revolts, in Italy and Sicily, which were concentrated in a few generations in the Late Roman Republic, from the 130s to the 70s B.C.[8]—and which, incidentally, never involved more than a small fraction of the total slave population of the Roman world of that day. So what on earth did Marx and Engels mean when they spoke, in the *Communist Manifesto* and elsewhere, of *class struggles* involving ancient slaves?

Certainly anyone who supposes, mistakenly, that class consciousness and/or common political activity are indeed *necessary* hallmarks of class (as many people still do) is going to get into an impossible position if he accepts slaves as a class. I think it is perhaps for that very reason that almost all the contemporary Continental ancient historians I have read, including soi-disant Marxists, becoming aware that there is a dilemma here, have chosen the wrong way of escape from it and have decided that slaves cannot be treated as a class.[9] (I use the expression 'soi-disant' or 'self-styled' Marxists because it seems to me that anyone who refuses to regard slaves as a class is, for reasons I shall give presently, denying a basic principle of Marx's thought.) I was always made uneasy by the kind of writing I have just been describing; but it is only in the last few years that I have become able to understand why it is wrong. I would like to think that from a fairly early stage I suspected that if a man of such tremendous intellectual power as Marx wrote of slaves from the first as a class, in spite of the serious difficulties that seemed to create, he may have had a *different notion of class* from his modern commentators. But what was that notion? As we all know, Marx never provided a definition of class. At the very end of Volume III of *Das Kapital,* where the work breaks off, he was about to do . . . . not precisely that: not to define class as a general concept, but to give a definition of 'the three great social classes', the *individual* classes *of his own day.*[10]

THE PRIMACY OF EXPLOITATION

I must not delay any longer to explain exactly what I think Marx *primarily* meant by 'class': a concept which for me is absolutely fundamental in his thinking, and which I myself fully share. I regard the whole complex of thought of which class is the very kernel as the most useful and effective contribution ever made to the analysis of human society above the most primitive level. I have just spoken of 'what Marx *primarily* meant by "class" '—because it can be shown that he *occasionally* uses the expression in a very *different* sense (a *narrower* sense) from the one I am treating as fundamental. I would like to think that the most important contribution I have made in the theoretical portion of my Class Struggle book is to elucidate this basic sense of class in Marx,[11] and to distinguish it from some of his other uses of the term, where he has allowed his context to dictate a narrower significance to the word than it properly bears. As far as I know, no one has ever sufficiently insisted that out of a number of different usages there is just one that is primary: class is (to put it as succinctly as possible, perhaps rather more crudely than in my book) *a relationship of exploitation;* and the other senses in which Marx uses the word are all secondary and must be treated as aberrations, unless they are given the specific narrower sense which Marx intended on each occasion, as indeed the context often unmistakably reveals. As far as I know, my book is the first in any language *both* to work out this theory in full *and* to apply it in detail to a very long period of history—some thirteen or fourteen hundred years, from the Archaic period of Greek history down to the Arab conquests of much of the Eastern part (the 'Greek' part) of the Roman empire: that is to say, from the eighth century B.C. to the 640s of the Christian era. Where an apparent dilemma is caused by Marx's inconsistent use of the terminology of class (especially in relation to class conflict, class struggle, *Klassenkampf*), many modern self-styled Marxists have ended, as I said a moment ago, by taking a wrong road and rejecting a fundamental part of Marx's theory. My position never obliges me to do that. Of course we must never follow Marx blindly; and we must never hesitate to correct him when he makes a wrong or inadequate judgment, as he does now and then, usually through insufficient knowledge of the historical evidence, which was sometimes not available in his day. But the Neo-Marxism or Pseudo-Marxism that has so many adherents in the contemporary world is often due to simple misunderstanding of what Marx actually said, as I hope I am showing today in relation to the meaning of 'class'.

To give more substance to my very brief definition—class (as I maintained in Chapter II Part ii of my book)[12] is the collective social expression of the fact of exploitation, the way in which exploitation is embodied in a social structure. (By 'exploitation', of course, I mean the appropriation of part of the product of the labour of others: in a commodity-producing society this is the appropriation of what Marx called 'surplus value'.) Class is essentially a *relationship*—just as *capital,* another of Marx's basic concepts, is specifically described by him, in some ten passages I have noted, as 'a relation', 'a social relation of production', and so forth.[13] And *a* class (a *particular* class) is a group of persons in a community identified by their position in the whole system of social production, defined above all according to their relationship (primarily in terms of the degree of *control*) to the conditions of production (that is to say, to the means and labour of production) and to other classes. The individuals constituting a given class may or may not be wholly or partly conscious of their own identity and common interests as a class, and they may or may not feel antagonism towards members of other classes as such. Class *conflict* (class struggle, *Klassenkampf*) is essentially the fundamental relationship between classes, involving *exploitation* and resistance to it, but not *necessarily* either class consciousness or collective activity in common, political or otherwise, although these features are likely to supervene when a class has reached a certain stage of development and become what Marx once (using a Hegelian idiom) called *'a class for itself'*.[14] The slaves of antiquity (and of later times) fit perfectly into this scheme. Not only do Marx and Engels refer repeatedly to ancient slaves as a class; in a whole series of passages[15] the slave in antiquity is given precisely the position of the free wage-worker under capitalism and of the serf in mediaeval times—as the proletarian is to the capitalist, and the serf to the feudal lord, so the slave is to the slaveowner. In each case the relationship is specifically a *class* relationship, involving class *conflict,* the essence of which is exploitation, *the appropriation of a surplus from the primary producer:* proletarian, serf or slave. That is the essence of class. Actually, in three of their early works, written during the 1840s, Marx and Engels commit what I have called in my book 'a minor methodological and conceptual error,'[16] by speaking of class struggle not, as they should have done, between slaves and *slaveowners,* but between slaves and free men, or citizens. That is clearly a mistake, because the great majority of free men, and even citizens, owned no slaves; and of course the distinction between slave and free man or citizen, however important, is a distinction not of class but merely of status, or 'order'. Fortunately, Marx and Engels did not repeat this error after 1848, as far as I know—if anyone is aware of a later example, I shall be glad to have the reference.

This theoretical position, which I arrived at in the 1970s, solves all the problems I mentioned earlier. It removes all difficulties in regarding slaves as a class. And it is strikingly helpful in the modern world. Its application to Thatcherite Britain is only too obvious. The fact that the British working class is very far from being uniformly self-conscious or a political unity becomes irrelevant. What is significant is that the government is overwhelmingly on the side of the propertied classes, and is eager—in so far as it can fulfil its objectives without driving itself out of office at the next election—to keep up the profits that go primarily to the propertied class and to keep down the wages that go to the workers, who are constantly told that if they show 'greediness' (through their trade unions above all), *they* will price *'us'* out of the market.

And above all, the theoretical position I have described helps us to understand a sinister major phenomenon of the contemporary world: capitalist exploitation on a world scale, which has taken on vast new dimensions in the past few decades, with the increasing export of capital from advanced countries to less developed areas, in particular to those which in the absence of democracy can be subjected to a high degree of control and coercion over their work-force—the oppressive American-backed dictatorships in Central and South America, for example, and of course that archetype of twentieth-century oligarchy, South Africa, which plays a great part in the minds of many influential people in this country, as a bastion of what they are pleased to call 'the free world'. As we all know, the objective of this global movement is to produce the highest possible profit for investors, members of the propertied classes, with the lowest possible wages for workers—exploitation in the fullest sense. As part of what I have called in my book 'the class struggle on the ideological plane',[17] this whole process is given a bogus air of respectability and indeed inevitability by being referred to as the beneficial operation of 'enterprise' through 'the free market', which of course can be relied upon, as a consequence of its very nature, to distribute its benefits, in the form of profits, to those above all who produce as cheaply as possible, and have no undue tenderness about their workers' wages.

POLITICAL ACTIVITY AND CONSCIOUSNESS

The theoretical position I have been describing has the very great advantage of enabling us to employ the concept of class consistently, with the same meaning, over the whole range of class society, from prehistoric times to the present day. I hope I have now brought out the fact that it was really becoming an ancient historian that enabled me to solve the problems that had long perplexed me. It was specifically the study of Greek and Roman slavery that enabled me to realise the nature of class in Marx's fundamental thought. As I said earlier, he always thought of slaves as a class. But this is the most extreme case: if ancient slaves are indeed to be regarded as a class, then neither class consciousness nor political activity in common (both of which were far beyond the capacity of ancient slaves) can possibly have the right to be considered *necessary* elements in class, in Marx's scheme of things; and this also provides a solution of the difficulties about class in modern society that had worried me since the 1930s.

Let me turn aside for a moment to say that many different concepts of class have been developed, and that of course it is perfectly open to anyone, if he thinks it produces more fruitful results, to adopt a conception of class that is quite different from the one held by Marx. (My one reservation is that he must not then try to foist his own peculiar notions on to Marx and to pretend that his conception represents that of Marx.) Probably the treatment of this subject most familiar to sociologists is the one by Max Weber,[18] whose definition of class was very far from anything that can be attributed to Marx. For example, Weber would not allow slaves to be a class at all 'in the technical sense of the term' (that is to say, according to Weber's own peculiar definition of class), because, as he put it (and I quote), 'the fate of slaves is not determined by the chance of using goods or services for themselves *on the market'*.[19] For Weber, ' "class situation" is ultimately "market situation" '; and of course slaves do not operate on the market: they are therefore, for Weber, not a class but a *Stand,* a status group. I should like to repeat today my expression of astonishment, in my Class Struggle book,[20] at not being able to find anywhere in Weber's work—all the relevant parts of which I think I have gone through—any serious consideration of Marx's fundamentally different concept of class. (If I have missed something, I hope someone will enlighten me.) But I suggest that there may have been a simple reason for this: Weber, like so many other people, was perhaps never quite able to make up his mind precisely what Marx's concept was!

There is a little more than I feel it is necessary to say about the concept of class in Marx. A major difference between my own attitude and that of many others who have written on this subject, as I have already indicated, is that I have not given *equal weight* to all the various passages (there are hundreds of them) in which Marx says something that may be taken as an indication of his conception of class. The point that many people miss is that these statements of Marx *cannot all be reconciled* as they stand. Instead of trying to assimilate them all, and picking out on each separate occasion a particular statement that happens to suit a specific argument, I have singled out a *basic* sense of the term 'class' which suits all but a very few of its occurrences in Marx; and I insist that the passages which are in *conflict* with that fundamental meaning must be treated as aberrant, and carefully examined, to discover how their *context*— which always turns out to be the cause of the aberration—has given the passage a peculiar meaning. In relation to the ancient world in particular, the aberrations can immediately be understood in several cases if it is realised that when Marx refers to 'class' or 'class conflict' he is, on those occasions, thinking primarily if not entirely of *political* struggles.

An example from the nineteenth century that no one can possibly gainsay is the statement in *The Eighteenth Brumaire of Louis Bonaparte,* in relation to the very end of 1850, that 'the bourgeoisie had done away with the *Klassenkampf* for the moment by abolishing universal suffrage'.[21] (A law restricting the right of suffrage had been passed some seven months earlier.) Taken literally, the statement is simply ridiculous as it stands, but it can be turned into perfectly good sense if we make it say, as indeed the context demands, that the abolition of general suffrage had for the time being banished French *parliamentary* class conflict. In a few other passages Marx even speaks, in striking contrast with the position he takes up elsewhere, as if workers in a capitalist society could not be considered a class at all until they had 'taken *political* shape' or 'been *organised* as a class'.[22] In a much-quoted passage in *The Eighteenth Brumaire* Marx says of the French smallholding peasants that in certain respects they do form a class and in certain other respects they do not.[23] The concept happens to require the second statement to receive all the emphasis, and I have known that second statement to be quoted by itself and the first simply ignored,[24] although it is absolutely clear from many other passages in *The Eighteenth Brumaire* and other works of Marx that he did consider peasant smallholders to be a class.[25]

Those who deny that the slaves of antiquity could constitute a class commonly quote two passages in Marx, referring specifically to *Klassenkampf,* one of which says (not very accurately, on any interpretation) that 'the class struggles of the ancient world took the form chiefly of a contest between debtors and creditors',[26] and the other that 'In ancient Rome the class struggle took place only within a privileged minority, between the free rich and the free poor, while the great productive mass of the population, the slaves, formed the purely passive pedestal for these combatants.'[27] The solution is that Marx is thinking entirely in both cases of *political* struggles; and the mere insertion of the word 'political' in each case before 'class struggle' brings both statements into line with his basic thought, and allows us to accept his other statements in their natural sense. We then have no reason at all to refuse to recognise Roman slaves as a class, engaged in continuous class struggle on the economic plane.

I suppose it is only fair that I should give some references to those historians, Marxist and non-Marxist, who argue or (more often) assume that slaves must not be considered a class. I shall confine myself to the few who are best known. (You will find some references in Chapter III Part ii of my Class Struggle book, with a brief but sufficient refutation;[28] the whole question is dealt with more thoroughly in my paper for the Paris 'Colloque Marx'.) There is an article by a leading French ancient historian, Professor Pierre Vidal-Naquet, which is often quoted and has received enthusiastic endorsement from Sir Moses Finley,[29] and a joint source-book in both French and English by Dr Michel Austin (of the University of St. Andrews) and Vidal-Naquet, containing a long Introduction by Austin. I am told that this is much read by British undergraduates in the improved English version of the book, which has the title *Economic and Social History of Ancient Greece*.[30] Although none of the three scholars I have just mentioned is in any sense a Marxist, or regards himself as such, they are mainly purporting to characterize the position of Marx. Their arguments (if I can call them that) seem to me entirely without substance against those I myself have just been sketching; but if you are interested, you will be able to read them and make up your own minds.

Nor do the Italians do any better. I have time to mention only Professor Andrea Carandini, one of the best of Italian archaeologists, who is a Marxist and shows more acquaintance with the works of Marx than the others I have mentioned, although I must say that on this particular subject he seems strangely unaware of the great mass of evidence against him.[31] His book, mainly about pre-capitalist economic formations, was not available to me when I was writing my Class Struggle book, so I must mention the cryptic title, the significance of which is likely to be understood at once (I am afraid) only by those who know their *Grundrisse:*[32] it is *L'anatomia della scimmia*. Some years ago at Oxford I had a Greats pupil who was looking in a bookshop (I forget which) for Rice Holmes's work on the Emperor Augustus, called *The Architect of the Roman Empire:* he told me he found it in the section labelled 'Architecture'. I am tempted to wonder where, in such a bookshop, one might expect to find this work of Carandini's: his 'Monkey book', as I tend to call it—without, let me hasten to say, intending the least disrespect to such an outstandingly able scholar. I suppose the fairly obvious *'anatomia'* would be likely to consign it to the Medical section, under 'Anatomy'. But perhaps, if the bookseller knew what *'scimmia'* meant, he might be more likely to put it under 'Zoology'.

PEASANTS AND EXPLOITATION

I want now to deal with a problem of Marxist class theory which gave me a great deal of trouble at one time, and the solution of which took me longer to work out, perhaps, than anything else. It concerns those who were actually a majority of the population of the Greek and Roman world for many centuries, but about whom (because of the nature of our sources) we know infinitely less than about the upper classes: I refer to the free independent producers, the vast majority of whom were of course peasants. And that makes what I am about to say of greater general interest than if I were just speaking about Graeco-Roman antiquity, because, as Teodor Shanin has well said, 'It is worth remembering that—as in the past, so in the present—peasants are the majority of mankind.'[33] A large literature on peasants has grown up in the past few decades, much of it written by sociologists and anthropologists who may be able to deal most effectively with the contemporary world but are helpless in the face of antiquity unless they can cope with the often very difficult source material, the ancient evidence, as few can.[34]

My own particular problem here, as an ancient historian, began to dawn upon me in my undergraduate days in the late 1940s, but I could not produce a satisfactory solution until the 1970s. The problem, in a nutshell, can be put as follows. Ancient slaves and serfs and debt bondsmen suffered exploitation in perfectly obvious ways, and so did a certain number of peasants, including leaseholders who were rack-rented and fell into arrears with their rents, and even freeholders who, when their crops failed, had to borrow at mortgage on usurious terms: both these groups might be ejected from their holdings, or subjected to debt bondage. But what about the great majority of small *freehold* peasants, who at least managed to scrape a living from their farms, handed down from generation to generation? In what ways were they exploited?

I have answered this in my book by distinguishing between two different kinds of exploitation: one I call 'direct and individual', the other 'indirect and collective'.[35] The first ('direct and individual') is of wage-labourers, slaves, serfs and debt bondsmen, and also of tenants and ordinary debtors, by particular employers, masters, landowners or moneylenders; and it presents no difficulties. Exploitation may be said to be 'indirect and collective' when a State (including, for example, the Roman imperial government or that of a Greek or Roman city), which represents primarily the interests of a superior class or classes, imposes burdens disproportionately upon a particular subject class or classes. These burdens divide up conveniently under three headings: taxation, military conscription, and forced labour or personal services. I will take each of these three in turn, very briefly. *Taxation,* often astonishingly light in the Classical Greek city-states and the Roman Republic, increased enormously under the Roman Empire, and in the Later Empire absorbed a high proportion of the total product of the peasantry: see in particular the last chapter of my Class Struggle book and of course A.H.M. Jones's magnum opus on the Later Roman Empire.[36] The incidence of *military conscription* varied greatly in antiquity: sometimes the poorest classes got off very lightly; but in the third and second centuries B.C. (as all historians of the Roman Republic will know) conscription was a fearful burden on the peasantry of Roman Italy, and many poor farmers lost their land as a result. The last of my three categories, *compul-*

sory services, has had far less attention paid to it than the other two, so I will give one or two examples of it which will be familiar to everyone, from the New Testament. We all know about Simon of Cyrene, who was compelled by the Romans to carry the cross of Jesus to the place of execution; but even Classical scholars are often unaware that in relation to this incident both Mark and Matthew use the correct Greek technical term for such impositions: a form of the verb *angareuein.*[37] The Greek *angareia* and Latin *angaria* descend from a word long used in the Persian empire for transport services, which was taken over by the Hellenistic kingdoms and came to be applied to similar and allied impositions for the benefit of the State or the municipalities in the Roman period.[38] Only an understanding of the *angareia*-system makes sense of one of the sayings of Jesus in the 'Sermon on the Mount': 'Whosoever shall compel thee to go a mile, go with him twain'; here again the Greek word is a form of the verb *angareuein.*[39] (I suggest that this passage deserves more attention than it usually receives in discussions of the attitude of Jesus to the political authorities of his day. I think it *may* have been one of the texts which contributed to forming the passive political attitude of St. Paul, as expressed in a disastrous group of texts which can be summed up in the words of the *Epistle to the Romans:* 'The powers that be are ordained of God.')[40] It is perhaps worth mentioning that the philosopher Epictetus (an ex-slave, incidentally) was a good deal less enthusiastic than Jesus about co-operation with officials exacting *angareia:* he says pragmatically that it is good sense to comply with a soldier's requisition of one's donkey. If one objects, he says, the result is likely to be a beating, and the animal will be taken just the same.[41]

I must add that after working out the theory of the forms of exploitation I have just been describing, I was encouraged to find that Marx himself had partly formulated it, in one of his series of articles for the *Neue Rheinische Zeitung* during 1850, which in their collective form are referred to as *The Class Struggles in France.* Marx says there of the condition of the French peasants of his day: 'Their exploitation differs only in *form* from the exploitation of the industrial proletariat. . . . The exploiter is the same: *capital.* The individual capitalists exploit the individual peasants through *mortgages* and *usury;* the capitalist class exploits the peasant class through the *State taxes.*'[42]

SLAVE SOCIETIES?

There is one other aspect of Marxist class theory which I want to deal with, as it may give rise to perplexity if it is not cleared up. It is a problem which may arise in relation to any class society but is particularly acute in regard to ancient slavery. What it needs essentially for its solution is simply a recognition of what Marx himself says in a series of passages in all three volumes of *Capital* which I have discussed in Chapter II Part ii of my book.[43] (It may be that someone has dealt thoroughly with this subject in general terms recently, but I do not happen to know of any satisfactory treatment.) In modern times some Marxists, knowing that Marx and Engels consistently regarded the Greek and

Roman world as a 'slave society', have thought it necessary to maintain that in that world *most of the actual production* was done by slaves. But this opinion is demonstrably false: the greater part of production, especially in agriculture (by far the most important sector of the ancient economy), was done by peasants who were at least nominally free, even if, from the early fourth century of the Christian era onwards, more and more of them were brought into forms of serfdom;[44] and much manufacture also was always done by free workers. The adoption of the position I have attacked has brought much criticism upon those who have held it, and rightly; but unfortunately many people have also supposed that the view in question is an inevitable consequence of accepting a Marxist analysis of ancient society, as it is not. I would not deny that Marx himself may *possibly* have believed that in much of Italy and Sicily during the Late Roman Republic (say, roughly the last century and a half B.C.) slaves did do most of the work. (That position, although mistaken, would be far from absurd.) But according to the principles Marx himself laid down in the passages in *Capital* which I have alluded to, the nature of a given mode of production is decided, not according to *who does most of the work of production,* but according to *the method of surplus-appropriation,* the way in which the dominant classes extract their surplus from the primary producers. In at least the most developed parts of the Greek and Roman world, while (as I have said) it was free peasants and craftsmen who were responsible for the bulk of production, *the propertied classes* obtained the great bulk of their regular *surplus* from *labour which was unfree.*[45] (The propertied classes, in my terminology, are those who can, if they wish, live without actually working for their daily livelihood: they may work or not, but they do not have to. They may have accounted for *perhaps* something between two or three and ten or fifteen per cent of the free population in Greek and Roman antiquity, according to place and period. The lower figure must generally have been nearer the reality, I think, especially in the Roman period.)

Now, unfree labour was not entirely that of slaves: first, forms of serfdom (the Spartan Helots, for example) existed here and there in the Greek world as rare exceptions;[46] and secondly, debt bondage existed in most places throughout the Greek and Roman world (democratic Athens is the one great exception) on a far larger scale than the vast majority of ancient historians have recognised. (I have shown this by producing a large quantity of evidence in Chapter III Part iv of my Class Struggle book.)[47] Thirdly, after about A.D.300 it seems to me likely that the propertied classes derived their surplus (always primarily agricultural in character) more from peasant serfs than from actual slaves, although slavery continued to be important. However, this is a fearsomely difficult question, which I have tried to discuss in detail in Chapter IV Part iii of my book,[48] and I must not go on about it now. I will only say that in my opinion the most useful single statement by Marx on this subject is one in the *Grundrisse,* to the effect that the ancient world was characterised by 'direkte Zwangsarbeit', direct compulsory labour.[49] The Greek and Roman world—at any rate down to the seventh century of the Christian era, which is as far as my own knowledge of the source material allows me to go—was indeed a *society dependent upon unfree labour,* in the sense that its propertied classes always derived the bulk of their regular surplus from unfree labour.

THE VERSATILITY OF MARX'S CONCEPTS

My time is nearly at an end, but you will perhaps expect me, before I finish, to say a few words about rival theories of historical interpretation, to set beside Marx's historical materialism. There are just two I will briefly mention: Structuralism, and the essentially Weberian type of approach associated with Sir Moses Finley and his followers.

Structuralism, as represented above all in the work of Claude Lévi-Strauss and his school, is thought by many people to have made a contribution of the greatest importance to anthropology; but its application to history seems to me to have brought as much darkness as light, although some of its practitioners, notably the French Byzantinist Evelyne Patlagean, are much admired in some circles. I will only recommend what seems to me a very good Marxist analysis of Structuralism as a historical method by John Haldon, of the Birmingham University Centre for Byzantine Studies, in English, in the Czech periodical *Byzantinoslavica* for 1981.[50] While paying tribute to Patlagean's work, Dr. Haldon brings out the weakness of Structuralism as a *historical* method both in its inability to handle successfully diachronic phenomena (as the historian must always be doing) and in its characteristic failure to go beyond mere description and provide explanations.

A well-known ancient social and economic historian who for some thirty years has been working in this country, and who has made some distinguished contributions to his subject, Sir Moses Finley, put a gulf between himself and Marx in his best-known book, *The Ancient Economy* (1973), by totally rejecting, as tools of historical analysis, both class and exploitation. In that book Sir Moses specifically dismisses in the most cavalier way, in a few lines, Marx's concept of class, of which he shows no comprehension. In place of it he chooses a highly subjective category, that of status—in the Weberian sense, although I think he never says that explicitly.[51] (I call status a 'subjective category' because it depends primarily upon the esteem accorded by others—what Aristotle called *time*, in fact: a term which, by the way, he banished almost entirely from his great work on *Politics,* reserving it mainly for his ethical writings.)[52] Sir Moses, in his *Ancient Economy,* is also disinclined to make serious use of the concept of exploitation, apparently on the ground that, like imperialism, it is 'in the end, too broad as a category of analysis'.[53] In two later works, published in 1981 and 1982, Sir Moses has had recourse to a particular piece of status-terminology, namely 'élites', in his attempt to define (as he had not done in his *Ancient Economy*) what he means by describing ancient Greek and Roman society as 'a slave economy': he now says that slaves 'provided the bulk of the immediate income from property . . . of the élites, economic, social and political'.[54] Now, 'élites' is one of the most imprecise of sociological obfuscations, which may sometimes have its uses but surely ought to be strictly avoided in a definition. And quite apart from the unnecessary imprecision inevitably introduced by the word 'élites' (made worse, if anything, by calling them 'economic, social and political' élites), that term is not at all a good choice in this particular case, for slave-owning certainly extended well below the lowest level at which 'élites' could be thought an appropriate description. Many well-to-do peasants whom it would be absurd to number among an 'élite' owned slaves to do their farm-work, and so did some quite humble people engaged in manufacture and trade. My own formula, you will remember from a few moments ago, is that *the propertied classes* (people who were able to live without themselves working for their livelihood) derived the bulk of their regular surplus from slave labour and other unfree labour.[55]

Now, I have no difficulty in understanding why so many people become uncomfortable and unhappy when they are seriously confronted with Marx. As I like to think I have shown in my Class Struggle book, Marx's analysis of society, although devised in the course of an effort to understand the mid-nineteenth-century capitalist world, resulted in the construction of a set of concepts which work remarkably well when applied even to the Greek and Roman world and can be used to *explain* many of its features and developments—the total destruction of Greek democracy over some five or six centuries,[56] for example, and even the age-old problem of 'the decline and fall of the Roman empire', or let us say rather, 'the disintegration of quite a large portion of the Roman empire between the fourth and eighth centuries.'[57] It is this very versatility and general applicability of Marxist historical method and concepts, I suggest, that makes so many members of late-twentieth-century capitalist society so reluctant to have anything to do with Marxism. I was particularly pleased, by the way, when a prominent Roman historian, who is not a Marxist, reviewing my book in a learned journal,[58] ended by asking whether it was possible to find my 'categories of analysis convincing without drawing disturbing inferences for contemporary society', as I have done.

And now to conclude. As early as 1845, in the eleventh of his *Theses on Feuerbach,* Marx wrote, 'The philosophers have only interpreted the world in various ways; the point however is to change it.'[59] Of course before the world can be changed, it must first be thoroughly understood; and we must *begin* this process by providing ourselves with a set of concepts that will enable us to understand and explain it—and thus to participate in the work to which Marx's own life was single-mindedly devoted: changing the world indeed, by putting an end to class society, and thus (as Marx himself put it, in a splendidly optimistic phrase in the 1859 Preface) 'bringing the prehistory of human society to a close'.[60]

NOTES

In the notes, the abbreviation CSAGW = *The Class Struggle in the Ancient Greek World* (Duckworth, 1981; corrected paperback reprint, 1983). References to works by Marx and Engels are according to the standard editions: the English MCEW, and the German MEW, MEGA[1] and MEGA[2], for all of which see CSAGW, pp. 684–5.

[1] 'Greek and Roman accounting', in *Studies in the History of Accounting,* ed. A. C. Littleton and B. S. Yamey (1956), pp. 14–74.

[2] For this important invention (spreading the risks of commerce over the much wealthier noncommercial classes) see my 'Ancient Greek and Roman Maritime Loans', in *Debits, Credits, Finance and Profits* [Essays in Honour of W. T. Baxter], ed. Harold Edey and B. S. Yamey (1974), pp. 41–59.

[3] For my 'Class Struggle book' (CSAGW here) see n. above. The proceedings of the 'Colloque Marx' have been edited by Bernard Chavance, *Marx en perspective, Actes du Colloque Marx de l'Ecole des Hautes Etudes en Sciences Sociales* (Paris, December 1983), in Editions de l'EHESS, Paris, 1985. My contribution is entitled 'Karl Marx and the Interpretation of Ancient and Modern History', pp. 159–87.

[4] See CSAGW, p. 31.

[5] I realise, of course, that my use of this quotation does not convey the meaning intended by Wittgenstein, and that a more realistic translation of the famous remark at the end of the *Tractatus* would be something like 'We must pass over in silence what we *cannot formulate in language*'!

[6] I deal with this in my contribution to the proceedings of the 'Colloque Marx': See n.3 above.

[7] CSAGW p. 146, cf. pp. 65–6.

[8] See CSAGW p. 146, with p. 564 n. 15.

[9] See my contribution to the proceedings of the 'Colloque Marx'.

[10] Marx, *Capital* III, pp. 885–6 = MEW XXV, pp. 862–3.

[11] See CSAGW II, ii–iii, esp. the definitions on pp. 43–4.

[12] CSAGW p. 43.

[13] Marx, *Capital* III, p. 814 (= MEW XXV, pp. 822–3), with I, p. 534, cited in CSAGW p. 547 n. 1; and many other passages, e.g. *Cap.* 1, p. 766 & n. 3; MECW IX, p. 212; *Grundrisse,* in the edition which is now standard, MEGA² II, i, 1 (1976) pp. 228, 229 = *Grundrisse. Foundations of the Critique of Political Economy,* Eng. trans. by Martin Nicolaus (Pelican Marx Library, 1973) pp. 309, 310. Of course, capital for Marx was also a *process* and 'not a *simple* relation' MEGA² II, i, 1, p. 180 = Eng. trans. p. 258.

[14] See CSAGW p. 60, with references to MECW VI, p. 211 and the French original in MEGA¹.

[15] These are cited in my contribution to the proceedings of the 'Colloque Marx' (n. 3 above).

[16] See CSAGW p. 66, referring to MECW V, pp. 33, 432; VI, p. 482.

[17] See CSAGW pp. 409–52 (Chapter VII).

[18] See CSAGW pp. 80–91, with 696–7 for the bibliographical references.

[19] CSAGW p. 89.

[20] CSAGW p. 90.

[21] MECW XI. p. 153 = MEW VIII, p. 165.

[22] E.g. MECW VI pp. 167 & 211, 318 & 332, 498 & 493.

[23] See CSAGW pp. 60–1.

[24] As by P. Vidal-Naquet, 'Les esclaves grecs étaient-ils une class?' in *Raison présente* 6 (1968) 103–12, at 103; twice reprinted, on the second occasion with the inclusion of the first half of Marx's statement, thus destroying the argument founded on its omission. See my contribution to the 'Colloque Marx', n. 3 above.

[25] Peasants are very well analyzed in an article by Engels, 'The Peasant Question in France and Germany', mentioned in CSAGW p. 211. For excellent discussions of mediaeval peasants, see the works of Rodney Hilton cited in CSAGW p. 680.

[26] Marx, *Capital* I, p. 135 = MEW XXIII, pp. 149–50.

[27] Marx, Preface to the second (1869) edition of *The Eighteenth Brumaire,* in MEW VIII, 560 = XVI, pp. 359–60.

[28] CSAGW pp. 63–6.

[29] See n. 24 above, with M. I. Finley, *The Ancient Economy* (1973) pp. 49 & 186 n. 32; and *Ancient Slavery and Modern Ideology* (1980; Pelican 1983) pp. 77 & 165 n. 29.

[30] See CSAGW pp. 64–5.

[31] I deal with this in my contribution to the proceedings of the 'Colloque Marx' (see n. 3 above).

[32] See the relevant passages in MEGA² II, i, 1, p. 40 = *Grundrisse,* Eng. trans. p. 105 (cf-n 13 above).

[33] *Peasants and Peasant Societies,* ed. T. Shanin, 1971, p. 17.

[34] See CSAGW pp. 208–26 (= IV, ii) on ancient peasants.

[35] CSAGW pp. 205–8 (= IV, i).

[36] CSAGW VIII, ii–iii, esp. pp. 473–503; and A.H.M. Jones, *The Later Roman Empire 284–602* (1964), esp. II, pp. 767–823 (Chapter XX).

[37] See CSAGW p. 15, on Mk XV, 21; Mt. XXVII, 32.

[38] See CSAGW p. 14–16.

[39] See CSAGW p. 15, on Mt. V, 41.

[40] See CSAGW p. 398, citing Rom. XIII, 1–7 and other passages.

[41] See CSAGW p. 15, citing Epict., *Diss.* IV, i, 79.

[42] See CSAGW p. 206, citing MECW X, p. 22.

[43] CSAGW pp. 50–2.

[44] See CSAGW IV, iii, esp. pp. 249–59.

[45] See CSAGW pp. 52–4. 133–4, 140 ff.; cf. III, vi, esp. pp. 179–82, etc.

[46] See CSAGW pp. 135–6, 147–58.

[47] CSAGW pp. 136–7, 162–70; cf. p. 282.

[48] CSAGW IV, iii, esp. pp. 255–9.

[49] See CSAGW p. 54; cf. pp. 52, 133.

[50] John F. Haldon, 'On the structuralist approach to the social history of Byzantium', in *Byzantinoslavica,* 42 (1981) pp. 203–11: a review-article on two books by Evelyne Patlagean, *Pauvreté économique et pauvreté sociale à Byzance, 4–7 siècles* (Paris, 1977), and *Structure sociale, famille, chrétienté à Byzance, IV–XI siècle* (London, 1981). Perhaps I should add that Structuralism, at least in the strict Lévi-Straussian sense, now seems to be in general retreat; and according to a review by Rodney Needham, in 4228 *Times Lit. Suppl.* (13th April 1984) p. 393, Lévi-Strauss himself writes of it in his most recent book, *Le Regard éloigné,* as 'having passed out of fashion'. Through its influence on Louis Althusser and his followers, Structuralism seems to me to have done serious damage to the study of Marxism in France. I am not acquainted with the works that are sometimes broadly described as 'post-structuralist', for which see, briefly, Perry Anderson, *In the Tracks of Historical Materialism* (The Wellek Library Lectures, delivered at the University of California at Irvine), Verso/NLB, London 1983, and published in London, 1983) pp. 39–57.

[51] See CSAGW pp. 58–9, 91–4.

[52] See CSAGW p. 80, with p. 551 n. 30. In view of M. I. Finley's light-hearted remark, in his *Politics in the Ancient World* (1983) p. 10 n. 1, that in my Class Struggle book I have 'turned Aristotle into a Marxist', perhaps I should point out here that what I have done is essentially to demonstrate in detail the important ways in which Aristotle's method of analysis of Greek politics closely resembles the approach adopted by Marx: see CSAGW pp. 69–80 (= II, iv).

[53] See CSAGW p. 91. And in Finley's later book, *Ancient Slavery and Modern Ideology* (see n. 29 above) I think that 'exploitation' hardly appears, apart from p. 78, except in the expression 'unit of exploitation' (e.g. pp. 133, 135, 136, 137).

[54] *Ancient Slavery and Modern Ideology* p. 82, repeated in Finley's 'Problems of Slave Society: Some Reflections on the Debate', in the first fascicule of the new Italian periodical, *Opus I* (1982) i. pp. 201-10, at p. 206. I cannot accept Finley's claim, which follows in the latter work. 'That definition can easily be translated into Marxist language': such a 'translation' would involve major conceptual changes.

[55] In his latest book, *Politics in the Ancient World* (1983), which I saw only after this lecture had been delivered, Finley seems to have abandoned his attachment to *status* concepts (though without, I think, admitting the fact) and to have begun to think in terms of *class:* see many passages (from pp. 2-3 onwards) in that book, the Index of which contains some 20 entries under 'class' (p. 147) but none under 'status' (or 'order'). Unfortunately, he refuses to be precise about what he means by 'class' and merely says he has 'used the term "class" loosely, as we customarily do in ordinary discourse' (p. 10). This reminds one of a reason he gave in 1973 for choosing status in preference to class as his prime tool of analysis: that it is 'an admirably vague word' (cf. my comment is CSAGW p. 92). We may hope that he will similarly discover the limited utility of employing yet another imprecise concept, and feel the need to define it properly.

[56] I have never been able to discover an adequate modern account of this process, and I therefore felt obliged to describe it in detail in CSAGW pp. 295-326, 518-37.

[57] See CSAGW VIII, esp. pp. 474-503.

[58] T. D. Barnes, in *Phoenix* 36 (1982) pp. 363-6, at p. 366.

[59] MECW V, pp. 5 & 8 (with 9) = MEW III, pp. 7 & 535; and see MECW V, p. 585 n. I.

[60] The standard German edition of the 1859 Preface to *A Contribution to the Critique of Political Economy* is now MEGA² II, ii (1980) pp. 99-103.

part SEVEN

ECONOMICS

The economic systems of communism and of capitalism both claim for themselves superiority in various vital areas of human concern. Communism will eliminate exploitation. Capitalism will leave people free to pursue their own happiness in the way best suited to them. But, some would argue, capitalism is exploitative, for it involves the benefiting of some classes at the expense of others! But, others would argue, communism limits civil liberties and does not really satisfy the needs and wants of the population!

Here we see numerous areas of controversy about the respective economic systems of capitalism and communism explored. The discussions will perhaps be most revealing for the light they shed on some of the lively debates on the international front. For even though neither the United States nor the USSR represent systems that are faithful to the ideals associated with them, the systems are still often referred to in terms of these ideals.

John Roemer

EXPLOITATION, PROPERTY RIGHTS, AND PREFERENCES

Marxists often hold that Marxism itself is open to change, just as is every other human endeavor, and John Roemer—Professor of Economics at the University of California, Davis, and author of A General Theory of Exploitation and Class *(1982)—argues that such a change in Marxism is overdue. Marxian ideas need to be based on a dimension of Marxian political philosophy and economics that relies on some of the standard features of contemporary neoclassical economic theory. Roemer first describes a social reason for this change: existing socialist systems are highly unsatisfactory, what with their lack of civil liberties and their failure to pay heed to consumer demand. And Roemer discusses the scientific recognition that when one tries to make Marxian economics more rigorous, one is pushed into treating preferences more seriously than they are treated in classical Marxian economics.*

1. INTRODUCTION

Economic theory based on the apparatus of subjective utility has long been attacked by Marxists as an apology for capitalism. In contrast, Marxism has been associated with a theory of objective needs, which, however, has never been made precise. The antagonism of Marxists toward subjective utility theory emerges in various places in economics. I will mention three here:

(1) The labor theory of value is a cost-based theory of price; it claims that equilibrium prices are determined by or equal to the costs of the labor needed to produce goods. Demand, and hence the role of preferences, is ignored (of course capital and interest are here ignored as well).

(2) Consumer sovereignty is attacked as having no compelling foundation due to the manipulation of preferences by capitalists who stand to make a profit from them. Marxists generally emphasize the endogeneity of preference; hence the ethical conclusions associated with welfare economics, weak as they are, evaporate, for if people's wants are not autonomously formed, what status does Pareto optimality have as a welfare concept?

(3) As a substitute for welfare economics, more generally, for any welfarist approach to evaluation of outcomes, Marxism substitutes the apparently objective (as opposed to subjective) concept of exploitation. Capitalism is condemnable by Marxism for a number of reasons; first among these is its dependence on exploitation. (I will try below to clarify what exploitation is and why it is considered a bad thing.)

I do not wish, here, to defend or criticize the classical Marxian antipathy towards utility theory. Rather I want to note that there is a growing strand of

This essay was prepared for the present volume.

Marxian political philosophy and economics today which pays much more attention to preference and subjective utility. I think there is a *social* and a *scientific* basis for this change in posture. The social basis is the history of existing socialism where scant attention has been paid to preferences and civil liberties; most people, Marxists included, find the results unappealing, and this has strengthened the preference-regarding and freedom-regarding strands in contemporary Marxism. There is a value in letting people choose, even if they do not choose what is good for them (for who is to decide what is good for them?). The scientific basis for the new respect for utility theory emerges from the attempt to make certain classical notions of Marxism rigorous, to understand what lies at their foundations; and in doing this, one is steered, over and over, towards the use of utility theory.

While some Marxists are relaxing their dogmatism against subjective utility, there is in contemporary non-Marxist political philosophy a significant move *away* from welfarism* and an emergence of various objective measures of need as a criterion for welfare or justice. John Rawls [1971] proposes a theory of justice in which the welfare criterion is to maximize the access to *primary goods* of the least well-off class of people. Primary goods are, for Rawls, explicitly not defined by subjective preference. Economists tend to bowdlerize Rawls, to encapsulate his welfare criterion as maximum utility, but it is not that. Rawls thinks there is something more basic than utility, and that is access to primary goods; this is the needs-based element in Rawls. Amartya Sen [1980], a leading critic of welfarism, calls for the realization of one's *basic capabilities* as the welfare goal, and distinguishes this from a utility-based theory. Ronald Dworkin [1981] asks what can equality mean if it is to have any interesting ethical status, and argues it cannot mean equality of utility or happiness, but rather it must mean equality of *resources*. Implicitly, he suggests equality of resources, therefore, as the welfare criterion, which is to be distinguished from a utility-based concept. These three concepts—primary goods, basic capabilities, and resources—are to be distinguished from the maximand of neoclassical welfare economics, which is utility, aggregated in some way over the population. A neoclassical welfare economist, in contrast, would argue the *final* good is utility, however the person measures it, and primary goods, resources, and basic capabilities are merely the inputs into the person's satisfaction-producing technology.

Thus there appears to be some convergence between contemporary Marxist and non-Marxist political philosophy. I will try and show this convergence is even closer than the vague antiutilitarian one indicated above. By taking preferences seriously, I will strip the Marxian theory of exploitation of what can be called its labor-fetishism, and show it is really an equality of resources theory. Having shown this, I will discuss a natural extension of resource egalitarian

---

* Welfarism is the philosophical position that the only information relevant for evaluating the desirability or justness of a state of world is the vector of utility levels of the population in that state. In particular, the process by which the state was reached, and the extent to which needs are fulfilled, are relevant only insofar as they are reflected in the utility levels of individuals.

theories: How would one go about equalizing opportunities by attempting the equalization of resources that are not alienable, but are embodied in people? As one would expect, preferences must be taken seriously in that discussion, and certain riddles emerge for political philosophy with which I will conclude.

2. THE CORN MODEL

I describe a model of an economy that shows that exploitation, as Marxists conceive of it, emerges simultaneously with four other phenomena: *domination* at the point of production, *alienation* of labor, *accumulation,* and *inequality* in the distribution of productive assets. This causes an identification problem with respect to our interest in exploitation as a social statistic.

First, the definition of exploitation must be recalled. A worker is said to be exploited, in the Marxian sense, if the labor embodied in the wage goods he receives is less than the labor he expended in production. Thus if a worker receives one bushel of corn as a wage for one day's labor, and produces three bushels of corn in a day when using capital and land (which may be owned by others), he is exploited. Think of the net national product produced by a society working on a certain capital stock in a certain period of time. That product is distributed to society's members, either as consumption or investment goods. A certain amount of labor was expended in producing the product. Some people, in general, will receive goods embodying more labor than they expended in production, and some will receive goods embodying less labor than they expended in production. The former group are exploiters and the latter are exploited, in the Marxian sense. Exploitation, thus described, occurs mainly because there is private ownership of the capital and land in the economy; the part of the net national product one receives is not related only to one's labor expenditure, but to one's ownership of other productive assets.

Imagine an economy with 1,000 people and two goods: corn and leisure. There are two technologies for producing corn, called the Farm and the Factory. The Farm is a labor-intensive technology in which no seed capital is required, but corn is produced from pure labor (perhaps by cultivating wild corn). The Factory technology produces corn with labor plus capital—the capital is seed corn. The technologies are given by:

Farm: 3 days labor → 1 corn output
Factory: 1 day labor + 1 seed corn → 2 corn output

Corn takes a week to grow (so the seed is tied up in the ground for that long). The total stock of seed corn in this society is 500 corn, and each agent owns ½ corn. The agents have identical preferences, which are the following: each wants to consume 1 corn *net* output per week. After consuming his one corn, the agent will consume leisure. If he can get more than one corn for no more labor, he will be even happier; but preferences are lexicographic in that each wishes to minimize labor expended subject to earning enough to be able to consume one corn per week, and not to run down his stock of capital.

There is an obvious equilibrium in this economy. The typical agent works up his ½ corn in the Factory in ½ day, which will bring him 1 corn at the end of the week. Having fully employed his seed capital, he must produce another ½ corn somewhere, to replace his capital stock: this he does by working in the Farm technology for 1½ days. Thus he works 2 days and produces 1 corn net output. Every agent does this. Indeed 2 days is the labor time socially necessary to produce a unit of corn, given that this society must produce 1,000 corn net each week. It is the labor embodied in a unit of corn. At this equilibrium there is no exploitation, since labor expended by each agent equals labor embodied in his share of the net output. Nor is there accumulation, for society has the same endowments at the beginning of next week; nor is there domination at the point of production, since no one works for anyone else; nor is there differential alienation of labor, since there is not even trade; and, of course, there is equality in initial assets. See Figure 1.

Now change the initial distribution of assets, so that each of 10 agents owns 50 seed corn, and the other 990 own nothing but their labor power (or, to be consistent with our former terminology, nothing but their leisure). Preferences remain as before. What is the competitive equilibrium? One possibility is that each of the 990 assetless agents works 3 days on the Farm, and each of the 10 wealthy ones works 1 day in the Factory. But this is not an equilibrium, since there is a lot of excess capital sitting around which can be put to productive use. In particular, the wealthy ones can offer to hire the assetless to work in the Factory on their capital stock. Suppose the "capitalists" offer a corn wage of 1 corn for 2 days labor. Then each capitalist can employ 25 workers, each for 2 days, on his 50 seed corn capital. Each worker produces 4 corn in the Factory with 2 days labor. Thus each capitalist has corn revenues of 100

PANEL 1   Egalitarian Corn Model

Farm: 3 days + 0 corn → 1 corn
Factory: 1 day + 1 corn → 2 corn gross or 1 corn net
                     1-week production period

Subsistence Preferences: Minimize labor expended, to consume 1 corn, and not run down initial stock. More corn is desired if labor cost is zero.
                     N = 1,000   K = 500

EGALITARIAN DISTRIBUTION OF CAPITAL

Each agent owns ½ corn.

Equilibrium: Each works ½ day in Factory, 1½ days on Farm.
          Socially Necessary Labor Time (SNLT): 2 days

Exploitation occurs when some work > SNLT and some work < SNLT.

corn: of that, 50 corn replaces the seed used up, 25 is paid in wages, and 25 remains as profits. Capital is now fully employed. But this may or may not be an equilibrium wage: only $10 \times 25 = 250$ workers have been employed, and perhaps the other 740 peasants would prefer to work in the Factory for a real wage of ½ corn per day instead of slaving on the Farm at a real wage of ⅓ corn per day. If so, the real wage in the Factory will be bid down until the assetless agents are indifferent between doing unalienated, undominated labor on the Farm, and alienated, dominated labor in the Factory. Let us say, for the sake of simplicity, this equilibrating real wage is 1 corn for 3 days of Factory labor. (In the absence of a preference for Farm life over Factory life, the real wage will equilibrate at 1 corn for 3 days labor, that is, at the peasant's labor opportunity cost of corn, since in this economy there is a scarcity of capital relative to the labor that it could efficiently employ.) Now we have *accumulation* (or at least much more production than before, which I assume is not all eaten by the capitalists), since each capitalist gets a profit of $100 - 50 - 16⅔ = 33⅓$ corn net, and each worker or peasant gets, as in the first economy, 1 corn net. Hence total net product is $990 + (10 \times 33⅓) = 1,323⅓$ corn, instead of 1,000 corn as before. We also have *domination* since some agents are employed by others, and by hypothesis, this gives rise to domination at the point of production. *Differential alienation* has emerged, since some agents (the workers) alienate a large part of their labor to the capitalists, while the capitalists and the peasants alienate no labor (although they work different amounts of time). *Exploitation* has emerged since the workers and peasants all expend more labor than is "embodied" in the corn they get, while the 10 capitalists work zero days and each gets 33⅓ corn. For a summary, see Figure 2.

PANEL 2   Inegalitarian Distribution of Capital

Agents 1, 2, . . . , 10 each own 50 corn
Other 990 own only their labor power

Equilibrium wage: ⅓ corn/day in Factory

Total Factory employment (capitalist sector): 500 worker-days or 166⅔ workers for 3 days

Thus: 166⅔ proletarians work 3 days for 1 corn
      823⅔ peasants work 3 days on Farm for 1 corn
      10 capitalists work 0 days for 33⅓ corn each

Total profits: ⅔ corn per worker-day, or $⅔ \times 500 = 333⅓$ corn

Exploitation emerges along with accumulation, domination, alienation, inequality in distribution of assets.

Hence, the three phenomena in question emerge simultaneously with exploitation, in the passage from the "egalitarian" economy to the "capitalist" economy. With respect to expropriation, we might also say that it has emerged in the second economy.

3. WHY BE INTERESTED IN EXPLOITATION?

As I have observed, exploitation emerges simultaneously with four other phenomena: (1) accumulation, (2) domination, (3) alienation, and (4) inequality in the ownership of the means of production, of assets. Why be interested in exploitation as a statistic? What does it measure? Some justification must be given for an interest in the rather obscure calculation that measures the hours of labor embodied in the bundle of goods a person can purchase with his income, and compares this to the hours of labor he expended in production. I think exploitation is not significant in itself; it is only interesting if it is a proxy for something of palpable ethical relevance. Indeed, the history of the concept of exploitation associates it with the four phenomena I listed. Exploitation is interesting, or significant, if it is a statistic for accumulation, domination, alienation, or inequality of ownership of productive assets. I will argue, necessarily very briefly here, that the Marxian interest in exploitation cannot be justified by the association of exploitation with accumulation, domination, or alienation. This will leave inequality of ownership of the means of production as the possible root for an interest in exploitation.

First, accumulation. As the corn model showed, accumulation does emerge with exploitation of labor. Indeed, the equivalence of labor exploitation and a positive rate of profit is what has been dubbed by Michio Morishima [1973] the Fundamental Marxian Theorem, from which many have concluded that the exploitation of labor *explains* profits and accumulation. Although the Fundamental Marxian Theorem is correct, the inference that exploitation of labor explains profits is false. For, it turns out, one can take any commodity, such as oil or steel or corn, in a productive economy, and define embodied oil or steel or corn values of all other commodities, and it can be proved that profits are positive if and only if *each* commodity is exploited when it is chosen as the numeraire for denominating embodied value. Thus labor is not special in this regard. Our reason to choose labor as the commodity numeraire for value and exploitation must be different: It does not derive its uniqueness from its exploitability. For a further discussion of how steel or oil is "exploited" in a productive economy, see my book, *A General Theory of Exploitation and Class*.

What about domination? Certainly labor is unique in this regard—it is not convincing to speak of the domination of steel or oil. So if exploitation of labor were a good statistic for its domination, that would be an argument for an interest in exploitation. Unfortunately, this turns out not to be the case. Imagine an economy, the corn economy if you will, where there is no labor market, but only a capital market. Agents can lend corn capital to each other at interest, but they cannot hire or sell labor power. The equilibria of this capital market economy are identical with the equilibria of the labor market economy: what before was a profit rate now becomes an interest rate. The allocation of labor and corn in the two economies is identical. Indeed, the exploitation properties are identical. Each agent who was exploited in one economy will be exploited in the other. But in the capital market economy, labor hires capital instead of capital hiring labor. I think most Marxists would be, on ethical grounds, just as opposed to the distributional results in the capital market economy as they are to those in the labor market economy, although there is no domination of man by man in the labor process on "Capital Market Island." Indeed, such economies exist. In small-scale agriculture, often the capital market is the important market, not the labor market.

An even more austere example may be given, although this one requires there be at least two different goods which are traded, not just corn. Imagine trade takes place, as well as production, but there is no labor or capital market. Agents engage in production that is constrained by their wealth. They can trade production inputs with each other and final output, but not labor or capital (that is, no lending). In this economy, there will in general be exploitation,* although there are no relations between agents except trade of conventional commodities. This, if you will, is a model of trade between countries where labor and capital do not flow across borders. Marxists have shown an antipathy towards this kind of international exploitation, which they call "unequal exchange," although domination of the labor by one nation over the other is not at issue. These examples show that exploitation can exist without domination, and that when it does, Marxists are usually still opposed to it. Finally, I would argue that domination in workplaces is necessary because of the impossibility of writing a perfect contract for the exchange of labor for the wage. If labor contracts were perfectly delineable and costlessly enforceable, domination would not be necessary, but exploitation would still exist. So although domination in the process of production may be objectionable, it is so for reasons other than exploitation. We must search for the true rationale for an interest in exploitation elsewhere.

I think the argument for an interest in exploitation as an indicator of alienation is even less compelling, because I think alienation of one's labor in commodity production is not a compelling ethical concept. I have given the argument elsewhere, and due to its marginal importance, I skip it here. For further discussion of the topics in this section, the reader is referred to Roemer [1985a].

4. EXPLOITATION AS INEQUALITY OF OWNERSHIP OF THE MEANS OF PRODUCTION

This leaves inequality in ownership of assets as the real reason for justifying an interest in exploitation theory. Thus the Marxian claims against exploitation

---

* That is, some agents will consume goods embodying more labor than they expended, and some agents will consume goods embodying less labor than they expended, although no one hires or lends to anyone else. This exploitation is a consequence of unequal distribution of wealth.

become claims against inequality in distribution of wealth, and the Marxian theory begins to look much more like the various contemporary non-Marxist theories I mentioned earlier, which emphasize equality of resources, in various forms, as the important criterion of justice or welfare.

I will now go farther. I think the Marxian notion of exploitation as the unequal exchange of labor in general evaporates as an interesting notion, *if* we take seriously the preferences that people have. That is, even the inequality of ownership in the means of production is not always properly reflected by the statistic of exploitation. If we admit general preferences, an unrestricted domain of preferences, then it is not always true that the rich exploit the poor. The poor may exploit the rich! When this happens, the Marxist is forced to answer the question, What is your true moral concern: Inequality of ownership of productive assets, or the unequal exchange of labor (exploitation)?

I will outline an example illustrating the divergence between exploitation and inequality of assets. I postulate the same Farm and Factory technologies as before:

Farm: 3 days labor (and no capital) produces 1 bushel of corn
Factory: 1 day labor plus 1 bushel seed corn produces 2 bushels corn

Karl has an initial endowment of 1 corn and Adam of 3 corn. Denote a bundle of corn and labor as (C,L). Thus (1,1) represents the consumption of 1 corn and the provision of 1 day's labor. I assume that each agent is not willing to run down his initial stock of corn (because he might die at any time, and he wishes, at least, not to deprive his one child of the same endowment that his parent passed down to him). Suppose we know at least this about Adam's and Karl's preferences:

$$\left. \begin{array}{l} (\tfrac{2}{3},0) \; > K \; (1,1) \\ (3\tfrac{1}{3},4) \; > A \; (3,3) \end{array} \right\} (*)$$

To translate, the first line says Karl would strictly prefer to consume $\tfrac{2}{3}$ bushel of corn and not to work at all than to work 1 day and consume 1 bushel. Now note that Karl can achieve (1,1) by working up his 1 corn in the Factory in 1 day; he consumes 1 of the bushels produced, and starts week 2 with his initial 1 bushel. Likewise, Adam can achieve (3,3) by working up his 3 bushels in the Factory with 3 days' labor; he consumes 3 of the 6 bushels produced, and replaces his initial stock for week 2. But this solution is not Pareto optimal. For now suppose Karl lends his 1 bushel to Adam. Adam works up the total of 4 bushels in 4 days in the Factory, produces 8 bushels, and pays back Karl his original bushel plus $\tfrac{2}{3}$ bushel as interest for the loan. This leaves Adam with $3\tfrac{1}{3}$ bushels, after replacing his 3 bushels of initial stock. Thus Karl can consume $\tfrac{2}{3}$ bushel and not work at all, which he prefers to (1,1), and Adam consumes the bundle $(3\tfrac{1}{3},4)$ which he prefers to (3,3). We have a strict Pareto improvement. (The interest rate charged is the competitive one; for if Adam, instead of borrowing from Karl, worked on the Farm for an extra day he would make precisely $\tfrac{1}{3}$ bushel of corn.) This arrangement may continue forever: Karl never works and lives off the interest from Adam's labor. According to the surplus labor definition of exploitation, there is no shadow of a doubt that Karl exploits Adam. However, Adam is richer than Karl. On what basis can we condemn this exploitation? Not on the basis of domination or alienation (we have decided), and surely not on the basis of differential ownership of the means of production, since the exploitation is going the "wrong way." Indeed, eliminating inequality in the ownership of the means of production should improve the lot of the exploited at the expense of the exploiter. But in this case an equalization of the initial assets at 2 bushels of corn for each renders the exploiter (Karl) better off, and the exploited (Adam) worse off! See Figure 3.

It should be remarked that the preferences postulated in this example for Karl and Adam are not perverse in the sense that they can be embedded in a full preference relation which has convex indifference curves of the usual sort, in corn-leisure space. It is even the case that the preference ordering specified in (*) can be embedded in one convex preference profile. Thus Karl and Adam can be thought of as having the same preferences.

If we have reason for calling unjust the postulated inequality in the original distribution of seed corn assets, then it is Karl who is suffering an injustice in the previous example, and not Adam; but according to exploitation theory, Karl exploits Adam. As I have said, I think the most consistent Marxian ethical position is against inequality in the initial distribution of productive assets; when surplus labor accounts reflect the unequal distribution of productive assets in the proper way (that the rich exploit the poor), that is what makes

---

PANEL 3   How the Poor Can Exploit the Rich

Karl and Adam have these preferences for bundles of (Corn, Labor):

    Karl: $(\frac{2}{3},0) >_K (1,1)$
    Adam: $(3\frac{1}{3},4) >_A (3,3)$

  Farm: 3 days $\longrightarrow$ 1 corn
Factory: 1 day + 1 corn $\longrightarrow$ 1 corn net

Initial endowment:
    Karl: 1 corn, 7 days labor power (or leisure)
    Adam: 3 corn, 7 days labor power (or leisure)

"Competitive" wage is $\frac{1}{3}$ corn/day

Hence equilibrium is:
    K: $(\frac{2}{3},0)$ A: $(3\frac{1}{3},4)$

Karl hires Adam to work up K's corn stock for 1 day at wage of $\frac{1}{3}$.
Thus, poor Karl "exploits" rich Adam.

exploitation theory attractive. But if that correlation can fail, as it has, then no foundation remains for a justification of exploitation theory.

My conclusion from this discussion is, first, that the ethical bite of the exploitation concept lies not in its association with domination or alienation, but with inequality of resources. And secondly, that when the association between inequality of resources and exploitation fails, it is the inequality concept that is compelling, not exploitation. Thus we can strip exploitation theory of its labor fetishism of comparing live labor to dead labor, of thinking there is some immediate mandate for condemnation of a system characterized by unequal exchange of labor, and what remains is a concept that may be appealing: a condemnation of a system based on unequal ownership of the means of production, *tout court*.

It is perhaps worthwhile, due to the many attacks on Marxian economic theory on account of its apparent reliance on the labor theory of value, to mention that exploitation as I now conceive of it, as that inequality of incomes following from unequal distribution of the productive assets, is a sensible concept independently of the labor theory of value. Indeed, I think the labor theory of value is false, it is useless baggage. But exploitation, although originally defined as the unequal exchange of labor, can be redefined entirely in terms of property relations, as I have indicated. I pursue this project more carefully elsewhere (Roemer [1982]), where general equilibrium and game theoretic models are used to propose a definition of exploitation that formalizes the idea presented here. In those models, exploitation is well defined and labor value is never mentioned; indeed, exploitation continues to be definable even when labor is heterogeneous, when joint production exists, when there are many primary factors—the various scourges that have plagued the labor theory of value.

So exploitation can be redefined, in a way I do not pursue here, as inequality that is the consequence of unequal initial distributions of productive assets. Exploitation, so conceived, should only be bothersome if unequal distribution of the means of production is bothersome. Indeed the next question must be: If there is an unequal distribution of the productive assets, how did that come to be? If it came about as a consequence of some people working harder than others, or voluntarily taking more risks than others, is that distribution unjust or undesirable? Investment is a risky business; a small fraction of the people who take socially desirable risks succeed, and accumulate capital, and the rest of us are exploited by them through market arrangements; but our surplus labor is just the insurance premium we pay for not having to take these risks ourselves. That is one common story.

Another story has to do with different rates of time preference. Imagine Karl and Adam each starting off with ½ corn. Each lives and consumes for many weeks. (Recall, a week is the time period required in each case to bring corn to fruition, although the amount of labor expended during the week differs in the two processes.) Karl is highly averse to performing work in the present—he desires only to consume one bushel of corn per week, subject to the requirement that he not run down his seed stock. In the first week, he therefore works ½ day in the Factory (fully utilizing his seed corn) and 1½ days on the Farm, producing a total of 1½ bushels, one of which he consumes at harvest time, leaving him with ½ bushel to start with in week 2. Adam accumulates; he works ½ day in the Factory, utilizing his seed, and 4½ days on the Farm, producing 2½ bushels gross. After consuming one bushel, he has 1½ bushels left to start week 2. In week 2, Karl works up his own seed stock in ½ day in the Factory producing 1 bushel; then, instead of going to the Farm, Karl borrows or rents Adam's 1½ bushels of seed and works it up in the Factory. This takes Karl precisely 1½ days, and he produces 3 bushels gross in the factory. Of the 3 bushels he keeps ½ bushel, and returns 2½ bushels to Adam (Adam's principal of 1½ bushels plus interest of 1 bushel). Indeed, Karl is quite content with this arrangement, for he has worked for a total of 2 days and received 1½ bushels, just as in week 1, when he had to use the inferior Farm technology. Adam, on the other hand, receives a profit of 1 bushel from Karl's labor, which he consumes, and is left again to begin week 3 with 1½ bushels. He has not worked at all in week 2. This arrangement can continue forever, with Karl working 2 days each week and consuming 1 bushel, and Adam working 5 days during the first week, and zero days thereafter. Clearly there is exploitation in the classical Marxian sense in this story, in all weeks after the first, but its genesis is in the differential preferences Karl and Adam have for the consumption of corn and leisure over their lives. Thus exploitation cannot be blamed, in this story, on differential initial ownership of the means of production, nor can the situation be condemned on Paretian grounds, as no other arrangement would suit Karl and Adam more. They chose this path of consumption/leisure streams from an initial unequal distribution of corn. Indeed during any week Karl could decide to work on the Farm and accumulate more seed corn, thus enabling him to cut his working hours in future weeks. (I am assuming he is *able* to do so; if he is not, then Karl is handicapped, and the ethical verdict is certainly more complicated.) But he does not. See Figure 4.

Now if Karl and Adam each have a right to the exercise of their preferences, who can quarrel with the outcome of exploitation? What results is, in fact, a Pareto-optimal steam of consumption-leisure paths for the two of them. If the socialist state forbade exploitation, the hiring of Karl by Adam, it would necessarily condemn the two of them to a Pareto-suboptimal allocation. In fact, the Farm technology would have to be used every period, if no hiring or lending were allowed, and so the solution would obviously be inefficient.

I think there may be grounds for interfering in capitalist acts betwen consenting adults (that's Robert Nozick's line). We might ask: Under what conditions were their preferences formed? Suppose Karl's myopic preferences were formed when he grew up in a poor family, a starving family, where perhaps it was rational to have a very high rate of time discount. Now, under the new conditions of initial equality, his preferences are not well suited to the environment. If preferences, therefore, are endogenous and a consequence of not having wealth in the past, then the consequences of exercising these prefer-

PANEL 4   Differential Rates of Time Preference

Farm: 3 days $\rightarrow$ 1 corn
Factory: 1 day + 1 corn $\rightarrow$ 1 corn net

Karl and Adam each start with ½ corn.

WEEK 1:   **K** works 1½ day on the Farm, ½ day in Factory.
Consumes 1 corn.
Begins Week 2 with ½ corn.

A works ½ day in Factory, 4½ days on Farm.
Consumes 1 corn.
Begins Week 2 with 1½ corn.

WEEK 2:   **K** works ½ day in his Factory.
A hires K at wage of ⅓ corn/day to work in A's factory.
Karl works: ½ day + 1½ day $\rightarrow$ 1 corn net
Adam works: 0 days $\rightarrow$ 1 corn net

WEEK	KARL WORKS	ADAM WORKS
1	2 days	5 days
2	2 days	0 days
3	2 days	0 days
4	2 days	0 days
5	2 days	0 days

Each consumes 1 corn each week.
After Week 1, Socially Necessary Labor Time is 1 day per person.

Adam exploits Karl; but the path of consumption-leisure bundles is Pareto optimal.

ences are due to the past inequality in the ownership of productive assets, and the outcome can be viewed as exploitative. Karl's intellectual formation was not autonomous in the sense relevant for evaluating the justice of the outcome. There may be other problems of ignorance that can justify forbidding capitalist acts. The many Karls whom Adam hires as his wealth grows may not realize that the concentration of wealth they are creating in Adam's hands may give rise to an uneven distribution of political power that they would not endorse. Concentration of wealth may be a public bad, and there is a free rider problem. It does not help if any one person refuses to work for a capitalist like Adam, and so a rule against contracts that give rise to concentration of wealth may be necessary.

But I do not wish to belabor these points here, germane as they may be. Let us accept for the sake of argument that there are differences between people that are respectable, autonomously formed, but will give rise to inequality in ownership of productive assets, with the exercise of free markets. Call these skills, or more properly talents (talent being an inborn quality, and skill the consequence of applying time and labor to a talent). What approach should an egalitarian—and I take Rawls, Dworkin, Sen, and most Marxists to be egalitarians for this purpose—take towards the existence of differential talent?

5. PROPERTY THROUGH HISTORY

By this point, I hope to have indicated how Marxian ethical theory and substantial sections of non-Marxian ethical theory have come to the same point. I have made no attempt to defend egalitarianism, but have simply observed that concerns of those animated by exploitation boil down to the same concerns as those motivated by equality of primary goods, equality of resources, and so on. The key issues, I think, which face political philosophers and economists today who worry about these problems are incentives and self-ownership. By the problem of self-ownership I mean: What part of oneself should one own?

To put this in perspective, here is a quick discourse on changing property rights since the early modern period. Imagine, under feudalism, that an agent has various assets: feudal assets (which is to say property in the labor of other people, the right to corvée and demesne labor), capital assets (alienable means of production), and what I will call socialist assets (skills, talents). In the feudal period, it is legitimate to own all these assets and profit from them. Gradually, over a several-hundred-year period, feudal assets become eroded as a consequence of class struggle internal to feudalism, and emerging capitalism; eventually, an ideology evolves, let us say encapsulated by the bourgeois revolutionaries of the late eighteenth century, by Jean-Jacques Rousseau, in economics by David Ricardo and Adam Smith, that views the ills of precapitalist society as due to the existence of feudal property. Indeed feudal property is seen to give rise to injustice and exploitation. Feudal property is responsible for gross inequality, and inefficiency is blamed also on its existence. Eventually, feudal property is abolished by law. It becomes illegal for consenting adults to enter into feudal acts. You can make money from your capitalist and socialist property, but you aren't allowed to feudalize it, to enserf people, even with their volition. Thus the jurisdiction of private property was circumscribed in the bourgeois revolution. (This, of course, had happened other times, when, for instance, slave property was made illegal.)

The elimination of feudal property did increase efficiency in the long run, though doubtless there were short-run inefficiencies due to restricted contracting. Whether inequality lessened is unclear; indeed, some felt it got more severe. "Liberté, égalité, fraternité" did not clearly emerge with the abolition of feudal property. And so, by 1848, some European thinkers were placing the blame on capitalist property. Marx suggested that the elimination of capitalist property would increase efficiency and equality, would bring about the conditions for the free development of each and the free development of all. Now exploitation was blamed on the existence of private capitalist property. Beginning in 1870 (the Paris Commune) or 1917, various societies made revolutions outlawing capitalist property. Socialist property (skills) remained legal—one could earn differential wages with differential skill—but one was not allowed to capitalize socialist earnings, just as, under capitalism, one was not allowed to feudalize capitalist earnings.

The efficiency story on socialism is not clear (I would say it is too early to reach a verdict, given the historical conditions in which socialism has emerged), and certainly socialist equality is not so great as many thought it would be: Various kinds of property become important when capitalist property is no longer legal—not only property in skills, but property in position. There are rents for occupying certain positions that are associated with what can be called positional or status property. In existing socialism, many people such as those in the Polish Solidarity movement identify a kind of exploitation with the existence of private property in position, what can be called status exploitation.

Socialist countries are now grappling with some of the inefficiencies associated with having legal socialist property but illegal capitalist property. To wit, they are allowing small-scale entrepreneurship (in Hungary, one can organize a firm and hire up to thirty people; in Yugoslavia, somewhat fewer, and China has recently unleashed small-scale capitalist enterprise).

Property rights since the early modern period have become progressively circumscribed. The types of property that have been deemed appropriately held in private hands have decreased in number, and the concomitant form of associated exploitation has changed with the evolution in property rights. Slave and feudal property have been largely eliminated, and we are now in the era of the whittling away of capitalist property—not only in socialist countries, but in social democratic countries, by means of increased taxation, nationalization, and regulation. There is, usually, both an efficiency and an equity argument for the changing conception of legitimate property. Many neoclassical economists take the historically myopic view that the property rights of capitalism are the eternal ones, even as this position is eroded from within, by the nagging issues of externalities, indivisibilities, and increasing returns to scale. (Historical materialism, incidentally, maintains that property rights evolve not for ethical reasons but for ones of efficiency: a system of property relations lasts only so long as it fosters economic growth.)

These remarks intend to show that property of various kinds has been abolished or socialized through history; generally the ills of an era are viewed as a consequence of the characteristic private property of that era. When that form of property is abolished, new ills come to the fore, and the erstwhile revolutionaries are seen to have been myopic in assuming that abolition of their peculiar property form (be it feudal or capitalist) would bring about the new man.

Conservatives are fond of pointing out the inconsistency, or let us say inefficiency, in socializing alienable means of production but allowing inalienable property (skills, talents, ambition) to be privately owned, in the sense that people are allowed to earn returns to these assets in the form of differential wages. As in the example of Figure 4, why not let people invest their differential wages differently, thus giving them also private ownership of their different rates of time preference? I imagine such arguments have always been given when a form of property is abolished. The conservative line is to postulate private ownership of talent and personal resources and then to deduce the necessary private ownership of alienable capital. One might call this the Lockean position. The radical or egalitarian line is to ask: How might we establish communal property rights in personal inalienable resources? How might we socialize talent or what I have called socialist property? I don't wish here to discuss the virtue of doing this, but rather to ask a more mechanical question. If that were the aim, and I have argued there is some reason to believe history is moving in that direction, then how might one even conceive of equality of resoures when those resources include inalienable ones attached to the person?

One should note it is possible to separate ownership from possession of skill, just as it is possible to separate ownership from possession of a capital asset. Indeed, if private property in capital is socialized, that does not mean each of us *possesses* 1/n of all the factories; it means we have a 1/n share in the profits. In the same way we can discuss the socialization of skill: possession will remain in the body of a person, but the fruits of its exercise can be divided up in different ways. There may be incentive problems with separating ownership from possession of skills—but this is not new. There are incentive problems in separating ownership and possession of factories also. Managers and workers, who possess but do not own factories, have somehow to be induced to operate them efficiently.

6. EQUALITY OF TALENT

I wish to examine the simplest possible model to show some issues that arise in trying to equalize talents. We are in Karl and Adam's world, where there are two consumable goods, corn and leisure. But now Karl and Adam have different talents, with which they are born. Talent is the ability to convert leisure into corn at a certain rate. Let us say, to make things sharp, that Adam and Karl have the same preferences for corn and leisure, and indeed they have interpersonally comparable utility. They derive identical amounts of satisfaction from the same bundle of corn and leisure. I view the talent endowment as an act of nature; so that if luck does not entitle one to ownership of an asset, then neither Karl nor Adam is entitled to the talent he draws by luck in the birth lottery. This is a quick justification for desiring a redistribution of talent, an equalization of talent, so to speak. We cannot, of course, redistribute talent, but we can redistribute corn. (I might note libertarians like Nozick do not agree that luck is a nonmoral way of acquiring wealth, or talents, more specifically. It is not my goal here to justify an egalitarian philosophy, but merely to ask how one might even *define* equality when inalienable resources are the object of redivision.)

I want to examine two institutions one might adopt to compensate the one who is unlucky in the birth lottery, both of which have some appeal. Each of these institutions provides a possible way of "equalizing talent." Let us assume either Adam or Karl will be born with High talent and the other one with Low. The first institution is an insurance market. Suppose Adam and Karl had the opportunity to insure themselves against an unlucky draw in the birth lottery for talent. Insurance would take the following form. The one who is born with High talent agrees to transfer a certain amount of corn to the one who is born with Low talent. Since behind the veil of ignorance before the birth lottery occurs they are identical, each will choose the same insurance policy. Let us assume they are rational agents; the insurance contract they choose is the one that will maximize their expected utility across the two states (of being born High or Low), from among the feasible insurance schemes. These insurance schemes are determined by the productivity of the agents and the incentive effects on production from knowing how much of a transfer one will receive or give if born with the Low or High talent level. The result of this exercise is that, if the utility function is separable in corn and leisure, then the High talent person always ends up worse off in utility than the Low, *ex post*. Indeed, the agents will insure that each consumes the same amount of corn, but High talent works longer (and hence enjoys less leisure) than Low talent. This is perhaps disturbing; in an attempt to compensate Low for his bad luck, he appears to be overcompensated. This insurance proposal is a formalization of a suggestion by Ronald Dworkin [1981] in his work on equality of resources. It is important to notice that although the insurance market proposed is conceived of as a method for achieving equality of *resources,* in this case personal ones, such equality is defined by recourse to the agents' *preferences,* since the insurance policy is arrived at by maximizing expected utility.

Here is a second institution for compensating talent differentials. Instead of using insurance, let us simply assign property rights in everyone's leisure to everyone else. Thus each of Adam and Karl owns ½ of the other's stock of leisure, and ½ of his own leisure, valued by the real wage each is capable of earning. Each person's real wage is known; there is no possibility of hiding it. Call this the "mutual slavery institution." We then allow markets to operate to distribute corn. In the equilibrium allocation, it will again be true that Karl, born with Low talent, is happier than Adam—the unlucky one seems to exploit the lucky one. The intuition here is clear. Karl and Adam have the same assets—namely, they each come into the world with no corn, and ½ of the leisure stock of each. So they have the same wealth. Karl wants to consume two goods: corn and his cheap leisure. Adam wants to consume two goods: corn and his dear leisure. (Adam's leisure is dear because the lost opportunity for him, when he takes leisure, is to exercise his highly valued talent.) Since they have the same wealth, Adam's budget set lies inside Karl's and so he will be worse off at equilibrium, since they have the same preferences. See Figure 5. What I have called mutual slavery has been discussed in the literature on envy. Hal Varian [1974] calls the resulting allocation "income-fair."

What I hope the reader finds disturbing about these examples is the growing confrontation between the equality of resources position, the kind of egalitarianism which I said is increasingly prevalent in modern political philosophy, and equality of welfare. In our attempt to equalize resources, the one born lucky, in possession of a good endowment of resources, ends up unlucky in utility.

PANEL 5   Mutual Slavery in Talents

Karl and Adam each own ½ of each other's leisure stock, valued at real wages h and l. Thus each have same "income."

Budget sets:

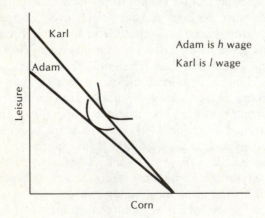

Adam is h wage

Karl is l wage

Thus Karl is happier than Adam.

Why exactly are these results problematical for ethics? The attacks on welfarism that have been posed by proponents of nonutilitarian theories of distributional justice are based, in large part, on the assumption that people have different preferences. Some people may have expensive tastes, which society should not subsidize, as it would with a utilitarian social welfare function. The proposals for equality of resources, or equality of primary goods, or equality of basic capabilities, or fulfillment of basic needs, are intended as a more objective and perhaps less arbitrary basis for distribution than is provided by recourse to utility indicators. But *if* all people have the same preferences, these criticisms of welfarism evaporate. In a world where all people have the same cardinal, interpersonally comparable utility function, the implementation of equality-of-resources should imply equality of utility. But the two institutions or mechanisms for equalizing inalienable resources that I have examined give unequal utilities, in the special pleasant case of identical preferences that I have outlined. This seems to impugn the equality of resources approach—or at least the two mechanisms discussed here for implementing such an approach.

Here is an example with differential preferences, which further strains our moral intuitions. There is one consumable good, corn; but Karl and Adam have different preferences for corn, they derive different amounts of pleasure from it. There must be a reason they do—let us say it is because they possess different amounts of endorphins in their bodies, which provide them different degrees of satisfaction from life. Adam has more endorphins than Karl, and so he gets more pleasure than Karl from any given amount of corn. If we put endorphins into the utility function, as a parameter, then Karl and Adam have the same preferences—it's just that they are consuming different amounts of endorphins. Suppose that Adam's utility schedule in corn rises more steeply than Karl's from the origin. At any level of corn, Adam derives greater marginal utility than Karl, due to his greater endowment of endorphins. See Panel 6.

An equality-of-resources approach would suggest we view both corn and endorphins as within the scope of redistribution. If Karl and Adam are not responsible for the endorphins they were born with, then a bad draw of endorphins should be something for which an equality-of-resources ethic compensates them. Let us see what happens by applying the insurance scheme to this problem. Behind the veil of ignorance, before one knows whether one will get the high or the low lot of endorphins, one chooses insurance, which takes the form of a contract to distribute corn in a certain way. The rational insurer, who cannot alter *ex post* his endowment of endorphins, will distribute the corn to himself in the two states so as to maximize his expected utility. This requires equalizing marginal utility of corn in the two states of the world. But by hypothesis, if he contracts to take the *same* amount of corn if he is Karl or Adam, then as Adam, he gets higher marginal utility than as Karl—and so the optimal insurance policy is to give still *more* corn to Adam (see Figure 6). Thus the one who draws the lucky lot of endorphins in fact will get more corn as well! In our attempt to equalize the resources, to compensate Karl for his

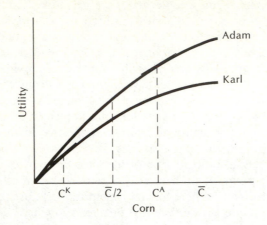

PANEL 6:   **Insurance against Endorphin Hazard**

- Adam gets higher absolute and marginal utility than Karl at any amount of corn consumption, due to higher level of endorphins he is internally consuming.
- Insurance behind the veil of ignorance, before endorphin level is known, will lead agents to distribute in amounts C^K to Karl and C^A to Adam, to equalize marginal utilities.
- Thus Karl ends up worse off under insurance than with equal split of corn.

bad draw in endorphins, he is made worse off than if we did not put endorphins within the jurisdiction of equality of resources. If there were no veil of ignorance, and there were just random lots of corn being drawn by Karl and Adam, whose identities are already known, then Karl and Adam will each insure to have the *same amount* of corn, regardless of how the lots fall. Thus withdrawing behind the veil of ignorance associated with a radical conception of equality of resources makes the unlucky one *worse* off than he would be if we did not try to compensate him for his low endorphin level.

If we use the mutual slavery institution, then we assign property rights as follows. Each of Karl and Adam owns one-half the corn, one-half of his endorphins, and one-half of the other fellow's endorphins. Markets operate to set the prices of corn and endorphins of both kinds. Notice there are three goods: corn, Karl's endorphins, and Adam's endorphins. Now Karl's endorphins are scarce, and in a competitive market, given the symmetry of preferences of the two agents, the price of Karl's endorphins will be greater than the price of Adam's. Karl and Adam have the same income, since they own identical property, but Karl will buy back his expensive endorphins, while Adam will buy back his cheap endorphins. Since the equilibrium must be Pareto efficient, we know each will in fact buy back all of his own endorphins. Whether or not Karl spends more of his income than Adam buying back his endorphins depends on the utility function; but for many utility functions, Karl will indeed spend more than Adam on endorphins. In that case, Karl has less income left to buy corn than Adam. Thus Karl ends up with all his own endorphins, but with less corn than Adam. Again, Adam is better off, twice over. The mutual slavery institution gives qualitatively the same result as the insurance institution.

We have the seemingly perverse result, that in our attempt to push back further the jurisdiction of private ownership, in our attempt to compensate the one who is unlucky in his endowment of an inalienable asset, the institutions that seem natural to adopt in the effort to equalize resources render the unlucky one even worse off than he would be with a less radical approach to resource equalization. Karl would be better off if we just equalized the corn, and didn't worry about his bad draw of endorphins.

The reason this occurs is that there is a fundamental difference between Karl and Adam: they in fact have preferences for *different goods*. Adam gets no kick whatsoever from Karl's endorphins, and Karl gets no kick from Adam's. Even if we equalize all three "resources," their preferences remain fundamentally different, for that reason. And because of that, it is not at all clear that we are doing Karl a favor by calling for equality of all resources. The situation is just like the corn-leisure-skill model. There are three goods: corn, Karl's leisure, and Adam's leisure. Neither gets any kick from consuming the other one's leisure. The one who is born with the high talent is in fact unlucky in an equality-of-resources world, since he has a taste for an expensive good, namely, his own leisure, which he must buy back from the rest of society.

7. CONCLUSION

Let me conclude by reviewing the path to this point. The call against exploitation, I have claimed, is nothing other than a call for equality of certain kinds of resources, alienable productive assets. In this sense, Marxism is or was the ethical philosophy of the late capitalist period, just as bourgeois philosophy of 1789, calling for the abolition of feudal assets, was the ethical philosophy of the late feudal period. In the reaction against utilitarianism and welfarism, both Marxist and non-Marxist political philosophy have emphasized as an alternative equality of resources of various kinds. In pursuing equality of opportunity and resources, I think one must discuss schemes for compensating people with an unlucky draw in the lottery for personal talents. But in equalizing personal inalienable resources, one is led inexorably to considerations of subjective utility. Moreover in that radical egalitarian attempt, it often happens that the people who have a bad lot of the distribution of personal resources become *worse* off in welfare terms than they would have been with a less radical egalitarianism that did not attempt to compensate them for their bad draw in personal endowments. This appears seriously to impugn the ethical appeal of equality-of-resource proposals. For a more thorough and technical discussion of these ideas, see Roemer [1985b, 1986].

Indeed, the distinction between resources and preferences becomes ephemeral. One might characterize a person by a long vector of parameters, which lists his endowment of various body chemicals, a description of his neural pathways and synaptic connections—a Cartesian decomposition of his mind. The very preferences and ambitions of a person, as well as his talents, are described by this list of personal resources, which he "consumes." Where do we draw the line between those components of the list that should be considered resources, and hence are within the jurisdiction of social redistribution, and those components that are his personal traits, which he may privately own and benefit from? Both the institutions for achieving equality of resources that I have discussed force upon us unpleasant confrontations with our ethical intuitions when this question is pursued. Dividing up the property in inalienable resources equally is motivated by a desire to improve the welfare of those who are unlucky in the lot of personal resources they possess; but quite the opposite result can be achieved by these egalitarian property rights. The nonwelfarist theories of resource equality prevalent in contemporary political philosophy become problematical once inalienable endowments are admitted to be within the jurisdiction of socializable property. We are driven back to a central consideration of subjective preference. Can we draw a meaningful divide on the slippery slope of personal traits that separates a person's resources from his preferences? What does it mean, in the next several centuries of evolving property rights, to be an egalitarian?

REFERENCES

Dworkin, Ronald, "What is Equality? Part 1: Equality of Welfare," *Philosophy and Public Affairs* X (Summer 1981), 185–246.

Dworkin, Ronald, "What is Equality? Part 2: Equality of Resources," *Philosophy and Public Affairs* X (Fall 1981), 283–345.

Morishima, Michio, *Marx's Economics,* Cambridge: Cambridge University Press, 1973.

Rawls, John, *A Theory of Justice* (Cambridge, MA: Belknap, 1971).

Roemer, John E., *A General Theory of Exploitation and Class* (Cambridge, MA: Harvard University Press, 1981).

Roemer, John E., "Should Marxists be Interested in Exploitation," *Philosophy and Public Affairs* 14, No. 1, Winter 1985a.

Roemer, John E., "Equality of Talent," *Economics and Philosophy* I (1985b), 151–86.

Roemer, John E., "Equality of Resources Implies Equality of Welfare," *Quarterly Journal of Economics,* 1986.

Sen, Amartya, "Equality of What?" in *Tanner Lectures on Human Values* I, S. McMurrin, ed. (Cambridge, England: Cambridge University Press, 1980).

Varian, Hal, "Distributive Justice, Welfare Economics and the Theory of Fairness," *Philosophy and Public Affairs* 4, No. 3, Spring 1975.

ROBERT NOZICK

EQUALITY, ENVY, AND EXPLOITATION

Critics of capitalism often lament the system's lack of concern with equality of conditions among human beings. Both as it is advanced in theory and as it leaves its mark on this or that actual society, capitalism is said to be unfair and inegalitarian. Robert Nozick—a philosopher at Harvard University and author of Anarchy, State, and Utopia (1974) *and* Philosophical Explanations (1983)—*argues that there need be nothing immoral in the system because of inequality. Why should there be some special preference for equality of conditions among human beings? Few arguments have been offered for these egalitarian assumptions. Perhaps the idea rests on the suspect feeling of envy, the desire to see others who do well brought down, if one cannot share their accomplishments and good fortune? In discussing these issues Nozick undertakes a detailed criticism of several important anticapitalist and Marxian ideas.*

EQUALITY

The legitimacy of altering social institutions to achieve greater equality of material condition is, though often assumed, rarely *argued* for. Writers note that in a given country the wealthiest *n* percent of the population holds more than that percentage of the wealth, and the poorest *n* percent holds less; that to get to the wealth of the top *n* percent from the poorest, one must look at the bottom *p* percent (where *p* is vastly greater than *n*), and so forth. They then proceed immediately to discuss how this might be altered. On the entitlement conception of justice in holdings, one *cannot* decide whether the state must do something to alter the situation merely by looking at a distributional profile or at facts such as these. It depends upon how the distribution came about. Some processes yielding these results would be legitimate, and the various parties would be entitled to their respective holdings. If these distributional facts *did* arise by a legitimate process, then they themselves are legitimate. This is, of course, *not* to say that they may not be changed, provided this can be done without violating people's entitlements. Any persons who favor a particular end-state pattern may choose to transfer some or all of their own holdings so as (at least temporarily) more nearly to realize their desired pattern.

The entitlement conception of justice in holdings makes no presumption in favor of equality, or any other overall end state or patterning. It cannot merely be *assumed* that equality must be built into any theory of justice. There is a surprising dearth of arguments for equality capable of coming to grips with the considerations that underlie a nonglobal and nonpatterned conception of justice in holdings.[1] (However, there is no lack of unsupported statements of a presumption in favor of equality.) I shall consider the argument

Reprinted from *Anarchy, State, and Utopia* by Robert Nozick (New York: Basic Books). Copyright 1974 by Basic Books, Inc., Publishers. Reprinted by permission of the publisher.

which has received the most attention from philosophers in recent years; that offered by Bernard Williams in his influential essay "The Idea of Equality."[2] (No doubt many readers will feel that all hangs on some other argument; I would like to see *that* argument precisely set out, in detail.)

Leaving aside preventive medicine, the proper ground of distribution of medical care is ill health: this is a necessary truth. Now in very many societies, while ill health may work as a necessary condition of receiving treatment, it does not work as a sufficient condition, since such treatment costs money, and not all who are ill have the money; hence the possession of sufficient money becomes in fact an additional necessary condition of actually receiving treatment. . . . When we have the situation in which, for instance, wealth is a further necessary condition of the receipt of medical treatment, we can once more apply the notions of equality and inequality: not now in connection with the inequality between the well and the ill, but in connection with the inequality between the rich ill and the poor ill, since we have straightforwardly the situation of those whose needs are the same not receiving the same treatment, though the needs are the ground of the treatment. This is an irrational state of affairs . . . it is a situation in which reasons are insufficiently operative; it is a situation insufficiently controlled by reasons—and hence by reason itself.[3]

Williams seems to be arguing that if among the different descriptions applying to an activity, there is one that contains an "internal goal" of the activity, then (it is a necessary truth that) the only proper grounds for the performance of the activity, or its allocation if it is scarce, are connected with the effective achievement of the internal goal. If the activity is done upon others, the only proper criterion for distributing the activity is their need for it, if any. Thus it is that Williams says (it is a necessary truth that) the only proper criterion for the distribution of medical care is medical need. Presumably, then, the only proper criterion for the distribution of barbering services is barbering need. But why must the internal goal of the activity take precedence over, for example, the person's particular purpose in performing the activity? (We ignore the question of whether one activity can fall under two different descriptions involving different internal goals.) If someone becomes a barber because he likes talking to a variety of different people, and so on, is it unjust of him to allocate his services to those he most likes to talk to? Or if he works as a barber in order to earn money to pay tuition at school, may he cut the hair of only those who pay or tip well? Why may not a barber use exactly the same criteria in allocating his services as someone else whose activities have no internal goal involving others? Need a gardener allocate his services to those lawns which need him most?

In what way does the situation of a doctor differ? Why must his activities be allocated via the internal goal of medical care? (If there was no "shortage," could some *then* be allocated using other criteria as well?) It seems clear that *he* needn't do that; just because he has this skill, why should *he* bear the costs of the desired allocation, why is he less entitled to pursue his own goals, within the special circumstances of practicing medicine, than everyone else? So it is *society* that, somehow, is to arrange things so that the doctor, in pursuing his own goals, allocates according to need; for example, the society pays him to do this. But why must the society do this? (Should they do it for barbering as well?) Presumably, because medical care is important, people need it very much. This is true of food as well, though farming does *not* have an internal goal that refers to other people in the way doctoring does. When the layers of Williams' argument are peeled away, what we arrive at is the claim that society (that is, each of us acting together in some organized fashion) should make provision for the important needs of all of its members. This claim, of course, has been stated many times before. Despite appearances, Williams presents no argument for it.* Like others, Williams looks only to questions of allocation. He ignores the question of where the things or actions to be allocated and distributed come from. Consequently, he does not consider whether they come already tied to people who have entitlements over them (surely the case for service activities, which are people's *actions*), people who therefore may decide for themselves to whom they will give the thing and on what grounds.

EQUALITY OF OPPORTUNITY

Equality of opportunity has seemed to many writers to be the minimal egalitarian goal, questionable (if at all) only for being too weak. (Many writers also have seen how the existence of the family prevents fully achieving this goal.) There are two ways to attempt to provide such equality: by directly worsening the situations of those more favored with opportunity, or by improving the situation of those less well-favored. The latter requires the use of resources, and so it too involves worsening the situation of some: those from whom holdings are taken in order to improve the situation of others. But holdings to which these people are entitled may not be seized, even to provide equality of opportunity for others. In the absence of magic wands, the remaining means toward equality of opportunity is convincing persons each to choose to devote some of their holdings to achieving it.

The model of a race for a prize is often used in discussions of equality of opportunity. A race where some started closer to the finish line than others would be unfair, as would a race where some were forced to carry heavy weights, or run with pebbles in their sneakers. But life is not a race in which we all compete for a prize which someone has established; there is no unified race, with some person judging swiftness. Instead, there are different persons separately giving other persons different things. Those who do the giving

---

* We have discussed Williams' position without introducing an essentialist view that some activities necessarily involve certain goals. Instead we have tied the goals to *descriptions* of the activities. For essentialist issues only becloud the discussion, and they still leave open the question of why the only proper ground for allocating the activity is its essentialist goal. The motive for making such an essentialist claim would be to avoid someone's saying: let "schmoctoring" be an activity just like doctoring except that *its* goal is to earn money for the practitioner; has Williams presented any reason why *schmoctoring* services should be allocated according to need?

(each of us, at times) usually do not care about desert or about the handicaps labored under; they care simply about what they actually get. No centralized process judges people's use of the opportunities they had; that is not what the processes of social cooperation and exchange are *for*.

There is a reason why some inequality of opportunity might seem *unfair*, rather than merely unfortunate in that some do not have every opportunity (which would be true even if no one else had greater advantage). Often the person entitled to transfer a holding has no special desire to transfer it to a particular person; this contrasts with a bequest to a child or a gift to a particular person. He chooses to transfer to someone who satisfies a certain condition (for example, who can provide him with a certain good or service in exchange, who can do a certain job, who can pay a certain salary), and he would be equally willing to transfer to anyone else who satisfied that condition. Isn't it unfair for one party to receive the transfer, rather than another who had less opportunity to satisfy the condition the transferrer used? Since the giver doesn't care to whom he transfers, provided the recipient satisfies a certain general condition, equality of opportunity to be a recipient in such circumstances would violate no entitlement of the giver. Nor would it violate any entitlement of the person with the greater opportunity; while entitled to what he has, he has no entitlement that it be more than another has. Wouldn't it be *better* if the person with less opportunity had an equal opportunity? If one so could equip him without violating anyone else's entitlements (the magic wand?) shouldn't one do so? Wouldn't it be fairer? If it *would* be fairer, can such fairness also justify overriding some people's entitlements in order to acquire the resources to boost those having poorer opportunities into a more equal competitive position?

The process is competitive in the following way. If the person with greater opportunity didn't exist, the transferrer might deal with some person having lesser opportunity who then would be, under those circumstances, the best person available to deal with. This differs from a situation in which unconnected but similar beings living on different planets confront different difficulties and have different opportunities to realize various of their goals. There, the situation of one does *not* affect that of another; though it would be better if the worse planet were better endowed than it is (it also would be better if the better planet were better endowed than *it* is), it wouldn't be *fairer*. It also differs from a situation in which a person does not, though he could, choose to *improve* the situation of another. In the particular circumstances under discussion, a person having lesser opportunities would be better off if some particular person having better opportunities didn't exist. The person having better opportunities can be viewed not merely as someone better off, or as someone not choosing to aid, but as someone *blocking* or *impeding* the person having lesser opportunities from becoming better off.[4] Impeding another by being a more alluring alternative partner in exchange is not to be compared to directly *worsening* the situation of another, as by stealing from him. But still, cannot the person with lesser opportunity justifiably complain at being so impeded by another who does not *deserve* his better opportunity to satisfy certain conditions? (Let us ignore any similar complaints another might make about *him*.)

While feeling the power of the questions of the previous two paragraphs (it is *I* who ask them), I do not believe they overturn a thoroughgoing entitlement conception. If the woman who later became my wife rejected another suitor (whom she otherwise would have married) for me, partially because (I leave aside my lovable nature) of my keen intelligence and good looks, neither of which did I earn, would the rejected less intelligent and less handsome suitor have a legitimate complaint about unfairness? Would my thus impeding the other suitor's winning the hand of fair lady justify taking some resources from others to pay for cosmetic surgery for him and special intellectual training, or to pay to develop in him some sterling trait that I lack in order to equalize our chances of being chosen? (I here take for granted the impermissibility of worsening the situation of the person having better opportunities so as to equalize opportunity; in this sort of case by disfiguring him or injecting drugs or playing noises which prevent him from fully using his intelligence.[5]) *No such consequences follow.* (Against whom would the rejected suitor have a legitimate complaint? Against what?) Nor are things different if the differential opportunities arise from the accumulated effects of people's acting or transferring their entitlement as they choose. The case is even easier for consumption goods which cannot plausibly be claimed to have any such triadic impeding effect. *Is* it unfair that a child be raised in a home with a swimming pool, using it daily even though he is no more *deserving* than another child whose home is without one? Should such a situation be prohibited? Why then should there be objection to the transfer of the swimming pool to an adult by bequest?

The major objection to speaking of everyone's having a right *to* various things such as equality of opportunity, life, and so on, and enforcing this right, is that these "rights" require a substructure of things and materials and actions; and *other* people may have rights and entitlements over these. No one has a right to something whose realization requires certain uses of things and activities that other people have rights and entitlements over.[6] Other people's rights and entitlements to *particular things* (*that* pencil, *their* body, and so on) and how they choose to exercise these rights and entitlements fix the external environment of any given individual and the means that will be available to him. If his goal requires the use of means which others have rights over, he must enlist their voluntary cooperation. Even to *exercise* his right to determine how something he owns is to be used may require other means he must acquire a right to, for example, food to keep him alive; he must put together, with the cooperation of others, a feasible package.

There are particular rights over particular things held by particular persons, and particular rights to reach agreements with others, *if* you and they together can acquire the means to reach an agreement. (No one has to supply you with a telephone so that you may reach an agreement with another.) No rights exist in conflict with this substructure of particular rights. Since no neatly contoured right to achieve a goal will avoid incompatibility with this substructure, no such rights exist. The particular rights over things fill the space of rights, leaving no room for general rights to be in a certain material condition. The reverse theory would place only such universally held general "rights to" achieve goals or to be in a certain material condition into its substructure so as to determine all else; to my knowledge no serious attempt has been made to state this "reverse" theory.

SELF-ESTEEM AND ENVY

It is plausible to connect equality with self-esteem.[7] The envious person, if he cannot (also) possess a thing (talent, and so on) that someone else has, prefers that the other person not have it either. The envious man prefers neither one having it, to the other's having it and his not having it.*

People often have claimed that envy underlies egalitarianism. And others have replied that since egalitarian principles are separately justifiable, we need attribute no disreputable psychology to the egalitarian; he desires merely that correct principles be realized. In view of the great ingenuity with which people dream up principles to rationalize their emotions, and given the great difficulty in discovering *arguments* for equality as a value in itself, this reply is, to

---

* With regard to you, another person, and having a kind of object or attribute, these are four possibilities:

	HE	YOU
1.	has it	have it
2.	has it	don't have it
3.	doesn't have it	have it
4.	doesn't have it	don't have it

You are *envious* (with regard to him and that kind of object or attribute; I suppress the relativization in what follows) if you prefer 4 to 2, while preferring 3 to 4. (The "while" is the "and" of conjunction.) You are *jealous* if you prefer 1 to 2, while being indifferent between 3 and 4. The root idea is that you are jealous if you want it because he has it. The condition formulated says you want it solely because he has it. A weaker condition would say that you are jealous if you want it more because he has it; that is, if you prefer 1 to 2 more than you prefer 3 to 4. Similarly we can formulate a less strong condition for envy. A strongly envious man prefers the other not have the thing if he himself doesn't. A partially envious man may be willing for the other to have the thing even though he himself cannot, but he prefers this less strongly than he prefers that the other have the thing if he himself does; that is, he prefers 2 to 4 less than he prefers 1 to 3. You are *begrudging* if you prefer 3 to 1, while preferring 3 to 4. You are *spiteful* if you prefer 4 to 1, while preferring 3 to 4. You are *competitive* if you prefer 3 to 4, while being indifferent between 1 and 4.

A competitive person is begrudging. A spiteful person is begrudging. There are envious people who are not jealous (in the sense of the weaker condition). Though it is not a theorem, it is a plausible psychological conjecture that most jealous people are envious. And surely it is a psychological law that spiteful people are envious.

Compare the similar though somewhat different distinctions that Rawls draws (*Theory of Justice*, sect. 80). Rawls' notion of envy is stronger than ours. We can formulate a close equivalent of his, by letting $i(X)$ be the ith row in the above matrix for something X; $i(Y)$ be the ith row for something Y. You are envious in Rawls' strong sense if you prefer $4(X)$ and $4(Y)$ to $2(X)$ and $1(Y)$; that is, if you prefer that neither of you have either X or Y, rather than that he have both X and Y while you have only Y. You are willing to give up something to erase the differential. Rawls uses both "jealous" and "begrudging" for our "begrudging" and has nothing corresponding to our "jealous." Our notion of spite here is stronger than his, and he has no notion corresponding to our "competitive."

say the least, unproven. (Nor is it proven by the fact that once people accept egalitarian principles, they might support the worsening of their own position as an application of these general principles.)

Here I prefer to focus on the *strangeness* of the emotion of envy. Why do some people *prefer* that others not have their better score on some dimension, rather than being pleased at another's being well-off or having good fortune; why don't they at least just shrug it off? One line seems especially worth pursuing: A person with a score along some dimension would rather another person with a higher score *H* had scored less well than *H*, even though this will not raise his own score, in those cases when the other person's having a higher score than himself threatens or undermines his own self-esteem and makes him feel inferior to the other in some important way. How can another's activities, or characteristics, affect one's own self-esteem? Shouldn't my self-esteem, feeling of worth, and so forth, depend only upon facts about me? If it is me that I'm evaluating in some way, how *can* facts about other persons play a role? The answer, of course, is that we evaluate how *well* we do something by comparing our performance to others, to what others can do. A man living in an isolated mountain village can sink 15 jump shots with a basketball out of 150 tries. He thinks (as do the others) that he's very good at it. One day, along comes Jerry West. Or, a mathematician works *very* hard and occasionally thinks up an interesting conjecture, nicely proves a theorem, and so on. He then discovers a whole group of whizzes at mathematics. He dreams up a conjecture, and they quickly prove or disprove it (not in all possible cases, because of Church's theorem), constructing very elegant proofs; they themselves also think up very deep theorems, and so on.

In each of these cases, the person will conclude that he wasn't *very good* or *adept* at the thing after all. There is no standard of doing something well, independent of how it is or can be done by others. At the end of his book *Literature and Revolution,* in describing what man will be like (eventually) in a communist society, Leon Trotsky says:

Man will become immeasurably stronger, wiser, and subtler; his body will become more harmonized, his movements more rhythmic, his voice more musical. The forms of life will become dynamically dramatic. The average human type will rise to the heights of an Aristotle, a Goethe, or a Marx. And above this ridge new peaks will rise.

If this were to occur, the average person, at the level *only* of Aristotle, Goethe, or Marx, wouldn't think he was very good or adept at those activities. He would have problems of self-esteem! Someone in the circumstances of the described basketball player or mathematician might prefer that the other persons lacked their talents, or prefer that they stop continually demonstrating their worth, at least in front of him; that way his self-esteem will avoid battering and can be shored up.

This would be *one* possible explanation of why certain inequalities in income, or position of authority within an industry, or of an entrepreneur as compared to his employees, *rankle* so; *not* due to the feeling that this superior position is undeserved, but to the feeling that it *is* deserved and earned. It may injure one's self-esteem and make one feel less worthy as a person to know of someone else who has accomplished more or risen higher. Workers in a factory started only recently by someone else previously a worker will be constantly *confronted* by the following thoughts: why not me? why am I only here? Whereas one can manage to ignore much more easily the knowledge that someone else somewhere has done more, if one is not confronted daily with him. The point, though sharper then, does not depend upon another's deserving his superior ranking along some dimension. That there is someone else who is a good dancer will affect your estimate of how good you yourself are at dancing, even if you think that a large part of grace in dancing depends upon unearned natural assets.

As a framework for discussion that embodies these considerations (and *not* as a contribution to psychological theory), consider the following *simple* model. There are a number of different dimensions, dimensional attributes along which people can vary, $D1, \ldots, D_n$, that people hold to be valuable. People may differ as to what dimensions they think valuable, and they may differ as to the (nonzero) weights they give to the dimensions they agree in considering valuable. For each person, there will be a *factual profile* that presents his objective position along each dimension; for example, on the jump-shot dimension, we might have "able regularly to score ___ jump shots out of 100 tries from 20 feet out," and a person's score might be 20, or 34, or 67.

For simplicity, let us assume that a person's beliefs about his factual profile are reasonably accurate. Also there will be an *evaluative profile* to represent how the person evaluates his own scores on the factual profile. There will be evaluative classifications (for example, excellent, good, satisfactory, poor, awful) representing his evaluation of himself for each dimension. These individual evaluations, how he gets from the factual score to the evaluations, will depend upon his factual beliefs about the factual profiles of other similar beings (the "reference group"), the goals he was given as a child, and so on. All shape his level of aspiration, which itself will vary over time in roughly specifiable ways. Each person will make some overall estimate of himself; in the simplest case this will depend solely on his evaluative profile and his weighting of the dimensions. *How* it depends upon this may vary from individual to individual. Some may take the weighted sum of their scores over all the dimensions; others may evaluate themselves as OK if they do well on some reasonably important dimension; still others may think that if they fall down on any important dimension they stink.

In a society where people generally agree that some dimensions are very important, and there are differences in how people fall along these dimensions, and some institutions publicly group people in accordance with their place along these dimensions, then those who score low may feel inferior to those with higher scores; they may feel inferior as persons. (Thus, *poor* people might come to think they are poor *people.*) One might try to avoid such feelings of inferiority by changing the society so that either those dimensions which served to distinguish people are downgraded in importance, or so that people do not have an opportunity publicly to exercise their capacities along these dimensions or to learn how others score on them.*

It might appear obvious that if people feel inferior because they do poorly along some dimensions, then if these dimensions are downgraded in importance or if scores along them are equalized, people no longer will feel inferior. (*"Of course!"*) The very reason they have for feeling inferior is removed. But it may well be that other dimensions would replace the one eliminated with the same effects (on different persons). If, after downgrading or equalizing one dimension, say wealth, the society comes generally to agree that some *other* dimension is most important, for example, aesthetic appreciativeness, aesthetic attractiveness, intelligence, athletic prowess, physical grace, degree of sympathy with other persons, quality of orgasm, then the phenomenon will repeat itself.[8]

People generally judge themselves by how they fall along the most important dimensions in which they *differ* from others. People do not gain self-esteem from their common human capacities by comparing themselves to animals who lack them. ("I'm pretty good; I have an opposable thumb and can speak some language.") Nor do people gain or maintain self-esteem by considering that they possess the right to vote for political leaders, though when the franchise was not widely distributed things may have been different. Nor do people in the United States today have a sense of worth because they are able to read and write, though in many other societies in history this has served. When everyone, or almost everyone, has some thing or attribute, it does not function as a basis for self-esteem. Self-esteem is based on *differentiating characteristics;* that's why it's *self*-esteem. And as sociologists of reference groups are fond of pointing out, who the *others* are changes. First-year students at prestige colleges may have a sense of individual worth based on attending those schools. This feeling is more pronounced, indeed, during their last two months of high school. But when *everyone* they associate with is in a similar position, the fact of going to these schools no longer serves as a basis for self-esteem, except perhaps when they return home during vacation (or in thought) *to those not there.*

Consider how you would set about to bolster the self-esteem of an individual who, perhaps from limited capacity, scored lower than all others on all the dimensions others considered important (and who scored better on no dimension one plausibly could argue was important or valuable). You might tell the person that though his absolute scores were low, he had done well (given his limited capacities). He had realized a greater proportion of his capacities than

---

* If a society's most important dimension, by common consensus, is undetectable in that it cannot directly be determined where along it a person falls, people will come to believe that a person's score on this dimension is correlated with his score on another dimension along which they *can* determine relative positions (the halo effect). Thus, people for whom the presence of divine grace is the most important dimension will come to believe other worthy detectable facts indicate its presence; for example, worldly success.

most and fulfilled more of his potential than others do; considering where he had started, and with what, he had accomplished a great deal. This would reintroduce comparative evaluation, by citing another important (meta)dimension along which he *does* do well as compared to others.*

These considerations make one *somewhat* skeptical of the chances of equalizing self-esteem and reducing envy by equalizing positions along that particular dimension upon which self-esteem is (happens to be) importantly based. Think of the varied attributes one can *envy* another's having, and one will realize the vast opportunities for differential self-esteem. Recall now Trotsky's speculation that under communism everyone would reach the level of Aristotle, Goethe, or Marx, and from his ridge new peaks would rise. Being at this ridge would no more give everyone self-esteem and a feeling of individual worth than does the ability to speak a language or the possession of hands able to grasp things. Some simple and natural assumptions might even lead to a principle of the conservation of envy. And one might worry, *if* the number of dimensions is not unlimited and if great strides are made to eliminate differences, that as the number of differentiating dimensions shrinks, envy will become more severe. For with a small number of differentiating dimensions, many people will find they don't do well on *any* of them. Though the weighted sum of a number of independently varying normal distributions itself will be normal, if each individual (who knows his score on each dimension) weights the dimensions differently from the way other persons do, the total sum of all the different individuals' differently weighted combinations need not itself be a normal distribution, even though the scores on each dimension are normally distributed. Everyone might view themselves as at the upper end of a distribution (even of a normal distribution) since each sees the distribution through the perspective of the particular weights he assigns. The fewer the dimensions, the less the opportunity for an individual successfully to use as a basis for self-esteem a nonuniform weighting strategy that gives greater weight to a dimension he scores highly in. (This suggests that envy can be reduced only by a fell-swoop elimination of all differences.)

Even if envy is more tractable than our considerations imply, it would be objectionable to intervene to reduce someone's situation in order to lessen the

---

* Is there any important dimension along which it is inappropriate to judge oneself comparatively? Consider the following statement by Timothy Leary: "It's my ambition to be the holiest, wisest, most beneficial man alive today. Now this may sound megalomaniac, but I don't see why. I don't see why . . . every person who lives in the world, shouldn't have that ambition. What else should you try to be? The president of the board, or the chairman of the department, or the owner of this and that?" *The Politics of Ecstasy* (New York: College Notes and Texts, Inc., 1968), p. 218. There certainly is no objection to wanting to be as holy, wise, and beneficial as possible, yet an ambition to be the holiest, wisest, and most beneficial person alive today is bizarre. Similarly, one can want to be as enlightened as possible (in the sense of Eastern traditions), but it would be bizarre to want especially to be the most enlightened person alive, or to be more enlightened than someone else. How one values one's degree of enlightenment depends only upon it, whatever others are like. This suggests that the absolutely most important things do not lend themselves to such comparative evaluation; if so, the comparative theory in the text would not hold universally. However, given the nature of the exceptions, this fact would be of limited sociological (though of great personal) interest. Also, those who do not evaluate themselves comparatively will not need equalization to take place along certain dimensions as a support for their self-esteem.

envy and unhappiness others feel in knowing of his situation. Such a policy is comparable to one that forbids some act (for example, racially mixed couples walking holding hands) because the mere knowledge that it is being done makes others unhappy. The *same kind* of externality is involved. The most promising ways for a society to avoid widespread differences in self-esteem would be to have no common weighting of dimensions; instead it would have a diversity of different lists of dimensions and of weightings. This would enhance each person's chance of finding dimensions that *some* others also think important, along which he does reasonably well, and so to make a nonidiosyncratic favorable estimate of himself. Such a fragmentation of a common social weighting is not to be achieved by some centralized effort to remove certain dimensions as important. The more central and widely supported the effort, the more contributions to *it* will come to the fore as the commonly agreed upon dimension on which will be based people's self-esteem.

MEANINGFUL WORK

Often it is claimed that being subordinate in a work scheme adversely affects self-esteem in accordance with a social-psychological law or fundamental generalization such as the following: A long period of being frequently ordered about and under the authority of others, unselected by you, lowers your self-esteem and makes you feel inferior; whereas this is avoided if you play some role in democratically selecting these authorities and in a constant process of advising them, voting on their decisions, and so on.

But members of a symphony orchestra constantly are ordered about by their conductor (often capriciously and arbitrarily and with temper flareups) and are not consulted about the overall interpretation of their works. Yet they retain high self-esteem and do not feel that they are inferior beings. Draftees in armies are constantly ordered about, told how to dress, what to keep in their lockers, and so on, yet they do not come to feel they are inferior beings. Socialist organizers in factories received the same orders and were subject to the same authority as others, yet they did not lose their self-esteem. Persons on the way up organizational ladders spend much time taking orders without coming to feel inferior. In view of the many exceptions to the generalization that "order following in a subordinate position produces low self-esteem" we must consider the possibility that subordinates with low self-esteem begin that way or are forced by their position to face the facts of their existence and to consider upon what their estimate of their own worth and value as a unique person is based, with no easy answers forthcoming. They will be especially hard pressed for an answer if they believe that others who give them orders have a right to do so that can be based only upon some *personal* superiority. On an entitlement theory, of course, this need not be so. People may be entitled to decide about certain resources, the terms on which others may use them, and so on, through no sterling qualities of their own; such entitlements may have been transferred to them. Perhaps readers concerned about differential self-esteem will help to make the entitlement theory better known, and thereby undercut one ground for lesser self-esteem. This will not, of course, remove all such grounds. Sometimes a person's entitlements clearly *will* stem from his own attributes and previous activities, and in these cases comparisons will be unpleasant to face.

The issue of meaningful and satisfying work is often merged with discussions of self-esteem. Meaningful and satisfying work is said to include: (1) an opportunity to exercise one's talents and capacities, to face challenges and situations that require independent initiative and self-direction (and which therefore is not boring and repetitive work); (2) in an activity thought to be of worth by the individual involved; (3) in which he understands the role his activity plays in the achievement of some overall goal; and (4) such that sometimes, in deciding upon his activity, he has to take into account something about the larger process in which he acts. Such an individual, it is said, can take pride in what he's doing and in doing it well; he can feel that he is a person of worth, making a contribution of value. Further, it is said that apart from the intrinsic desirability of such kinds of work and productivity, performing other sorts of work deadens individuals and leads them to be less fulfilled persons in *all* areas of their lives.

Normative sociology, the study of what the causes of problems *ought to be,* greatly fascinates all of us. If X is bad, and Y which also is bad can be tied to X via a plausible story, it is very hard to resist the conclusion that one causes the other. We *want* one bad thing to be caused by another. If people *ought* to do meaningful work, if that's what we want people to be like,[9] and if via some story we can tie the absence of such work (which is bad) to another bad thing (lack of initiative generally, passive leisure activities, and so on), then we happily *leap* to the conclusion that the second evil is *caused by* the first. These other bad things, of course, may exist *for other reasons;* and indeed, given selective entry into certain sorts of jobs, the correlation may be due to the fact that those predisposed to show low independent activity are just those who are most willing to take and remain with certain jobs involving little opportunity for independent flowering.

It often has been noted that fragmentation of tasks, rote activity, and detailed specification of activity which leaves little room for the exercise of independent initiative are not problems special to capitalist modes of production; it seems to go with industrial society. How does and could capitalism respond to workers' desires for meaningful work? If the productivity of the workers in a factory *rises* when the work tasks are segmented so as to be more meaningful, then individual owners pursuing profits so will reorganize the productive process. If the productivity of workers *remains the same* under such meaningful division of labor, then in the process of competing for laborers firms will alter their internal work organization.

So the only interesting case to consider is that in which dividing a firm's work tasks into meaningful segments, rotation of labor, and so forth, is *less efficient (as judged by market criteria)*, than the less meaningful division of labor. This lessened efficiency can be borne in three ways (or in combinations of them). First, the workers in the factories themselves might desire meaningful work. It has all of the virtues its theorists ascribe to it, the workers realize this, and they are willing to give up something (some wages) in order to work at meaningfully segmented jobs. They work for lower wages, but they view their total work package (lower wages plus the satisfactions of meaningful work) as more desirable than less meaningful work at higher wages. They make a trade-off of some wages for some increase in the meaningfulness of their work, increased self-esteem, and so forth. Many persons do very similar things: They do not choose their occupations solely by the discounted value of expected future monetary earnings. They consider social relationships, opportunities for individual development, interestingness, job security, the fatiguing quality of the work, the amount of free time, and so on. (Many college teachers could earn more money working in industry. Secretaries in universities forgo the higher pay of industry for a less stressful and, in their view, more interesting environment. Many other examples could be cited.) Not everyone wants the same things, or wants them as strongly. They choose among their employment activities on the basis of the overall package of benefits it gives them. Similarly, workers to whom a different organization of work mattered might choose to forgo some wages in order to get it; and no doubt those to whom it *most* matters actually do so in choosing among the jobs available to them. The rhythm of a farmer's life differs from that of assembly-line workers (who total less than 5 percent of U.S. manual workers), whose income and life differ from that of a store clerk, and so on.

But suppose that a more meaningful job isn't worth that much to a worker; he will not take lower wages in order to get it. (*When* in his life isn't it worth this? If at the beginning, then his scale of values is not *itself* the product of doing nonmeaningful work, and we should be wary of attributing his later character to his work experiences.)

Mightn't someone *else* bear the monetary costs of the lessened efficiency? They might do so because they believe the cause is important, even though not important enough to the individual worker himself so that *he* will choose to bear the *monetary* costs. So, secondly, perhaps individual consumers will bear the costs by *paying more* for what they buy. A group of us may band together into a buyers cooperative and buy only from factories whose work tasks are segmented meaningfully; or individually we may decide to do this. How much we do so will depend on how much the support of such activities is worth to *us* as compared to buying more of other goods, or to buying the items less expensively from factories whose work tasks are not segmented meaningfully and using the saved money to support other worthy causes—for example, medical research or aid to struggling artists or to war victims in other countries.

But what if it's not worth enough either to individual workers or to individual consumers (including the members of social democratic movements)? What alternative remains? The third possibility is that workers might be forbidden to work in factories whose work tasks are not meaningfully segmented, or consumers might be forbidden to purchase the products of such factories.

(Each prohibition would enact the other, *de facto,* in the absence of illegal markets.) Or the money to float the meaningfully segmented enterprise might be taken out of entrepreneurial profits. The last raises a large subject which I must leave for another occasion. But notice that there still would be the problem of how work tasks are to be organized even if there were no private owners and all firms were owned by their workers. In organizing its production, some firms would decide to divide jointly the increased monetary profits. Other firms either would have to do likewise, or would have to set lower yearly income per worker, or would have to persuade some consumers to pay higher prices for their products. Perhaps a socialist government, in such a setup, *would* forbid nonmeaningful work; but apart from the question of how it would phrase the legislation, on what grounds could it *impose* its views on all those workers who would choose to achieve other ends?

WORKERS' CONTROL

Firms in a capitalist system might provide meaningful jobs to those who wanted them enough. Could it similarly supply internally democratic authority structures? To some extent, certainly. But if the demand for democratic decisionmaking extends to powers like ownership, then it cannot. Of course, as an alternative, persons may form their own democratically-run *cooperative* firms. It is open to any wealthy radical or group of workers to buy an existing factory or establish a new one, and to institute their favorite microindustrial scheme; for example, worker-controlled, democratically-run firms. The factory then could sell its products directly into the market. Here we have possibilities similar to those we canvassed earlier. It may be that the internal procedures in such a factory will not lessen efficiency as judged by market criteria. For even though fewer hours are spent at work (some hours go into the activities of the process of democratic decisionmaking), in those hours the workers may work so efficiently and industriously for their own factory on projects they had a voice in shaping that they are superior, by market standards, to their more orthodox competitors (cf. the views of Louis Blanc). In which case there should be little difficulty in establishing financially successful factories of this sort. I here ignore familiar difficulties about how a system of such workers' control is to operate. If decisions are made by the vote of workers in the factory, this will lead to underinvestment in projects whose returns will come much later when many of the presently voting workers won't benefit enough to outweigh withholding money from current distribution, either because they no longer work there and get nothing or because they then will have only a few years left. This underinvestment (and consequent worsening of the position of future workers) can be avoided if each worker *owns* a share in the factory which he can sell or bequeath, for then future expectations of earnings will raise the current value of his ownership share. (But then. . . .) If each new worker acquires a right to an equal percentage of the annual net profit (or an equal ownership share), this will affect the group's decisions to bring in new workers. Current workers, and therefore the factory, will have a strong incentive to choose to maximize *average* profits (profits per worker) rather than *total* profits, thereby employing fewer persons than a factory that employed everyone who profitably could be employed.* How will extra capital for expansion be acquired? Will there be differences of income within factories? (How will the differences be determined?) And so on. Since a system of syndicalist factories would involve great inequalities of income among workers in different factories (with different amounts of capital per worker and different profitability), it is difficult to see why people who favor certain egalitarian end-state patterns think this a suitable realization of their vision.

If the worker-controlled factory so organized will be less efficient by market criteria, so that it will not be able to sell articles as inexpensively as a factory geared mainly to inexpensive production with other values playing a secondary role or being absent altogether, this difficulty, as before, is handled easily in one of two ways (or a combination of them). First, the worker-controlled factory can pay each worker less; that is, through whatever joint decisionmaking apparatus they use, they can pay themselves less than those employed in the more orthodox factories receive, thus are not so altruistic. They act in their personal and not their class interests. On the other hand, how sufficient resources could be gathered in a state system to begin a private enterprise, supposing there were people willing to be laborers and consumers, is a more troublesome question.

Even if it is more difficult to obtain external investment than the previous paragraph makes out, union treasuries now contain sufficient funds to capitalize many such worker-controlled firms which can repay the money with interest, as many private owners do with bank loans, and even with loans from labor unions. Why is it that some unions or groups of workers don't start *their own* business? What an *easy* way to give workers access to the means of production: buy machinery and rent space, and so forth, just as a private entrepreneur does. It is illuminating to consider why unions don't start new businesses, and why workers don't pool their resources to do so.

MARXIAN EXPLOITATION

This question is of importance for what remains of Marxist economic theory. With the crumbling of the labor theory of value, the underpinning of its particular theory of exploitation dissolves. And the charm and simplicity of this theory's *definition* of exploitation is lost when it is realized that according to the definition there will be exploitation in *any* society in which investment takes place for a greater future product (perhaps because of population growth); and in *any* society in which those unable to work, or to work productively, are *subsidized* by the labor of others. But at bottom, Marxist theory

---

* Since workers acting in their own individual interests will thwart the efficient operation of worker-controlled factories, perhaps broadly based revolutionary movements should try to staff such factories with their "unselfish" members.

explains the phenomenon of exploitation by reference to the workers not having access to the means of production. The workers have to sell their labor (labor power) to the capitalists, for they must use the means of production to produce, and cannot produce alone. A worker, or groups of them, cannot hire means of production and wait to sell the product some months later; they lack the cash reserves to obtain access to machinery or to wait until later when revenue will be received from the future sale of the product now being worked on. For workers must eat in the meantime.* Hence (the story goes) the worker is forced to deal with the capitalist. (And the reserve army of unemployed labor makes unnecessary the capitalists' competing for workers and bidding up the price of labor.)

Note that once the rest of the theory, properly, is dropped, and it is this crucial fact of nonaccess to the means of production that underlies exploitation, it *follows* that in a society in which the workers are *not* forced to deal with the capitalist, exploitation of laborers will be absent. (We pass over the question of whether workers are forced to deal with some other, less decentralized group.) So, if there is a sector of publicly owned and controlled (what you will) means of production that is expandable so that all who wish to may work in it, then this is sufficient to eliminate the exploitation of laborers. And in particular, if in addition to this public sector there is a sector of privately owned means of production that employs wage laborers who *choose* to work in this sector, then these workers are *not* being exploited. (Perhaps they choose to work there, despite attempts to convince them to do otherwise, because they get higher wages or returns in this sector.) For they are not forced to deal with the private owners of means of production.

Let us linger for a moment upon this case. Suppose that the private sector were to expand, and the public sector became weaker and weaker. More and more workers, let us suppose, choose to work in the private sector. Wages in the private sector are greater than in the public sector, and are rising continually. Now imagine that after a period of time this weak public sector becomes completely insignificant; perhaps it disappears altogether. Will there be any concomitant change in the private sector? (Since the public sector was already small, by hypothesis, the new workers who come to the private sector will not affect wages much.) The theory of exploitation seems committed to saying that there would be some important change; which statement is *very* implausible. (There's no good theoretical argument for it.) If there would not be a change in the level or the upward movement of wages in the private sector, are workers in the private sector, heretofore unexploited, now being exploited? Though they don't even know that the public sector is gone, having paid scant attention to it, are they now *forced* to work in the private sector and to go to the private capitalist for work, and hence are they *ipso facto exploited?* So the theory would seem to be committed to maintaining.

---

* Where did the means of production come from? Who earlier forwent current consumption then in order to gain or produce them? Who now forgoes current consumption in paying wages and factor prices and thus gets returns only after the finished product is sold? Whose entrepreneurial alertness operated throughout?

Whatever may have been the truth of the nonaccess view at one time, *in our society* large sections of the working force now have cash reserves in personal property, and there are also large cash reserves in union pension funds. These workers can wait, and they *can* invest. This raises the question of why this money isn't used to establish worker-controlled factories. Why haven't radicals and social democrats urged this?

The workers may lack the entrepreneurial ability to identify promising opportunities for profitable activity, and to organize firms to respond to these opportunities. In this case, the workers can try to *hire* entrepreneurs and managers to start a firm for them and then turn the authority functions over to the workers (who are the owners) after one year. (Though, as Kirzner emphasizes, entrepreneurial alertness would also be needed in deciding whom to hire.) Different groups of workers would compete for entrepreneurial talent, bidding up the price of such services, while entrepreneurs with capital attempted to hire workers under traditional ownership arrangements. Let us ignore the question of what the equilibrium in this market would look like to ask why groups of workers aren't doing this now.

It's *risky* starting a new firm. One can't identify easily new entrepreneurial talent, and much depends on estimates of future demand and of availability of resources, on unforeseen obstacles, on chance, and so forth. Specialized investment institutions and sources of venture capital develop to run just these risks. Some persons don't want to run these risks of investing or backing new ventures, or starting ventures themselves. Capitalist society allows the separation of the bearing of these risks from other activities. The workers in the Edsel branch of the Ford Motor Company did not bear the risks of the venture, and when it lost money they did not pay back a portion of their salary. In a socialist society, either one *must* share in the risks of the enterprise one works in, or everybody shares in the risks of the investment decisions of the central investment managers. There is no way to *divest* oneself of these risks or to choose to carry some such risks but not others (acquiring specialized knowledge in some areas), as one can do in a capitalist society.

Often people who do not wish to bear risks feel entitled to rewards from those who do and win; yet these same people do not feel obligated to help out by sharing the losses of those who bear risks and lose. For example, croupiers at gambling casinos expect to be well-tipped by big winners, but they do not expect to be asked to help bear some of the losses of the losers. The case for such asymmetrical sharing is even weaker for businesses where success is not a random matter. Why do some feel they may stand back to see whose ventures turn out well (by *hindsight* determine who has survived the risks and run profitably) and then claim a share of the success; though they do not feel they must bear the losses if things turn out poorly, or feel that if they wish to share in the profits or the control of the enterprise, they should invest and run the risks also?

To compare how Marxist theory treats such risks, we must take a brief excursion through the theory. Marx's theory is one form of the productive resources theory of value. Such a theory holds that the value V of a thing X

equals the sum total of society's productive resources embodied in X. Put in a more useful form, the ratio of the value of two things $V(X)/V(Y)$ is equal to the ratio of the amount of productive resources embodied in them, M (resources in X)/M (resources in Y), where M is a measure of the amount. Such a theory requires a measure M whose values are determined independently of the V ratios to be explained. If we conjoin to the productive resources theory of value, the labor theory of productive resources, which holds that labor is the only productive resource, we obtain the labor theory of value. Many of the objections which have been directed toward the labor theory of value apply to any productive resources theory.

An alternative to the productive resources theory of value might say that the *value* of productive resources is determined by the value of the final products that arise from them (can be made from them), where the value of the final product is determined in some way *other* than by the value of the resources used in it. If one machine can be used to make X (and nothing else) and another can be used to make Y, and each uses the same raw materials in the same amounts to make a unit of its product, and X is more valuable than Y, then the first machine is more valuable than the second, even if each machine contains the same raw materials and took the same amount of time to make. The first machine, having a more valuable final product, will command a higher price than the second. This may give rise to the illusion that its products are more valuable because *it* is more valuable. But this gets things backwards. It is more valuable because its products are.

But the productive resources theory of value doesn't talk about the value of the productive resources, only about their amounts. If there were only one factor of production, and it were homogeneous, the productive resources theory at least could be noncircularly stated. But with more than one factor, *or one factor of different kinds,* there is a problem in setting up the measure M to get the theory stated in a noncircular way. For it must be determined how much of one productive factor is to count as equivalent to a given amount of another. *One* procedure would be to set up the measure by reference to the *values* of the final products, solving the ratio equations. But this procedure would define the measure on the basis of information about final values, and so could not be used to *explain* final values on the basis of information about the amounts of inputs.* An *alternative* procedure would be to find some *common* thing that can be produced by X, and Y, in different quantities, and to use the ratio of the *quantities* of final product to determine the *quantities* of input. This avoids the circularity of looking at final *values* first; one begins by looking at final *quantities* of something, and then uses this information to determine quantities of input (to define the measure M). But even if there is a common product, it may not be what the different factors are best suited for making; and so using

* However if given the values of *some* final products (with great latitude about which ones would serve) the ratio equations could be used to specify the measure M and that could be used to yield the values for the other final products, then the theory would have some content.

it to compare them may give a misleading ratio. One has to compare the different factors at their individual best functions. Also, if two different *things* can be made by each resource, and the ratios of the amounts *differ,* there is the problem of which ratio is to be picked to provide the constant of proportionality between the resources.

We can illustrate these difficulties by considering Paul Sweezy's exposition of the concept of simple, undifferentiated labor time.[10] Sweezy considers how skilled labor and unskilled labor are to be equated and agrees that it would be *circular* to do so on the basis of the value of the final product, since that's what's to be explained. Sweezy then says that skill depends on two things: training and natural differences. Sweezy equates training with the number of *hours* spent in training, without looking to the skill of the teacher, even as crudely measured by how many hours the teacher spent in training (and how many hours *his* teacher did?). Sweezy suggests getting at natural differences by having two persons make the same thing, and seeing how the quantities differ, thus finding the ratio to equate them. But if skilled labor of some sort is not best viewed as a faster way of producing the same product that unskilled labor produces, but rather as a way of producing a *better* product, then this method of defining the measure M won't work. (In comparing Rembrandt's skill with mine, the crucial fact is not that he paints pictures *faster* than I do.) It would be tedious to rehearse the standard counterexamples to the labor theory of value: found natural objects (valued above the labor necessary to get them); rare goods (letters from Napoleon) that cannot be reproduced in unlimited quantities; differences in value between identical objects at different places; ferences skilled labor makes; changes caused by fluctuations in supply and demand; aged objects whose producing requires much time to pass (old wines), and so on.[11]

The issues thus far mentioned concern the nature of simple undifferentiated labor time, which is to provide the *unit* against which all else is to be measured. We now must introduce an additional complication. For Marxist theory does *not* hold that the value of an object is proportional to the number of simple undifferentiated labor hours that went into its production; rather, the theory holds that the value of an object is proportional to the number of simple undifferentiated *socially necessary* labor hours that went into its production.* Why the additional requirement that the labor hours be socially necessary? Let us proceed slowly.

---

* "The labour time socially necessary is that required to produce an article under the normal conditions of production, and with the average degree of skill and intensity of labor prevalent at the time in a given society." Karl Marx, *Capital,* vol. I (New York: Modern Library, n.d.), p. 46. Note that we also want to explain why normal conditions of production are as they are, and why a particular skill and intensity of labor is used on *that* particular product. For it is not the average degree of skill prevalent in a society that is relevant. Most persons may be more skilled at making the product yet might have something even more important to do, leaving only those of less than average skill at work on it. What is relevant would have to be the skill of those who actually *work at making* the product. One wants a theory also to explain what determines which persons of varying skills work at making a particular product. I mention these questions, of course, because they *can* be answered by an alternative theory.

The requirement that an object have utility is a necessary component of the labor theory of value, if it is to avoid certain objections. Suppose a person works on something absolutely useless that no one wants. For example, he spends hours efficiently making a big knot; no one else can do it more quickly. Will this object be that many hours valuable? A theory should not have this consequence. Marx avoids it as follows: "Nothing can have value without being an object of utility. If a thing is useless so is the labor contained in it; the labor does not count as labor, and therefore creates no value."[12] Isn't this an *ad hoc* restriction? Given the rest of the theory, who does it apply? Why doesn't *all* efficiently done labor create value? If one has to bring in the fact that it's of use to people and *actually wanted* (suppose it were of use, but no one wanted it), then perhaps by looking only at wants, *which have to be brought in anyway*, one can get a *complete* theory of value.

Even with the *ad hoc* constraint that the object must be of *some* use, there remain problems. For, suppose someone works for 563 hours on something of some very *slight* utility (and there is no way to make it more efficiently). This satisfies the necessary condition for value that the object have *some* utility. Is its value now determined by the *amount* of labor, yielding the consequence that it is incredibly valuable? No. "For the labor spent on them (commodities) counts effectively only insofar as it is spent in a form that is useful to others."[13] Marx goes on to say: "Whether that labor is useful for others, and its product consequently capable of satisfying the wants of others, can be proved only by the act of exchange." If we interpret Marx as saying, *not* that utility is a necessary condition and that (once satisfied) the amount of labor determines value, but rather that the *degree* of utility will determine how much (useful) labor has been expended on the object, then we have a theory very different from a labor theory of value.

We can approach this issue from another direction. Suppose that useful things are produced as efficiently as they can be, but that too many of them are produced to sell at a certain price. The price that clears the market is lower than the apparent labor values of the objects; a greater number of efficient hours went into producing them than people are willing to pay for (at a certain price per hour). Does this show that the number of average hours devoted to making an object of significant utility doesn't determine its value? Marx's reply is that if there is such overproduction so that the market doesn't clear at a particular price, then the labor was inefficiently used (less of the thing should have been made), even though the labor itself wasn't inefficient. Hence not all of those labor hours constituted socially necessary labor time. The object does not have a value less than the number of socially necessary labor hours expended upon it, for there were fewer socially necessary labor hours expended upon it than meet the eye.

Suppose that every piece of linen in the market contains no more labor-time than is socially necessary. In spite of this, all the pieces taken as a whole may have had superfluous labor-time spent upon them. If the market cannot stomach the whole quantity at the normal price of 2 shillings a yard, this proves that too great a portion of the total labor of the community has been expended in the form of weaving. The effect is the same as if each weaver had expended more labor-time upon his particular product than is socially necessary.[14]

Thus Marx holds that this labor isn't all socially necessary. *What* is socially necessary, and how much of it is, will be determined by what happens on the market!![15] There is no longer any labor theory of value; the central notion of socially necessary labor time is *itself defined* in terms of the processes and exchange ratios of a competitive market![16]

We have returned to our earlier topic, the risks of investment and production, which we see transforms the labor theory of value into one defined in terms of the results of competitive markets. Consider now a system of payment in accordance with simple, undifferentiated, socially necessary labor hours worked. Under this system, the risks associated with a process of production are borne by each worker participating in the process. However many hours he works at whatever degree of efficiency, he will not know how many socially necessary labor hours he has worked until it is seen how many people are willing to buy the products at what price. A system of payment in accordance with the number of socially necessary labor hours worked therefore would pay some hard-working laborers almost not at all (those who worked for hula hoop manufacturers after the fad had passed, or those who worked in the Edsel plant of the Ford Motor Company), and would pay others very little. (Given the great and nonaccidental incompetence of the investment and production decisions in a socialist society, it would be very surprising if the rulers of such a society dared to pay workers explicitly in accordance with the number of "socially necessary" labor hours they work!) Such a system would compel each individual to attempt to predict the future market for the product he works on; this would be quite inefficient and would induce those who are dubious about the future success of a product to forgo a job they can do well, even though others are confident enough of its success to risk much on it. Clearly there are advantages to a system which allows persons to shift risks they themselves do not wish to bear, and allows them to be paid a fixed amount, whatever the outcome of the risky processes.* There are great advantages to allowing opportunities for such specialization in risk-bearing; these opportunities lead to the typical gamut of capitalist institutions.

Marx attempts to answer the following Kantian-type question: how are profits possible?[17] How can there be profits if everything gets its full value, if

---

* Such risks could not be insured against for every project. There will be different estimates of these risks; and once having insured against them there will be less incentive to act fully to bring about the favorable alternative. So an insurer would have to watch over or monitor one's activities to avoid what is termed the "moral hazard." See Kenneth Arrow, *Essays in the Theory of Risk-Bearing* (Chicago: Markham, 1971.) Alchian and Demsetz, *American Economic Review* (1972), pp. 777–795, discuss monitoring activities; they arrive at the subject through considering problems about estimating marginal product in joint activities through monitoring *input,* rather than through considerations about risk and insurance.

no *cheating* goes on? The answer for Marx lies in the unique character of labor power; *its* value is the cost of producing it (the labor that goes into it), yet it itself is capable of producing more value than it has. (This is true of machines as well.) Putting a certain amount of labor L into making a human organism produces something capable of expending an amount of labor *greater* than L. Because individuals lack the resources to wait for the return from the sale of the products of their labor (see above), they cannot gather these benefits of their own capacities and are forced to deal with the capitalists. In view of the difficulties with Marxist economic theory, one would expect Marxists to study carefully alternative theories of the existence of profit, including those formulated by "bourgeois" economists. Though I have concentrated here on issues about risk and uncertainty, I should also mention innovation (Schumpeter) and, very importantly, the alertness to and search for new opportunities for arbitrage (broadly conceived) which others have not yet noticed.[18] An alternative explanatory theory, if adequate, presumably would remove much of the scientific motivation underlying Marxist economic theory; one might be left with the view that Marxian exploitation is the exploitation of people's lack of understanding of economics.

VOLUNTARY EXCHANGE

Some readers will object to my speaking frequently of voluntary exchanges on the grounds that some actions (for example, workers accepting a wage position) are not really voluntary because one party faces severely limited options, with all the others being much worse than the one he chooses. Whether a person's actions are voluntary depends on what it is that limits his alternatives. If facts of nature do so, the actions are voluntary. (I may voluntarily walk to someplace I would prefer to fly to unaided.) Other people's actions place limits on one's available opportunities. Whether this makes one's resulting action non-voluntary depends upon whether these others had the right to act as they did.

Consider the following example. Suppose there are twenty-six women and twenty-six men each wanting to be married. For each sex, all of that sex agree on the same ranking of the twenty-six members of the opposite sex in terms of desirability as marriage partners: call them A to Z and A' to Z' respectively in decreasing preferential order. A and A' voluntarily choose to get married, each preferring the other to any other partner. B would most prefer to marry A', and B' would most prefer to marry A, but by their choices A and A' have removed these options. When B and B' marry, their choices are not made non-voluntary merely by the fact that there is something else they each would rather do. This other most preferred option requires the cooperation of others who have chosen, as is their right, not to cooperate. B and B' chose among fewer options than did A and A'. This contraction of the range of options continues down the line until we come to Z and Z', who each face a choice between marrying the other or remaining unmarried. Each prefers any one of the twenty-five other partners who by their choices have removed themselves from consideration by Z and Z'. Z and Z' voluntarily choose to marry each other. The fact that their only other alternative is (in their view) much worse, and the fact that others chose to exercise their rights in certain ways, thereby shaping the external environment of options in which Z and Z' choose, does not mean they did not marry voluntarily.

Similar considerations apply to market exchanges between workers and owners of capital. Z is faced with working or starving; the choices and actions of all other persons do not add up to providing Z with some other option. (He may have various options about what job to take.) Does Z choose to work voluntarily? (Does someone on a desert island who must work to survive?) Z does choose voluntarily if the other individuals A through Y each acted voluntarily and within their rights. We then have to ask the question about the others. We ask it up the line until we reach A, or A and B, who chose to act in certain ways thereby shaping the external choice environment in which C chooses. We move back down the line with A through C's voluntary choice affecting D's choice environment, and A through D's choices affecting E's choice environment, and so on back down to Z. A person's choice among differing degrees of unpalatable alternatives is not rendered nonvoluntary by the fact that others voluntarily chose and acted within their rights in a way that did not provide him with a more palatable alternative.

We should note an interesting feature of the structure of rights to engage in relationships with others, including voluntary exchanges.* The right to engage in a certain relationship is not a right to engage in it with anyone, or even with anyone who wants to or would choose to, but rather it is a right to do it with anyone who has the right to engage in it (with someone who has the right to engage in it . . .). Rights to engage in relationships or transactions have hooks on them, which must attach to the corresponding hook of another's right that comes out to meet theirs. My right of free speech is not violated by a prisoner's being kept in solitary confinement so that he cannot hear me, and my right to hear information is not violated if this prisoner is prevented from communicating with me. The rights of members of the press are not violated if Edward Everett Hale's "man without a country" is not permitted to read some of their writings, nor are the rights of readers violated if Josef Goebbels is executed and thereby prevented from providing them with additional reading material. In each case, the right is a right to a relationship with someone else who *also* has the right to be the other party in such a relationship. Adults normally will have the right to such a relationship with any other consenting adult who has this right, but the right *may* be forfeited in punishment for wrongful acts. This complication of hooks on rights will *not* be relevant to any cases we discuss. But it does have implications; for example it complicates an immediate condemnation of the disruption of speakers in a

---

* Since I am unsure of this point, I put this paragraph forward very tentatively, as an interesting conjecture.

public place, solely on the grounds that this disruption violates the rights of other people to *hear* whatever opinions they choose to listen to. If rights to engage in relationships go out only half-way, these others do have a right to hear whatever opinions they please, but only from persons who have a right to communicate them. Hearers' rights are not violated *if* the speaker has no hook to reach out to join up with theirs. (The speaker can lack a hooked right only because of something he has done, not because of the *content* of what he is about to say.) My reflections here are not intended to justify disruption, merely to warn against the too simple grounds for condemnation which I myself have been prone to use.

NOTES

[1] For a useful consideration of various arguments for equality which are not at the most fundamental level, see Walter J. Blum and Harry Kalven, Jr., *The Uneasy Case for Progressive Taxation,* 2nd ed. (Chicago: University of Chicago Press, 1963).

[2] Bernard Williams, "The Idea of Equality," in *Philosophy, Politics, and Society,* 2nd ser., ed. Peter Laslett and W. G. Runciman (Oxford: Blackwell, 1962), pp. 110–131; reprinted in Joel Feinberg, ed., *Moral Concepts* (New York: Oxford University Press, 1969).

[3] Williams, "The Idea of Equality," pp. 121–122.

[4] Perhaps we should understand Rawls' focus on social cooperation as based upon this triadic notion of one person, by dealing with a second, blocking a third person from dealing with the second.

[5] See Kurt Vonnegut's story "Harrison Bergeron" in his collection *Welcome to the Monkey House* (New York: Dell, 1970).

[6] See on this point, Judith Jarvis Thomson, "A Defense of Abortion," *Philosophy & Public Affairs,* 1, no. 1 (Fall 1971), 55–56.

[7] "Men are, in great measure, what they feel themselves to be, and they think of themselves as they are thought of by their fellows. The advance in individual self-respect and in social amenity caused by the softening of the more barbarous inequalities of the past is a contribution to civilization as genuine as the improvement in material conditions." R. H. Tawney, *Equality* (New York: Barnes & Noble, 1964), p. 171. The slightly different connection I shall trace between equality and self-esteem does not go in the first instance through other persons' views.

[8] Compare L. P. Hartley's novel, *Facial Justice;* and Blum and Kalven, *The Uneasy Case for Progressive Taxation,* p. 74: "Every experience seems to confirm the dismal hypothesis that envy will find other, and possibly less attractive, places in which to take root." See also Helmut Schoeck, *Envy,* trans. M. Glenny and B. Ross (New York: Harcourt, Brace, Jovanovich, 1972).

[9] Might some thrive on no work at all, others on repetitive work that does not demand constant attention and leaves many opportunities for daydreaming?

[10] *The Theory of Capitalist Development* (New York: Monthly Review Press, 1956). See also R. L. Meek, *Studies in the Labour Theory of Value* (London: Lawrence & Wishart, 1958), pp. 168–173.

[11] See Eugene Von Böhm-Bawerk, *Capital and Interest,* vol. I (South Holland, Ill.: Libertarian Press, 1959), chap. 12; and his *Karl Marx and the Close of His System* (Clifton, N.J.: Augustus M. Kelley, 1949).

[12] *Capital,* Part I, Chapter I, Section I, page 48.

[13] Marx, *Capital,* Vol. I, Chapter 2, pp. 97–98.

[14] Marx, *Capital,* p. 120. Why "stomach"?

[15] Compare Ernest Mandel, *Marxist Economic Theory,* vol. I (New York: Monthly Review Press, 1969), p. 161. "It is precisely through competition that it is discovered whether the amount of labor embodied in a commodity constitutes a *socially necessary* amount *or not....* When the supply of a certain commodity exceeds the demand for it, that means that more human labor has been spent altogether on producing this commodity than was socially necessary at the given period.... When, however, supply is less than demand, that means that less human labor has been expended on producing the commodity in question than was socially necessary."

[16] Compare the discussion of this issue in Meek, *Studies in the Labour Theory of Value,* pp. 178–179.

[17] See the detailed discussion of his theory in Marc Blaug, *Economic Theory in Retrospect* (Homewood, Ill.: Irwin, 1962), pp. 207–271.

[18] See Israel Kirzner, *Competition and Entrepreneurship* (Chicago: University of Chicago Press, 1973).

David Schweickart

CAPITALISM, CONTRIBUTION, AND SACRIFICE

Do capitalists earn their wealth? Do they forego value to obtain value—do they make contributions for which their wealth is just compensation? These and related questions concern David Schweickart, an Associate Professor of Philosophy at Loyola University, Chicago, Illinois, who has written extensively on matters of social and political philosophy. We are exploring the views which give communism and capitalism their philosophical and moral attraction. Schweickart contests one of the most widely held beliefs supporting capitalism. He argues that the picture of the capitalist as a dedicated servant of the public interest is false. To make his point, he dissects the technical argument invoking the marginal productivity of capital and the popular arguments appealing to the entrepreneurial activity of the capitalist and the sacrifice of the saver.

It has often been alleged that the distribution of wealth under capitalism accords substantially with the canon of productive contribution. The American economist John Bates Clark (1847–1938) was an early exponent of this view. The Marxian charge that capitalism is based on exploitation is false, he writes, for it can be shown that "the natural effect of competition is ... to give to each producer the amount of wealth he specifically brings into existence."[1]

Political economists and social philosophers of the libertarian tradition tend to agree. The fundamental question, says Friedrick von Hayek, is "whether it is desirable that people should enjoy advantages in proportion to the benefits which their fellows derive from their activity, or whether the distribution of advantages should be based on other men's views of their merit." The first alternative, he argues, is the foundation of a "free" (capitalist) society.[2] Nozick takes exception to Hayek, citing "inheritance, gifts for arbitrary reasons, and charity" as countervailing considerations, but he concurs that "distribution according to benefit to others *is* a major patterned strand in a free capitalist society."[3]

In this paper we will demonstrate that capitalist distribution, even in an ideal world free of Nozickean exceptions (gifts, etc.) and those of monopoly and related forms of imperfect competition, cannot be justified by the ethical canon of productive contribution. Specifically, we will argue that *property* income, i.e., income derived from the ownership of productive assets, cannot be legitimized by the canon that "justice consists in the treatment of people according to their actual contribution to the group."[4] We do not dispute the canon itself (though we recognize that it is problematic), but we deny that a defense of capitalism can be built upon it.

Reprinted, with permission, from *The Philosophical Forum*. First published in *The Philosophical Forum*, Volume VII, number 3–4, Spring/Summer 1976.

Any defense of capitalism which appeals to "productive contribution" must provide a definition of contribution that is subject to at least three constraints: (1) it must be formulated without reference to the market mechanism (to avoid circularity); (2) it must allow for quantitative interpersonal comparisons and (3) it must accord reasonably well with ordinary usage of the term in ethical contexts. The defense must then show (4): some plausible version of capitalism does distribute in accordance with this notion of contribution.

We will consider three such defenses of capitalism: the neoclassical one formulated by Clark, another derived from Joseph Schumpeter's conception of capitalism as a process of "creative destruction," and a third gleaned from Alfred Marshall's famous dictum, "capital is the product of labor and waiting." We will show that none of these arguments are valid. Clark's founders on condition (3); Schumpeter's cannot reconcile (2) and (4); Marshall's, to the extent that it appeals to contribution as its ethical foundation, reduces to Clark's. It can also be regarded as appealing to a different ethical canon, that of sacrifice. But this formulation, as we shall see, avoids one fatal criticism only by exposing itself to another. If our analysis is correct, it should be evident that no defense of capitalism which appeals to either traditional canon is likely to be sound. A defense may still be attempted on utilitarian, Rawlsian or neo-Lockean grounds, but care must be taken to avoid seriously misconstruing the nature of a capitalist's "contribution" or "sacrifice."

CAPITALIST CONTRIBUTION AS THE MARGINAL PRODUCT OF CAPITAL

Milton Friedman provides a succinct formulation of the principle of capitalist distribution: "to each according to what he or the instruments he owns produces."[5] Since it is characteristic of capitalism that those who own the means of production are generally not those who operate them, the claim that capitalism distributes according to contribution presupposes that one can quantitatively distinguish the contribution of the instrument from the contribution of the operator. This is what Paul Samuelson calls "the riddle of the sphinx"— how to allocate the joint total product among the factors of production (land, labor and capital). He credits Clark with discovering the answer.[6]

The modern, textbook version of Clark's solution begins with a definition of *production function* and then neatly invokes Euler's Theorem. A production function is a technical function specifying the maximum productive output for each and every quantity of relevant technical input, given a particular technology. Suppose, for example, that corn is the joint product of labor and land, each of which is homogeneous in quality.[7] The production function can be represented as $z = P(x,y)$ where z is the maximum number of bushels of corn that can be produced by x laborers working y acres of land. Now, the question is, what are the "distinct contributions" of labor and land when in fact neither operating alone can produce any corn at all?

The key to the solution is the notion of *marginal product*. The marginal product of a particular productive factor is defined to be the extra output resulting from the addition of *one extra unit* of that factor while all others are held constant. For example, the marginal product of labor, given ten laborers and five acres of land, is $P(11,5)-P(10,5)$. The marginal product of land in the same case is $P(10,6)-P(10,5)$. When the quantities involved are large, the marginal product of a factor is essentially the partial derivative of the production function with respect to that factor: i.e., $P(x+1,y)-P(x,y)$ is approximated by $\partial P/\partial x$, and $P(x,y+1)-P(x,y)$ by $\partial P/\partial y$.

Now enters Euler's Theorem: If $P(x,y)$ is a "well-behaved" function[8] then $P(x,y) = (\partial P/\partial x)x + (\partial P/\partial y)y$. Thus, if we define the *contribution* of each laborer to be $\partial P/\partial x$ and that of each acre of land to be $\partial P/\partial y$, the total contribution of labor $(\partial P/\partial x)x$, plus the total contribution of land, $(\partial P/\partial y)y$ comes out to be precisely equal to the total product. This yields a "natural" division of the total product into the contribution of labor and the contribution of land, computed from purely technical information, without reference to private property, capitalism, or the market.

Armed with this definition of contribution, the neoclassical economist can now ask whether or not capitalism (a specific, socio-economic arrangement) distributes the total product accordingly. The answer is: not always. Monopolistic practices distort distribution. However, in a state of "perfect competition" where uniform goods and services command uniform prices, and where no monopolistic collusion exists, the distribution resulting from each individual's efforts to maximize his own economic well-being will be precisely that proposed by Euler's theorem. In a society of n equally skilled laborers and m acres of equally fertile land, the wage rate (per worker) will be $\partial P/\partial x$ evaluated at (n,m)—i.e., the marginal product of the nth worker. The ground rent (per acre) will be $\partial P/\partial y$ evaluated at (n,m)—i.e., the marginal product of the mth acre of land.[9]

Does this establish that perfectly competitive capitalism distributes according to the canon of contribution? Is it true that each person receives in proportion to what he produces? Clark himself has no doubts:

If each productive factor is paid for according to the amount of its product, then each man gets what he himself produces. If he works, he gets what he creates by working; if he also provides capital, he gets what his capital produces, and if, further, he renders services by coordinating labor and capital, he gets the product that can be traced separately to that function. Only in one of these three ways can a man produce anything. If he receives all that he brings into existence through any of these three functions, he receives all that he creates at all.[10]

For Clark this conclusion has enormous ethical and social import:

The welfare of the laboring class depends on whether they get much or little; but their attitude toward other classes—and therefore the stability of society—depends chiefly on the question, whether the amount they get, be it large or small, is what they produce. If they create a small amount of wealth and get the whole of it, they may not seek to revolutionize society; but if it were to appear that they produce an ample amount and get only a part of it, many of them would become revolutionists and all would have the right to do so.[11]

In fact Clark has *not* shown that perfectly competitive capitalism distributes according to contribution, not if "contribution" is to be taken in the sense that it is in the ethical canon. All Clark has shown is that a partition of the total product can be defined independently of the market mechanism, and that capitalism distributes according to this partition. But it remains to be argued that this notion of "contribution" is equivalent to that employed by the ethical canon.

To decide this question, let us consider Clark's analysis more closely. Why is a laborer said to receive exactly what he has produced? The neoclassical answer: if he ceases to work, the total product will decline by precisely the value of his wage. Does it follow that should two laborers quit together the total product will decline by exactly the value of their wages? Not at all—the total product will decline by more than that. The wage *each* worker receives is the marginal product of the *last* laborer. But the neoclassical argument presumes a *declining* marginal productivity; i.e., the marginal product of the tenth laborer is less than that of the ninth, that of the ninth less than that of the eighth, etc.[12] These differences preclude the total contribution of labor from equalling the total product, and hence establish a basis for the "contribution" of land— and therefore of landowners.

What exactly is the "contribution" of the latter? Clark claims (in the passage quoted above) that a person can create wealth in three ways: by working, by providing capital and by coordinating labor and capital. The third function is, for Clark, that of the *entrepreneur* who borrows money from the capitalist and hires laborers.[13] This activity is problematic as a universal wealth-creating activity, for it is tied by definition to a specific socio-economic system. But we will not pursue this problem here because there is a deeper confusion in Clark's analysis. Let us simply construe the "coordination of labor and capital" as a managerial function, a human activity directly related to the production process. Thus understood, laboring and coordinating labor and capital are *productive activities* in a perfectly straightforward sense: should laborers or managers cease their mental and physical work, the production of wealth would likewise cease—the economy would grind to a halt.

Now consider Clark's third way of creating wealth—"providing capital." The neoclassical model is a *static* model. Contributions are calculated from a production function defined in terms of a *fixed* technology.[14] In what "activity" does "providing capital" consist? In this setting, it can only mean one thing—"allowing it to be used." The "contribution" of the capitalist is his act of granting permission, of letting laborers till his soil or otherwise utilize his means of production. But "granting permission" is a different sort of activity altogether from laboring or coordinating production. It is tied conceptually to a mode of economic organization which recognizes individual ownership of means of production, and hence cannot be regarded as a universal "productive activity." If laborers ceased to labor, production would cease in any society. But if owners ceased to grant permission, then production would cease *only if* their ownership claims were recognized and enforced. If they ceased to grant permission because their authority over the means of production was no longer acknowledged, then production need not be affected at all.

Granting permission, in short, is not a productive activity in the usual sense of the phrase. We do not say, "his permission to till the fields produced the corn." We might say, "his land produced it," but not "his ownership of the land produced it." Land is necessary to grow corn, but not land-owners.

Clark's analysis exhibits a serious confusion of three distinct concepts. In any economic organization, non-human material things enter into the production of objects that human beings desire. We might, I suppose, speak of these *productive resources* as "contributing" to the final product, though this is an odd way of talking, one clearly devoid of ethical import. We do not ordinarily say, having baked a cake, that the flour and the oven have contributed a share, much less that they deserve a slice.

Human labor, be it mental or physical, managerial or manual, also enters into the productive process, and may also be said to "contribute" to the final product. This productive activity does, in most contexts, have ethical import. If a human being expends his mental and physical energy in cooperating with other human beings to produce an object of material wealth, he is ordinarily thought to be entitled to a share of it. A *prima facie* claim, at least, is established.

Ownership of a productive factor is a third concept, a social category specifying a relationship between a human being (or a group of human beings), a set of material (and sometimes non-material) things, and other human beings. Ownership is a concept with considerable ethical import, but it is not a productive activity.

We observe that what Clark has done is conflate the first and third concepts, and then give the combination a linguistic form which suggests productive activity. A *productive resource* may be said to "contribute," though in a non-ethical sense, to the production of wealth, and ownership is an ethical category. By confusing the two and calling the result *providing capital,* he thinks he has uncovered a distinctive "way of creating wealth."[15]

The marginal product definition of "contribution" is clearly inadequate to the task of showing that capitalism distributes in accordance with the ethical canon of contribution. It provides us with a criterion for judging the assertion, "X% of the product was the contribution of labor, Y% of land, and so on," but it does so at the cost of severing the "contribution" of the owner of a factor from anything but a legal relation to the factor itself. In Clark's static, perfectly competitive world, capitalists *qua* capitalists take no risks, do not innovate, do not sacrifice, do not engage in any productive activity whatsoever. The abstraction from individual activity which allows one to define the contribution of a factor in a precise mathematical sense also removes from consideration any reason one might wish to give for claiming that the "contribution" of the factor is the contribution of the owner. If one is to defend capitalist distribution, one must either redefine "capitalist contribution" or abandon the social contribution canon as its justification. However mathematically elegant marginal product theory may be, it cannot serve as the basis of an ethical argument.[16]

CAPITALIST CONTRIBUTION AS ENTREPRENEURIAL ACTIVITY

The marginal definition of contribution fails to agree with ethical usage because it abstracts completely from all characteristic activities of property owners. An alternative definition which does not suffer this defect is suggested by Joseph Schumpeter's well-known critique of the neoclassical static equilibrium model we have been considering:

The essential point to grasp is that in dealing with capitalism we are dealing with an evolutionary process. It may seem strange that anyone can fail to see so obvious a fact which moreover was long ago emphasized by Karl Marx. Yet that fragmentary analysis which yields the bulk of our propositions about the functioning of modern capitalism persistently neglects it. . . .

The fundamental impulse that sets and keeps the capitalist engine in motion comes from new consumer goods, the new markets, the new forms of industrial organization that capitalist enterprise creates.[17]

If it is true, as Schumpeter and Marx propose, that the fundamental feature of capitalism is its dynamism, then it would be more appropriate in determining the respective contributions of laborers and capitalists to compare society at *different* points in time instead of at a fixed point (represented by a fixed production function). Insofar as an increase in output can be attributed to the activities of capitalists, we can perhaps define the contribution of the capitalists to be this increase. A simple model illustrates this definition. Suppose a capitalist-landowner employs ten people to grow corn. Under prevailing technology these workers could, let us say, produce 1500 bushels a year. But suppose a particular capitalist-landowner reorganizes production, innovates, with the result that his workers can now produce 2000 bushels. The extra 500 bushels, by our new definition, is *his* contribution.

A difficulty appears at once with this definition (if we wish to use the canon of contribution to justify capitalism) since under most "prevailing conditions" the market will return *more* than 500 bushels of corn to the capitalist. As the neoclassical analysis makes clear, the market will return to the capitalist a portion of the original 1500 even without innovation. Thus a capitalist entrepreneur will be rewarded for two kinds of "contribution," one determined by the increase he effected, and the other by the marginal productivity of his land, the latter being ethically irrelevant.

Perhaps we can avoid appealing to the marginalist definition by returning to the dawn of capitalist production. Here, maybe, we have the relevant base-point upon which to establish the contribution of capitalists. When we look at society at a later time, a certain portion of the capitalists' income seems solely due to ownership of means of production. But it might be argued, appearances are misleading, for this portion can be traced to creative capitalist innovation in the manner suggested by the following scenario:[18] During year zero, just prior to the dawn of capitalist production, laborers produce a certain quantity of goods and consume them all. An entrepreneur emerges and introduces an innovation which increases the total product, this increase being his contribution. The next year a second innovation takes place, the third year a third, and so on, each supplementing the increase already in effect. The contribution of the capitalist steadily mounts.

This account is obviously oversimplified, but at least it links the "contribution" of the capitalist to a specific productive function, namely, innovation. We are not concerned about whether this account accurately reflects the historical genesis of capitalism, nor will we ask what portion of the increase in the total was due to the increasing skill and education of the workers. Our concern is with this definition of "contribution" as an *ethical* notion. The essential difficulty appears to involve not the relative sizes of the respective contributions of labor and capital, but the comparative *natures* of each.

The problem lies in the *duration* of capitalist "contribution." Consider an elaboration of our example. Suppose a capitalist enters the scene at year one, when ten laborers, using rude implements, produce 1500 bushels of corn per year. Suppose he introduces an innovative concept for a new kind of plow. He sets two of his workers[19] into motion building the plow according to his specifications, and he reorganizes the remainder efficiently. At the end of the year his workers harvest 2000 bushels, 500 of which constitute his "contribution."

Now this concept of contribution seems unambiguous and straightforwardly ethical. But a complication arises in the second year. The process can now repeat itself, but with one important difference: no *new* invention is necessary. The blueprint for the plow, the reorganization scheme, the technology for a 2000 bushel harvest is now in existence. Even if the particular plows constructed during the first year have worn out, the workers can build new ones. Suppose they employ the existing technology to produce 2000 bushels of corn. Who, we must ask, contributed *this* 2000 bushels? In a sense the capitalist still contributed 500, since the increase, measured from basepoint zero, is 500, and is due to his activity, for without the technology only 1500 bushels could have been produced. If we measure from year one, however, there is no increase, so the capitalist has "contributed" nothing, a conclusion consistent with our assumption that he has introduced no *new* innovation during this second period. Which sense of capitalist "contribution" do we intend when we define his contribution as the increase in production which can be attributed to his activities?

The latter sense cannot be intended, for it depends on an arbitrary specification of time interval. If we specify one year, then our entrepreneur "contributes" 500 bushels; if two, he "contributes" 1000; if twenty, 10,000. There is surely no "natural" time interval beyond which the "contribution" ceases to be that of the capitalist and becomes that of the workers.[20] On the other hand, if we do not specify a limit, we have a definition of "contribution" which entails that certain "contributors" are perpetual, while others are by nature only transitory. The capitalist and his laborers expend mental and physical energy during the first year and each makes a "contribution," the laborers 150 bushels each and the capitalist 500. However, the "contribution" of the capitalist continues into the next year, and then into the next. If he innovates anew he will be entitled (according to the canon of contribution) to the increase brought about by the new innovation, as well as to the 500 effected by the earlier one. The "contribution" of the laborer, however, and his entitlement to a share of the product cease with his labor.

Let us consider the notion of "perpetual contribution" more closely. If distribution under capitalism accords with contribution, then a "perpetual contribution" requires a "perpetual reward." But is there any sense in which capitalism does in fact "perpetually reward" the capitalist?

If we look at capitalist reality, indeed we find a plethora of institutions which do reward "perpetually." A stock of capital, however acquired, may be invested by an individual as he sees fit. He may put it in a savings account, or buy government or corporate bonds with it; in such cases he can collect interest indefinitely. He may purchase stock and collect yearly dividends. Such rewards are quite independent of the fate of the original innovation (if there was one) to which the original stock of capital is traceable, and independent as well of his present activities. Galbraith's remark points to this phenomenon:

No grant of feudal privilege has even equalled, for effortless return, that of the grandparent who bought and endowed his descendants with a thousand shares of General Motors or General Electric. The beneficiaries of this foresight have become and remain rich by no exercise of effort or intelligence beyond the decision to do nothing, embracing as it did the decision not to sell.[21]

It must be admitted then that under capitalism some rewards are "perpetual" in an ethically significant sense.[22] If one wishes to defend capitalist distribution by an appeal to the contribution canon, one must therefore defend the contention that some *contributions* are perpetual, and hence deserving of perpetual reward. Perhaps this is not implausible. Innovations, even when they are supplanted by others, have often served as the basis for the new technology, and so in some sense their effects persist. (Einstein stood on Newton's shoulders.) Surely there is nothing ethically objectionable about rewarding lasting contributions lastingly.

To see the problem with this argument, let us return briefly to our original entrepreneur and his new kind of plow. What exactly was the nature of the "contribution" that qualified it as "perpetual"? The seemingly obvious answer that he has created a new kind of productive instrument, and reorganized production in an efficient manner will not do, not if such activities are to serve to justify his reward under capitalism, for he need not have done these *himself*. He could have hired a scientist or an engineer to create the plow, and a managerial expert to reorganize his farm. Such people are regularly employed as wage laborers in a capitalist society. If capitalism rewards according to contribution, then such technical activities cannot be "perpetual" contributions, for they are not rewarded perpetually. Nor will it do to say that the *idea* to construct the new plow belongs to the capitalist, for the idea itself could have originated in our capitalists' research and development division. Ideas and their execution frequently originate in such places in modern capitalist society. A "perpetual" reward may follow from the idea, but it does not necessarily go to the originator.

It is tempting to say that the capitalist *supplies the money*. This is certainly his distinctive "service" *qua* capitalist. But this cannot be his "contribution," for supplying money or providing capital is no more a *productive activity* in this dynamic situation than it was in the static case analyzed earlier. The workers to be hired already exist, as do the food, clothing and shelter which their wages will buy. Other workers have made them, just as other workers have dug from the ground the coal to fire the factories, and still others have provided the raw materials.

It is true that the capitalist serves to allocate resources. His decision to supply money for a particular project results in setting a certain portion of the workforce to work in that activity rather than another, but so do the decisions of hired executives, managers, and foremen. There is nothing distinctive in a *technical* sense about this activity when performed by a capitalist.[23]

The fact of the matter is that it is impossible to find a distinctive productive activity (or class of activities) definable independently of the socio-economic system which is engaged in exclusively (or even predominantly) by capitalists. Yet such distinctive activity is essential to a defense of capitalism which is grounded on the contribution canon, for such a defense implies, as we have seen, that the "contribution" of the capitalist is distinctively perpetual, while that of the worker is not. Therefore we conclude that our second definition of capitalist contribution—the increase effected by him over time—fares no better than the marginal product definition in establishing that capitalism distributes in proportion to contribution. The marginal product definition fails to establish an ethically relevant link between the technically defined "contribution" of the productive factor and the productive activity of the owner of the factor. The "entrepreneurial" definition attempts such a connection, but it fails to survive analysis. Although one might define an "entrepreneur" independently of the socio-economic system, one cannot do so in such a way as to make the class of entrepreneurs coextensive with the class of capitalists.

Such coextensiveness might once have been roughly the case, but it scarcely seems so today. Nor is there anything in the structure of capitalism which suggests that this divergence is an aberration. It seems more reasonable to suppose, as Schumpeter himself does, that such a divergence will become more pronounced as capitalism continues to develop:

For, on the one hand, it is much easier now than it has been in the past to do things that lie outside the familiar routine—innovation itself is being reduced to routine. Technological progress is increasingly becoming the business of trained specialists who turn out what is required of them and make it work in predictable ways. . . .

On the other hand, personality and will power must count for less in environments which have become accustomed to change—best instanced by an incessant stream of new consumers' and producers' goods—and which instead of resisting accepts it as a matter of course. The resistance which comes from interests threatened by innovations in the productive process is not likely to die out as long as the capitalist order persists. . . . But every other kind of resistance—the resistance in particular of consumers and producers to a kind of thing because it is new—has well-nigh vanished already.[24]

INTEREST AS REWARD FOR WAITING

The basic problem in trying to justify capitalism by an appeal to contribution is the impossibility of identifying an activity or set of activities which could be called "contributions" in an ethically relevant sense, engaged in by almost all capitalists, and only by them. It is true that some capitalists innovate, reorganize, invent; but it is also true that many do not. This fact is readily acknowledged by economists, and is reflected in their distinction between "interest" and "profit."[25] *Interest* is the "natural" return to capital, the reward for owning property. Profit includes interest, but also the rewards for risk and entrepreneurial achievement. Samuelson's definition of the market rate of interest exemplifies this distinction:

The market rate of interest is that percentage of return per year which has to be paid on any safe loan of money, which has to be yielded on any safe bond or other security, and which has to be earned on the value of any capital asset (such as a machine, a hotel building, a patent right) in any competitive market where there are no risks or where all the risk factors have already been taken care of by special premium payments to protect against any risks.[26]

Thus, in trying to justify capitalism by an appeal to contribution, we must justify *interest,* a reward which does not require any entrepreneurial activity on the part of its recipient. If interest is not the reward for such activity, what is it a reward for? Alfred Marshall, the most prominent pre-Keynsian of this century, responds with a basic neoclassical justification: interest is the reward for waiting.

It is not true that the spinning of yarn in a factory, after allowance has been made for the wear and tear of the machinery, is the product of the labor of the operatives. It is the product of their labor, together with that of the employer and subordinate managers, and of the capital employed; and that capital itself is the product of labor and waiting. If we admit it is the product of labor alone, and not of labor and waiting, we can no doubt be compelled by an inexorable logic to admit that there is no justification of interest, the reward of waiting; for the conclusion is implied in the premises. . . .

To put the same thing in other words, if it be true that the postponement of gratification involves *in general* a sacrifice on the part of him who postpones, just as additional effort does on the part of him who labors, and if it be true that this postponement enables man to use methods of production of which the first cost is great but by which the aggregate of enjoyment is increased, as certainly as it would be by an increase of labor, then it cannot be true that the value of a thing depends simply on the amount of labor spent on it. Every attempt to establish this premise has necessarily assumed implicitly that the service performed by capital is a "free good," rendered without sacrifice, and therefore needing no interest as a reward for its continuance.[27]

Marshall suggests two distinct justifications of capitalism, one based on the canon of contribution and another on the canon of sacrifice. Insofar as this passage is an argument concerning contribution, it fails for the reasons set out in the first section of this paper. Marshall does not observe the distinction, crucial to the ethical argument, between the "contribution" of capital and the activity of the capitalist. This is striking in the last sentence, for the premise he means to destroy, that the "service of capital" is rendered without sacrifice and therefore needs no interest as a reward for its continuance, is surely *true*. One does not induce a field to grow corn by paying it interest. The spinning wheel does not need to be rewarded for turning cotton into yarn.

Marshall's argument need not be construed so simply, for it also appeals to the *sacrifice* of the capitalist, and to the increase in the "aggregate of enjoyment" due to this sacrifice. The ethical appeal presumably is this: the creation of the social product requires sacrifice on the part of each member of society; hence it is fair that one's share be proportional to one's sacrifice.

A defense of capitalist distribution based on sacrifice requires three steps: one must specify the nature of the sacrifice of each member; one must find a common standard by which to measure respective sacrifices; and finally, one must show that capitalism does indeed distribute income more or less in proportion to sacrifice so measured.

The sacrifice of laborers seems relatively clear: they sacrifice their leisure; to a greater or lesser degree, they undergo physical and mental discomfort. What sacrifice on the part of the capitalist is comparable to this? Marshall's answer seems straightforward: he postpones gratification. When choosing between consuming his wealth at once and deferring consumption, he generally finds it painful to postpone gratification, and this pain is not completely compensated for by the later consumption of the same amount.

But how does one quantify sacrifice so as to allow interpersonal comparisons? One cannot *define* the quantity of sacrifice to be the increase in production due to that sacrifice, for this reduces what seems to be an appeal to the canon of sacrifice to a disguised (and confused) appeal to the canon of contribution. Marshall is perhaps suggesting that it is an *empirical fact* rather than a matter of definition that the quantity of pain and discomfort is proportional to the size of the increase effected by the sacrifice. If such a proposition is true, then Marshall has provided an ethically relevant link (such as we are unable to discover in our analysis of appeals to contribution) between the owner of property and the productive contribution of that property.

Before questioning the plausibility of this empirical assertion, let us consider its rationale. Interest rates, according to Marshall, are determined by the "money market" which brings entrepreneurs in search of capital face to face with households tempted to save. The market is in equilibrium when interest rates are such that they call forth exactly as much savings as entrepreneurs are desirous of borrowing. Suppose, for example, that the market is in equilibrium at 4%. This means that the average saver[28] will not lend money at less than 4%, thus indicating that he requires a 4% premium as a "reward for waiting" to compensate for the sacrifice of immediate gratification. With the market in equilibrium there is an entrepreneur willing to borrow at 4% what a saver is willing to save at that rate. The person with $1000 who will save it if compensated with $40 will find an entrepreneur eager for that money for he (the entrepreneur) can reasonably expect to increase productivity enough to pay the $40 premium and still have sufficient excess to reward himself for his risk and entrepreneurial skills. Thus we have the required quantitative connection between the pain and suffering of deferred gratification and the productive contribution of the $1000.

There are at least two kinds of criticism that can be levelled against this account. One can deny that this paradigm is applicable to economic reality, or one can argue that the model, if descriptively accurate, entails the exact opposite of the intended ethical conclusion. A Marxist is inclined to take the first approach. The Marshall model depicts society as divided into two groups, households which consume and save, and entrepreneurs who borrow and innovate. The plausibility of regarding the pain of deferred gratification as something akin to the discomfort of labor rests on the implicit assumption that the typical savings unit is a small- or medium-income household, for it is not implausible that in such a setting a worker would require some monetary incentive to entice him into depositing a portion of his paycheck into a savings account, a sum which makes up for the pain of postponed consumption.[29] But if one assumes, as a Marxist does, that it is more realistic to see society as composed of two classes, one, comprising the large majority, which saves but little, and another, the class of capitalists, which does the bulk of saving and investing, then the comparability of the "sacrifice" of postponement with the "sacrifice" of labor evaporates.[30] Marx makes the obvious point.

The more, therefore, capital increases by successive accumulations, the more does the sum of value increase which is divided into consumption-fund and accumulation-fund. The capitalist can, therefore, live a more jolly life and at the same time practice more "abstinence."[31]

This Marxian objection derives from a denial of the applicability of Marshall's model to reality. Such a denial, though in my view correct, is unnecessary for disposing of Marshall's argument. For even if this model accurately depicts reality, the ethical conclusion that capitalism distributes in proportion to sacrifice does not follow. To see this, let us grant the basic assumption that the premium an individual requires to entice him into saving accurately measures the pain he feels in sacrificing immediate gratification. Let us assume also that society consists of households and entrepreneurs, whose interactions determine interest rates in accordance with Marshall's general theory. One can deduce from these premises that capitalism does not distribute according to the canon of sacrifice.

Suppose the money market is in equilibrium, the interest rate, say 4%, just right to balance the supply of money from households with the demand for money by entrepreneurs. The neoclassical theory of interest determination, to which Marshall subscribes, holds that the equilibrium rate of interest is determined by the marginal utility of capital. The 4% rate (in our example) is required to entice that *last portion* of money from the pockets of savers necessary to bring total savings into equilibrium with total investment. Now, unless it should be the case that *nobody* would save at a lower rate of interest (scarcely a plausible assumption, nor one consistent with neoclassical theory), then some people would save at 3%, though presumably fewer, some at 2%, and so on. Some, the wealthy, might even *pay* to have their wealth safely guarded. Given our original assumption that the premium a person requires to make him save measures the pain of his sacrifice, we deduce that these people have evaluated the pain of postponement at a lower figure than the prevailing market rate of interest, and hence they are being *over*compensated for their pain. Therefore, distribution is *not* according to the canon of sacrifice.

To be sure there is a core of truth to the notion that capital is the "product of waiting." Capital accumulation is generally a necessary condition for increasing productivity. Such accumulation is possible only if consumption is "deferred" in a certain sense: In order to bring physical capital into existence—say, a factory designed to manufacture tractors—certain human beings must spend their time building it. If instead those workers had spent their time tilling the fields, society would have had somewhat more corn immediately, but in order to have a *larger* increase at a later date, some potential present consumption must be sacrificed. In this sense capital is the result of "deferred" consumption, and is the product of "labor and waiting."

The market mechanism indeed channels the workforce in such a way that consumption is "sacrificed" in this sense. Some workers are directed into areas that will yield an increase in productivity only at a later date. But if this sacrifice correlates at all with actually experienced pain, the pain is surely not experienced primarily by the capitalists, the recipients of the "compensation."

It is true, therefore, that capital accumulation requires the postponement of consumption, and it is no doubt true that the interests of society are best served by sacrificing some such consumption. But these facts no more justify the claim that capitalist distribution is proportional to sacrifice than the fact that innovative activities contribute to production justifies the contention that it is proportional to contribution. A serious defense of capitalism must foreswear appeals to either of these traditional canons. However important they may have been to the capitalist apology, and however valid they may be as ethical principles, they are incapable of providing an intellectually sound basis for such a defense today.

NOTES

[1] John Bates Clark, *The Distribution of Wealth* (New York, 1956), p. 5.

[2] Friedrich Hayek, *The Constitution of Liberty* (Chicago, 1960), p. 94.

[3] Robert Nozick, *Anarchy, State and Utopia* (New York, 1974), p. 158.

[4] Nicholas Rescher, *Distributive Justice* (New York, 1966), p. 78. This canon is called variously the canon of "productivity," "social contribution," "productive contribution," or simply "contribution." We will use these terms interchangeably.

[5] Milton Friedman, *Capitalism and Freedom* (Chicago, 1962), p. 166.

[6] Paul Samuelson, *Economics* (New York, 1973), p. 539.

[7] For the sake of simplicity we will carry through our analysis in terms of a two-variable function instead of the more traditional three-variable one (land, labor and capital). We will ignore the "Cambridge Controversy" surrounding the neoclassical treatment of capital as a factor of production on par with land and labor, and simply identify capital with land. The Cambridge (England) critique of the neoclassical argument is independent of our own. (For details consult G. C. Harcourt, *Some Cambridge Controversies in the Theory of Capital* (Cambridge, 1972).)

[8] It is sufficient that $P(x,y)$ be smooth and homogeneous of order one. This latter condition (in mathematical terms, $P(ax,ay) = aP(x,y)$ for all a) translates into the economic condition that there be constant returns to scale. Increasing *all* the production factors by a% results in an a% increase in the total product. The former condition requires that a smooth variation in input factors produce a smooth variation in output.

[9] Wages will be *at least* as high as the marginal product of the last laborer, for if they were lower, each landowner would try to entice laborers away from his neighbors. Wages will not be any *higher* than that, for that would involve paying the last person more than he yields. Cf. Samelson, p. 539, for details.

[10] Clark, p. 7.

[11] *Ibid.,* p. 4.

[12] This law of diminishing returns can be derived from the assumed characteristics of the production function: constant returns to scale, smoothness, and positive marginal products. It does *not* depend on any assumptions about declining skills; all workers in fact are presumed equally skilled.

[13] Clark, p. 3.

[14] Innovation, if there is any, is traceable to the entrepreneur, not to the capitalist.

[15] The peculiarity of this notion of "providing capital" becomes even more apparent if we try to apply it to other forms of society in order to ascertain who creates what, and whether dis-

tribution in that society accords with "contribution." A feudal lord, for example, who owns far more land than his peasants can till, creates, in "providing land," no wealth at all, because the marginal product of his last acre is zero. But as his peasant population grows, and with it the marginal product of that last acre, his "contribution" increases. The tribute once unjustly extracted becomes fair, even philanthropic, as the share of the wealth "he creates" expands.
[16] Contemporary neoclassical economists of a more liberal persuasion than Hayek are reasonably sensitive to the spuriousness of Clark's ethical argument, (Cf., for example, H. G. Johnson, *The Theory of Income Distribution* (London, 1973), p. 37.) But they persist in using "contribution" without scare-quotes, a misleading convention which tends to direct the ethical debate toward the validity of the ethical canon itself (Should one get what one contributes? Should some other canon, need perhaps, also be considered?) rather than toward a concrete analysis of the nature of factor "contribution." The problem is not that contribution is not the *whole* story. Neoclassical "contribution" should not be *any part* of the ethical debate.

[17] Joseph Schumpeter, *Capitalism, Socialism and Democracy* (New York, 1962), p. 83.

[18] Nozick suggests this line of reasoning in a slightly different context. Cf. p. 177.

[19] How the workers became *his* workers is a question we will not consider. To avoid ethical complications, we will assume that they are being paid somewhat more than the 150 bushels they could reap on their own, so that it is in their own self-interest (we will presume for the sake of argument) to work for him.

[20] The natural life of the capitalist might seem to be a plausible candidate, a thought which perhaps underlies arguments for a confiscatory inheritance tax. We will not consider the question of inheritance, however, for it distracts from the real problem with capitalist contribution, which would be present even if capitalists lived forever.

[21] John Kenneth Galbraith, *The New Industrial State* (Boston, 1967), p. 394.

[22] We do not maintain, needless to say, that the reward is *necessarily* eternal. We mean that its continuance is linked neither in theory or practice to the continuance of the innovative activity which served (perhaps) as its foundation.

[23] It should be noted that one cannot appeal here to *risk,* since taking a financial risk is not a productive activity that can be defined independently of the social system. Society need not be so structured that one need risk one's fortune to innovate. Such appeals go beyond the bounds of the contribution canon.

[24] Schumpeter, p. 133.

[25] The terminology is not standard among economists, but the distinction is invariably made. Some refer to Net Interest and Gross Interest; some use "profit" to refer to what others call "pure profit," the difference between profit (in the inclusive sense) and interest.

[26] Samuelson, p. 599.

[27] Alfred Marshall, *Principles of Economics,* 8th ed. (New York, 1948), p. 587.

[28] Actually Marshall's theory holds that the saver at the margin, not the average saver, requires this compensation. We use "average saver" here to give the story more ethical plausibility, but we will return to this distinction below.

[29] It is also plausible that interest rates have little to do with a moderate-income household's choice between saving and consuming, but we will waive this objection.

[30] This assumption seems closer to reality. As Simon Kuznets observes, "according to all recent studies, only the upper income groups save; the total savings of groups below the top decile are fairly close to zero." *Economic Growth and Structure* (New York, 1965), p. 263.

[31] Karl Marx, *Capital* (New York, 1906), p. 667.

ERIC MACK

IN DEFENSE OF "UNBRIDLED" FREEDOM OF CONTRACT

One of the central tenets of capitalist theory is that exchange of property, including the property that one may have in a skill or craft (labor), ought not to be controlled by anyone other than those taking part in the exchange. Anything from a minor transaction involving trade between a plumber and a homeowner, to a buyout of a major corporation, should be on terms set by those involved. But why? What justifies this belief, if anything at all? Eric Mack—professor of philosophy at Tulane University—advances the case for such "unbridled" freedom of contract by arguing that it rests on a more basic natural rights idea.

I
INTRODUCTION

If one merely stumbled across the phrase, "freedom of contract," one's best guess would be that this phrase referred to a very general doctrine to the effect that each individual is to be free to join with any number of individuals in any form of association or exchange on any terms that are mutually agreed to. That is, no outside party may prohibit or restrict individuals in the types of relationships they establish among themselves by mutual consent. It would be a corollary of such a view that no individual should be required, against his consent, to partake of any relationship with others. According to this corollary, no outside party may impose any relationship or any terms within a relationship upon two or more other parties and no party to a relationship may coercively impose that relationship or any terms of that relationship upon another. Subsequently I shall expand, clarify, and defend this general doctrine. It will, for instance, be important to explain what is to count as *coercive* imposition.

But before pursuing this explication and defense we must note that the actual historical doctrine referred to by the phrase "freedom of contract" represents the implications of this general philosophical doctrine merely within a narrow range of cases. The general doctrine would clearly classify as improper all victimless crime legislation, all coercive restrictions on free market relationships, and even all involuntary taxation. In contrast, the narrower historical doctrine classified as improper restrictions by an outside party (specifically, the State) on the specific terms of employment within legally and socially accepted economic activities. The historical doctrine opposed outside restriction upon who might perform how arduous a task and it opposed restrictions upon what form of payment might be made for agreed upon tasks. Thus, the narrower historical doctrine was among the legal doctrines invoked against laws restricting

Reprinted with some additions and with permission from *The American Journal of Economics and Sociology*, 10 (January 1981).

employment in certain occupations to those of a certain age or sex, against laws restricting the number of hours for which a person could agree to work, and against laws requiring that employees be paid in legal tender (as opposed to company scrip).[1] So, while the advocates of the narrower historical doctrine of liberty of contract are considered to have been radical laissez-fairists, their views were timidly moderate from the perspective of the general philosophical doctrine. In this more modest version freedom of contract probably reached its highwater mark as constitutional doctrine in *Coppage v. Kansas* (decided in 1915). In this decision the Supreme Court majority held unconstitutional a Kansas statute which forbade employers from requiring that their employees agree not to join labor unions as a condition of their employment. The court held that in insisting upon this clause in its employment contracts an employer engages in no "actual or implied coercion or duress." Rather the employer is merely insisting "upon its right to prescribe terms upon which alone it would consent to a continuance of the relationship of employer and employee."[2] The opinions offered in *Coppage v. Kansas* will provide illustrations for many of the arguments and positions discussed in this paper.

Since the less bold historical doctrine, even in its constitutionally most ambitious form, is the result of arbitrarily limiting the scope of the general philosophical doctrine, there is no clearcut set of cases to which it applies. But it would seem to be pretty much in the spirit of the narrow historical doctrine to invoke it against laws imposing minimum wages or maximum wages. Besides being applied only to employment contracts and not, *e.g.,* contracts to lend money[3] the doctrine was qualified in a variety of ambiguous ways. The purportedly absolute right to make what contracts one chose was described as a right ". . . to make *reasonable and proper* contracts in conducting a legitimate business."[4] And it seems to have been common practice to attach a rider to the effect that freedom of contract was contingent upon the contract not being a threat to "the safety, health or moral welfare of the public."[5] Clearly such an ambiguous rider is sufficient to thoroughly blunt the force of the doctrine whenever this suits the court's conception of the welfare of the public or whenever it suits the conception of the public welfare possessed by the legislative body to which the court was prepared to defer.

In *Coppage v. Kansas,* for instance, the majority held that, even though the Kansas statute suppressed noncoercive acts, it would have been constitutional had it fostered or protected "the public health, safety, morals or general welfare." The majority simply denied that the act in fact fostered or protected any of these ends. Their underlying, unstated, reason seems to have been that a legislative act could count as fostering the public or general welfare only if it benefited everyone or, at least, benefited some while harming none, while the law at issue benefited *some at the expense of others.* But their main explicit argument was simply that the unions which the act was designed to strengthen were "not public institutions, charged by law with public or governmental duties."[6] In the dissenting opinion, the claim that "the right of contract is not absolute and unyielding, but is subject to limitation and restraint in the interest of public health, safety and welfare" is repeated. And it is added that "such limitations may be declared in legislation of the State indeed, that, "each act of legislation has the support of the presumption that it is an exercise in the interest of the public."[7]

Philosophically, there is no satisfactory way to defend the narrower, more hesitant, historical view except by defending the general, unbridled, view of which it is a logical part. Furthermore, anything less than a defense of the unbridled view allows some limitations on freedom of contract which, in turn, will be employed as precedents for further limitations. For example, in *Coppage v. Kansas,* the dissenting opinion cites the prohibition on the sale of lottery tickets[8] as a legitimate and constitutional curtailment of liberty of contract and, hence, as a sign that other legitimate curtailments are likely to be found. In order to stay off the slippery slope which descends toward the admission of more and more constraints as legitimate, the freedom of contract advocate must reject the legitimacy of any genuine curtailment.[9] It must be remembered, however, that the setting aside of those contracts or clauses of contracts which have resulted from rights violating activities such as threats, deceptions, and (in some cases) "undue influence" will not count as genuine curtailments of freedom of contract. For it is only in terms of a recognition of the rights that are violated by such threats and deceptions that the doctrine of freedom of contract is defined and advanced. Furthermore, an apparent contract may be set aside on the basis of the contractual incompetence of one or more of the parties to it. What is crucial for the advocate of freedom of contract is not that nothing having the appearance of a contract be set aside but, rather, that contracts not be set aside simply *on the basis of their substantive terms.*[10]

II
NATURAL RIGHTS VERSUS SOCIAL GOALS

The moral philosophical perspective from which this essay proceeds is essentially Lockean.[11] Among individuals there are no natural moral slaves and no natural moral masters. No one's purposes or goals take moral precedence over the purposes and goals of any other person in a way which would justify the complete or partial subordination of any individual to any other individual or to any group of individuals. For there is a moral equality among persons. But this moral equality does not merely consist of an equal presence in a morally empty universe—a universe in which no values are objective and in which acts of aggression and subjugation, while not right, are also not wrong. The moral equality of persons includes the equal ultimacy of the value of each person's life. Each individual's life is an ultimate value—to him whose life it is. For each person that which is of fundamental value and is the rational goal of his action and planning is the fulfillment of his best (available) plan of life, i.e., the most harmonious lifetime satisfaction of his desires, interests, and capacities. The value of the fulfillment of a rational life plan or of the elements contributing to such a plan is objective, but agent-relative or positional.[12] It is for him who stands in relationship to a fulfilled rational plan of life as its agent and subject that this fulfillment is ultimately valuable. It is objectively the case that the fulfillment of any given rational plan of life is ultimately valuable to someone (and quite possibly of nonultimate value to other individuals). But the someone for whom it is fundamentally desirable is the party in the position of living and undergoing that life.

This individualistic conception of the equally (but noncommeasurably) ultimate value of each person's respective harmonious fulfillment of his desires, interests, and capacities has crucial implications for how individuals must act (or refrain from acting) toward others. These implications constitute individuals' fundamental natural rights and obligations. In maintaining that each person's well-being is an ultimate value, *the* ultimate value with respect to *that* agent, one is not only maintaining that people constitute a multiplicity of points or even receptacles in which value can be achieved and lodged. For the "receptacles" themselves, i.e., these individuals, respectively occupy moral space not merely as depots for the storage of well-being but as embodied, active, choosing beings having the achievement of their well-being as their respective rational purposes. Given that each person has a specific and separate rational end of his own, his faculties and capacities for choice and action, and his choices and actions, are not like natural resources which are equally morally available to whomever desires to put them to use. Rather, the possession of a separate moral purpose removes each person as an embodied, active, choosing being from the domain of objects which simply exist as possible material for the use of this or that contingently determined individual.

Since a person is an active, choosing being and his faculties and capacities are, morally speaking, uniquely *for* his own well-being, his person and faculties are uniquely a means to this end. One cannot coherently affirm that the well-being of each is his separate and distinctive end without affirming also that some things stand distinctly as means to that end, and hence, as means not available to others. On the most fundamental level, it is the person himself, his existence as an embodied, living, purposive being, which stands as a means to the end which is his well-being and, hence, as material which is morally out of bounds for other people's exploitation.

Since each person is an end-in-himself in the sense that the most cohesive realization of his person, desires, and capacities is the distinctive rational ultimate value (for him), each person is a means to that separate ultimate value which is his successful life and, therefore, no person is a means for anyone else's life or purposes. This is our reading and explication of the Kantian slogan that because each is an end-in-himself, each has a moral immunity against being treated as a means.[13] A person's moral sovereignty over himself involves claims, i.e., rights, to life and liberty, to property in his own body, and to other property permissibly acquired. There are correlative obligations in all others not to (non-consensually) deprive him of life, liberty, and legitimate property. These (natural) moral rights and obligations exist independent of and prior to any agreements among persons and independent of the social utility or positive legality of recognizing these rights and obligations. These rights and obligations, subject of course to modification through individuals' free relationships with one another, provide the basic extralegal standards for what forms of conduct may be legally prohibited and what forms of conduct must be legally permitted.

In a limited sense, then, there are natural sovereigns—each being a natural sovereign over himself. And persons are not ethereal beings. A person's sovereignty over himself involves a claim to his body and whatever other objects he acquires as instruments of his purposes without violating the like sovereignty of others. His sovereignty involves a claim, a right, to life and liberty, to property in his own body, and to other property permissibly acquired. And its right involves a correlative obligation in all others not to (non-consensually) deprive him of life, liberty, and legitimate property. Understanding "coercion" as constraining a person against his will in a way that involves some violation of his rights, we can speak generally of a right against coercion possessed by each person and an obligation upon all persons not to coerce. These are the (natural) moral rights and obligations of individuals which exist independent of and prior to any agreements among persons and independent of the social utility or positive legality of recognizing these rights and obligations.

In one important respect these are very modest rights and obligations. While each person has a right against all others not to be coerced this right will be satisfied simply by that person's being left alone. As long as an individual is not made to act in ways which do not accord with his purposes he is uncoerced and his right against coercion is being respected. Each person can fulfill his obligation not to coerce by merely leaving others alone. Hence, these natural rights and obligations are negative. That is, Smith's rights require only that Jones *not* coerce him. They require no positive act from Jones. Jones' obligation is fulfilled in *not* coercing others. He needn't perform any positive act in order to fulfill his natural obligations.

This view of natural rights and obligations should be accompanied by a full theory of property rights in external objects. Such a theory would present something like the following structure. A person comes to possess a property right to an object when, through noncoercive activities, he comes to be so related to that object as an instrument of his purposes that subsequently to deprive him of that object without his agreement is to deprive him also of something to which he already has an acknowledged right, *e.g.*, to control over the time, effort, and skill which he has invested in the newly acquired and transformed object. If I have labored on a previously unowned field in order to clear it for planting and then it is seized by others for their purposes, my actions have been disposed of for the purposes of others which I do not share. I and my activities have been treated as resources at the disposal of others. Such a seizure (unless it is done in accordance with previous contractual agreement or as an act of restitution for a previous unjustified seizure) presupposes that the laborer is naturally subservient to and owned by those who seize his product. Nozick points out:

Seizing the results of someone's labor is equivalent to seizing hours from him and directing him to carry on various activities. If people force you to do certain work, or unrewarded work, for a certain period of time, they decide what you are to do and what purposes your work is to serve apart from your decisions. This process whereby they take this decision from you makes them a *part-owner* of you; it gives them a [legal, but morally unjustified] property right in you. Just as having such partial control and power of decision, by right, over an animal or inanimate object would be to have a property right in it.[14]

Such a seizure is coercive. The natural obligation not to coerce requires, then, that no individual ever be deprived of his legitimate property without his consent. And, of course, it is always within an individual's right to retain his property since in merely retaining it he cannot be coercing another. His obligation not to coerce never requires (in the absence of contract) that he surrender his legitimate property to anyone or any group.

Of course, in any human *society* individuals do more than merely leave each other alone. Almost all individuals receive all sorts of goods and services from other individuals. Yet any disposal of the time, activity or property of Jones requires Jones' agreement. He must willingly make or allow that disposal (and he may will or allow anything noncoercive). In order to insure the provision of goods and services by others, each of us seeks pledges from others that desired goods or services will be forthcoming. A pledge from Smith to Jones to provide a certain service generates a positive right in Jones to have that service performed and a positive obligation in Smith to perform that service. Characteristically, of course, such a pledge from Smith to Jones will be elicited in return for a rights-generating pledge from Jones to Smith, *e.g.*, a pledge to pay Smith a certain fee for his service. All the special (positive) rights that individuals have beyond the (general) negative right against coercion and all the special (positive) obligations that individuals have beyond the (general) negative obligation not to coerce are the products of contractual relationships. Each person, then, has a right to accept any contractual offer (except for payments to coerce others). But no one has a right to be made any particular offer.[15] So, Smith must elicit contractual offers from Jones by means of the goods or services Smith can counter-offer to Jones. And it is the fact that Jones has no right to any particular counter-offer by Smith which requires that Jones adjust his offers to Smith's preferences just as Smith adjusts his counter-offers to Jones. In emphasizing this symmetry of rights to withhold agreement to exchanges, the majority in *Coppage v. Kansas* asserted that,

The right of a person to sell his labor upon such terms as he deems proper is, in its essence, the same as the right of the purchaser of labor to prescribe the conditions upon which he will accept such labor from the person offering to sell it.[16]

Strictly speaking, however, neither party has a (pre-contractual) right to an exchange on any particular terms. Each simply has a right not to have terms of exchange imposed upon him. The actual terms of exchange in a noncoerced agreement must, then, represent a mutual accommodation among the contracting parties.

These symmetrically ascribed rights are violated by, *e.g.,* minimum wage laws. Suppose employee Jones, who in the absence of minimum wage laws would contract to work for Smith for $2.50 per hour, becomes subject to a $3.00 per hour minimum wage law. There are two alternative cases: either Jones will no longer be employed or he will be offered and will accept a contract at $3.00 per hour. The first case was, it seems, largely ignored by the courts in freedom of contract cases. Yet it is when this alternative is realized that Jones' freedom of contract is most clearly and grievously violated. For in this case Jones would want to offer his services at $2.50 per hour and would be coercively prevented from doing so. Suppose, in contrast, that Jones remains employed at $3.00 per hour. Characteristically, courts invoking the freedom of contract doctrine would say that here too Jones has been denied his freedom of contract. Now although this is true—Jones was not free to accept $2.50 per hour and an increased risk of unemployment was coercively imposed upon him—it also seems a bit disingenuous. For in these circumstances the only act which Jones is coercively forbidden to do (*viz.,* offering to work at $2.50 per hour) is one which, by hypothesis, Jones does not want to do (at least after he knows that he will still be employed at $3.00 per hour).[17] The real victim in this instance is Smith who is coercively required to make an offer which he has a right not to make and which, except for being coerced not to make a lower offer, he would not make. The right not to make contractual offers, which includes the right not to make the more pleasing (to others) offers which would not be made in the absence of coercion, is just as central to freedom of contract as the right to tender and accept offers. (Of course, any restriction such as a minimal wage which applies to a class of employees is likely to produce victims of both sorts, *viz.,* those relatively unseen victims who are unemployed because the mandated terms of employment are too favorable to them and those more visible victims upon whom greater costs are imposed than would have resulted from unregulated negotiation.)

The type of individualistic and pluralistic natural rights view I have sketched has been labeled a "moral side-constraint" view. For on this view, the only constraints on an individual's actions are constraints against employing certain means in the pursuit of one's goals—whatever those goals be. Individuals are morally constrained from taking paths to their goals which involve the violation of others' natural or contractual rights, *i.e.,* which involve coercion or default on promised actions. What a person must aim at with his life and time is in no way constrained (except in the trivial sense of being constrained from acting with the violation of moral side-constraints as his end). Such an approach in social and legal philosophy is to be contrasted with what I call the social goal approach. According to each version of the social goal approach there is some single, overall, social goal *e.g.,* utility maximization, equality, stability, etc. or some mixture of these, to which each person's life and effort should be devoted. Each person is so obligated to pursue this or that favored social goal that he may properly be coerced into doing whatever most accords with realizing that goal. Persons are to look at themselves and others as resources to be devoted to this common social project. If particular coercive acts are not conducive to the greatest realization of the favored goal, then they should not be done. But, according to this approach, an individual's claim against being manipulated and used must always be made out by showing that this utilization of this individual at this time is, in terms of the favored goal, an ineffective utilization of a social resource. Similarly, on this approach, an individual's claim to any freedom or object or service is valid only insofar as his being permitted that freedom or provided with that object or service remains part of the most effective overall program for generating the sanctified social goal. Many objections to principled defenses of freedom—including defenses of freedom of contract—proceed from one social goal theory or another. But, to put it briefly, none of these objections are sound since no social goal theory is true since the moral side-constraint view is true. There are moral constraints on how we must treat other individuals which do not leave room for our thinking of people as (even partial) unclaimed resources permissibly to be used for "our" or "society's" purposes. There is no collective social purpose and no specially ordained individual purposes which can justify the forceful subordination of individuals and their (noncoercive) life-plans.[18]

III
OBJECTIONS TO UNBRIDLED FREEDOM OF CONTRACT

Having clarified the doctrine of freedom of contract and having, in the name of Lockean natural rights, dismissed objections to liberty of contract which are explicitly based on social goal theories, we may now consider four recurring objections to unbridled freedom of contract each of which adopts the language of freedom, noncoercion or just exchange.

According to one objection, belief in unbridled freedom of contract results from slipping into a faultily empty conception of freedom. It is claimed that noncoercion should be valued only insofar as it is a condition for freedom in the sense of persons having abilities and opportunities to do what they want (or what would make them happy, or what they should do). One historically important advocate of this conception of freedom, T. H. Green, gives as the initial characterization of such "positive freedom": "a positive power or capacity of doing or enjoying something worth doing or enjoying."[19] The further claim is that if the promotion of such freedom is the valued goal, then although we might *sometimes* allow freedom of contract as a means to this goal, we should also be prepared to interfere with the terms of a (potential) contract if that interference would maximize positive freedom. While some forcible intervention against Jones, *i.e.,* some deprivation of Jones' negative liberty, may carry with it some loss of positive freedom for Jones, we are to favor it if it also brings a greater gain of positive freedom, for, *e.g.,* Smith. Many thinkers have pointed out that the theory of positive freedom blurs the useful distinctions between a person's being free to do X, his having the opportunity to do X, his having the ability to do X, etc. At the very least the advocate of positive liberty must acknowledge that he really is promoting some ill-defined mixture of (negative) freedom, opportunity, capacity, etc. More importantly, he turns out to be just another version of a social goal theorist. For his theory will take one of two possible forms. He may advocate a utilitarianism of positive freedom, *i.e.,* that everyone should be seen as a social resource for maximizing the sum of positive freedom. As with all types of utilitarianism, this approach will require that individuals be deprived of their positive freedom when and to the extent that such deprivations yield larger gains in positive freedom for others. Whereas one individual's enjoyment of negative freedom (*i.e.,* of freedom from coercion as previously defined) never requires that any other person surrender his enjoyment of negative freedom, one individual's possession of the opportunities and abilities which make up positive freedom may well require that others be denied or deprived of opportunities and abilities which are necessary for *their* positive freedom. In shifting to positive freedom, then, one becomes entangled in determining the relative moral weights of alternative combinations of positive freedoms with the aim of favoring the most socially weighty combination. If one wants to obscure the fact that some persons' freedoms are thereby to be sacrificed for larger gains in other individuals' freedoms, one can insist that only the freedoms which are part of the socially best combination of freedoms are true freedoms. To avoid acknowledging the clash of positive freedoms, one may whittle down what counts as freedom by declaring that true positive freedom is only displayed in actions which serve or partake of some sanctioned social goal, *e.g.,* "the common good." This, for example, is exactly the tack taken by T. H. Green, for whom the social realization of positive freedom is finally said to be ". . . the liberation of the powers of all men *equally for contributions to a common good.*" We are told that "no one has a right to do what he will with his own in such a way as to contravene *this* end."[20] Here, perhaps even more explicitly than in the utilitarianism of positive freedom, we have an abandonment of individual rights and the moral side-constraints they impose for a collective social goal orientation.

Two objections to the general doctrine of freedom of contract stem from the claim that on some occasions such a freedom sanctions coercion. The first of these two objections focuses especially on "necessitous" persons. It is claimed that persons who are in dire circumstances are not really acting freely in forming the contractual ties which will remove them from those dire circumstances. Thus, to take one familiar example, imagine that Jones comes across Smith hanging from the edge of a cliff. If Jones has no positive obligation to save Smith, then he can refuse to save Smith unless Smith contractually obligates himself to transfer all his worldly possessions to Jones. Suppose that such an agreement is reached and Smith is saved. It might then be argued that the obligation to Jones should be set aside or moderated because Smith was not truly free when it was made. But this argument once again confuses lack of freedom in the sense of incapacity in the face of natural facts to do certain things (pull oneself up over the edge of the cliff) and lack of freedom in the sense of being coerced, *i.e.,* being non-consensually deprived by another of something to which one has a right. As Smith is hanging over the edge he is perfectly uncoerced—unless Jones is standing on his fingers. He is no more in a state of being coerced than he would be if no one else were within 100 miles of him. Similarly Smith is not being threatened with the violation of his right against coercion. Even his trip to the foot of the cliff, should it occur, will not be caused by Jones (unless Jones stamps on his fingers).[21] Hence, although he may be very eager to elicit Jones' help, what he agrees to do in return for that help is not agreed to *under duress.* Smith's eagerness for the agreement is a measure of the value (to him) of the service which Jones can perform for him. When we are inclined to say that Jones takes advantage of Smith we should at least recall that, in Smith's eyes, the service Jones renders him is more valuable than what Smith surrenders for this service.

A third objection to freedom of contract asserts that attractive offers coerce persons into entering contractual relationships. In the face of an alluring offer an individual is "threatened" with the loss of the (offered) benefit. There are many ways to answer this charge. We can begin by noting that an attractive offer induces Smith to do something he wouldn't otherwise do *by means of appealing* to other purposes and aims of Smith. Smith places only negative value on standing on his head until, in light of an offer of monetary payment, he sees that standing on his head will be a means to a dinner at Antoine's. Rather than subverting the direction of a person's actions by his own aims and purposes, such offers provide new avenues by which a person can pursue his own relatively highly valued aims and purposes. Furthermore, it is misleading to say that Smith acts under the threat of losing (not getting) the payment. For the payment is not something to which he has a right (prior to a contractual agreement). Assuming that there is no prior contract, nothing is inflicted upon Smith by his simply not being provided with that payment. Hence, holding out the prospect of his not getting that payment does not constitute a threat of inflicting something on Smith. The program of respecting each person's rights, of coercing no (peaceful) individuals, is in no way compromised by "seductive" offers or by individuals being moved by a desire not to miss a chance of being seduced. Note, finally, the interesting tension between the second and the third objections. In the case of the second objection the sign that a person is unfree is that he gets "too little" (for what he gives) while in the case of the third objection his getting as much as he does is taken to be a sign of his having been coerced!

Finally there is an objection that is directed against the claim that all free contracts are just in that each party *ex ante* advances his interests by means of each of his contractual relationships, *i.e.,* within a given relationship no party ever benefits at the expense of another party. Against this endorsement of free contractual relationships, it is often claimed that justice in an exchange requires an equitable division (usually conceived of as an equal division) of the benefits of exchange and that in some cases unregulated terms of exchange result in inequitable (specifically, unequal) divisions of the benefits. That the terms of a given contract involve an unequal "distribution" of the benefits of that contractual exchange is itself traced to the unequal economic status, and hence, to the unequal "bargaining power" of the parties to that agreed upon exchange. Now the logical inference to draw from these claims would seem to be that bargaining parties should be made equal and then allowed utter freedom of contract. But such an inference is not usually drawn and understandably so. For a program of continually bringing people back to the egalitarian starting point which free contracts would disrupt would be equivalent to a program of continuous regulation of the terms of contractual relationships. The inference which is drawn is that certain specific restrictions (*e.g.,* minimum wage laws) should be continuously imposed upon all relevant contracts—restrictions which would rule out supposedly blatantly inequitable terms. There are many problems with this view. One major problem is the lack of any basis for the claim that justice requires equality (or any other specific proportion) of benefits. Each person gains from free exchange. Each party gets some good or service from the other which he would not have gotten except for their mutual agreement. On what conceivable basis can it be known that the sum of benefits ought to be equally divided? The more plausible view is that these benefits should be divided in accordance with the terms freely agreed to by the parties to the exchange. Besides, the demand that the benefits of the exchange be divided in a particular way presupposes that we could give a cardinal reading to the utility advance of each of the parties so as to know what the sum of the benefits are. Such determinations may be in principle impossible. They are at least systematically unattainable in practice. But if this is so, by what standards are we to judge that a particular term of a contract (*e.g.,* a certain wage-rate) should be banned because it reflects an unequal division of the total benefits?

Finally, the whole idea of unequal bargaining power leading to inequitable divisions of benefits is, at best, obscure. For the "stronger" bargaining power is simply the party who is the position to satisfy what are seen as another party's vital or vitally felt needs. But if a bargain is struck, then those purportedly most vital needs will be satisfied.[22] So the powerfully positioned bargainer is just the one who, if an exchange is allowed, renders what appears to be the more vital service. All that stands in the way of seeing the exchange from *this* perspective is the supposition that the less well positioned party really has a prior right to the services or goods of the better endowed party. Given this supposition, the free contractual outcome will be seen as inequitable since it reflects the failure of the well-positioned to fulfill his supposed (pre-contractual) obligation toward the less-positioned person. But in the absence of any previous agreement to provide his services or goods no person, however well-positioned, has such obligations. Each has only the negative obligation not to coerce others. And this obligation is fulfilled by the well positioned party.

Let us return to the horrendous cliff-hanging example to put this defense of "unbridled" freedom of contract within a broader moral perspective. The point of focusing on such extreme examples is to engage the opponent of freedom of contract on his (intuitively) strongest ground. It is to grant that there are extreme cases and to indicate the reasons why, on principle, even in these instances, the theoretical case for freedom of contract still stands. The theoretical motivation of the defender of freedom of contract is to block exceptions to this freedom which might then serve as bases for further, and far more costly and counterproductive, *legally imposed* encroachments on the freedom of contract. The principled advocate of freedom of contract need no more delight in Jones's exercise of his right to demand great payments from Smith than the principled advocate of freedom of speech need delight in the racist's exercise of his freedom of speech.

Indeed, in both cases, the advocate of the right in question may view its particular exercise as morally despicable, as profoundly contrary to the advocate's conception of worthy human life. It is sometimes claimed that the libertarian's individualistic (agent-relative) conception of value precludes even a *moral* condemnation of, for example, the person who only sees another's distress as an attractive bargaining situation. But such claims, I think, ultimately rest on the idea that it is contrary to an individual's well-being to empathetically appreciate the value of others' lives and purposes and to be moved by such sentiments as sympathy and generosity or on the idea that an insistence upon people's libertarian rights will harden people and make them less able to empathize with others and less likely to be moved by sympathy and generosity. I believe that both of these ideas are profoundly mistaken. They are, after all, the flip sides of the implausible ideas that collectivist moralities enhance people's appreciation of the value of others' separate lives and purposes and that collectivist politics enhances people's sympathies and generous impulses. So the individualist libertarian is far from precluded from condemning *as a matter of morality* mean-spirited exercises of the rights he asserts as a matter of political philosophy. But he does assert those rights, including the right of freedom of contract, as defining the legitimate legal framework within which individual ambitions and social cooperation may be pursued.

NOTES

[1] Roscoe Pound, "Liberty of Contract," *Yale Law Journal* (May 1909): 417.
[2] *Coppage* v. *Kansas* 236 U.S. 8 (1915).
[3] Pound, "Liberty of Contract," p. 472.
[4] Ibid., p. 461.
[5] *Coppage* v. *Kansas* 16.
[6] *Coppage* v. *Kansas* 28.
[7] *Coppage* v. *Kansas* 29. Dissenting Justices Day and Hughes go so far as to declare that, "We cannot put our judgment in place of that of the legislature. . . ." (38).
[8] *Coppage* v. *Kansas* 28.
[9] The dissenting judges in *Coppage* v. *Kansas* pose hard questions for the advocate of freedom

of contract. They ask, e.g., whether it can "be successfully contended that the State may not, in the public interest, prohibit an agreement to forego [milita] enlistment as against public policy?" And they ask whether the State may not prohibit an agreement "to forego affiliation with a particular political party, or the support of a particular candidate for office?" (37). To reject such proposed genuine curtailments, the advocates of unbridled freedom of contract must argue that: there can be no legitimate "public policy" over and above the protection of individual rights (including the rights involved in liberty of contract); no violations of some individuals' rights (i.e., prohibiting parties from agreeing not to enlist) can be justified in terms of these violations' being the means for protecting others' rights; engaging in political activities is (at most) on a par with other rightful activities and hence, as in the case of these other activities, one can permissibly sell one's abstention from it.

[10] For an illuminating emphasis on the distinction between substantive and procedural defects and an insistence that contract may be set aside or prohibited only on the basis of procedural defects, see Richard Epstein, "Unconscionability: A Critical Reappraisal," *Journal of Law and Economics* (October 1975). The insistence that substantively contracts not be "unconscionable" is the form taken by most recent attacks on freedom of contract. See Epstein for references to this literature.

[11] Since a full defense of the general freedom of contract perspective would be a task for several volumes, it is my intention here to sketch some of the features of this defense, and to note why the social philosophy that embodies the general doctrine of freedom of contract is more plausible than each of its fundamental competitors. If these competing social philosophies are rejected, then many possible objections to universal freedom of contract are rejected also. For instance, if utilitarianism is dismissed, then so too will be the objections to liberty of contract that are based on claims that this or that set of restrictions on freedom of contract would enhance social utility. Similarly, if egalitarianism is dismissed, then so too will be objections to liberty of contract based on the inequality of outcomes that freedom of contract in general or free contract in specific tend to yield. However, as we shall see, the most common objections to unbridled freedom of contract—objections directed at restricting this freedom in special cases, not at utterly abolishing it—appear to come from within the philosophical perspective that generates the (initial) universal doctrine. For this perspective centers on the value of realizing individualistic conceptions of liberty and justice and the most common objections to unbridled freedom of contract assert that, in special cases, such a freedom leads to or sanctifies coercion or injustice. From the point of view of these objections, there is something inconsistent in and unstable about unbridled freedom of contract. For, the view goes, if one really values liberty or justice, then in the name of these values one must avoid the mechanical application of the doctrine to all possible cases, whatever the special features of the case. We shall turn to these specific, apparently internal, objections to unbridled freedom of contract after briefly considering the philosophical foundations for freedom of contract and the character of competing philosophical perspectives. For the next several paragraphs, I draw on my essay, "The Ethics of Taxation: Rights Versus Public Goods," in D. R. Lee, ed., *Taxation and the Deficit Economy* (San Francisco: Pacific Institute, 1986).

[12] For a recent account of this conception of objective, albeit relational, value, see Amartya Sen's "Evaluator Relativity and Consequential Evaluation," *Philosophy and Public Affairs* (Spring 1983).

[13] But this is not intended as an explication of what Kant himself actually meant.

[14] Robert Nozick, *Anarchy, State, and Utopia* (New York: Basic Books, 1974), p. 172.

[15] In *Coppage* v. *Kansas* this principle is exemplified in the majority view that: "Concerning the full right of the individual to join the union, he has no inherent right to do this and still

remain in the employ of one who is unwilling to employ a union man, any more than the same individual has a right to join the union without the consent of that organization. Can it be doubted that a labor organization—a voluntary association of working men—has the inherent and constitutional right to deny membership to any man who will not agree that during such membership he will not accept or retain employment in company with non-union men? Or that a union man has the constitutional right to decline proffered employment unless the employer will agree not to employ any non-union man?" (19–20). Note that this opinion assigns a constitutional liberty to unions that is violated by current right-to-work constraints on unions.

[16] *Coppage* v. *Kansas* 10. As noted in the text, this passage is potentially misleading. It should be read in conjunction with the passage in note 16.

[17] Although one does not have to want to do something in order to have a right to do it, and one's wanting to do something certainly does not give one a right to do it, it is odd to attach great *importance* to a person's being forbidden a rightful act that, by the nature of the case, he would not perform anyway.

[18] For the rejections of all the types of theories I have labelled "social goal" theories on the basis of a Lockean view of individual entitlements, see Chapter 7 ("Distributive Justice") in Nozick, *Anarchy, State, and Utopia,* and my essays, "Distribution versus Justice," in *Ethics* (January 1976), and "Liberty and Justice" in J. Arthur and B. Shaw, eds., *Justice and Economic Distribution* (Englewood Cliffs, NJ: Prentice-Hall, 1978).

[19] T. H. Green, "Freedom of Contract," in J. R. Rodman, ed., *The Political Theory of T. H. Green* (New York: Appleton-Century-Crofts, 1964), p. 51.

[20] Ibid., p. 53.

[21] See Eric Mack, "Bad Samaritanism and the Causation of Harm," *Philosophy and Public Affairs* (Summer 1980).

[22] Thus, in *Coppage* v. *Kansas,* we find ". . . each party when contracting is inevitably more or less influenced by the question of whether he has much property, or little, or none; for the contract is made to the very end that each may gain something that he needs or desires more urgently than that which he proposes to give in exchange."

part EIGHT

IMPERIALISM

Both communism and capitalism have been accused of being imperialistic. Capitalism is supposed to require foreign markets for capitalists to sell their products once the home consumers have stopped being able to purchase them. Communism is supposed to involve the spreading of revolution, so that a truly universal society can be created where all the workers are fully liberated.

Is capitalism guilty as charged? Is communism? While the historical controversies will have to be discussed elsewhere, some of the more philosophical questions about whether existing conditions of poverty and abundance are due to the ills of one or the other system can be touched on here. The following essays will also address the question as to which system should be implemented in developing nations. That is perhaps one of the most politically vital questions facing us on the global front.

KAI NIELSEN

GLOBAL JUSTICE, CAPITALISM, AND THE THIRD WORLD

Marxism may not be egalitarian in the sense of its being a moral exhortation in favor of enforcing universal equality for human social life, but in a certain sense the Marxian promise of the ultimate elimination of classes and the realization of the principle of "From each according to his ability, to each according to his need" is arguably not far from what egalitarianism morally requires. Kai Nielsen—who teaches philosophy at the University of Calgary, Alberta, Canada, and has written, among numerous other works, Equality and Liberty *(1985)—would agree. He defends, from a largely Marxian ethical and geopolitical frame of reference, the ideal of global redistribution, though, as Nielsen makes clear in his* Equality and Liberty, *while he hopes his views are compatible with those of Marx, his arguments are not grounded on distinctly Marxian premises. He sees the peoples of the Third World as the victims of capitalism and argues that the only sensible and just alternative is to bring into place a democratic socialist replacement of capitalism, which can finally with the development of the productive force make feasible an egalitarian world order.*

I

Let us start with some stark empirical realities. Approximately 10,000 people starve every day. There was a severe drought last year (1983) in Africa and about twenty million people, spread through 18 countries, face severe shortages of food: shortages that will in some instances bring on starvation and in others, for very many people, will bring about debilitating malnutrition—a malnutrition that sometimes will permanently and seriously damage them. The Brandt Report of 1980 estimates that 800 million people cannot afford an adequate diet. This means that millions are constantly hungry, that millions suffer from deficiency diseases and from infections that they could resist with a more adequate diet. Approximately fifteen million children die each year from the combined effects of malnutrition and infection. In some areas of the world half the children born will die before their fifth birthday. Life for not a few of us in the industriously developed world is indeed, in various ways, grim. But our level of deprivation hardly begins to approximate to the level of poverty and utter misery that nearly 40% of the people in the Third World face.

As Robert McNamara, who is surely no spokesman for the Left, put it, there are these masses of "severely deprived human beings struggling to survive in a set of squalid and degraded circumstances almost beyond the power of sophisticated imaginations and privileged circumstances to conceive."[1] Human misery is very much concentrated in the southern hemisphere (hereafter "the South") and by any reasonable standard of justice there is a global imbalance

Reprinted, with permission, from *The Journal of Applied Philosophy* 1 (1984).

of the benefits and burdens of life—the resources available to people—that calls for an extensive redistribution of resources from the industrial countries of the northern hemisphere ("the North") to the South.

This, of course, assumes that there is something properly called global justice and this, in certain quarters, will be resisted as a mirage or as being an incoherent conception. We can properly speak of justice within a society with a common labour market, but we cannot speak of justice for the world community as a whole. We cannot say, some claim, of the world community as a whole that it is just or unjust. Justice is only possible, the claim goes, where there are common bonds of reciprocity. There are no such bonds between a Taude of Highland New Guinea and a farmer in Manitoba. In general there are no such bonds between people at great distances from each other and with no cultural ties, so, given what justice is, we cannot correctly speak of global justice. I think this is a mistaken way of construing things and I shall return to it in a moment.

The call for a massive redistribution of resources also assumes, what Neo-Malthusians will not grant, namely that we can carry this out without still greater harm resulting.[2] Part of the demand for the redistribution of resources is in the redistribution of food and in the resources (including the technology and the technological know-how) to realize agricultural potential. Neo-Malthusians believe that this redistribution, at least for the worst-off parts of the Third World, is suicidal.

It is a moral truism, but for all of that true, that it would be better, if no greater harm would follow from our achieving it, if we had a world in which no one starved and no one suffered from malnutrition. But, some Neo-Malthusians argue, greater harm would in fact follow if starvation were prevented in the really desperate parts of the world, for with the world's extensive population-explosion resulting from improved medicine and the like, the earth, if population growth is not severely checked, will exceed its carrying capacity. An analogy is made with a lifeboat. Suppose the sea is full of desperate swimmers and the only available lifeboat can only take on a certain number. It has, after all, a very definite carrying capacity. If too many are taken on the lifeboat it will swamp and everyone will drown. So the thing is not to go beyond the maximum carrying capacity of the lifeboat.

We are, Neo-Malthusians claim, in a similar position *vis-à-vis* the earth. It is like a lifeboat and if the population goes out of control and gets too large in relation to the carrying capacity of the earth there will be mass starvation and an unsettlement bringing on a suffering vastly exceeding the already terrible suffering that is upon us. Sometimes our choices are between evils and, where this is so, the rational and morally appropriate choice is to choose the lesser evil. It may be true that we may never do evil that good may come, but faced with the choice between two certain evils we should choose the lesser evil. Better four dead than twenty. But, some Neo-Malthusians claim, *vis-à-vis* famine relief, this is just the terrible situation we are in.

Parts of the earth have already, they claim, exceeded their carrying capacity. The population there is too great for the region to yield enough food for its expanding population. Yet it is in the poorer parts of the world that the population continues to swell and, it is terrible but still necessary to recognise, it is the above horrendous situation that we are facing in many parts of the world.

Neo-Malthusians maintain that if we do not check this population explosion in a rather drastic way the whole earth will in time be in the desperate position of the Sahel. Redistributive reform is softhearted and softheaded, encouraging the poor to increase their numbers and with that to increase the sum total of misery in the world.

I shall talk about Neo-Malthusianism first and then, after I have considered the International Food Order, turn to a consideration of whether we have a coherent conception of global justice. Neo-Malthusianism, I shall argue, is a pseudo-realism making dramatics out of a severe and tragic morality of triage when the facts in the case will not rationally warrant such dramatics—will not warrant in these circumstances a morality of triage.

In the first place, while lifeboats have a determinate carrying capacity, we have no clear conception of what this means with respect to the earth. What population density makes for commodious living is very subjective indeed; technological innovations continually improve crop yield and could do so even more adequately if more scientific effort were set in that direction.

Secondly, for the foreseeable future we have plenty of available fertile land and the agricultural potential adequately to feed a very much larger world population than we actually have.[3] Less than half of the available fertile land of the world is being used for any type of food production. In Africa, for example, as everyone knows, there are severe famine conditions and radical underdevelopment, but African agriculture has been declining for the last twenty years.[4] Farmers are paid as little as possible, masses of people have gone into the large urban centres where industrialization is going on. Domestic food production is falling while a lot of food is imported at prices that a very large number of people in the Third World cannot afford to pay. Yet Africa has half the unused farm land in the world. If it were only utilized, Africa could readily feed itself and be a large exporter of food.[5] The principal problem is not overpopulation or even drought but man-made problems, problems on which I will elaborate in a moment when I discuss the Postwar International Food Order.

Thirdly, the land that is used is very frequently used in incredibly inefficient ways. The *latifundia* system in Latin America is a case in point.[6] In Latin America as a whole, and by conservative estimates, landless families form 40% of all farm families. One percent of all farm families control, again by conservative estimates, 50% of all farm land. This landed elite has incredible power in Latin America and they use this power to keep the peasantry poor, disorganized and dependent. The *latifundia* system is an autocratic system, but—and this is what is most relevant for our purposes—it is also a very inefficient system of agricultural production. The landowner, not infrequently through his farm manager, has firm control over the running of the farm and over the destinies of his farm labourers. The *latifundios* are very large estates and the land on them is underworked. Much of it is used for pasture. Only 4% of all the land in large estates is actually in crops. There is more fallow land, that is land not even used for pasture but held idle, than there is land in crops. If the *latifundia* land were redistributed to peasants and they were allowed to work it intensively and particularly if they formed into peasant cooperatives, the food production would be increased enormously. Again, it isn't the lack of land or the size of the population that is the problem but the way the land is used.

Fourthly, there is the problem of cash crops: crops such as peanuts, strawberries, bananas, mangos, artichokes, and the like. Key farm land, once used by local residents for subsistence farming, is now used for these cash crops, driving subsistence farmers off the best land into increasingly marginal land and, in many instances, forcing them to purchase food at very high prices, prices they often cannot afford to pay. The result has been increasing malnutrition and starvation and impoverishment. Previously in New Guinea most of the tribal peoples had a reasonably adequate diet. Now, with the incursion of the multinationals and the introduction of cash crops, severe malnutrition is rife. The good land is used for cash crops and the farming for local consumption is on the marginal land. Mexican peasants, to take another example, did reasonably well on a staple diet of corn and beans. With the advent of multinational food producers, they became a rural, but typically underemployed, proletariat, in one not atypical instance, planting, harvesting and processing in freezing plants strawberries for export and importing food to replace the staple food they had previously grown themselves.[7] The catch was that the food they purchased was typically less nutritious and was at prices they could hardly afford. Again, in those Mexican communities malnutrition is rife but the principal cause here, just as in New Guinea, is in the socio-economic system and not in droughts or population explosion.

In fine, against Neo-Malthusians, it is not the case that the basic cause of famine is the failure of the food supply relative to the population. Rather the basic cause of famine is poverty and certain economic policies. People who are not poor are not hungry. We look at North-South imbalance and it is plain as anything can be that this is the result of the workings of the world economic system and a clear indicator of that is the food economy. A stark difference between North and South is in the vast malnutrition and starvation which is principally a phenomenon of the South. But these famine conditions result from the working of the economic system in allocating the ability of people to acquire goods.[8] As Amartya Sen has shown for the great Bengal famine of 1943–1944, a famine in which around three million people died, it was not the result of any great crop failure or population explosion.[9] In 1942 there had been an extraordinary harvest but the 1943 crop was only somewhat lower and was in fact higher than the crop of 1941 which was not a famine year. Sen's figures show that the 1943 crop was only 10% less than the average of the five preceding years. Yet 1943 was a famine year of gigantic proportions. Why? The answer lies in people's economic position.[10] People have entitlements to a range of goods that they can acquire. Whether they have such entitlements, whether they can command the goods they need, depends on the workings of the economic system. Given—to take a current (1983) example—the minimum wage in Brazil (something for which approximately 1/3 of the work force labours), if that situation persists, many workers will not have the entitlement to the food they need to survive. In fact, right now a day's wage enables them only to command a kilo of beans. They can, that is, only purchase a kilo of beans for a day's work at the minimum wage. So people in such circumstances, understandably, reasonably and indeed rightly, take considerable risks to loot supermarkets and the like. People starve when their entitlements are not sufficiently large to buy the food necessary to keep them alive. That, to return to Sen's example of the great famine in Bengal, is precisely what happened in Bengal in 1943–44 and is happening again in Brazil and, with greater severity, in a not inconsiderable number of other places.

The food available to people is a matter of income distribution and that, in the capitalist system, is fundamentally rooted in their ability to provide services that people in the economy are willing to pay for. In poorer countries for many people about two-thirds of their total income goes for expenditures on food. Where there is some rapid industrialization newly employed workers are likely, with increased entitlements, to spend more on food. This, under a capitalist system, will force food prices up and it is very likely as a result that the entitlements of very poor agricultural labourers—labourers who own no land and have only their labor power to sell—will fall, until, even with a constant supply of food in their environment, they will no longer be able to purchase food to meet their minimum needs. Where people are on the margin of sustainable life, a famine may be created by such an increase of demand with little or no decline in the food supply.[11] What we need to recognise is that hunger, malnutrition and famine are fundamentally questions of distribution of income and the entitlements to food. And here, of course, we have plainly questions of justice and, I shall argue in Section III, questions of global justice. But in trying to achieve a moral assessment of what should be done in the face of such extensive starvation and malnutrition, Neo-Malthusian accounts are very wide of the mark, principally because of their failure to understand what causes and sustains such misery.

II

In order to make more perspicuous my discussion of global justice and to make even clearer why we should *not* regard the starvation and malnutrition facing the South as a matter of actual food shortages caused by or at least exacerbated by population explosion, I want to do a bit of political sociology and describe—an interpretative description if you like—the rise and fall of the Postwar International Food Order.[12] Since the early 1970s the perception of scarcity and disaster because of that scarcity has been a popular refrain of much of our discussion of the world food economy. But this, as I in effect indicated in the previous section, is more ideology than fact. To understand what is going on, we need to come to understand the political economy of food as it was developed after World War II in the capitalist world. The capitalist world, after the last great war, went from the gold standard to the dollar standard with the United States clearly becoming the preponderant world power. In the 1950s and 1960s, the American State, reflecting plainly the interests of its capitalists, developed a policy of food aid to Third World countries. These were countries which were often trying rapidly to industrialise. This food aid, at one and the same time, provided a lot of cheap food for their new and very inexpensive industrial labour force and a respite for the American farmers with their, relative to the market, overproduction. (We must remember that since the Roosevelt years the farmers had come to be a powerful lobby.) But it should also be noted that this food aid program helped turn self-sufficient agrarian countries into economically dependent countries dependent on food aid. It led to a commodification of food and to placing structurally these Third World countries in the commodity exchange system of the capitalist order.

The easiest way to see how the postwar food order developed and declined is to chart the fate of wheat in the world economy. In the 1950s and 1960s the surplus in wheat in the United States was sustained both for domestic-political reasons and to pull the newly emerging Third World countries firmly into the capitalist orbit. It was an astute way to help make the world safe for the flourishing of capitalism. Cheap food exported and subsidised from America encouraged in Third World countries the growth, in the process of industrialisation, of urban populations. It encouraged, that is, the formation of a proletariat and a lumpen-proletariat from a previously peasant population—a proletariat and a lumpen-proletariat dependent on cheap food sold to them principally as a commodity. A previously self-sufficient agriculture in Third World countries radically declined and ceased to be self-sufficient. Much of the rural population, in a state of impoverishment, as a huge reserve industrial army, was in effect driven into the cities and in tandem with that, as rural production declined, rural life became ever more impoverished.

Though there were in the 1950s and 1960s great hardships for both the new urban workers and the peasants in the countryside, nonetheless the system based on the export of cheap food from America worked in some reasonable fashion until the early 1970s. Then it began to come apart. This International Food Order "encouraged a massive increase in the numbers of people in all countries separated from direct ties to agriculture."[13] In such a situation an increase in grain prices will trigger an increase in scarcity, though the scarcity is not rooted in what "can technically be produced but in what people with constant or declining real monetary incomes can buy."[14] What we had facing us in the 1960s was an "extraordinary growth of urban populations—an aspect of proletarianisation—and agricultural underdevelopment."[15] The capitalist rationale for this activity was plain, food aid was intended to assist capitalist development in the Third World while appeasing the farm lobby in America. The thing was to integrate these Third World societies into the capitalist economic system: a system which was becoming a world system. Cheap foreign wheat facilitated this by facilitating the growth of urban populations, but it also contributed to underemployment and poverty in the countryside in these very same countries. But in the 1970s the International Food Order began to break down. Grain surpluses dwindled, prices rose, food aid was cut back. The food aid program gradually ceased to have a capitalist rationale. What had happend was that the food aid program had in the course of time made commercial markets work. In virtue of its very success, food aid became increasingly superfluous from a capitalist perspective. Some of the urban workers could now afford to buy food under market conditions, though many in the urban centers (those marginally employed or unemployed) had the *need* for the food but in a market system no longer had the *entitlement*. Similar things obtained for rural farm labourers rotting in the countryside where agricultural production had been cut back. The difficulty for Third World countries in continuing to get cheap food was exacerbated by the huge Russian/American grain deals of 1972 and 1973. Consumerism and a meat diet American Style became a goal in the Soviet Union and in Eastern Europe. And even though détente is now a thing of the past, or at least temporarily shelved, the grain sales to the Soviet Union still go on. But food aid to the Third World has almost vanished, the western agricultural sector continues to decline, farmers become fewer, now pitted against consumers, and food prices continue to rise so that the many poor in Third World countries lose their entitlements. Capitalism, of course, needs a workforce that can reproduce itself but with newly developed industrial enterprises in the Third World a little starvation and malnutrition will not hurt, will not affect the efficiency of capitalist production, as long as they have, as they indeed have, a huge labour pool to draw upon. Individual workers can starve as long as there are plenty of replacements. Things like this happened with the industrialisation of the Western World under capitalism in the nineteenth century. It is now being repeated in the Third World in the twentieth century.

III

With this sketch of political sociology before us, we can now return to the topic of global justice. There are some who would maintain that talk of justice can only coherently be applied within particular societies or at best between societies similarly situated and in a condition of mutual cooperation. I want to show why this doctrine is false and why it is quite morally imperative for us to speak of global justice and injustice and to characterise these notions in a perspicuous fashion.

Those who would argue against extending justice arguments into a North-South context and into the international arena generally, will argue that when we talk about what is to be done here we need to recognise that we are beyond the circumstances of justice. For considerations of justice coherently to arise there must, between the people involved, be (a) a rough equality in the powers and capacities of persons, (b) be a situation where people do cooperate but largely on the basis of reciprocal advantage and (c) a situation where all parties are in a condition of moderate scarcity.[16] It is, many have argued, only in such circumstances that issues of justice are at home. Only in such circumstances, the claim goes, can we appeal to principles of justice to adjudicate conflicting claims on moderately scarce goods. For principles of justice to function, there must be enough reciprocity around for people to find some balance of reciprocal advantage. If they cannot find that, they have no basis for regulating their conduct in accordance with the principles of justice.

However, if these really are the circumstances of justice, it looks at least as if we can have no global justice, for the richest nations do not seem to be related to the poorest ones in such a way that the rich nations secure a reciprocal advantage if justice is done. It very likely makes more sense for them to go on cruelly exploiting the poor nations as they have done in the past. There is, in short, in most circumstances at least, little in it for them if they would do, what in circumstances of greater equality, we would uncontroversially say is the just thing to do.

The mistake here, I believe, is in sticking with the existence of a skein of actual cooperative reciprocity as essential for the circumstances of justice. The world is certainly not a cooperative scheme. We do not have in place internationally schemes for mutual support. It is even rather far-fetched, given the class nature of our own societies, to regard discrete societies as cooperative partnerships, but certainly the world is not. We do not have in place there the cooperative reciprocal interdependency which, some say, is essential for justice.

However, this condition for the very possibility of justice is too strong. That this is so can be seen from the following considerations. There is a world-wide network of international trade; poor countries stand to rich countries in complex relations of interdependence, indeed in an interdependency relation that places poor countries in a position of dependence. The rich nations, functioning as instruments for gigantic capitalist enterprises, have dominated and exploited underdeveloped countries using their resources and markets on unfair terms. Between North and South—between rich and poor nations—there are conflicts of interest and competing claims under conditions not so far from moderate scarcity such that conditions giving scope for arguments of justice obtain. In intrastate situations we do not need conditions of actual reciprocity of mutual advantage for issues of justice to be in place. The Australian aborigine population could be too small, too weak, and too marginal to mainstream life in Australia for the non-aboriginal population to gain any advantage from *not* seizing their lands and driving them from them without any compensation. But such an action would not only be plainly wrong it would be grossly unjust. Yet it is quite possible that the non-aboriginal population would stand to gain rather than lose from such an action. Still, that would not make such an action one whit the less unjust. What we need to invoke instead is a *moral reciprocity* not resting on actual schemes of cooperation for mutual advantage but instead on a broadly Kantian conception of moral equality in which justice requires that we all treat each other as equals, namely, we are to treat all people as persons and in doing so treat them as we would reasonably wish to be treated ourselves.[17] In other words, we must, in reasoning justly, be willing to universalise and to engage in role reversal. It does not take much moral imagination for us, if we are relatively privileged members of the so-called First World, to realise that we would not wish to live the marginal existence of many people in the Third World. We would, that is, not wish to starve or have our children starve or to be in one way or another crippled by malnutrition or live, where this could be avoided, without anything like an adequate education or without adequate housing and the like. We would not accept role reversal here. If our feet, that is, were in their shoes, we would not take as morally tolerable, where such conditions could be avoided, such conditions of life for ourselves. But there is no relevant difference here between ourselves and them. If, in such circumstances, we would not will it for ourselves, we cannot will it for them either.

In the light of our conception of the moral equality of people, we could not accept such inequalities as just. Yet it is just such inequalities that the International Food Order, a deliberate policy objective of the United States, acting for the capitalist order, has brought about in the postwar years. Even given Nozickian notions of justice in rectification, it would be correct to say that many people in Third World countries are not being treated justly. However, the injustice of such an order is even more evident if we develop a conception of justice as fair reciprocity. People, through conquest, domination and exploitation, have been made worse off than they were before these relations were brought into place. They had been driven into bargains they would not have made if they had not been driven to the wall. They are plainly being coerced and they are surely not being treated as moral equals.

If we start with an idea of moral reciprocity in which all human beings are treated as equals, we cannot accept the relations that stand between North and South as something that has even the simulacrum of justice. But any tolerably adequate understanding of what morality requires of us will not allow us to accept anything less than a commitment to relations of moral equality. Starting from there we can see that global justice is a plain extension of domestic justice when we remember that in the international arena as well as in the domestic arena we stand (a) in conditions of interdependence, (b) in conditions of moderate scarcity (if we pool our resources) and (c) in conditions where our interests sometimes conflict. Moreover, by any plausible principles of global justice we might enunciate, the relations between North and South are so unjust that extensive redistributions of resources are in order. Whatever critical standards we use to regulate conflicting claims over scarce goods, we cannot, if we have any tolerably good knowledge of the facts in the case and a sense of fairness, but think the present relations are unjust and require rectification. There is not even in the various states of the North a fair access to basic natural and cultural resources, but viewed globally to speak of anything like a fair access to basic natural and cultural resources, where people are being treated as equals, can be nothing but a cruel and rather stupid joke.

If we start from a premise of *moral* equality as the vast majority of social theorists and moral philosophers right across the political spectrum do, from Robert Nozick to G. A. Cohen, we will believe that the interest of everyone matters and matters equally. There is no not believing in that, if we believe in *moral* equality.

For liberal egalitarians, such as Ronald Dworkin, this will involve a commitment to attain, not equality of condition but equality of resources, while for a radical egalitarian it will involve, as well, under conditions of productive abundance, a commitment to try to move as close as we reasonably can to an equality of condition. While rejecting all such egalitarian readings of *moral* equality, Nozick, with most other philosophers and economists on the right, thinks of moral equality as consisting most essentially in protecting individual rights to non-interference. Individuals in a just social order must be protected in their rights peacefully to pursue their own interests without interference from government, Church or anyone else. Even if the kind of redistribution from North to South I am advocating did not bring about financial hari-kari for people in the North, it would still involve an interference with their right peacefully to pursue their own interests where they are not harming anyone. Thus such a redistribution would still be wrong.

There are at least two responses that should be made here. The first is to assert that such capitalist behaviour has in fact harmed people. Sometimes this has been intentional, often not. But in any event, harm has been done. This is a factual issue, but if the factual descriptions I have given are near to the mark, and particularly if I have accurately described the workings of the international food order, the capitalist order centered in the West has indeed harmed, and continues to harm, very deeply many people in the Third World. (I do not mean to imply that it only harms people in the Third World.) But in our historical circumstances this is unnecessary for we could have an economic system whose underlying rationale was production to meet human needs and which was controlled democratically. Moreover, we now have the technical capacity to develop our productive powers so that the needs of people could be met. But the capitalist order has been massively supported in a very large part of the North and a not inconsiderable number of people in the North have been the beneficiaries of a socio-economic order that did so exploit. (Of course, there are others in the North who are just victims of that order.) This being so, even Nozickian notions of justice in rectification would require redistribution between North and South.

However, a second response seems to me more fundamental, less puritanical and less concerned with blaming people. To see best what is at issue we should proceed rather indirectly. We not only have rights to non-interference, we also have rights to fair cooperation and these rights can conflict. A very important liberty is the liberty to be able to guide one's own life in accordance with one's own unmystified preferences. Central to liberty is the capacity and opportunity to make rational choices and to be able to act on those rational choices.[18] This is much broader than to construe liberty as simply the absence of restrictions or interference, though it certainly includes that. What is vital to see here is that liberty will not be adequately protected if we limit our rights to the protection of rights to non-interference. We must also give central weight to the rights of fair cooperation. If the right of all to effective participation in government and, more generally, to effective direction of their lives is to be attained, there must be in place in our social organisations a respect for the right of everyone to fair cooperation. It is, of course, evident that respect for this right is not very widespread in the world. It will not only not be in place where there is subordination and domination, it will also not be effective where there is widespread starvation, malnutrition, exploitation and ignorance. What is unavoidable is that in class-based societies rights to fair cooperation and rights to non-interference will conflict. To move toward correcting the imbalances between North and South, we will have to move to a collective ownership and control of the means of production, for otherwise economic power becomes concentrated in the hands of a few and they will dominate and exploit others. But moving to collective ownership will in turn have the effect of overriding the rights to non-interference of Horatio Alger types who, capitalistically inclined, seek to acquire productive property through hard work and honest bargains. (It is hardly accurate or fair to say that there are no capitalists like that, particularly small capitalists.) In following their entirely peaceful interests—they have no wish to dominate or impoverish anyone—they wish to invest, buy and sell, and own productive property. If we are to protect their rights to non-interference, these activities can hardly be stopped, but if they are allowed to go on, the institutional stage is set, whatever the particular agent's own inclinations may be, for the undermining of rights to fair cooperation. So we have a fundamental clash of rights: rights of non-subordination with rights to non-interference.

To overcome the great disparities between North and South, even to put an end to the conditions of immiseration in the South—starvation, malnutrition, lack of work, extreme poverty—there would have to be significant and varied redistribution from North to South. In doing this we would have to give rather more weight to the rights of fair cooperation than to rights of non-interference. But—and here is what is alleged to be the catch—there is no significant consensus concerning which rights are to be overriding when they conflict.

I think that there would be a consensus if we came to command a clear view of these rights and their relations, along with some other powerful moral considerations and came, as well, to command a clear view of the relevant social realities. Surely people have a right to pursue their interests without interference. But there are interests and interests. (Indeed rights are most paradigmatically linked to our vital interests.) There is, among these interests, our interest in maintaining our bodily and moral integrity. To require, for example, that a person (say a quite ordinary person), quite against her wishes, donate a kidney to keep someone alive whose value to the society is extensive is, that fact notwithstanding, still an intolerable intrusion on that involuntary donor's bodily integrity; to require a person to give up her religion or political convictions to enhance social harmony or even peace is another intolerable intrusion in that person's life—it simply runs roughshod over her civil liberties. But the interference with the peaceful pursuit of a person's interests that would go with a collective ownership of the means of production would not touch such vital interests. Rather what would be touched is her freedom to buy and sell, to invest and to bequeath *productive* property. But these interests are not nearly as vital as the above type of interests which genuinely are vital for our personal integrity. When the price for overriding those less vital interests is, as it is in the North/South situation, the overcoming of starvation, malnutrition, domination, subordination, great poverty and ignorance (certainly vital interests for any person), there is no serious doubt about in which direction the tradeoffs should go. That there is not a massive consensus about this results, I believe, not from deeply embedded moral differences between people but from disputes or at least from different beliefs about what is in fact the case and about what in fact can come to be the case.[19] Ideological mystification leads us to believe that there is nothing significant that could be done about these matters or nothing that could be done short of impoverishing us all or undermining our civil liberties. But that is just ideological mystification.

IV

So we know that from the moral point of view, justice, or at least humanity, requires an extensive redistribution between North and South. We also know, if we have anything of a sense of *realpolitik,* that nothing like this is going to happen within the present socio-economic order. We can, as I have tried to indicate, know something of what morality requires here but what is far more important to know, and much less obvious, is what are the mechanisms by which this conception of moral requiredness can become a reality in the lives of people so that our societies can be turned around. You may think that what I am about to say is too *parti pris* or perhaps you will even believe it to be vulgar, but it seems to me to be plainly true all that notwithstanding. And, even if it is vulgar, it is better to say something which if true is importantly true than to be evasive out of a sense of nicety or out of fear of saying something obvious.

What I think is plainly true is this: our capitalist masters, in principal control of the consciousness industry, have a plain interest in maintaining something not very different from the present North-South state of affairs.[20] To stabilise things they might, in certain circumstances, where they envisage a threat, favour some minor redistribution of wealth, but it would be very much against their interests, and that of a tiny stratum beholden to them, to make any extensive redistributions—redistributions that would touch their secure power base. Capitalism requires, and indeed can accept, at most a somewhat improved and more efficient version of the present and that, in turn, requires great injustice and inhumanity. It could only marginally improve our lot. A necessary but not a sufficient condition for attaining the end of such global injustice and inhumanity is the shedding of capitalism. As long, that is, as we live in a capitalist system, we are going to have such injustices. At most we might lessen their severity a bit.

If we are morally serious and not ideologically blinkered, we will realise that it is our central social task to get rid of capitalism. But concretely how this is to be done, given capitalist dominance in Western industrial societies, is anything but obvious. (This is exacerbated by the technological sophistication of these societies—by their awesome means of surveillance and control.) However, that the way or the ways are not obvious does not mean, if our efforts are over the long haul, that it cannot be done or that we should settle, as many do, for some reformist tinkering inside bourgeois parameters. We are not going to get justice or even a reign of common humanity that way. Recognising that there are no quick fixes, we need to continue to struggle, without hiding from ourselves the sobering and indeed depressing recognition that things are probably going to get much worse before they get better.

NOTES

[1] Robert McNamara as cited by Peter Singer (1979) *Practical Ethics* (London, Cambridge University Press), p. 159.

[2] Hardin, Garrett "Lifeboat ethics: the case against helping the poor" and Fletcher, Joseph "Give if it helps but not if it hurts," both in: Aiken, William & La Follette, Hugh (Eds) (1977) *World Hunger and Moral Obligation* (Englewood Cliffs, N.J., Prentice-Hall).

[3] Friedmann, Harriet (1982) The political economy of food: the rise and fall of the postwar International Food Order, in: Burawoy, Michael & Skocpol, Theda (Eds) *Marxist Inquiries* (Chicago, University of Chicago Press), pp. 248–286.

[4] Ibid.

[5] Ibid.

[6] Feder, Ernest (1971) Latifundia and agricultural labour in Latin America, in: Shanin, Teodor (Ed.) *Peasants and Peasant Societies* (Harmondsworth, Penguin), pp. 83–102.

[7] Moore Lappé, Frances & Collins, Joseph (1977) *Food First: Beyond the myth of scarcity* (Boston: Houghton Mifflin), pp. 256–258, 278–281; Feder, Ernest (1978) *Strawberry Imperialism: An enquiry into the mechanisms of dependency in Mexican agriculture* (The Hague, Institute of Social Studies).

[8] Sen, Amartya (1981) *Poverty and Famines: An essay on entitlement and deprivation.* (Oxford, Clarendon Press); Arrow, Kenneth J. Why people go hungry, *New York Review of Books,* Vol. XXIX, No. 12 (15 July 1982), pp. 24–26.

[9] Sen, op. cit., pp. 52–83.

[10] Ibid.

[11] Ibid., pp. 24–37.

[12] My account here is indebted to Harriet Friedman's masterful account of this order. See Friedman, op. cit., pp. 248–286.

[13] Ibid., p. 250.

[14] Ibid.

[15] Ibid., p. 268.

[16] Hume, David (1964), in: Selby-Brigge, L. A. (Ed.) *A Treatise of Human Nature* (Oxford,

Clarendon Press), pp. 485–495; Rawls, John (1971) *A Theory of Justice* (Cambridge, Mass., Harvard University Press), pp. 126–130; Barry, Brian Circumstances of justice and future generations, in: Sikora, R. I. & Barry, Brian (1978) (Eds) *Obligations to Future Generations* (Philadelphia, Temple University Press), pp. 204–248.

[17] Richards, David A. J. (1982) International distributive justice, in: Pennock, Roland J. & Chapman, John W. (Eds) *Nomos,* Vol. XXIV (New York, New York University Press), pp. 275–295; Nagel, Thomas (1979) *Mortal Questions* (Cambridge, Cambridge University Press), pp. 111–112.

[18] Norman, Richard (1981) Liberty, equality, property, *Aristotelian Society,* Supplementary Volume, LV (1981), pp. 199–202.

[19] This is powerfully argued by Andrew Collier in Scientific socialism and the question of socialist values, in: Nielsen, Kai & Patten, Steven (Eds) (1981) *Marx and Morality* (Guelph, Ontario, Canadian Association for Publishing in Philosophy), pp. 121–154.

[20] Enzensberger, Hans Magnus (1974) *The Consciousness Industry* (New York, Seabury Press), pp. 3–25.

P. T. BAUER

WESTERN GUILT AND THIRD WORLD POVERTY

Those critical of free markets in Western societies also indict these societies for their alleged exploitation of the Third World. Peter T. Bauer—Professor of Economics at the London School of Economics and a member of the House of Lords of England—will have none of it. For him the Western influence, to the extent that it has adhered loyally to free-market principles—not to colonialism per se, or to racism—has been all to the good for the peoples of the Third World. And because this good influence is predicated on the existence of inequality, the ideal of total equality cannot be a moral primary. According to Bauer, the free market is not a depriver but a provider. It does not pretend to offer something that is impossible and unwise, namely, universal equality of economic and related beneficial conditions. The West need not feel guilty for its free-market dealings with the Third World and the Third World can only benefit from encouraging these dealings further.

> Come, fix upon me that accusing eye.
> I thirst for accusation.

W. B. YEATS

1

Yeats' words might indeed have been written to describe the wide, even welcome, acceptance by the West of the accusation that it is responsible for the poverty of the Third World (i.e. most of Asia, Africa and Latin America).[1] Western responsibility for Third World backwardness is a persistent theme of the United Nations and its many affiliates.[2] It has been welcomed by spokesmen of the Third World and of the Communist bloc, notably so at international gatherings where it is often endorsed by official representatives of the West, especially the United States. It is also widely canvassed in the universities, the churches and the media the world over.

Acceptance of emphatic routine allegations that the West is responsible for Third World poverty reflects and reinforces Western feelings of guilt. It has enfeebled Western diplomacy, both towards the ideologically much more aggressive Soviet bloc and also towards the Third World. And the West has come to abase itself before countries with negligible resources and no real power. Yet the allegations can be shown to be without foundation. They are readily accepted because of widespread feelings of guilt. The West has never had it so good, and has never felt so bad about it.

Reprinted by permission of the publishers from *Equality, the Third World and Economic Delusion* by P. T. Bauer, Cambridge, Mass.: Harvard University Press, and George Weidenfeld & Nicolson Ltd., © 1981 by P. T. Bauer.

2

A few characteristic examples will illustrate the general theme of Western responsibility. To begin with academics. The late Paul A. Baran, Professor of Economics at Stanford, was a highly regarded development economist. He was a prominent and influential exponent of Western guilt in the early days of contemporary development economics. He contributed the chapter on economic development to the *Survey of Contemporary Economics* published by the American Economic Association, and his book *The Political Economy of Growth* is a widely prescribed university textbook. In it Baran wrote:

To the dead weight of stagnation characteristic of pre-industrial society was added the entire restrictive impact of monopoly capitalism. The economic surplus appropriated in lavish amounts by monopolistic concerns in backward countries is not employed for productive purposes. It is neither plowed back into their own enterprises nor does it serve to develop others.[3]

This categorical statement is wholly and obviously untrue because throughout the underdeveloped world large agricultural, mineral, commercial and industrial complexes have been built up through profits re-invested locally.

Professor Peter Townsend of Essex University is perhaps the most prominent British academic writer on poverty. In his book, *The Concept of Poverty,* he wrote:

I argued that the poverty of deprived nations is comprehensible only if we attribute it substantially to the existence of a system of international social stratification, a hierarchy of societies with vastly different resources in which the wealth of some is linked historically and contemporaneously to the poverty of others. This system operated crudely in the era of colonial domination, and continues to operate today, though more subtly, through systems of trade, education, political relations, military alliances, and industrial corporations.[4]

This again cannot be so. The poorest and most backward countries have until recently had no external economic contacts and often have never been Western colonies. It is therefore obvious that their backwardness cannot be explained by colonial domination or international social stratification. And there are no industrial corporations in the least developed countries of the Third World (the so-called Fourth World) such as Afghanistan, Chad, Bhutan, Burundi, Nepal and Sikkim.

In this realm of discourse university students echo what they have learnt from their mentors. About ten years ago a student group at Cambridge published a pamphlet on the subject of the moral obligations of the West to the Third World. The following was its key passage:

We took the rubber from Malaya, the tea from India, raw materials from all over the world and gave almost nothing in return.

This is as nearly the opposite of the truth as one can find. The British took the rubber *to* Malaya and the tea *to* India. There were no rubber trees in Malaya or anywhere in Asia (as suggested by their botanical name, *Hevea braziliensis*) until about 100 years ago, when the British took the first rubber seeds there out of the Amazon jungle. From these sprang the huge rubber industry—now very largely Asian-owned. Tea-plants were brought to India by the British somewhat earlier; their origin is shown in the botanical name *Camilla sinensis,* as well as in the phrase "all the tea in China."

Mr. Charles Clarke, a former President of the National Union of Students, said in his presidential address delivered in December 1976: "For over a hundred years British industry has been draining wealth away from those countries." Far from draining wealth from the less developed countries, British industry helped to create it there, as external commerce promoted economic advance in large areas of the Third World where there was no wealth to be drained.

Western churches and charities are on the same bandwagon. Professor Ronald J. Sider is a prominent American churchman. In an article entitled "How We Oppress the Poor" in *Christianity Today* (16 July 1976), an influential Evangelical magazine, he wrote about the "stranglehold which the developed West has kept on the economic throats of the Third World" and then went on to say, "It would be wrong to suggest that 210 million Americans bear sole responsibility for all the hunger and injustice in today's world. All the rich developed countries are directly involved . . . we are participants in a system that dooms even more people to agony and death than the slave system did." These are evident fantasies. Famines occur in Third World countries largely isolated from the West. So far from condemning Third World people to death, Western contacts have been behind the large increase in life expectation in the Third World, so often deplored as the population explosion by the same critics.

Many charities have come to think it advantageous to play on the theme of Western responsibility. According to a widely publicized Oxfam advertisement of 1972:

Coffee is grown in poor developing countries like Brazil, Colombia and Uganda. But that does not stop rich countries like Britain exploiting their economic weakness by paying as little for their raw coffee as we can get away with. On top of this, we keep charging more and more for the manufactured goods they need to buy from us. So? We get richer at their expense. Business is Business.

A similar advertisement was run about cocoa. Both advertisements were subsequently dropped in the face of protests by actual and potential subscribers. The allegations in these advertisements are largely meaningless, and they are also unrelated to reality. The world prices of coffee and cocoa, which were as it happens very high in the 1970s, are determined by market forces and not prescribed by the West. On the other hand, the farmers in many of the exporting countries receive far less than the market prices, because they are subject to very high export taxes and similar government levies. The insistence on the allegedly low prices paid by the West to the producers and the lack of any reference to the penal taxation of the producers locally are examples that this guilt literature is concerned more with the flagellation of the West than with improving the conditions of the local population.

The intellectuals outside the academies and churches are also well to the fore. Cyril Connolly wrote in an article entitled "Black Man's Burden" (*Sunday Times,* London, 23 February 1969):

It is a wonder that the white man is not more thoroughly detested than he is. . . . In our dealings with every single country, greed, masked by hypocrisy, led to unscrupulous coercion of the native inhabitants. . . . Cruelty, greed and arrogance . . . characterized what can be summed up in one word, exploitation. . . .

If this were true, Third World countries would now be poorer than they were before Western contacts. In fact, they are generally much better off.

Insistence that the West has caused Third World poverty is collective self-accusation. The notion itself originated in the West. For instance, Marxism is a Western ideology, as is the belief that economic differences are anomalous and unjust, and that they reflect exploitation. But people in the Third World, especially articulate people with contacts with the West, readily believed what they were told by prominent academics and other intellectuals, the more so because the idea accorded with their interests and inclinations.

Inspired by the West, Third World politicians have come habitually to insist that the West has exploited and still exploits their countries. Dr. Nkrumah, a major Third World figure of the 1950s and 1960s, was a well-known exponent of this view. He described Western capitalism as "a world system of financial enslavement and colonial oppression and exploitation of a vast majority of the population of the earth by a handful of the so-called civilized nations."[5] In fact, until the advent of Dr. Nkrumah, Ghana (the former Gold Coast) was a prosperous country as a result of cocoa exports to the West, with the cocoa farmers the most prosperous and the subsistence producers the poorest groups there.

Julius Nyerere, President of Tanzania, is a highly regarded, almost venerated, world figure.[6] He said in the course of a State visit to London in 1975: "If the rich nations go on getting richer and richer at the expense of the poor, the poor of the world must demand a change. . . ." When the West established substantial contact with Tanganyika (effectively the present Tanzania) in the nineteenth century, this was an empty region, thinly populated with tribal people exposed to Arab slavers. Its relatively modest progress since then has been the work primarily of Asians and Europeans.

The notions of Western exploitation of the Third World is standard in publications and statements emanating from the Soviet Union and other Communist countries. Here is one example. The late Soviet Academician Potekhin was a prominent Soviet authority on Africa. He is worth quoting because Soviet economic writings are taken seriously in Western universities:

Why is there little capital in Africa? The reply is evident. A considerable part of the national income which is supposed to make up the accumulation fund and to serve as the material basis of progress is exported outside Africa without any equivalent.[7]

No funds are exported from the poorest parts of Africa. Such remittances as there are from the more prosperous parts of the continent (generally very modest in the case of Black Africa, to which Potekhin refers) are partial returns on the resources supplied. In the most backward areas there are no foreigners and no foreign capital. It is the opposite of the truth to say that the reason there is little capital in Africa is that much of the national income is "exported . . . without any equivalent." In Africa as elsewhere in the Third World, the most prosperous areas are those with most commercial contacts with the West.

I could cite many more such allegations, but the foregoing should suffice to illustrate the general theme. In subsequent sections I shall note more specific allegations, some of them even more virulent than those already quoted.

3

Far from the West having caused the poverty in the Third World, contact with the West has been the principal agent of material progress there. The materially more advanced societies and regions of the Third World are those with which the West established the most numerous, diversified and extensive contacts: the cash-crop producing areas and entrepôt ports of South-East Asia, West Africa and Latin America; the mineral-producing areas of Africa and the Middle East; and cities and ports throughout Asia, Africa, the Caribbean and Latin America. The level of material achievement usually diminishes as one moves away from the foci of Western impact. The poorest and most backward people have few or no external contacts; witness the aborigines, pygmies and desert peoples.

All this is neither new nor surprising, since the spread of material progress from more to less advanced regions is a commonplace of history. In medieval Europe, for instance, the more advanced regions of Central and Eastern Europe and Scandinavia were the areas with most contacts with France, the Low Countries and Italy, the most advanced parts of Europe at the time. The West was materially far ahead of the present Third World countries when it established extensive and diverse economic contacts with them in the nineteenth and twentieth centuries. It was through these contacts that human and material resources, skills, capital and new ideas, including the idea of material progress itself (and, incidentally, that of Western guilt too) flowed from the West to the Third World.

In recent times the role of external contacts in promoting economic advance in the Third World has been much more significant than that of similar contacts in the earlier history of Europe. To begin with, and as just noted, the very idea of material progress in the sense of sustained, steady and increasing control over man's environment is a Western concept. People in the Third World did not think of these terms before the advent of Western man. Scholars of such widely differing philosophical and political persuasion as, for instance, J. B. Bury and Christopher Dawson, have for long recognized the Western origin of the idea of material progress. The Western impulse behind economic advance in the Third World has also been acknowledged by writers who recognized this progress but warned against the disturbing, even corrosive, results of the sudden impact of contact with materially much more advanced societies.[8]

The West developed multifarious contacts with the Third World in the nineteenth and twentieth centuries, when the difference in economic attainment between the West and these regions was very wide, much wider than such differences had been in the past. Thus these contacts offered correspondingly greater opportunities, especially in view of the great improvements in transport and communications over the last two hundred years or so.

Since the middle of the nineteenth century commercial contacts established by the West have improved material conditions out of all recognition over much of the Third World, notably in South-East Asia; parts of the Middle East; much of Africa, especially West Africa and parts of East and Southern Africa; and very large parts of Latin America, including Mexico, Guatemala, Venezuela, Colombia, Peru, Chile, Brazil, Uruguay and Argentina. The transformation of Malaya (the present Malaysia) is instructive. In the 1890s it was a sparsely populated area of Malay hamlets and fishing villages. By the 1930s it had become the hub of the world's rubber and tin industries. By then there were large cities and excellent communications in a country where millions of Malays, Chinese and Indians now lived much longer and better than they had formerly, either in their countries of origin or in Malaya.

Large parts of West Africa were also transformed over roughly the same period as a result of Western contacts. Before 1890 there was no cocoa production in the Gold Coast or Nigeria, only very small production of cotton and groundnuts, and small exports of palm oil and palm kernels. By the 1950s all these had become staples of world trade. They were produced by Africans on African-owned properties. But this was originally made possible by Westerners who established public security and introduced modern methods of transport and communications. Over this period imports both of capital goods and of mass consumer goods for African use also rose from insignificant amounts to huge volumes. The changes were reflected in government revenues, literacy rates, school attendance, public health, life expectation, infant mortality and many other indicators.

Statistics by themselves can hardly convey the far-reaching transformation which took place over this period in West Africa and elsewhere in the Third World. In West Africa, for instance, slave trading and slavery were still widespread at the end of the First World War. Many of the worst endemic and epidemic diseases for which West Africa was notorious throughout the nineteenth century had disappeared by the Second World War. External contacts also brought about similar far-reaching changes over much of Latin America.

The role of Western contacts in the material progress of Black Africa deserves further notice. As late as the second half of the nineteenth century Black Africa was without even the simplest, most basic ingredients of modern social and economic life. These were brought there by Westerners over the last hundred years or so. This is true of such fundamentals as public security and law and order; wheeled traffic (Black Africa never invented the wheel) and mechanical transport (before the arrival of Westerners, transport in Black Africa was almost entirely by human muscle); roads, railways and man-made ports; the application of science and technology to economic activity; towns with substantial buildings, clean water and sewerage facilities; public health care, hospitals and the control of endemic and epidemic diseases; formal education. These advances resulted from peaceful commercial contacts. These contacts also made easier the elimination of the Atlantic slave trade, the virtual elimination of the slave trade from Africa to the Middle East, and even the elimination of slavery within Africa.

Although peaceful commercial contacts had nothing to do with the Atlantic slave trade, in the contemporary climate it is impossible not to refer to that trade in a discussion of Western responsibility for Third World poverty. Horrible and destructive as was the Atlantic slave trade, it cannot be claimed legitimately as a cause of African backwardness, still less of Third World poverty. Asia was altogether untouched by it. The most backward parts of Africa, such as the interior of Central and Southern Africa and most of East Africa, were largely unaffected by it.[9]

The slave trade between Africa and the Middle East ante-dated the Atlantic slave trade by centuries, and far outlasted it. Slavery was endemic over much of Africa long before the emergence of the Atlantic slave trade, and it was eventually stamped out by the West. Arabs and Africans do not seem to feel guilty about slavery and the slave trade; but Western Europeans and Americans often do and are made to do so. And yet it was due to their efforts that these practices were largely eliminated. Guilt is a prerogative of the West.

Western activities—supplemented at times by those of non-Western immigrants, notably Chinese, Indians and Levantines whose large-scale migration was made possible by Western initiative—have thus transformed material conditions in many parts of the Third World. All this is not to say that over the past hundred years there has been substantial material advance uniformly throughout the Third World. Large areas, especially in the interior of the Third World, have had few contacts with the West. Moreover, in much of the Third World the political, social and personal determinants of economic performance are often uncongenial to economic achievement. And the policies of many governments plainly obstruct economic achievement and progress. Again, people often refuse to abandon attitudes and mores which obstruct economic performance. They are not prepared to give up their established ways for the sake of greater prosperity. This is a preference which is neither unjustified nor reprehensible.

Such considerations in no way warrant the allegations that Western contacts have obstructed or retarded Third World progress. Wherever local conditions have permitted it, commercial contacts with the West, and generally established by the West, have eliminated the worst diseases, reduced or even eliminated famine, extended life expectation and improved living standards.

4

Many of the assertions of Western responsibility for Third World poverty imply that the prosperity of relatively well-to-do persons, groups and societies is achieved at the expense of the less well-off. These assertions express the misconception emphasized in chapter 1 that the incomes of the well-to-do have been taken from others. In fact, with a few clearly definable exceptions, which do not apply to the relations between the West and the Third World, incomes whether of the rich or of the poor are earned by their recipients. In the Third World it is an article of faith of the most influential and articulate groups that their societies have been exploited by the West, both by Western individuals and Western companies, and also by locally resident ethnic minorities such as the Chinese in South-East Asia, Asians in East Africa, and Levantines in West Africa. The appeal of these misconceptions is all too familiar. They are especially useful to politicians who have promised a prosperity which they cannot deliver. But they are also useful to other influential local groups who expect to benefit from policies inspired by these ideas, especially from the expropriation of foreign enterprises or discrimination against minorities.

In recent decades certain readily recognizable influences have reinforced the notion that the prosperity of some group means that others have been exploited. The impact of Marxist-Leninist ideology has been one such influence. In this ideology any return on private capital implies exploitation, and service industries are regarded as unproductive. Thus, earnings of foreign capital and the incomes of foreigners or ethnic minorities in the service industries are evidence of forms of exploitation. Further, neo-Marxist literature has extended the concept of the proletariat to the peoples of the Third World, most of whom are in fact small-scale cultivators. In this literature, moreover, a proletariat is exploited by definition, and is poor because it is exploited.[10]

The idea of Western responsibility for Third World poverty has also been promoted by the belief in a universal basic equality of people's economic capacities and motivations. This belief is closely related to egalitarian ideology and policy which have experienced a great upsurge in recent decades. If people's attributes and motivations are the same everywhere and yet some societies are richer than others, this suggests that the former have exploited the rest.[11] Because the public in the West has little direct contact with the Third World, it is often easy to put across the idea that Western conduct and policies have caused poverty in the Third World.

The recent practice of referring to the poor as deprived or under-privileged again helps the notion that the rich owe their prosperity to the exploitation of the poor. Yet how could the incomes of, for example, people in Switzerland or North America have been taken from, say, the aborigines of Papua, or the desert peoples or pygmies of Africa? Indeed, who deprived these groups and of what?[12]

5

The principal assumption behind the idea of Western responsibility for Third World poverty is that the prosperity of individuals and societies generally reflects the exploitation of others. Some variants or derivatives of this theme are often heard, usually geared to particular audiences. One of these variants is that colonialism has caused the poverty of Asia and Africa. It has particular appeal in the United States where hostility to colonialism is traditional. For a different and indeed opposite reason, it is at times effective in stirring up guilt in Britain, the foremost ex-colonial power.

Whatever one thinks of colonialism, it cannot be held responsible for Third World poverty. Some of the most backward countries never were colonies, as for instance Afghanistan, Tibet, Nepal, Liberia. Ethiopia is perhaps an even more telling example (it was an Italian colony for only six years in its long history). Again, many of the Asian and African colonies progressed very rapidly during colonial rule, much more so than the independent countries in the same area. At present one of the few remaining European colonies is Hong Kong—whose prosperity and progress should be familiar.[13] It is plain that colonial rule has not been the cause of Third World poverty.

Nor is the prosperity of the West the result of colonialism. The most advanced and the richest countries never had colonies, including Switzerland and the Scandinavian countries; and some were colonies of others and were already very prosperous as colonies, as for instance North America and Australasia. The prosperity of the West was generated by its own peoples and was not taken from others. The European countries were already materially far ahead of the areas where they established colonies.

In recent years the charges that colonialism causes Third World poverty have been expanded to cover "colonialism in all its forms." The terms "economic colonialism" and "neo-colonialism" have sprung up to cover external private investment, the activities of multinational companies, and indeed almost any form of economic relationship between relatively rich and relatively poor regions or groups. Reference to "colonialism in all its forms" as a cause of Third World poverty is a major theme at UNCTAD meetings. This terminology has become common currency in both academic literature and in the media. It regularly confuses poverty with colonial status, a concept which has normally meant lack of political sovereignty.

One unusually direct formulation of these ideas (which are normally expressed in much more convoluted form in the academic and official literature) was provided in an editorial in the June 1978 issue of *Poverty and Power* published by War on Want, a British charity:

We see poverty in the Third World as a result of colonial looting in the past and neo-colonial exploitation in the present.

The demise of political colonialism has probably been another important factor behind the shift in terminology. Disappearance of colonial rule has forced the accusers of the West to find new ground for their charges. Hence the terminology of neo-colonialism and economic colonialism. The usage represents a shift in the basis of accusation and at the same time it retains the benefits of the older, familiar terminology. The influence of Marxist-Leninist doctrine has also promoted the new terminology. According to Marxist-Leninist ideology, colonial status and foreign investment are by definition evidence of exploitation. In fact, foreign private investment and the activities of the multinational companies have expanded opportunities and raised incomes and government revenues in the Third World. Reference to economic colonialism and neo-colonialism both debase the language and distort the truth.[14]

6

The West is now widely accused of manipulating international trade to the detriment of the Third World. This accusation is a major theme of the demands for a New International Economic Order. In particular, the West is supposed to inflict unfavourable and persistently deteriorating terms of trade on the Third World. Among other untoward results, this influence is said to have resulted in a decline in the share of the Third World in total world trade, and also in a large volume of Third World foreign debt. These allegations are again irrelevant, unfounded and often the opposite of the truth.[15]

The poorest areas of the Third World have no external trade. Their condition shows that the causes of backwardness are domestic and that external commercial contacts are beneficial. Even if the terms of trade were unfavourable on some criterion or other, this would only mean that people do not benefit from foreign trade as much as they would if the terms of trade were more favourable. People benefit from the widening of opportunities which external trade represents. Besides this last and basic conclusion, there are many other objections to the notion that the terms of trade are somehow inherently unfavourable to the Third World, and external commercial contacts damaging to it.

As the Third World comprises most of the world, the aggregation of the terms of trade of all its countries has a very limited meaning. The terms of trade of some Third World countries and groups of countries move differently and often in opposite directions from those of others; the effect of the OPEC price increases on many Third World countries is only one recent and familiar example.

Again, except over very short periods, changes in the terms of trade as conventionally measured are of little welfare significance without reference to changes in the cost of production of exports, the range and quality of imports, and the volume of trade. In so far as changes in the terms of trade do affect development and welfare, what matters is the amount of imports which can be purchased with a unit of domestic resources. This figure cannot be inferred simply from the ratio of import and export prices because these do not take into account the cost of production of exports. (In technical language, the comparisons relevant to economic welfare and development are the factoral terms of trade, which allow for changes in the cost of production, and not the simple ratio between import and export prices, i.e. crude commodity terms.) Further, expressions such as unfavourable terms of trade are meaningless except by reference to a base period. In recent decades, however, even the crude commodity terms of trade of Third World countries have been exceptionally favourable. When changes in the cost of production, the great improvement in the range and quality of imports, and the huge increase in the volume of trade are taken into account, the external purchasing power of Third World exports is now relatively high, probably more so than ever before. This situation has made it easier for governments to retain a larger proportion of export earnings through major increases in mining royalty rates, export taxes and corporation taxes. The imposition of substantial export taxes, often very high in the Third World, makes clear that the terms of trade of a country do not determine people's ability to buy imports, much less their living standards.

The exponents of the idea that the terms of trade of the Third World deteriorate persistently rarely specify the period they envisage for this process. Yet it must come to an end at some stage before the terms of trade decline to zero.[16] Nor is it usually made clear why there should be such a deterioration. It is often implied that the West can somehow manipulate international prices to the disadvantage of the Third World. But the West cannot prescribe international prices. These prices are the outcome of innumerable individual decisions of market participants. They are not prescribed by a single individual decision-maker, or even by a handful of people acting in collusion.[17]

The share of a country or group of countries in total world trade is by itself no index of prosperity or welfare. Similarly, reduction in this share has by itself no adverse economic implications. It often reflects the expansion of economic activity and trade elsewhere, which does not normally damage but usually benefits those whose relative share has declined. For instance, since the 1950s the large increase in the foreign trade of Japan, the reconstruction of Europe, and the liberalization of intra-European trade have brought about a decline in the share of other groups in world trade, including that of the United States and the United Kingdom. Furthermore, the share of a country or group of countries in world trade is often reduced by domestic developments, and in particular by policies unrelated to external circumstances such as increased domestic use of previously exported products, or domestic inflation, or special taxation of exporters, or the intensification of protectionist policies. Merely as an aside, it is worth noting that since the Second World War the Third World's share of total world trade has in fact much increased compared with earlier times. It is evident that this share has increased hugely under Western influence in the modern period. Before then, the areas forming the present Third World had little external trade. Of course, if international trade harmed the peoples of the Third World as the critics of the West so often allege, then a decline in the share of the Third World in this trade would be beneficial. Ultimate economic bliss would be attained when the Third World no longer had external economic relations, at any rate with the West.

The external debts of the Third World are not the result or reflection of exploitation. They represent resources supplied. Indeed, much of the current indebtedness of Third World governments consists of soft loans under various aid agreements, frequently supplemented by outright grants. With the world-wide rise in prices, including those of Third World exports, the cost even of these soft loans has diminished greatly. Difficulties of servicing these debts do not reflect external exploitation or unfavourable terms of trade. They are the result of wasteful use of the capital supplied, or inappropriate monetary and fiscal policies. Again, the persistent balance of payments deficits of some Third World countries do not mean that they are being exploited or impoverished by the West. Such deficits are inevitable if the government of a country, whether rich or poor, advancing or stagnating, lives beyond its resources and pursues inflationary policies while attempting to maintain overvalued exchange rates. Persistent balance of payments difficulties mean that external resources are being lent to the country over these periods.

The decline of particular economic activities, as for instance the Indian textile industry in the eighteenth century as a result of competition from cheap imports, is habitually instanced as an example of the damage caused to the Third World by trade with the West. This argument identifies the decline of one activity with the decline of the economy as a whole, and the economic interests of one sectional group with those of all members of a society. Cheap imports extend the choice and economic opportunities of people in poor countries. These imports are usually accompanied by the expansion of other activities. If this were not so, the population would be unable to pay for the imports.

The so-called brain drain, the migration of qualified personnel from the Third World to the West, is another allegation of Western responsibility for Third World poverty or stagnation. This is a somewhat more complex issue than those noted so far, but it certainly does not substantiate the familiar)accusation. The training of many of the emigrants was financed by the West. Again, formal education is not an indispensable instrument nor even a major instrument of emergence from personal poverty or economic backwardness—witness the rapid progress to prosperity of untrained or even illiterate people in many Third World countries. The enforced exodus or outright expulsion of many enterprising and skilled people from many Third World countries, the maltreatment of ethnic minorities or tribal groups, and the refusal of many

Third World governments to allow foreigners to work inhibit development much more than do voluntary departures. And many of these emigrants leave because their own governments cannot or will not use their services. It is not the West nor the emigrants who deprive the society of productive resources: it is these Third World governments.[18]

The West is also said to have damaged the Third World by ethnic discrimination. But the countries in which such discrimination occurred were those where material progress was initiated or promoted by contact with the West. The most backward groups in the Third World (aborigines, desert peoples, nomads and other tribesfolk) were quite unaffected by ethnic discrimination on the part of Europeans. Many communities against which discrimination was often practised—the Chinese in South-East Asia, Indians in parts of South-East Asia, Asians in Africa, and others—have progressed greatly. In any case, discrimination on the basis of colour or race is not a European invention. In much of Africa and Asia and notably in India it has been endemic for many centuries. Finally, any ethnic discrimination by Europeans was negligible compared with the massive and sometimes brutal persecution of ethnic and tribal groups systematically practised by the governments of many independent Asian and African states.

Altogether, it is anomalous or even perverse to suggest that external commercial relations are damaging to development or to the living standards of the people of the Third World. They act as channels for the flow of human and financial resources and for new ideas, methods and crops. They benefit people by providing a large and diverse source of imports and by opening up markets for exports. Because of the vast expansion of world trade in recent decades, and the development of technology in the West, the material advantages from external contacts are now greater than ever before. The suggestion that these relations are detrimental is not only unfounded but also damaging. For instance, it has often served as a specious but plausible justification for official restrictions on the volume or diversity of these relations.

The basic realities of the results of external contacts have been obfuscated by the practice, rife both in public discussion and in the contemporary development literature, of confusing governments, or elites with the population at large.[19] Many Third World governments and their local allies do indeed often benefit from state economic controls, and in particular from the restrictions on external commerce. Such restrictions enable governments to control their subjects more closely, a situation from which the rulers benefit politically and materially. Other articulate and influential local groups also benefit politically and financially from organizing or administering economic controls. These realities are concealed in allegations that the West had forced imports on Third World countries. It is, of course, the rulers who object to the imports desired by their subjects.

The allegations that external trade, and especially imports from the West, are damaging to the populations of the Third World reveal a barely disguised condescension towards the ordinary people there, and even contempt for them.

The people, of course, want the imports. If they did not the imported goods could not be sold. Similarly, the people are prepared to produce for export to pay for these imported goods. To say that these processes are damaging is to argue that people's preferences are of no account in organizing their own lives.

The disparagement of external contacts is relatively recent. Before the Second World War the role of these contacts as instruments of economic advance was widely recognized in academic and public discussion. Their role in providing both external markets and incentive goods, as well as transforming people's attitudes, was a conspicuous theme of the classical economists, including writers as different in their outlook as Adam Smith, John Stuart Mill and Marx.

7

Apart from the damage allegedly caused to the Third World by external trade, it is frequently said nowadays that the mere existence and day-to-day activities of the peoples of the West also harm the Third World.

Cheap consumer goods developed and used in the West and available also in the Third World are said to obstruct development there because these goods supposedly encourage spending at the expense of saving. The mainstream development literature calls this the international demonstration effect. This contention disregards the level of consumption and the extension of choice as criteria of development. Yet these matters are what economic development is about. The notion of a damaging international demonstration effect also ignores the role of external contacts as an instrument of development. It overlooks the fact that the new consumer goods have to be paid for, which usually requires improved economic performance including such things as more work, additional saving and investment, and readiness to produce for sale instead of for subsistence. Thus this accusation neglects the obvious consideration that a higher and more varied level of consumption is both the principal justification for material progress and an inducement to further economic advance.[20]

An updated version of the international demonstration effect proposes that the eager acceptance of Western consumer goods in the Third World is a form of cultural dependence engendered by Western business. The implication here is that the peoples of the Third World lack the ability to decide for themselves how best to spend their incomes. They are looked on as children, or even as mere puppets manipulated by foreigners at will. In fact, however, Western goods have been accepted selectively and not indiscriminately in the Third World where they have been of massive benefit to millions of people. This charge of cultural dependence is often accompanied by the accusation that the West also damages the Third World through its patent laws. Thus, both the provision of Western goods and also the alleged withholding of them are said to be damaging.

As is not surprising, allegedly lavish consumption habits and the pollution and plunder of the environment in the West have also been pressed into ideological service. A standard formulation is that per capita consumption of food and energy in the United States is many times that in India, so that the American consumer despoils his Indian opposite number on a large scale. Professor Tibor Mende is an influential and widely-quoted writer on development. A few years ago he wrote: "According to one estimate, each American has twenty-five times the impact on the environment—as a consumer and polluter—as an Indian" (*Newsweek,* 23 October 1972). Note the reference to each American as consumer and polluter, but not as a producer.

Even babies are drafted into the campaign to promote Western guilt, notably in the familiar pictures of babies with distended bellies. An article entitled "The Greed of the Super Rich" in the London *Sunday Times,* 20 August 1978, opens as follows:

One American baby consumes fifty times more of the world's resources than an Indian baby. . . . The wheat need of the people in Africa's Sahel region could have been met by a twentieth of the wheat European countries use each year to feed cattle.

The West has even come to be accused of mass cannibalism. According to Professor René Dumont, the widely-known French agronomist and consultant to international organizations: ". . . in over-consuming meat, which wasted the cereals which could have saved them, we ate the little children of Sahel, of Ethiopia, and of Bangladesh."[21] This grotesque allegation has come to be widely echoed in the West. According to Miss Jill Tweedie of *The Guardian* (London): "A quarter of the world's population lives, quite literally, by killing the other three-quarters" (*The Guardian,* 3 January 1977). And another article prominently featured in *The Guardian* of 11 June 1979 referred to the

social cannibalism which has reduced over three-quarters of mankind to beggary, poverty and death, not because they don't work, but because their wealth goes to feed, clothe, and shelter a few idle classes in America, Europe, and Japan . . . money-mongers in London and New York and in other Western seats of barons living on profit snatched from the peasants and workers of the world.[22]

Such ridiculous statements could be multiplied many times over. Their expression by prominent academics and by journalists in the so-called quality press tells much about the contemporary intellectual scene.

The West has not caused the famines in the Third World. These have occurred in backward regions with practically no external commerce. The absence of external trading links is often one aspect of the backwardness of these regions. At times it reflects the policies of the rulers who are hostile to traders, especially to non-indigenous traders, and often even to private property. As a matter of interest, it has proved difficult to get emergency supplies to some of the Sahelian areas because of poor communications and official apathy or hostility. Attempts permanently to support the populations of such backward areas with Western official donations would inhibit the development of viable agriculture there.

Contrary to the various allegations and accusations noted in this section, the higher level of consumption in the West is not achieved by depriving others of what they have produced. Western consumption is more than paid for by Western production. This production not only finances domestic consumption but also provides the capital for domestic and foreign investment as well as foreign aid. Thus the gap between production in the West and in the Third World is even greater than the gap in consumption.

8

The West has indeed contributed to Third World poverty, in two senses. These, however, differ radically from the familiar assertions.

First, Western activities since the Second World War have done much to politicize economic life in the Third World. In the terminal years of British colonial rule the traditional policy of relatively limited government was abandoned in favour of close official economic controls. As a result of this change in policy in most British colonies outside the Far East and South-East Asia, a ready-made framework for state-controlled economies or even for totalitarian states was presented to the incoming independent governments. The operation of official Western aid to Third World governments, reinforced by certain strands in its advocacy and by the criteria of its allocation, has also served to politicize life in the Third World.[23] These controls have wasted resources, restricted social and economic mobility and also external contacts. They have also provoked fierce political and social strife. These consequences in turn have brought about poverty and even large-scale suffering.

Many independent Third World governments would presumably have attempted in any case to politicize their economies extensively, because this greatly enhances the power of the rulers. But they are unlikely to have gone so far as they have in recent years, or to have succeeded in their attempts, without Western influence and assistance. But all this does not validate the position of the exponents of Western guilt. The most vocal and influential critics both of colonial rule and of Western contacts with the Third World have emphatically urged large-scale economic controls and other forms of politicization of life in the Third World. Indeed, they have blamed colonial governments and Western influence for not promoting such policies sooner and more vigorously.

Second, Western contacts with the Third World have helped bring about the sharp decline in mortality in the Third World which is behind the recent rapid population growth there. These Western contacts have therefore enabled many more poor people to survive and have thus increased apparent poverty. But, as I have argued in chapter 3, this outcome represents an improvement in the condition of people, and is not the result of deprivation.

9

The allegations that external contacts damage the Third World are plainly condescending. They clearly imply that Third World people do not know what is good for them, nor even what they want. The image of the Third

World as a uniform stagnant mass devoid of distinctive character is another aspect of this condescension. It reflects a stereotype which denies identity, character, personality and responsibility to the individuals and societies of the Third World. Because the Third World is defined as the whole world with the exception of the West and a handful of Westernized societies (such as Japan and South Africa) it is regarded as if it were all much of a muchness. Time and again the guilt merchants envisage the Third World as an undifferentiated, passive entity, helplessly at the mercy of its environment and of the powerful West.

The exponents of Western guilt further patronize the Third World by suggesting that its economic fortunes past, present and prospective, are determined by the West; that past exploitation by the West explains Third World backwardness; that manipulation of international trade by the West and other forms of Western misconduct account for persistent poverty; that the economic future of the Third World depends largely on Western donations. According to this set of ideas, whatever happens to the Third World is largely our doing. Such ideas make us feel superior even while we beat our breasts.

A curious mixture of guilt and condescension is also discernible behind the toleration or even support of inhuman policies of many Third World governments. The brutalities of the rulers are often excused on the ostensible ground that they are only following examples set by the West. For instance, when Asian or African governments massively persecute ethnic minorities, they are excused by their Western sympathizers as doing no more than adopting a local variant of ethnic discrimination by Europeans. Similarly, the most offensive and baseless utterances of Third World spokesmen need not be taken seriously because they are only Third World statements, a licence which has been extended to their supporters in the West. In this general scheme of things, neither Third World rulers nor their peoples have minds or wills of their own; they are envisaged as creatures moulded by the West or, at best, as being at the mercy of their own environment. Moreover, like children, they are not altogether responsible for what they do. In any case, we must support them to atone for alleged wrongs which our supposed ancestors may have perpetrated on their supposed ancestors.[24] And economic aid is also necessary to help these children grow up.

Insistence on Western foreign aid is a major theme of the recent literature of Western guilt. But whether or not linked to patronization (and it usually is so linked), the idea of Western guilt is not only unfounded but is also a singularly inappropriate basis for aid. It leads to a disregard of the effects of aid in the recipient countries and of the conduct of the recipient governments. It discourages even cursory examination of the likely political, social and economic results of Western alms. The prime concern is with divesting the West of resources, not with the effects of its donations.

A feeling of guilt has nothing to do with a sense of responsibility or a sense of compassion. Exponents of guilt are concerned with their own emotional state and that of their fellow citizens, and not with the results of the policies inspired by such sentiments. These policies damage the West. They damage the ordinary people in the Third World even more.

NOTES

[1] In current usage the Third World means most of Asia except Japan and Israel, most of Africa except white southern Africa, and Latin America. Classification of the oil-producing countries is often vague—sometimes they are included in the Third World, sometimes not.

[2] Throughout this essay, Western responsibility refers to the accusation that the West has inflicted backwardness or poverty on the Third World. This usage again accords with standard practice. The different question of moral responsibility for the relief of poverty is examined elsewhere. See note 23.

[3] Paul A. Baron, *The Political Economy of Growth,* New York, Monthly Review Press, 1957, p. 177.

[4] Peter Townsend, *The Concept of Poverty,* London, Heinemann, 1970, pp. 41–2.

[5] Kwame Nkrumah, *Towards Colonial Freedom,* London, Heinemann, 1962. Cf. also P. T. Bauer, *Dissent on Development,* op. cit., chapters 3 and 4.

[6] An adulatory profile in *The Observer* (23 November 1975) cosily referred to Nyerere as "St. Julius." An article in the *Financial Times* (11 August 1975) described him as "Africa's senior statesman and a man of formidable intellect."

[7] I. Potekhin, *Problems of Economic Independence of African Countries,* Moscow, Academy of Sciences, 1962, pp. 14–15.

[8] A list of such warnings and objections will be found in *Dissent on Development* op. cit.

[9] In fact, the areas most involved in the Atlantic slave trade, particularly West Africa, have become the economically most advanced areas in Black Africa. A recent study of pre-colonial South-Eastern Nigeria examines the economic development promoted by the slave trade which "... led to sufficient economic development of the region" to enable the profitable trade in palm-oil to burgeon in the early nineteenth century. David Northrup, *Trade Without Rulers: Pre-colonial Economic Development in South-Eastern Nigeria,* Oxford, Clarendon Press, 1978, p. 176.

[10] This extension of Marxist-Leninist ideology is reflected, for instance, in the passage from the Soviet Academician Potekhin, section 2 above. Marxist-Leninist statements are apt to be designed for political purposes. Thus, in Potekhin's booklet, the passage I have quoted is followed immediately by the injunction that Western enterprises in Africa should be expropriated and economic activity collectivized. This injunction is now accepted by a number of African states.

[11] This relationship was noted in P. T. Bauer, *Equality, the Third World and Economic Decision,* Cambridge, Mass., Harvard University Press, 1983, chapter 1.

[12] Underprivileged is a nonsense expression akin to under- or overfed. Privilege connotes special advantages conferred on some people and denied to others.

[13] See Bauer, *Equality, the Third World and Economic Decision,* chapter 10.

[14] A convenient recent example is a statement by the Ayatollah Khomeini in January 1979: "Our people are weary of it (colonial domination). Following their example other countries will free themselves from the colonial grip." *Daily Telegraph,* 10 January 1979. In its long history Iran never was a Western colony. Further examples of this usage are noted in *Dissent on Development,* chapter 3, "The Economics of Resentment."

[15] These allegations and the demand for a New International Economic Order are discussed

at some length in several essays in Karl Brunner (ed.) *The First World and the Third World*, University of Rochester, N.Y., 1978. See especially essays by Karl Brunner, Harry G. Johnson, Peter T. Bauer and Basil S. Yamey.

[16] When some ostensible evidence is produced in support of these allegations, it usually turns out to involve shifts in base periods or in the aggregates under discussion. I have examined these matters in some detail in *Dissent on Development,* chapter 6: "A Critique of UNCTAD."

[17] Even if the West had the market power implied in many of these discussions, this would not account for a deterioration of the terms of trade, unless the effectiveness of this power increased persistently. Any such idea would be quite unrelated to reality.

[18] An article in *The Observer* (22 July 1979) was entitled "The boat people's 'brain drain' punishes Vietnam." The article suggested that the refugees from Vietnam were selfish and unpatriotic people who left because they could earn more elsewhere, and because they would not accept the new socialist order. It suggested further that this brain drain deprived the country of much-needed skills, especially medical skills. The article used the terms *brain drain, exodus* and *loss* to describe what was in fact a well-documented example of a huge mass expulsion—a revealing misuse of language.

[19] The distinction which applies in many contexts is pertinent also to an assessment of changes in a country's terms of trade. As noted earlier in this section, changes in the terms of trade do not necessarily correspond to the ability of people to buy imports.

[20] At the official level, a damaging international demonstration effect may indeed operate by encouraging show projects and unsuitable technologies financed with public funds. But this is not usually what the exponents of the international demonstration effect have in mind. Nor is it appropriate to blame the West for the policies of Third World governments in their adoption of unsuitable external models.

[21] Quoted by Daniel P. Moynihan, "The United States in Opposition," *Commentary,* March 1975.

[22] The article, written by Ngugi wa Thiang'O, opened a special survey of Kenya.

[23] These implications and results of official foreign aid are examined at greater length in chapter 5 of my *Equality, the Third World and Economic Decision.*

[24] Ibid., chapter 5, section 13.

INDEX

Accumulation, and exploitation, 366, 368, 369
Action, *see* Virtuous action
Adler-Karlsson, Gunnar, 266
Adorno, T. W., 26–27
Agenthood, 101, 285
  rational, 287–288
Agent-type control, and sensation, 275–278
Albert, Hans, 21
Alienation, 62–81, 97, 324, 326–328
  and capitalism, 64, 68–74, 79–81
  and exploitation, 366, 368, 370
  and historical materialism, 331–334
  and information, 95
  and labor, 94–95, 334–339, 366, 368, 370
  and others, 96.
  and personal identity, 76–78
Allen, Fred, 101
Ambition, and motives, 171
Anarchy, State and Utopia (Nozick), 273, 275
Anatomia della scimmia, L' (Carandini), 353
Ancient Economy, The (Finley), 357
Anscombe, G. E. M., 164, 167
Anti-Semitism, 30, 106
Anxiety, and separateness, 66–67
Aquinas, St. Thomas, 93, 97–98
Archimedes, 289
  influence of, 54
Arendt, Hannah, 127, 128
Areopagitica (Milton), 235
Aristotle, 19, 89, 140, 142, 143, 145, 148, 151, 200, 210, 233–234, 236–239, 245, 256, 357, 391, 394

influence of, 8, 14, 42, 50, 53, 67, 258
Art of Loving, The (Fromm), 65, 67
Augustus, Emperor, 353
Austin, Dr. Michel, 353
Autonomy
  and feedback, 126
  and self-realization, 119

Bakunin, Michael, 33, 194
Baran, Paul A., 455
Bargaining power, and freedom of contract, 435
Barker, Ernest, 256–257, 258, 259
Bauer, Peter T., 454
Baxter, Will, 344
Benign practices, 99–101
Benn, Tony, 254
Berlin, Isaiah, 221, 227
Bernstein, Eduard, 34
Billet, Leonard, 292
Binder, Julius, 29
Bismarck, Otto von, 29
Blake, William, 120
Blanc, Louis, 398
Blanqui, Auguste, 194
Blanquists, 192, 194
Body rights
  natural, 273–278
  as property rights, 272–286
Branden, Nathaniel, 62
Brandt Report (1980), 440
Bukharin, Nikolai, 26
Burdens, relief of, 201–202
Bury, J. B., 459

Calculation problem, 85–87, 92, 97, 157
Capital, 298–299, 300–301
Capital (Marx), 185, 191, 193, 224, 327, 332, 343–338, 348, 355, 356, 403n
Capitalism
    and alienation, 64, 68–74, 79–81
    and contribution, 410–419, 421
    and dialectical approach, 6–7
    and egoism, 139–158
    vs. freedom, 217–231
    and global justice, 451–452
    manipulation in, 227–231
    morality of, 84–106
    sacrifice in, 411, 420–423
    and Third World, 445–446
    workers under, 134–135
    see also Private gain
Capital-labor partnership, 255–259
Carandini, Andrea, 353
Cardenas Lázaro, 267
Carter, Jimmy, 253
Cartesians, 384
Causality, 142
Censorship, 181–182
Ceremonial rules, 240–241, 243
Chartist movement, 188
Choice, 211
    dimensions of, 221–222, 226–227
    see also Free choice
Cicero, Marcus Tullius, 263
Civil liberties, 451
Clark, John Bates, 410–415
Clarke, Charles, 456
Class, 344–358
    and exploitation, 348–351
    peasants, 353–355
    and political activity, 351–353
    slave societies, 355–357
Classical egoism, *see* Egoism
Class Struggle in the Ancient Greek World, The (St. Croix), 345
Class Struggles in France, The (Marx), 355
Coercion, 204–205, 213, 220, 429
    and freedom of contract, 425, 433–434
    overt, 222–224
    and relationships, 209–210
    systematic, 222–226, 227
    and totalitarianism, 207–208
Cohen, G. A., 449
Colonialism, 306–308, 462–463
Commodities, 332, 333, 335–338
Communes, 91
Communism, 97, 183
    advanced stage of, 323
    cooperative production in, 193–194
    first phase of, 321–322

and individual freedom, 190–191
Communist man, 58–59
Communist Manifesto (Marx), 183, 184, 187, 188, 191, 311, 348
Community
    and freedom, 319
    and self-realization, 129–132
Competition, 174
    and capitalism, 229–230
Compulsory services, 354–355
Concept of Poverty, The (Townsend), 455
Conceptual level of consciousness, 72
Conflicts, and dialectical approach, 7
Conjectures and Refutations (Popper), 8
Connolly, Cyril, 457
Conscious being, man as, 46–47
Constant, Benjamin, 128
Consumption, 117, 321, 364
    sacrifice of, 422–423
    vs. self-realization, 111–114, 118–119
Contract, *see* Freedom of contract
Contradiction, and dialectical approach, 5–9, 13, 15
Contribution, and capitalism, 410–419, 421
Contribution to the Critique of Political Economy, A (Marx), 335
Control, and property rights, 260–265
    see also Agent-type control; Manipulation
Cooperation, and markets, 90–92
    see also Fair cooperation
Cooperative production, in communism, 193–194
Coppage v. Kansas, 426–427, 430
Corporate property, 250
Corporation, 296–297
Critique of the Gotha Program (Marx), 194, 321, 323
Critique of Political Economy (Marx), 334, 337
Critique of Pure Reason (Kant), 90
Culture, 55, 565

Damiani, St. Petrus, 23
Dawson, Christopher, 459
Death, threat of, 222
Declaration of Independence (U.S.), 189
Declaration of 1793 (France), 188
Democracy, 133
    participatory vs. representative, 131–132
Democracy in America (Tocqueville), 126
Deontological defense, of markets, 88–89, 91, 93, 99, 102
Deutscher, Isaac, 344
Dialectical approach, 2–16, 19–36
    and contradiction, 5–9, 13, 15
    derivations of, 28–30, 35–36
    and Enlightenment, 19–21

and individual, 10–11
and manipulation, 24–28
and science, 11–13, 22–23
sources of, 31–35
and thinking, 13–15
Dialectical integration, 53–58
Diesing, Paul, 8
Dignity, 259
Discrimination, forms of, 103–106, 466
Distribution, 266
in capitalism, 411–415
unequal, 373–374
Distributive justice, 321–324
Domination, and exploitation, 366, 368–370
Downs, Anthony, 127
Dumont, René, 468
Dworkin, Ronald, 119, 365, 376, 379, 449

Easton, Loyd, 180
Economic abundance, 218–219, 228–229
Economic and Philosophic Manuscripts of 1844, The (Marx), 184, 190, 322–335, 337, 339–340
Economic and Social History of Ancient Greece (Austin / Vidal-Naquet), 353
Egalitarianism, and envy, 390–391
Egoism, 328
and capitalism, 139–158
criticisms of, 153–156
Hobbesian vs. classical, 143–145
implications of, 156–158
and morality, 145–147
and natural rights, 151–153
questions about, 150–151
revised, 147–150
Eighteenth Brumaire of Louis Bonaparte, The (Marx), 352
Einstein, Albert, 417
Elites, 357–358
Elster, Jon, 111
Emancipation, 329
Engels, Friedrich, 33, 41, 83, 156, 183, 190, 194, 297, 338, 341, 347, 348, 350, 355–356
Enlightenment, and dialectical approach, 19–21
Entitlements, 385–390, 395–396, 443–444
Entrepreneurs, 401, 415–418, 421
Envy, and self-esteem, 390–395
Epictetus, 355
Equality, 385–390
of opportunity, 387–390
Equality of resources theory, 365–368, 370–376, 378–384
Estrangement, *see* Alienation

Ethical egoism, *see* Egoism
Ethical Foundations of Marxism, The (Kamenka), 341
Ethnic discrimination, 103, 106, 466
Euclid, 289
Euler, Leonhard, 411, 412
Exchange, 298–299, 316, 336
and freedom of contract, 434–435
market, 84–85
voluntary, 406–408
Excusing, 211–212
Exploitation, 321, 364–376, 399–400, 406
and alienation, 366, 368, 370
and class, 348–351
and inequality, 366, 368, 370–376
and peasants, 353–355

Fair cooperation, 450
Fairness ethics, 73
Fanny Hill, 90
Federalist Papers, 307
Fetishism, commodity, 268–269
Feuerbach, Ludwig, 25, 40, 41, 45, 46, 48–51, 57, 180, 184, 185, 188–189, 341
Fichte, Johann, 8, 40, 41, 45, 181
influence of, 49–50
Finley, Sir Moses, 128, 353, 357
Fisk, Milton, 250
Fourier, Charles, 122
"Frankfurt School," 26, 27, 35
Fraser, Douglas, 254
Fraud, 101–102
Frederick II, 20
Free being, man as, 47
Free choice, and survival, 225
Freedom, 75, 80, 298, 326
vs. capitalism, 217–231
and coercion, 207–210, 213, 220, 222–226
and individual/social property, 317–320
and manipulation, 227–229
positive and negative, 228, 432–433
primary and secondary, 201–204, 205
and responsibility, 235
of self-realization, 115
and virtue, 200–213
see also Individual freedom; Liberty
Freedom of contract, 425–436
natural rights vs. social goals, 427–432
objections to, 432–436
Free market, 295–454
Free-riding, and self-realization, 121–122, 135
French Revolution, 189
Freud, Sigmund, 15
influence of, 63

Friedman, Milton, 200, 220, 221, 224, 411
Fries, Jakob Friedrich, 31
Fromm, Erich, 62, 65–75, 80, 228
Fung Yu-lan, 20

Galbraith, John Kenneth, 417
General Theory of Exploitation and Class, A (Roemer), 369
German Ideology, The (Marx / Engels), 52, 185, 190, 341
Gibbard, Alan, 273, 278
Gibbon, Edward, 347
Global justice, 440–441, 446–452
Goebbels, Josef, 407
Goethe, Johann von, 24, 391, 394
Gompers, Samuel, 258
Good life, and capital-labor partnership, 256–259
Government, role of, 301–306
Gradualist socialism, and property rights, 265–268
Green, T. H., 432, 433
Grundrisse (Marx), 2, 10, 122, 315, 332n, 353, 356

Habermas, Dr. Jürgen, 21, 26–28, 126
Hackman, J. Richard, 125
Haldon, Dr. John, 357
Hale, Edward Everett, 407
Hamilton, Thomas, 188
Hammen, Oscar J., 339–340
Happiness, 150–151, 155
Harman, Gilbert, 153–154, 155
Harrington, Michael, 265
Hartmann, Eduard von, 28
Hayek, Friedrich A. von, 200, 410
Hegel, Georg Wilhelm, 67, 129, 324
  and alienation, 63
  and dialectical approach, 4–6, 8–9, 19, 22–25, 29–33, 35, 36, 180–190, 193, 195
  humanism of, 40, 41, 46, 50
  influence of, 47, 119, 313, 350
Heidegger, Martin, 22
Heilbroner, Robert, 2, 298
Heraclitus, 3, 4
Hess, Moses, 33
Hierarchy, vs. peer group, 133–134
Historical materialism
  and alienation, 331–334
  and property rights, 378
Hitler, Adolf, 24, 29
Hobbes, Thomas, 41, 154, 260
  influence of, 140, 142, 143–145

Hodges, Donald C., 155–156
Holmes, Rice, 353
Holmes, Stephen, 128
Holy Family, The (Marx), 185
Honoring the Self (Branden), 81
Houseman, A. E., 62
Human being, man as, 46–53
Human development, 257
Humanization, of nature, 54–58
Human nature, 142, 148–150
Hunger, 44
Hunt, Lester, 233
Hunt, Richard, 188

Identity, *see* Personal identity
Ilting, Karl-Heinz, 31
Immoral situations, in market, 101–103
Individual, 58
  and dialectical approach, 10–11
Individual and the Crowd, The—A Study of Identity in America (Ruitenbeck), 62
Individual freedom, 180–196
Individualism, 68, 69, 129, 152
  see also Egoism
Individual/social property, 315–329
  and freedom, 317–320
  and justice, 321–324
  and self-realization, 324–329
Industry, 55
  self-realization in, 124–126
Inequality, and exploitation, 366, 368, 370–376
Inferiority feelings, 392–393
Initiatory coercion, 204, 210
Innovation, 416, 417, 419
Inquiry into the Nature and Causes of the Wealth of Nations, An (Smith), 85, 292–297, 300–303, 306, 308
Institutional conditions, and self-realization, 132–135
Intentions, and motives, 170
Interest, as reward, 419–422
Interests, 450–451
International demonstration effect, 467
Intimacy, 91
Introspection, and motives, 168, 170
Intuitive thought, 15

Jackson, Jesse, 106
Jefferson, Thomas, 189
Jesus, 355
Jews, 30
John Paul II, Pope, 258–259
Jones, A. H. M., 347, 354

Jungians, 63
Justice, 292–309
    and capital, 298–299, 300–301
    and colonialism, 306–308
    and corporation, 296–297
    and freedom of contract, 434–435
    and government role, 301–306
    and individual/social property, 321–324
    and labor, 297–301
    and land ownership, 295–296
    and liberty, 293–294
    and market economy, 295
    and self-interest, 294–295
    and wealth, 296
    see also Distributive justice; Entitlements;
        Global justice
Just price, 97–99

Kamenka, Eugene, 340–341
Kamptz, Herr von, 31
Kant, Immanuel, 19–20, 31, 90, 96, 103,
    143, 181, 245, 287, 323, 341
    influence of, 210, 234, 405, 428, 447–448
Kelsen, Hans, 25
Keyes, Thomas, 311
Keynes, John Maynard, 93, 252
Keynesians, 252
Knight, Frank, 163, 164
Kolakowski, Leszek, 342
Kolm, Serge, 123
Kramer, Michael, 27

Labor, 315, 320–323, 414
    and alienation, 94–95, 334–339, 366, 368,
        370
    and necessity, 318–319
    as self-realization, 324–326
    and survival, 226
    value of, 297–301
    see also Capital-labor partnership
Laborem Exercens, 259
Labor theory of value, 364, 373, 402, 404,
    405
Labor time, simple undifferentiated, 403
Land ownership, 295–296
Latifundia system, 442–443
Leary, Timothy, 394n
Lee, J. Roger, 84
Legitimate rights, 258
Legitimation, 282
Leibniz, Gottfried Wilhelm von, 116, 129
Leisure, 71
Lenin, Vladimir Ilyich, 34, 35, 192, 269, 339,
    340, 341

Leninism, 340
Leo XIII, Pope, 258
Lévi-Strauss, Claude, 357
Liberty, 449–450
    and justice, 293–294
    see also Freedom
Liebenfels, Jörg Lanz von, 36
Lindgren, J. R., 295
Literature and Revolution (Trotsky), 391
Locke, John, 139, 140, 154–155, 189, 260
    influence of, 273, 378, 427, 432
Logic (Hegel), 195
Logic, and dialectical approach, 11–12,
    14–16
Logical contradiction, 5, 8
Lorenz, Konrad, 22
Love, 67–68
    and capitalism, 73, 74
Lübbe, Hermann, 20–21

Machan, Tibor, 139
Mack, Eric, 425
McLaughlin, Andrew, 217
McNamara, Robert, 440
Malnutrition, in Third World, 440–446
Man, 40–59
    Communist, 58–59
    and dialectical integration, 53–58
    as human being, 46–53
    as natural being, 41–46
Man for Himself (Fromm), 65, 67
Manipulation
    in capitalism, 227–231
    and dialectical approach, 24–28
Mann, Thomas, 27
Marginal product, 412–415, 418
Mark, Saint, 355
Market, 134
    benign practices, 99–101
    calculation problem, 85–87, 92, 97, 157
    and cooperation, 90–92
    criticisms of, 93–99
    deontological defense of, 88–89, 91, 93,
        99, 102
    discrimination in, 103–106
    exchange, 84–85
    immoral situations in, 101–103
    morality of, 84–106
    personal flourishing tradition, 89–90
    and property rights, 268–269
    public goods problem, 92–93
    and utilitarianism, 85, 87–88, 93
    see also Free market; Prices
Market economy, 295

Marshall, Alfred, 411, 419–422
Marx, Karl, 67, 83, 130, 157, 266, 297, 391, 394, 401, 467
  and alienation, 63, 69, 80, 94–97, 322–339
  and capital, 300
  and capitalism, 98, 162, 226, 415, 421–422, 440
  and central economic planning, 331
  and class, 155, 344–353, 355–358
  and commodity fetishism, 268, 269
  and dialectical approach, 2, 4, 6, 7–13, 15, 22, 24–26, 29, 31–35
  on egoism, 140
  and freedom, 180–196, 217, 224, 317–320
  as humanist, 339–342
  and human nature, 149, 233
  and individual/social property, 315, 316
  and justice, 309, 321–324
  and labor, 298, 404–406
  and labor time, 403n
  and market, 93
  and political economy, 1, 291, 299
  and production, 226, 316
  and property, 250, 311–316, 377
  and self-determination, 156
  and self-realization, 111, 114, 116, 122, 124, 126, 129, 324–329
  and social production, 316
  theory of man, 40–59
Marxism, 98, 385, 440
  and alienation, 62, 80, 81, 337–339
  and capitalism, 421–422
  and central economic planning, 331
  and class, 344–349, 353, 355–356, 358
  determinism of, 156
  and dialectical approach, 1, 2–13, 15–16, 19, 21, 22, 26, 32, 34, 35
  as egalitarian, 376
  and equality of resources, 383
  and ethics, 155
  and exploitation, 364, 366, 369, 370, 374, 399–400, 406, 410
  and freedom, 179, 180, 200
  and good will, 340
  and humanism, 342
  and human nature, 40
  and inequality, 372
  and labor theory of value, 373
  and labor time, 403
  and political economy, 291
  and preferences, 365
  and productive resources theory of value, 401
  and property, 249, 250, 316

scientific character of, 341
  and self-realization, 111–112, 114, 122, 126, 129
  and value judgments, 83
  as Western ideology, 457
  and "whole man," 233
Marxist-Leninists, 306, 461, 463
Materialism, and capitalism, 229, 230
Matthew, Saint, 355
"Meaning is use" theory, 288
Meidner Plan, 254–255
Mende, Tibor, 468
Middle Ages, 68–69, 72, 79
Middleman, 99, 101
Military conscription, 354
Mill, James, 58
Mill, John Stuart, 88, 163, 165, 200, 467
Milton, John, 129, 235–236, 243
Minima Moralia (Adorno), 27
Mises, Ludwig von, 64
Money, and alienation, 94–95
Montesquieu, Charles de Secondat de, 298
Moral equality, 427–429, 449
Moral good, 148–150
Morality
  action vs. agent, 210–211
  of capitalism, 84–106
  and egoism, 145–147
  reciprocal, 448
  rules of, 240
  see also Virtue
Morishima, Michio, 369
Motives, 165–166, 175
  and causes, 163–164
  distinguishing, 166–172
Myopia, and self-realization, 120, 135

Napoleon, 33, 34, 403
Natural being, man as, 41–46
Natural rights, 139–141, 152–153
  and egoism, 151–153
  Lockean, 154–155
  vs. social goals, 427–432
Nature
  and dialectical approach, 8–9
  humanization of, 54–58
Necessity, 325
  and freedom, 318–320
Need
  and distributive justice, 322–323
  production for, 226
Negative freedom, 228, 433
Negative rights, 153–154
Neill, A. S., 231

Neo-Aristotelians, 139, 142
Neo-Lockeans, 411
Neo-Malthusians, 441–444
Neo-Marxism, 349
Neumann, Franz, 269
Newton, Isaac, 417
Nielsen, Kai, 440
Nkrumah, Dr., 457
Nock, Albert J., 235, 236, 237, 239, 243
Nock, Arthur Darby, 347
Non-interference, rights to, 449–450
Nozick, Robert, 152, 273, 275, 295, 374, 379, 385, 410, 429–430
    influence of, 448, 449
Nyerere, Julius, 457

Object, creation of, 58
O'Brien, G. E., 125
Ollman, Bertell, 15
On Liberty (J. S. Mill), 200
Others, and self-realization, 129–132

Paine, Thomas, 233, 234
Paradise Lost (Milton), 129
Parekh, Bhikhu, 40
Pareto, Vilfredo, 15, 364, 371, 374, 375, 383
Paris Commune (1871), 187–188, 191–195, 377
Participatory democracy, and self-realization, 131–132
Pashukanis, Evgeny B., 268, 269
Passion, 45
Patlagean, Evelyne, 357
Paul, Saint, 355
Peasants, and exploitation, 353–355
Peer group, vs. hierarchy, 133–134
Permission, seeking, 242
"Perpetual" contributions, 417–418
Personal identity, and alienation, 76–78
Personal flourishing tradition, 89–90
Personal property, 250–251
Phaedo (Plato), 143
Piaget, Jean, 14
Planning, central, 134
Plato, 3, 19, 89, 143, 293
    influence of, 148, 210
Political activity, and class, 351–353
Political Economy of Growth, The (Baran), 455
Political means, 234–236, 243–245
Political Theory of Bolshevism, The (Kelsen), 25
Politics (Aristotle), 357
Politics, and self-realization, 126–129
Popper, Sir Karl, 8

Population, 441–443
Positive freedom, 432–433
Positivism, and dialectical approach, 11–12
Potekhin, I., 457–458
Poverty, 218–219
    in Third World, 455–458, 461–463, 468–469
Preferences, 112, 364–368, 371–372, 374–376, 379–384
    adaptive, 132–133, 135
Prices, 157
    market, 86–87
    see also Just price
Private gain, desire for, 162–165, 172–175
Private property, 251, 328
    capitalist, 313–316
Private sector, 400
Production, 46, 327, 334
    and alienation, 332–333
    for need, 226
    ownership of, 320–324, 414
    and property, 311–312
    and self-realization, 130–131
    and slave societies, 356
    see also Cooperative production; Marginal product
Production relations, apart from property rights, 265–269
Productive resources theory of value, 401–402
Profit, 298–299
Promise-breaking, 103
Property, 298
    inequality of, 300
    and production, 311–312
    see also Individual/social property; Personal property; Private property
Property rights, 250–270, 376–378, 384
    apart from production relations, 265–269
    as body rights, 272–286
    capital-labor partnership, 255–259
    as functional, 259–265
    and social institutions, 286–288
Proudhon, Pierre Joseph, 185
Proudhonists, 192
Pseudo-Marxism, 349
Psychology of Self-Esteem, The (Branden), 78
Public choice theory, 157
Public goods problem, 92–93
Public sector, 400
Pyatakov, Grigori, 340

Racial discrimination, 103–106
Rand, Ayn, 101, 152

Rationality, 152
Rawls, John, 92, 112, 145, 251, 257–258, 365, 376, 390n
  influence of, 411
Reagan, Ronald, 252, 253
Rechtsphilosophie (Hegel), 32
Redistribution, 219, 381, 441–443, 449, 451
Relationships, 72
  and coercion, 209–210
Rembrandt, 403
Rerum Novarum, 258
Resources, *see* Equality of resources theory; Productive resources theory of value
Responsibility, 204–207
  and freedom, 235
  and virtue, 235
Retaliatory coercion, 204, 210
Ricardo, David, 187, 376
Rights, 389–390
  see also Entitlements; Negative rights; Property rights; Transfer rights
Risk-aversion, and self-realization, 120–121
Roberts, Paul Craig, 331
Robespierre, Maximilien, 182
Rockefeller, John D., Jr., 255–256
Roemer, John, 364, 370, 373, 384
Roosevelt administration (U.S.), 445
Rousseau, Jean-Jacques, 189, 200, 376
Routine, 125
Rückseite des Spiegels, Die (Lorenz), 22
Ruitenbeek, Hendrik M., 62
Rules, 240–243, 244–245

Sacrifice, in capitalism, 411, 420–423
Samuelson, Paul, 411, 419
Schleiermacher, Friedrich, 31
Schmitt, Carl, 32
Schmitt, Richard, 162
Schumpeter, Joseph, 406, 411, 415, 419
Schweikart, David, 410
Science, and dialectical approach, 11–13, 22–23
Self-actualization, 115–119
Self-alienation, 77–78, 81
Self-determination, 89, 294
Self-esteem, 119
  and envy, 390–395
  and meaningful work, 395–396
Self-externalization, 116
Self-interest, economic, 294–295
Self-love, 145
Self-realization, 111–135
  classification of, 113–114
  and community, 129–132

  definition of, 114–116
  freedom of, 115
  fullness of, 114–115
  and individual/social property, 324–329
  and institutional conditions, 132–135
  and others, 129–132
  and politics, 126–129
  resistance to, 120–122
  value of, 116, 118–119
  and work, 122–126
Sen, Amartya, 365, 376, 443, 444
Sensation, and agent-type control, 275–278
Separateness, and anxiety, 66–67
Sexual discrimination, 103, 104, 105, 106
Sexuality, 44, 45
Sexual liberation, 231
Shanin, Teodor, 354
Sider, Ronald, J., 456
Simon of Cyrene, 355
Size, of group, 133
Skills, 126, 378
Skinner, Andrew, 301
Slave societies, 355–357
Slave trading, 459–460
Smith, Adam, 1, 83, 85, 87, 116, 139, 291, 376, 467
  and freedom, 318
  and human nature, 140
  and justice, 292–309
  and labor, 98
  and "self-love," 162–163, 165
  and virtue, 156–157
  and work, 122
Social choice paradox, 157
Social Contract (Rousseau), 200
Social convention, 236, 239, 240, 245
Social goals, vs. natural rights, 427–432
Social institutions, and property rights, 286–288
Socialism, workers under, 134–135
  see also Gradualist socialism
Socialization, *see* Manipulation
Social production, 316
Socrates, 3, 22
Solomon-Corbit theory of "opponent process," 116
Solzhenitsyn, Alexander, 26
Species-being, man as, 47–53
Speculators, 99–101
Spengler, Oswald, 302
Spinoza, Baruch, 181, 200
Stalin, Joseph, 25–26, 29, 35, 340, 341
Stalinism, 340
Starvation, in Third World, 440–446

State property, 251, 329
Statism and Anarchy (Marx), 194
Ste. Croix, Geoffrey de, 344
Stephenson, Matthew A., 331
Stojanovic, Svetozar, 34
Subjective utility theory, 364–365
Substantive rules, 240–244
Surpluses, and agenthood, 285
Survey of Contemporary Economics, 455
Survival
   and free choice, 225
   and labor, 226
Sweezy, Paul, 403
Sykes, Gerald, 63

Taft, William Howard, 253
Talent, equality of, 378–380
Tawney, R. H., 230
Taxation, 354
Technology, 218
Techow, Lieutenant, 32–33
Thatcher, Margaret, 252
Thatcherites, 350
Theory of Justice (Rawls), 390n
Theory of Moral Sentiments, The (Smith),
   292–293
Theses on Feuerbach (Marx), 358
Thinking, and dialectical approach, 13–15
Third World, 440–452, 454–471
   capitalism and, 445–446
   and colonialism, 462–463
   debts in, 465
   and ethnic discrimination, 466
   external contacts in, 466–467
   and international demonstration effect,
      467
   malnutrition in, 440–446
   poverty in, 445–458, 461–463, 468–469
   and slave trading, 459–460
   starvation in, 440–446
   and terms of trade, 463–465
   see also Global justice
Tocqueville, Alexis de, 126, 188
Topitsch, Ernst, 19
Totalitarianism, and coercion, 207–208
Townsend, Peter, 455
Tractatus (Spinoza), 181
Trade (terms of), and Third World,
   463–465
Transactions, immoral, 101–103
Transcendence, 185
Transfer rights, 282–284
Transfers, 388–389
Trotsky, Leon, 391, 394

Tucker, Robert C., 333
Twain, Mark, 236
Tweedie, Jill, 468

Underdevelopment, *see* Third World
Unfreedom, 224
Unions, and property rights, 253–255
Universal being, man as, 47
Universality, 57
Use-values, 336
Utilitarianism, 212–213
   and market, 85, 87–88, 93
   of positive freedom, 433
Utility, and proprty rights, 281–282
Uyl, Douglas Den, 200

Values, 77, 228
   and capitalism, 229–230
   see also Labor theory of value; Productive
      resources theory of value
Varian, Hal, 380
Vidal-Naquet, Pierre, 353
Viner, Jacob, 302
Virtue, 235–236, 245
   and freedom, 200–213
Virtuous action, 236–239
Vyshinsky, Andrey, 26

War, 128
Wealth, 87, 296, 297, 326
Weber, Max, 260, 351
   influence of, 357
Welfare, 364
   and property rights, 251–253
Welfarism, 365, 381
West, Jerry, 391
Western societies, and Third World,
   454–471
Wheeler, Samuel, 272
Williams, Bernard, 386, 387
Williamson, Oliver, 133
Wilson, Woodrow, 162
Windelband, Wilhelm, 25
Winpisinger, William, 254
Work
   disutility of, 122–123
   marginal utility of, 123–124
   meaningful, 395–398
   and self-realization, 122–126
Workers' control, 398–399
Wundt, Max, 30
Wynn, William, 254

Yeats, W. B., 454

ABOUT THE EDITOR

TIBOR R. MACHAN is professor of philosophy at Auburn University in Alabama. He was smuggled out of Hungary in 1953 and, after emigrating to the United States, served in the U.S. Air Force. He then went on to earn his B.A. (Claremont McKenna College), M.A. (New York University), and Ph.D. (University of California at Santa Barbara) degrees in philosophy.

Machan wrote *The Pseudo-Science of B. F. Skinner* (1974) and *Human Rights and Human Liberties* (1975) and edited *The Libertarian Alternative* (1974) and *The Libertarian Reader* (1982), among other works. He has contributed to numerous scholarly journals, including *The American Philosophical Quarterly, Theory and Decision, The Southern Economic Review, The Journal of Applied Philosophy,* and *The American Journal of Jurisprudence.*

Machan is co-founder and senior editor of *Reason* magazine, is editor of *Reason Papers,* and is scheduled to host the television political philosophy series "Vision of Social Order."